Dr. Dobb's Toolbook of 80286/80386 Programming

M&T BOOKS

Dr. Dobb's Toolbook of 80286/80386 Programming

Editors of *Dr. Dobb's Journal*

M&T BOOKS

M&T Publishing, Inc.
Redwood City, California

M&T Books
A Division of M&T Publishing, Inc.
501 Galveston Drive
Redwood City, CA 94063

M&T Books
General Manager, Ellen Ablow
Project Manager, Michelle Hudun
Editors, David Rosenthal, Ann Lee, Sally Brenton
Illustrator, Lynn Sanford
Cover Designer, Barbara Mautz

Library of Congress Cataloging in Publication Data

Dr. Dobb's toolbook of 80286/80386 programming / Robinson, Phillip. -- 1st ed.
    p.   cm.
    ISBN 0-934375-42-9 : $24.95
    1. Intel 80286 (Microprocessor)--Programming. 2. Intel 80386
(Microprocessor)--Programming.   I. Dr. Dobb's journal. II. Title:
Doctor Dobb's toolbook of 80286/80386 programming.
QA76.8.I2927D7 1988
005.265--dc19   88-17559
                                          CIP

92 91 90 89 88   5 4 3 2 1

Limits of Liability and Disclaimer of Warranty

How to Order the Accompanying Disk

All the programs in **Dr. Dobb's Toolbook of 80286/80386 Programming** are available on disk with full source code. You'll find programs that illustrate the ideas discussed in the book, code that shows you how to use 80X86 in protected mode, example programs that employ the mathematical capabilities of the 80X87 chips, examples of multitasking code, programs for listing what processor a program is using, examples of windows and presentation manager manipulation, and much more.

The disk price is $20.00. California residents must add the appropriate sales tax. Order by sending a check, or credit card number (VISA, MasterCard, or American Express) and expiration date, to:

Dr. Dobb's Toolbook of 80286/80386 Disk
M&T Books
501 Galveston Drive
Redwood City, CA 94063

Or, you may order by calling our toll-free number between 8 A.M. and 5:00 P.M., Monday through Friday, Pacific Standard Time: 800/533-4372 (800/356-2002 in California). Ask for Item **#54-2**.

Contents

Introduction

Microprocessors have been around long enough now to have evolved through several generations. Back in 1975, programming a microprocessor chip meant squeezing the most out of a tiny set of registers, rudimentary instructions, and cramped memory space. A few years later the era of the Z80, 6800, and 6502 relaxed the boundaries a bit. Then the IBM PC endorsed Intel's 8080 family of microprocessors and made 8088/8086 programming a daily diet for thousands of engineers. The 8088 and 8086 weren't very different from the previous generation, but they did allow even more memory and 16-bit operations. (The 1 MB memory space of the 8086—tied down further to 640K by the DOS operating system—once seemed like a lot, particularly compared to the 64K of many CP/M systems. The 68000 chip found in the Apple Macintosh had similar improvements, although its memory space was a capacious 16 MB.) With more memory and more powerful instructions, programmers were able to create some impressive programs. Still, nearly all microprocessor and microcomputer software stuck to a straightforward and simple world of single-tasking and direct use of available physical memory.

Then the 80286 chip appeared, the next step in Intel's 8080 family. At first it was employed as a fast 8086 in the IBM AT and compatibles. But it was more than that—the 80286 included sophisticated new "modes" and "memory protection" hardware that were borrowed from the world of minicomputers and mainframes. These were not put to use immediately because the attraction of compatibility with the 8088/8086 generation was so strong—those chips had the largest library of software in the world. Making the 80286 run 8086 software as well as its own, more advanced software was not simple. Then Intel released the next generation chip—the 80386—that took the 80286's sophistication and added yet more speed, more minicomputer technology, and 8086 compatibility. At the same time, Microsoft began to release details and initial samples of a new operating system—OS/2—that exercised the 80286's advanced features. (Microsoft was the firm responsible for the DOS operating system that was absolutely dominant on the 8088/8086/80286 systems from IBM and its competitors. Because of that clout, OS/2 had a huge head start in the OS/2 market over any competing operating system. In fact, the most popular competitor was UNIX, and Microsoft was also home to the most widely used variation of UNIX for microcomputers—XENIX.)

Programming the 80286 could be done in several different ways. You could just write programs to the 8086 generation, and run them on the faster 80286. You could write to the 80286's strength—its protected mode that could work with far more memory and so with multiple programs, as well. In essence, that choice meant writing for DOS (along with its related environments such as Windows) for OS/2 (with its related Presentation Manager environment).

Programming for the 80386 is yet another kettle of fish. You can again use it as just a very fast 8088/8086 and write to DOS, or you can pretend to some extent that it is an 80286 and write to OS/2. But the 80386 can also do more than that. It has a special compatibility mode for 8086 software that can allow you to run several 8086 programs side-by-side. (It does not have such a mode for 80286 software, unfortunately.) Some DOS environments—such as Windows/386—take advantage of this mode. The 80386 is also fast enough and has the memory protection hardware to work with vast physical memory spaces and even vaster "virtual memory," where the physical memory is logically magnified to thousands of times its real size. Combine that speed and virtual memory and the 80386 is an ideal platform for multitasking—running more than one program or even more than one operating system simultaneously, sharing the processor power between them.

Yet another wrinkle that has been added to programming in the 286/386 era is the coprocessor. These specialized processor chips were once somewhat rare—used only by arcane applications software and programmed by a few specialized code sharks. Today, many computers rely on math coprocessors, graphics coprocessors, and even memory-management coprocessors for unloading important but tedious special tasks from the main microprocessor. Intel has surrounded the 80286 and 80386 with a family of coprocessors, including the 80287 and 80387 math chips, the 82786 graphics coprocessor, the 82385 cache controller, and the 82380 DMA controller. Other companies, such as Weitek, make their own coprocessors to accompany the Intel line.

Programming the 80286 and 80386 chips can be as simple as writing 8086 programs and watching them run fast, or as complex as crafting operating systems that would do a million-dollar mainframe computer proud. The two chips have many characteristics in common, but they also have some distinct differences. Of course you should have a basic book about the chip you're tackling—in fact, you should probably team Intel's own documentation with one of the 286 or 386 books that are now crowding bookstore shelves. These describe the registers, instruction set, memory addressing, and other fundamentals of the chips. (Intel also offers some books aimed at systems programming concerns.)

However, in my humble opinion, you should also pick up a book just like this one, a book that will give you real-world opinions on the environments, operating systems, tricks, clues, and pitfalls of 80286 and 80386 programming. I searched through technical computer magazines, cadged every piece of literature I could from Intel, and asked 286/386 experts to suggest stuff they would like to have known when they started programming this new generation of chips. The material is written by people from big companies such as Lotus and Microsoft and from little companies or consultant operations. After reading and comparing all the texts, I winnowed them down, pulling out pieces that were too old or were redundant. Some of the articles in this collection overlap with other articles, but they give the information from a different point of view, with different emphases, explanations, and details.

This is not the kind of book you'll want to read from front to back, though you may want to read a couple of articles in each section as you work from the introductory material on toward the more specialized stuff. It is certainly the kind of book we hope you'll want to keep on your shelf. There are lists of tips, descriptions of important memory addresses, code fragments and programs for manipulating or testing chip modes, and explanations of operating system concepts—all things you would have to otherwise dig out of a shelf full of expensive books and magazines.

The first few articles describe the general history and architecture of the 80286 and 80386. Then there is a section devoted to writing transportable programs that can operate in the 8088 and 80286 environments. The following articles make the first move into the sophisticated 286 abilities: changing the 286 to the protected mode and exercising it in that state. Memory is the subject of the next section— virtual memory, 80386 memory addressing, and Expanded/Extended memory in DOS.

Operating Systems (such as OS/2, DOS, XENIX, UNIX, VM/386, and Concurrent DOS) and environments (such as Windows, Desqview, and PC-MOS/386) come to the plate next. OS/2 gets a lot of play, because many developers will be moving programs from the DOS world to OS/2. Experiences in porting both from DOS to OS/2 and from Windows to the Presentation Manager are described. Multitasking and the special operating system strengths of the 386 are explained and illustrated.

Then a series of articles describes the practical elements of 386 development today—tools for converting DOS programs to reach its memory space and schemes for native debugging of 386 software.

Finally, the coprocessors, particularly the 80287 and 80387 math chips, are dissected and compared. Schemes for taking advantage of their abilities and descriptions of the 82786 graphics coprocessor and 82385 cache coprocessor follow. Because most of the 80286 and 80386 programs will run on IBM PC, PS/2, and competing compatible computers, the tail of this book is a chart that compares the BIOS foundations of those computers. Knowing the BIOS changes is part and parcel with general 286/386 knowledge in writing programs that are as powerful as possible and as portable as is practical.

Clearly some of the material will be old news in a year or two (especially the parts on environments) while other stuff (such as the coprocessor information) will remain useful for much longer. I hope this book is a reference that will last on your shelf until you're busy converting from the 80486 to whatever generation follows it.

PHILLIP ROBINSON

I
Architecture and
Implications of the 80386

1
Anatomy of a 386 [*]

Winn L. Rosch

In more than a few ways, 80386-based computers are all like fine wines. To the uninitiated, they all seem the same. The feeling is bred by the thriving market for cheap, almost generic 8088-based XT clones and 80286-equipped AT compatibles. The advanced state of today's carbon-paper engineering almost guarantees that you can substitute one brand (or lack of brand) of AT clone for another with little or no change in either operation or performance.

Indeed, as with wines, the only apparent difference between 80386-equipped computers is the shape of the bottle—different chassis designs that might prefer one placement of disk drives over another. But it's what's inside that counts, and, with computers, the subtleties of taste and nuances of design can have a real effect—not just on how fast you can get things done, but on what you can do.

The point was driven home with the introduction of *Microsoft Windows/386*. In its initial release, the new operating environment was compatible (according to Microsoft) solely with Compaq's 80386-based computer lineup. A more generalized version was scheduled for release later.

Some of the differences between computers are intangible. For instance, certain PCs have snob appeal based on brand name alone. Dropping one on your desk is like putting a Cherokee in your driveway or Romane-Conti on your table. The IBM PS/2 Model 80 or Compaq Deskpro 386/20 on your desk says you can afford the best.

Along with the notoriety, name-brand machines can bring real, tangible benefits, too. For instance, part of the manufacturer's reputation is based on a commitment to support, processing speed, construction quality, and the simple reassurance that a reputable company probably won't close up shop and leave you holding a bag full of malfunctioning microprocessors.

No single 80386-based PC ranks as best on all counts. You don't get status and low price in the same package, for instance. All practical computer packages inevitably embody some compromises.

Because of the higher prices of the technically advanced parts needed to boost performance to its limits, faster machines, inevitably tend to be more expensive. (The relationship between speed and price is not always proportional, however, nor is the more expensive machine necessarily faster.) Other equipment may incorporate features that will endear it to you in particular situations. For instance, big fast hard disks can work wonders for a network, and built-in communications ports can benefit a multiuser installation.

Finally, not everyone needs an 80386-based computer. If you plan on using a computer for just one job—for instance, keeping books or making them—you won't need the multitasking power of the 80386. If you're looking for the most performance per dollar spent, mail-order high-speed At compatibles are still among the best bargains around.

But if you're concerned about the future, the PCs equipped with the 83086 microprocessor are the only way to go. Not just faster, they are architecturally superior to everything that's come before in the IBM environment. Settle for something less today, and you'll rue your decision tomorrow.

Watching the Clock

Undeniably, the biggest allure of 80386-based PCs is performance. A machine that runs twice as fast as an ordinary 80286-based AT will potentially get your work done in half the time. Once applications that use 32-bit code become available, that performance level will likely double again on the same equipment without any other change.

But when it comes to performance, all 80386-based PCs are not created equal. While the latest heavy-duty 80386 hardware promises to triple or quadruple the throughput of plain ATs on ordinary DOS software, some systems won't even double the AT level of performance.

No one factor can explain these surprising differences. The performance of 80386-based computers varies with clock speed, memory type, and overall system architecture.

The most obvious—and most publicized—difference between various 80386-based computers and PCs in general is clock speed. Advertisements are full of claims quoting number of megahertz; in today's commercial 80386-based PCs the bottom end is encountered at about 14 MHz and the top at 20.

The clock in question has little to do with the time of day—it counts nanoseconds instead of hours. Its function is to keep the computer's electronic thoughts straight. It works more like a metronome, beating time to keep all the parts of the machine humming along in harmony.

The clock is necessary because computers process information in the form of very brief electrical pulses. Each pulse is dealt with separately, in a linear sequence, one after another. The computer understands a digital state—the smallest piece of information: a bit—as the presence or absence of a pulse at a given instant.

Although electricity moves quickly, it doesn't move instantaneously. Circuit resistance slows the pulse and stretches it out because a pulse has to overcome both the resistance and reactance (mostly capacitance) of the computer circuits and components. Consequently, some discrete period is required for the full power of a pulse to travel from one part of a computer to another—and different lengths of time are required for moving between different parts of the computer.

The system clock synchronizes all the pulses by allotting a given period for moving the electrical charges, then triggering the various computer parts to see what they have—whether they have received the electrical equivalent to a logical one or zero—at the instant of the clock trigger. Once all the pulses everywhere in the system are registered, the system can begin to shift signals around anew.

The rate at which these clock beats recur thus determines how fast information can move through the system. The faster the clock, the quicker bits are recognized and processed. But the speed of the clock cannot be increased without limit. At some point, increasing the clock speed may call on the computer to register information before all the pulses in the computer have reached their destinations. In addition, a faster clock operates at a higher frequency (by definition), and higher frequencies are more likely to leak between connections and register false results. Both of these conditions can cause errors.

Computer chips, too, are rated to operate at certain clock rates, limited in speed by their internal resistances and reactances as well as by their power consumption and ability to dissipate heat. A clock that's too fast can confuse the chips and make them work unreliably.

Clock speed is measured in megahertz: millions of cycles (or pulses) per second. The 80386 microprocessor is designed to operate in its slowest form at 12.5 MHz. Faster versions are rated to run at 16 or 20 MHz. This rating is mostly a recommendation. The 80386 chip can, in general, run faster than the rating screened on its case, but reliability decreases (often dramatically) as the clock speed is increased.

The clock speed inside most personal computers is determined by the very precise vibrations of a thin slice of quartz crystal. This crystal may be in a metal package by itself on the computer system board or it may be combined with other circuits into an oscillator module. In either case, in 80386-based computer systems the crystal and oscillator frequency is twice the speed at which the microprocessor operates. The chip itself cuts the clock speed in half internally before using it. In other words, an 80386 that operates at 16 MHz actually requires a system clock that can operate at 32 MHz.

With rare candor, every maker of 80386-based PCs reports the actual operating speed of the microprocessor chip and not the system clock speed on the computer bus.

All else being equal, the throughput of a computer—how much information it can actually process—is directly related to its clock speed. A machine that runs at 16 MHz will find answers twice as fast as one operating at 8 MHz.

Of course, all else is rarely equal. Different microprocessor designs running at the same clock speed can work through problems at different rates. Factors that influence processing speed include the size of internal registers (where calculations actually take place inside the microprocessor) and the microcode used by the chip.

The more bits in a register, the bigger the chunk of a problem that can be worked through in a given processing cycle. In theory, a 16-bit computer can do twice as much work per clock cycle as can an 8-bit machine. A 32-bit chip like the 80386 would be faster still.

Such speed projections assume that all the bits of a register are put to use. PC-DOS poses a problem for the 32-bit 80386, however, because it uses at most half the space in a 32-bit register. When working on PC-DOS programs, the 32-bit architecture of the 80386 is really of no benefit.

Even chips that have the same size registers solve problems at different rates. The microcode of a microprocessor determines what bit patterns cause the chip to carry out what operation and how that operation is performed. While one microprocessor might require 7 simple operations to carry out a complex task like adding two numbers, another chip design may require 17.

For instance, although the 80286 microprocessor in the AT has the same size registers as its predecessor, the 8086, it can perform roughly five times as much work at less than twice the clock speed. Clock rates are thus only a rough guideline that should be used to directly compare similar chip models operating in similar environments.

Moving Memory

In 80386-based computer systems, the clock speed is one indication of how fast a given machine can perform. But in many high-performance computers, including most 80386-based PCs, the clock speed determines only how fast information is processed inside the microprocessor chip itself.

The speed at which the information is sent to and taken away from the microprocessor—both from memory and from mass-storage and other system peripherals—is another factor that affects the performance of the total computer system.

The 80386 microprocessor operates so quickly that most memory chips cannot keep up with it. To prevent the microprocessor from outrunning the memory chips, most 80386-based computer systems periodically force the chip to stop whatever it's doing to give the memory a chance to catch up. Because the microprocessor is essentially doing nothing but waiting around, these pauses are called "wait states."

The number of wait states is counted for each memory cycle. A memory cycle normally requires three microprocessor cycles—one for the microprocessor to send out an instruction telling the memory system which bytes it wants to read, another to find the bytes, and a third cycle for the memory system to send the requested information back to the microprocessor. Adding one wait state will increase each memory access from three to four cycles, slowing down the system by 33 percent. Some 80386-based computers may, at times, have to endure 2 or 3 wait states per memory cycle when accessing system board memory and sometimes 16 or more wait states when they read from memory expansion boards.

The reason that wait states are necessary at all is that most PC designs use Dynamic Random Access Memory (DRAM) chips. DRAMs store information as minuscule electrical charges, akin to the static electricity that bites your hand when you touch a doorknob during dry winter months. As with static electricity, the charges stored in DRAM chips tend to drain off on their own. To prevent this brain drain, DRAM chips are periodically refreshed. Each stored charge is given a small boost to keep it from fading. Computers can devote from 6 to 12 percent of their time to refreshing memory, even if their memory chips are never accessed.

In addition, the very act of reading a bit of memory tends to weaken its charge, and in many cases the chip must be refreshed before it can be read again. Recharging a memory chip requires a small but substantial amount of time, roughly from 100 to 500 nanoseconds (billionths of a second). If the microprocessor attempts to read from a DRAM chip before it has been completely refreshed, it may gather erroneous data. So the microprocessor waits.

Most people are familiar with the speed ratings of memory chips, given in nanoseconds. Perform some simple math, and you might think you could calculate the speed rating necessary for a computer—three cycles of a 16-MHz clock requires 187.5 ns. But 200-ns chips won't work with zero wait states in a 16-MHz 80386 computer. In fact, such a machine requires memory chips that are rated faster than 80 ns.

"Every DRAM chip has an access time specification that relates to how fast you can get data after you ask for it. That's the number on top of the chip that people are familiar with," explains David Lunsford, systems architect, Dell Computer Corp., Austin, Texas. "All chips also have a cycle time which describes how often you can ask for data. With dynamic RAM the cycle time is much longer than access time. For example, an 80-nanosecond DRAM chip has a cycle time of 190 nanoseconds, so the most often you can ask for data is every 190 nanoseconds."

One way to avoid the wait is obvious: make the DRAM chips faster. Faster chips are, however, more expensive and may not be readily available. In fact, few DRAM chips are quick enough to keep up with an 80386 operating full-tilt at 16 MHz, and those that are tend to be expensive. Nevertheless, NCR Corp. achieves zero wait states in its Model 916 through the use of 70-ns DRAM chips.

A different style of memory chip, called Static Random Access Memory (SRAM), can achieve substantially faster cycle times. Static RAM chips work on a different principle than their dynamic cousins. Rather than storing information as static-like charges, each memory cell of an SRAM chip works like a two-way switch, latching itself in one position or another. A tiny charge of electricity is constantly supplied to each cell to keep the switch locked in its particular position. Because current is constantly supplied, the chips does not need to be refreshed. It does away with both the refresh time the computer requires and the need for wait states to recharge the RAM.

Without the need to refresh, the cycle time is no longer important. "With static RAM, the access time and the cycle time are exactly the same, so you can ask for data from an 80-nanosecond chip every 80 nanoseconds," says Lunsford.

To achieve zero-wait-state operation, the PC's Limited 386-16 uses fast static RAM for all of the main memory of the system. The static RAM of the 386-16 also eliminates the need for memory refresh, speeding performance a few more percent.

However, static RAM has a major disadvantage: it's much more expensive than DRAM, and the chips don't hold as much information.

Static Subterfuge

To sidestep the need for huge banks of expensive static RAM chips, computer makers can use several strategies to make DRAM memory appear to work faster. These techniques are based on the principle that most memory accesses that computers make tend to be confined to a narrow range of addresses, often sequential. Only a few software commands—those to jump to a new memory area and those that call subroutines—break away from sequential operation. By optimizing the speed at which a computer can read sequential bytes, overall system throughput with modest-performance DRAMs can be raised to nearly the level afforded by SRAM.

The most straightforward of these strategies is the fast memory cache, often using SRAM chips. This technique uses normal DRAM chips but adds a block of extremely fast memory chips that serve as a buffer between the microprocessor and main memory banks. When the microprocessor requires a certain byte of memory, it is read directly from the DRAM and loaded into both the microprocessor and the fast cache. Alternately, a whole block of bytes can be read into the cache whenever a memory request is made. If a subsequent memory request asks for a byte that's kept in the cache, it can be retrieved with zero wait states. The only time wait states are encountered is when the next instruction cannot be found within the memory cache.

The odds are in favor of bytes being in the cache, according to Gary Stimac, vice president of systems engineering for Compaq Computer Corp., Houston. "Almost all programs are designed to loop with respect to frequently used data. For instance, in Lotus 1-2-3 the actual calculation of cells is a loop that just gets duplicated time and time again," he says.

The "hit ratio"—the percentage of the time that the microprocessor actually finds the bytes it needed in the high-speed cache—varies somewhat with the number of bytes in the cache itself. The cache may be as small as a couple of kilobytes or as large as 64K, the size used by the PC Designs GV-386. Caches much larger than that don't make sense because they approach the size of main memory.

Even with modest cache sizes, manufacturers claim hit ratios has high as 90 percent—Compaq claims 95 percent for its 80386-controlled 32K cache of its Deskpro 386/20 Model 300—although the actual value depends on the software you're running. With an adequately large cache and amenable applications, a system equipped with cache memory can run nearly as fast as one with no wait states.

The caching technique is preferred by most manufacturers of 80386-based turbo boards (expansion boards that add an extra high-performance microprocessor into an existing computer) and allows them to nearly double the performance of the host computer. The fast cache memory operates at 16 MHz along with the turbo board 80386 microprocessor, while the cache is stocked with bytes from the host's slow 8 MHz memory banks.

Some manufacturers have reservations about memory caching, seeing it as a Band-Aid solution that works for some software but may have significant drawbacks in future applications.

"Caching is a very usable technique. It's very good as long as you can keep your code or data segments residing in the cache," notes Dell Computer's Lunsford. "But once we move into the OS/2 environment where a microprocessor must handle multiple concurrent processes, a problem called thrashing can arise. Every time the chip needs code for a different process, it will have to reload the cache. Moving code back and forth like that will impede performance."

Others are more reserved in their opinions.

"Caching is a standard architectural approach to all the minicomputers, which are almost always used in multiuser, multi-tasking applications. It's a well-accepted approach," counters John Patterson, senior vice president, Tandy Computer, Fort Worth. "The honest truth is that nobody knows what will happen with OS/2. Although we have the code, we don't have any applications. Nobody knows what will speed it up or slow it down."

Problems can arise with memory caches. For instance, a program may alter bytes in main memory that have also been copied to the cache. If the cache is not updated, then using its unchanged byte can result in errors.
Compaq uses a new support chip for the 80386 microprocessor called the 82385

cache controller.

"The 82385 helps us to achieve data coherency and high data integrity. The chip prevents the cache memory and main memory from ever getting out of sync," says Stimac. The 82385 has "snooping" capability, he explains. It can determine whether bytes in the main memory of the system are changed, for instance, when a hard disk is read. The 82385 ensures that those changes made in main memory aren't missed when the bytes from the same location are drawn from the cache.

In addition, the 82385 has the capability to buffer memory writes as well as reads. Consequently, the system can write to RAM with zero wait states. The 82385 then transfers the changed bytes to the main memory of the system. According to Stimac, caching memory writes can improve overall system performance by about 10 percent.

Weaving Memories

A different technique breaks the whole memory of a computer system into a number of individual sections that each operate as a small cache. Implementing this technique requires special RAM chips that can divide their address range into a page or a group of rows and columns. These special chips allow very fast access in one of the two directions of their organization. Called page-mode access, this technique cuts the number of wait states in much the same way that a cache does.

"Essentially, page-mode access is a function of the type of RAM chips you use," explains James D. Rogers, product manager, Monolithic Systems Corp., Englewood, Colorado. "Once you access any location within a page, any other location in that page is accessible with no wait states. When you cross that boundary, you encounter wait states."

The special chips are called static-column or page-mode RAM. Although the two terms describe distinct chip technologies, in PCs their application is the same.

In the static-column RAM arrangement, sequential memory bytes are organized in adjacent rows within a single column. As long as the microprocessor attempts to access sequential memory bytes, it can retrieve information without wait states. When it dashes across columns for the information it needs, however, the microprocessor will require wait states to allow the memory to keep up.

Page-mode memory arranges memory in individual pages and allows back-to-back accesses made within a given page at zero wait states. Jumps outside the page impose wait states.

As with true caching, the performance of static-column or page-mode memory systems depends on the page or column size that makes up the individual "cache." The larger the cache, the higher the hit ratio and the better the performance. The static-column RAM of the Compaq Deskpro 386/16, for example, cuts the system from two wait states to about 0.8.

Another clever technique called "interleaved memory" also earns speed gains on sequential accesses but is not limited to a small page. In an interleaved memory system, the RAM is divided into two or more banks, and the microprocessor alternates between banks when it reads sequential bytes.

Typically, memory will be divided into two banks, and for sequential bytes the microprocessor will first read from one, then from the other, then again from the first. While one bank is being read, the other has time to refresh itself. As long as the microprocessor reads sequential bytes, it will encounter no wait states.

When bytes are not sequential, the microprocessor has a 50-50 chance of reading from the bank that is ready. Otherwise, the microprocessor will encounter one or more wait states while the requested bank is refreshed. Because of this, there's a 50 percent chance of making a hit with no sequential bytes. A four-way interleave can reduce wait states by 75 percent. In addition, interleaving is often combined with page-mode addressing to further improve performance.

Of course, the only way to eliminate wait states is to use memory that's fast enough to keep up with the microprocessor. In terms of practical microcircuits today, that means using SRAMs or very fast DRAMs for all system memory. Although it is the most expensive alternative, when performance counts, it's also the best.

Coprocessor Choice

As an extension of the 80286 microprocessor, the 80386 is designed to work with all of its predecessor's software and hardware. Also included in its compatibility is the ability to make use of the 80287 numeric coprocessor.

A numeric coprocessor is a special form of microprocessor designed to do exactly one thing well: arithmetic. It can multiply floating-point numbers very quickly, hundreds of times faster than a general-purpose microprocessor like the 80386— and with much greater accuracy.

Because the 80287 is a separate microprocessor, it takes its own special program code to run. Thus, software must be specially written to use the 80287. It offers no benefit to programs that are not written to accommodate its needs.

Many 80386-based PCs include sockets for installing an 80287. In many cases, just any 80287 won't do. The chip comes in various speed ratings, from 4 to 12 MHz. Some systems only support particular speeds. Obviously, the faster the 80287 operates, the better the performance it will deliver.

Better than the 80287 is the numeric coprocessor designed as a companion to the 80386, the 80387. Not only is the 80387 capable of operating at the full microprocessor speed of the 80386 (both chips come in speed ratings from 12.5 to 20 MHz), but also its design is much improved over the 80287. In fact, it's so much improved that it can deliver performance four times better than an 80287. The 80387 is code-compatible with the 80287 and will operate with any software that supports the earlier chip.

But the 80387 is not the ultimate in numeric coprocessors Another new chip called the Weitek coprocessor has been developed for the dedicated workstations that are used in computer-aided engineering (CAE). Compaq has adapted the Weitek coprocessor to some of the machines in its line of 80386-based PCs.

"The Weitek chip uses memory-mapped architecture and is a lot faster than the 80387 chip. Compared to the 80387, it's about ten times faster at the micro level," says Stimac.

The Weitek coprocessor achieves its high performance with a design completely different from that of the 80287 and 80387. Consequently, it requires its own special software. "The Weitek coprocessor is not compatible with code written for the 80287," notes Stimac. "But Compaq has worked with different compiler manufacturers, who are in turn working with people like Autodesk, so that they can recompile their programs to support the Weitek coprocessor. In the near future you will get very tremendous performance improvement in CAD applications," he says.

Compatibility Concerns

In the early days of PCs, the term "compatibility" mostly indicated whether the computer in question could run Microsoft's *Flight Simulator*, a troublesome program that took direct hardware control of several system functions. Today, a more suitable concern might appear to be whether a specific machine will run Lotus 1-

2-3—or whatever program you will rely upon for the majority of your daily livelihood.

With the advent of proven, independently written (from IBM) BIOS codes, many of the old compatibility concerns have been put to rest. BIOS routines (the initials stand for Basic Input/Output System) link software to the hardware of the computer, matching the hardware-specific port addresses through which many system features are addressed with simple firmware-coded utility routines.

When a program wants to read a character from the keyboard, for instance, it may call a BIOS function that queries the proper input port, reads the character, and resets the port for the next character input. The software never needs to know exactly where the character came from, so it can be written without regard to the system on which it will run.

Phoenix Technologies is credited with creating the first BIOS that achieved excellent IBM compatibility and was available to the general market of manufacturers. Using the Phoenix code, a company had a quick way of making its hardware truly compatible. Its availability is one of the cornerstones of the compatible computer industry.

Several newer BIOS systems have become available in the last couple of years, most importantly from Award Software and AMI, which have quickly earned reputations for compatibility with IBM chips. Because of these BIOS chip sets, this level of compatibility is almost a nonissue among 80386-based PCs.

But the BIOS alone is not enough to free 80386-based systems from compatibility problems. Many systems stumble with nontraditional software. Some hardware enhancements won't work with some 80386-based PCs. And specific 80386-based machines themselves are generally incompatible with the memory-expansion options of other 80386-based PCs.

The newly discovered software troubles concern the use of specific 80386 features never before present in personal computers. With no guiding standard, manufacturers have implemented features and interfaces in their own styles. As a result, some software that reaches down to 80386 hardware may work with one system and not with others.

The issue of hardware compatibility has two sides: the ability to make use of internal accessories developed for earlier-generation PCs, and the ability to interchange 32-bit expansion options with other 80386-based computers.

All 80386-based personal computers, with the exception of the IBM PS/2 Model 80, incorporate 8-and 16-bit internal bus structures generally compatible with those used by IBM's PC-XT and PC AT lines of personal computers. Although they don't have to be that way, this compatibility enables them to make use of off-the-shelf expansion cards such as disk controllers, video adapters, and memory boards. This degree of compatibility gives both you and the system manufacturer the surest way to low-cost system expansion and access to the widest possible array of options.

To accommodate such expansion, most 80386-based computers operate their internal expansion buses at less than the clock speed of their microprocessors, 8 MHz (for compatibility with AT expansion options) being the preferred performance level.

The lower speed is necessary because most expansion cards won't operate much faster than 10 or 12 MHz. Of course, this lower bus speed means that accessing any expansion cards will reduce system throughput, sometimes severely.

To wring more performance out of their systems, some manufacturers allow you the option of running the expansion buses of their machines at higher speed. For example, the PC's Limited 386-16 jazzes up bus speed to 12 MHz on demand, selected through the system setup procedure. Some expansion products may not operate at this rate.

Other, more subtle incompatibilities may arise. For instance, the PC's Limited 286 series of computers uses a memory bus structure that varies slightly from that of the IBM's PC AT. Some third-party memory expansion cards won't work in those machines. Similar problems may arise with other manufacturers' computers and expansion products as well.

More vexing is the lack of consensus for 32-bit expansion of 80386-based computers. Without a doubt full 32-bit expansion is the only way to achieve top performance with add-in products for these machines. But a lack of standardization has prevented the influx of 32-bit-based boards.

One facet of the problem is purely physical. Different manufacturers locate the additional connections for the extra 16 lines of the data path in different places. Some, notably Intel, extend the connectors of the standard AT bus to accommodate memory expansion. Others add extra connectors at various places on the system board that solely accommodate memory expansion. The former technique, while providing for more memory, also permits the possibility of adding other 32-bit components, for instance, a wide-bus hard disk controller.

Intel adopted this strategy for its AT-compatible iSBC-386AT OEM system board, which is used by more than half a dozen machine manufacturers. The popularity of this board has led to its acceptance as a de facto standard of sorts for 32-bit expansion, with at least one non-Intel board using the same structure for its wide bus slots.

The expansion slot architecture is dependent on the underlying structure of the host computer's memory bus. Thus, it is unlikely that systems using different memory techniques can share memory expansion boards. Products with four-way interleaving would not work with systems that have two-way interleaves. Dynamic memory boards won't work in static RAM systems. Caching systems, however, hold the potential of working with other techniques, depending on their underlying structure.

Bus architecture can affect performance as well as expansion. Two examples are IBM's Micro Channel and Compaq's Flex Architecture. Both systems allow, in their own ways, information to be shifted differently—in particular, faster—than in earlier PCs.

Because IBM is treading new ground with the Micro Channel, it need not abide by traditional standards or worry about hardware incompatibilities. Consequently, the Micro Channel runs faster and more intelligently. For instance, the PS/2 Model 50 is able to transfer information from hard disk nearly twice as fast as an AT despite having a clock speed which is only 20 percent faster.

Compaq retains PC compatibility on its bus but splits it into two parts, one side for memory and one side for system I/O. The two sides can operate independently and concurrently, and each can be optimized for its own particular purpose. On hard disk operations, the Compaq architecture is nearly as fast as the Micro Channel, even though it operates at a lower clock speed.

Mass Storage

Nearly all 80386-based computers come with some sort of high-speed mass-storage system. After all, the supercharged performance of an 80386-based PC would be hardly worthwhile if you have to spend 90 percent of your time shuffling floppies and waiting for programs to load.

At one time, nearly everyone lumped all hard disks together. They were simply better and faster than floppies. The AT changed the hard disk perspective by putting increased emphasis on average access time, the speed at which the hard disk could locate any given byte in its memory domain. All disks were classed as either AT-specification (with an average access time of 40 milliseconds and quicker) or cheap stuff (more laggardly drives).

While a swift disk with a low average access time is of even more importance for 80386-based PCs (the quicker the better—speeds under 28 ms. are the most desirable, and 16-ms. drives are available), another figure of hard disk merit also demands attention: the data transfer rate. This specification indicates how quickly the processor can shift blocks of data from magnetic memory into system RAM.

Use of 80386 technology makes data transfer rate important because computers can, for the first time, deal with data that moves faster than bytes can be peeled off the conventional hard disk. Although the 5-MHz data transfer rate of the traditional hard disk seems fast enough, PCs and XTs were not capable of dealing with information at that rate. Even ATs could not accommodate it quickly enough. Hence the actual throughput of a mass-storage system, the speed at which data could actually be put in memory and used, lagged far behind the rated 5 MHz.

Computers based on the 80386 microprocessor are more than fast enough to accept information at the pack rate at which standard hard disks can deliver it. At the same time, 80386-based PCs tend to work on bigger, more complex problems involving larger numbers and bigger blocks of data. The new machines demand faster and more efficient mass-storage handling to facilitate the type of high-volume work they will be doing.

Several techniques have been used for improving hard disk data transfer performance. One impediment to better performance is the data channel barrier. All PCs based on the original IBM design have severe design weaknesses in moving information from disk to memory, which is the primary limit on throughput. All computers designed to be compatible with the original PC are inherently handicapped by this architecture.

The Micro Channel architecture of the IBM PS/2 Model 80 avoids this encumbrance by starting with a clean design slate, totally redefining the bus structure. It's effective enough to more than double the throughput of PS/2 systems compared with those based on PC architecture, all else being equal.

Another technique used for boosting data transfer speed is to speed up the disk itself by using a different disk-to-computer interface. Both the SCSI (Small Computer System Interface) and ESDI (Enhanced Small Device Interface) offer faster data transfer speeds than the 5 MHz of the conventional connection—speeds that the 80386 microprocessor can put to use. Consequently, manufacturers are adding these newer disk interfaces to their products. IBM, Compaq, and PC's Limited offer systems with ESDI-interfaced hard disks, while Zeos International has built an SCSI interface into its 386 replacement motherboard.

No single feature is enough to make one 80386-based computer better than another. As with vintage wines, a truly great PC is a combination of elements that must work together. It must have balance, with no one factor dominating.

Indeed, today's 80386-based PCs show great promise, and they may just have achieved an early—and an excellent—maturity.

2

Upward to the 80386 [*]

Caldwell Crosswy and _Mike Perez_

From its beginnings in the 8086 and 8088, the growth of the Intel processor family has been characterized by full upward compatibility and significant advances in function and performance. While providing functional advances, every new member of the family has retained a full instruction set and operational compatibility with its predecessors, affording protection of the investment made on software for the previous microprocessors. In the case of the 8086/88, this investment has been formidable.

It is therefore significant that Intel's latest microprocessor, the powerful 32-bit 80386, brings even greater function and performance while also providing for a smooth transition from the programming environment of the 8086/88 and 80286.

This newest Intel family member features internal enhancements, such as instruction and bus pipelining, a larger prefetch queue, and a 32-entry page table cache for memory paging functions, which, coupled with the 16-MHz clock rate, provide a level of performance that is traditionally associated with central processing units in minicomputer products.

The most significant advances of the 80386 are those with the potential for removing the barriers that operating system and application developers have encountered in its predecessors. These new advances include the 32-bit instruction set enhancements, the memory paging functions, the enhanced I/O permission features, and the large linear address (4GB) programming model.

Most of all, and most important, is that these advances have been incorporated in a superset manner in order to maintain full compatibility with software products developed for the 8086/88 and 80286. Table 2-1 summarizes the functional superset provided by each member of the Intel microprocessor family.

[*] © 1987, 1988 Ziff Communications Company, _PC Tech Journal_, February 1987, p. 51

FEATURES	8088/8086 80386		80286
Maximum physical memory	1MB	16MB	4GB
Maximum virtual memory	1MB	1GB	64TB
Maximum segment size	64KB	64KB	64KB or 4GB
Paging hardware	No	No	Yes
Operand sizes (bits)	8, 16	8, 16	8, 16, 32
Register sizes (bits)	8, 16	8, 16	8, 16, 32
Memory-I/O protection	No	Yes	Yes
Coprocessor support	8087	80287	80287/80387
Prefetch queue (bytes)	4/6	6	12

Table 2-1: Intel Family Functional Aspects
Newer members of the Intel microprocessor family are designed to add functionality and performance while providing compatibility with older family members.

Solid Foundations

The 8086/88 microprocessors are the foundation of industry-standard personal computing. They provide the functional base from which the Intel microprocessor family has continued to evolve in function and performance, and they have set the programming standards used to develop the large number of software products available today for personal computers. However, innovation in the software industry has outgrown the 8086/88 architecture. The performance and function provided by this architecture have become an impediment to the development of more powerful software applications.

The 8086 and 8088 both use a 16-bit internal architecture and provide 16-bit registers and a 16-bit instruction set. The only difference between the two processors is that the 8086 uses a 16-bit external bus to reference memory, whereas the 8088 uses an 8-bit external bus. Their addressing mechanism is a simple one. During program memory references, the contents of the segment register are shifted left by 4 bits and added to the offset to form a 20-bit physical memory address. This address provides software programs with direct access to 1 MB of physical memory.

The 8086/88 programming model is based on a segmented memory model in which the code and data portions of a program are partitioned into variable length segments up to 64KB in size. In this model, the 8086/88 microprocessors provide an environment appropriate for developing relatively simple operating systems and applications.

As applications have increased in sophistication, the limits of the 8086/88 architecture have become evident. The 1 MB physical memory constraint has forced some applications to resort to complex memory management techniques, such as overlays, that typically place performance and function limitations on those applications. In addition, operating systems with the required functions to support the complexity of new applications have been limited due to the memory size constraints and the direct accessibility of physical memory and I/O devices by applications.

80286 Expands Limits

The next step in the evolution of Intel microprocessors was the 80286, also based on a 16-bit architecture, but with significant improvements in the areas limited by the 8086/88. The 80286 provides two different modes of operation: real and protected. In real mode, the 16-bit instruction set, the segmented programming model, addressing mechanism, and 1 MB physical memory limitations are identical to those provided by the 8086/88. This compatibility allows most application programs developed for the 8086/88 to execute on the 80286. Execution of these applications in real mode benefits primarily from the faster execution speed offered by the 80286-based computers.

The 80286's protected mode addresses up to 16 MB of physical memory and implements a hierarchical memory protection model that is necessary for the implementation of more sophisticated operating systems. Unfortunately, a basic incompatibility between real and protected modes has hindered development of protected mode operating systems that make available to applications the new capabilities of protected mode while also allowing real mode applications to execute.

The protected mode's memory protection model is based on four privilege levels (0 to 3) that can be used to manage access to system memory and I/O devices. Typically, the operating system executes at the highest privilege level (0) and has the ability to access all system memory and I/O resources. Applications, on the other hand, usually execute at the lowest privilege level in which access to memory and I/O resources is limited.

Applications can, however, access operating system and other higher-privilege services that have access to a wider range of system resources by transferring control to those services via *gates*. Gates are used to transfer execution between routines at different privilege levels. For example, call gates can provide access to operating system services that allow applications to access protected system resources indirectly. Other gates—interrupt, trap, and task—are used for interprivilege-level transfers, such as those of execution between tasks and interrupt handlers.

Memory protection is accomplished by assigning to each memory segment a privilege level that is placed in the segment's descriptor entry. This level determines the minimum privilege a program must have to access that segment. An I/O privilege level is also assigned in the flags register to define the level of privilege necessary for a program to perform direct I/O to devices. Combined, the memory and I/O privilege levels assigned to system resources by the operating system define which programs can access these resources.

Similarly, the operating system assigns to each application a privilege level of execution. This privilege level is placed in the least two significant bits of the program *code segment* (CS) register. Programs that are assigned a lower privilege (higher numerical value) than that required to access a memory segment are prevented by the 80286 from accessing that segment. If such a program attempts to access a memory segment of higher privilege level, a general protection fault (interrupt 0DH) occurs. Similar results occur if a program whose privilege level is lower than that assigned to *I/O devices* (IOPL) attempts to access an I/O device directly.

By using the least significant bits of the segment registers to contain the privilege level of the executing program, the memory-addressing mechanism is made to function differently in protected mode than in real mode. As a result, the vast number of applications developed for the 8086/88 cannot be executed in protected mode and thus cannot take advantage of the increased memory capacity of the 80286.

Figures 2-1 and 2-2 show the addressing mechanism used in the protected mode of both the 80286 and the 80386. In this mode, the content of the segment registers is used, during a memory access, as an index into one of several descriptor tables that define how the physical memory is partitioned in the system. Using the three least significant bits in the segment registers to define the privilege level (0 to 3) and descriptor table (global or local) make the use of the segment register contents incompatible with that of the 8086/88 and 80286 real mode. For example, in the 8086/88, general data, unrelated to segment information, can be stored in the segment registers. Some 8086 programs use their knowledge of segment/offset addressing by placing the value 0 in a segment register. On an 8086, this provides access to the low 64KB of memory. On an 80286 in protected mode, this typically results in a memory protection fault, because the segment register bits have different meanings.

The 80286 also offers task management facilities via the *task state segment* (TSS) data structure, which allows an operating system to assign a TSS to each task in the system and to store in the TSS the execution state (for example, register contents and flags) associated with that task. The TSS functions make an efficient transition from one task to another by saving the current task's execution parameters quickly in the TSS and restoring the execution parameters of the new task from its corresponding TSS data structure.

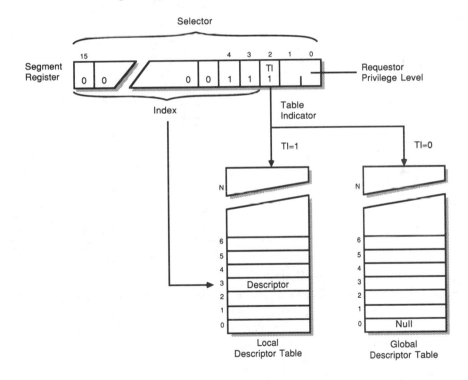

Figure 2-1: Segment Registers in 80286/80386 Protected Mode
A 16-bit segment register selects the segment by indexing either the global (GDT) or local (LDT) descriptor table. Typically, each task has its own LDT.

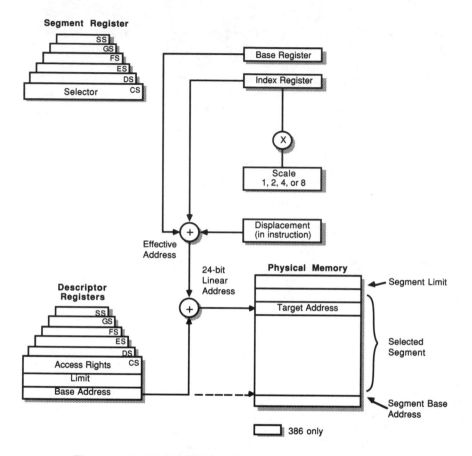

Figure 2-2: 80286/80386 Protected Mode Addressing
Both the 80286 and 80386 allow addressing through a combination of displacement and base/index registers. The 80386 provides additional segment registers FS and GS and allows the index registers to be scaled (multiplied) by 1, 2, 4, or 8.

A Few Constraints

Powerful applications that have been especially developed to run in protected mode face a number of constraints in the 80286 segmented programming model. For large applications, such as artificial-intelligence-based expert systems, the 64KB segment size limitation forces the developer to partition an application into multiple code and data segments. Thus, the operating system cannot relieve the application (or its source language) from the burden of managing code and data segments).

The segmentation model of the 80286 also hinders the porting of applications developed for microprocessors that use a large linear address programming model, such as the Motorola 68000. Porting such an application to the Intel family would probably require a major redesign of the application in order to partition it into multiple code and data segments.

Other constraints in the 80286 functions have also slowed certain areas of operating system development. For example, the 80286 lacks some of the functions needed to implement an effective virtual memory system. The advantage of such a system is the ability concurrently to execute single or multiple applications, the total memory requirement of which exceeds the total amount of physical memory installed in the system.

Such sophisticated memory management techniques have long been used in mainframe and minicomputer products and are becoming essential for microcomputers. The requirement in certain environments for running multiple applications concurrently has increased the need for these memory management techniques.

Stepping up to 32 Bits

Given these limitations of the 80286, the time seemed right for yet another advancement in microprocessors—and Intel introduced the 80386. It is built on a 32-bit internal and external bus architecture and features a full complement of 32-bit registers (see Figure 2-3), a subset of which can be used to perform 16-bit operations compatible with those of the 8086/88 and the 80286.

All 16-bit registers present on the 80286 can be accessed on the 80386 by the same names (*AX*, *BX*, etc.). Their 32-bit counterparts are accessed as extensions of the 16-bit registers (*EAX*, *EBX*, etc.).

All instruction prefetch operations are made on a 32-bit basis, thus taking full advantage of the bandwidth of the memory bus. As a result of this more effective prefetching method and for optimization with the larger average instruction size, the size of the prefetch queue has been increased from that of previous microprocessors to hold three double words (12 bytes).

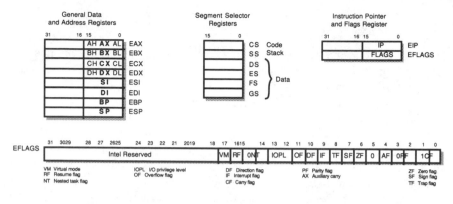

Figure 2-3: 80386 General Registers and Flags

Most registers are expanded to 32 bits in the 80386. Instruction prefix bytes determine if the 16- or 32-bit register is used.

The instruction pipelining capability allows the parallel fetching, decoding, and execution of instructions. The execution unit can execute an instruction while the instruction decode unit is decoding the following instruction and the bus control unit is prefetching yet a third instruction. Similarly, for instructions that require memory or I/O bus cycles, the bus control unit can generally perform bus cycles simultaneously with the execution of internal cycles that do not require bus activity.

An example of the efficiency of instruction pipelining is found in the execution of an iteration of the repeat move string (*REP MOVS*) instruction. An iteration (not the first execution of the repeated *MOVS* instruction) of this instruction requires four execution cycles and two memory bus accesses (one to read and one to write). In a system with a pipelined zero-wait-state memory architecture, where each 32-bit memory bus access is performed in two cycles, the four bus cycles are performed in parallel with the four CPU execution cycles. The parallel execution of internal and bus cycles yields a 32-bit memory move time of 250 nanoseconds (ns), or four 62.5-ns cycles at 16 MHz.

Bus pipelining is also an important advance of the 80386. It maximizes memory bus activity and allows 80386-based designs to use more cost-effective memory subsystems than equivalent 80286-based systems. With bus pipelining, the 80386 places the control and address signals of the next bus cycle on its external bus while the current bus cycle is still in progress. This allows the memory subsystem to start decoding the next bus operation while the current operation is completing. As a result, the memory control circuitry and memory devices have a longer time to decode memory cycles.

Using bus pipelining, a 32-bit memory access can be accomplished, depending on the speed and design of the memory subsystem, as fast as 125 ns (two 62.5-ns cycles in a 16-MHz zero-wait-state bus operation). This access time compares favorably with the 1 microsecond (16 cycles at 62.5 ns) required to access 32 bits of information via the 8-MHz one-wait-state, 16-bit-bus of typical 80286 computers. Figure 2-4 shows the operation of bus pipelining. The memory subsystem indicates to the 80386 via the next address signal (*NA#*) that it is ready to accept the address and control signals for the second cycle while the first cycle is still in progress (the # symbol indicates the signal is active in its low state). The 80386 places the control (*BE0#-BE3#*, *M/IO#*, *D/C#*, *W/R#*) and address (A2-A31) signals on the bus and indicates the validity of these signals with a negative transition of address status (*ADS#*). The memory subsystem uses this transition of *ADS#* to latch the control and address signals and to start decoding the operation for the next bus cycle (cycle 2). When cycle 1 completes, the memory subsystem then activates the *READY#* signal to indicate to the 80386 that it is ready to start cycle 2, the address and control signals of which have already been decoded during the execution of cycle 1. Having the decoding already accomplished allows the memory system to complete the memory bus cycle time in two CPU clock cycles.

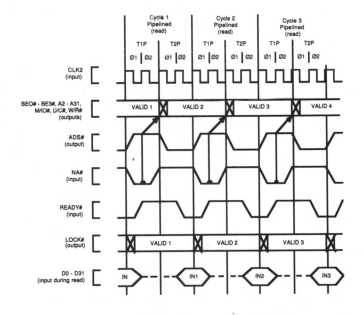

Figure 2-4: Bus Pipelining Operation

A fast memory subsystem can use the next address (NA#) line to overlap the fetching of one operand with the address decoding of the next operand.

Instruction Enhancements

The instruction set of the 80386 is a superset of that found in the 8086/88 and 80286 microprocessors. Its highlights are as follows:

- Instructions such as *multiply* (MUL) have been optimized by using an early-out algorithm in which the most significant bits of the multiplier are 0. This allows a multiply instruction to execute in 0.56 microsecond (that is, 9 cycles * 62.5 ns at 16 MHz).

- The scaled index address mode has been added for instructions using memory references. This address mode permits the contents of an index register to be scaled—that is, multiplied by 1, 2, 4, or 8—before being added to the base. This allows for efficient indexing into data arrays with multiple-byte entries. For example, the instruction:

```
MOV EAX, [EDI*8][EBX]
```

can retrieve into *EAX* a double word from a data array with its base address stored in *EBX*. The number of the entry to be accessed (0 = first entry) is stored in *EDI* with the multiplier, in this case indicating an array with eight bytes per entry.

- A 64-bit barrel shifter in the 80386 execution unit optimizes shift, multiply, and divide operations. With the barrel shifter, multiple-bit shift operations can be executed in one clock cycle. The new *shift right double* (SHRD) and *shift left double* (SHLD) instructions use this capability to allow bit string manipulations typically found in BITBLT graphics routines. The SHRD and SHLD instructions use two 32-bit registers to allow a 64-bit string to be shifted multiple positions in a single CPU clock cycle. These instructions allow BITBLT operations to execute on the 80386 in a small fraction of the time possible on the 80286 using multiple shift operations.

- Support for 32-bit operands and addresses has been added to the instruction set. The 32-bit operand capabilities are available in all modes of the 80386. In real mode, the default size of the operands and addresses is 16 bits, but can be overridden by a prefix byte. This is necessary to maintain full compatibility with programs developed for the 8086/88 and 80286. In protected mode, operand and address size is governed by a bit in the segment descriptor. Use of the 32-bit operands and addresses in each 80386 mode is covered later.

A 4 GB Improvement

Protected mode of the 80386 features a large linear address programming model. Using this facility, the maximum size of a segment can be increased to 4 GB from the traditional 64KB. In this programming model, large applications can reside in a single protected mode segment, thus eliminating the need for the application to manage multiple code and data segments.

Protected mode operating systems such as Xenix/386 provide the linear address programming model to applications. The operating system sets the maximum size of an application segment by specifying a 20-bit segment limit and setting the granularity bit in the segment descriptor (see Figure 2-5). When this bit is set to 0, the segment limit is specified in bytes and yields a maximum segment size of 1 MB. Byte granularity is the default value in the descriptor and allows compatibility with programs written for the 80286. When the granularity bit is set to 1, the segment granularity is in pages (4KB per page). This granularity yields a maximum segment size of 4GB.

											Byte Address
31									0		
Segment Base 15...0				Segment Limit 15...0							0
Base 31...0	G	D	0	0	Limit 19...16	P	DPL	S	TYPE	A	Base 23...16	+4

Base	Base address of the segment	A	Accessed bit
Limit	The length of the segment	G	Granularity bit: 1 = segment length is page
DPL	Descriptor privilege level: 0 - 3		granular; 0 = segment length is byte granular
S	Segment descriptor: 0 = system descriptor	D	Default operation size (recognized in code
	1 = code or data segment descriptor		segment descriptors only): 1 = 32-bit segment;
TYPE	If system descriptor, TYPE indicates TSS, LDT, or		0 = 16-bit segment
	GATE; if code or data descriptor, TYPE indicates	P	Present bit: 1 = present; 0 = not present
	reading, writing, or executing privileges	0	Bit must be zero for compatibility with future processors

Figure 2-5: 80386 Segment Descriptor
A segment's starting memory address, size (up to 4GB), and attributes are all given by its segment descriptor.

Intel has added memory paging functions to the 80386 to allow linear addresses (as seen by programs) to be mapped to physical memory addresses. This facility allows the efficient implementation of virtual memory systems. In virtual memory systems, the operating system creates an environment that allows execution of single or multiple applications that are larger than the installed physical memory. The operating system stores on disk the portions of the application that are least recently used. Then, as code or data portions of the application are needed for execution, the operating system brings them into memory from disk, while restoring to disk the contents of the least recently used portions of memory. This operation occurs transparently to the application, which perceives the entire program as being memory-resident.

With memory paging support, such as that implemented in the 80386 with a 4KB page size, the operating system can easily allocate contiguous memory to an application simply by mapping a number of noncontiguous physical memory pages into the requested logical program space. This mapping is performed by updating the page directory and tables. Figure 2-6 shows how the page directory and tables are used to translate the 32-bit linear address that the program sees into a noncontiguous set of physical memory pages.

A set of control registers, shown in Figure 2-7, governs the operation of memory paging. Paging is enabled by setting a bit 31 in control register *CR3*. Another control register (*CR3*) is set by the operating system software to point to the location in memory that contains the base of the page directory table. This table, together with the page tables, defines the translation between the 32-bit linear address that is derived from the segmentation model and a 32-bit physical memory address.

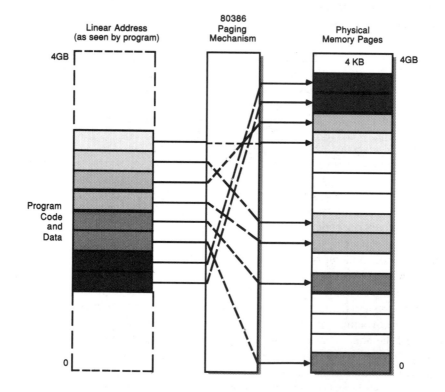

Figure 2-6: Linear to Physical Address Conversion

The 80386 paging mechanism maps the program's linear address space into physical memory. The operating system decides how pages are mapped.

The page directory is 4KB in size. This table size allows up to 1,024 page directory entries, each containing the address of a 4KB page frame in physical memory. Figure 2-8 shows how the memory paging mechanism generates a 32-bit physical address from the 32-bit linear address output by the segmentation unit.

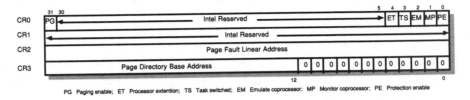

Figure 2-7: 80386 Control Registers

CR0 regulates memory management and coprocessor handling. CR1 is reserved by Intel. CR2 is set by the 80386 to the linear address that last generated a page default. CR3 is the physical address of the page directory, which is always page-aligned.

The page table entries also contain bits that are updated by the 80386 in order to help the operating system manage the memory pages. A *dirty flag* is set to 1 by the 80386 whenever a page is written to. This lets the operating system know that the contents of the page have been modified since the last time it was brought in from disk. An *accessed bit* also is set by the 80386 whenever a page is read or written to. This bit allows the operating system to determine which memory pages have been most recently accessed.

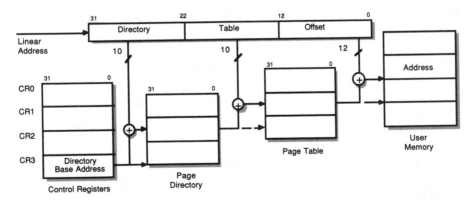

Figure 2-8: 80386 Memory Paging Mechanism

A two-level scheme is used to access a page.. In a linear address, bits 22–31 act as an index into the page directory, selecting a page table. Bits 12–21 index into the selected page table to designate the page. Bits 0–11 give the offset onto the 4,096-byte page. A page cache is used to avoid this look-up for commonly used pages.

Another feature that helps the operating system implement memory management functions is the use of the *present bit* in the page table entries. When a page is swapped to disk, the operating system marks the page table entry as not present. If an access occurs to a page that is not present in memory, the 80386 generates a page fault. The fault signals the operating system that the page whose linear address is stored in control register 2 should be brought into memory. As the page is brought into memory, the operating system updates the page table entry as present and returns from the page fault to perform the desired memory access.

To support the memory paging functions without accessing the page directory tables on each memory access, the 80386 contains an internal 32-entry cache called the *translation lookaside buffer* (TLB). This cache automatically keeps the address of the 32 most recently used page table entries for speedy look-up during memory accesses. The operating system must flush the contents of the cache whenever a page table entry is marked not present in order to maintain coherency between the cache and the pages present in memory. The contents of the cache are flushed whenever CR3 is written to.

When the TSS data structures are used by the operating system to perform task management functions, the address of the page directory (*CR3*) associated with a task is saved in its TSS when a task context switch is performed. Because a single page directory entry has the capacity to address a full page table of 1,024 entries (4MB of memory), it is doubtful that an entire page directory would be assigned to each task. A single page directory entry per task should suffice in most cases.

The 80386 offers I/O permission functions that are an extension of the I/O protection level (IOPL) mechanism found on the 80286. The basic IOPL mechanism prevents applications with low privilege levels from accessing any I/O device without the intervention of the operating system. This mechanism has been extended on the 80386 to allow the operating system to specify the I/O devices (I/O addresses) that it wants to protect from direct access by applications. This capability is useful in the 80386's virtual-8086 mode (described later) where it prevents direct access to I/O devices by 8086/88 applications and simulates low-bandwidth I/O devices.

The I/O devices to be protected by an operating system are specified via the I/O permission bit map, a variable length map where each bit corresponds to a byte I/O port address. When I/O operations are performed to a device address whose corresponding I/O permission bit is 1, control is transferred by the 80386 to the operating system via a general protection fault. The operating system then can take the appropriate action to protect or simulate a specific I/O device at the accessed I/O address. The base address of the I/O permission bit map is contained in the active TSS and is automatically saved on a task context switch. Because each task is likely to have access to different devices, each task should normally have its own I/O permission bit map.

Modes of Operation

Real mode is the default mode of the 80386 upon reset. This allows the 80386 to begin execution in a manner compatible with the 8086/88 and 80286. The memory addressing mechanism, 1MB memory limitation, and 64KB-maximum segmented programming model are identical to real mode in the 80286. Most programs written for the 8086/88 and 80286 should run without modification. For a discussion of trouble areas, see the accompanying section "Programming Considerations for the Intel Family."

The key distinction between 80386 real mode and that of its predecessors is its support of 32-bit operands and addresses in the instruction set. By using override instruction prefixes for operand size and address size, the 16-bit default nature of instruction operands and addresses can be specified to be 32 bits in size. The specification of 32-bit operands yields significant performance benefits in arithmetic and memory transfer operations. The 32-bit addressing feature is less important in real mode due to the maximum segment limit of 64KB and the 1MB physical address limitation, but it does allow the use of the extended addressing specifications, such as scaled indexing with the full register set available as base and index.

The operand size prefix (66H), when used preceding an instruction in real mode, indicates that the operands to be used are 32 bits. For example, when the instruction *MOV AX,BX* is preceded by the operand size prefix, the result is an instruction that moves the 32-bit register *EAX* to *EAX*. Similarly, the address size prefix (67H) can be used on individual instructions to specify extended addressing and can be used in combination with the operand size prefix. With both the operand size and address size override prefixes, an instruction can be created, such as:

```
MOV EBX, [EAX][ESI*4]ARRAY + 80
```

This specifies a base value (*EAX*), a scaled index value (*ESI*$*), and a displacement (*ARRAY + 80*) that are combined to form an offset, the 32-bit contents of which are placed into the *EBX* register. Other improvements are available in

80386 real mode. For more information, see the accompanying section "Making the Most of the 80386 Today."

Protected mode in the 80386 offers a superset of the functions found in that mode in the 80286. The privilege-level-based memory and I/O protection system, 8-and 16-bit operand modes, and 64KB-maximum segmented programming model of the 80286 are supported in the 80386's protected mode. In addition, memory paging, large linear address space, and the I/O permission bit map can be used in protected mode.

The TSS, introduced in the 80286, now includes data defined by the operating system software as well as the hardware registers. The 80386 I/O permission bit map, which allows precise control over I/O port usage, is also contained in the new TSS.

The 80386 protected mode includes a more effective mechanism to switch to real mode. In the 80286, protected mode is entered by setting the protection enable (PE) bit in the machine status word. Once set, the PE bit in the 80286 cannot be reset. The 80286 must be reset to return to real mode, an operation taking hundreds of microseconds. The 80386 can be returned to real mode simply by resetting the PE bit in control register 0.

The 80386 protected mode provides a programming environment fully compatible with that of the 80286; 16-bit protected mode applications can be executed because the segment descriptors function the same as those on the 80286 when initialized for use by programs for the 80286. For example, when initialized for use by such a program, the granularity (G bit) in the segment descriptors (see Figure 2-5) is set to 0, indicating byte granularity. This yields memory segments compatible with the 64KB maximum limit of the 80286. Similarly, the default operation size (D bit) is set to 0, indicating the use of 16-bit operands and addresses equivalent to those of the 80286.

When 80386 descriptors are initialized for use by programs developed for the 80386, the additional capabilities of protected mode can be enabled to create a 32-bit programming environment. Full 32-bit applications (using 32-bit operands and addresses) can execute without instruction prefixes, as is the case in real mode. In addition, the 32-bit programming environment provides data segments of 4GB maximum size by selecting the page granularity in the corresponding descriptors.

Combined, the 16-bit compatibility features and additional functions of 80386 protected mode make it ideal for multitasking operating systems supporting a variety of programming environments. An operating system can provide a virtual memory multitasking environment capable of concurrently executing 16-and 32-bit protected mode applications. The nature of each application (16-or 32-bit) is determined by the configuration of its segment descriptors.

Full Family Compatibility

When combined with virtual-8086 mode (an extension of protected mode), the 80386 provides compatibility with applications developed for the 8086/88 while simultaneously providing a full, 32-bit large linear address programming environment in its protected mode. With this capability an operating system can provide a multiplicity of programming environments that span those in the entire Intel microprocessor family. This family compatibility makes virtual-8086 mode one of the most significant advances of the 80386. (Virtual in this context refers to a technique whereby an entire processor environment, or machine, is transparently simulated; the term should not be confused with virtual memory techniques used in demand-paged operating systems.)

Virtual environments have historically been used as bridges to provide upward compatibility with existing applications while offering a new environment with enhanced functions and performance. An example of this concept is IBM's virtual machine (VM) operating system architecture for its mainframe systems. VM allows existing applications to be used for production work while new applications that take full advantage of the features of the new machines are being developed.

Virtual-8086 mode allows virtualization of only a real mode environment. Applications for the 8086/88 can execute transparently in virtual-8086 mode under control of a protected mode operating system. These applications perceive that they are running in real mode while actually executing in virtual-8086 mode. Virtual-8086 mode, however, does not provide for execution of 80286 or 80386 protected mode software under supervision of a higher-level program—no level exists that is logically higher in privilege than 0. The 80386 does not allow a protected mode operating system to execute under the control of another like system.

Technically, virtual-8086 mode is a subset of protected mode and is enabled by setting the VM bit in the flags register (see Figure 2-3). In a multitasking, protected mode operating system, virtual-8086 mode is enabled when an 8086/88 application is executed. The primary difference between virtual-8086 and protected modes is in the interpretation of the segment registers. In virtual-8086 mode, the normal protected mode segmentation unit is bypassed and the linear address is calculated as it is in real mode—the segment register value is shifted left by 4 bits and added to the offset. Although the 32-bit addressing modes are allowed in virtual-8086 mode (by use of instruction prefixes), segments are still limited to 64KB, limiting the value of 32-bit addressing. The 64KB limitation also means that virtual-8086 mode addressing is confined to the same 1 MB physical address of the 8086/88.

Applications that are designed for the 8086/88 execute transparently in virtual-8086 mode. The main difference between execution in virtual-8086 and real modes is that in virtual-8086 mode all interrupts are vectored through the protected mode *interrupt descriptor table* (IDT). When a hardware, software, or processor trap interrupt occurs, the IDT entry for that interrupt, typically an interrupt or task gate initialized by the protected mode operating system, causes the VM bit to be reset. The interrupt handler, executing in protected mode, can either take care of the interrupt itself or reflect the interrupt back to the code that normally would have been invoked in the 8086/88 application. This reflection is accomplished by retrieving the appropriate target address from the 8086-equivalent interrupt vectors (the table of 4-byte vectors starting at virtual address 00000000), manipulating the stack frame to contain the address of the 8086/88 interrupt handler, and returning to virtual-8086 mode. The interception and reflection of interrupts is one of the basic functions of a protected mode operating system supervising the execution of an 8086/88 application in virtual-8086 mode.

The other differences between virtual-8086 and real modes involve privileged instructions, IOPL sensitivity, and I/O permission. The ability to control the use of privileged instructions and access to I/O devices in virtual-8086 mode allows the operating system to maintain concurrency between 8086 and protected mode applications. Privileged instructions cause a general protection fault if executed at a privilege level other than 0. Because code executes at privilege level 3 in virtual-8086 mode (real mode implicitly executes at level 0), these instructions trap to the operating system, which executes at level 0. *Load machine status word* (LMSW) and *load global descriptor table* (LGDT) are examples of privileged instructions. Execution of these instructions typically indicates a program's intent to enter protected mode. An application that executes these instructions is usually aborted by the operating system because protected mode applications are not allowed to execute in virtual-8086 mode.

Sensitive instructions are those whose operation is affected by the current IOPL. Again because virtual-8086 mode code runs at privilege level 3, the 2-bit IOPL field in the flags register (Figure 2-3) must be set to 3 to avoid traps on these instructions. The sensitive instructions in virtual-8086 mode are software interrupt (*INT*), interrupt return (*IRET*), and push and pop flags (*PUSHF/POPF*). Though

INT is IOPL-sensitive in both protected and virtual-8086 mode, *PUSHF*, *POPF*, and *IRET* are sensitive only in virtual-8086 mode. This allows the operating system to keep track of and virtualize the interrupt flag. For example, an 8086/88 application can attempt to disable hardware interrupts with the clear interrupt flag (*CLI*) instruction. The operating system can make interrupts appear disabled to the application and continue to handle hardware interrupts necessary for operating system administrative functions (such as system timers) and other concurrent protected mode applications.

The I/O permission facility allows the operating system to control selected I/O ports. The operating system can set up an I/O permission bit map in the TSS corresponding to the virtual-8086 mode application. The bit map can define specific I/O ports as protected. Any *IN* or *OUT* instructions that refer to a protected I/O port will trap to the operating system, which can either emulate or directly execute the instruction.

In all these cases, the operating system decides whether or not a particular instruction will appear to be executed. This action is totally transparent to the program running in virtual-8086 mode—as far as the program is concerned, an emulated instruction appears to have been executed by the 80386 microprocessor. The only potential difference is that simulated instructions or operations may take longer to execute. Through the use of the 80386's paged memory management features, an operating system can allow more than one 8086/88 machine to be simulated at a time, thus permitting multiple 8086/88 applications to coexist with each other as well as with 32-bit applications. This capability would typically be used in concert with hardware simulation so that each application would see an entire machine, complete with the simulated, peripheral hardware.

To simulate the programming environment of one or more 8086/88 machines, the operating system would provide support for interrupt handling and for the instruction and I/O emulation just as outlined above. In the case of a single, virtual-8086 environment, memory paging would not be enabled and the single virtual-8086 machine would execute in the first physical megabyte of memory, just as it would in real mode. The operating system would normally reside in memory past the first (physical) megabyte or in reserved and/or protected memory within the first megabyte of memory. If multiple 8086/88 machine simulations are desired, or if it is necessary to execute a single 8086/88 machine in a physical location other than the first megabyte, then the paging mechanism must be enabled.

Because the segmentation unit is bypassed in virtual-8086 mode, the paging unit is the only memory management method available to virtual-8086 mode programs. The paging mechanism allows the 1 MB address space of virtual-8086 mode to be simulated anywhere in physical memory. Via memory paging the 1 MB contiguous memory space of virtual-8086 mode can be created from up to 256 physical memory pages (1MB address space/4KB per page). Each of these pages can be located anywhere within the 4GB physical address space of the 80386 and need not by physically contiguous, allowing great flexibility. Using the 80386 memory paging functions, a demand-paged operating system can manage memory for multiple virtual-8086 mode machine simulations concurrently with protected mode applications. Memory paging also can be used to allow each 8086/88 machine simulation to have access to common routines and data, such as a system ROM, by making the physical ROM appear in the memory space of each simulated machine. Actually, only one ROM exists, but each machine sees it at the expected address within its 1 MB address space. Figure 2-9 shows how the 80386 paging mechanism enables multiple virtual-86 machines to be managed; a single copy of the 8086/88 operating system is made to appear in the address space of both machines.

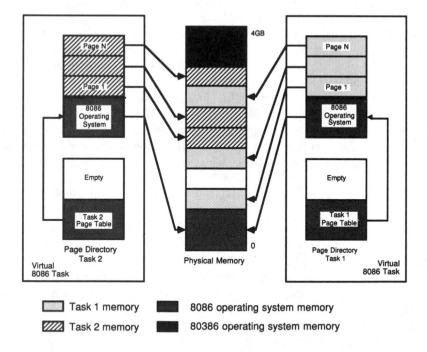

Figure 2-9: Virtual-8086 Mode Memory Management

The paging mechanism gives each virtual-8086 task a 1MB linear address space. Read-only areas, such as the 8086 operating system, can reside on shared pages used by all virtual-8086 tasks. Unused pages can be omitted from physical memory.

For further reference, the following literature can be obtained from the Intel Corporation by calling this toll-free number: 800/548-4725.

PROCESSOR	NUMBER	Order TITLE PRICE		
8086/88	The iAPX 88 Book	210200	$20.95
80286	Introduction to the iAPX 286	210308	No charge
	iAPX 286 Programmer's Reference	210498	20.95
	iAPX 286 Hardware Reference	210760	20.95
	iAPX 286 Operating System Writer's Guide	121960	50.00
80386	Introduction to the 80386 (including the 80386 Data Sheet)	231746	No charge
	80386 Programmer's Reference	230985	25.00
	80386 Hardware Reference	231732	25.00
	80386 System Software Writer's Guide	231499	23.00
	80386 Data Sheet	231630	No charge

Intel References
For further reference, the following literature can be obtained from the Intel Corporation by calling this toll-free number: 800/548-4725.

Virtual Performance

The performance of applications executed in virtual-8086 mode is typically lower than in real mode in the same processor, because an operating system is intervening to handle interrupts and emulate certain instructions. The trap operation alone usually takes significantly longer to execute than the instruction that cause it. To this is added the execution time of the code that saves and restores machine state and emulates the instruction. Fortunately, the instructions that must be emulated are relatively few in number and frequency of occurrence. The primary impact is in interrupt-intensive programs, because straight code tends to execute unimpeded in virtual-8086 mode.

Like the instructions themselves, simulated hardware should not be expected to have the same performance as the actual hardware. Differences in performance depend upon the device used. Performance is also affected when simulating more than one 8086/88 machine at a time.

The 80386 provides unprecedented compatibility with previous members of the Intel family while providing the advanced functions required for the development of sophisticated virtual memory operating systems in which 8086/88 applications can coexist with 16-and 32-bit protected mode applications. Even without such advanced operating system software, it is possible to take advantage of the 80386 by using its new instructions and 32-bit data manipulations. Future software advances will unlock the full power of the 80386.

Programming Considerations for the Intel Family

In general, software developed for one member of the Intel microprocessor family executes without modification on the others. However, when a software product is under development, the developer should follow a few rules to ensure the product's upward compatibility and its migration to the higher-performance members of the family. Some generally accepted guidelines are listed here.

- A program that is intended to run on all Intel processors should be written to the least common denominator, the 8086/88.

- Any use, implicit or explicit, of the values of registers, flags, or data structures that are declared undefined or reserved in the Intel documentation should be avoided. For example, a program that uses the reserved fields of an 80286 descriptor most likely will not run on an 80386. The multiply (*MUL*) instruction provides another example; the state of the zero flag is listed as undefined following the execution of *MUL*. A program that depends on the state of the zero flag after *MUL* is executed on one member of the family may behave differently when run on another member.

- A program should not depend on the power-on state of the processor registers. The value of the various registers and flags after reset is different on the different processors. The program should explicitly load the required register values.

- Instruction opcodes that are not explicitly documented in the Intel literature should not be used. An opcode that is not part of the supported instruction set for a particular processor may be defined differently in a later processor, even if the opcode appeared to have a function in the earlier processor.

- An application should not contain self-modifying code. Due to the difference in prefetch queue length for the various processors, an instruction modification sequence that works correctly on one processor may not modify the target instruction until after it has been prefetched on a different processor. In this case, the unmodified instruction would be executed rather than the modified instruction.

- Because of increases in clock speed and optimizations in the architecture, the 80286 and 80386 tend to execute specific code sequences significantly faster than the 8086/88. In addition, systems based on the same processor may run at different clock speeds. Any code that interacts with realtime events or depends on its execution time to perform its function should use a timing source that is independent of the processor clock speed. Execution-speed-independent timing services are typically provided by the operating system and/or a hardware timer.

- Each peripheral chip or controller in a system has a minimum I/O recovery time—that is, the time required by that peripheral between successive I/O cycles. If a peripheral was designed for operation in an 8086/88 system, this minimum I/O recovery time may be violated when the peripheral is used in the pipelined bus architecture of an 80286-or 80386-based system. In general, 8086/88 I/O speed can be simulated by inserting a *JMP $+2* instruction between successive I/O cycles to the same peripheral.

- Routines for the 80286 and 80386 should not be sensitive to the state of the PE bit in the machine status word. Although the 80386 virtual-8086 mode runs with real-mode semantics, it executes with the PE bit set in the machine status word indicating protected mode. The visibility of the PE bit via the store machine status word (SMSW) instruction may cause problems for dual-mode code—that is, code that attempts to act differently based on whether the processor is executing in real or protected mode.

Most of these guidelines are based on common sense; nonetheless, many applications violate one or more of them and therefore fail on one of the Intel processors. One reason may be that the application has been debugged and tested on one processor before another processor is available. In all cases, the appropriate Intel literature should be consulted.

Making the Most of the 80386 Today

Although operating systems that fully support the features of the 80386 may not be available today, the programmer can take advantage of many 80386 features in real-mode programs now.

Many instructions such as the immediate forms of *ADD* and *SUB*tract have been optimized by directly decreasing the number of cycles required for execution. Others such as *MUL*tiply execute in fewer average cycles due to internal algorithm optimizations. Nothing special is required of the programmer to invoke these improvements; they are built into the 80386 architecture.

The operand size prefix (66H) can be used to achieve 32-bit data operations. This allows the programmer to take advantage of the extended 32-bit register set for 32-bit arithmetic and logic operations. For example, *DB 66H/ADD AX,BX* is equivalent to *ADD EAX,EBX*. The operand size prefix also can be used to speed data manipulations by taking advantage of the full 32-bit width of the 80386 internal and external data paths. One of the most dramatic improvements to existing code can be realized by the use of a 32-bit repeated string move instruction (*REP MOVS*) in block move operations.

Two additional segment registers, *FS* and *GS*, are available along with the instructions needed to manipulate them. No explanation of the desirability of extra segment registers is necessary to anyone who has programmed the Intel family.

The new double-shift instructions, SHLD/SHRD, allow the manipulation of full-width (32-bit) bit strings within a double-width (64-bit) bit space. This allows the efficient implementation of such graphics primitives as BITBLT. Because the maximum shift entity on the 8086/88 and the 80286 has been 16 bits, routines such as BITBLT have typically been limited to 8-bit manipulations.

A full set of conditional jumps with 16-bit displacements is provided. This eliminates the awkward instruction sequence often required (jumping around a jump) when the destination of a conditional jump is more than 127 bytes away.

The move with sign-extension (*MOVSX*) and move with zero-extension (*MOVZX*) instructions allow small operands to be moved into larger ones in a single instruction with automatic size conversion. The high-order part of the destination is filled with the high bit of the source or zeroes. These may be most useful in manipulating the 32-bit register set, but they also allow functions such as *MOVZX DI,AL* to be done in a single instruction.

A complete set of single-bit instructions alleviates the time-consuming masking and test-and-set/reset operations that characterize many operating system primitives, such as manipulating the bits in a task's status word. Having a single-instruction implementation assures the indivisible execution of these functions, freeing the programmer from the overhead of framing the operation with the typical *CLI/STI*.

The byte set on condition instructions set the destination operand to 0 or 1 depending on the setting of the specified condition flag. This is a useful function for high-level language interfaces that pass status information in registers or memory rather than in the CPU flags. These instructions provide direct translation from CPU status to a byte register or memory operand.

Although addressing is limited by real-mode semantics to 64KB segments and a 1MB address space, the address size prefix (67H) allows the use of the extended addressing modes of the 80386 in real mode. When the address size prefix is used, any register can be used as base and index registers, with or without the scaling options. The coding of the Mod R/M byte is different in this case, making manual encoding difficult.

A single-precision uncharacterized multiply instruction complements the immediate form of IMUL that was added to the 80286, but removes the implicit register characterization; therefore, the destination operand can be specified as something other than the *AX* register.

New debug registers allow the implementation of a software debugger with hardware debugging capabilities. The debug registers can be programmed to cause a trap when a specific memory location is read or written or when an instruction is executed at that address. This capability previously required external breakpoint hardware.

Selective use of these features can result in applications that achieve high performance relative to the 8086/88 and 80286. It may be desirable, however, for the same application to execute on all members of the Intel family. One approach is to optimize portions of an application that benefit most from the features of the 80386. These optimized portions would be executed only when the application is run on an 80386-based system.

3
Programming on the 80386 [*]

_____ *Ross Nelson*_____

Intel recently introduced the 80386, its entry into the 32-bit microprocessor derby. The 80386 can run all programs developed for the 80286, which in turn runs programs designed for the 8086 and 8088. Because of this compatibility with its widely used predecessors, the 80386 is likely to be very popular. The 80386 (or 386 for short) is not merely bigger and faster, however; Intel has made some significant architectural changes as well. The enhancements that I'll examine in this chapter include the elimination of the 64K segment restriction; enhanced instruction set and operand addressing; the ability to run 32-bit and 16-bit software simulataneously; and virtual memory support, including paging.

Operating Modes

Like its predecessor the 286, the 386 operates in either real address mode or protected virtual address mode, usually just called real mode and protected mode, respectively. In real mode, the 386 is practically indistinguishable from an 8088 or an 8086. Real mode carries with it all the restrictions of the 8086—most important, only 1 megabyte of memory is directly addressable. As in the 8086, physical addresses are created by multiplying the segment register value by 16 and adding an offset.

Object-code compatible with the 286, the 386 also operates in protected mode. Unlike the 286, however, it also performs 32-bit operations. All the architectural enhancements of the 386 are available when running 32-bit instructions in protected mode. This is the way the processor was designed to run and is therefore called its native mode. The other modes (real mode, 16-bit protected mode, and virtual 8086 mode) are called emulation modes. The basic protection mechanism of the 386 is identical to that of the 286. It is outside the scope of this chapter to describe the full protection model of the 286 and 386; therefore, I will essentially ignore gate descriptors, tasking, and privilege levels. The extensions to the 386 are primarily in memory addressing, so it's appropriate to review protected mode addressing in the 286.

_____

[*] © M&T Publishing, Inc., *Dr. Dobb's Journal*, October 1986, p.28

In protected mode, there is a dramatic change in the way the processor behaves. In real mode, the program currently executing interprets memory values, and the processor is merely the vehicle for manipulation of the data provided by the program. In protected mode, however, the processor assigns semantic meaning to certain blocks of memory independently of whatever program may be running. Each block of memory the processor recognizes I call a *system object*. The most common system object is the *descriptor*. Other objects include *descriptor tables*, which contain descriptors; *segments*, which are blocks of memory; and *gates*, which restrict access to segments and help enforce the protection rules. Each segment, gate, and table has an 8-byte descriptor that defines it. Descriptors contain information about the object, such as its size, type, location in memory, and protection attributes. Figure 3-1 shows a typical segment descriptor for the 286.

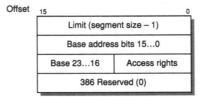

Figure 3-1: 286 Segment Descriptor

In protected mode, memory is accessed via a descriptor. The contents of segment registers do not point to specific memory paragraphs but are treated as indices into descriptor tables. The processor requires the existence of a *global descriptor table* (GDT) and an *interrupt descriptor table* (IDT). It also allows optional *local descriptor tables* (LDTs) to be present. The GDTR and IDTR registers point to the GDT and IDT, respectively. All other system objects, including segments, LDTs, and gates, are pointed to by descriptors. Figure 3-2 outlines the hierarchy of pointers to system objects.

When a memory reference instruction, such as *MOV AX*, [200], is executed, the base address from the descriptor selected by the DS register is added to the offset from the instruction (in this case 0200H) to generate the linear address. In the 286, the linear address becomes the physical address that goes out over the processor bus. In the 386, however, the linear address passes through the paging mechanism, which generates the final physical address. I will examine paging a little later. First, I'll look at how descriptors have been changed in the 386. In the 286, the last 2 bytes of the descriptor must be 0. In the 386, though, these bytes can take on other values. Figure 3-3 shows the fields in the last 16 bits of a descriptor on the 386. Eight of the bits have been used to extend the linear address space to 32 bits, another 4 bits go toward extending the limit field, 2 bits are used as flags, and another 2 bits are

The 286/386 Protection Model

Intel's protected mode processors, the 80286 and 80386, use a variety of methods to safeguard the security of data belonging to one process from corruption by another process. By making all memory references indirect (through a descriptor), the CPU can verify that the operations specified are valid.

The access rights (*AR*) byte of a descriptor contains the key to the operations that are legal for the object. Bits in the *AR* byte specify whether the object is currently present in memory, the privilege level of the object, and the type of object.

When a program is running, the privilege level of the code segment is set to the process's *current privilege level* (CPL). There are four privilege levels, ranging from level 0 (most privileged) to level 3 (least privileged). No process is allowed to access an object more privileged than itself. Typically, the operating system will consist of segments of higher privilege than applications, and it will therefore be protected from accidental or malicious attempts at modification.

In the interest of efficiency, certain routines are often shared tetween processes. I/O libraries, for example, are often part of the operating system but are usable by all applications. The protection model provides an object called a *gate* to deal with this situation. A *gate* is a descriptor that points to a code segment and off-set of a valid operating system entry point. Because the gate is a descriptor, it has a privilege level of its own, separate from that of the code segment. A program requests access to a gate by issuing a *FAR* call or jump to the gate. If no privilege violation occurs, the CPL of the executing process is set to the privilege of the new code segment, and execution continues at the privilege level of the operating system so that they canot be modiefied by the caller. When the called routine executes a *FAR* return, the CPL is reset to that of the caller.

To prevent applications at the same privilege level from corrupting one another, the architecture provides *task state segments* (TSSs) and *local descriptor tables* (LDTs). TSSs provide direct hardware support for multitasking. When a call or interrupt is executed through a task gate, all the registers for the current process are saved in its TSS, and all the registers are reloaded with new values from the TSS pointed to by the task gate. One of the registers is the *LDTR*, which points to an LDT for the task. If the code and data segment descriptors for each task are stored in its own LDT, then there is no way that one task can get access to memory belonging to another task because it has no way to reference the other task's descriptors.

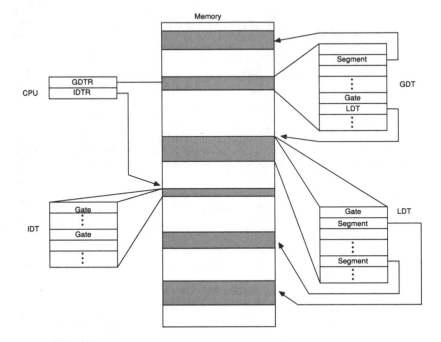

Figure 3-2: Descriptor Hierarchy

reserved for some future processor. At first glance, these extensions grant you a physical address space of 232, as expected, with a maximum segment size of 220, or 1 megabyte.

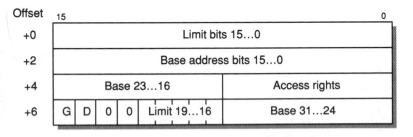

Figure 3-3: 386 Segment Descriptor

Have you been saddled with a new segment limitation? Fortunately, no. The G bit stands for segment granularity. When reset to 0, as in 286 code, the size of a segment (as indicated by the limit field) is measured in bytes. But when the G bit is set to 1, the segment size is measured in pages. Each page is 212 bytes (4K) long. Therefore, the maximum segment size is 220 pages times 212 bytes per page, or 232 bytes. The *D* bit, which Intel calls the *default bit*, is active only in executable segment descriptors. When set to 1, it means that the native mode, 32-bit instruction set is to be used. When reset, the processor interprets opcodes as if it were a 286.

Native Architecture and Instruction Set.

The 386 microprocessor holds 34 different registers, grouped into four classes. These registers are illustrated in Figure 3-4. The first group, general-purpose registers, are the ones most commonly dealt with. They act as accumulators and index registers, and their names are derived from the corresponding registers of the previous generations of processors.

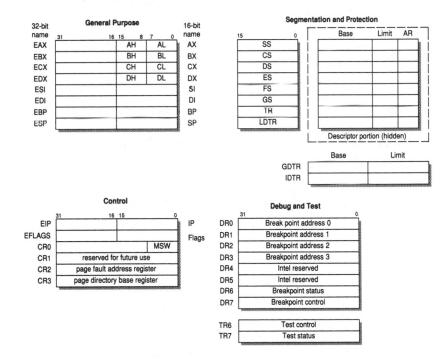

Figure 3-4: 386 CPU Registers

The next register class, segmentation and protection, is also familiar from the 286, although there are two new entries. In addition to the *SS*, *CS*, *DS*, and *ES* segment registers, there are the *FS* and *GS*. These segment registers are used only when the special segment override prefixes FS: and GS: are found in the intruction stream. Associated with most of the registers in this class is a special on-chip cache that holds the descriptor information associated with each segment. This precludes the necessity of reading the descriptor table every time an access to a given segment occurs.

The registers in the control class are partially familiar. *EIP* is the 32-bit extension of the instruction pointer, and *EFLAGS* contains two additional flag bits. The control registers (*CR0-CR7*) are new to the 386, but *CR0* contains what was called the *machine status word* (MSW) on the 286. These control registers contain information necessary for controlling processor extensions (80387) and paging.

The final class of registers, test and debug, are completely new. The debug registers (*DR0-DR7*) allow a software debugger to set the kind of breakpoints that used to require an expensive emulator to generate. I'll describe use of these registers in more detail later. The test registers, *TR6* and *TR7*, are used to verify that the paging cache is working correctly.

In addition to expanding the address space and register set of the processor, Intel has also expanded the addressing modes of the instruction set. The instruction format of the previous generations of processors was an opcode byte, followed by the *modr/m* byte, followed by any operands required. Because only a limited number of addressing modes could be encoded in the *modr/m* byte, certain registers took on dedicated functions. Only *BX*, *SI*, *DI*, and *BP* could be used for indexing or indirection and only in certain combinations. These restrictions have been greatly relaxed in the 386 with the addition of another address mode byte following the *modr/m*.

This new byte, called *s-i-b*, for scale-index-base, extends the addressing capabilities of the 386 in two significant ways. First, it allows any of the eight general-purpose registers to be used as base or index registers, in any combination. This makes the job of compiler writers much easier because they no longer have to worry about having the results of address computations in the proper register. Any of the registers is proper.

In addition, the scale portion of the *s-i-b* byte can be used to eliminate array index computation altogether in some cases. As an example, assume that array *FOO* contains several 32-bit floating-point numbers. The instruction sequence generated by the high-level language statement *SQRT (FOO[1+3])* is shown for the 8086, the 286, and the 386 in Table 3-1, below. Automatic scaling is allowed only for arrays whose elements are 2, 4, or 8 bytes long.

In the 8086 and 286 instruction sets, the most common operations affected either byte or word operands. The same is true of the 386 except that the *D* bit of the executing code segment is checked to see if the machine word is 32 bits long (*D=1*) or 16 bits long (*D=0*). The *MOVSW* instruction, for example, will copy a 16-bit quantity when *D* is 0 and a 32-bit quantity when *D* is 1. To allow a program running in the native (32-bit) mode to access a 16-bit quantity, an override instruction (*066H*) is provided, which toggles the default operand size for the next instruction. While running in 16-bit mode, this opcode has the inverse effect—it allows access to 32-bit registers and memory operands.

```
8086                  286                  386
MOV   AX,1            MOV   AX,1           MOV   EAX,1
ADD   AX,3            ADD   AX,3           ADD   EAX,3
MOV   BX,AX          MOV   BX,AX          FLD   FOO[EAX * 4]
MOV   CL,2            SHR   BX,2           FSQRT
SHR   BX,CL          FLD   [BX]
FLD   [BX]           FSQRT
FSQRT
```

Table 3-1: Implementation of SQRT (FOO[1 + 3]) on 8086/286/386

The instruction repertoire of the 386 has been enhanced as well. Opcodes have been added to allow access to the new control, breakpoint, and debug registers, and new conditional and bit operators have been added. There are now double-precision shift operators and move byte with sign extension or zero extension. Table 3-2, below, lists the new mnemonics.

MOVSX	move byte to word, sign extended
MOVZX	move byte to word, zero extended
LFS,LGS	load pointer, new segment register
SHLD,SHRD	double word shift
BT	bit test
BTC	bit test and complement
BTS	bit test and set
BTR	bit test and reset
BSF	bit scan forward
BSR	bit scan reverse
SETcc	set byte if condition code
	(cc same as Jcc in conditional jumps)

Table 3-2: Instruction set additions for the 386

Paging

Paging has long been the most popular method of implementing virtual memory. Although virtual memory can be achieved with segmentation alone (as in the 286), paging methods are usually faster and simpler because the fixed page size maps easily onto the fixed sector sizes of disks, the most common secondary storage medium. The page size of the *memory management unit* (MMU) of the 386 is 2^{12} bytes, or 4K. It is no coincidence that the granularity bit of the segment descriptors deals with pages of the same size.

The low-order 12 bits are reserved to address within a page, leaving 20 or the 32 physical address bits to select the page. The additional 20 bits could be used as an index into an array of linear (virtual) to physical addresses, but this would require a table of more than 1 million entries (2^{20}) to be in memory constantly for each task. Instead, the upper 20 bits are divided into two 10-bit numbers. The highest order value is used to select one of 1,024 (2^{10}) page table directories. Each directory entry points to a page table containing 1,024 physical page addresses. The advantage of using this method is that only the directory entries must be guaranteed to be in memory at all times, whereas the page tables themselves may be swapped out to save working storage space. Note that, with 1,024 entries of 32 bits each, a page table is 4K long.

One of the control registers (*CR3*) points to the starting location of the page table directories. A copy of *CR3* is stored for each task in 386 native mode. Figure 3-5 illustrates translation from linear to physical address. Because the directory pointers and the page table pointer both reference a 4K page, only 20 bits of the 32-bit word

80386 Development Tools

In addition to the standard Intel development tools that have been available for some time, new products (both software and hardware) that can significantly speed 386 development tasks are starting to appear.

One such product is called the 386 Translator. It's a plug-in piggyback card that replaces the 80286 in a standard IBM PC/AT with an 80386 and some support circuitry. The new board allows developers to createshat takes advantage of the 386's ability to run simultaneously in several different lmodes. The only penalty seems to be that an AT with the 386 Translator board runs about 10 percent slower than an unmodified machine because of the wait states that must be inserted for 386 memory accesses.

The 386 Translator is available from American Computer & Peripheral Inc., 2720 Croddy Way, Santa Ana, CA 92704; (714) 545-2004.

are used as a page address by the MMU. This frees up the 12 low-order bits for other uses. The lowest-order bit (called the *P* bit) is used to mark whether the page is actually present in physical memory. If a memory reference occurs and either the page table or the physical page is marked "not present," a page fault (*int 14*) occurs, and the operating system is responsible for reading the page into physical memory. The other 11 bits have various uses; some are used by the hardware to mark whether pages have been used and to provide a simple user/supervisor protection scheme, and three of the bits can be used by the operating system. Note that whenever the *P* bit is 0 or "not present," the pointer does not contain a physical memory address and the operating system can use the other 31 bits as it chooses—typically to hold the disk sector that contains the primary storage memory image.

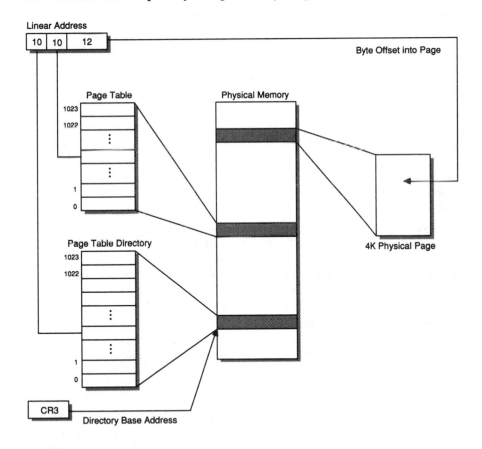

Figure 3-5: Linear-to-Physical-Address Translation

From this discussion, it would seem that every memory-reference instruction executed while paging was enabled would actually require three memory fetches to complete: the first to fetch the page directory, the next to fetch the page table, and the third to finally read the operand itself. To prevent this slowdown, the 386 contains a cache, called the *translation lookaside buffer* (TLB), which holds the 32 most commonly referenced page table entries. If a cache "hit" occurs, no lookup penalty will be exacted. Intel estimates that only 2 percent of address lookups will require the three-state memory references. As a further performance optimization, the MMU is on-chip. Microprocessor systems with an external MMU often require delays equivalent to one wait state while the MMU determines whether a page fault has occurred.

Performance

Instruction durations for the 386 are measured by the number of clock cycles required for an instruction to complete. When coupled with the processor clock rate, an instruction time (in nanoseconds or microseconds) can be generated.

For the most part, the number of clocks required for a given instruction on the 386 is the same as it was on the 286. When the 286 was first available, however, it ran at clock rates of 6 and 8 MHz. The 386 can run at speeds of 12.5 and 16 MHz, approximately twice as fast. It must be emphasized that clock rate alone is an inadequate measure of performance. For one thing, the bandwidth of the 386 is also twice that of the 286; that is, each 386 instruction is capable of processing 32 bits of data, whereas the 286 processes only 16 bits. Programs written in high-level languages that are recompiled for native mode can also see performance gains based on the use of new instructions and addressing modes.

As a general rule, you can assume that programs running in emulation mode will see a performance gain equivalent to the change in clock rate between the two computers being compared. Assuming you are comparing a 6-MHz 286 with a 12-MHz 386, this means a speedup of two times, all other things being equal. Comparing a 286 program against a 386 native mode program, two times should be the minimum performance improvement. Depending on the application, gains of four to five times are easily attainable.

Additional Features

One unique feature of the 386 architecture is its support for the programmer. In addition to the single-step interrupt (*int 1*) and software breakpoint interrupt (*int 3*), also found on the 8086 and 286, the 386 provides four breakpoint registers that can be set to match on instruction execution, data accessed, or data written for a given address. This feature allows debuggers written for the 386 to implement commands such as *GO til variable ZOT modified.*

Another selling point for the processor is the virtual 8086 mode. With this option, an operating system that runs in the native mode (Unix, for example) would be able to run MS-DOS and DOS applications as subtasks. Because programs running in this mode actually generate the same linear addresses as an 8086 (0-1 megabytes), this option is useful only in an operating system running with paging enabled so that the addresses of multiple DOS tasks can be mapped to their different physical memory locations.

Also, for those who cannot abide segmentation of any sort, the 386 can masquerade as a linear-address-space machine. By initializing the CS, DS, and SS registers with a descriptor that points to one gigantic 4-gigabyte segment, users will never have to load another segment register. A slight variation on this can permit a simple user/ supervisor protection model that fits in well with the paging mechanism.

Even with all the features and enhancements found in the 386, though, there is still some room for improvement. It still has no "store pointer" instruction counterpart to the *LDS reg, [memory]* instruction for loading pointers. A set of conditional "skip" instructions would be much more efficient in compiled code than are the conditional jumps that are currently available. Compilers often have to generate the following sequence of code when processing if statements:

```
        jnz     LAB1
        jmp     ELSE_CLAUSE
LAB1:           ; then clause
```

The jump-not-zero forces the instruction queue to be flushed, which degrades performance. Replacing the *jnz* with a *skipnz* would be more efficient.

Finally, for use in tightly coupled multiprocessor applications, Intel should have provided a hardware signal that would force the TLB to be flushed. With the current implementation, if one processor modifies a page table entry in RAM, another processor may be using the entry stored in its on-chip TLB, which could contain some invalid information.

Summary

Despite the quibbles noted above, the 80386 has been well designed. Elimination of the 64K segment size restriction makes it a pleasure to program rather than a pain.

The enhanced architecture makes it easier for compilers to generate efficient code, and the machine itself is fast. The ability to run 8086 code, 286 code, and native code simultaneously means that a large software base will be available. Programmers also will appreciate the availability of new development tools.

Because of the complexity of the processor, I have been able only to highlight some of its most important new features. I hope I have spurred your interest. This chip is sure to have an important effect on microcomputing in the near future.

Bibliography

Intel Corp. *80386 Microprocessor Data Book*, 1985.
Intel Corp. *iAPX 286 Programmer's Reference Manual*. 1985.

II
Moving Up from the 8088 and Real Mode to the 286/386 Generation and Protected Mode

4
Determining CPU Type *

Bob Felts

With the advent of OS/2, a protected-mode operating system, it is useful to have a function to determine CPU type, regardless of CPU operating mode. Many previously published procedures of this kind work only in real mode because they write to the code segment. The function listed here, *cputype*, can be called by DOS and OS/2 programs in either real or protected mode. It returns a value of 86, 186, 286, or 386 in real mode, and -286 or -386 in protected mode. For brevity, the test to distinguish between the 8086 and 8088 classes of chip is not included.

The first test is a *PUSH SP* instruction to differentiate between 8086/80186 and 80286/80386 CPUs. If the value on the stack is the same as the *SP* value after the push, then the CPU is either an 8086 or an 80186. These chips are distinguished by their response to a shift instruction. For a 32-bit shift count, the 8086 will shift 32 bits, clearing the shifted register, whereas the 80186 will not shift at all, leaving the value in the register unchanged.

The next test determines whether the CPU is using 16- or 32-bit operands. This is done by pushing the flags, then testing the change in the SP register to determine whether two or four bytes were pushed. In the latter case, the CPU is an 80386 executing in a 32-bit segment. To load a two-byte immediate value into *AX*, the *MOV* instruction must be preceded by an operand-length override prefix. MASM version 4 has no mnemonic for this, so it is generated with a *DB* instruction at the label *is32bit*.

The distinction between an 80386 that uses 16-bit operands and an 80286 is made by storing the global descriptor table register (GDTR) to a six-byte field in memory. The 80286 stores a -1 to the last byte of this field, whereas an 80386 stores either a 0 or a 1. The space for holding the GDTR value is allocated on the stack (by subtracting from *SP*), because in protected mode that is the only one of the four segments guaranteed to be writable.

The CPU operating mode (real or protected) is indicated by the low-order bit of

* © 1987, 1988 Ziff Communications Company, *PC Tech Journal*, November 1987, p. 51

the machine status word (MSW). At label *testprot*, the MSW is loaded into a register, the mode bit is shifted into the carry flag, and, if that sets *CF*, the returned value is negated to indicate that the CPU is in protected mode.

The function follows Microsoft mixed-language naming conventions, because it has no parameters, it needs no declarations to specify the calling sequence. If called from a C program, it must be declared far.

Listing 4-1

```
;
;       determine CPU type.  works in
;       both real and protected modes.
;
;       in:
;               none
;
;       out:
;               ax      :       processor type
;                               86 => 8086
;                               186 => 80186
;                               286 => 80286 (real mode)
;                               -286 => 80286 (protected mode)
;                               386 => 80386 (real mode)
;                               -386 => 80386 (protected mode)
;
;       destroyed:
;               upper 16 bits of eax if executed
;               in a 32 bit 80386 code segment
;

        .286p                                   ; must be assembled in 16-bit code segment


        public  _cputype


_cputype        proc    near            ; "far" for large model programs


        pushf                                   ; save original flags
        push    cx                              ;    and registers
        push    bp
```

```
        mov     ax,sp                           ; 86/186 or 286/386?
        push    sp                               ; 86/186 will push sp-2
        pop     cx                               ;    others will push sp

        cmp     ax,cx
        jz      short cpu_2386          ; if 80286/80386


        mov     ax,186                          ; distinguish between 86 and 186
        mov     cl,32                           ; 8086 will shift 32 bits
        shl     ax,cl                           ; 80186 will shift 0 bits
        jnz     short cpu_exit          ; NZ implies 80186


        mov     ax,86                           ; it's an 8086
        jmp     short cpu_exit

cpu_2386:
        pushf                                   ; 286/386.  32 or 16 bit operand size?
        mov     cx,sp                       ; if pushf pushed 2 bytes then
        popf                                    ;    16 bit operand size
        inc     cx                          ; assume 2 bytes
        inc     cx
        cmp     cx,ax
        jnz     short cpu_386_32    ; jmp/4 bytes, => 32-bit 80386

;
;       either 286 or 386 with 16 bit operands
;
        sub     sp,6                            ; allocate room for SGDT
        mov     bp,sp

        ifndef  PWORD
        sgdt    FWORD PTR ss:[bp]       ; for 286 assemblers
        else
        sgdt    PWORD PTR ss:[bp]       ; for 386 assemblers
        endif

        add     sp,4                            ; trash limit and base (low word)
        pop     ax
        inc     ah                              ; 286 stores -1, 386 stores 0 or 1
        jnz     short cpu_386_16

        mov     ax,286                          ; it's a 286
        jmp     short cpu_prot          ; go check for protected mode
```

```
cpu_386_32:
        db          066h                                        ; 386 in 32 bit code segment
        mov         ax,386                                      ; 066h (override) to force 16 bit move
        jmp         short cpu_prot          ; into ax

cpu_386_16:
        mov         ax,386                                      ; 386 in 16 bit code segment

cpu_prot:
        smsw        cx                                          ; check for protected mode
        ror         cx,1
        jnc         short cpu_exit          ; if PE == 0 then real mode

        neg         ax                                          ; else flag protected mode

cpu_exit:
        pop         bp
        pop         cx
        popf
        ret


_cputype    endp
```

5

Performance Programming [*]

_____*Joel Rosenblum* and *Dan Jacobs*_____

If you create programs for the IBM PC, you often need to sell separate versions of your software for particular "compatible" machines. The wide variety of so-called PC compatibles creates problems for you as a software engineer trying to write one version of your program that operates on as many machines as possible.

As many buyers have already discovered, some IBM PC clones are not true clones at all. These machines either are enhanced with features that give them a marketing edge over the original IBM machine or are so restricted that they have trouble using common existing software such as Lotus 1-2-3 and dBASE III. All this hardware incompatibility makes it more difficult to design and sell your programs to everyone who can use them. Your customers send you back to the salt mines to develop 16 different versions of the same software product.

Defining Performance Programming

We have developed a methodology that lets you design "generic" software; it will operate with most IBM-compatible machines that use MS-DOS.

Best of all, our procedures will let your programs automatically take advantage of PC hardware features. Your programs will know when they can write directly to video memory or access the IBM BIOS low-memory variables. If you program encounters a machine it doesn't know, it can decide whether certain features exist for it to use or whether it should treat the new machine as generic until you can incorporate that machine's features into the next release of your software. We will also describe some methods that allow user-selectable compatibility so your customers won't have to wait for your next software release. Now you can sell only one version of your program. However, that version is special because you create it using a method we call performance programming.

---

[*] © McGraw-Hill Information Systems Company, *Byte*, 1986 Extra Edition

We will explain how to program for performance while maintaining compatibility. Our approach is twofold. First, we define a generic PC as a model on which to base your program. Then we define and use a features table that automatically determines IBM PC compatibility by reading the manufacturer's copyright notice contained in the machine's BIOS ROMs. We next look at how you can use the presence of other equipment to set "performance bits" and how you can incorporate that information into your overall program design. Finally, we will give some examples relating to processor detection and speed determination, video capability, extended character set presence, ANSI cursor addressing, and use of other set bits in your program.

Defining the Generic PC

We define a generic PC as a computer that is only minimally compatible with the IBM PC. The requirements of our theoretical generic PC design are the presence of an Intel 8088 or equivalent processor, the ability to read/write either IBM PC 5.25-inch or 3.5-inch disks, MS-DOS, the ability to display 25 lines of either 40- or 80- column text, and an ASCII keyboard without cursor and function keys.

Our generic PC does not include the following features present in a true IBM PC: an IBM extended character set, direct cursor-key positioning, bit-mapped screen graphics, the ability to use BIOS calls and corresponding access to low-memory variables, and the ability to access hardware directly.

We assume that a generic PC has a text-only screen display that supports only the standard ASCII character set and has a keyboard without cursor-positioning or function keys. You might note that the Zenith Z-100 is close to qualifying as our theoretical generic PC. Also, the generic system does not have an IBM- compatible BIOS even though it supports MS-DOS. This implies that all operating system function calls for a generic PC must occur at the highest level, which in this case is by using DOS system interrupt calls 20h through 27h. More information about these OS interrupt calls appears in *IBM's Disk Operating System Technical Reference*, available through IBM dealers or directly from IBM.

The advantages of generic PC software are threefold. From your standpoint as a programmer, your software will work on most IBM PCs and compatibles. As a software publisher and dealer, you have to stock and sell only one version of a program. Finally, as a user, you do not need to be concerned about program compatibility or special steps to install the software on your IBM PC- compatible hardware.

On the other hand, generic software cannot take advantage of the advanced features present in the original IBM PC and some compatibles. Software with only scrolling generic screens and no graphics capability is not acceptable for some users. Here the second part of our methodology, the features table, comes into play.

Defining a Features Table

A features table lets your programs take advantage of a particular compatible's features by determining the equipment your program is operating on. Your software automatically enhances itself for certain compatibles, so your program runs faster and more efficiently and has an improved user interface.

If your program is to operate with this type of intelligence, it must reliably determine the equipment. Your software can't read the label on the outside of your compatible, so we rely primarily on the copyright notice contained inside the machine's BIOS ROMs.

When an engineer designs a PC compatible, he or she incorporates into that machine's ROMs a set of routines that directly control the hardware. Those routines are the BIOS. A manufacturer of PC compatibles can write his or her own BIOS or purchase a BIOS from another manufacturer such as Phoenix Software Associates or Faraday Electronics.

The manufacturer can also market a machine that is made by an OEM. The OEM usually brands its machines by placing a copyright notice within the BIOS code. An example is the AT&T PC 6300, which is manufactured by Olivetti. Olivetti purchases the BIOS for its machine from Phoenix Software Associates. So what is the resulting copyright notice inside the user's 6300? It is the string "OLIVETTI," followed by some text.

Copyright notices thus far have been an unofficial method of determining a machine's manufacturer. The method is not 100 percent reliable, however, since the manufacturer might decide, for whatever reason, to change the location or actual string of the copyright notice. To prevent problems with your users, we have provided some software escape hatches. When your program cannot locate the copyright, the software will default to its generic-machine mode. However, some of your users might not be satisfied with the resulting loss of performance, so we also suggest that you incorporate into your program a method for the user to set the machine's compatibility level. Here are three examples of how to do that.

First, you can let your user input a slash option such as */IBM* when invoking your software with its command string, as in:

```
yourprm /IBM
```

A good example of a program that uses the slash-option approach is Microsoft's SYMDEB.

Second, you can incorporate an "It's a compatible" override as part of an optional installation process. Finally, you can let your user set compatibility as part of the DOS environment. For example:

```
set compatibility = IBM
```

The use of any of these methods in your program lets those users who need more performance obtain it. When a new machine appears on the market, advanced users will be able to use that machine to its fullest potential.

An example of a C-language implementation of a features table is presented in Listing 5-1. In that example, machine characteristics are defined as bit flags in the variables *FEATURES* and *VIDEO_FEATURES*.

You should develop your own set of bit flags for the features your program needs to use. These bit flags are bits that you can set either off or on and that exist within a word. For example, if we set bits 1, 4, and 8 of a word "on" while leaving the remaining bits "off," the value of that word is 13 hexadecimal. Since we are interested in determining only if particular bits within the word are set, the value of the word is not important. Instead, we extract the bits that we are interested in by using a mask. Our sample programs in the listings illustrate how the mask is used.

Some of your programs might require information about the compatible's operating system version or the availability of certain BIOS calls. We will not discuss the detection of this additional information here, but we have provided a summary of some bit-field considerations for use in the *FEATURES* variable in Table 5-1.

The definitions are then followed by the copyright notices that appear in a structure containing the location and unique identifying string for some sample machine BIOS ROMs. Note that each defined machine in the table contains its own set of characteristics that are then placed in the bit-flag variable.

CPU-related features:
  - detection of the primary processor in the machine
  - detection of the processor's speed
  - detection and use of coprocessors

Video-related features:
  - present video type(s)
  - present video mode
  - installation of ANSI.SYS video device driver
  - ability to use IBM expanded-video character set

Operating system-related features
  - availability of certain BIOS-level calls
  - DOS version check

Disk-related use and detection
  - floppy and/or hard disk drive type
  - floppy and/or hard disk drive size
  - detection of floppy disk drive mode
  - ability to use interrupt 13h calls
  - DMA detection

Table 5-1: Summary of Bit-Field Considerations

Two machines, the Wang PC and the TI Professional, are important examples of how you can use the table to deal with some unusual compatibility considerations. For example, the Wang PC requires clearing the direction flag before making disk I/O calls from assembly language routines. This problem does not occur when making the I/O calls from most high-level languages since, in these languages, the direction flag is usually left in the increment position. The TI Professional requires a substitution of interrupt 4Eh in place of any assembly language interrupt 13h direct disk I/O calls. Thus, Listing 5-1 defines the special bit flags *WANG* and *TIPROF*. If your program needed to use any of these calls on one of these two machines, the defined bit flag would handle the branch within your program. Some examples of use of the bit-flag branch to control program performance optimization are contained in the "Detecting Video Type" section of this article.

The sample features table in Listing 5-1 also shows how you might determine the presence of a turbo board. The copyright notice was given for an STD turbo board used in an IBM or Compaq PC. Again, once it detects the board, your program could act accordingly. Of course, your program could also incorporate detection for other installed circuit cards using their copyright notices.

In summary, the equipment features table places all the burden of compatibility and machine optimization in one convenient place. If a computer is not on the list, the program assumes it is generic. Otherwise, the capabilities of the machine are already "known" and your program would automatically use them. For new or previously unknown machines, your user must either accept the automatic generic-machine mode or over ride it by providing the program with performance optimization. Therefore, as a service to your users who prefer to use software as it comes off the shelf, you have a responsibility to keep your features table as up-to-date as possible. Perhaps the features table will become a public domain standard for use by all programmers.

Listing 5-1: Sample Features Table

```
/*
*/
/*

    This code contains a C language Features Table which contains the location and copyright

    string that uniquely identify a machine.  In addition to the copyrights, the bit fields

    for the FEATURES and VIDEO_FEATURES variables are defined.  Note that this code is

    compiled with the Lattice C Compiler version 2.15, using -md -n options.  Copyright ©

    1986 Don Jacobs and Joel Rosenblum for public, unrestricted use.

*/
/* bit flags for FEATURES */


#define IBMPC          0x0100     /* IBM PC, XT, portable, */

#define IBMPCAT        0x0200     /* IBM AT */

#define IBMCOMPAT      0x0400     /* IBM PC BIOS Compatible */

#define IBM_CONVERT    0x0800     /* IBM Convertible */

#define GENERIC        0x1000     /* Assumed generic PC */

#define NO_DMA         0x2000     /* Machine has no DMA */

#define WANG           0x4000     /* Wang PC special case */

#define TIPROF         0x8000     /* TI Professional PC special case */

#define CPU>88         0x0001     /* 8088, 8086 processor */

#define CPU_186        0x0002     /* 80188, 80186 processor */

#define CPU_286        0x0004     /* 80286 processor */

#define CPU_V20        0x0008     /* V20, V30 processor */
```

```
#define NDP                 0x0010      /* 8087, 80287 math coprocessor */


/* bit flags for VIDEO_FEATURES */


#define CGA                 0x0001      /* IBM Color Graphics Adapter */

#define MONO                0x0002      /* IBM Monchrome Adapter */

#define HERCULES            0x0004      /* Hercules Monochrome Adapter Card */

#define PGA                 0x0008      /* IBM Professional Graphics Adapter */

#define EGA_MONO            0x0010      /* w/Monochrome Monitor */

#define EGA_COLOR           0x0020      /* w/Color Monitor */

#define EGA_HIGH            0x0040      /* w/High Resolution Color Monitor */

#define UNKNOWN             0x0080      /* Unknown graphics type */

#define ANSI                0x0100      /* ANSI.SYS installed */


/* Additional bit fields may also be defined, please see TABLE 5-1 for suggestions */


struct machine_info {
     char      *logo;  /* Unique copyright string */
     long      addr;   /* String memory location */
               /* Note:  actually (char *) must be (long) to pass Lattice C */
     int type;  /* Machine attributes */
} feature_table[] = {

/*      copyright notice, physical address, pctype */

     { "IBM", 0xFE00EL, IBMPC|IBMCOMPAT},     /* All IBMs */
     { "COMPAQ", 0xFFFEAL, IBMCOMPAT},        /* All Compaqs */
     { "Corona", 0xFE00F, IBMCOMPAT},         /* Old Version Corona */
     { "Corona", 0xFE01A, IBMCOMPAT},         /* Version 3.10 ROM Corona (also Phillips) */
     { "M.P.C.", 0xFDB2D, IBMCOMPAT},         /* New Columbia */
     { "Columbia", 0xFF768, IBMCOMPAT},       /* Old Columbia */
     { "Eagle PC", 0xFFFAA, IBMCOMPAT},       /* Eagle PC */
     { "Eagle PC", 0xFF810, IBMCOMPAT},       /* Eagle PC Plus */
     { "Zenith", 0xFB000, IBMCOMPAT},         /* Zenith Data Systems */
     { "Zenith", 0xFC2FF, GENERIC},           /* Zenith 100 */
     { "MITSUBISHI", 0xFC02A, IBMCOMPAT},     /* Sperry PC and Leading Edge */
     { "TVS", 0xFE003, IBMCOMPAT},            /* TeleVideo */
     { "OSM", 0xFFFF5, IBMCOMPAT},            /* OSM Rom Version 3.6 or later */
     { "OLIVETTI", 0xFC050, IBMCOMPAT},       /* AT&T-IS PC 300 and Xerox */
                                              /* NOTE: AT&T is not supporting V1.0 ROMs */
     { "WANG", 0xFFFC2, WANG|GENERIC},        /* WANG Professional */
     { "ADDS", 0xFC050, IBMCOMPAT},           /* Applied Data Digital Systems Model PC/I */
     { "CROS", 0xFE000, IBMCOMPAT},           /* Seattle Telecom Turbo Boards */
     { "PCPI", 0xFE00F, IBMCOMPAT},           /* Personal Computer Products */
     { "TAVA", 0xFE018, IBMCOMPAT},           /* TAVA PC */
     { "Tandy", 0xFC02B, IBMCOMPAT|NO-DMA},   /* Tandy 1000 has no DMA without memory upgrade */
     { "Tandon", 0xFC013, IBMCOMPAT},         /* Tandy 1200 */
     { "Texas", 0xFE022, TIPROF},             /* TI Professional V1.23 & V2.11 SYSROM */
     { "American", 0xFE004, IBMCOMPAT},       /* American PC lookalike */
```

```
{ "STD", 0xFE00EL, IBMCOMPAT},          /* STD Turbo Boards in IBMs */
{ "STD", 0xFFFEAL, IBMCOMPAT},          /* STD Turbo Boards in COMPAQS */
{ "TOMCAT", 0xFE028, IBMCOMPAT},        /* Tomcat AT clone */
{ "WYSE", 0xFC003, IBMCOMPAT},          /* WYSE PC BIOS Version 1.08 */
{ "Hewlett-Packard", 0xF0024, IBMCOMPAT}, /* Hewlett-Packard Vectra AT Compatible */
{ "Morrow", 0xFE073, IBMCOMPAT},        /* Morrow Pivot II & Zenith 171 Desktops */

/* Additional machines are added to the list starting here */

{ NULL, NULL, 0}
};
```

Using the Features Table

Now that you have developed a features table, how do you use it in your code? Listing 5-2 contains a C-language routine that uses the features-table structure defined in Listing 5-1 to determine machine compatibilities. The routine reads the copyright notice, if it can locate one, and sets the bits within the variable *FEATURES*. The routine also calls separate functions that set additional bits within *FEATURES* and *VIDEO_FEATURES*. Your program's code then checks the appropriate bit within the variable to determine if a particular ability exists for the machine on which your software is currently operating.

It is important that the routines in your program that use the features variables exist at the lowest level of your code. The reason for this is so that the rest of your program will sit above the machine's hardware and be oblivious to the equipment present. Your program will execute the appropriate routines based on the information contained within the variables. For example, suppose your software could speed up its disk access by using BIOS interrupt 13h calls. If *FEATURES* indicated that the machine your software is currently operating on is 100 percent IBM- compatible, then you would use the BIOS interrupt; otherwise, you would use DOS interrupt calls 25h and 26h to access the disk. In effect, you create a device-independent interface for your program. If you later find that you need to define another *FEATURES* bit or you need to extend the length of the *FEATURES* variable, you will be able to make the change with a minimum of recoding.

Now that we have defined the bits that make up the variables, the next sections will show you the details behind setting those flags. These examples illustrate how your programs can detect such features of your machine as its processor, effective clock speed, and video display. These routines are the foundation for the creation of your own hardware-independent modules.

Listing 5-2: A C-Language Routine

```
/*
*/
/*
    This code shows how the Features Table is used to set up
    the bit flags in the FEATURES variable,  Once FEATURES
    is set for the current machine, your other program
    modules can use it to determine what section of code
    should be executed to yield the best program performance.

    Copyright (c) 1986 Dan Jacobs and Joel Rosenblum

    Compiled using Lattice C ver 2.15, using -md -n options
*/

unsigned int video_features;    /* global variable which holds video attributes */

unsigned int set_features()
{
    char *cp;                   /* Pointer */
    struct machine info *p;     /* Features Table Structure */
    unsigned int feature;       /* FEATURES bit field variable */

    /* Assume the PC is generic to start */
    feature = GENERIC;          /* default to generic */

/*
    A pseudo code example of how to override the automatic set of FEATURES
    assuming that either a slash option or a DOS environment variable is
    set.  Your actual code will depend upon how you do the parsing.  See
    the section on using the machine's copyright notice to determine
    compatibility in our text.

begin pseudo code example --

    if ((/IBM entered on command line) |
        (compatibility = IBM is in the environment)) {
        feature = IBMCOMPAT;
        goto cpu_test;
    }
-- end pseudo code example */

    for (p = feature_table; p->addr != NULL; p++) /* If next table entry is NULL, end loop */
        if (strncmp((char *) p->addr, p->logo, strlen(p->logo)) == 0) {
            feature = p->type;
            break;
        }

    if (feature & IBMPC) {          /* IBM Personal Computers */
        cp = (char *) 0xFFFFE;      /* physical address 0FFFF:E */
        switch (*cp) {
            case 0xF9:  /* IBM Convertible */
                feature |= IBM_CONVERT;
```

```
            break;
    case 0xFC:      /* IBM AT */
        feature|= IBMPCAT | CPU_286;
        break;
    case 0xFD:  /* IBM PC JR */
        feature |= NO_DMA;
        break;
    case 0xFE:  /* IBM XT or Portable */
    case 0xFF:  /* IBM PC */
        break;
    default:
        break;  /* unknown IBM type */
    }
}


/* add the cpu type to FEATURES -- see listing 3 */
feature = cputest(feature);

    /* check for numeric data processor -- see listing 4 */
    feature = test_ndp(feature);

    /* add the video display type to VIDEO_FEATURES -- see listing 6 */
    video_features = video_test(feature);

    /* check if ANSI.SYS is present -- see listing 7 */
    if (check_ansi()) {
            video_features |= ANSI;
    } else {
            putch(0x0D);  /* This cleans up any garbage left on the screen */
            putch(' ');   /* by the ANSI check if ANSI.SYS  is not present */
            putch(' ');
            putch(' ');
            putch(' ');
            putch(0x0A);
            putch(0x0D);
    }

        return (feature);
    }
```

Determining CPU Type

Software that is dependent upon processor type needs to determine under which processor it is operating. Examples include operating system software that might require the use of certain processor modes such as the Intel 80286's protected mode or the use of the *PUSHA* instruction on the 80186.

Listing 5-3 gives a C-callable assembly language routine that you can use to determine the presence of the Intel 8088/8086, 80186, and 80286 processors and the NEC V20 and V30 processors, so you can set the corresponding bit in

FEATURES.

Your program's performance might improve by detecting and using a math coprocessor. Examples include programs with heavy trigonometric or floating-point operations such as statistical analysis and speech-processing software. Two methods for detecting a math coprocessor are in Listing 5-4. Finally, it might be important to determine the processor's clock speed. Timing loops are an important part of communications software, and the assembly language procedure in Listing 5-5a lets you set processor- speed-independent timing loops. Listing 5-5b shows an example of how to use the timing routine.

Listing 5-3: A C-Callable Assembly Language Routine

```
; Cputest.asm is the Lattice C-callable assembly language routine that determines
; the machine's processor type. Copyright (c) 1986 Dan Jacobs and Joel Rosenblum

        name    cputest         ;determine CPU type
        include dos.mac         ; Lattice C memory model configuration macro
                                ; In this case it is a copy of dm8086.mac

; processor type equates
CPU_88    equ 01H       ; Intel 8088 - 8086
CPU_186   equ 02H       ; Intel 80188 - 80186
CPU_286   equ 04H       ; Intel 80286
CPU_V20   equ 08H       ; NEC V20 - V30

        PSEG

comment\*******************************************************************

NAME
        cputest
SYNOPSIS
            unsigned int cputest (features)
            unsigned int features;        see definition of machine type
DESCRIPTION
            returns features with the proper active CPU type or'ed in

***************************************************************************\

            public  cputest
cputest     proc    near

            push    BP              ; save the frame pointer (if called from C)
            mov     BP, SP
                                    ; next, save the passed existing features
            mov     AX, 4[BP]
            push    AX
        ; check for  8088 or 8086 by using the SHR instruction since the
        ; 8088 and 8086 do not mask cl with 07H before executing the shift.
```

```
                mov     CL, 20H
                mov     AX, 1
                shr     AX, CL
                test    AX, AX          ; if after the shift AX is the same
                                        ; as before, it's an 8088 - 8086 or V20 - V30
                jnz     check_80186     ; else, continue checking other Intel CPUs
        ; check for V20 or V30 by detecting if PUSHA is a valid instruction
        ; on the NEC CPUs
                mov     BX, SP          ; save SP
                pusha
                cmp     BX, SP          ; if SP has not been decremented, then
                je      is_88           ; it's an 8088 - 8086
                popa                    ; else, we restore registers
                mov     AX, CPU_V20
                jmp     return
is_88:          mov     AX, CPU_88
                jmp     return
check_80186:
        ; check for the 80188 or 80186 by detecting if SP is updated
        ; before or after it is pushed.
                push    SP
                pop     BX
                cmp     BX, SP
                je      is_286          ; if updated after, it's an 80286
                mov     AX, CPU_186     ; else, it's an 80186 or 80188
                jmp     short return
is_286:         mov     AX, CPU_286

return:         pop     BX              ; recall saved features
                or      AX, BX          ; and or cputype into other features bits
                pop     BP
                ret
cputest         endp
                ENDPS
                end
```

Listing 5-4: Detecting Math Co-Processor

```
; testndp.asm is the Lattice C-callable assembly language routine that
; determines the presence of an 8087 or 80287 math  co-processer chip.

; assembeled using Microsoft MASM v4.0

; Copyright (c) 1986 Dan Jacobs and Joel Rosenblum

; portions copyrighted by MicroWay, Inc.

        name    test_ndp

        include dos.mac         ; Lattice C memory model configuration macro
                                ; In this case it is a copy of dm8086.mac
```

```
; We have to code the instructions for the NDP as dbs as the assembler
; generates an unwanted WAIT instruction

FINIT_MAC       MACRO
                db          0DBH, 0E3H
                ENDM


FSTCW_MAC       MACRO    address
                db          0D9H, 03EH
                dw          offset DGROUP:address
                ENDM




; bit mask for coprocessor in FEATURES
NDP             equ      0010H    ; a coprocessor is present

        DSEG
ndp_word        dw       0        ; a storage location for the ndp to use for test
        ENDDS

        PSEG

comment\*************************************************************************

NAME
        testndp

SYNOPSIS
                Check to see if a  8087 or 80287  numeric data processor is
                present in the machine.  Here, we present two methods which
                you may select based  upon how you set  CHOOSE in the  code:
                First,  IBM's  recommended  procedure  which does an  int 11
                (equipment determination)  BIOS call.  The problem with this
                method is that it only  works on IBMs and  100% compatibles.
                Note that in the PC and XT the returned value is  determined
                by reading the  switch setting.   Unfortunately, all of the
                early "guide to operations" manuals  informed you to set the
                switch  the  coprocessor the wrong way, rendering it usless.
                Second,  MicroWay's  recommended  procedure  checks for the
                coprocessor directly.  We believe that this method should be
                used since it is more universal.  We leave the choice to you
                depending how you set the equ for CHOOSE  below:

                  1 to use int 11
                or
                  0 for direct check

SYNOPSIS
                unsigned int test_ndp (features);
                unsigned features;              see definition of machine type
```

```
RETURN VALUE
        the passed features variable with the NDP bit or'ed in

*************************************************************************\

CHOOSE   equ     0        ; 0 = direct ndp check, 1 = IBM int 11 bios call

                public  test_ndp

test_ndp        proc    near

        assume  ds:DGROUP

        push    bp                ; save the frame pointer (if called from C)
        mov     bp, sp

        ; next, save the passed existing features
        mov     ax, 4[bp]
        push    ax

if CHOOSE ; use bios int check
        int     11H                     ; equipment determination call
        and     ax, 2                   ; coprocessor present
        jz      no_ndp
else ; use direct ndp check ala MicroWay
        FINIT_MAC                       ; initilize the coprocessor
        mov     ndp_word, 0
        FSTCW_MAC <ndp_word>            ; fstcw ndp_word
                                        ; move control word to ndp_word
        mov     cx, 064H                ; count for wait loop
l1:     push    dx
        pop     dx
        loop    l1
        and     ndp_word, 03BFH         ; mask to bits we want
        cmp     ndp_word, 03BFH         ; all the correct bits set
        jne     no_ndp

        mov     ndp_word, 0
        FSTCW_MAC <ndp_word>            ; fstcw ndp_word
                                        ; move control word to ndp_word
        mov     cx, 064H                ; count for wait loop
l2:     push    dx
        pop     dx
        loop    l2
        and     ndp_word, 1F3FH         ; mask to bits we want
        cmp     ndp_word, 033FH         ; all the correct bits set
        jne     no_ndp

endif
        mov     bx, NDP                 ; mask to turn on coprocessor bit
        jmp     short ndp_exit
```

```
no_ndp: mov     bx, 0                   ; nothing to mask in

ndp_exit:
        pop     ax                      ; get saved passed features
        or      ax, bx                  ; and or in bit for ndp

        pop     bp                      ; restore frame pointer to return to C caller

        ret

test_ndp        endp

        ENDPS
        end
```

Listing 5-5a: Calculating Timing Loops

```
; Cal.asm is an assembly language routine that provides a standard
; delay independent of clock speed.  It may be called from a C
; routine in your software as illustrated in listing 5b.

; Note: The PC's timer interrupt is assumed set to the standard ~18.2Hz

; Copyright (c) 1986 Howie Marshall, Applied Reasoning Corp.

pgroup  group   prog
dgroup  group   data

bios_data       segment at 40H
                org     06cH
low_time        dw      ?
bios_data       ends

data            segment public 'data'
                extrn   us500:word, ms2:word
dummy           dw      0               ; a dummy to compare against
data            ends

prog    segment byte public 'prog'
;
; delaycal - calibrate the delay loop
;
; temp = delaycal(delay_time) from C.  Returns delay_count
;
        assume  cs:pgroup
        public  delaycal
delaycal proc   near
        assume  ds:dgroup
```

```
        push    bp
        push    ds
        mov     bp,sp
        mov     ax,bios_data
        mov     ds,ax
        assume  ds:bios_data
;
; wait for the timer to tick over
;
        mov     di,low_time
timwait:
        cmp     di,low_time
        je      timwait
;
        xor     ax,ax
        xor     dx,dx
        add     di,6                ; wait for 5 more ticks
;**************************************************************
timloop:
        add     ax,1
        adc     dx,0
        cmp     di,low_time     ; have 5 ticks occurred yet?
        ja      timloop         ; no, continue looping
;**************************************************************
;
;  5 ticks @ 18.2 ticks/sec => 270272 microseconds in 5 ticks
;
;  270272 = 16 * 16892
;
        mov     bx,16
        div     bx              ; cut down to single word
        mov     bx,6[bp]        ; get desired delay time
        mul     bx
        mov     bx,16892
        div     bx              ; finish divide-by-270272
        or      ax,ax
        jnz     timok
        inc     ax              ; do at least one loop
timok:
        mov     sp,bp
        pop     ds
        assume  ds:dgroup
        pop     bp
        ret
delaycal endp
;
;  DELAY SUBROUTINES:
;
;  This routine delays for 500 microseconds.
;
        public  del500u
```

```
del500u proc    near
        assume  ds:dgroup
        mov     ax,us500
        neg     ax
;
;  This loop contains the same instructions as the calibration loop
;  in delaycal above, but in a different order.  The first two are
;  do not actually affect the loop, other than taking the same number
;  of cycles as the corresponding portion of the loop in delaycal.
;
;  Note that both loops consist of:
;       ADD, ADC, CMP, Jcond
;
;***************************************************************
loop1:
        adc     dx,0            ; kill some time
        cmp     dx,dummy        ; and some more
        add     ax,1            ; increment our count
        jnz     loop1           ; no, continue looping
;***************************************************************
        ret
del500u endp
;
;  This is essentially the same as del500u, except that a different
;  count value is used to delay for 2 milliseconds.
;
        public  del2m
del2m   proc    near
        assume  ds:dgroup
        mov     ax,ms2
        neg     ax
;***************************************************************
loop2:
        adc     dx,0            ; kill some time
        cmp     dx,dummy        ; and some more
        add     ax,1            ; increment our count
        jnz     loop2           ; no, continue looping
;***************************************************************
        ret
del2m   endp
prog    ends
        end
```

Listing 5-5b: Illustration of Timing Delays, C Calling Routine

```
*/

/*
    This driver provides an example of how to use  cal.asm  for
    delay calibrate routines.  The routine will print the delay
    according to the speed  of the processor.   The   closer you
    make the loops to your actual code,  the more  accurate the
    calculation will be.   You should  then adjust  your actual
    program delay proportional to the results of this test.
*/

#include <stdio.h>

static char id[] = "#PROGRAM: calibrate driver (hzm)";

/*
 * Global variables:
 */

        int     us500;
        int     ms2;
/*
 *  init -- calibrate the delay counters
 */

static
init()
{
        us500 = delaycal(500);
        ms2   = delaycal(2000);
        printf("%d loops equals 500 microseconds.\n", us500);
        printf("%d loops equals 2 milliseconds.\n", ms2);
}

/*
 *  delay1 -- delay for .5 sec (= 1000 * 500 usec)
 */

static
delay1()
{
        char    before[4];
        char    after[4];
        int     i;

        printf("\nNow, delay 1000 * 500 usec...\n");
        dostime(&before);
```

```
        for (i = 0; i < 1000; i++) del500u();
        dostime(&after);
        printf("  Start: %02d:%02d:%02d.%02d\n",
                before[1], before[0], before[3], before[2]);
        printf("  End:   %02d:%02d:%02d.%02d\n",
                after[1], after[0], after[3], after[2]);
}


/*
 *  delay2 -- delay for 4.0 sec (= 2000 * 2000 usec)
 */

static
delay2()
{
        char    before[4];
        char    after[4];
        int     i;

        printf("\nNow, delay 2000 * 2000 usec...\n");
        dostime(&before);
        for (i = 0; i < 2000; i++) del2m();
        dostime(&after);
        printf("  Start: %02d:%02d:%02d.%02d\n",
                before[1], before[0], before[3], before[2]);
        printf("  End:   %02d:%02d:%02d.%02d\n",
                after[1], after[0], after[3], after[2]);
}

/*
 * driver main program:
 */

main(argc, argv)
int argc; char *argv[];
{
        init();
        delay1();
        delay2();
        exit(0);
}
```

Detecting Video Type

Automatic video detection should be an almost universal part of your software if
you want to display any of the IBM extended character set or bit-mapped graphics
on the video display. Further, automatic display-type determination eliminates

placing the burden of video-display installation on the user. Of course, a feature that lets users override this display determination, similar to the ones described in the copyright-notice section of our article, could be incorporated into your program.

Video detection starts with determination of the active display- adapter type. The five major adapter types are IBM Monochrome Adapter, Hercules Graphics Card, IBM Color Graphics Adapter (CGA), IBM Enhanced Graphics Adapter (EGA), and IBM Professional Graphics Adapters (PGA). The procedure in Listing 5-6 detects these adapter types and sets the appropriate performance bits in the variable *VIDEO_FEATURES*.

Listing 5-6: Detecting Video Type

```
; Video.asm is the Lattice C-callable assembly language routine that determines
; the presence of video screen adapter cards and displays in an  IBM compatible
; system.
; *NOTE* The timing loops have only been validated on 6 Mhz. AT

; Copyright (c) 1986 Dan Jacobs and Joel Rosenblum

; portions copyrighted by Hercules Corp. and International Business Machines Corp.

; For a more complete test of the EGA adapter card see IBM Seminar Proceedings
; Vol. 2, No. 11-1

        name    video_test      ;determine video adapter card

        include dos.mac         ; Lattice C memory model configuration macro
                                ; In this case it is a copy of dm8086.mac

; *NOTE* all the below equates must be the same as list1.c

; video mode equates
CGA             equ     01H     ; IBM Color graphics adapter (CGA)
MONO            equ     02H     ; IBM Monochrome card
HERCULES        equ     04H     ; Hercules monochrome graphics card
PGA             equ     08H     ; Professional graphics controller (PGA)
EGA_MONO        equ     10H     ; IBM Enhanced graphics adapter (EGA) w/monochrome display
EGA_COLOR       equ     20H     ; EGA w/color display
EGA_HIGH        equ     40H     ; EGA w/high resolution color display
UNKNOWN         equ     80H     ; Unknown board type

; machine type equates
IBMCOMPAT       equ     0100H
IBMPC           equ     0200H
```

```
IBMPCAT         equ     0400H
IBM_CONVERT     equ     0800H

; global equates
VIDEO_IO        equ     10H     ; BIOS video i/o interrupt number
GET_MODE        equ     0FH     ; video i/o get mode function

        DSEG

video_type      db      ?       ; place to accumulate the video type
t_features      dw      ?       ; machine discriptor passed to function

        ENDDS

        PSEG

comment\*********************************************************************

NAME
        Video_test - checks to see which video adapter and display are used

SYNOPSIS
        unsigned int Video_test (features);
        unsigned features;                      see definition of machine type

RETURN VALUE
        type of video board used
                01H = Color graphics adapter
                02H = Monochrome card
                04H = Hercules card
                08H = Professional graphics adapter
                10H = EGA w/monocrome display
                20H = EGA w/color display
                40H = EGA w/high resolution color display
                80H = Unknown video card

*********************************************************************\

                public  video_test

video_test      proc    near

        push    bp              ; save the frame pointer (if called from C)
        mov     bp, sp

        ; next, save the passed existing features
        mov     ax, 4[bp]
        mov     t_features, ax

check_ega:
        ; Unfortunately this method of checking the EGA requires the use of
```

```
                    ; BIOS routines.  Therefore, it can only be used on compatible
                    ; machines. We first, however, determine if we can make the BIOS call.

                    ; We use FEATURES to check if the BIOS int 10
                    ; is available for use.

            test    t_features, IBMCOMPAT + IBMPC + IBMPCAT
            jz      ega_done                ; can only do this test on compatible

            mov     ax, 1200H               ; video alternate select
            mov     bl, 10H                 ; return EGA info
            mov     bh, 0FFH                ; invalid data for test
            mov     cl, 0FH                 ; reserved switch setting
            int     VIDEO_IO                ; returns with bh = color or mono mode
                                            ;            bl = memory value
                                            ;            ch = feature bits
                                            ;            cl = switch setting

            cmp     cl, 0CH                 ; test switch setting
            jge     ega_done                ; above max setting
            cmp     bh, 01H                 ; test range 0 - 1
            jg      ega_done                ; above range
            cmp     bl, 03H                 ; check memory value for 0 - 3 range
            jg      ega_done                ; above range

            ; if it gets here, there is a EGA card present
            ; now test for the attached monitor

            and     cl, 0EH                 ; trim the switch to the bits we need
            cmp     cl, 1010B               ; monochrome monitor attached ?
            je      is_m
            cmp     cl, 0100B               ; secondary mono setting ?
            jne     color                   ; nope check color display
is_m:       or      video_type, EGA_MONO    ; set EGA card with monochrome display
            jmp     short ega_done
color:      cmp     cl, 1000B               ; primary color display ?
            je      is_c
            cmp     cl, 1110B               ; secondary color ?
            jne     enh_d                   ; check for high resolution display
is_c:       or      video_type, EGA_COLOR   ; EGA card with color display
            jmp     short ega_done
enh_d:      cmp     cl, 1100B               ; primary high resolution display ?
            je      is_enh
            cmp     cl, 0110B               ; secondary high resolution display ?
            jne     ega_done
is_enh:     or      video_type, EGA_HIGH    ; EGA card with high resolution color display

ega_done:

            ; check for Hercules card is present by checking the status port
            ; at 3BAH for the vertical retrace bit.
```

```
        ; **NOTE** you can also tell the mode the card is in and set the card
        ; mode.  For more information, contact Hercules technical support.

        mov     dx,3BAH                 ; address of status port
        in      al,dx
        and     al,80h                  ; vertical retrace bit
        mov     ah,al                   ; Save bit 7 for test

        mov     cx,8000h                ; count for delay loop
examine:
        in      al,dx                   ; Take another reading
        and     al,80h                  ; Isolate bit 7
        cmp     al,ah
        jne     is_hercules             ; If bit 7 changes then it
        loop    examine                 ; is a Hercules Graphics Card

        jmp     check_color             ; After this long, it must be
                                        ; something else.
is_hercules:
        or      video_type, HERCULES
        jmp     short check_pga         ; don't check for mono or color
                                        ; board if Hercules present

check_color:
        test    video_type, EGA_COLOR + EGA_HIGH
        jnz     check_mono              ; can't have a color card with
                                        ; EGA in color mode

        ; next check for a Color Graphics Adapter by the checking for the
        ; presence of the cursor register at 0x3D4
        mov     dx, 03D4H
        call    cursor_reg              ; carry flag set if not there
        jc      check_mono
        or      video_type, CGA         ; there is a color graphics adapter

check_mono:
        test    video_type, EGA_MONO    ; can't have mono card in machine
        jnz     check_pga               ; with EGA in mono

        ; first check for a monochrome board by checking for the
        ; presence of the cursor register at 0x3B4
        mov     dx, 03B4H
        call    cursor_reg              ; carry flag set if not there
        jc      check_pga
        or      video_type, MONO        ; there is a monochrome adapter card

check_pga:
        ; now test for a Professional Graphics Adapter by checking the cursor
        ; status register which is memory mapped to address C600:03DB

        push    es
```

```
        mov     ax, 0C600H              ; load segment
        mov     es, ax
        mov     di, 03DBH               ; load offset
        mov     ah, es:[di]             ; save the original value
        mov     byte ptr es:[di], 5AH   ; test value
        mov     al, byte ptr es:[di]    ; read it back
        mov     byte ptr es:[di], ah    ; restore original
        cmp     al, 5AH
        pop     es                      ; clear stack
        jne     check_done              ; no PGA adapter
        or      video_type, PGA         ; yes, it's there

check_done:
        cmp     video_type, 0           ; When all else fails...
        jne     exit                    ; can't recognize any card
        mov     video_type, UNKNOWN

exit:   xor     ax, ax                  ; clear ah
        mov     al, video_type

        pop     bp                      ; restore frame pointer to return to C caller

        ret

video_test      endp


comment\**********************************************************************

NAME
        cursor_reg

SYNOPSIS
        checks to see if there is a cursor register at the
        address passed in dx

RETURN VALUE
        carry clear - if cursor register present
        carry set   - no cursor register here

**********************************************************************\
cursor_reg      proc    near

        mov     al, 0FH         ; set the index to the cursor register
        out     dx, al
        inc     dx              ; increment to data register
        in      al, dx          ; get the original value
        xchg    al, ah          ; save it for later
        mov     al, 5AH         ; test value
        out     dx, al          ; set cursor control register
        jmp     $+2             ; waste some time
```

```
        jmp     $+2
        jmp     $+2
        in      al, dx
        cmp     al, 5AH         ; same as written ?
        xchg    al, ah          ; restore saved value
        out     dx, al
        je      yup             ; it was the control register
        stc                     ; no cursor return code
        ret
yup:    clc                     ; is there return code
        ret


cursor_reg      endp


        ENDPS
        end
```

The performance bits in *VIDEO_FEATURES* activate code within your program, which can then take advantage of the selected display adapter's features. Programs that allow use of the EGA's colors, for instance, could be set active when that adapter type is detected. You could also use *VIDEO_FEATURES* bit flags to politely notify your user that a particular display is not present if, for instance, your software absolutely requires the use of that display.

If none of the above display adapters is in the compatible's hardware, the display might still have the ability to position the cursor directly on the screen. Direct cursor positioning lets screen displays appear without scrolling. Displays with this capability are ANSI-compatible. ANSI compatibility implies that the *ANSI.SYS* device driver has been installed by the user as part of the *CONFIG.SYS* file on the compatible machine. If you incorporate the code contained in Listing 5-7 into your program, the program will be able to directly check whether *ANSI.SYS* has been installed on the user's machine.

Listing 5-7: Test for Presence of ANSI.SYS

```
/*
    This code contains the check for the presence of ANSI.SYS.    If
    found, the appropriate bit in VIDEO_FEATURES is set.  This code
    is called from listing 2 and is  compatible with the  Lattice C
    Compiler.

    Copyright (c) 1986 Dan Jacobs and Joel Rosenblum

    Compiled using Lattice C ver 2.15, using -md -n options
```

```
*/

#include "dos.h"

#define FAIL   1
#define OK     0

#define ANSI      1
#define NOT_ANSI  0

int line, line2, column, column2;
union REGS in, out;      /* defined in dos.h file of Lattice C Compiler */

/***************************************************************************

NAME
    check_ansi

SYNOPSIS
    Checks to see if ANSI.SYS is installed on your machine
    by doing an ansi "report cursor position"  call  twice
    in a row to make sure each call returns a value,   and
    that the values match for  two successive calls.   For
    further  information  on  ANSI.SYS,  see  the  IBM DOS
    technical reference.

RETURN VALUE
    1 if ansi.sys is installed
    0 otherwise

****************************************************************************/

check_ansi()
{

    dump_key_buffer();
    cputs("\x1B[6n");   /* report cursor position command */
    if (get_line_column()) {
        dump_key_buffer();
        return NOT_ANSI;    /* no cursor position came in */
    }
    line2 = line;       /* save the reported values */
    column2 = column;

    dump_key_buffer();
    cputs("\x1B[6n");   /* try it one more time */
    if (get_line_column()) {
        dump_key_buffer();
        return NOT_ANSI;
    }
```

```
        dump_key_buffer();

        if (line2 != line || column2 != column) return NOT_ANSI;

        return ANSI;
}
```

```
/****************************************************************************

NAME
        get_line_column

SYNOPSIS
        checks to see if there are two keystokes
        the keyboard buffer (K.B.) and if so,
        them in the global variables line
        column.

****************************************************************************/
```

```
get_line_column()

{
    if (!(line = check_key())) return FAIL;
    if (!(column = check_key())) return FAIL;
    return OK;
}
```

```
/****************************************************************************

NAME
        check_key

SYNOPSIS
        returns keystroke left in K.B. if a keystroke exists there

****************************************************************************/
```

```
check_key()
{
    int c;

    for (c = 0; c < 100; c++)
        ; /* do nothing but wait */

    in.h.dl = 0xFF;
    in.h.ah = 0x6;
    c = intdos(&in, &out);

    if (c & 0x40) return 0;
```

```
        return (int)out.h.al;
}

/***************************************************************************

NAME

        dump_key_buffer

SYNOPSIS

        clears K.B.

***************************************************************************/


dump_key_buffer()
{
    in.h.dl = 0xFF;
    in.h.al = 0x06;
    in.h.ah = 0x0C;
    intdos(&in, &out);
}
```

In addition to determining ANSI compatibility, you might want to take advantage of the IBM extended character set so that you can design screen displays and menus to look better. Screen enhancements such as character blinking, underlining, and boldface might also be possible. We assume that a machine has an extended character set if it has the *IBMCOMPAT* bit set in the variable *FEATURES*.

The sample program in Listing 5-8 shows how to draw a simple box that could take advantage of the machine's ability to use the IBM extended character set. The *draw_box* routine uses the *IBMCOMPAT* bit flag contained in *FEATURES* to determine which character set can be displayed. Figure 5-1 shows the difference between boxes drawn with the two sets.

Listing 5-8: Example Video Character Output Routine

```
/*
    This code contains a C language example that uses the bit
    fields contained within the FEATURES variable to determine
    if it is possible to display the IBM extended character
    set on the machine.  We assume these characters may be
    displayed if the machine is IBMCOMPAT.  Note that this
    may be called from other modules in your program without
    regard to hardware considerations.
```

```
    Compiled using Lattice C ver 2.15, using -md -n options
*/


extern unsigned int features;        /* see definition */


/* position of characters in box_char */
#define TOP_LEFT          0
#define TOP_SIDE          1
#define TOP_RIGHT         2
#define SIDES             3
#define BOTTOM_LEFT       4
#define BOTTOM_SIDE       5
#define BOTTOM_RIGHT      6


char box_char[2][7] = {
        {0xDA, 0xC4, 0xBF, 0xB3, 0xC0, 0xC4, 0xD9}, /* expanded char codes */
        {0x2B, 0x2D, 0x2B, 0x7C, 0x2B, 0x2D, 0x2D}  /* replacement char codes
                                                       to use when no extended
                                                       codes can be used */

    };


/**************************************************************************

NAME
        draw_box

SYNOPSIS
        Draws a box of size, length, and width at the row
        and column specified.  Notice how the characters
        used for the box are changed based on the
        availability of the  extended  set.   (Those
        characters only exist on IBM compatibles).

**************************************************************************/


draw_box(row, column, length, depth)
int row, column, length, depth;
{
    int i;
    int char_set;  /* tells which row of box_char to use based
                      on the the IBMCOMPAT bit in features, use row
                      0, which contains extended chars, if IBMCOMPAT
                      otherwise, use row 1 which contains standard
                      ASCII replacements for the extended set */


    char_set = features & IBMCOMPAT ? 0 : 1;


    move_cursor(row, column);   /* First, draw left corner */
```

```
/* Move_curser is in listing 9.  It moves the cursor to row, column
   by determining the machine's video features contained in the bit
   flags in FEATURES.  You notice that your program does not need
   to worry about the details of how to move the cursor depending
   upon which machine is used.  That leaves you free to solve more
   important problems */


putchars(box_char[char_set][TOP_LEFT], 1);

/* Putchars is a routine which puts the char passed in the first arg
   out to the screen the number of times specified by the second arg.
   Putchar also decides which method it will use to output that char
   based on the type of equiptment installed on your machine.  See
   listing 9 for move_cursor detail */

move_cursor(row, column+1);     /* now the top side */
putchars(box_char[char_set][TOP_SIDE], length-2);

move_cursor(row, column+length-1); /* next top right corner */
putchars(box_char[char_set][TOP_RIGHT], 1);

for(i = 1; i < length-1; i++)  {  /* Vertical sides */
    move_cursor(row+i, column);
    putchars(box_char[char_set][SIDES], 1);
    move_cursor(row+i, column+length-1);
    putchars(box_char[char_set][SIDES], 1);
}

move_cursor(row+length-1, column); /* bottom left corner */
putchars(box_char[char_set][BOTTOM_LEFT], 1);

move_cursor(row+length-1, column+1 ); /* bottom side */
putchars(box_char[char_set][BOTTOM_SIDE], length-2);

move_cursor(row+length-1, column+length-1); /* bottom right corner */
putchars(box_char[char_set][BOTTOM_RIGHT], 1);

}
```

The draw-box routine uses a routine called *move_cursor*, which is contained in Listing 5-9. Whereas draw_box uses a bit flag set in *FEATURES*, move_cursor relies more directly upon the video hardware. Thus, it uses bit flags set in *VIDEO_FEATURES*, as well as a bit set in *FEATURES*. Move_cursor then moves the cursor to the position row, column. It decides which method is needed to move the cursor on your particular machine without burdening the calling program with the task.

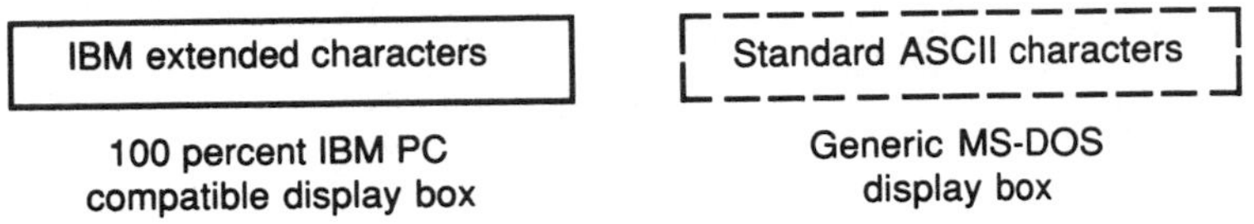

IBM extended characters		Standard ASCII characters

100 percent IBM PC
compatible display box

Generic MS-DOS
display box

Figure 5-1: Two boxes drawn by the routine in Listing 5-8, on a system that has the IBM extended character set available (left) and on a system that does not and uses only ASCII characters (right).

Listing 5-9: Example Video Cursor Positioning Routine

```
/*

    This routine handles the details of  cursor positioning  based on
    the bits set in the variables  FEATURES and  VIDEO_FEATURES.    It
    is called from the draw_box routine in listing 8, and illustrates
    how common machine dependent routines  should  be written.    Note
    a similar type of routine  should exist in your program to handle
    bit-mapped graphics-related calls.

    Compiled using Lattice C ver 2.15, using -md -n options
*/

extern unsigned int features;       /* global variable which holds machine features */
extern unsigned int video_features; /* global variable which holds video-related features */


char *screen_buff; /* pointer to buffer of 2000 (80*25) chars which is big
                      enough to hold the ASCII  charactures for a complete
                      video page */
char *screen_pos;  /* pointer into screen_buff at current cursor position */

char page_no;      /* previously set video page number */

char string[80];   /* string to use for ASCII calls */

/*****************************************************************************

NAME
    move_cursor

SYNOPSIS
    moves the cursor to row, column on the video  display
    note  that  the  routine decides which method to  use
    based on bits set in both FEATURES and VIDEO_FEATURES
```

```
*************************************************************************/

move_cursor(row, column)
int row, column;
{
    union REGS inregs, outregs;          /* defined in dos.h */

    if (features & IBMCOMPAT) {          /* use int 10 video bios */
        inregs.h.ah = 2;                 /* set cursor position */
        inregs.h.dl = column;
        inregs.h.dh = row;
        inregs.h.bh = page_no;           /* page number */
        int86(0x10, &inregs, &outregs);     /* do bios int 10 */
    } else if (video_features & ANSI) {   /* need to do ansi calls */
        sprintf(string, "\x1B[%d;%df$", ++row, ++column);
        dos_puts(string); /* dos_puts is a routine that calls dos and
                            prints string using function 9, print string */
    } else { /* dos generic mode */
        screen_pos = screen_buff + row * 80 + column;
    }

        /* NOTE: In DOS generic mode we keep a buffer (screen_buff)
            big enough to hold one video page of ASCII text.  In all
            of the calls that write to video, we move the chars into
            screen_buf at the pheudo cursor position, screen_pos.
            When we have completed updating the memory-based page,
            we write the ASCII chars from the memory buffer to the
            actual screen using standard dos calls */
}
```

Note that if your program detects the presence of *ANSI.SYS* operating on a machine that is *IBMCOMPAT* and sets screen attributes using BIOS-level video calls, then it should not use the low-level video DOS calls to display additional text. To do so will overwrite the attributes you have just set with what *ANSI.SYS* believes the attributes to be. Complicated problems like this are easier to solve with the availability of some of the seemingly unrelated bit flags. Parts of your program gain compatibility and performance on some machines but not on others. Here's a scenario.

Incorporating processor- and speed-detection procedures into your program allows for run-time performance determination of the PC compatible. Based on that run-time analysis, you could enable sections of optimizing code in the program by setting your program's "performance bit flags." For example, a multiuser spreadsheet program that allows for multiple users only if operating on an 80286-based system could determine if the processor type was an 80286. If so, a flag within the software could be set that allows multiuser capability.

6

Moving from the 8088 *
to the 80286

_____ *William J. Claff* _____

This guide to writing assembly-language code for the IBM PC family pays particular attention to the impact of the 80286 on current programming methods. With the growing number of 80286-based machines, including the IBM PC AT (and probably the anticipated IBM "PC2"), the differences between the 80286 and the 8088 become quite important to the software developer. This is especially true when multitasking and multiuser operating systems acquire a larger installed base. These differences also highlight the ever-present need to structure programs for change.

This article is not a primer. It assumes that you are familiar with assembly-language concepts and does not cover the expanded instruction set of the 80286 or how to write systems software. Its primary aim is to acquaint you with the specific differences between the 80286 and the 8088. It also attempts to convey that change is inevitable and programs must be structured accordingly.

The 8088 Microprocessor

Figure 6-1 shows an elementary block diagram of the 8088. This processor has two separate processing units: the execution unit (*EU*), which executes instructions, and the bus interface unit (*BIU*), which is responsible for the 8088's communication with the outside world. The *EU* provides a logical address to the *BIU*, which translates it into a physical address. This translation, called the physical-address computation, uses two 16-bit quantities: a segment register and an offset. The notation used for logical addresses is *segment:offset*. The segment registers (parts of the *BIU*) are code segment (*CS*), data segment (*DS*), stack segment (*SS*), and extra segment (*ES*). The offset is usually supplied by the *EU*.

To compute the physical address, the 8088 shifts the segment register left 4 bits

_____

* © McGraw-Hill Information Systems Company, *BYTE*, Fall 1985, p. 93

and adds the offset in the *BIU*'s dedicated adder, Σ. Segments are 64K-byte relocatable pieces of the 1-megabyte physical-address space. They are located on 16-byte boundaries called paragraphs. Since assembly-language programs are written in logical segments, the placement of these segments in memory is a function of the linker and DOS. They can be overlapped, contiguous, or disjointed.

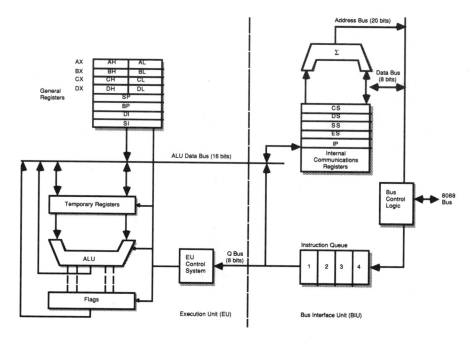

Figure 6-1: An 8088 Elementary Block Diagram

The address of the next instruction to be executed is *CS:IP* (code segment:instruction pointer). For increased efficiency, the *BIU* pipelines bytes (prefetches them and puts them into a queue). To facilitate this calculation, the instruction-pointer register is kept in the *BIU*.

The *EU* contains eight 16-bit registers, any of which can be used in computations. Four of these registers comprise the data group. They are the accumulator (*AX*), base (*BX*), count (*CX*), and data (*DX*) registers. The 8088 can also access the high and low 8 bits of each data register. The two halves of the accumulator register, for example, are *AH* (accumulator high) and AL (accumulator low). The respective halves of the *BX*, *CX*, and *DX* registers are similarly named.

The next two general registers, the stack pointer (*SP*) and the base pointer (*BP*), constitute the pointer group. These registers manipulate the stack. When a sub-routine is invoked, *SS:SP* (stack segment:stack pointer) stores the return address on the stack. *SP* points to the top of the stack and *BP* to the base. *SP* is auto-matically decremented by calls and incremented by returns. The stack is also used to pass subroutine parameters. *BP* accesses these parameters.

Two other general registers, the destination index (*DI*) and the source index (*SI*) make up the index group and are used primarily in string operations. Two seg-ment registers are required to perform moves or comparisons on memory more than 64K bytes apart. This is why there is an *ES* in the *BIU* in addition to the *DS*. The destination in a string operation is always *ES:DI* (extra segment: desti-nation index).

Many of the registers in the *EU* have special uses. Table 6-1 shows these regis-ters and their uses.

Register	Operations
AX	Word multiply, word divide, word I/O
AL	Byte multiply, byte divide, byte I/O, translate, decimal arithmetic
AH	Byte multiply, byte divide
BX	Translate
CX	String operations, loops
CL	Variable shift, variable rotate
DX	Word multiply, word divide, indirect I/O
SP	Stack operations
I	String operations
DI	String operations

Table 6-1: 8088's Implicit Use of General Registers

8088 Addressing

The *EU* generates an effective address (offset) using one of several methods called addressing modes. An effective address has one or more of the following: base, index, and displacement. A base can be *BX* or *BP*; an index can be either *SI* or *DI*; and a displacement is a 16-bit signed number.

If you do not specify a segment register, the 8088 uses the *DS* register. If you specify the *BP* register as the base, it uses *SP* as the segment register. Supplying a segment register other than the default is called using a segment-override prefix.

However, you cannot override the *IP*, *SP*, or *DI* register in string operations. Figure 6-2 shows how the various addressing modes in the *EU* and the *BIU* combine to form the physical address.

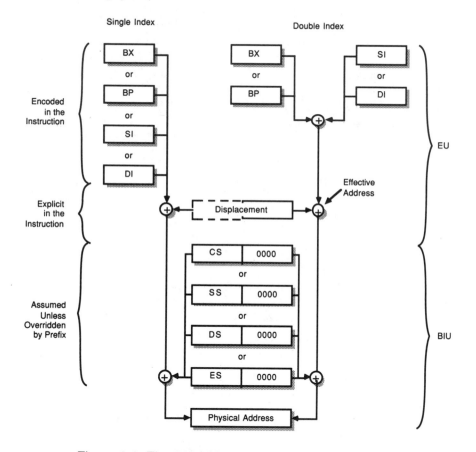

Figure 6-2: The 8088 Memory-Address Computation

8088 Interrupts

The 8088 does not distinguish between interrupts invoked by the assembly-language instruction *INT* and those generated by the hardware. There are 256 interrupts, vectored through a table of double words found at location 00000:00000 hexadecimal. Each double-word entry in the table corresponds to the *CS:IP* of the subroutine that the interrupt invokes. The 8088 uses interrupts 000 through 004 hexadecimal for the following errors: divide by zero, single step, nonmaskable interrupt, breakpoint, and overflow.

The 80286 Central Processing Unit

Figure 6-3 shows an elementary block diagram of the 80286. This processor has four separate processing units: the *EU*, the bus unit (*BU*), the instruction unit (*IU*) and the address unit (*AU*). The 80286 operates in either real-address mode or protected virtual-address mode (protected mode). Bits in a new register, the machine status word (MSW), control the processor mode. The machine status word also activates a feature of the 80286 that allows for the emulation of coprocessors such as the 80287. Let's examine the components as they operate in real-address mode first.

The *IU* is a further refinement of pipelining. The *BU* prefetches up to 6 bytes of instructions; however, instead of being decoded by the *EU* as in the 8088, the *IU* decodes them in parallel execution with the *EU*. This improves the speed of the 80286 but has no impact on programming.

The 80286's *BU* and *AU* operate in essentially the same way as the 8088's *BIU* does. Specifically, the *AU* calculates the physical addresses in the same manner.

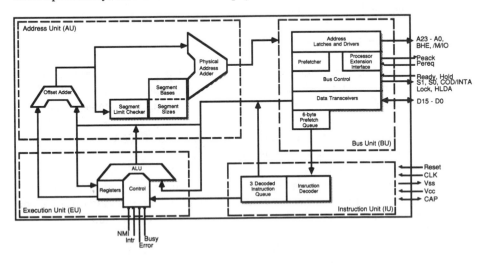

Figure 6-3: An 80286 Internal Block Diagram

80286 Execution Unit

While the *EU* executes a superset of the 8088 instruction set, some instructions operate slightly differently, posing a compatibility problem. These differences are summarized as follows, but are of no consequence in most applications programming:

- Shift counts are masked to reduce the maximum instruction time. The *CL* register is masked when it is used as a shift or rotate count.

- *PUSH SP* works differently. Due to protected mode, the value of *PUSH SP* is different on the 80286. If this is important, you should use the following instructions:

```
PUSH BP
MOV  BP,SP
XCHG BP,[SP]
```

- Flag word has a different value. The upper 4 bits of the flag word are 1111 on an 8088 and 0000 on an 80286 operating in real-address mode. (Note: This provides a way of telling these processors apart programmatically.)

- Quotients of 80 or 8000 hexadecimal are possible.

- Divide error is restartable.

- Segment wraparound causes exception *D* hexadecimal.

- External interrupt handlers cannot be single stepped. The priority of the single-step interrupt has been changed. This keeps an external interrupt from being single-stepped if it occurs while single-stepping through a program.

- Interrupts can occur after *MOV/POP DS/ES*. The 80286 only ignores interrupts after a *MOV/POP SS* instruction.

- Do not rely on NMI (nonmaskable interrupt) interrupting the NMI handler. The 80286 disables NMI and processor-extension interrupts after recognizing an NMI; they remain disabled until the first *IRET* is executed.

- Place a far jump at FFFF0 hexadecimal. The 80286 starts execution at F000:FFF0 hexadecimal as opposed to the FFFF:0000 for the 8088.

- Do not duplicate prefixes. The prefetch and instruction unit imposes a 10-byte instruction-length limit that you can reach only if you code redundant prefixes.

- Do not use undefined op codes, in particular *POP CS* or *MOV CS,op* or *POP/PUSH mem* with undefined encodings.

- Self-modifying code may not work. Since the 80286 can prefetch further ahead, you should jump to self-modifying code. (Note: Self-modifying code will not be compatible with the 80386 microprocessor.)

- The numeric-exception handler must use interrupt 10 hexadecimal.

- The numeric-exception handler must not use the 8259A-chip *INT* signal.

- *FNDISI* and *FDISI* do not disable numeric interrupts.

- Do not perform I/O (input/output) to ports F8-FD hexadecimal.

- Avoid operations that the *iAPX 286* may restrict to ensure system integrity, low interrupt latency, or low bus-request latencies (for example, shift/rotate with shift count greater than 31, locked *CMPS/STOS/SCAS/LODS*, *STI*, *CLI*, *HALT*, and I/O instructions).

- Do not rely on the value pushed onto the stack by *PUSH SP*.

- Do not rely on processor instruction-execution times.

80286 Interrupts

Another difference between the 8088 and the 80286 operating in real-address mode is in their handling of interrupt vectors. Table 6-2 lists the 80286's predefined interrupt vectors. These new interrupt vectors would not be a problem if IBM had avoided using Intel's reserved interrupts in designing the PC. For example, a processor-extension error (interrupt 10 hexadecimal for the 80286 in Table 6-2) causes a random video interrupt (the IBM PC's use of interrupt 10 hexadecimal) to occur. These new interrupts are unlikely to occur in real-address mode, and you can trap them in protected mode, so this may not turn out to be as great a problem as it appears.

00	Divide-error exception
01	Single-step interrupt
02	Nonmaskable interrupt
03	Breakpoint interrupt
04	INTO detected overflow exception
05	Bound RANGE exceeded exception
06	Invalid op-code exception
07	Processor-extension not-present trap
08	Double protection exception
09	Processor-extension segment overrun exception
0A	Task segment format exception
0B	Segment not-present exception
0C	Stack under-/overflow exception
0D	General protection exception
0E-0F	Reserved
10	Processor-extension-error interrupt
11-1F	Reserved

Table 6-2: The 80286's Predefined Interrupt Vectors

Protected Mode

Examination of the processor components as they operate in protected mode brings the most significant difference between the 8088 and the 80286 to light. Since most 80286-based systems are currently operating in real-address mode, this difference has not yet become a major problem.

Figure 6-4 shows the complete 80286 register set when operating in protected mode. There are several new registers, some of which are not programmer accessible. In protected mode the *AU* provides full memory management, protection, and virtual-memory support. To do this, the *AU* sets up operating-system control tables in memory that describe all of the machine's memory, and then the hardware enforces the information in these tables.

The 80286 extends the 8088's 16-bit segment registers into 64-bit segment selectors by appending a 48-bit segment descriptor taken from a descriptor table that uses the segment register as an index. Using the segment descriptor to hold this information is called an *explicit cache*. This is more efficient since the indexing takes place only when you set the segment-register value, rather than

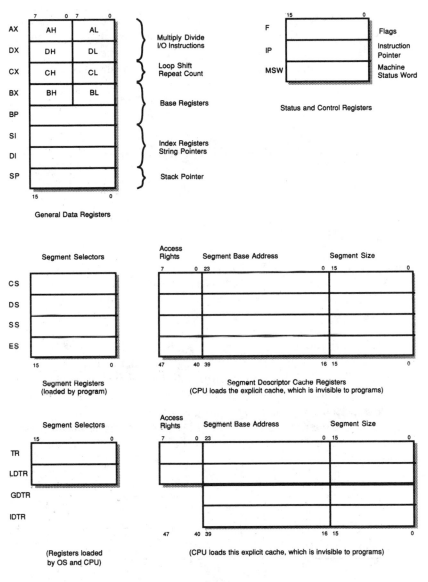

Figure 6-4: The Full Register Set for the 80286

each time you use it.

Figure 6-5 shows the format of the selector. The requested privilege level refers to reducing the privilege level required to access a particular segment. The table indicator lets you choose between using the global descriptor table (GDT) and the currently active local descriptor table (LDT). There is only one global descriptor table; it is established when you enter protected mode. The currently active local descriptor table, if any, is a segment within the global descriptor table. The 14-bit index portion of the selector and the 16-bit offset combine to allow a 1-gigabyte logical-address space.

15							8	7						2		0
			Index											TI	RPL	

Figure 6-5: The format of a selector, where TI means table indicator and RPL means requested privilege level.

Descriptor tables are segments and can contain up to 8192 8-byte descriptors. There are four types of descriptors: data-segment, executable-segment, system-segment, and gate. Figures 6-6a through 6-6d contain the formats of these descriptors.

Data-segment descriptors contain system or application data including stacks. Executable-segment descriptors refer only to segments that contain instructions. System-segment descriptors contain data structures that are recognized directly by the hardware such as the descriptor tables themselves. A gate descriptor provides a pointer to an exported entry point. The call gate offers an additional level very much like a software interrupt. A particular call gate can represent the entry point of an operating-system function by number so that no explicit binding of addresses is required.

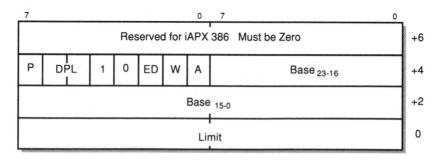

Figure 6-6a: Data-segment descriptor, where P means present bit; DPL, descriptor privilege level; ED, expansion direction; W, writable; and A, accessed

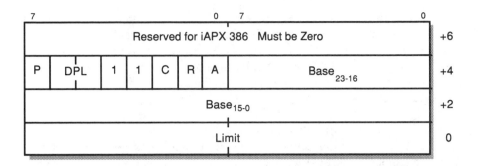

Figure 6-6b: Executable-segment descriptor, where P means present bit; DPL, descriptor privilege level; C, conforming; R, readable; and A, accessed

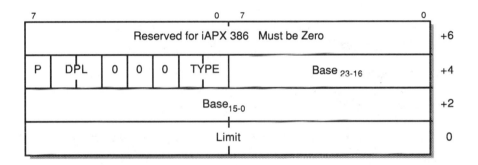

Figure 6-6c: System-segment descriptor, where P means present bit and DPL means descriptor privilege level

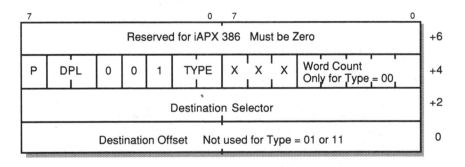

Figure 6-6d: Gate descriptor, where P means present bit; DPL, despcriptor privilege level; and X, *not used*

The present bit (P) and the accessed bit (A) are used in implementing virtual memory. The other bits hold protection and privilege information of interest if you are writing operating systems. The 24-bit base address for a segment means that the 1-gigabyte logical-address space is mapped into a 16-megabyte physical-address space. The 16-bit limit means that segments in the 80286 address space can be less than 64K bytes.

There is also an interrupt-descriptor table (IDT). This makes it possible for different tasks in a multitasking environment to have their own interrupt handlers. This table is conceptually like the real-address mode vector tables except that the entries are descriptors and not double words. Inspecting or changing interrupt vectors in protected mode is necessarily an operating-system function.

Differences

The different view of memory that each of these machines takes implies several rules for programming on the 80286.

- Since segments can be less than 64K bytes, keep all references within the logical-segment boundary. For example, do not use a label at the end of a data segment as if it were the offset to free memory.

- Keep all data and code references within logical-segment boundaries and consistent with the segment's attributes.

- Do not rely on the *iAPX 86* relationship between the value in a segment register and the selected physical memory. Programs should be as independent of the physical-memory address in which they reside as possible.

- Do not write self-modifying code.

- Do not use overlapping segments.

- Do not store temporary values in segment registers.

- Use intersegment calls to invoke operating-system functions.

Conclusion

By applying good programming techniques and by paying attention to the differences between the 8088 and the 80286, you can greatly simplify the writing of easily transportable programs. As microcomputers become more complicated, proper programming structure and practice become more important. You should write modular programs that use operating-system-provided facilities as heavily as possible. For the 80286 this is especially true of memory-management and I/O facilities. Many software developers have already adopted this approach because it results in "well-behaved" programs in the IBM TopView and Microsoft Windows environments. Your modifications are more likely to be localized and well defined if you take this approach.

References

1. *iAPX 86,88 User's Manual*. Santa Clara, CA; Intel Corp. 1981.

2. *iAPX 286 Hardware Reference Manual*. Santa Clara, CA; Intel Corp. 1983.

3. *Introduction to the iAPX 286*. Santa Clara, CA; Intel Corp., 1982.

4. *iAPX 286 Operating Systems Writer's Guide*. Santa Clara, CA; Intel Corp., 1983.

7

Experimenting with Protected *
Mode on the AT

_____*Marshall Brain*_____

For most users, the IBM AT and its compatibles are nothing more than accelerated PCs. The AT has the same 640K memory limit as the PC and runs DOS
programs exactly the same way the PC does, but it does its work three or four
times faster than the older system.

The AT's CPU chip, the 80286, can actually do a great deal more than simply
emulate the 8088 used in the PC, because the 80286 has two separate modes of
operation. It has a Real mode in which the 80286 behaves just like an 8088 or
8086. This mode allows the AT to act like a fast PC. The 80286 also has a
Protected mode in which the chip behaves like a main frame CPU. DOS currently
runs only in the Real mode, so the extra capabilities of the 80286 are never seen
by the normal user.

This chapter discusses the differences between the Real mode and the Protected
mode. It explains the requirements of Protected mode operation, and uses a simple
Turbo Pascal program to demonstrate taking the AT into Protected mode and back
out to Real mode. This chapter assumes that you have some knowledge of assembly language programming techniques on the 8088. You may also wish to
consult the books and articles listed in the bibliography for additional information
on the AT BIOS calls used and for more information about the Protected mode.

Differences Between the PC and the AT

The AT system board has three features that distinguish it from the PC system
board. First, the AT system board has not only the main CPU chip, but also a
second complete microprocessor called the 8042. This microprocessor is used
primarily as a keyboard interface, but it has other capabilities that are important
to using the Protected mode on the AT. Second, the AT has a CMOS
clock/RAM chip built onto the system board; this chip is used to provide a soft-

_____

© M&T Publishing, Inc., *Micro/Systems Journal*, January/February 1987, p. 34

5

ware equivalent for the DIP switches found on the PC system board, but it also has memory locations needed when you work in Protected mode. Finally, the AT system board contains an 80286 processor instead of the PC's 8088.

The presence of the 80286 gives the AT its speed boost in three ways: the 80286 runs at a higher clock rate; the 80286 has a 16-bit data bus compared to the 8088's 8 bit bus; and the 80286 has internal pipelining that speeds up instruction execution. When running in Real mode, the AT uses all of these advantages to provide noticeably better performance than the PC.

The very fact of the 80286's existence also gives the AT Protected mode capabilities. Once the 80286 is switched to Protected mode, the programmer is able to access the following features: (1) a 16Mb address space, as opposed to the Real mode's 1Mb space; (2) virtual memory support; (3) hardware multitasking support for context switching and task separation; and (4) an impermeable protection mechanism that isolates different tasks from one another. The AT has all of the essential features of a mainframe or super-minicomputer built in, due to the presence of the 80286.

Segment Registers

The main difference between the Real mode and the Protected mode on the AT lies in their use of the segment registers. A new use for segment registers is the key to the capabilities of the Protected mode. On the 8088, and on a 80286 running in Real mode, the segment registers are used simply to address a memory space greater than the 64K that would be allowed by the 16-bit width of the registers and instruction pointer. Whenever a memory access takes place, it is always done relative to one of four 16-bit segment registers; the value of the appropriate segment register is multiplied by 16 and added to the 16-bit offset value. This allows the CPU to reference any location in a 1 Mb address space.

In the Protected mode, you are able to access up to 16 Mb of physical memory (and up to several billion bytes of virtual memory), because the segment registers are used in a new way. Instead of being used as a physical memory pointer, the segment registers are used as 13-bit pointers that point into tables of "descriptors." Descriptors are 8-byte (64-bit)-long values that are used to describe a segment. Such a description includes the segment's location in physical memory, the segment's length, and the segment's access rights.

Many different types of descriptors are possible, because many different types of segments are defined in Protected mode. There are code segments, data segments, and task-state segments. In general, though, there are two main types of segments (and therefore segment descriptors): memory descriptors and control descriptors. This chapter concentrates on memory descriptors. Control descriptors are used to implement protection and multitasking features of the 80286, and will be largely ignored in this chapter.

To access descriptors, you use 16-bit segment register values to point into descriptor tables. These tables can be thought of as arrays of descriptors, with each descriptor being an 8-byte-long element of the array. There are three different types of tables defined. The Global Descriptor Table (GDT) is potentially accessible by any task in the system (although access may be denied). A Local Descriptor Table (LDT) can be defined for each task and is private to the task. An Interrupt Descriptor Table (IDT) is also defined and replaces the 256 vector pointers found in the first 1000 bytes on the 8088. These tables are stored in memory and are actually another type of segment themselves.

This chapter concentrates on memory descriptors in the GDT. Just remember that, in Protected mode, any segment register is used to point into a descriptor table so that a segment descriptor can be retrieved. The information contained in the segment descriptor is used to access memory.

How Descriptor Tables Work

Think about the following statements when they are made in Real mode or on the 8088:

```
MOV   AX,  40H
MOV   DS,  AX
```

They seem almost insignificant. A 16-bit value is moved to *AX*, and then this 16-bit value is moved to the data segment register *DS*. These statements allow you to access data beginning at memory location 400H.

In Protected mode, this instruction pair works very differently. *AX* gets loaded as usual, but the loading of *DS* sets in motion the following chain of events:

1) The upper 13 bits of the segment register are used as an index into the appropriate descriptor table.

2) The 8-byte descriptor is retrieved and placed into a descriptor cache for the appropriate segment register. On the 80286, all four segment

registers have the same 16 bit segment register found on the 8088, but there is also a hidden 8 byte register that holds the current segment descriptor for that segment register.

3) The cached information is then used any time a reference is made to the given segment.

This chain of events shown in Figure 7-1 occurs whenever any segment register is loaded with a new 16-bit value. Many instructions load segment registers, including *MOV* (as shown), *POP*, *LDS*, far *CALLs* and *JMPs*.

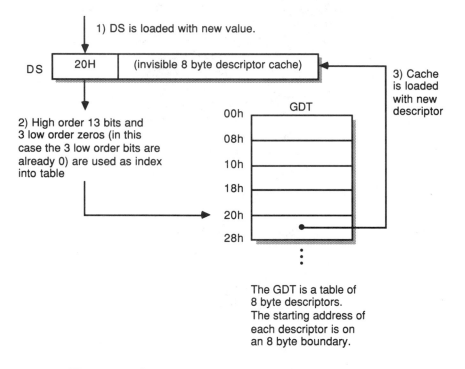

Figure 7-1: Sequence of events used whenever a new value is loaded into a segment register.

Figure 7-2 describes the format of information contained in segment registers and descriptors in Protected mode. As can be seen, it is the descriptor that actually contains the physical memory address for the segment. The descriptor also contains the length of the segment, and access rights. When you try to access information using a given segment, all of this cached information comes into play. For example, assume that the following instruction is executed:

```
MOV AX,DS[69H]
```

The following events take place:

1) The 80286 makes sure that 69H is within the length of the segment. If the segment is only 10 bytes long, a processor fault will occur.

2) The 80286 adds the 24 bit physical memory address found in the cache to the offset value 69H.

3) The memory location addressed by this sum is loaded into *AX*.

All of this takes place in hardware, using information that has already been loaded, so there is no time penalty for the extra work done in Protected mode. The only speed penalty occurs when a segment register is loaded. At that point, the 8-byte descriptor value must be retrieved and moved from the appropriate table in memory into the cache register.

Descriptors give the Protected mode its flexibility. For example, assume that *DS* is loaded with 40H at one point. At this time, the descriptor may indicate that this segment is located at memory location 1000H. At a later time, however, 40H might be moved into DS again, and this time the retrieved descriptor might indicate a physical address of 74500H. The program has no idea that the segment has been moved, because it used 40H to reference the data in both cases. It is also important to note that each segment is treated as a specific, fixed length entity, which can be moved or altered. This is somewhat different from the way segments are treated on the 8088.

Getting Into Protected Mode

To take advantage of the capabilities of Protected mode, the 80286 has to be running in Protected mode. Fortunately this is fairly easy, because the AT BIOS contains a call that will switch the 80286 into Protected mode. Before this call can be used, however, some preparation is required.

For the 80286 to work in Protected mode, it must have a GDT. The GDT is needed because the first thing that the 80286 does when it gets to Protected mode is to try to get the descriptor for the *CS* register. Without this it cannot execute any instructions. Also, the first instructions executed once in Protected mode are instructions that load the *SS*, *DS*, and *ES* registers, so that the program can access data and make subroutine calls. These four descriptors will be found in the

Segment register

INDEX | TI | RPL

15   3   2   1   0

Bits	Name	Description
0-1	RPL	Requested Privilege Level.
2	TI	Table Index. 0=GDT, 1=LDT. Tells the 80286 which table to get the descriptor from.
3-15	INDEX	Index into the descriptor table. Three zeros are placed in the 3 low order bits when the table is actually indexed.

Memory Descriptor

RESERVED | RGHTS | BASE | LIMIT

byte   7   6   5   4   3   2   1   0

Bytes	Name	Description
0-1	LIMIT	Maximum size of the segment. 1 to 64K bytes.
2-4	BASE	Location of the segment in physical memory. This is a 24 bit value to allow addressing across the entire 16 Meg address space.
5	RGHTS	Access rights byte. See below.
6-7	RESERVED	Reserved for use on the 80386.

Access Rights Byte for a data segment

P | DPL | 1 | E | X | W | A

bit   7   6   5   4   3   2   1   0

Bits	Name	Description
0	Accessed	1 Indicates that segment has been accessed.
1	Writable	For a data segment, 1=writable, 0=read only. For a code segment (bit 3 = 1), 1=readable, 0=execute only.
2	eXpansion	1=expand down, 0=expand up.
3	Executable	1=executable segment, 0=data segment.
4		Indicates Memory descriptor (as opposed to Control)
5-6	DPL	Descriptor privilege level.
7	Present	Indicates that segment is present in memory. 1=Present.

Figure 7-2: On the 80286, a segment register consists of the 16 byte segment register found on the 8088, as well as 8 bytes of cached information from a descriptor table. The individual bits of each of these values are defined as shown.

GDT, so the GDT must be set up in the Real mode before the switch to Protected mode is made. Once these four descriptors are cached, the 80286 can work on its own in Protected mode by creating or modifying descriptor tables to give it access to any memory location. The Protected mode needs the Real mode, though, to get things started.

To switch to Protected mode, an AT BIOS routine can be used. This routine is accessed using interrupt 15H, function 89H. As shown in the AT *Technical Reference Manual*, this routine requires that a GDT be set up before it is called. It also requires that an IDT be created. Normally, the IDT is set to handle at least the 14 processor faults possible on the 80286. These processor faults are shown in Table 7-1. A problem arises with these faults, however, because the original PC architecture defined hardware and software interrupts at many of these locations. The BIOS routine therefore allows the programmer to remap the hardware-interrupt controllers so that their vectors don't occur within the first 14 interrupts.

Number	Description
* 0	Divide Error
* 1	Single Step interrupt
* 2	Non-Maskable interrupt
* 3	Breakpoint interrupt
* 4	INTO Overflow
5	Bound Range Exceeded exception
6	Invalid Opcode exception
7	Processor Extension Unavailable
8	Double Exception Detected
9	Processor Extension Segment Overrun
10	Invalid Task State Segment
11	Segment Not Present
12	Stack Segment Overflow or Not Present
13	General Protection Error

*same as 8088

Table 7-1: Processor Faults on the 80286. Taken from the Intel Manual

This is all that is required to go to Protected mode. It would be nice, however, to be able to get back to Real mode eventually through software, rather than having to turn the machine off and back on to get back to DOS. Unfortunately, the 80286 has no provision for getting back to Real mode from Protected mode. Apparently the designers assumed that the Real mode would be used once to initialize a GDT and IDT, and that there would be no reason to return.

To get around this problem, a sort of Rube Goldberg machine was built into the AT that allows it to return to Real mode. It is used by the VDISK utility, for example, to allow it to access expanded memory. VDISK switches to Protected mode so that it can access the full 16M address space, stores or recalls information above the 1M memory limit of Real mode, and then returns to Real mode. To take advantage of this mechanism, it must be set up before entering Protected mode.

The mechanism works like this: To get back to Real mode from Protected mode, the 80286 sends a message to the 8042 microprocessor on the AT system board. This message says, "Reset the machine." The 8042 does this, sending a hardware reset across the AT system board. This is essentially the same signal as the signal created by powering off and back on. The 80286 resets, and the BIOS starts executing its normal power-on sequence in Real mode. (Whenever the 80286 is reset, it comes up in Real mode). Just before it starts its power-on self-test routines, however, it looks into the CMOS RAM. If it finds one of several different values in location 0FH of that RAM (the CMOS RAM has its own address space), it knows that the reset signal was not a "power on" signal, but instead a "returning from Protected mode" signal. The value 05H in location 0FH tells the BIOS to do a far jump directly to whatever location it finds in memory at 467H and 469H.

To use this mechanism, the programmer is required to set the CMOS RAM so that an 05H appears in its location 0FH and must also set up 467H and 469H (locations in the BIOS reserved memory area) to contain the address of the code that should begin executing when the computer returns to Real mode. If this is done correctly, the 80286 can go to Protected mode and then go back to Real mode without any problems.

An Example Program

Keeping all of this in mind, examine the example program. The main routine spells out the steps necessary to get into Protected mode.

The first statement sets up the GDT. The BIOS call being used requires eight descriptors, as described in Table 7-2. This routine simply sets the physical memory address, segment size, and appropriate access-rights byte into each descriptor. For most, the value 92H in the access-rights byte indicates that the segment is present, has a privilege level of 0 (used for the protection features—0 is the highest level), is not executable, and is both readable and writable. For the code segment, the access-rights byte indicates that the segment is present, has a privilege level of 0, is executable (the 80286 will not allow data segments to be executed, or code segments to be written into), and is readable (you can make code segments nonreadable to keep other routines from stealing the code). For more information, refer to the Intel manual in the bibliography.

Number	Name	Description
0	Dummy	Segment 0 is invalid, so initialize to 0.
1	GDT Alias	Since the GDT is itself a segment, there must be a descriptor available if it is to be changed. A descriptor created to access a segment that would not normally be accessible is called an "alias".
2	IDT Alias	Alias for interrupt table.
3	Data Seg	Descriptor to point to the user's data segment.
4	Extra Seg	Descriptor to point to user's extra segment.
5	Stack Seg	Descriptor to point to user's stack segment.
6	User Code Seg	Descriptor to point to user's code segment.
7	BIOS Code Seg	The BIOS routine fills this descriptor so that its code can continue executing once the jump to protected mode occurs. Once in protected mode, the BIOS routine loads the segment registers with the user defined values, and then jumps to the user's code.

Table 7-2: Segments expected to be found in the GDT by the AT BIOS call Interrupt 15H, function 89H

The next step is to set up the IDT for the 14 processor fault vectors. The descriptors here are used as "call gates" (a type of control descriptor). For example, the statement "SET_IDT_DESC(0,...)" sets up the IDT descriptor 0 (also vector 0 and fault 0), so that an interrupt 0 goes to the routine *FAULT* in the code segment. The "+7" makes sure that the code put in place by Turbo Pascal to allow local variable access is ignored. Don't try to access local variables from the fault routine (once *FAULT* calls something else, the called routine can access local variables). All fault routines currently point to the same fault handler that beeps the speaker twice.

The next step saves the segment registers needed to run in Real mode (*SS*, *DS*, and *ES*). When you return to the Real mode, these values are reloaded into the appropriate segment registers. Once this is done, Turbo never knows that it was ever out of Real mode. These values are stored in typed constants, which reside in the code segment. This allows the values to be accessed, since *DS* and *SS* are unknown.

When the BIOS call for Protected mode executes, it remaps the hardware interrupts to whatever location is requested. It also masks off all hardware interrupts so that they can't get in to bother the 80286 while it is in Protected mode. When returning to Real mode, the interrupts are remapped to their normal positions, but they remain masked off. To allow them to work again, you must set the masks in the interrupt-controller chips back to their original states. The *SAVE_8259_REGS* routine saves the contents of the mask registers so that they can be correctly restored upon return to Real mode.

The next routine sets 05H into location 0FH of the CMOS RAM. It sends the address 0FH to port 70H (the CMOS RAM address port, which gives this RAM its own address space), and then writes the value O5H into port 71H. This causes the CMOS RAM chip to move the 05H into location 0FH.

Next, locations 467H and 469H are set to the address of the exit-point routine that will be used when the return to Real mode occurs. Again, the "+7" is used to circumvent the local-variable-address setup code. The exit-point routine cannot access local variables.

Finally, the 80286 can be taken to Protected mode. A small piece of inline code is used to set the registers to their appropriate values and call the interrupt. You cannot use the *INTR* here because the BIOS call destroys *BP*, and *INTR* tries to use it.

Once you enter Protected mode, all of its capabilities are opened to you—the 16M address space is available, as well as virtual memory support, protection, etc. So why then, after all of this work, does the program simply beep once and drop back to Real mode? This occurs for several reasons. First, the hardware interrupts are off, so the keyboard does not work. The screen cannot be accessed because the video BIOS call is not entered in the IDT, and a descriptor for the video memory space does not exist. The disk drives don't work for a variety of reasons. Essentially, the AT becomes a naked machine, and the speaker is the only accessible output device. While in Protected mode, you can do most non-I/O and things unrelated to the heap that you normally do in Turbo Pascal, although the results of any calculations must be sent out in beeps.

To get out of Protected mode, the 8042 is told to create a hardware reset by sending 0FEH to port 64H. The HLT command halts the processor until the reset can take effect. The Rube Goldberg machine then takes over and eventually begins executing the program again at the exit-point routine. This routine restores all segment registers, replaces the mask registers, and returns. If you make a drawing of the stack contents through all of this, you will find that what is on the stack at the time of the exit point's return is the address of the caller of GOTO_PROTECTED_MODE. The exit point routine returns to the main routine, which returns to DOS.

There are several things you should bear in mind while Turbo Pascal is running in Protected mode. First, no screen, keyboard, or disk I/O is possible for the reasons mentioned above. In addition, no BIOS or DOS function calls are available. You cannot access the heap because the heap manager loads many segment values that have no entries in the GDT. The compiler directives shown must be off, or the program will not work. Typed constants (whose values are stored in the code segment) cannot be written to while in Protected mode, because the 80286 guards against any modification of executable code segments. Finally, local variables or parameters should not be used in the routines mentioned above, because the BP register is either lost or destroyed. Any routines called by these routines, however, can have local variables and parameters.

Experimenting

Once you have the Protected mode program working—that is, it runs, beeps once, and returns to the Turbo Pascal environment—you can try several easy modifications and experiments. One of the first might be to create processor faults while in Protected mode.

You can create processor faults in several ways, but the easiest involves the creation of a nonpresent segment. For example, the access-rights byte for the Data descriptor in the GDT (descriptor 3 in Table 7-2 and in the SETUP_GDT procedure) has an access rights byte of 92H, or 10010010. Figure 7-2 shows that bit 7 is used as a "present" bit; you can mark a segment "not present" by changing bit 7 to zero. This is normally done in a virtual memory system. When a segment is swapped out to disk, the descriptor is marked "not present." The next time that segment is referenced, a "not present fault" (fault 11) occurs, which allows the operating system to pull that segment back into physical memory, set the descriptor to indicate "present", and then restart the faulting instruction.

To try this, simply change the access-rights byte of descriptor 3 in the GDT from 92H to 12H. Now, when the program executes, it will try to load the descriptor for DS, and a "not present fault" will occur. You will hear two beeps instead of one to indicate that the fault took place.

You can also do this with the extra and stack segments. The stack segment will use fault 12 instead of 11, although you won't hear any difference. Do not try this on the code segment, however. If you change the code segment descriptor to 1AH, the program will crash. This occurs because the 80286 never gets a code segment descriptor loaded and can therefore do nothing.

When experimenting with faults, or when debugging, it is nice to know exactly which fault is occurring. You may wish to create 14 different fault routines—one for each possible fault. Fault 0 might beep once, fault 1 twice, etc., so that you know exactly which fault occurred. Create the 14 routines, and then change the descriptors in SETUP_IDT so that each one points to the appropriate fault routine instead of to the generic fault routine. Then recompile the program. (A note on compiling: All tests for this chapter were done using an IBM AT and Turbo Pascal Version 3.00B. It is unknown how the program will behave on AT compatibles, or on older versions of Turbo Pascal.)

It would be nice to have some output device other than the speaker. You may have noticed that an extra descriptor is included in SETUP_GDT. The TEST_SCREEN routine can use this descriptor to access the screen as an output device from Protected mode. To make use of this routine, first remove the comment braces from around the TEST_SCREEN call. Then modify the physical address for descriptor 8 in the GDT to match your system. If your system uses an EGA or CGA board, the call to ADDR24 should use the value $B800 for the physical address. If you use a monochrome adaptor, the address should be $B000.

Once you have made these changes, compile the program and run it. It should print "HELLO FROM PROTECTED MODE" onto your screen several times. This routine takes full advantage of the redirectability of segments to access the screen. An absolute array SCREEN is declared at the beginning of the program. It has been declared to point to $40:0. If you decode 40H in light of the Protected mode use of segment values, you will find that this corresponds to descriptor 8. Descriptor 8 has been directed (in the GDT) to point at the physical memory address that contains the screen memory buffer. The routine DISPLAY simply writes information into the appropriate address in the screen buffer by accessing the segment value $40. The absolute address feature of Turbo is very convenient in this case. Whenever the screen array is accessed, the segment value $40 is loaded into a segment register. This retrieves the descriptor needed to actually access the screen.

You can use the DISPLAY routine to create a CLRSCR procedure for Protected mode. Simply display 25 lines of spaces on the screen.

Conclusion

This chapter has shown how to get Turbo Pascal to run, with limitations, in Protected mode, but it has barely scratched the surface of the Protected mode's capabilities. You will find that you can use Turbo Pascal to create a comfortable environment for further experimentation with Protected mode features.

References

Claff, William J., "Moving From the 8088 to the 80286; Important Differences You Need to Know to Make Your Programs Transportable," *Byte* Special Issue, "Inside the IBM PCs," Volume 10, Number 11, 1985.

IBM Corporation, *IBM Technical Reference Personal Computer AT*, 1984.

Intel Corporation, *iAPX 286 Programmer's Reference Manual*, 1985.

Quendens, Guy, and Gary Webb, "Switching Modes; Getting Into and Out of the iAPX 286's Protected Virtual Mode Helps Take Full Advantage of the AT's Power," *PC Tech Journal*, August 1985.

```
program protected_mode_and_back;
{$u-,k-}  {These directives MUST be set off like this}

{Marshall Brain    Version 1.0    September 15, 1986}
{This program demonstrates what is required to go into protected
mode, and then come back to real mode. Interrupt 15, function
89 is used to get into protected mode. See article or AT ROM BIOS
listing for details.
    The program will beep once (low tone) from protected mode and
return to DOS if everything works correctly. A processor fault
will cause 2 beeps (high tone) and halt the system.}

const
   gdt_size=8;    {Max number of descriptors in GDT minus 1}
   idt_size=13;   {Max number of descriptors in IDT minus 1}
   code_desc={6*8}48; {Code segment selector is #6 in GDT}
const    {typed constants are variables in the code segment}
   data_seg:integer  = 0; {storage space for segment registers}
   stack_seg:integer = 0;
   extra_seg:integer = 0;
type
```

```
   descriptor=record     {from AT Bios listing}
     seg_limit:integer;         {segment limit (1-65536 bytes)}
     base_lo_word:integer;      { 24 bit physical address (0-(16M-1))}
     base_hi_byte:byte;
     data_acc_rights:byte;      {access rights byte}
     data_reserved:integer      {reserved for 80386 compatability}
   end;
   string80=string[80];
var
   gdt:array[0..gdt_size] of descriptor; {Global descriptor table}
   idt:array[0..idt_size] of descriptor; {interrupt dscrptr table}
   result:record ax,bx,cx,dx,bp,si,di,ds,es,flags:integer; end;
   mask1_8259,mask2_8259:byte;  {storage space for 8259 masks}
   screen:array[0..$2000] of byte absolute $40:0;

procedure setup_error;
{Displays a message if you try to setup a descriptor outside the
 boundries of a descriptor table.}
begin
   writeln;writeln('There has been an error during setup of ',
                   'descriptor tables.');
   halt;
end;

procedure set_gdt_desc(num,seg_lim,base_lo:integer;
                       base_hi,acc_rights:byte);
{This procedure sets up descriptor number NUM in the GDT with the
 values that are passed.}
begin
   if (num>=0) and (num<=gdt_size) then
   begin
     with gdt[num] do
      begin
        seg_limit:=seg_lim;
        base_lo_word:=base_lo;
        base_hi_byte:=base_hi;
        data_acc_rights:=acc_rights;
        data_reserved:=0;
      end;
   end else setup_error;
end;

procedure set_idt_desc(num,seg_lim,base_lo:integer;
                       base_hi,acc_rights:byte);
{This procedure sets up descriptor number NUM in the IDT with the
 values that are passed.}
begin
   if (num>=0) and (num<=idt_size) then
   begin
     with idt[num] do
     begin
        seg_limit:=seg_lim;
        base_lo_word:=base_lo;
        base_hi_byte:=base_hi;
        data_acc_rights:=acc_rights;
        data_reserved:=0;
```

```
      end;
  end else setup_error;
end;

procedure beep;
{beeps the speaker.}
begin
  sound(300);delay(400);nosound;delay(400);
end;

procedure errbeep;
begin
  sound(2000);delay(400);nosound;delay(400);
end;

procedure fault;
{This routine is entered if a processor fault occurs while in
 protected mode.}
begin
  errbeep;
  errbeep;
  {pop the 4 words put on the stack when fault occured.}
  inline($5b/$5b/$5b/$5b);  {pop BX 4 times.}
  port[$64]:=$fe;  {return to real mode}
  inline($f4);       {Halt to wait for reset to take effect.}
end;

procedure setup_idt;
{this procedure loads the idt with the appropriate values to handle
 all 80286 processor faults.}
var x:integer;
begin
  {The first 14 selectors are all 80286 faults, and are directed to
   the fault routine for now.}
  set_idt_desc(0,ofs(fault)+7,code_desc,0,$86);
  set_idt_desc(1,ofs(fault)+7,code_desc,0,$86);
  set_idt_desc(2,ofs(fault)+7,code_desc,0,$86);
  set_idt_desc(3,ofs(fault)+7,code_desc,0,$86);
  set_idt_desc(4,ofs(fault)+7,code_desc,0,$86);
  set_idt_desc(5,ofs(fault)+7,code_desc,0,$86);
  set_idt_desc(6,ofs(fault)+7,code_desc,0,$86);
  set_idt_desc(7,ofs(fault)+7,code_desc,0,$86);
  set_idt_desc(8,ofs(fault)+7,code_desc,0,$86);
  set_idt_desc(9,ofs(fault)+7,code_desc,0,$86);
  set_idt_desc(10,ofs(fault)+7,code_desc,0,$86);
  set_idt_desc(11,ofs(fault)+7,code_desc,0,$86);
  set_idt_desc(12,ofs(fault)+7,code_desc,0,$86);
  set_idt_desc(13,ofs(fault)+7,code_desc,0,$86);
end;

procedure addr24(segment,offset:integer; var a24w:integer; var a24b:byte);
{To work in protected mode, physical addresses must be expressed
 in 24 bit values. Addr24 puts the lower 16 bits of the 24
 bit address in a24w, and puts the upper 8 bits in a24b.}
var x:integer;y:byte;
begin
```

```
  inline(
  $8B/$86/segment/      {mov  ax,segment[bp]                               }
  $BA/$10/$00/          {mov  dx,16        ; move segment over 4 bits}
  $F7/$E2/              {mul  dx                                          }
  $03/$86/offset/       {add  ax,offset[bp]; add offset and send          }
  $83/$D2/$00/          {adc  dl,0         ; carry bit to dl              }
  $88/$96/y/            {mov  y[bp],dl     ; save result                  }
  $89/$86/x);           {mov  x[bp],ax     ; save result                  }
  a24w:=x;
  a24b:=y;
end;

procedure setup_gdt;
{This procedure sets up the GDT with the descriptors required by
 Int 15, function 89.}
var a24w:integer;a24b:byte; {24 bit physical addr storage}
begin
                                            {# Function         }
  set_gdt_desc(0,0,0,0,0);                  {0 dummy descriptor}
  addr24(dseg,ofs(gdt),a24w,a24b);
  set_gdt_desc(1,sizeof(gdt),a24w,a24b,$92); {1 GDT alias       }
  addr24(dseg,ofs(idt),a24w,a24b);
  set_gdt_desc(2,sizeof(idt),a24w,a24b,$92); {2 IDT alias       }
  addr24(dseg,0,a24w,a24b);
  set_gdt_desc(3,$ffff,a24w,a24b,$92);       {3 Data descriptor }
  set_gdt_desc(4,$ffff,a24w,a24b,$92);       {4 Extra descriptor}
  addr24(sseg,0,a24w,a24b);
  set_gdt_desc(5,$ffff,a24w,a24b,$92);       {5 Stack descriptor}
  addr24(cseg,0,a24w,a24b);
  set_gdt_desc(6,$ffff,a24w,a24b,$9a);       {6 Code descriptor }
  set_gdt_desc(7,0,0,0,0);                   {7 Temp Bios CS    }
  {the following is an additional descr used to access the screen.}
  addr24($b800,0,a24w,a24b);
  set_gdt_desc(8,$2000,a24w,a24b,$92);       {8 Screen descriptor }
end;

procedure save_segs;
{Saves the current segment values in typed constants so they can
 be retrieved when program returns from protected mode.}
begin
  data_seg:=dseg;
  extra_seg:=dseg;
  stack_seg:=sseg;
end;

procedure save_8259_regs;
{Saves current 8259 masks so they can be replaced on return to
 real mode.}
begin
  mask1_8259:=port[$21];
  mask2_8259:=port[$a1];
end;

procedure set_cmos_for_shutdown;
{sets cmos ram so that the reset that brings this program back to
 DOS jumps to the correct address in this program.}
```

```
begin
  port[$70]:=$0f;
  port[$71]:=$05;
end;

procedure protected_mode_exitpoint;
{When program returns to real mode, if comes here.}
begin
  {recover segment registers}
  inline(
    $2E/$A1/data_seg/        {mov  ax,cs:data_seg }
    $8E/$D8/                 {mov  ds,ax          }
    $2E/$A1/extra_seg/       {mov  ax,cs:extra_seg}
    $8E/$C0/                 {mov  es,ax          }
    $2E/$A1/stack_seg/       {mov  ax,cs:stack_seg}
    $8E/$D0);                {mov  ss,ax          }
  {reset 8259 masks}
  port[$21]:=mask1_8259;
  port[$a1]:=mask2_8259;
  {when this procedure returns, it will return to the place where
   goto_protected_mode was called from (see last line of pgm).}
end;

procedure setup_jump_locations;
{set up appropriate memory locations with address of routine
 to use when returning to real mode.}
begin
  memw[$0040:$67]:=ofs(protected_mode_exitpoint)+7;
  memw[$0040:$69]:=cseg;
end;

procedure display(col,row:byte;ln:string80);
{routine to display information on the screen by writing directly
 into screen memory. Col,row express the coords that LN should be
 displayed at.}
var x,addr:integer;
begin
  addr:=row*80+col;
  for x:=0 to length(ln)-1 do
    screen[(x+addr)*2]:=ord(ln[x+1]);
end;

procedure test_screen;
{writes a message on the screen.}
var x:integer;
begin
  for x:= 1 to 5 do
    display(5,x,'HELLO FROM PROTECTED MODE.');
end;

procedure goto_protected_mode;
{Take program into protected mode and perform whatever routines
 are needed while in protected mode. Returns to real mode when
 done. Do not use any turbo function requiring BP register in this
 routine.}
begin
```

```
  {Call interrupt 15, function 89}
  inline(     {do interrupt 15h, function 89h to get to protected mode}
    $8c/$d8/         {mov ax,ds }    {load address of GDT into es:si}
    $8e/$c0/         {mov es,ax }
    $be/gdt/         {mov si,ofs(gdt)}
    $b7/$08/         {mov bh,8}       {bh,bl contain new location for}
    $b3/$08/         {mov bl,8}       {hardware interrupt vectors}
    $b4/$89/         {mov ah,89h}
    $cd/$15);        {int 15h}
  {procedures to be executed in protected mode should go here}
    beep;
    {test_screen;}
  port[$64]:=$fe;   {return to real mode}
  inline($f4);      {Halt to wait for reset to take effect.}
end;


begin {main routine}
  setup_idt;
  setup_gdt;
  save_segs;
  save_8259_regs;
  set_cmos_for_shutdown;
  setup_jump_locations;
  goto_protected_mode;
  {protected_mode_exitpoint will return to here.}
end.
```

8

A Protected-Mode Program[*] for the PC AT

_____ _Ross Nelson_ _____

The computer industry usually ties new-generation hardware to the older hardware by making it compatible with existing software. To take advantage of the machine's newer features, you must write software for its native mode. Such is the case with the IBM PC AT's central processor, the Intel 80286, which runs software written for the 8086/8088 processors.

Due to lack of operating system support, very little software has appeared for the 80286's native mode, called the _protected virtual address mode_, leaving the processor's power largely untapped in current microcomputer systems. Ironically, applications programs that adhere to a few simple rules will run unmodified in the native mode, but only if you dramatically modify the operating system. I've written a program, _PM_AT.EXE_, that places an IBM PC AT in its protected mode and provides a base for future expansion and experimentation with the protected mode in the 80286.

Processor Overview

In the 8086 emulation mode (which is equivalent to the standard operating modes of the 8088, 8086, 80188, and 80186), the 80286 has one type of system object, the segment. The processor grants access to a segment when a value is loaded into a segment register. The processor then allows direct access to the 64K-byte block of memory beginning at location <value> x 16.

In protected mode, the processor views the system much the same as an operating system would. The processor "knows" about objects other than memory segments. Each object is referenced by a descriptor, which contains information about the object. When the system is in protected mode, the value loaded into the segment register does not point to the object itself, but to a table of descriptors where the object is described. From that table, the physical address and size of the object (assuming it is a memory segment) are extracted. Memory segments can range from 1K to 64K bytes in size, and the processor verifies that every memory

---

[*] © McGraw-Hill Information Systems Company, _BYTE_, 1986 Extra Edition, p. 123

access is within the bounds of the segment size (see Figure 8-1).

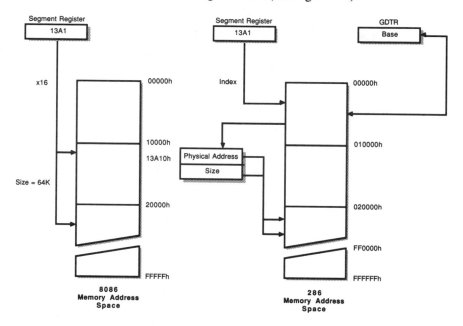

Figure 8-1: Direct addressing of real-address mode versus the indirect addressing of protected mode

In addition to segments, the 80286 works with *descriptor tables*, *task segments*, and *gates*. A particular type of descriptor is used to reference each object (see Figure 8-2). The processor uses descriptors to ensure that system security is not violated. To prevent a valuable program from being disassembled, the processor would use an execute-only descriptor for the code segment; any program that tried to read that segment as data would fail.

The 80286 requires two tables of descriptors whenever the system is running protected mode: the *global descriptor table* (GDT) and the *interrupt descriptor table* (IDT). A number of *local descriptor tables* (LDTs) can also exist. LDTs are associated with the 80286 task implementation. The GDT and LDTs contain descriptors for code and data segments. The IDT is analogous to the 8086 interrupt vector table and contains special code descriptors known as gates.

In 80286 parlance, the 16-bit value loaded into the segment register is called a selector. A selector accesses a system object by selecting the descriptor for the object. A selector has three components: the *table indicator* (TI), which selects either the GDT or the currently active LDT; the desired descriptor within the table (Index); and a *requested privilege level* (RPL). Normally, the RPL is the same as the operating privilege of the currently executing code. The 16 bits that

144

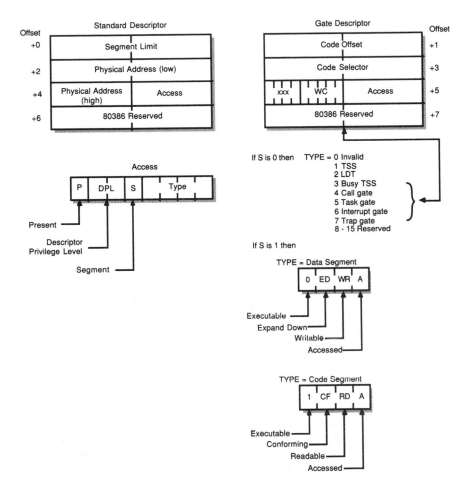

Figure 8-2: The Format of a Descriptor

are loaded into the segment register have the following format:

For example, the processor interprets the value 13A1 hexadecimal in a segment register as a request to access descriptor 274 hexadecimal in the GDT with a privilege of 1.

Protection

In protected mode, as the name implies, the 80286 is concerned with system integrity. It makes every effort to ensure that the flow of execution is well behaved. To prevent corruption of code or of constant data, it can mark segments as execute-only or read-only.

The processor also provides isolation between coresident processes, either via the task mechanism (discussed below) or by the execution privilege level. The 80286 provides four levels of security, numbered from 0 (most secure) to 3 (least secure). A program may access any descriptor with a descriptor privilege level that is numerically equal to or higher (less secure) than its own execution level. Typically, operating system code executes at the most privileged levels, and the applications execute at less privileged levels.

This arrangement presents a problem when an application attempts to execute subroutines that are part of the operating system, such as I/O requests. The code segments should be protected from corruption, but less privileged applications should still be allowed access. The 80286 provides two mechanisms to deal with this problem. The first is the conforming code segment, used when the shared code does not need to access restricted elements of the system, such as hardware I/O ports. Libraries of routines that perform data conversion between ASCII and binary or floating-point, for example, could take advantage of conforming segments.

The other mechanism is a descriptor called the gate, which provides a passageway to a more privileged execution level. It does this with an additional level of indirection. A gate has a privilege level that is separate from the privilege level of the code segment to which it points (see Figure 8-3). For example, a call gate that has a descriptor privilege level of 3 could point to a code segment with a descriptor privilege level of 0. This means that any executing code segment could issue a call through the gate because 3 is the least privileged level. Since the gate points to a level-0 segment, the 80286 would change the privilege of the currently executing task to level 0 to match the new segment. Thus, the application runs at a higher privilege level, but only while executing the operating system's secure code. It then returns to its original level after the return instruction.

The 80286 architecture also provides interrupt and trap gates for handling hardware and software interrupts.

The notion of a task is built into the 80286 architecture. Loosely defined, a task is a set of segments required to perform a particular series of operations. The 80286 creates this union of segments with the help of two descriptors, the task-state segment and the LDT.

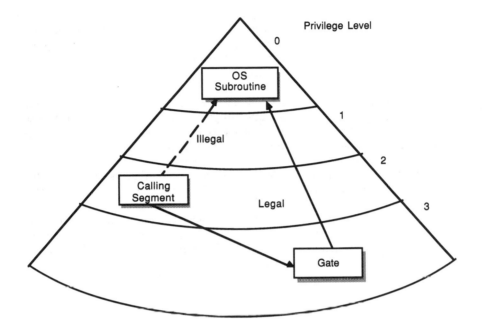

Figure 8-3: A call gate that has a descriptor privilege level of 3 but points to a code segment with a descriptor privilege level of 0

It is often helpful to think of tasks as separate programs executing on their own individual microprocessors. The task-state segment provides a good simulation of this notion, since each task-state segment holds a copy of all the machine registers used by the task. Because in most cases a single processor handles all the tasks in a system, the operating system switches between the tasks, executing one for a period of time, then another. In this way, a multitasking system appears to be running many programs concurrently. When a task-switch operation is performed on the 80286, the current values of all the registers are stored in the task-state segment of the executing segment; the registers are then loaded from the task-state segment of a new task, which begins execution based on the new value of the instruction pointer.

The segment descriptors in the task's LDT are available only to that task; another task cannot access them. This isolation provides an excellent form of protection.

The Protected-Mode Program

My program, PM_AT, places the IBM PC AT into protected mode and provides support scaffolding for further experimentation with protected mode. The program illustrates various features of the 80286's native mode and includes examples of fault handlers, conforming code segments, gates, and task switching.

I wrote the program using the IBM Macro Assembler version 2.0. Since this product was designed for the 8086 family of processors, it does not support some features of protected mode. In some cases, I have resorted to programming tricks to provide a reasonable approximation of the missing features.

The PROTECT.INC listing contains a set of macros that let the user assemble 80286 protected-mode instructions. The 80286's instruction set contains two kinds of enhancements over the 8086 family: the addition of new instructions such as *PUSH* <data> and *ENTER*, and the protected-mode instruction set. The IBM Macro Assembler version 2.0 supports the first group of new instructions, but not the second. When you include PROTECT.INC, macros simulate the unsupported op codes such as *LGDT* and *ARPL*.

Tables

Three macros help build the descriptor tables. Each segment in the program is defined with either a *memory-segment* (MSEG) or a *system-segment* (SSEG) macro. These two macros create assembler variables that contain information necessary for building a descriptor. A third macro, the *descriptor* (DSCRP) macro, builds a descriptor from the variables when given the name of a segment. The DSCRP macro also accepts an optional export name that is used as a selector for the descriptor. This trick works because the format of a level-0 GDT selector is equivalent to the index multiplied by eight. Since each descriptor takes up 8 bytes, the byte offset of the descriptor equals the index times eight.

The GDT begins with the line

```
DESCRIP <0,0,0,0>
```

which builds the first GDT entry via the DESCRIP data structure. The system can never access descriptor 0 in the GDT; therefore, it is null. Descriptors 1 through 7 are set up to meet the requirements of the INT 15h function call. Descriptor 8 provides a task-state segment for the initialization code. The INT 15h protocol does not require the creation of a task, but a task fault will occur at the first task switch if the task register has not been loaded.

The next four descriptors are for the portion of code that I call the MiniBIOS. The MiniBIOS handles the hardware interrupts and provides screen-handling routines similar to those normally found in the standard *ROM BIOS*; however, the *ROM* functions will not execute correctly when the processor is in protected mode. When you invoke the MiniBIOS functions (via a trap gate at INT 30h), the privilege of the executing task is set to 0 for the duration of the function.

The next nine descriptors point to the fault handlers I have implemented. As you add new code to the system, it is inevitable that at some point a routine will fail. The handlers that are a part of PM_AT will indicate the type of fault and the location in the program where the fault occurred. The descriptors provide code, data, and task segments for the fault-handling code. The last of these descriptors is initially unused but available for the fault-handling routines to modify as needed.

The next two descriptors provide access to a library of ASCII/binary-conversion routines. The first descriptor, *shlib_code*, is a level-0 conforming code segment. Programs with a lower privilege can gain access to this code via the *CALL_GATE* descriptor, which has a privilege level of 3. Since the code segment is conforming, the privilege of the calling task does not change when executing the code in *shlib_code*.

The next descriptors provide the system-level descriptors for a second task to illustrate the 80286's task-switching capabilities.

The final four descriptors are null and are available for future expansion. Normally, an operating system will provide functions such as *CREATE_TASK*, *ALLOC_SEGMENT*, and *FREE_SEGMENT*, which create new descriptors or free up entries in the GDT for later use. The operating system would have access to the GDT as if it were a standard data segment (via descriptor 1). Obviously, this sort of access to the GDT must be limited to only the most secure portions of the operating system.

The GDT requires the physical starting address of the segment as a part of segment descriptors. The assembler places the 16-bit (real address mode) segment address in the prototype GDT. A subroutine in the program's initialization portion adjusts all the addresses, multiplying them by 16. It assumes all data resides in the first 1 megabyte of memory.

The IDT contains a set of gates that point to the routines that handle interrupts and faults. It contains only trap, interrupt, or task gates. Trap gates handle software-interrupt requests, and interrupt gates handle hardware interrupts. You can invoke a task gate by hardware or software; it causes an immediate task switch.

As defined under DOS, the interrupt structure of the PC AT resembles that of the standard PC or XT. Unfortunately, IBM chose to use some of the interrupts that Intel designated as reserved. In the AT, this causes a conflict between the way DOS wants to use the interrupts and the way the processor wants to use them. In my program, I followed the Intel specification and allocated the first 32 interrupts for exceptions and fault handling, mapping the hardware interrupts to vectors 32 (20 hexadecimal) and above (see Table 8-1).

Vector	Function	DOS Equivalent
00	Divide fault	0
01	Trap (single step)	1
02	NMI	2
03	BRKPT (INT 3)	3
04	Interrupt on overflow	4
05	Bound interrupt	
07	80287 not available	
08	Double fault	
09	80287 segment overrun	
10	Invalid TSS fault	
11	Not present fault	
12	Stack fault	
13	General protection fault	
16	80287 error	
17 ... 31	Reserved	
32	Timer	08
33	Keyboard interrupt	09
35	Com port 1	11
36	Com port 2	12
37	Printer 2	13
38	Floppy disk	14
39	Printer 1	15
40	Real-time clock	
45	80287 request	
46	Hard disk	

Table 8-1: The interrupt vector mapping used in PM_AT contrasted with DOS

Descriptors 0 through 31 handle processor faults. All these gates are interrupt gates except for 8, 10, and 12, which are task gates. Task gates are required because the failures that cause these interrupts are so serious that the processor must load an entirely new machine state to continue running.

The hardware interrupts are found at vectors 20 to 2F hexadecimal. The change from the DOS vector locations is accomplished by programming the 8259A interrupt controller. In the PC AT, the BIOS call INT 15h takes care of this detail.

Interrupt vectors 30 and 31 hexadecimal have been allocated to the MiniBIOS. Since INT 30h provides display services, its privilege level is set to 3 so that any task may request its services.

The last page of the program contains an LDT for the second task. The code and data segments for the second task are in the LDT rather than the GDT. When an LDT is used for each task, the GDT will contain only a task-state segment and an LDT descriptor for the task. The descriptors for the code and data segments need not appear in the GDT.

Initialization

After MS-DOS loads PM_AT, execution begins at the label *START*. The program then calls the subroutine *ADJUST_ADDR* to fix up the physical addresses in the GDT and LDT, converting them from 16-bit real address mode segments to 24-bit physical addresses. It then calls the *ROM BIOS* to request protected mode.

The PC AT BIOS provides a function (code 89 hexadecimal of INT 15h) that places the processor into protected mode. To do this, it loads the GDT and IDT base registers, programs the 8259A interrupt controller with the hardware vector locations, and frees up the A20 address bit. (Due to a design oversight at Intel, the 80286 occasionally generates addresses beyond 1 megabyte. The PC AT includes hardware to force the A20 bit to 0 while running in emulation mode.) It then sets the protected-mode bit in the *machine status word* (MSW) register of the processor and returns to the calling program.

Protected-Mode Execution

The only setup required after the program returns from the INT 15h call is to load the task register. The task-state segment for the initial task contains no data but must be present for a task switch to occur.

Program execution is very simple. The program beeps once to let you know that all is well, clears the interrupt-register masks, enables interrupts, and goes into a loop. The main task prints the number of clock ticks that have occurred since interrupts were enabled. It then invokes a second task, which merely displays a message and returns. The program loops until you generate a keyboard interrupt; it will then halt and reset the system.

The second task runs at privilege level 3, the way most applications would in a standard operating system. Its execution privilege level is determined by the privilege of its code-segment descriptor found in the task's LDT. When it invokes the display services via INT 30h, however, its execution privilege is changed to level 0 for the duration of the call. To prevent an errant program from corrupting the local variables and return addresses of the level-0 code, the 80286 changes to a level-0 stack before it begins level-0 execution. A level-0 memory segment is provided for this purpose in the task's LDT and task-state segment.

The executing tasks use two small libraries of code. One is the set of routines that does ASCII/binary conversion. They are located in a conforming code segment, and any task can call them via the *CALL_EX* macro. This macro takes an export name and a privilege level and creates a *FAR* call to the object. It can be used with any export segment or gate. The other set of routines provides display services and is part of the MiniBIOS. Since these routines require access to hardware, they will execute at privilege level 0 and are invoked via the gate at interrupt 30h.

The ASCII/binary-conversion library is located in the *shlib_code* segment. This library provides the following 16-bit conversion functions: ASCII hexadecimal to binary, binary to ASCII hexadecimal. ASCII signed integer to binary, binary to ASCII signed integer, ASCII unsigned integer to binary, and binary to ASCII unsigned integer. The actual calling sequences are documented in the code.

PM_AT provides a set of rudimentary display utilities for character and line output and cursor manipulation. These are invoked via the trap gate at INT 30h. The current implementation of the program supports only the IBM monochrome display. To support the color adapter, you replace the *DEV_MONO* literal with *DEV_COLOR*. To prevent snow on the display, a color implementation should also loop and wait for a retrace before writing any characters to the display.

Fault Handlers

If you use this program as a basis for your own experiments with protected mode, the fault handlers are important. Whenever the 80286 detects a violation of its protection rules, it issues an interrupt that will vector through the IDT to the appropriate fault-handling routine. My fault handlers display the fault type and the address of the instruction that caused the fault. They will also display the fault code for the "general protection" fault and other faults that provide an error code. The format of the address is <selector>:<offset>. You will have to extract the selector's index portion to determine which code segment was executing when the fault occurred.

In a complete operating system, the different faults would be handled differently. For example, the "not present" fault (INT 11h) would probably cause the operating system to load the referenced segment from virtual memory and restart the instruction that caused the fault; the "general protection" fault (INT13h) would normally cause termination of the offending task and the logging of a message to the appropriate terminal.

My program assumes that any fault is a programmer error. It will display the location and type of fault on the display, pause, and reboot the system. Should you attempt to make the fault handlers more sophisticated, you might run across two other conditions: double fault and shutdown. Double fault (INT 8) occurs when the system is attempting to process a fault but is prevented from doing so by another protection violation. The double-fault handler, therefore, should be an isolated task that makes as few assumptions as possible. Should the processor detect another violation while attempting to handle the double-fault condition, it will give up entirely and shut down. The PC AT includes hardware that detects the shutdown status on the bus and resets the processor.

Suggestions for Expansion

To understand all the complex interactions of the protected mode, you will almost certainly need Intel's iAPX 286 Programmer's Reference Manual. This manual includes a pseudocode description of the processor microcode for instructions such as *INT* or *CALL FAR*. Unfortunately, in the latest edition (1985), some of the steps are missing. After you've worked with the processor for a while, however, you should get a feel for the types of operations being carried out.

The next logical step in developing the code is adding a keyboard driver. After you get this working, you will have a small interactive system to build on and could add a debugger/monitor. This would let you recover more gracefully from certain errors rather than reset the system.

The complexity of the native-mode 80286 is an order of magnitude greater than that of the previous generation of microprocessors. But as powerful support for secure multitasking operating systems, it will be much appreciated by designers of the next generation of operating systems.

Bibliography

iAPX 286 Operating Systems Writer's Guide. Intel Corporation. 1983.

iAPX 286 Programmer's Reference Manual. Intel Corporation. 1985.

IBM PC AT Technical Reference. IBM Corporation. 1984.

```
          NAME    PM_AT
          PAGE    60, 132
          .286P
;
;   PM/AT - A program to place the PC/AT into Protected Mode
;   Copyright 1985, Ross P. Nelson
;
```

```
;   Updated to work with MASM 5.0
;

; Data structure definitions
DESCRIP         STRUC                               ; generic descriptor format
  limit         DW      ?                           ; offset if gate
  phys_addr_lo          DW      ?                       ; selector if gate
  phys_addr_hi          DB      ?                       ; wc if gate
  access        DB      ?                           ; access rights
                DW      0                           ; reserved for 386
DESCRIP         ENDS


TSS_BLOCK       STRUC                               ; format of a TSS
  back_link     DW      ?                           ; previously active TSS
  rSP0                  DW      ?                       ; level 0 stack
  rSS0                  DW      ?
  rSP1                  DW      ?                       ; level 1 stack
  rSS1                  DW      ?
  rSP2                  DW      ?                       ; level 2 stack
  rSS2                  DW      ?
  rIP                   DW      ?
  FLAGS         DW      ?
  rAX                   DW      ?
  rCX                   DW      ?
  rDX                   DW      ?
  rBX                   DW      ?
  rSP                   DW      ?
  rBP                   DW      ?
  rSI                   DW      ?
  rDI                   DW      ?
  rES                   DW      ?
  rCS                   DW      ?
  rSS                   DW      ?                   ; active stack segment
  rDS                   DW      ?
  task_LDT      DW      ?                           ; LDT selector
TSS_BLOCK       ENDS

; Literal values for descriptor types
TSS                     EQU     1
LDT                     EQU     2
TSS_BUSY        EQU     3
CALL_GATE       EQU     4
TASK_GATE       EQU     5
INT_GATE        EQU     6
TRAP_GATE       EQU     7


RDONLY                  EQU     0                   ; read only
RD_WR                   EQU     1                   ; read/write
RD_WR_XD        EQU     3                       ; read/write expand down
EXONLY                  EQU     4                       ; execute only
EX_RD                   EQU     5                       ; execute/readable
EXONLY_CF       EQU     6                   ; execute only/conforming
EX_RD_CF        EQU     7                   ; execute/readable/conforming


TSS_LIMIT       EQU     43
```

```
; Segment building macros
MSEG                    MACRO     name,type,priv,combine    ;; start a memory segment
name                    SEGMENT PARA combine                ;; MASM directive
zero = $                                                    ;; for ALIGN macro
&name&_start = $                                            ;; origin
&name&_ar = 90h OR (priv SHL 5) OR (type SHL 1) ;; access rights
            ENDM


SSEG                    MACRO     name,type,priv            ;; start a system segment
name                    SEGMENT PARA                        ;; MASM directive
zero = $                                                    ;; for ALIGN macro
&name&_start = $                                            ;; origin
&name&_ar = 80h OR (priv SHL 5) OR type     ;; access rights
            ENDM


ENDSEG                  MACRO     name                      ;; terminate a segment
&name&_limit = $ - &name&_start - 1         ;; create variable for seg limit
name                    ENDS                                ;; limit <- size-1  (0-FFFFh)
            ENDM


; Descriptor building macros
DSCRP                   MACRO     export,name               ;; build descrip for segment
            IFDIF       <export>,<>                         ;; check for export name
export                  LABEL     WORD
            ENDIF
            DW          &name&_limit                        ;; segment limit
            DW          name                                ;; 16-bit segment addr
            DB          0                                   ;; high order addr
            DB          &name&_ar                           ;; access rights
            DW          0                                   ;; reserved
            ENDM


GATE                    MACRO     export,offset,select,wc,type,priv   ;; build descriptor
            IFDIF       <export>,<>                         ;; check for export name
export                  LABEL     WORD
            ENDIF
            DW          offset                              ;; offset
            DW          select                              ;; segment selector
            DB          wc                                  ;; word count
            DB          80h OR (priv SHL 5) + type     ;; access rights
            DW          0                                   ;; reserved
            ENDM


; Selector creating macros for Task segments
GDT_SEL     MACRO       sel,priv
            DW          sel + priv                          ;; assume sel = index * 8
            ENDM


LDT_SEL     MACRO       sel,priv
            DW          sel + 4 + priv                      ;; like GDT but TI bit set
            ENDM


; Utility macros
CALL_EX     MACRO       sel,rpl                             ;; call exported item
            DB          9Ah                                 ;; FAR call
            DW          0                                   ;; no offset
```

```
                DW      sel + rpl                       ;; selector with req. priv.
                ENDM


                PAGE
;   This segment contains the Global Descriptor Table

                MSEG    GDT,RD_WR,0
; Required by INT 15
    DESCRIP <0,0,0,0>                       ; GDT(0) always blank
    DSCRP       int15_gdt_dat,GDT               ; DATA -> GDT
    DSCRP       int15_idt_dat,IDT               ; DATA -> IDT
    DSCRP       ,DSC                            ; DATA -> DS
    DSCRP       ,DSC                            ; DATA -> ES
    DSCRP       ,DSC                            ; STACK -> SS
    DSCRP       ,INIT                           ; CODE -> CS
    DESCRIP <0,0,0,0>                       ; CODE -> BIOS/int 15 reserved
    DSCRP       setup_tss,INIT_TSS              ; TSS -> initial task
; Mini BIOS
    DSCRP       bio_dat,MBDAT                   ; DATA -> mini bios
    DSCRP       bios_seg,BIOS                   ; CODE -> mini bios
    DSCRP       disp_mono,MONO_RAM              ; DATA -> monochrome display
    DSCRP       disp_color,COLOR_RAM            ; DATA -> color display
; Fault handlers
    DSCRP       task_df,FTASK8                  ; TSS  -> double fault
xtra8           DESCRIP <ftask8_limit,FTASK8,0,92h> ; writable DATA alias for TSS
    DSCRP       task_tf,FTASK10                 ; TSS  -> task fault
xtra10          DESCRIP <ftask10_limit,FTASK10,0,92h>  ; writable DATA alias for TSS
    DSCRP       task_sf,FTASK12                 ; TSS  -> task fault
xtra12          DESCRIP <ftask12_limit,FTASK12,0,92h>  ; writable DATA alias for TSS
    DSCRP       fault_dat,FDAT                  ; DATA -> handler
    DSCRP       fhandler,HAND                   ; CODE -> handler
    DSCRP       falias,FDAT                     ; free for fault handler use
; Shared library
    DSCRP       share_lib,SHLIB                 ; CODE -> shared
    GATE        share_gate,shlib_start,share_lib,0,CALL_GATE,3      ; GATE to code
; Second task
    DSCRP       task2_tss,TASK2                 ; TSS for 2nd task
    DSCRP       task2_ldt,T2LDT                 ; LDT for 2nd task
; Future use
    DESCRIP <0,0,0,0>                   ; available
    DESCRIP <0,0,0,0>                   ; available
    DESCRIP <0,0,0,0>                   ; available
    DESCRIP <0,0,0,0>                   ; available
                ENDSEG  GDT


                PAGE
;   This segment contains the Interrupt Descriptor Table.

                MSEG    IDT,RD_WR,0
; Chip level interrupts (0 - 1Fh)
    GATE        ,fault_00,fhandler,0,TRAP_GATE,0    ; DIVIDE
    GATE        ,fault_01,fhandler,0,TRAP_GATE,0    ; TRAP
    GATE        ,fault_02,fhandler,0,TRAP_GATE,0    ; NMI
    GATE        ,fault_03,fhandler,0,TRAP_GATE,3    ; BRKPT
    GATE        ,fault_04,fhandler,0,TRAP_GATE,0    ; INTO
    GATE        ,fault_05,fhandler,0,TRAP_GATE,0    ; BOUND
```

```
        GATE        ,fault_06,fhandler,0,TRAP_GATE,0      ; undef
        GATE        ,fault_07,fhandler,0,TRAP_GATE,0      ; 287 NAVAIL
        GATE        ,0,task_df,0,TASK_GATE,0          ; DBL FAULT
        GATE        ,fault_09,fhandler,0,TRAP_GATE,0      ; 287 OVRRUN
        GATE        ,0,task_tf,0,TASK_GATE,0        ; TSS FAULT
        GATE        ,fault_11,fhandler,0,TRAP_GATE,0      ; NP FAULT
        GATE        ,0,task_sf,0,TASK_GATE,0        ; STACK FAULT
        GATE        ,fault_13,fhandler,0,TRAP_GATE,0      ; GP FAULT
        GATE        ,unknown,fhandler,0,TRAP_GATE,0
        GATE        ,unknown,fhandler,0,TRAP_GATE,0
        GATE        ,fault_16,fhandler,0,TRAP_GATE,0     ; 287 ERROR
        GATE        ,unknown,fhandler,0,TRAP_GATE,0
        GATE        ,unknown,fhandler,0,TRAP_GATE,0
        GATE        ,unknown,fhandler,0,TRAP_GATE,0
        GATE        ,unknown,fhandler,0,TRAP_GATE,0
        GATE        ,unknown,fhandler,0,TRAP_GATE,0
        GATE        ,unknown,fhandler,0,TRAP_GATE,0
        GATE        ,unknown,fhandler,0,TRAP_GATE,0
        GATE        ,unknown,fhandler,0,TRAP_GATE,0
        GATE        ,unknown,fhandler,0,TRAP_GATE,0
        GATE        ,unknown,fhandler,0,TRAP_GATE,0
        GATE        ,unknown,fhandler,0,TRAP_GATE,0
        GATE        ,unknown,fhandler,0,TRAP_GATE,0
        GATE        ,unknown,fhandler,0,TRAP_GATE,0
        GATE        ,unknown,fhandler,0,TRAP_GATE,0
; System interrupts
;    Hardware Level 0 (20-27)               DOS equivalent vector
        GATE        ,timer_int,bios_seg,0,INT_GATE,0    ;  8
        GATE        ,kb_int,bios_seg,0,INT_GATE,0              ;  9
        GATE        ,rsrv_int,bios_seg,0,INT_GATE,0        ;  A
        GATE        ,com1_int,bios_seg,0,INT_GATE,0        ;  B
        GATE        ,com2_int,bios_seg,0,INT_GATE,0        ;  C
        GATE        ,prn2_int,bios_seg,0,INT_GATE,0        ;  D
        GATE        ,fd_int,bios_seg,0,INT_GATE,0            ;  E
        GATE        ,prn1_int,bios_seg,0,INT_GATE,0        ;  F
;    Hardware Level 1 (28-2F)
        GATE        ,rtc_int,bios_seg,0,INT_GATE,0            ;  70
        GATE        ,rsrv_int,bios_seg,0,INT_GATE,0        ;  71
        GATE        ,rsrv_int,bios_seg,0,INT_GATE,0        ;  72
        GATE        ,rsrv_int,bios_seg,0,INT_GATE,0        ;  73
        GATE        ,rsrv_int,bios_seg,0,INT_GATE,0        ;  74
        GATE        ,n287_int,bios_seg,0,INT_GATE,0        ;  75
        GATE        ,hd_int,bios_seg,0,INT_GATE,0            ;  76
        GATE        ,rsrv_int,bios_seg,0,INT_GATE,0        ;  77
;   Mini BIOS (30 - 31)
        GATE        ,int_30,bios_seg,0,TRAP_GATE,3
        GATE        ,sw_reset,bios_seg,0,TRAP_GATE,0
                ENDSEG    IDT


                PAGE
;    Mini BIOS
;       This section contains the "miniBIOS," a collection of
;       routines for hardware support, including the interrupt
;       handlers, and user-callable display routines.
```

```
; PC/AT Hardware Control
            MSEG     MONO_RAM,RD_WR,0,<AT 0B000h>
            ORG      4000                          ; end of monochrome RAM
            ENDSEG   MONO_RAM

            MSEG     COLOR_RAM,RD_WR,0,<AT 0B800h>
            ORG      16 * 1024                     ; end of color RAM
            ENDSEG   COLOR_RAM

MASTER               EQU      20h                      ; master 8259A
SLAVE                EQU      0A0h                     ; slave 8259A
DEV_COLOR    EQU     3D4h                    ; color port
RETRACE_PORT EQU     3DAh                    ; port for horiz/vert retrace
DEV_MONO     EQU     3B4h                    ; monochrome port
DEV_RTC      EQU     70h                     ; real-time-clock port

EOI                  EQU      20h                  ; end of interrupt command

WR_DEVICE    MACRO   device,unit,data  ; write to rtc or crt devices
             IFDIF   <device>,<>
             mov     dx, device
             ENDIF
             mov     al, unit
             out     dx, al
             inc     dx
             mov     al, data
             out     dx, al
             dec     dx
             ENDM


             MSEG    MBDAT,RD_WR,0

tick_ctr     DD      0                            ; incremented by timer int
kb_ctr               DW       -2                  ; keyboard interrupts
;   NOTE:  This program is setup to run on a monochrome system only
;    This pointer must be modified to support a color display.
display_ptr  LABEL   DWORD                        ; points to display RAM
             DW      0                                ; offset
             DW      disp_mono                        ; selector (MONOCHROME)
cursor               LABEL    word
cursor_x     DB      0                       ; column
cursor_y     DB      0                       ; row
attrib               DB       7
             ENDSEG  MBDAT

             MSEG    BIOS,EXONLY,0
             ASSUME  CS:BIOS, DS:NOTHING

; INTERRUPT HANDLERS
;    This is where the MINIBIOS comes when it gets a hardware interrupt.
;    In this implementation, the only interrupt which is handled is
;    the timer tick.  The keyboard interrupt is also used as a signal
;    to exit protected mode.  The other handlers are left as an
;    exercise for the user.
; Level 0 interrupts
```

```
timer_int:
                push    ax
                push    ds
                mov     ax, OFFSET bio_dat          ; data seg selector
                mov     ds, ax
                ASSUME  DS:MBDAT
                inc     WORD PTR tick_ctr  ; bump counter
                adc     WORD PTR tick_ctr[2], 0
                mov     al, EOI                      ; signal 8259A
                out     MASTER, al
                pop     ds
                ASSUME  DS:NOTHING
                pop     ax
                iret

kb_int:
                push    ax
                mov     al, EOI
                out     MASTER, al
                pop     ax
                int     31h                          ; RESET system
                iret

com1_int:
                push    ax
                mov     al, EOI
                out     MASTER, al
                pop     ax
                iret

com2_int:
                push    ax
                mov     al, EOI
                out     MASTER, al
                pop     ax
                iret

prn2_int:
                push    ax
                mov     al, EOI
                out     MASTER, al
                pop     ax
                iret

fd_int:
                push    ax
                mov     al, EOI
                out     MASTER, al
                pop     ax
                iret

prn1_int:
                push    ax
                mov     al, EOI
                out     MASTER, al
                pop     ax
```

```
                iret

; Level 1 interrupts - must EOI both the SLAVE and MASTER 8259As
rtc_int:
                push    ax
                mov     al, EOI
                out     SLAVE, al
                out     MASTER, al
                pop     ax
                iret


n287_int:
                push    ax
                mov     al, EOI
                out     SLAVE, al
                out     MASTER, al
                pop     ax
                iret


hd_int:
                push    ax
                mov     al, EOI
                out     SLAVE, al
                out     MASTER, al
                pop     ax
                iret


rsrv_int:
                int     1Fh                             ; cause failure

                PAGE

; MiniBIOS user callable function codes
MBIOS_WR_CHAR           EQU     0
MBIOS_WR_STRING EQU     1
MBIOS_WR_CRSR EQU       2
MBIOS_WR_ATTR           EQU     3
MBIOS_BELL      EQU     4
MBIOS_CLS       EQU     5

; USER CALLABLE FUNCTIONS
;   INT 30h
;   Write to display   -- All registers but AX preserved
;               FN:     AH = 0          Write character
;               Input:  AL = char
;
;               FN:     AH = 1          Write ASCIIZ string
;               Input   DS:SI -> string
;
;               FN:     AH = 2          Set cursor
;               Input:  DH = row
;                       DL = column
;
;               FN:     AH = 3          Set attribute
;               Input:  AL = attribute
;
```

```
;               FN:     AH = 4          Bell
;
;               FN      AH = 5          Clear Screen
;
int_30:
                cld
                or      ah, ah          ; determine function
                jz      co
                dec     ah
                jnz     $ + 5
                jmp     linout
                dec     ah
                jnz     $ + 5
                jmp     set_cursor
                dec     ah
                jnz     $ + 5
                jmp     set_attrib
                dec     ah
                jnz     $ + 5
                jmp     bell
                dec     ah
                jnz     $ + 5
                jmp     cls
                iret

wr_cursor       PROC    NEAR
; Write HW cursor - cursor in DX, trashes AX, CX, DX
                mov     ax, 80                  ; convert to 16 bit
                mul     dh
                xor     dh, dh
                add     dx, ax
                mov     cx, dx
                WR_DEVICE DEV_MONO,14,ch   ; write hardware
                WR_DEVICE ,15,cl
                ret
wr_cursor       ENDP

co:
                push    cx                      ; save state
                push    di
                push    ds
                push    es
                mov     cx, OFFSET bio_dat      ; bios data segment
                mov     ds, cx
                ASSUME  DS:MBDAT
                les     di, display_ptr
                mov     ch, al                  ; save character
                mov     ax, 80 * 2              ; number of columns/row
                mov     cl, cursor_y            ; time #rows
                mul     cl
                add     di, ax                  ; update offset
                xor     ax, ax                  ; zero
                mov     al, cursor_x            ; column
                shl     al, 1                   ; * 2
                add     di, ax                  ; update offset
                mov     al, ch                  ; restore character
```

```
                mov     ah, attrib              ; get data
                stosw
                inc     cursor_x                ; ajust cursor position
                cmp     cursor_x, 80
                jb      co_done
                sub     cursor_x, 80
                inc     cursor_y
co_done:        push    dx
                mov     dx, cursor
                call    wr_cursor
                pop     dx
                pop     es
                pop     ds
                ASSUME  DS:NOTHING
                pop     di
                pop     cx
                iret


linout:
                push    es                      ; save state
                push    si
                push    di
                push    cx
                push    ds
                mov     cx, OFFSET bio_dat      ; bios data segment
                mov     ds, cx
                ASSUME  DS:MBDAT
                les     di, display_ptr   ; get screen pointer
                mov     ax, 80 * 2              ; number of columns/row
                mov     cl, cursor_y            ; time #rows
                mul     cl
                add     di, ax                  ; update offset
                xor     ax, ax                  ; zero
                mov     al, cursor_x            ; column
                shl     al, 1                   ; * 2
                add     di, ax                  ; update offset
                mov     ah, attrib              ; screen attribute
                pop     ds                      ; user data
                ASSUME  DS:NOTHING
                xor     cx, cx                  ; count
                cld
linout_loop:    lodsb
                or      al, al                  ; end of string?
                jz      line_done               ; yes - quit loop
                stosw                           ; no - write char/attrib
                inc     cx
                jmp     linout_loop             ; write next char
line_done:      push    ds
                mov     ax, OFFSET bio_dat      ; bios data segment
                mov     ds, ax
                ASSUME  DS:MBDAT
                mov     ax, cx                  ; count
                mov     cl, 80
                div     cl                      ; al = rows, ah = columns
                add     cursor_x, ah
                cmp     cursor_x, 80            ; overflow?
```

```
                jb      update_row              ; no
                sub     cursor_x, 80            ; else adjust
                inc     al
update_row:     add     cursor_y, al
                push    dx
                mov     dx, cursor
                call    wr_cursor
                pop     dx
                pop     ds
                ASSUME  DS:NOTHING
                pop     cx
                pop     di                      ; start of chars written
                pop     si                      ; restore state
                pop     es
                iret                            ; and return

set_cursor:
                push    cx
                push    dx
                push    ds
                mov     ax, OFFSET bio_dat      ; bios data segment
                mov     ds, ax
                ASSUME  DS:MBDAT
                mov     cursor, dx              ; save new cursor
                call    wr_cursor
                pop     ds
                ASSUME  DS:NOTHING
                pop     dx
                pop     cx
                iret

set_attrib:
                push    cx
                push    ds
                mov     cx, OFFSET bio_dat      ; bios data segment
                mov     ds, cx
                ASSUME  DS:MBDAT
                mov     attrib, al
                pop     ds
                ASSUME  DS:NOTHING
                pop     cx
                iret

bell:
                push    ax
                push    bx
                push    cx
                mov     bx, 200
                in      al, 61h                 ; get current state
                push    ax                      ; save it
bell_loop:      and     al, 0FCh                ; speaker off
                out     61h, al
                mov     cx, 60
idle1:          loop    idle1
                or      al, 002h                ; speaker on
                out     61h, al
```

163

```
                mov     cx, 180                 ; duty cycle 1:3
idle2:          loop    idle2
                dec     bx                      ; test major loop
                jnz     bell_loop
                pop     ax
                out     61h, al                 ; restore state
                pop     cx
                pop     bx
                pop     ax
                iret

cls:
                push    cx                      ; save state
                push    dx
                push    di
                push    ds
                push    es
                mov     cx, OFFSET bio_dat      ; bios data segment
                mov     ds, cx
                ASSUME  DS:MBDAT
                les     di, display_ptr
                mov     ah, attrib
                mov     al, ' '
                mov     cx, 80 * 25
                cld
                rep stosw
                xor     dx, cx
                mov     cursor, dx
                call    wr_cursor
                pop     es
                pop     ds
                pop     di
                pop     dx
                pop     cx
                iret


;
;   INT 31
;   Reset processor
;
sw_reset        PROC    FAR
                WR_DEVICE DEV_RTC,0Fh,0    ; write SHUTDOWN code to RTC
                mov     al, 0FEh                        ; HW SHUTDOWN
                out     64h, al                         ; HW STATUS
halt:           hlt
                jmp     halt
sw_reset        ENDP
                ENDSEG  BIOS


                PAGE
; FAULT HANDLERS
;   In this prototype system, all the fault handler does is to display
;   the name and location of the fault on the screen for a short period
;   of time before resetting the system.  This should provide the user
;   with enough information to correct the problem.
```

```
; TSS for #DF - double fault handler
; #DF must have its own task to prevent shutdown
            SSEG    FTASK8,TSS,0
            DW      0                           ; back link
            DW      0, 0                         ; SS0:SP - unneeded/CPL=0
            DW      0, 0                         ; SS1:SP
            DW      0, 0                         ; SS2:SP
            DW      fault_ts                    ; IP
            DW      0                           ; flags
            DW      4 DUP (0)                   ; AX/CX/DX/BX
            DW      fhandler_stack              ; SP
            DW      fhandler_stack              ; BP
            DW      msg_08, 0                   ; SI/DI
            GDT_SEL xtra8,0                     ; ES
            GDT_SEL fhandler,0                  ; CS
            GDT_SEL fault_dat,0                 ; SS
            GDT_SEL fault_dat,0                 ; DS
            DW      0                           ; LDT selector
            ENDSEG  FTASK8

; TSS for #TF - task fault handler
; #TF must have its own task to ensure a valid machine state
            SSEG    FTASK10,TSS,0
            DW      0                           ; back link
            DW      0, 0                         ; SS0:SP - unneeded/CPL=0
            DW      0, 0                         ; SS1:SP
            DW      0, 0                         ; SS2:SP
            DW      fault_ts                    ; IP
            DW      0                           ; flags
            DW      4 DUP (0)                   ; AX/CX/DX/BX
            DW      fhandler_stack              ; SP
            DW      fhandler_stack              ; BP
            DW      msg_10, 0                   ; SI/DI
            GDT_SEL xtra10,0                    ; ES
            GDT_SEL fhandler,0                  ; CS
            GDT_SEL fault_dat,0                 ; SS
            GDT_SEL fault_dat,0                 ; DS
            DW      0                           ; LDT selector
            ENDSEG  FTASK10

; TSS for #SF - stack fault handler
; #SF requires its own task to prevent #DF in certain occasions
            SSEG    FTASK12,TSS,0
            DW      0                           ; back link
            DW      0, 0                         ; SS0:SP - unneeded/CPL=0
            DW      0, 0                         ; SS1:SP
            DW      0, 0                         ; SS2:SP
            DW      fault_ts                    ; IP
            DW      0                           ; flags
            DW      4 DUP (0)                   ; AX/CX/DX/BX
            DW      fhandler_stack              ; SP
            DW      fhandler_stack              ; BP
            DW      msg_12, 0                   ; SI/DI
            GDT_SEL xtra12,0                    ; ES
            GDT_SEL fhandler,0                  ; CS
            GDT_SEL fault_dat,0                 ; SS
```

```
                GDT_SEL  fault_dat,0                      ; DS
                DW       0                                ; LDT selector
                ENDSEG   FTASK12

                MSEG     FDAT,RD_WR,0
; Data for fault handlers
msg_00                   DB       "*** DIVIDE FAULT ***", 0
msg_01                   DB       "*** SINGLE STEP TRAP ***", 0
msg_02                   DB       "*** NMI ***", 0
msg_03                   DB       "*** INT 3 ***", 0
msg_04                   DB       "*** OVERFLOW EXCEPTION ***", 0
msg_05                   DB       "*** BOUND EXCEPTION ***", 0
msg_06                   DB       "*** UNDEFINED OPCODE ***", 0
msg_07                   DB       "*** 287 NOT AVAILABLE ***", 0
msg_08                   DB       "*** DOUBLE FAULT ***", 0
msg_09                   DB       "*** 287 SEGMENT OVERRUN ***", 0
msg_10                   DB       "*** ILLEGAL TSS FAULT ***", 0
msg_11                   DB       "*** NOT PRESENT FAULT ***", 0
msg_12                   DB       "*** STACK FAULT ***", 0
msg_13                   DB       "*** GENERAL PROTECTION FAULT ***", 0
msg_16                   DB       "*** 287 EXCEPTION ***", 0
msg_fcode       DB       "*** Fault code = ",0
msg_faddr       DB       "*** Fault address = ",0
msg_unknown     DB       "*** UNKNOWN EXCEPTION ***", 0
msg_buffer      DB       40 DUP (0)

                ALIGN    2                                ; force stack to word boundary
                DW       64 DUP (0)
fhandler_stack           LABEL    WORD

                ENDSEG   FDAT

                MSEG     HAND,EXONLY,0
; Code for fault handlers
                ASSUME   CS:HAND, DS:FDAT

fault_00:       mov      si, OFFSET msg_00
                jmp      fail

fault_01:       mov      si, OFFSET msg_01
                jmp      fail

fault_02:       mov      si, OFFSET msg_02
                jmp      fail

fault_03:       mov      si, OFFSET msg_03
                jmp      fail

fault_04:       mov      si, OFFSET msg_04
                jmp      fail

fault_05:       mov      si, OFFSET msg_05
                jmp      fail

fault_06:       mov      si, OFFSET msg_06
                jmp      fail
```

```
fault_07:       mov     si, OFFSET msg_07
                jmp     fail

fault_08:       mov     si, OFFSET msg_08
                jmp     fail

fault_09:       mov     si, OFFSET msg_09
                jmp     fail

fault_10:       mov     si, OFFSET msg_10
                jmp     fail

fault_11:       mov     si, OFFSET msg_11
                jmp     fail

fault_12:       mov     si, OFFSET msg_12
                jmp     fail

fault_13:       mov     si, OFFSET msg_13
                jmp     fail

fault_16:       mov     si, OFFSET msg_16
                jmp     fail

unknown:        mov     si, OFFSET msg_unknown
                jmp     fail

; All fault handlers that have a task switch come here
fault_ts:
                pop     ax                          ; error code
                mov     bx, ES:[back_link]          ; selector of faulting task
                lar     dx, bx                      ; check if accessable
                jnz     fake_data                   ; invalid
                test    dh, 80h                     ; check present bit
                jz      fake_data                   ; invalid
                and     dh, 1Fh                     ; mask - leaving type info
                cmp     dh, TSS_BUSY                ; should point to user TSS
                jne     fake_data                   ; invalid
                lsl     dx, bx                      ; get segment size
                cmp     dx, TSS_LIMIT              ; ensure size OK
                jb      fake_data                   ; branch too small
; At this point, we know that the back link points to a
; valid TSS, we now wish to create a readable data segment
; that points to the same physical location as the TSS so
; we can extract some information from it.  Since this segment
; is created pointing to the same address as a previously
; existing segment, it is called an ALIAS
                mov     di, OFFSET falias ; offset of free descriptor
                mov     dx, OFFSET int15_gdt_dat; selector for GDT as
                mov     es, dx                      ; if it were a data seg
                and     bx, 0FFF8h                  ; convert selector to offset
                mov     cx, ES:[bx].phys_addr_lo; get phys addr of user TSS
                mov     ES:[di].phys_addr_lo, cx; store in free descriptor
                mov     cl, ES:[bx].phys_addr_hi; continue with high byte
                mov     ES:[di].phys_addr_hi, cl
```

```
                mov     ES:[di].limit, TSS_LIMIT; complete free descriptor
                mov     es, di                  ; use as selector to segment
                push    ES:[rCS]                ; push task's CS
                push    ES:[rIP]                ; push task's IP
                push    ax                      ; error code
                jmp     fail


fake_data:      push    WORD PTR 0FFFFh    ; can't get real info
                push    WORD PTR 0FFFEh    ; push false CS, IP
                push    ax                      ; error code
                jmp     fail


pause                   PROC    NEAR
                mov     bx, 10
ploop:                  mov     cx, 0FFFFh
                loop    $
                dec     bx
                jnz     ploop
                ret
pause                   ENDP

fail:                   mov     ax, OFFSET fault_dat    ; get legal DS
                mov     ds, ax
                mov     es, ax
                mov     dx, 0                   ; cursor x=0/y=0
                mov     ah, MBIOS_WR_CRSR  ; home cursor
                int     30h
                mov     ah, MBIOS_WR_STRING     ; write msg
                int     30h
                mov     dx, 0100h               ; cursor x=0/y=1
                mov     ah, MBIOS_WR_CRSR  ; home cursor
                int     30h
                ; check if error code on stack
                cmp     si, OFFSET msg_08  ; was DF fault?
                je      show_code
                cmp     si, OFFSET msg_10  ; was TF fault?
                je      show_code
                cmp     si, OFFSET msg_11  ; was NP fault?
                je      show_code
                cmp     si, OFFSET msg_12  ; was SF fault?
                je      show_code
                cmp     si, OFFSET msg_13  ; was GP fault?
                jne     show_addr
show_code:      mov     si, OFFSET msg_fcode       ; print code message
                mov     ah, MBIOS_WR_STRING
                int     30h
                pop     dx                  ; get code from stack
                mov     di, OFFSET msg_buffer
                mov     ah, LIB_BIN_HEX    ; convert to hex
                CALL_EX share_gate,0
                mov     si, OFFSET msg_buffer      ; and print
                mov     ah, MBIOS_WR_STRING
                int     30h
                mov     dx, 0200h               ; cursor x=0/y=2
```

```
                mov     ah, MBIOS_WR_CRSR  ; home cursor
                int     30h
show_addr:
                mov     si, OFFSET msg_faddr        ; print addr message
                mov     ah, MBIOS_WR_STRING
                int     30h
                pop     bx                          ; get offset
                pop     dx                          ; get segment
                push    bx                          ; save offset
                mov     di, OFFSET msg_buffer
                mov     ah, LIB_BIN_HEX
                CALL_EX share_gate,0
                mov     si, OFFSET msg_buffer
                mov     ah, MBIOS_WR_STRING
                int     30h
                mov     al, ':'
                mov     ah, MBIOS_WR_CHAR
                int     30h
                pop     dx                          ; offset
                mov     di, OFFSET msg_buffer
                mov     ah, LIB_BIN_HEX
                CALL_EX share_gate,0
                mov     si, OFFSET msg_buffer
                mov     ah, MBIOS_WR_STRING
                int     30h
                call    pause                       ; wait
                call    pause
                call    pause
                mov     ah, MBIOS_BELL              ; bell
                int     30h
                call    pause
                mov     ah, MBIOS_BELL              ; bell
                int     30h
                call    pause
                mov     ah, MBIOS_BELL              ; bell
                int     30h
                call    pause                       ; wait
                call    pause
                call    pause
                call    pause
                int     31h                         ; reset processor
                ENDSEG  HAND

                PAGE
                MSEG    SHLIB,EX_RD_CF,0
;
;   This segment implements a library of shared functions that may be
;   invoked through gate "share_gate". The segment is conforming, so its
;   code will run at the same privelege as the caller. The calling
;   sequence is merely to set up the registers and CALL the gate. If an
;   illegal function number is called, the system issues a DIVIDE BY 0.
;   Only registers BP, SP, CS, DS, ES, and SS are guaranteed preserved.
;
                ASSUME  CS:SHLIB, DS:NOTHING, ES:NOTHING

LIB_SINT_BIN    EQU     0
```

```
LIB_UINT_BIN    EQU     1
LIB_HEX_BIN     EQU     2
LIB_BIN_SINT    EQU     3
LIB_BIN_UINT    EQU     4
LIB_BIN_HEX     EQU     5


shlib_code      PROC    FAR
                cld                             ; set direction for string fns
                cmp     ah, 5                   ; beyond last function?
                jbe     index                   ; no - do indexing
                xor     ax, ax                  ; zero ax
                div     al                      ; force divide fault

index:          mov     bl, ah                  ; get FN code
                xor     bh, bh                  ; clear high order
                shl     bx, 1                   ; convert FN to index
                add     bx, OFFSET table
                jmp     WORD PTR CS:[bx]   ; invoke function.

table           DW      sint_bin
                DW      uint_bin
                DW      hex_bin
                DW      bin_sint
                DW      bin_uint
                DW      bin_hex

;   Function 0 / ASCII SIGNED INT to BINARY conversion
;       AH = 0
;       DS:SI -> Null terminated string of digits
;   Returns:
;       AX <- 16-bit signed integer
;       CY <- set if error
;
sint_bin:
                mov     cx, 10                  ; multiply constant
                xor     ax, ax                  ; initialize accumulator
                xor     dx, dx
                xor     bh, bh                  ; sign flag FALSE
                cmp     BYTE PTR [si], '-'       ; signed?
                jne     get_schar               ; no
                inc     si                      ; next char
                inc     bh                      ; set signed flag
get_schar:      mov     bl, [si]                ; get input character
                inc     si                      ; bump ptr
                or      bl, bl                  ; end of string?
                jz      set_sign
                cmp     bl, '0'                  ; check valid
                jb      err_ret
                cmp     bl, '9'
                ja      err_ret
                sub     bl, '0'                  ; convert digit to binary
                mul     cx                      ; decimal shift left
                add     al, bl                  ; new digit
                adc     ah, 0                   ; propogate carry
                js      err_ret                 ; quit if sign overflow
                adc     dx, 0
```

```
                jnz     err_ret                 ; quit if overflow
                jmp     get_schar
set_sign:       or      bh, bh                  ; sign flag on
                jz      done                    ; no - return
                neg     ax                      ; else complement
done:           clc                             ;  no error
                ret
err_ret:        stc                             ; CY is error flag
                ret

;   Function 1 / ASCII UNSIGNED INT to BINARY conversion
;       AH = 1
;       DS:SI -> Null terminated string of digits
;   Returns:
;       AX <- 16-bit unsigned integer
;       CY <- set if error
;
uint_bin:
                mov     cx, 10                  ; multiply constant
                xor     ax, ax                  ; initialize accumulator
                xor     dx, dx
get_uchar:      mov     bl, [si]                ; get input character
                inc     si                      ; bump ptr
                or      bl, bl                  ; end of string?
                jz      done                    ; yes - return
                cmp     bl, '0'                 ;  check valid
                jb      err_ret
                cmp     bl, '9'
                ja      err_ret
                sub     bl, '0'                 ;  convert digit to binary
                mul     cx                      ; decimal shift left
                add     al, bl                  ; new digit
                adc     ah, 0                   ; propogate carry
                adc     dx, 0
                jnz     err_ret                 ; quit if overflow
                jmp     get_uchar

;   Function 2 / ASCII HEX to BINARY conversion
;       AH = 2
;       DS:SI -> Null terminated string of digits
;   Returns:
;       AX <- 16-bit unsigned
;       CY <- set if error
;
hex_bin:
                xor     dx, dx                  ; init accumulator
get_hchar:      lodsb                           ; get character
                or      al, al                  ; last char?
                jnz     test_hchars
                mov     ax, dx
                ret                             ; CY cleared by OR
test_hchars:    cmp     al, '0'                 ;  check valid digit
                jb      err_ret
                cmp     al, '9'
                jbe     got_valid
                or      al, 20h                 ; must be alpha - force lower
```

```
                cmp     al, 'a'                     ; check valid char
                jb      err_ret
                cmp     al, 'f'
                ja      err_ret
                sub     al, 27h                     ; adjust range
got_valid:      sub     al, '0'                     ; convert digit to binary
                cmp     dx, 0FFFh                   ; test overflow
                ja      err_ret
                shl     dx, 4                       ; hex shift left
                add     dl, al                      ; insert new digit
                jmp     get_hchar

;   Function 3 / BINARY to ASCII SIGNED INT conversion
;       AH = 3
;       DX -> 16-bit signed
;       ES:DI -> Buffer for ascii string
;   Returns:
;       Null terminated ASCII string at ES:DI
;
bin_sint:       test    dh, 80h                     ; sign bit?
                jz      bin_uint                    ; no - treat as unsigned
                mov     al, '-'                     ; else write sign
                stosb
                neg     dx                          ; and complement
                jmp     bin_uint

div_tab         DW      10000
                DW      1000
                DW      100
                DW      10
                DW      1

;   Function 4 / BINARY to ASCII UNSIGNED INT conversion
;       AH = 4
;       DX -> 16-bit unsigned
;       ES:DI -> Buffer for ascii string
;   Returns:
;       Null terminated ASCII string at ES:DI
;
bin_uint:       mov     si, OFFSET div_tab          ; index
                xor     bx, bx                      ; bh is zero suppress flag
                mov     ax, dx                      ; value
u_loop:         cmp     WORD PTR CS:[si], 1         ; last divisor?
                je      u_out                       ; yes - output last digit
                xor     dx, dx                      ; high order zero
                div     WORD PTR CS:[si]   ; DX:AX/10^n
                or      ax, bx                      ; quotient == 0 || ! suppress?
                jz      u_loop
                mov     bh, 1                       ; turn off zero suppress flag
                add     al, '0'                     ; quotient always single digit
                stosb
                mov     ax, dx                      ; restore AX with remainder
                inc     si
                inc     si                          ; next divisor
                jmp     u_loop
u_out:          add     al, '0'                     ; last digit
```

```
                stosb
                xor     al, al                      ; ASCII null
                stosb
                ret

;   Function 5 / BINARY to ASCII HEX conversion
;       AH = 5
;       DX -> 16-bit unsigned
;       ES:DI -> Buffer for ascii
;   Returns:
;       Null terminated 4 character ASCII string at ES:DI
;
bin_hex:        mov     al, dh                  ; high order byte
                shr     al, 4                   ; high nybble
                add     al, '0'                   ; convert to ASCII
                cmp     al, '9'                   ; test value > '9'
                jbe     bin_h1
                add     al, 7                   ; ajust alpha
bin_h1:         stosb
                mov     al, dh                  ; high order byte
                and     al, 0Fh                 ; low nybble
                add     al, '0'                   ; convert to ASCII
                cmp     al, '9'                   ; test value > '9'
                jbe     bin_h2
                add     al, 7                   ; ajust alpha
bin_h2:         stosb
                mov     al, dl                  ; low order byte
                shr     al, 4                   ; high nybble
                add     al, '0'                   ; convert to ASCII
                cmp     al, '9'                   ; test value > '9'
                jbe     bin_h3
                add     al, 7                   ; ajust alpha
bin_h3:         stosb
                mov     al, dl                  ; low order byte
                and     al, 0Fh                 ; low nybble
                add     al, '0'                   ; convert to ASCII
                cmp     al, '9'                   ; test value > '9'
                jbe     bin_h4
                add     al, 7                   ; ajust alpha
bin_h4:         stosb
                xor     al, al
                stosb                           ; ASCII null
                ret


shlib_code      ENDP
                ENDSEG  SHLIB


                PAGE
;
;   This section contains the main code and data.  We come here initially
;   in Real Address Mode, perform necessary setup, and enter Protected
;   Virtual Address Mode.  The data segment has combine type STACK
;   so that the linker will initialize SS:SP.
;
                MSEG    DSC,RD_WR,0,STACK
```

```
no_pm_msg     DB        '*** Unable to enter protected mode ***$'
blank_line    DB        80 DUP (' ')
              DB        0
msg                     DB        'Testing',0

              ALIGN     2                          ; force stack to word bound
              DW        100 DUP (?)                ; stack
              ENDSEG    DSC

              SSEG      INIT_TSS,TSS,0
              TSS_BLOCK <>                          ; uninitialized
              ENDSEG    INIT_TSS

              MSEG      INIT,EXONLY,0
              ASSUME    CS:INIT, DS:DSC

adjust_addr   PROC      NEAR
; This subroutine marches through a descriptor table to fixup 16-bit
; segment addresses to full 24-bit physical addresses.  Since the
; segment fixups were done by the DOS linker in Real Address Mode,
; all we need to do is multiply by 16.   We assume the high order 8
; bits are zero, i.e., all addresses are in the first 1Mb.
; Called with ES:0 pointing to table, CX is number of entries.
              xor       bx, bx                     ; initial offset
l1:                     mov       al, ES:[bx].access   ; get access rights byte
              test      al, 10h                    ; is descriptor a segment?
              jnz       got_seg                    ; yes
              and       al, 0Fh                    ; extract type
              cmp       al, 3                      ; gate?
              ja        update_next                ; yes - skip segment adjust
got_seg:      mov       ax, ES:[bx].phys_addr_lo; get segment
              mov       dx, 16
              mul       dx                         ; convert to phys addr
              mov       ES:[bx].phys_addr_lo, ax; store
              mov       ES:[bx].phys_addr_hi, dl; 24 bits
update_next:  add       bx, 8                      ; incr to next descrip
              loop      l1
              ret
adjust_addr   ENDP

start:
              mov       ax, DSC                    ; set up DS
              mov       ds, ax
              sti

; When DOS created the prototype descriptors, it placed segment addresses
; in the physical address portion of the segment descriptors.  We must
; fix up all descirptor tables which contain segment descriptors.
              mov       ax, T2LDT
              mov       es, ax                     ; point to proto LDT
              mov       cx, t2ldt_limit   ; get limit
              inc       cx                         ; bump to size in bytes
              shr       cx, 3                      ; convert to # entries
              call      adjust_addr

              mov       ax, GDT
```

```
        mov     es, ax                      ; point to proto GDT
        mov     cx, gdt_limit
        inc     cx
        shr     cx, 3                       ; gdt entries
        call    adjust_addr
```

```
;   Now we ask the BIOS to place us in protected mode.  The BIOS requires
.;  the first 7 descriptors of the GDT to be setup as we have done.  This
;   gives it enough information to load GDTR and IDTR and setup a new
;   code and data segment for the calling routine.  The BIOS will also
;   program the 8259A to our requested interrupt vectors.  Additionally, it
;   sets up the internal AT hardware to allow addresses > 1Mb to go out
;   over the bus (frees A20 line).
```

```
        xor     si, si                      ; ES:SI -> proto GDT
        mov     bh, 20h                     ; int level 1 start
        mov     bl, 28h                     ; int level 2 start
        mov     ah, 89h                     ; enter PM request
        mov     cx, 0FFFFh                  ; idle here to ensure all
        loop    $                           ; DOS keybd ints processed
        int     15h                         ; BIOS call
        jnc     vm                          ; successful if no CY bit

        mov     ah, 9                       ; no - print message
        mov     dx, OFFSET no_pm_msg
        int     21h
        mov     ax, 4C01h                   ; failure
        int     21h                         ; exit
```

```
;;; NOW IN PROCTED MODE -- INTS DISABLED
```

```
vm:
        mov     bp, sp                      ; setup registers
        mov     ax, ds
        mov     es, ax
        mov     ax, OFFSET setup_tss        ; active task
        ltr     ax
```

```
pm_init_done:
        mov     ah, MBIOS_BELL              ; bell
        int     30h
        call    idle

        mov     ah, MBIOS_CLS               ; cls
        int     30h
```

```
; Enable ints
        xor     al, al                      ; no ints masked
        out     MASTER+1, al
        out     SLAVE+1, al
        sti
```

```
; Print number of ticks so far
print_ticks:
        mov     ah, MBIOS_CLS               ; clear screen
        int     30h
        mov     dx, 0010h
```

```
                mov     ah, MBIOS_WR_CRSR
                int     30h
                mov     ax, OFFSET bio_dat
                mov     es, ax
                cli
                mov     dx, WORD PTR ES:tick_ctr     ; get tick counter
                mov     ax, WORD PTR ES:tick_ctr[2]
                sti
                push    dx
                call    pr_hex_word                  ; print high order
                pop     ax
                call    pr_hex_word                  ; print low order
                call    idle                         ; pause

                CALL_EX task2_tss,0                  ; invoke task 2

                call    idle
                call    idle
                mov     ah, MBIOS_BELL               ; bell
                int     30h
                jmp     print_ticks                  ; loop forever


idle                    PROC    NEAR
                push    bx
                push    cx
                mov     bx, 10
iloop:                  mov     cx, 0FFFFh
                loop    $
                dec     bx
                jnz     iloop
                pop     cx
                pop     bx
                ret
idle                    ENDP

pr_hex_word     PROC
;   Print word in AX
                push    bp
                mov     bp, sp
                sub     sp, 10                       ; space for string on stack
                push    ds
                pop     es                           ; es = ds
                lea     di, [bp-10]                  ; destination
                mov     dx, ax                       ; value
                mov     ah, LIB_BIN_HEX     ; function
                CALL_EX share_gate,0                 ; shared code
                lea     si, [bp-10]                  ; hex string ptr
                mov     ah, MBIOS_WR_STRING          ; function
                int     30h                          ; print string
                mov     sp, bp
                pop     bp
                ret
pr_hex_word     ENDP
                ENDSEG  INIT
```

```
                PAGE
;   Finally, we have a small second task, which will alternate execution
;   with the initial task.    It runs at privelege level 3, which means it
;   has access only to its code segment, data segment, the shared library
;   gate and INT 30h.

                SSEG    T2LDT,LDT,0
; All memory segments for this task reside in a local descriptor table.
        DSCRP   task2_cs,CODE2                  ; CS for 2nd task
        DSCRP   task2_dsc,DSC2                  ; DS/SS for 2nd task
        DSCRP   task2_stk0,STK2_0               ; Level 0 stack for OS calls
                ENDSEG  T2LDT

                SSEG    TASK2,TSS,0
                DW      0                       ; back link
                DW      STK2_0_limit + 1   ; SP0
                LDT_SEL task2_stk0,0            ; SS0
                DW      0, 0                     ; SS1:SP
                DW      0, 0                     ; SS2:SP
                DW      top                     ; initial IP
                DW      200h                    ; flags - INTs enabled
                DW      4 DUP (0)               ; AX/CX/DX/BX
                DW      stack2                  ; SP
                DW      stack2                  ; BP
                DW      2 DUP (0)               ; SI/DI
                LDT_SEL task2_dsc,3            ; ES - segments all in LDT
                LDT_SEL task2_cs,3             ; CS
                LDT_SEL task2_dsc,3            ; SS
                LDT_SEL task2_dsc,3            ; DS
                GDT_SEL task2_ldt,0            ; LDT selector
                ENDSEG  TASK2

                MSEG    STK2_0,RD_WR,0
                DW      128 DUP (?)             ; stack for level 0 execution
                ENDSEG  STK2_0

                MSEG    DSC2,RD_WR,3
; Data and stack segment for 2nd task
t2_msg                  DB      "Task 2 running",0

                ALIGN   2                       ; stack on word boundary
                DW      128 DUP (?)
stack2                  LABEL   WORD

                ENDSEG  DSC2

                MSEG    CODE2,EXONLY,3
                ASSUME  CS:CODE2, DS:DSC2
top:                                            ; task starts here first time
                mov     dx, 0032h
                mov     ah, MBIOS_WR_CRSR
                int     30h                     ; cursor to "safe" location
                mov     si, OFFSET t2_msg
                mov     ah, MBIOS_WR_STRING
                int     30h                     ; print message
                iret                            ; return to previous task
```

```
        jmp     top                 ; when task invoked again,
                                    ; CS:IP points here (after IRET)
        ENDSEG  CODE2

        END     start
```

9

286/386 Protected-Mode [*] Programming

_____*Joel Barnum*_____

There's no such thing as a free lunch. Some pitfalls await you when you try to update real-mode programs to protected mode. With the release of OS/2, a protected-mode operating system for 80286- and 80386-based computers, you might want to rewrite existing real-mode programs or write new programs that execute under protected mode. While it is generally more reliable, protected mode is not totally compatible with real mode and places additional restrictions on programs. This article deals with those restrictions, but first I will discuss the various modes and how they work.

Modes of Operation

Real mode is the "power-on" mode of the 80286 and 80386 processors, in which the processor emulates the 8086 and 8088 microprocessors. Real mode has no memory protection, and the maximum amount of physical address space is 1 megabyte. Currently, PC-DOS and MS-DOS operate in real mode on the IBM PC AT and compatibles.

To switch to protected mode, the operating system sets the least-signif the *machine-status word* (MSW). In protected mode, the processor v memory access so that one program can't corrupt memory belongir Protected mode also enables multitasking support and virtual mem imum amount of physical memory that an 80286 operating in pro address is 16 megabytes; on an 80386, this number increases to

The 80386 also includes virtual 8086 mode (VM86), whic 80386 protected-mode operating systems to execute unmod guest tasks.

179

The Segment Descriptor

Regardless of mode, well-behaved programs use symbolic names to address segments. For example, Listing 9-1 uses the name of a segment, *DATA*, to initialize the DS (data segment) register. In real mode, *DATA* refers to the segment's address, and the program loader fills in the correct value at load time. In protected mode, however, the program loader fills in a 16-bit number, called a selector, that points to the segment indirectly via an 8-byte data structure called a descriptor.

Listing 9-1: If you use symbolic segment names to create well-behaved programs, your code should work equally well in real or protected mode

```
DATA SEGMENT
    var1 DB ?
DATA ENDS
CODE SEGMENT
    ASSUME CS: CODE,DS:DATA
    MOV AX,DATA              ;symbolic segment name
    MOV DS,AX                ;point to data segment
    MOV var1,1               ;sample access
CODE ENDS
```

The program loader creates the descriptor, which contains information describing the segment. Figure 9-1 shows a segment descriptor. The base address is the segment's starting address; that is, where the program loader put it. The processor uses this address to locate the segment; it is comparable to the segment address in real mode.

8 bytes

16 bits	24 bits	8 bits	16 bits
imit	Base Address	Access Rights	Used only by 80386

The 80286 segment descriptor contains the offset limit segment's base address and access rights.

num offset allowed in that segment. If a program tries to

use an offset greater than the limit, the processor prevents the instruction from executing. This ensures that one program is unable to modify another program's memory.

The access-rights byte contains bit fields that indicate the type of the segment; it includes the *descriptor privilege level* (DPL). Each descriptor has a DPL ranging from 0 to 3, with 0 the most privileged. One segment cannot access another segment that has a higher privilege. These levels help protect system integrity; for example, they prevent applications programs from corrupting the operating system.

The access-rights byte also tells you what kind of access is allowed on the segment. For data-segment descriptors, the access rights indicate that the segment is either readable and writable, or readable only. For code-segment descriptors, the segment can be either executable and readable, or executable only.

The operating system organizes the descriptors into groups called descriptor tables, which contain a maximum of 8192 descriptors each, numbered from 0 to 8191. These tables are of two types: the *global-descriptor table* (GDT), which contains those descriptors that are available to all programs, and the *local-descriptor tables* (LDTs), which contain the descriptors for each task's own segments. While each task has an LDT, the system has only one GDT.

To access a segment, you load a segment register with the selector. Its index and *table indicator* (TI) fields (see Figure 9-2) point to a descriptor from the GDT or an LDT. During this load, the processor locates the descriptor and copies its base address, limit, and access rights into an extended version of the segment register. From then on, the extended segment register contains all the pertinent information about the segment.

Figure 9-2: The Selector Format: The index can range from 0 to 8191, and it points to the descriptor. The TI equals 0 if the selector refers to the GDT, or 1 if it refers to an LDT. The privilege level (RPL here) is described in Figure 9-3.

Thus, when a protected-mode program loads a segment register, the result is the same as in real mode--the segment register contains the segment's address. The difference is that the protected-mode segment register also contains the segment's limit and access rights so the processor can enforce memory protection. The example in Listing 9-1 should work the same in real or protected mode, because it is well-behaved and uses a symbolic name to refer to its data segment.

When a protected-mode program violates one of the protection rules, the processor generates an interrupt called an exception. An operating system can handle exceptions in various ways, but the most probably action is to terminate the faulting program.

Behavioral Problems

Real-mode programs that are poorly behaved (i.e., that use direct addressing) may not work properly in protected mode because a selector's value doesn't correspond to a segment's address. For example, consider the real-mode program in Listing 9-2, which writes to the IBM PC's color display memory. In real mode, 0B800 hexadecimal is the segment address of the color card's memory. In protected mode, however, a selector with value 0B800h refers to the GDT descriptor located at index equals 1700h. It's unlikely that there's a valid descriptor at that large an index, but even if there is, it's improbable that it's the right one. At best, the program won't display a character. At worst, it will incur a protection exception during the segment-load instruction, because the selector refers to an invalid descriptor.

Listing 9-2: If you use direct addressing to create poorly behaved programs, your code will have problems in protected mode.

```
MOV AX, 0B800H              ;segment address of color card
MOV ES,AX                   ;ES to display memory
MOV BYTE PTR ES: [0], 'A'   ;display a character A
```

Well-behaved programs avoid writing to fixed memory locations and use operating-system I/O services instead. You could upgrade Listing 9-2 more easily if it used the DOS display-character function *call* instead of writing directly to the color card. If you need to write directly to memory for performance reasons, you should restrict such accesses to a single procedure. Then you need to modify only one procedure, not your mainline code.

Another problem related to poor behavior arises if a program performs arithmetic on segment values. For example, a real-mode program with two contiguous 64K-byte segments might add 1000h to the segment address of the first in order to point to the second. Or, a program might calculate its load size by subtracting the segment address of the first from that of the second. In either case, the program would have problems in protected mode, because a selector doesn't correspond to the segment's base address. A protected-mode program should not rely on segment arithmetic.

In protected mode, the access-rights byte has enough bits to delineate two types of code segments: executable and readable, and execute only. However, there is no way to make code segments writable. Thus, a protected-mode program can never use a CS segment override as an instruction's destination.

For example, in both of the *MOV* instructions in Listing 9-3, the program accesses a variable, *var1*, inside the code segment. *MOV AL, var1* works fine as long as the code segment's descriptor says that the segment is readable. *MOV var1,AL* fails regardless of the descriptor type, however, because code segments are never writable in protected mode. To avoid this problem, you should define all variables within a data or stack segment.

Listing 9-3: Accessing code-segment variables

```
CODE  SEGMENT
      ASSUME CS:CODE
      var1 DB 1                 ;code segment variable
      start:
      MOV  AL,var1              ;works if execute and read access rights
      MOV  var1,AL              ;never works, can't write
CODE  ENDS
```

The interrupt-vector table is the source of another potential conversion problem. In real mode, the operating system stores the addresses of interrupt-service routines in the interrupt-vector table located at memory address 0000. In protected mode, the interrupt-descriptor table has a different format and doesn't have to reside at any specific address. Therefore, programs that directly manipulate the real-mode interrupt-vector table won't work in protected mode. You can avoid this problem by using DOS functions 25h and 35h to read and write entries in the interrupt table.

Sensitive and Privileged

To make a system as reliable as possible, the operating system can prevent you from executing so-called sensitive instructions (Table 9-1) while in protected mode. If you use these instructions incorrectly, your program can crash the system. For example, if you issued an invalid *OUT* instruction, you could turn off the PC's direct-memory-access controller and cause a memory parity error.

IN	Read a port
OUT	Write to a port
INS	Read a string from a port
OUTS	Write a string to a port
CLI	Disable interrupts
STI	Enable interrupts

Table 9-1: Protected-Mode Sensitive Instructions

The operating system controls who can execute sensitive instructions via the *I/O privilege level* (IOPL) bits in the program's flags. (Each program has its own set of flags.) To be allowed to execute sensitive instructions, the current code segment's privilege level, or CPL, must be higher (i.e., numerically lower) than the IOPL; otherwise, the processor will generate an exception (Figure 9-3).

Figure 9-3: The CPL is located in the last two bits of the code segment's selector. The IOPL is found in the program's flags. You can modify the IOPL only when CPL=0; you can execute sensitive instructions only if CPL<=IOPL.

Existing real-mode programs that use sensitive instructions may fault in protected mode, depending on how the operating system assigns CPL and IOPL. To avoid such faults, you can compare these values programmatically to determine whether a particular program can execute sensitive instructions. The procedure *check_sensitive* in Listing 9-4 performs this comparison.

Listing 9-4: This routine determines whether you can execute sensitive instructions. It takes no inputs. After execution, the carry flag will be 0 if you can use sensitive instructions at the segment's current privilege level, or 1 if their use will generate an exception.

```
check_sensitive              PROC
                             PUBLIC check_sensitive

        PUSH        AX
        PUSH        BX

        PUSHF                            ;save flags (IOPL) on stack
        POP         AX                   ;copy flags to AX
        AND         AX,3000H             ;mask all but IOPL
        SHR         AX,12                ;right-justify IOPL
        MOV         BX,CS                ;CPL resides in CS
        AND         BX,3                 ;mask all but CPL
        CMP         BX,AX                ;compare CPL and IOPL
        JA          no_sensitive         ;jump if CPL > IOPL
        CLC                              ;sensitive instructions OK
        JMP         SHORT cs_exit
no_sensitive:
        STC                              ;exception occurs on sensitive
cs_exit:
        POP         BX
        POP         AX
        RET

check_sensitive              ENDP
```

Only the operating system or other highly privileged programs with a CPL equal to 0 can execute privileged instructions; they would pose too great a risk in applications programs. Table 9-2 contains a list of privileged instructions. Of these, only the *HLT* instruction exists in real mode, so it's the only one you have to look for; you won't have upgrade problems with any of the others. New protected-mode programs can use the procedure *check_privileged* in Listing 9-5 to determine whether they can execute privileged instructions.

HLT	Halt the processor
LGDT	Load the GDT register
LIDT	Load the interrupt-descriptor-table register
LLDT	Load the LDT register
CLTS	Clear the task-switched flag
LMSW	Load the MSW
LTR	Load the task register

Table 9-2: Protected-Mode Privileged Instructions

Listing 9-5: This routine determines whether you can execute privileged instructions. It takes no input. After execution, the carry flag will be 0 if you can use privileged instructions at the segment's current privilege level, or 1 if their use will generate an exception.

```
check_privileged                    PROC
                                    PUBLIC check_privileged

        PUSH    AX
        MOV     AX,CS               ;CPL resides in CS
        AND     AX,3                ;mask all but CPL
        JNZ     no_privileged       ;jump if CPL <> 0
        CLC                         ;privileged instructions OK
        JMP     SHORT cp_exit
no_privileged:
        STC                         ;exception occurs on privileged
cp_exit:
        POP     AX
        RET

check_privileged                    ENDP
```

Living Within Limits

In real-mode programs, you can freely use offsets greater than the size of a segment. For example, if two small segments are contiguous, you can set a segment register to the first and use a large offset to access the second. If you try to access beyond a segment's limit in protected mode, however, the processor will generate an exception interrupt. To prevent these faults, a program--particularly a proce-

dure to which an offset is passed—can use the *load segment limit* (LSL) protected-mode instruction to verify that the offset lies within the segment's limit.

LSL requires two operands: a destination 16-bit register and a source selector in a
register or memory location. The instruction verifies that the source selector is
valid; it if is not, LSL clears the zero flag. A selector might be invalid for a variety of reasons, the most common of which is a privilege-level violation. If the
selector is valid, the processor copies the limit from the segment's descriptor into
the destination register. The *check_segment_limit* procedure in Listing 9-6 uses
LSL to determine whether a particular selector:offset address is valid.

**Listing 9-6: Routine to determine if an offset is usable within a segment.
The selector for the segment goes in BX, and the offset goes in CX. After
execution, the carry flag will be 0 if the selector:offset is fine, or 1 if its use
will generate an exception.**

```
check_segment_limit            PROC
                               PUBLIC check_segment_limit

        PUSH    DX
        LSL     DX,BX                          ;obtain the segment's limit
        JNZ     exception_return               ;exit if bad selector
        CMP     CX,DX                          ;compare offset and limit
        JA      exception_return               ;jump if offset above limit
        CLC                                    ;selector:offset OK
        JMP     SHORT csl_exit   ;return to caller
exception_return:
        STC                                    ;bad selector or offset
csl_exit:
        POP     DX
        RET

check_segment_limit            ENDP
```

Time to Pay the Piper

Protected-mode programs are more robust and reliable than real-mode programs
and can take advantage of larger memory addressability, but some problem areas
exist in converting programs from real mode to protected mode. These areas are
contained in the selector and the segment descriptor. The privilege level in the
selector controls the use of sensitive and privileged instructions. The protection
afforded by access rights, making sure that you don't write to a segment if you're
not supposed to, or even read it unless you have the right to, can cause problems

where you least expect them. The use of limits ensures that you are not jumping unintentionally (or intentionally) into another segment with offsets that exceed the size of the current segment.

Finally, one subject comes up again and again. It is what anyone and everyone with anything to say about programming will tell you: Write well-behaved programs. While performance considerations in the past may have dictated that you not always follow that advice, the time has come to pay the piper.

10
80286 and 80386 Programming [*]

Bud E. Smith

Until now, the usual rule in writing programs to run under DOS on the 80286 and 80386 has been simple: Use the same code originally written for the 8088. This was efficient in terms of programmer times and ease-of-use for the target audience since the same program would run on any PC-compatible, no matter what processor was inside. Users of AT-class and even 80386-based machines were so happy to get increased speed that they didn't demand improved programs as well. And DOS-enforced limitations, such as the 640K limit on available RAM, made the powers of the new chips pretty much inaccessible anyway.

Now new or newly popular operating systems (OS/2 and UNIX), extenders for DOS, and new programming tools allow 80286-specific and 80386-specific code to be written for programs.

In this article, we'll look at some of the reasons programs automatically run faster on the more powerful processors and then at the benefits you'll get if you bite the bullet and write (or compile to) 80286- or 80386-specific code. We'll also touch on some of the effects new compilers, assemblers, operating systems, and control programs will have on the PC programmer. Understanding these considerations will help you adapt to the more complicated PC environment now emerging. The discussion will focus on real mode programming in assembly language.

Higher Clock Speeds

Each new Intel processor does more than its predecessor--while running at higher clock speeds. The 8088 in the PC runs at 4.77 MHz; the early 80286s run at 6 or 8 MHz (the newer ones run up to twice as fast); and the 80386, only a year old, already runs at 16 or even 20 MHz. So a program written for the 8088 will run two to four times faster on one of the newer chips due to clock speed increases alone.

---

[*] © Oakley Publishing Co., _1988 Programmer's Journal 6.2_, p. 64

This processor speed increase is lost somewhat to waits for disk access or operator input. But as multitasking becomes more popular, the waiting time will be used for work by other programs, so the speed advantage comes to the fore again.

Fewer Clocks per Instruction

It's well known that each new Intel microprocessor runs all of the same instructions as its predecessor; many of the instructions also execute in fewer clock counts than before. A new chip's higher clock speed already means that there are perhaps twice as many clock ticks ("clocks" for short) available in a given second of wall time; add to this that many instructions need fewer clocks to execute, and throughput increases substantially. Table 10-1 shows the number of clock cycles and the amount of wall time needed to execute a series of instructions on the 8088, 80286, and 80386, respectively.

Instruction	Clocks			Wall Time (microseconds)		
	8088	80286	80386	8088	80286	80386
				(4.77 MHz)*	(8 MHz)	(20 MHz)
INC CL	3	2	2	.63	.25	.10
MOV, BX, one word	10	5	4	2.10	.62	.25
IMUL AX, <imed. byte>	(80-98)**	21	9-14***	(16.77-20.54)	2.62	.45-.70

  *1 MHz = 1 million (clock) cycles per second
  **This form is not allowed on the 8088. IMUL of a word by a byte takes 80-90 clocks.
  ***The "Early out" algorithm finishes faster for fewer significant bits in the rightmost operand..

Table 10-1: Sample instructions with clock counts and wall times for the 8088, 80286, and 80386

The assembly language programmer can do a lot to speed up programs by looking at the clock counts of various instructions. For instance, on an 8088 it's worthwhile to write special routines that use ADDs, or that load addresses with shifts and bit shifts for multiplying by a small integer, and that branch to an IMUL instruction only as a last resort. On the 80386, it's faster and easier simply to use an IMUL for any pair of reasonably sized integers.

Pipelining

Both the 80286 and the 80386 use pipelined architectures, in which several things are usually going on at once:

- One part of the chip uses spare bus cycles to grab instructions from RAM and store the instructions in an on-chip "prefetch queue."

- At the same time, another part of the chip decodes instructions from the prefetch queue and stores the result in the "decode queue."

- The execution unit actually carries out the prefetched, predecoded instructions from the decode queue.

Figure 10-1 demonstrates how the fetch, decode, and execute units work in parallel.

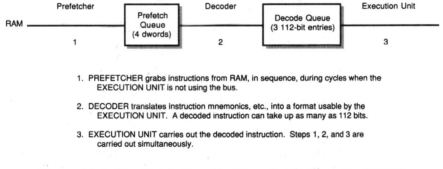

1. PREFETCHER grabs instructions from RAM, in sequence, during cycles when the EXECUTION UNIT is not using the bus.

2. DECODER translates instruction mnemonics, etc., into a format usable by the EXECUTION UNIT. A decoded instruction can take up as many as 112 bits.

3. EXECUTION UNIT carries out the decoded instruction. Steps 1, 2, and 3 are carried out simultaneously.

Figure 10-1: The Fetch-Decode-Execute Cycle on the 80386

One reason the 80386 is faster than the 80286 is that each prefetch (done when the currently executing instruction is not using the bus) can grab 32 bits of code, not just 16 bits. So fewer prefetches are needed to keep the queue full for the decoder, which can then keep the execution unit going at full speed.

A programmer can help or hinder pipelining in a couple different ways. The prefetcher grabs instructions in sequence; when a jump is taken or a subroutine CALL is executed, the sequence is disrupted and the prefetch and decode queues are cleared as a defensive measure to prevent the execution of no-longer-valid code. So minimizing jumps and calls helps pipelining. If the first instruction after the transfer of control is aligned on a 32-bit (*dword*) boundary, it can be fetched in fewer 32-bit memory accesses than if it is misaligned; your HLL or assembler may or may not contain a command to *dword-align* the next piece of code. After a transfer of control, the instruction unit of the 80286 or 80386 must wait while a new instruction is decoded; a short first instruction such as the ever-popular CLC runs so quickly that the execution unit must again wait for prefetching, or at least decoding, before another instruction is ready for it. So putting an easily decoded, slow to execute instruction, dword-aligned, at the top of a loop or subroutine will optimize the efficiency of pipelining.

Instruction timings for 80286 and 80386 instructions are based on the assumption that the instruction is already fetched and decoded when the processor is ready to execute it. The occasional extra cycles that occur while the fetch and decode queues fill again after a jump add a certain amount, estimated by Intel at about 5 percent, to the execution time of most programs.

It's easy to get carried away with optimizing code for speed when spending more time on program design or even the user interface might ultimately be more profitable. But it's worth noting that in a multitasking, or especially a multiuser, system, each program gets only part of the processor's time and must make good use of it or risk being perceived as slow.

New Instructions

A single new instruction can replace several or even a whole subroutine of 8088 code. We will discuss only instructions available in real (8088-type) mode--protected mode programming is a separate subject.

Several instructions available on both the 80286 and 80386 make it easier to write well behaved subroutines:

- *PUSH IMMEDIATE* pushes the immediate value onto the stack, replacing the normal *MOV AX,IMMED*, *PUSH AX* sequence.

- *BOUND* checks whether a pointer is keeping within the bounds of an array.

- *ENTER* and *LEAVE* create "stack frames" to speed entering into and exiting from deeply nested subroutines. These instructions are said to be "mostly for compiler writers," a challenge to any assembler programmer.

- *POPA* and *PUSHA* quickly pop or push all the general registers at once.

These new instructions speed things up in three ways:

1. Each new instruction can be used to replace a much longer and slower-to-execute group of instructions.

2. Less memory traffic is needed for fetching groups of instructions.

3. Coding and debugging are easier using the new instructions as simple, standard tools for arrays and subroutines.

But the really fun new instructions are found only on the 80386--the new bit-oriented test and set instructions. These will allow you to do things with bit arrays that are still technically illegal in 17 states and Canada.

The new real mode instructions on the 80386 are the bit test instructions, the set byte instructions, and a few commands for handling 32-bit data items including a long divide:

- *BSF* and *BSR* perform a bit scan of a word or doubleword, either forward or backward. The position of the first nonzero bit in the first operand is returned in the second. (Note to hardware hackers: This is the software version of the hardware function, "*priority encode:*.")

- *BT*, *BTC*, *BTR*, and *BTS* are all "bit test" instructions, which use their second operand as a pointer to a bit position in the first operand. The *Carry* flag is set if the indicated bit is set. Depending on which instruction is used, the tested bit is left unchanged, complemented (inverted), reset (made 0), or set (made 1), respectively. Intricate, easily updated bit tables can be constructed with these new instructions.

- In *SETcc*, *cc* indicates a "condition code" determined by the current settings of one or more flags. If the flag(s) has the status indicated by the command, the byte pointed to by the single operand is set to one; else it is cleared. This instruction type is a bit obscure; to spark interest, perhaps Intel should have a contest with a prize for the most creative use of *SETcc* instructions. One possible application is to transform code with lots of *Jcc*'s into code with several *SETcc* tests and a CASE-type structure at the end.

- *CWDE*, *CDQ*, *SHLD*, and *SHRD* will convert a word to a doubleword, extending the high bit; convert a doubleword to a quadword; or do a double shift either left or right (a shift where vacated bits in one operand are filled with values from a specified other operand). This is basically bookkeeping-type stuff for dealing with 32-bit data items.

Unless you write Ada compilers for fun, the most interesting instructions are the new bit instructions. It's too bad graphics coprocessors are becoming so popular because these new instructions and the absence of forced segmentation on the 80386 make it capable of handling large video displays. No matter--these instructions make it possible to write arrays that boggle the mind. The largest possible 80386 segment is 4 Gb; there are eight bits per byte, so an array with over 32 billion positions is possible. Short of that, programmers will no doubt come up with incomprehensibly complex multi-level indexing and other arrays before long. The new instructions make it possible to do operations nearly or completely unmanageable before in a few lines.

Speed Increases for the 80386 Only

The 80386 is a true 32-bit microprocessor--it has 32-bit addressing and 32-bit data paths, internally and externally. Using 32-bit data allows fast access to large data items or a group of smaller ones. This will decrease the time spent accessing data and increase the number of records, fields, etc., that a given program can support.

In protected mode (breaking my promise not to touch on that), segment size is programmer-definable, with a maximum size of 4 Gb per segment. A common programmer response to this opportunity has been to set all segment bases to 0, set the top of each segment to 4 Gb, and use the 4 Gb space as flat, unsegmented memory--as used on the 68000 series and other processors. The harsh limitations enforced up to now by the 64 Kb segment limit simply disappear. For programmers of number-crunching applications, this single change is reason enough to switch over completely to the 80386.

Several compilers that support huge arrays by using larger segments--especially FORTRAN compilers--are now coming out. The compilers incorporate DOS extenders that allow DOS programs to freely mix 16-bit, real-mode routines with 32-bit, protected-mode routines. If you currently have large arrays in your programs, they will run much faster once the end-of-segment checking is removed; if you've been forcing all your arrays to stay under the old limit, you can now run wild.

Why Assembler on the 80386?

In this chapter we discuss the differences between microprocessors in terms of benefits to the assembly language programmer, who can take direct advantage of the capabilities of a given chip.

A well-written compiler for a *high-level-language* (HLL) will create machine language optimized for a specific processor. But the degree to which a given compiler takes advantage of a given new instruction varies.

It's possible to use an HLL for initial coding, disassemble the resulting object code, then optimize the result by hand. But many of the new optimizing compilers produce object code that is possibly better than a human could quickly produce, but is certainly harder to follow, making optimization by hand difficult.

The best combination of ease of writing, ease of maintenance, and access to the full capabilities of a given processor may be to write the program in an HLL, then rewrite speed-critical and processor-dependent pieces of code in assembler. With a truly top-notch compiler, the HLL can be used for some or all of the work that would otherwise be done in assembler. But if you are already good at "real" programming and you have a large library of assembler routines at hand, the mixed HLL-plus-assembler approach may be the best solution for a long time to come.

Better 80386 Programs

Those poor souls who must program in constricted environments (CP/M, the Apple II, PROMs, etc.) often direct a "repent, for the end is near" attitude towards those DOS programmers who write large, sloppy programs that use RAM as if there were no tomorrow.

Well, tomorrow is here, in the form of OS/2 and control programs for the 80386. There are two main ways in which these new factors make small, tightly written programs look good.

1. *Virtual Machines*

    Under the DOS "control programs" now coming on the market, multiple applications can be run at once, with each running as a separate task or in its own "virtual machine." In a certain amount of memory, a user may be able to run three large, sprawling applications or four to five equally useful, tightly written ones. Guess which programs will get more use--and a reputation for efficiency?

2. *Virtual Memory*

Virtual memory is used by OS/2 and some 80386 control programs. In virtual memory, some of the code and data that would normally be in RAM is stored out on disk until needed. Under OS/2, 64 Kb-sized segments are swapped in and out; under an 80386 control program, 4 Kb pages are moved back and forth.

A pause occurs each time a program's execution causes it to jump to code or access data in a "swapped-out" (disk-stored) page or segment. A small, tightly written program will run with few such faults while a more sprawling program may cause the operating system to spend much of the time moving code and data from RAM to disk. (Note that assembler programmers have more control over code and data structures than HLL programmers.)

OS/2 and 80386 control programs are now largely in the hands of a small but influential group of programmers and power users. This group can be expected to voice its opinions loudly and frequently, pasting long-lasting labels, for good or ill, on certain programs and the companies that produce them.

III
Using More Memory:
Expanded and Virtual

11
Virtual Memory, Virtual Machines [*]

Jon Shiell

Virtual memory is a method for making the amount of memory that a program uses independent of the actual amount of RAM in the machine. In virtual memory systems, the disk memory effectively becomes the main memory, and the RAM becomes a temporary holding area for code and data that the processor is currently using. With virtual memory, the programmer doesn't care how much RAM (hereafter called real memory) the machine has. In fact, the program has no way of knowing how much real memory the system has. Instead, the program cares only about how big the virtual address space is.

The 8086 (which does not support virtual memory), the 80286, and the 80386 in real mode have a real address space of only 1 megabyte. The 80286 in protected mode has a virtual address space of 1 gigabyte and a real address space of 16 megabytes. The 80386 in protected mode has a virtual address space of 64 terabytes and a 4-gigabyte real address space. For comparison, IBM's latest mainframe architecture, 370/XA, can have virtual address spaces that add up to 128 terabytes and a real address space of 2 gigabytes. The 80286's 1-gigabyte virtual address space is composed of 16,000 segments of 64K bytes each. The 80386's 64-terabyte virtual address space is composed of 16,000 segments of 4 gigabytes each.

Virtual memory systems must provide hardware support for the translation of the virtual (or logical) addresses into real (or physical) addresses. During the translation, the hardware must be able to recognize those portions of code and data that are not resident in real memory. Such recognition is commonly called a fault. An interrupt must notify the operating system that such portions are needed and must be brought into real memory from the disk (Figure 11-1).

A virtual memory system must also be able to handle the situation where either the next instruction that is to execute or data that the current instruction needs is not resident. In such cases, the hardware has to fault to the operating system,

---

[*] © McGraw-Hill Information Systems Company, *BYTE*, Extra Edition, 1986, p. 111

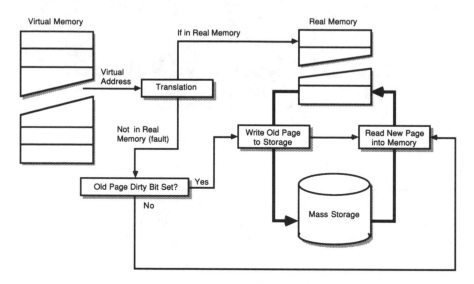

Figure 11-1: A Virtual Memory System

which then brings in the required code or data. Then the operating system must be able to resume execution of the program at the instruction where the fault occurred without the fault being visible to the program. In other words, the instructions must be restartable.

A couple of ways exist to make an instruction restartable. For those instructions that write a single result, you can have the instruction issue all its accesses before it attempts to write the result. For more complex instructions that store multiple results, you have two options. The instruction has to either test all result locations to make sure they are resident before it actually stores to any of them or it must be interruptible: It must save enough state information to be able to resume execution at the point at which it was stopped.

Virtual Memory Schemes

There are three kinds of *virtual memory* (VM) schemes. Segmenting schemes break memory into variable-length units called segments. Paging schemes divide memory into fixed-length units called pages. Finally, the hybrid scheme (like that in the 80386) uses variable-length segments that are divided into pages.

In virtual memory schemes, you have a trade-off between the amount of real memory in the system and the amount of virtual memory that it can support with reasonable performance. Typically, what you need is enough real memory to hold the working sets of a significant fraction of the programs that you want to run. Having less than this amount of real memory causes a tremendous increase in disk I/O due to paging or segment swapping. (Swapping of pages is called paging. Bringing something from a disk to real memory is a page-in operation; moving something from real memory to a disk is a page-out operation.) When the system reaches the point where a large amount of its time is spent paging in and paging out instead of executing programs, it is said to be thrashing.

The 8086/8088 microprocessors cannot implement virtual memory because they don't have the required address-translation hardware on-chip and they don't support an off-chip memory management unit. The only memory management that they can perform is overlays, which require that the program explicitly manage its own swapping of resident and disk code and data. Almost all big MS-DOS programs use overlays: Lotus 1-2-3 and WordStar are two examples. DOS provides explicit support for overlays via a DOS function call. Overlays have certain disadvantages. First, an individual section of an overlay can be no larger than some fraction of the available real memory. Second, the programmer is responsible for managing the overlays.

The IBM PC multitasking environments (like TopView, CCP/M, and DESQview) do not fully implement virtual memory in that each program can use only what real memory is available to it. But by using time-slicing and swapping, such systems make memory appear large enough to hold multiple programs. Because the 8086/8088 doesn't provide any memory protection, it is possible for a program to corrupt the operating system or anything else in memory.

The 80286 VM Scheme

One of Intel's major enhancements in defining the 80286 was a protected mode that includes the logic required to implement VM. (From now on, references to the 80286 or the 80386 are to their protected modes.) The virtual addresses in the 80286 are split into two 16-bit segments. The first half is a segment selector that specifies the segment to be used. The other half is the offset within the segment, thus permitting access to any byte within a 64K-byte address space. The format of these two halves is shown in Figure 11-2, along with the 8086/8088 addressing scheme.

Note that the format of an 80286 segment selector differs from that of the 8086. This is the major reason that many programs written for MS-DOS or other 8086 operating systems won't run in 80286 protected mode. The problem is that addresses in protected mode cannot be treated as 32-bit integers because of the T and

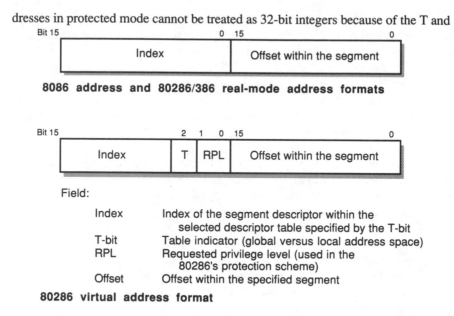

8086 address and 80286/386 real-mode address formats

Field:

Index	Index of the segment descriptor within the selected descriptor table specified by the T-bit
T-bit	Table indicator (global versus local address space)
RPL	Requested privilege level (used in the 80286's protection scheme)
Offset	Offset within the specified segment

80286 virtual address format

Figure 11-2: Addressing Formats for iAPX Microprocessors

RPL fields in the segment selector.

The presence of these fields means that the 8086 method of doing simple 32-bit arithmetic for addressing structures bigger than 64K bytes doesn't work in protected mode. A couple of methods that will work are detailed in Listing 11-1. Also note that the 80286's segments—like the 8086's—can be from 1K to 64K bytes long. However, the 8086 segments start on a 16-byte boundary; thus, the segment number can overlap the apparent offset (see Figure 11-3). The 80286's segment numbers do not overlap the offset values, so they appear on 64K-byte boundaries in the virtual address space.

Listing 11-1: Pseudocode example of address arithmetic in 80286 protected mode.

```
Adding a displacement of 16 bits or less: (offset in DX, displacement in AX)
        Add new displacement to DX.
        If carry-out then
          Move DS into BX.
          Add '0008'x to BX.     (add 1 to index field)
```

```
        Move BX back into DS.

Adding a displacement of more than 16 bits (offset in DX, displacement in BX:AX)

        Add new displacement to DX.   (DX <- DX + AX)

        Add carry-out to BX.

        Left-shift BX by 3.   (align with index field)

        Move DS into CX.

        Add CX to BX.         (add displacement high to index field)

        Move CX back into DS.


80386 handling of displacements of up to 32 bits in native mode; (offset in EDX,
displacement in EAX)


        Add EDX, EAX
```

Intel has solved this 8086 addressing compatibility problem in the 80386 by providing an 8086 virtual machine mode that I will discuss in more detail later. In this mode, even though the machine is running protected mode, the 80386 uses 8086-type selector and addressing.

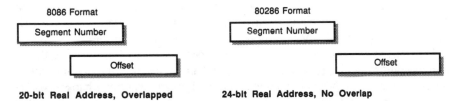

Figure 11-3: Differences in address translation between the 8086 and 80286

The 80286 (used in the IBM PC AT and its clones) implements virtual memory at the segment level—that is, by swapping whole segments. Thus, address translation in the 80286 consists of remapping segments from one spot within the virtual address space into another within the real memory (see Figure 11-4). This is done by providing a P-bit (present bit) in the segment descriptor that indicates whether or not the segment is present in real memory. When software attempts to load a segment register with a descriptor whose P-bit is 0, the hardware takes an interrupt of type 11 or, for stacks, interrupt type 12 (see Table 11-1).

30-bit Virtual Address (Note: The 2-bit RPL is not used in addressing.)

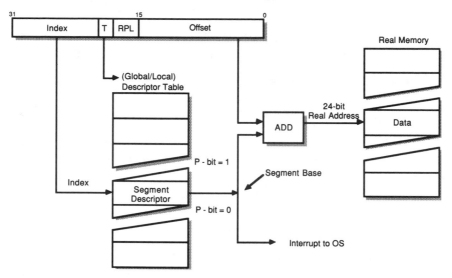

Figure 11-4: 80286 Virtual Address Translation

This interrupt lets the operating system fault handler load this segment into real memory, possibly overwriting a current segment. If the segment to be overwritten has been modified since being brought in from disk, the operating system will write the modified segment out to disk before overwriting it. Once the required segment has been brought in, the fault handler can return to the interrupted program, letting the program continue without knowing anything happened. The instruction pointer that is saved on the stack points to the first byte of the faulted instruction. This facilitates restarting the interrupted program from the fault handler via the *IRET* (interrupt return) instruction.

The 80386 VM Scheme

The 80386 overcomes the addressing compatibility problems between the 80286 and 8086 by implementing both of their addressing modes as well as its own 32-bit native addressing mode. There is no specific 80286 compatibility mode. Instead, each time the 80386 switches between tasks, it specifies the mode of its target program (see Figure 11-5) via the *TYPE* and *D* bit fields of the code-segment descriptor. Unlike the method used for 80286 compatibility, 8086 mode is explicitly specified by the *VM* bit in the processor's *FLAGS* register.

Function	Interrupt Number	Instruction That Can Cause Exception	Return Address Points to Faulting Instruction
Divide error	0	DIV, IDIV	Yes
Debug exception	1	Any instruction	Yes
NMI interrupt	2	INT 2 or NMI	No
1-byte interrupt	3	INT	No
Interrupt on overflow	4	INTO	No
Array bounds check	5	BOUND	Yes
Invalid op code	6	Any illegal instruction	Yes
Device not available	7	ESC, WAIT	Yes
Double fault	8	Any instruction that can generate an exception	
Invalid TSS	10	JMP, CALL, IRET, INT	Yes
Segment not present	11	Segment-register instructions	Yes
Stack fault	12	Stack references	Yes
General protection fault	13	Any memory reference	Yes
Page fault	14	Any memory access or code fetch	Yes
Coprocessor error	16	ESC, WAIT	Yes
Intel reserved	17-32		
2-byte interrupt	0-255	INT n	No

Table 11-1: 80386 Interrupt Vectors

In addition to the segment-level protection provided by the 80286, the 80386 provides page-level protection when paging is used. Since the 80386 first performs segment translation, followed by page translation, it is possible to have two or more small segments share a single page. In this case, the page-level protection would not be used. Note that the operating system can still use the paging scheme for memory management; however, care must be taken to ensure that the page is swapped out only when all the segments in the page are not in use.

The 80386 VM scheme implements virtual memory via mainframe-style paging schemes using two-level translation tables. The first level, pointed to by *CR3* (control register 3), is the page-directory table containing from 1 to 1024 page-directory entries of 4 bytes each. Each of these *PDE*s points to a page containing page-table entries of 4 bytes each, for up to 1024 pages. Each *PTE* contains the

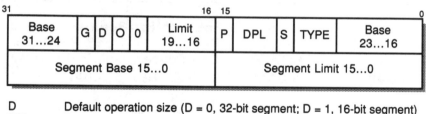

Base 31...24	G	D	O	0	Limit 19...16	P	DPL	S	TYPE	Base 23...16
Segment Base 15...0					Segment Limit 15...0					

D   Default operation size (D = 0, 32-bit segment; D = 1, 16-bit segment)
DPL   Descriptor privilege level (0 to 3)
G   Granularity (G = 0, segment lengths are byte granular;
             G = 1, segment lengths are page granular)
P   Present (P = 0, not present; P = 1, present in memory)
S   Segment descriptor (0 = system; 1 = code or data)
TYPE   See below

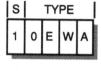

Data Segment:

E = expansion direction (0 = up; 1 = down)
W = writable (W = 0, read only; W = 1, read/write
A = accessed bit (A = 0, not accessed;
        A = 1, segment has been used)

Data Segment:

C = conforming segment (part of protection scheme)
R = readable (R = 0, execute only; R = 1, execute/read
A = accessed bit (A = 0, not accessed;
        A = 1, segment has been used)

Type:

0 Invalid	8 Invalid
1 Available 80286 TSS	9 Available 80386 TSS
2 LDT	10 Intel reserved
3 Busy 80286 TSS	11 Busy 80386 TSS
4 80286 call gate	12 80386 call gate
5 80286 task gate	13 Intel reserved
6 80286 interrupt gate	14 80386 interrupt gate
7 80286 trap gate	15 80386 trap gate

Figure 11-5: 80286/80386 Segment-Descriptor Format

address of a 4K-byte block in real memory called a page frame. Thus, a *PDE* points to *PTE*s describing up to 4 megabytes of real memory. Both the *PDT* and each page table will not exceed one page (4K bytes) in length and are aligned on page (4K-byte) boundaries. Also, the pointer in *CR3* and the pointers within the *PDE*s and *PTE*s are real addresses, not virtual addresses. If they were not real addresses, you would run the risk of your page tables being paged out, effectively hanging the system.

Figure 11-6 shows the format and contents of a *PTE*. The accessed and dirty bits of a *PTE* are used for memory management. The OS will use the accessed bit to keep track of how often a program uses a page and the dirty bit to tell whether the page must be copied out to the disk before the new page overwrites it. The standard method of tracking a program's page use is to have the operating system periodically clear the accessed bit of all pages a program has in real memory and then check, after a certain period, which pages have their accessed bits set. This information, collected over a period of time, tells which pages a program is currently using. This set of pages is called the program's current working set. Also, a P-bit indicates to the processor whether this page is present in real memory. If the bit is off, the processor takes a page fault to the operating system so it can bring in the page from disk. The process of bringing in a page when a program faults on it is called demand paging.

Bit 31		12	11	10	9	8	7	6	5	4	3	2	1	0
Page-Frame Address (PFA)			OS Res			0	0	D	A	0	0	U	R	P

Field:

PFA	Real address bits 31-12. If it's a directory entry, this is the real address of a page frame containing the page table. If it's a page table entry, this is the address of a page frame for program use.
OS Res	Reserved for operating system use.
D-bit	Dirty page bit. If a 1, the page has been modified; it's set when a write to an address in the page occurs.
A-bit	Accessed bit is set to 1 when any kind of access (read/write/execute) occurs to an address in the page.
U-bit	User access permitted. If a 1, access is permitted by level-3 programs. If a level-3 program attempts to access a page with a U-bit of 0, an exception occurs.
R-bit	Level-3 access control (assuming U-bit is 1). If a 0, only read/execute accesses are allowed; if the R-bit is a 1, writes are also permitted.
P-bit	Present bit. If P = 1, page is present in real memory; if P = 0, page is swapped out. An interrupt is generated when a program attempts to use this page. If P = 0, the rest of the word is undefined from hardware's point of view.

Figure 11-6: 80386 Page-Directory/Table-Entry Format

The translation of virtual addresses request two accesses—the first to get the *PDE* and the second to get the *PTE*—for each access done by the program. Rather than run at less than one-third of its potential speed, the 80386 uses an on-chip address cache called a translation-lookaside buffer. This cache, unlike a "normal" cache, returns a *PTE*—instead of a data word—when given an address. The 80386 has a 32-entry, four-way set (that is, four sets of eight *PTEs* each) associative *TLB*, which should give a hit rate of about 98 percent (see Figure 11-7). In other words, 98 percent of the time the *TLB* will contain the *PTE* that you need. The other 2 percent of the time, the processor must actually do the translation and then load the new *PTE* into the *TLB*.

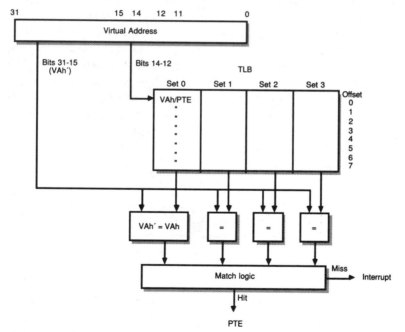

How a TLB works:

Use a portion of the VA, bits 14-12 in this case, as the index into the TLB arrays. Read out one entry per set in the TLB, four entries in this case. The entries that were read out consist of three parts: VA entry, PTE, and control information. Compare the VA in each entry with the VA you are looking up. If any matches, you have your translation (unless control indicates this entry is invalid). Otherwise, signal a TLB miss to the processor so it can get the correct translation.

Figure 11-7: Sample Diagram for a 32-Entry Translation-Lookaside Buffer

The dirty bit indicates that the page has been altered by the processor since being brought into real memory. When a program does a write to memory, the processor sets the dirty bit in the *PTE*. What actually occurs is that the 80386 sets the real dirty bit on the first write, because a copy of this bit is kept in the *TLB*. Note that the 80286 segment descriptor doesn't have a hardware dirty bit. The way that an 80286 operating system tells that a segment is dirty is to initially make all the program's segment descriptors write-protected when they are brought in from disk. When the program attempts to write (first time only) to the segment, an exception occurs and the operating system takes control. The operating system sets a software dirty bit, removes the write-protection from the segment, and restarts the task.

Effects of Virtual Memory

For a system based on segment swapping (the 80286), the only requirement is that I/O can't cross a segment boundary. The OS must load the starting real address into the direct-memory-access unit instead of the starting virtual address, unless the DMA unit is capable of handling the translation and knows where the tables are. In either case, the OS must not swap out the segment until I/O finishes. Thus, the operating system must "lock" a segment into memory. A software-only bit in the descriptor is normally used for this purpose.

For a paged system, things are further complicated by the fact that a segment can span more than one page. This leads to three possible ways to handle DMA. In the first and simplest (this is the case for PCs so far), the DMA unit doesn't know about paging and the processor must set up each page transfer separately. In the second way, the DMA unit knows how to handle a string of real addresses and counts that point to each page that I/O is to address and specify the number of bytes to be moved. Finally, the DMA unit itself can use virtual addressing, in which case it must be given a translation table address in addition to a starting address and count. Of course, the pages that I/O will be addressing should be locked.

An 80386 running in 8086 virtual machine mode treats segment descriptors as the 8086 does: They are simple 16-bit integers that are multiplied by 16, then added to the 16-bit offset to get a 20-bit virtual address. Unlike the 8086, the 80386 then performs page translation on the address. Thus, the 1-megabyte address space of an 8086 program is split into 256 4K-byte pages. Using paging to remap the address space permits the sharing of pages that are not written to. This reduces the real memory required to support multiple 8086 virtual machines. Also, the host operating system can use the remapping function to provide page-level protection for the guest operating system. It is even possible to support virtual expanded memory.

Virtual Machines

A virtual machine is the extension of the concept of virtual memory to an entire machine, including I/O devices and privilege levels, so that a program can't tell that it doesn't have a real machine—in this case an 8086—to itself. A virtual machine lets multiple operating systems (which may be incompatible) run concurrently with not modification or conflict. A program running in a virtual machine sees whatever memory and I/O the host operating system desires, not the amount of memory in or the I/O devices of the real machine. It is important to note that virtual machine is not an emulator, nor is a virtual machine as efficient as a real machine.

Why use virtual machines in the first place? Because this permits an 80386 system to run multiple PC-DOS programs unmodified in what appears to be their native environment. Thus, the need to modify existing programs so that they run in protected mode is avoided. This ability to run multiple operating systems lets the 80386 run an 8086-type UNIX or CP/M-86 at the same time, in addition to the native-mode user interface.

To support multiple virtual machines, a *control program* (CP) actually manages the real machine's resources (real memory, I/O, privilege levels). The CP creates and handles multiple virtual machines, distributing the real machine resources in an orderly fashion. The CP is not an operating system; it is a layer of software that mediates requests from the operating system to the hardware.

For a processor to support virtual machines, all instructions that would let a program be able to tell that it is running in user mode must be privileged. Access to some facilities, such as I/O and timers, must be restricted. There must be no possibility of a conflict between a guest address space and the host operating system's address space. This becomes especially evident when you attempt to run a copy of the CP in a virtual machine.

While the current 80386 supports virtual 8086 machines, it does not support virtual 80286 and 80386 machines. This is due to problems in handling the *PUSHF* and *POPF* instructions and the store-system-register instructions (*STR*, *SGDT*, *SLDT*, and *SMSW*) and to the fact that the address to which an interrupt transfers control is a virtual address using the local-descriptor tables and global-descriptor tables at the time the interrupt occurred. While the lack of ability to run a virtual machine other than an 8086 is a real limitation, it doesn't seem to be a fatal flaw. Intel might fix this in a later release of the chip.

The 80386 CP invokes an 8086 virtual machine by performing a task switch where a program's task-state segment has the 8086 virtual mode bit (bit 17) set in its copy of the *EFLAGS* register. Virtual 8086 programs run at the lowest privilege level, so to utilize specific privileged instructions, the I/O permission-level field in the *EFLAGS* register and the I/O permission bit map (located in the task-state segment) must also be set up. Now any interrupt or exception causes the 80386 to switch back into protected mode (native 80386 mode) before invoking the handler pointed to by the interrupt-descriptor table. Thus, the routines that are invoked must be 80386 native-mode routines. In most cases, these routines will emulate the operation requested by the virtual machine—for example, an *OUT* instruction—then return to 8086 virtual mode via an *IRET* instruction.

When the 80386 runs in virtual 8086 mode, it does address generation like an 8086 but the 20-bit address that is produced is a virtual address. The page-translation hardware then translates the virtual address into a page number and a starting offset within that page. This lets the 80386 CP use a page-level protection "below" the guest operating system, so that elements such as ROM can be emulated (just mark the page "read-only"). This same method lets the host share portions of memory between multiple virtual machines. So while the 8086 virtual machine can't use the segment-level protection that is available to both 80286 and 80386 mode programs, the 80386 CP can use protection at the page level to enhance real memory utilization of the guest machines.

The Wrap-Up

Virtual memory lets you run a program even if your system doesn't have enough real memory. It also makes multitasking much safer by providing the ability to isolate tasks from one another. The virtual machine mode will protect your investment in 8086 software while providing a relatively painless method of entrance to virtual memory, multitasking, and the 80386 itself. If Intel corrects the inability of the 80386 to "virtualize" itself and the 80286, the same path provided for 8086 software will be available for 80286 software such as XENIX and protected-mode DOS.

Why No 80386 Virtual Machine?

One reason the 80386 cannot "virtualize" itself is the asymmetric behavior in its instruction pairs, such as *PUSHF* and *POPF*. *PUSHF* saves the *REAL* flag values in protected mode. *POPF* will not cause a general-protection exception in protected mode. Even if an attempt is made to alter the I/O privilege level or interrupt flag bits without sufficient privilege level, no interrupt will occur for an unauthorized alteration attempt; it is simply ignored.

Consider the attempt to virtualize XENIX-286 under the current 386 architecture. The XENIX kernel may use the *POPF* instruction to alter the current *IF* bit. This works in native 286 mode (no VM). Under VM, the hardware will not allow the change, and no notification will occur (via a general-protection exception) that an attempt to alter the *IF* bit was made. As far as the host CP is concerned, the guest XENIX OS is still able to receive interrupts from the outside. If XENIX is in the middle of altering a critical area where interrupts can't be tolerated (such as stack changes or modifying the global-descriptor table) and the host CP has no way of knowing its guest's state, the interrupt is passed to XENIX at the wrong time, causing the guest to crash.

A similar problem exists with the task-register load and store instructions (*LTR/STR*). Again, consider the attempt to virtualize XENIX-286. It's normal for XENIX to store its current task register during preparation for a task switch (many operating systems do this). In the current 386 architecture, if XENIX attempted to load the task register, this would cause a GP exception and appropriate simulation by the CP could be done. However, when XENIX stores its task register (which has been virtualized), no GP exception occurs, and the real (CP) task register is stored. If XENIX had stored the TR with a value, say, or 21F (a XENIX task-register load), the *LOAD* might return a value of 1C (the real CP value). Any internal bookkeeping XENIX was doing that depended on *LTR/STR* being a matched set is destroyed, and bugs will result.

The final problem with virtualizing the 80386 relates to addressing problems. Part of the difficulty is that the CP must share the same address space with the guest. The other part of this problem deals with interrupts: For a virtual machine interrupt, the address that you transfer to is a virtual address. This causes the following problem when attempting to run an 80386 virtual machine. Say that a guest OS is using linear address 8000000 for some control information. Suppose that the host CP also uses that address for some purpose. Due to the nature of the 80386, the host CP cannot set up the page tables to prevent this, and data is overwritten.

12
Memory Addressing on the Intel 80386 [*]

Howard Vigorita

When Intel announced the 8086, I recall reading that its segmentation scheme of address formation was so abstract that only systems programmers and compiler writers were likely to grasp it. Similarly the 80386's operating modes are causing similar confusion. Recently it has been heard that unlike the 286, the "native mode" of the 386 is the protected mode. And from time to time, the 386 is claimed to have anywhere from two different operating modes on up.

There seem to be two fundamental modes on the 386: real 386 mode and protected 386 mode. The real 386 mode is a superset of the 8086, 186, and the real 286 modes of its predecessors, with some differences. If the differences are avoided, programs written for the older processors will be upwardly compatible and the 386 seen as simply a faster processor with added instructions and registers.

As on the 286, the 386 comes up in real mode on reset. At the same time, real 386 mode cannot take advantage of all the 386 features. Those features include 32-bit addressing, protection, paging, and hardware assisted task switching. The only major difference between the 286 and 386 in this area is that the 386 can return to real mode from protected mode without being reset. I suppose if they'd only told us about 286 native mode, OS/2 might have arrived a long time ago.

The 386's protected mode is characterized by 32-bit addresses and operands as well as the ability to provide multilevel rings of protection, virtual memory paging, and rapid task switching. The beauty of the 386's protected mode, is that 32-bit operation and paging can be enabled or disabled by default in any combination. That's four protected mode possibilities, plus real mode makes five modes.

The use of 32-bit addresses by default in a code segment is called a USE32 segment in Intel parlance. When 32-bit addresses and operands are disabled by default, 16-bit addresses and operands are presumed. This code segment is called a USE16 segment and emulates the 286's protected mode. Although the default address and

---

[*] © M&T Publishing, Inc., *Micro/Systems Journal,* November/December 1987

operand length can only be set together as a pair, the use of one byte instruction prefixes can override and reverse either on an individual instruction basis. That brings us up to nine modes of operation.

A variation of 286 mode is virtual 8086 emulation mode (V86 mode). V86 mode looks just like real 386 mode except that V86 mode can be entered and exited via task switching and peacefully coexists with protection and paging. Intel supports V86 mode with a piece of software called the V86 monitor. The monitor is intended to be bound to the system's 386 kernel. It allows whole 8086 operating systems to run as a V86 task with an 8086 application as a V86 sub-task. Through special software hooks into the CPU, the monitor intercepts I/O and interrupts but only engages the Task Gate overhead of calling the coresident 32-bit protected mode operating system when required. V86 mode, like real 386 mode, forms effective addresses in the same way as the 8086. Thus the V86 mode makes ten modes of operation.

Effective address formation is still at the heart of the Intel scheme of things. On the 8086, effective addresses are formed by taking the value in a segment register, multiplying it by 16 (shifting it left 4 bits) and then adding the result to a pointer register. The segment register can be considered a pointer itself, albeit to memory on a 16-byte boundary (often called a paragraph).

The 286 and 386 are an order of magnitude more unusual. In protected mode, the segment register is no longer a pointer to real user code or data. Instead it contains something called a "selector". Within the 16-bit selector, 13 bits constitute a record number for access to a database called a "descriptor table". The descriptor table is a little different from the databases familiar to most programmers . The records are all 8 bytes long, but they have a number of different formats. The code segment register selects an "executable segment descriptor", while other segment registers usually select "data segment descriptors" which may be of the "expand down" variety for optimal stack usage.

In addition, there are also 5 flavors of "gate descriptors". Gate descriptors are special descriptors which, instead of pointing directly to code segments, point to other executable descriptors which in turn point to code segments. Gate descriptors are generally used to provide regulated, indirect access to processes of a higher privilege level, or to other tasks. Far JMP and CALL instructions, which in real mode need a segment as part of the operand, select a call gate in protected mode. And then there are trap, interrupt, and task gates, not to mention a collection of system segment gates. In protected mode, the descriptor tables are where the action is.

Thus in protected mode, the 386 segment registers select records from a descriptor table. A linear address is formed by fetching, from the appropriate descriptor, a 32-bit segment base address and adding it to the user's pointer register. The descriptor also sets the segment size (from 1 byte to 4 gigabytes) and contains privilege information. Tests are performed to see if your intended memory reference will be permitted. The days of reading or writing to memory not allocated to you for that purpose will be history. That's protection. Once the linear address is in hand, the on-chip paging hardware does further translation to a physical address. This step is optional. If paging is implemented, the linear address is broken into three parts. A 12-bit "physical offset", a 10-bit "page table record", and a 10-bit "page directory record". Two tables are referenced, a "page directory table" and a "page table". The page directory record is fetched and points to one of many page tables. The page table record is fetched and contains a 20-bit page number as well as flags indicating whether the page has been written to (dirty bit) and is present in memory. Pages are 4K long. The final physical address is obtained by concatenating the page number (20-bits) to the physical offset (12-bits from the linear address). Pages can be swapped from disk or slower memory if not present. Figures 12-1 and 12-2 illustrate how translation works.

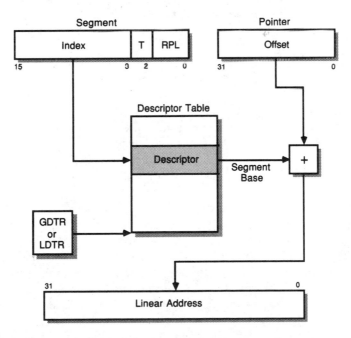

Figure 12-1: In protected mode, a linear address is formed by fetching a 32-bit segment base address from the appropriate descriptor and adding it to the user's pointer register.

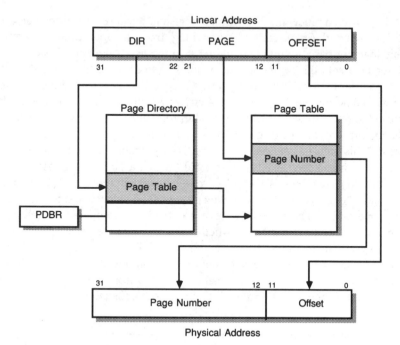

Figure 12-2: Once the linear address is formed, the on-chip paging hardware translates further to a physical address.

Address translation is the key to physical hardware independence. This is crucial in a multitasking environment. All segment, interrupt, and I/O requests undergo descriptor and/or page translation. Remapping by the operating system is done by simply patching a translation table. Concurrently running programs will never know it when the video RAM is switched out from under them.

With all this translation and checking going on, the 64K question is: What happens to processor performance in protected mode? Considering that the 386 does no on-chip instruction or data caching in the ordinary sense, its performance is remarkable. The buffering it does do is in connection with translation tables. The segment registers are unusual in that they are actually wider than they appear. Only a 16-bit portion is visible; a hidden portion acts as a descriptor buffer. Subsequent address calculations and privilege checks consume no additional cycles. Page table records are also retained in a 32-register cache called a "translation lookaside buffer". But there's no getting around it. Instructions that access descriptor or page tables for the first time are going to take longer.

Figure 12-3 lays out comparative cycle times for instructions which force an access to a descriptor table. They are all segment changing, I/O, or interrupt instructions. When comparing 286 and 386 instructions that purge the prefetch queue, note that the 386 fetches operands and addresses in one cycle, whether they're 8-, 16-, or 32-bits long. The 286 always fetches 1 byte per cycle.

	386 protected	V86 & 386 real	286 real
MOV seg,r16	18	2	2
MOV seg,mem16	19	5	5
POP seg	21	7	5
LDS	22	7	7
CALL imm32	34+m	17+m	13+n
CALL mem32	38+m	22+m	16+n
RET (far)	32+m	18+m	15+n
JMP imm32	27+m	12+m	11+n
JMP mem32	31+m	17+m	15+n
IN acc,imm	6(1) 26(2)	12	5
IN acc,DX	7(1) 27(2)	13	5
INT nn	59(3) 99(4) 316(5)	37	23+n

Notes: m = Target instruction component count
n = Target instruction byte count
1 = I/O privilege level permits port access
2 = Port access intercepted or V86 mode
3 = Via gate to same privilege level
4 = Via gate to different privilege level
5 = V86 to 386 protected mode via task gate

Figure 12-3: Here is a list of comparative cycle times for instructions that force access to a descriptor table.

Any other gotchas? I've already alluded that there are a few. 8086 or 286 code that uses the LOCK prefix may trigger an undefined opcode exception (INT 6) if used with other than a limited set of instructions. Noticeably absent from the acceptable set are the string instructions. And even when effective, the memory protected from coprocessor interference is now limited to the memory area defined by the destination operand of the instruction so prefixed, instead of the entire physical address space. This need only be of concern to designers of multiprocessor systems.

In V86 mode, page translation seems to be required if multiple V86 tasks are desired since descriptor translation is bypassed. And then there's the new instructions. Some of them overlap with the NEC V20 unique instructions. Intel's revenge!

All those protected mode 286 operating systems out there will probably need some adjustment if they're to run as a task under a full featured 386 kernel. The *Task State Segment* (TSS) is a structure in memory where the processor saves its registers when multitasking. TSSs are very different on the 286 and 386. After all, the 386 has more registers. If the 386 kernel is restricted to not changing registers that the 286 sub-operating system doesn't save and restore (e.g., Page Directory Base Register), it would be little more than a 286 system itself. The more practical approach would be to use 386 TSSs throughout.

What enhancements would I like to see on the 486? Tops on my list would be on chip data, code, and stack caches. And more data registers. And while we're at it, how about a Z80 styled alternate register array? There's no reason why there can't be a megabyte or two on-chip for registers and caches.

Regardless of how many modes you think the 386 has, one thing is clear. Intel is committed to upward compatibility throughout the 8086 family. With that, and its top notch performance, the 386 has an excellent chance of achieving what has so far eluded the 8086 family: parlaying the way from microcomputer dominance into the multiuser marketplace.

13

LIM EMS 4.0: A Definition for the Next Generation of Expanded Memory *

Marion Hansen and *John Driscoll*

Back in the bad old days, if your spreadsheet program returned a memory-full error, you were out of memory—and out of luck. All that changed in 1984, when Lotus Development Corp., Intel Corp., and Microsoft Corp. smashed the 640Kb conventional memory barrier with their Expanded Memory Specification (EMS). The EMS allowed the creation of another kind of memory: expanded memory.

Expanded resides on one or more add-in boards in the computer (Intel's Above Board and AST's Advantage! are examples). The EMS defines a segment of memory, located within the first 1Mb of memory, as the page frame. The page frame is a window into expanded memory.

Just after an application program starts executing, it can allocate a certain number of 16Kb pages of expanded memory for its own use. By mapping pages in and out of the frame, the program can access any area of expanded memory it has allocated for itself.

MS-DOS cannot access expanded memory directly; instead, the job of handling the extra memory goes to the Expanded Memory Manager (EMM), which is defined by the EMS. EMM functions can be added to any program to enable it to use expanded memory. To avoid confusion, remember that EMS is the Expanded Memory Specification, and that EMM is the Expanded Memory Manager. EMS (the spec) defines the EMM (the manager), and the EMM provides the functions that application programs need to use expanded memory.

In the fall of 1987 Lotus, Intel, and Microsoft released the latest EMS, Version 4.0. This chapter describes the enhancements to EMS 4.0 and how to use them for even greater expanded memory performance.

---

* © Microsoft Corporation, *Microsoft Systems Journal*, January 1988, p. 67

New Feature Set

Intel sent a free EMM 4.0 upgrade to all registered Above Board users. Except for faster execution of expanded memory tests at power-on, however, users will not see improved performance with their existing programs until they have access to new application programs written specifically to the EMS 4.0 spec. Even so, certain features of EMS 4.0 have generated excitement in the expanded memory world:

- With AST's endorsement, EMS 4.0 is now the expanded memory standard for the personal computer industry.

- The 15 new functions defined by EMS 4.0 provide faster performance and more efficient use of memory.

- EMS 4.0 supports a full 32Mb of expanded memory; earlier versions only supported up to 8Mb.

- The OS/2 systems don't run on 8088- or 8086-based computers. EMS 4.0 extends the useful life of existing MS-DOS-based applications on 8088-, 8086-, 80286-, and 80386-based computers.

- Many software vendors are already updating their programs (such as Lotus 1-2-3 Version 3.0 and Microsoft Windows 2.0) in order to take advantage of EMS 4.0's new features.

- Software written for earlier versions of the EMS is compatible with EMS 4.0.

- EMM 4.0 runs on existing hardware; you don't need new expanded memory boards to install EMM 4.0. However, not all expanded memory boards currently support every enhancement to EMM 4.0. For example, the AST RAMpage! board and the Intel Above Board 2 support placing the page frame in memory below 640Kb, while the Intel Above Board 286 currently does not.

EMS 4.0 Enhancements

The enhancements to EMS 4.0 improve performance and memory efficiency and make it easier to write programs that use expanded memory.

- With EMM 4.0, one calls maps in all logical pages that can be physically mapped to one page frame; earlier versions required each page to be mapped separately.

- New functions allow application programs to dynamically increase and decrease the amount of expanded memory allocated to them. With each program using just the amount of expanded memory it needs, multiple programs can share expanded memory more efficiently.

- Now you can name handles—the values that the EMM assigns and uses to identify a block of memory requested by an application program—so that data and code can be shared by application programs.

- EMS 4.0 adds special functions for operating systems (such as MS-DOS) and environments (such as Windows and DESQview) to allow programs to isolate themselves from all other software in the system, thus providing a safe environment for programs sharing expanded memory.

- New EMS functions directly support executing code in expanded memory. Earlier versions supported the execution of code in expanded memory, but implementation was cumbersome. For example, before EMS 4.0, terminate-and-stay-resident (TSR) programs required commands to explicitly map the new context into expanded memory when the TSR program was called up and to restore the previous context when the TSR returned control to the application program. Now the job of mapping and restoring contexts can be handled directly with EMS 4.0 functions, which allows for easier and more efficient execution of code.

- Earlier EMS versions put the page frame in an unused 64Kb block of memory between 640Kb and 1Mb. EMS 4.0 supports the page frame anywhere in the first 1Mb of memory. Hardware may limit the location of the page frame—in an 80286-based computer such as an IBM PC/AT, for example, the page frame can reside only between 256Kb and 1Mb. For an 80386-based computer or an IBM PS/2 computer with the Micro Channel, on the other hand, the page frame can be anywhere in the first 1Mb of memory.

- Before EMS 4.0, the page frame held four pages. Now you can define a page frame of up to eight pages in memory above 640Kb. The size of the page frame in memory below 640Kb is limited only by the amount of available memory. (In some implementations of the EMM, you can use all 640Kb for the page frame by putting the EMM itself into expanded memory.)

- Although the standard size of expanded memory pages is 16Kb, some expanded memory boards use smaller pages. EMS 4.0 supports both 16Kb pages and smaller-sized pages.

The Page Frame

Although EMM 4.0 supports locating a page frame in any available memory between 0Kb and 1Mb, how you plan to use the page frame determines whether you'll place it above or below 640Kb. For application programs, continue to locate the page frame above 640Kb because existing applications may not work when the page frame is located below 640Kb. Locate page frames used by most operating systems and environments in memory below 640Kb. (An exception to this is the Windows/386 EMM, which cannot use a page frame located below 640Kb.) In any case, you cannot create a page frame in memory below 640Kb unless you first create a page frame in memory above 640Kb.

New EMM Parameters

The LIM EMM 4.0 device driver has new parameters, one of which is of special interest to users who are concerned with speed and efficiency.

The handle count parameter lets you tell the EMM to support as many handles as a particular application program needs. (A handle is a value that the EMM assigns and uses to identify a block of memory requested by an application program.) The EMM allocates memory based on the number of handles requested by the application. By specifying a small handle count, you can save conventional memory and allow the EMM to run faster.

The EMM 4.0 handle count default is 64 handles; programs written for earlier versions use a maximum of 32 handles. If you are using older programs with EMM 4.0, consider changing the EMM handle count to 32 for faster execution. The maximum number of handles is 254.

The EMM Functions

The EMM functions provide the tools application programs need to use expanded memory. EMS 4.0 doubled the number of EMM functions. Table 13-1 lists all 30 functions; the new functions are shaded.

Functions 16 through 30 are new to EMM 4.0. This section describes each new function. Functions 26, 28, and 30 are for use by operating systems (such as MS-DOS) and environments (Windows and DESQview, for example); the rest are for application programs.

Program Functions

Get/Set Partial Page Map (Function 16) handles situations Functions 8, 9, and 15 cannot handle. Functions 8 and 9, respectively, handle only four-page page frames and can save and restore expanded memory pages only when the page frame is located between 640Kb and 1Mb. Function 15 saves and restores all pages (no matter how many pages are in the page frame), even pages located below 640Kb. Function 16 also saves and restores all pages anywhere between 0 and 1Mb, but, unlike Function 15, it lets you choose the pages you want to save or restore.

Function 16 has three subfunctions. The *Get Partial Page Map* subfunction saves a partial mapping context for specific mappable memory regions in a system. This subfunction can be faster than Function 15 because it saves only a subset of the entire mapping context and uses much less memory for the save area. You can use the *Get Partial Page Map* subfunction with or without a handle, while Function 8 requires a handle.

The *Set Partial Page Map* subfunction restores a partial mapping context for specific mappable memory regions in a system. Like *Get Partial Page Map*, this subfunction uses far less memory for the save area than Function 15, and you can use it with or without a handle.

The *Get Size* of *Partial Page Map Save Array* subfunction returns the storage requirements for the array passed by the *Get/Set Partial Page Map* subfunctions. Use this subfunction before the other two subfunctions.

Map/Unmap Multiple Handle Pages (Function 17) maps or unmaps (in one invocation) logical pages into as many physical pages as the system supports. This means less overhead than mapping pages one at a time (as required by EMS

Function Name	No.	Description
GET STATUS	1	Returns a status code to tell you whether the EMM is present and the hardware/software is working correctly.
GET PAGE FRAME ADDRESS	2	Gives the program the location of the page frame.
GET UNALLOCATED PAGE COUNT	3	Tells the program the total number of pages in expanded memory and the number of unallocated pages.
ALLOCATE PAGES	4	Allocates the number of expanded memory pages requested by the program; assigns a unique EMM handle to the set of pages allocated.
MAP HANDLE PAGE	5	Maps the specified logical page in expanded memory to the specified physical page within the page frame.
DEALLOCATE PAGES	6	Deallocates the pages currently allocated to an EMM handle.
GET EMM VERSION	7	Returns the version number of the EMM Software.
SAVE PAGE MAP	8	Saves the contents of the page mapping registers of all expanded memory boards.
RESTORE PAGE MAP	9	Restores the contents of the page mapping registers.
	10	Reserved.
	11	Reserved.
GET EMM HANDLE COUNT	12	Returns the number of active EMM handles.
GET EMM HANDLE PAGES	13	Returns the number of pages allocated to a specific EMM handle.
GET ALL EMM HANDLE PAGES	14	Returns the active EMM handles and the number of pages allocated to each one.
GET/SET PAGE MAP	15	Saves and restores the mapping context of the active EMM handle.
GET/SET PARTIAL PAGE MAP	16	Saves a partial mapping context for specific mappable memory regions in a system.
MAP/UNMAP MULTIPLE HANDLE PAGES	17	Maps/unmaps (in a single invocation) logical pages into as many physical pages as the system supports.

(continued on next page)

Function Name	No.	Description
REALLOCATE PAGES	18	Increases or decreases the amount of expanded memory allocated to a handle.
GET/SET HANDLE ATTRIBUTE	19	Lets an application determine and set a handle as volatile or nonvolatile.
GET/SET HANDLE NAME	20	Gets the eight-character name currently assigned to a handle; assigns an eight-character name to a handle.
GET HANDLE DIRECTORY	21	Returns information about active handles and the names assigned to each.
ALTER PAGE MAP AND JUMP	22	Alters the memory mapping context and transfers control to the specified address.
ALTER PAGE MAP AND CALL	23	Alters the specified mapping context and transfers control to the specified address. A return can then restore the context and return control to the caller.
MOVE/EXCHANGE MEMORY REGION	24	Copies or exchanges a region of memory from conventional to conventional memory, conventional to expanded memory, expanded to conventional memory, or expanded to expanded memory.
GET MAPPABLE PHYSICAL ADDRESS ARRAY	25	Returns an array with the segment address and physical page number for each mappable physical page in a system.
GET EXPANDED MEMORY HARDWARE INFORMATION	26	Returns an array containing the hardware capabilities of the expanded memory system.
ALLOCATE RAW PAGES	27	Allocates the number of nonstandard size pages that the operating system requests and assigns a unique EMM handle to these pages.
ALTERNATE MAP REGISTER SET	28	Lets an application program simulate alternate sets of hardware mapping registers.
PREPARE EXPANDED MEMORY HARDWARE FOR WARM BOOT	29	Prepares the expanded memory hardware for an impending warm boot.
ENABLE/DISABLE OS/E	30	Enables and disables EMM Functions designed for use by operating systems and environments (Functions 26, 28, and 30).

Table 13-1: EMM 4.0 Functions

versions before 4.0). Use this function instead of Function 5 for application programs that do a lot of page mapping.

Reallocate Pages (Function 18) allows an application program to dynamically increase or decrease the number of logical pages allocated to an EMM handle, so programs can share expanded memory more efficiently. Function 18 does not determine the number of pages a program needs; rather, the program itself must specify the number of pages to allocate or deallocate (depending on its needs at any one time).

Get/Set Handle Attribute (Function 19) defines a handle as volatile or nonvolatile. If it is nonvolatile, the handle, its name (if it has one), and the contents of the pages allocated to it are maintained after a warm boot. For example, this function saves the contents of a RAM disk in expanded memory after a warm boot. Function 19 is not supported by most hardware because it disables memory refresh signals for a long period of time.

Function 19 has three subfunctions. The *Get Handle Attribute* subfunction returns the attribute (volatile or non-volatile) associated with a handle. The *Set Handle Attribute* subfunction changes the attribute associated with a handle. Before using Function 19's other two subfunctions, you can use the *Get Attribute Capability* subfunction to determine whether the EMM supports the non-volatile attribute.

By naming the handle associated with a block of memory, *Get/Set Handle Name* (Function 20) lets application programs share the same area in expanded memory associated with a handle. Assigning a name to a handle also protects the memory specified by the handle because only a program that knows the handle name can get that handle and use the memory assigned to it. Function 20 has two subfunctions. The *Get Handle Name* subfunction gets the eight-character name assigned to a handle. The *Set Handle Name* subfunction assigns an eight-character name to a handle.

Get Handle Directory (Function 21) has three subfunctions. The *Get Handle Directory* subfunction returns an array which contains all active handles and their associated names (if any).

The *Search for Named Handle* subfunction searches the handle name directory for the specified handle name. If it finds the name, the subfunction then returns the handle number associated with the name. An application program is able to use this subfunction to determine if a shared handle exists.

The *Get Total Handles* subfunction returns the total number of handles that the EMM supports. (Different versions of EMM support different numbers of handles. EMM 4.0 supports up to 254 handles; earlier versions support just 32).

Functions 22 and 23 make executing code in expanded memory easier and more efficient. *Alter Page Map* and *Jump* (Function 22) changes the memory mapping context and transfers control to the specified address. The original memory is lost. This function is analogous to the *FAR JUMP* in the 8086 family architecture.

Alter Page Map and *Call* (Function 23) contains two subfunctions. The *Alter Page Map* and *Call* subfunction saves the current memory mapping context, alters the specified memory mapping context, transfers control to the specified address, and restores the state of the specified mapping context after the return. This subfunction is analogous to the *FAR CALL* in the 8086 family architecture.

The *Alter Page Map* and *Call* subfunction pushes information onto the stack. The *Get Page Map Stack Space Size* subfunction returns the number of bytes of stack space the *Alter Page Map* and *Call* subfunction needs to do this. Use the information provided by *Get Page Map Stack Space Size* to alter the stack size before using either Function 22 or the *Alter Page Map* and *Call* subfunction.

Move/Exchange Memory Region (Function 24) lets you move large amounts of memory without mapping and unmapping pages. You can move or exchange up to 84 pages without mapping any logical pages. Function 24 has two subfunctions. The *Move Memory Region* subfunction copies and the *Exchange Memory Region* subfunction exchanges: conventional memory to conventional memory, conventional memory to expanded memory, expanded memory to conventional memory, and expanded memory to expanded memory. The subfunctions maintain the current mapping context, so the program does not have to save and restore it.

Get Mappable Physical Address Array (Function 25) tells an application what physical memory is mappable. Function 2 (get page frame address) gives the segment address of the first four pages in the page frame. Use Function 25 to find the amount of mappable physical memory for page frames larger than four pages. Function 25 has two subfunctions. The *Get Mappable Physical Address Array* subfunction returns an array containing the segment address and physical page number for each mappable physical page in a system. The array is a cross reference between physical page numbers and the actual segment addresses for each mappable page in the system. The array is sorted by segment address in ascending order, but the physical page numbers associated with the segment address are not necessarily in ascending order.

The *Get Mappable Physical Address Array Entries* subfunction gets the number of entries needed by the array returned by the *Get Mappable Physical Address Array* subfunction. Before using the *Get Mappable Physical Address Array Entries* subfunction, use the *Get Mappable Physical Address Array* subfunction to determine how much memory to allocate for storing the physical address array.

Allocate Raw Pages (Function 27) with two subfunctions allocates the number of raw pages requested by the operating system or environment and assigns a unique EMM handle to these pages. (Some expanded memory boards have pages of less than the standard 16Kb. These non-standard sized memory pages are called raw pages.) Handles assigned to raw pages are called raw handles. Function 4 (*Allocate Pages*) allocates only 16Kb pages; it does not support raw pages.

Programs whose page frames are in conventional memory must use *Prepare Expanded Memory Hardware for Warm Boot* (Function 29) when they detect Ctrl-Alt-Del. This function prepares the expanded memory hardware for an impending warm boot.

Environment Functions

The following functions are for inclusion in operating system and environment programs so the operating system/environment knows the kind of hardware support available for expanded memory. Never use Function 26, 28, or 30 in application programs.

Get Expanded Memory Hardware Information (Function 26) is only for use by operating systems (such as DOS) and environments (such as Windows/386 and DESQview). The operating system/environment can disable Function 26 at any time. The function has two subfunctions. The *Get Hardware Configuration Array* subfunction returns an array containing expanded memory hardware configuration information for use by operating systems and environments. The operating system/environment uses this information to determine the hardware support for expanded memory, including raw page size, alternate register sets available, context save area size, and register sets for DMA channels.

Some expanded memory boards have pages of less than the standard 16Kb, called raw pages. Function 3 (*Get Unallocated Page Count*) returns only the number of 16Kb pages. The *Get Unallocated Raw Page Count* subfunction returns the number of unallocated raw mappable pages and the total number of raw mappable pages in expanded memory to the operating system/environment.

Alternate Map Register Set (Function 28) is for use by operating systems and environments only. It has nine subfunctions.

The *Get Alternate Map Register Set* subfunction responds in one of two ways, depending on the setting of the map register set which is active when the function is invoked. If the map register set is equal to zero, a pointer to a context save area is returned. If the map register set is greater than zero, the number of the alternate map register set is returned.

The *Set Alternate Map Register Set* subfunction responds in one of two ways, depending on the map register set specified. If the alternate map register set equals zero, map register set zero is activated, and the contents of the map register context save area is copied into register set zero on each expanded memory board in the system. If the alternate map register set specified is not zero, the alternate map register set specified is activated. The restore area, which the operating system is pointing to, is not used.

The *Get Alternate Map Save Array Size* subfunction returns the storage requirements for the map register context save area that is referenced by the other subfunctions.

If an alternate map register is available, the *Allocate Alternate Map Register Set* subfunction gets its number and copies the currently active alternate map register set's contents into the newly allocated alternate map register set's mapping registers. This does not change the alternate map register set in use but prepares the new alternate map register set for a subsequent *Set Alternate Map Register Set* subfunction. Operating systems can use this subfunction to quickly switch mapping contexts.

The *Deallocate Alternate Map Register Set* subfunction returns the alternate map register set to the memory manager. The memory manager can then reallocate the alternate map register set. This subfunction also makes the mapping context of the specified alternate map register unavailable for reading or writing, thus protecting the pages previously mapped in an alternate map register set by making them inaccessible. The current alternate map register set cannot be deallocated, so memory currently mapped into conventional and expanded memory is inaccessible.

The four DMA subfunctions let operating systems/environments use DMA register sets. (Hardware that supports these subfunctions is not yet available.) If a DMA register set is available, the *Allocate DMA Register Set* subfunction gets the current number of a DMA register set for an operating system/environment.

This subfunction is useful with multitasking operating systems, in which you would like to switch to another task when one task is waiting for DMA to complete. The *Deallocate DMA Register Set* subfunction deallocates the specified DMA register set.

The *Enable DMA* on *Alternate Map Register Set* subfunction allows DMA accesses on a specific DMA channel to be associated with a specific alternate map register set. This function is useful in a multitasking operating system, where you would like to switch to another task until the first task's DMA operation completes. The *Disable DMA* on *Alternate Map Register Set* subfunction disables DMA accesses for all DMA channels which were associated with a specific alternate map register set.

Enable/Disable OS/E Function Set (Function 30) is only used by operating systems and environments. It includes three subfunctions which are *Enable OS/E Function Set* subfunction that will enable Function 26 (*Get Expanded Memory Hardware Information*), Function 28 (*Alternate Map Register Sets*), and also Function 30 (*Enable/Disable Operating System Functions*).

The *Disable OS/E Function Set* subfunction disables Functions 26, 28, and 30.

The *Return Access Key* subfunction lets the operating system/environment return the access key to the EMM. Returning the access key to the EMM enables access to the operating system/environment function set.

Example Programs

The following two examples (written in Microsoft C, Version 5.0, and Microsoft MASM, Version 5.0) illustrate how functions new to EMS 4.0 can be implemented. The first example shows how expanded memory can be shared between two application programs. The first program (*SAVSCR.EXE*) saves the current screen, initializes a blank screen in expanded memory, and then exits (see Listing 13-1). The second program (*SWPSCR.EXE*) saves its current screen, displays the blank screen and the first program's current screen, and then restores its own current screen.

Listing 13-1: SAVSCR Main Program

```
#include <c:\msc\include\dos.h>
#include <c:\msc\include\memory.h>
#include <c:\msc\include\stdio.h>
```

```
#include <c:\emm\demo\emm.h>

/* set up size and base of video ram */
#define VIDEO_RAM_SIZE 4000
#define VIDEO_RAM_BASE OXB8000000
union REGS     inregs,    outregs;
struct SREGS       segregs ;

char far *video_ram_ptr = (VIDEO_RAM_BASE):  /* video start address
                                                (CGA)*/
unsigned long int video_ram_size =(4000):    /* bytes in video ram */
unsigned int emm_handle ;                    /* our emm handle */
char emm_device_name[]  = "EMMXXXXO";        /* Device Name of EMM */
char emm_handle_name[8] ="shared";           /* name for handle to be
                                                shared   */
char far *emm_ptr;                           /* pointer to page
                                                frame */
char far *(*page_ptr)  ;                      /* pointer to page in the
                                                frame */
int pages_needed = 4;
struct log_phys (
  int log_page_number;
  int phys_page_number;
      ) current_pages [4] ;
struct log_phys far *map_unmap_ptr ;
int result ; /* result passed back from function calls */

main ()
{
   check_emm_version_number() ;  /*Check for EMM > 4.0 */

   result = get_expanded_memory (&cmm_ptr, pages_needed,
                               &emm_handle, emm_handle_name);
   if (result != 0) exit(1);  /*exit if error */

   result= map_unmap_multiple_pages (current_pages, /* Map in */
                              emm_handle, 1); /* pages */

   move_exchg_to_expanded(MOVE_MEMORY_REGION,  /* Copy video screen
z3g                                            to */
                      video_ram_ptr,       /*  logical page 0 */
                      emm_handle, 0, video_ram_size);


   /*make a null video screen at logical page 1       */
   page_ptr = (emm_ptr + 0x4000);        /* make null screen at */
   memset (page_ptr, 0, VIDEO_RAM_SIZE); /* at logical page 1    */

 /* Unmap all pages so they are protected */
   result = map_unmap_multiple_pages (current_pages, emm_handle, 0);
```

Before it can use expanded memory, *SAVSCR.EXE* must first see if the EMM is present (by getting the device name from the device driver header). Because *SAVSCR.EXE* uses 4.0 functions, it also checks the EMM version (Function 7), and exits if EMM is earlier than version 4.0 (see Listing 13-2).

Listing 13-2: This function checks to see if the EMM is present and if the version number is >= 4.0. It uses EMM function 7, GET.VERSION NUMBER.

```
int check_emm_version_number()
{
    char *emm_device_name_ptr ;  .

    inregs.h.ah = 0x35; /* Use the DOS get interrupt function (0x35) to */
    inregs.h.al =EMM_INT;/* get the pointer at interrupt vector 0x67, */
    intdosx(&inregs, &outregs, &segregs);/* and check for device name. */
    emm_device_name_ptr = (segregs.es * 65536)  + 10;
    if (memcmp(emm_device_name, emm_device_name_ptr,8) !=0)
      {
        printf("Expanded memory manager not present\n");
        exit (1);
      }
    inregs.h.ah = GET_VERSION ;     /* set function code and check for  */
    int86(EMM_INT,&inregs,&outregs);/* version >= 4.0              */
    if (outregs.h.ah != 0) exit(1);
    if ((outregs.h.ah == 0) & (outregs.h.al < 0x40))
    {
        printf("Expanded memory manager does not support LIM 4.0");
        exit(1) ;
    }
}
```

SAVSCR.EXE next determines the number of unallocated pages in expanded memory (Function 3) and exits if there are fewer pages than it needs. Then the program allocates the expanded memory pages it needs and gets an EMM handle (Function 4), assigning the unique name *SHARED* to the handle (Function 20). This unique handle name will be used later by the second application program to find the handle so it can use the same expanded memory (see Listing 13-3).

Listing 13-3: This function gets the amount of expanded memory requested, returns a pointer to the page frame, and assigns the name to the handle.

```
int get_expanded_memory(emm_ptr_ptr, pages, emm_handle_ptr, name)
```

```
char *(*emm_ptr_ptr);          /* pointer to expanded memory page frame
*/
int pages;                     /* Number of pages to allocate */
unsigned int *emm_handle_ptr;  /* Pointer to emm handle */
char *name;

{
    inregs.h.ah = GET_UNALLOCATED_PAGE_COUNT ;   /* Check to see if
                                                    there */
    int86(EMM_INT, &inregs, &outregs); /* enough unallocated pages
                                          left.*/
    if (outregs.h.ah != 0) return(1);
    if (outregs.x.bx < pages) return(2);

    inregs.h.ah = ALLOCATE_PAGES ;   /* Get a handle and allocate */
    inregs.x.bx = pages;             /* the requested pages.*/
    int86(EMM_INT, &inregs, &outregs);
    if (outregs.h.ah != 0) return(3);
    *emm_handle_ptr = outregs.x.dx ;

    inregs.h.ah = GET_FRAME_ADDRESS; /* Get page frame segment
                                        address */
    int86(EMM_INT, &inregs, &outregs); /* and make it a pointer. */
    if (outregs.h.ah != 0) return(4);
    *emm_ptr_ptr = (unsigned long int) (outregs.x.bx *65536);


    inregs.x.ax = SET_HANDLE_NAME ; /* assign name to handle */
    inregs.x.dx = *emm_handle_ptr ;
    inregs.x.si = FP_OFF(name) ;
    segregs.ds = FP_SEG(name) ;
    int86x(EMM_INT, &inregs, &outregs, &segregs);
    if (outregs.h.ah != 0) return(5);

    return(0);
}
```

Next, *SAVSCR.EXE* uses the *Map/Unmap Multiple Handle* function (Function 17) to map the needed pages into the page frame. This is done with one function call; earlier versions of the EMM require one call for each page (see Listing 13-4).

Listing 13-4: Implementing the MAP/UNMAP MULTIPLE PAGES EMM Function

```
int map_unmap_multiple_pages (log_phys_pages,handle,map_unmap)

struct log_phys *log_phys_pages ;   /* Pointer to log_phys struct */
```

```
unsigned int handle;                /* Handle to map or unmap */
unsigned int map_unmap;             /* 0 = map, 1 = unmap */
{
 int i ;
 struct log_phys *temp_ptr;

 temp_ptr = log_phys_pages;

 for (i=0 ; i<=3; i++)
 {
 /* Setup the structure to Map or unmap the logical pages 0 to 3 */
   log_phys_pages->phys_page_number = i;
   if (map_unmap == 1)
    log_phys_pages->log_page_number = i;
   else
    log_phys_pages->log_page_number = 0xFFFF  ;

   log_phys_pages++ ;

 }

 inregs.x.ax = MAP_UNMAP_MULTIPLE_PAGES ;
 inregs.x.dx = handle;
 inrega.x.cx = 4;
 inrega.x.si = FP_OFF(temp_ptr);
 segregs.ds  = FP_SEG(temp_ptr);
 int86x(EMM_INT, &inregs, &outregs, &segregs);
 if (outregs.h.ah != 0) return(1);
 return(0);
}
```

Then the *SAVSCR.EXE* program copies the current screen to logical page 0 and physical page 0, using the *Move Memory Region* subfunction (Function 24). Although this particular move does not span any more than one expanded memory page, the same function call can transfer up to 1Mb of memory without mapping in any logical pages of expanded memory (see Listing 13-5).

Listing 13-5: This function implements the MOVE or EXCHANGE MEMORY REGION function to move or exchange conventional memory with expanded memory pages.

```
int move_exchg_to_expanded(function_number, conv_buffer,  handle,
page, length)
unsigned int function_number ;   /* Move or Exchange*/
char far *conv_buffer ;          /* conventional memory with */
int handle;                      /* EMM memory associated with this
handle */
int page ;                       /* at this physical page */
```

```
unsigned long int length;        /* and for this many bytes */

{
#pragma pack(1) /* Make sure the following structure
                is byte aligned */
struct move_exchg
 {
    unsigned long int region_length;
    char source_type ;
    unsigned int source_handle ;
    unsigned int source_offset ;
    unsigned int source_seg_page;
    char dest_type;
    unsigned int dest_handle;
    unsigned int dest_offset;
    unsigned int dest_seg_page;
  } move_exchg_struct;
struct move_exchg *move_exchg_ptr;

   move_exchg_struct.region_length  = length ;
   move_exchg_struct.soruce_type    = 0;
   move_exchg_struct.source_handle  = 0;
   move_exchg_struct.source_offset   = FP_OFF(conv_buffer);
   move_exchg_struct.source_seg_page = FP_SEG(conv_buffer);
   move_exchg_struct.dest_type      = 1;
   move_exchg_struct.dest_handle    = handle;
   move_exchg_struct.dest_offset    = 0 ;
   move_exchg_struct.dest_set_page  = page;

   inregs.x.ax = function_number;
   move_exchg_ptr = &move_exchg_struct;
   inregs.x.si = FP_OFF(move_exchg_ptr);
   segregs.ds  = FP_SEG(move_exchg_ptr);
   int86x(EMM_INT, &inregs, &outregs, &segregs);
   if (outregs.h.ah != 0) exit(1);

   return(outregs.x.as)  ;

}
```

Finally, *SAVSCR.EXE* unmaps all of the pages using the *Map/Unmap Multiple Handle Pages* function (Function 17) and then exits without returning the handle to the EMM (see Listing 13-4).

Expanded memory is now protected. The second program, *SWPSCR.EXE*, can find this same expanded memory by using the *Search for Named Handle* subfunction.

First, *SWPSCR.EXE* verifies that the EMM is present and is version 4.0 or greater, as the first program did. However, unlike the *SAVSCR.EXE* program,

SWPSCR.EXE does not need to allocate pages because it can use the same handle named *SHARED* that *SAVSCR.EXE* received.

SWPSCR.EXE uses the *Search for Named* handle subfunction (Function 21) to determine if the handle named *SHARED* is present. If the first program (*SAVSCR.EXE*), has not been executed already, *SWPSCR.EXE* will exit, because it could not find the handle named *SHARED*.

Finally, *SWPSCR.EXE* uses the *Exchange Memory Region* subfunction (Function 24) to: swap its current screen with the logical page that has the blank screen; swap the blank screen with the logical page that has the original screen; and then restore its own current screen. (Because the *Exchange Memory Region* subfunction handles all mapping, none of the logical pages have to be mapped before this call.)

SWPSCR.EXE unmaps all expanded memory pages before exiting (Function 17) as seen in Listing 13-6. *SWPSCR.EXE* illustrates how EMM 4.0 has simplified executing code in expanded memory.

Listing 13-6: The Main Program for SWPSCR

```
#include <c:\msc\include\dos.h>
#include <c;\msc\include\memory.h>
#include<c:\msc\include\stdio.h>
#include <c:\emm\demo\emm.h>
#define VIDEO_RAM_SIZE 4000
#define VIDEO_RAM_BASE 0XB8000000

union REGS      inregs,    outregs;
struct SREGS       segregs ;

char far *video_ram_ptr = (VIDEO_RAM_BASE); /* video start address
                                              (CGA)*/
unsigned long int video_ram_size =(4000);   /* bytes in video ram */
unsigned int emm_handle ;                   /* emm handle */
char emm_divice_name[] = "EMMXXXX0";        /* Devide Name of EMM */
char emm_handle_name[8] ="shared" ; /* name for handle to be shared*/
char far *(*expanded_memory_ptr) ; /* pointer to page frame */
char far *(*page_ptr) ;             /* pointer to page in the frame  */
long target_time,current_time ;
struct log_phys {       /* structure to hold the mapping of logical */
  int log_page_number; /* pages to physical pages */
  int phys_page_number;
      } current_pages [4] ;

main ()
{
```

```
    check_emm_version_number();

    search_for_handle(emm_handle_name, &emm_handle);

    /* Exchange screens*/
    move_exch_to_expanded(EXCHANGE_MEMORY_REGION,video_ram_ptr,
                          emm_handle, 1, video_ram_size);

    time(&current_time); /* Delay so user can see screen changes */
    target_time = current_time + 3;
    while (current_time < target_time) time(&current_time);

   /* Display Screen */
    move_exchg_to_expanded(EXCHANGE_MEMORY_REGION, video_ram_ptr,
                           emm_handle, 0, video_ram_size);
    time(&current_time); /* Delay so user can see screen change */
    target_time = current_time + 3;
    while (current_time < target_time) time(current_time);

    /* Restore original screen */
    move_exchg_to_expanded(EXCHANGE_MEMORY_REGION,video_ram_ptr,
                           emm_handle, 1, video_ram_size);

    result = map_unmap_multiple_pages (&current_pages, emm_handle, 0);

    exit (0) ;
}
```

As in the first example, *MAPCALL.EXE* (see Listing 13-7) checks for the version of EMM and allocates expanded memory. Then it uses the *MS-DOS Load Overlay* function to load two modules (*MODULE1.EXE* and *MODULE2.EXE*) into expanded memory (see Listing 13-8).

Listing 13-7: The Main Program for MAPCALL

```
#include <c:\msc\include\dos.h>
#include <c:\msc\include\memory.h>
#include <c:\msc\include\stdio.h>
#include <c:\emm\demo\emm.h>

union REGS      inregs,    outregs;
struct SREGS      segregs ;

unsigned int emm_handle ;
char emm_device_name[] = "EMMXXXX0";                /* Device Name
                                                       of EMM */

char far emm_handle_name [8] ="mapcall";        /* Name for
                                                   handle */
char far mod1_name[] ="c:\\emm\\demo\\module1.exe\0"; /* Name of
```

```
                                                        modules */
char far mod2_name[] ="c:\\emm\\demo\\module2.exe\0"; /* to be
                                                        loaded */

char far *emm_ptr ;
char far *(*page_ptr) ;
int pages_needed = 16 ;
struct log_phys {
  int log_page_number;
  int phys_page_number;
        } ;
struct log_phys far current_pages[4];
struct log_phys far map_call_pages ;
int result;

main ()
{


   check_emm_version_number();

   result = get_expanded_memory (&emm_ptr, pages_needed, &emm_handle,
                               emm_handle_name);
   if (result != 0) exit(1);

           /* Map in pages */
   result = map_unmap_multiple_pages (current_pages,
                                   emm_handle, 1);

   *page_ptr = emm_ptr;  /* Load Module 1 into logical page 0  */
   load_overlay(modi_name, page_ptr, 0); /* at physical page 0 */

         /*Load Module 2 into logical page 1 at physical page 1 */
   load_overlay(mod2_name, page_ptr, 1);

             /* Unmap all pages */
   result = map_unmap_multiple_pages (current_pages,
                                   em_handle, 0);

          /* Map and call to module in page 0 and physical page 1 */
    map_call_pages.log_page_number  =0;

    map_call_pages.phys_page_number =0;


    map_and_call(&map_call_pages, 1, &current_pages, 0, emm_handle);

    inregs.h.ah = DEALLOCATE_PAGES ; /* Release handle before
                                        exiting */
    inregs.x.ds = emm_handle ;
    int86(EMM_INT, &inregs, &outregs);

    exit (0);
}
```

Listing 13-8: Implementing the ALTER PAGE MAP AND CALL EMM Function

```
int map_and_call (new_map_ptr, new_length, old_map_ptr, old_length,
                          handle)
struct log_phys *new_map_ptr;
char new_length;
struct log_phys *old_map_ptr;
char old_length;
unsigned int handle;
{
# pragma pack (1) /* Make sure structure is byte aligned */
  struct map_call_struct {
     unsigned int offset_target_address ;
     unsigned int seg_target_address ;
     char new_page_map_length ;
     unsigned int offset_new_page_map ;
     unsigned int seg_new_page_map ;
     char old_page_map_length ;
     unsigned int offset_old_page_map;
     unsigned int seg_old_page_map ;
   } map_call;
   struct map_call_struct *map_call_ptr;

  map_call_ptr = &map_call ;
  map_call.offset_target_address = 0 ;
  map_call.seg_target_address      =0xd000;
  map_call.new_page_map_length   = new_length;
  map_call.offset_new_page_map   = FP_OFF (new_map_ptr);
  map_call.set_new_page_map      = FP_SEG (new_map_ptr);
  map_call.old_page_map_length   = old_length;
  map_call.offset_old_page_map   = FP_OFF (old_map_ptr);
  map_call.seg_old_page_map      = FP_SEG (old_map_ptr);

  inregs.h.ah +0x56; /* Setup for Alter page Map and Call EMM
  function */
  inregs.h.al = 0;
  inregs.x.dx = handle ;
  map_call_ptr = &map_call ;
  inregs.x.si = FP_OFF (map_call_ptr);
  segregs.ds = FP_SEG (map_call_ptr);
  int86x (EMM_INT,&inregs,&outregs,&segregs);
  if (outregs.h.ah != 0) return (1);

  return(0) ;
}
```

Next, *MAPCALL.EXE* uses the *Alter Page Map and Call* subfunction (Function 23) to execute *MODULE1.EXE* (see Listing 13-9).

Listing 13-9: This function implements the MS-DOS load function 4BH. It sets AL to 3 causing the function to load the file and apply the relocation factor without executing the file.

```
int load_overlay (load_file_name,relocation_ptr,page)
char *load_file_name ;
char *(*relocation_ptr);
unsigned int page; /* physical page at which to load */

{
struct reloc {
  unsigned int load_seg; /* Which segment to load file */
  unsigned int reloc_factor; /* Which segment to use for
                                relocation */
  } reloc_struct:
  struct reloc *reloc_struct_ptr;

  reloc_struct.load_seg = FP_SEG(*relocation_ptr) + (page * 0x400);
  reloc_struct.reloc_factor = FP_SEG(*relocation_ptr) + (page *
                                                   0x400);

  inregs.h.ah = 0x4B ; /* Dos Exec function code */
  inregs.h.al = 3;  /* load but do not execute */
  inregs.x.dx  = FP_OFF(load_file_name);
  segregs.ds   = FP_SEG(load_file_name);

  reloc_struct_ptr = &reloc_struct ;
  inregs.x.bx  = FP_OFF(reloc_struct_ptr);
  segregs.es  = FP_SEG(reloc_struct_ptr) ;

  intdosx(&inregs, &outregs, &segregs);

}
```

MODULE1.EXE in turn uses the *Search for Named Handle* subfunction to determine which handle to use and uses the *Alter Map Page* and *Call* subfunction to execute *MODULE2.EXE* (see Listing 13-10).

Listing 13-10: NAME Start

```
; Use the DOSEG directive to ensure that the code segment is the
; first segment in the module.  Since this piece of code will be
; loaded in at the page frame at D000;000H the Alter Page Map and
; Call will use D000:0000H as the entry point.
DOSSEG
```

```
data SEGMENT PUBLIC 'DATA'
Data ends

CODE SEGMENT PUBLIC "CODE'
        ASSUME CS:CODE, DS:DATA
start proc far
        push    ds
        PUSH    dx
        mov     DX,data ; setup data seg into ds
        mov     ds,dx
        pop     dx
        mov     ah, 09  ; set function code for DOS display string
        mov     dx, offset enter_mag
        int     21H
        mov     si, offset handle_name
        mov     ax, 5401H               ; set function to search for named
                                        ; handle
        int     67H                     ; and invoke EMM
        or ah, ah
        jnz exit

        mov     si, offset map_call ; Set up registers for Alter Page
                                    ; Map and Call
        mov     al, 0               ; indicate that values are pages
        mov     ah, 56H             ; set function to map and call
        int     67H                 ; invoke emm
        or ah, ah
        jnz exit

        mov     ah, 09              ; set function for DOS display
                                    ; string
        mov     dx, offset exit_msg
        int 21H
exit:
        pop     ds
        ret
start endp
CODE ENDS
data SEGMENT PUBLIC 'DATA'
;
cr      equ     ODh
1f      equ     OAH
;
log_phys_map_struct     STRUC
    log_page_number     DW ?
    phys_page_number    DW ?
log_phys_map_struct     ENDS

map_call_struct         STRUC
    target_address          DD ?  ; Pointer to which EMM will transfer
                                  ; control
    new_page_map_length DB ?      ; Number of new pages to be mapped on
                                  ; call.
    new_page_map_ptr        DD ?  ; Pointer to array of
                                  ; log_phys_map_struc.
    old_page_map_length DB ?      ; Number of pages to mapped on
```

```
                                  ;  return.
        old_page_map_ptr    DD ?  ;  pointer to array of
                                  ;  log _phys_map_struc
        reserved            DW 4 DUP  (?)
map_call_struct ENDS
;
new_map  log_phys_map_struct <1.1>    ;  mapping before call
old_map  log_phys_map_struct <0,0>    ;  mapping after call

map_call  map_call_struct <0D0004000H,1,new_map,1,old_map>

handle_name db 'mapcall' ,0          ; handle name is ascciz string
enter_msg   db 'Entering Module 1' ,cr,1f,'$'
exit_msg    db 'Exiting Module 1' ,cr,1f,'$'
Data ends
end start
```

MODULE2.EXE prints a message to the screen and does a far return. The far return causes the EMM to restore the mapping specified in the old map page
definition and return control to *MODULE1.EXE* (see Listing 13-11).

Listing 13-11: NAME Start (MODULE2.EXE)

```
DOSSEG

data SEGMENT PUBLIC 'DATA'
Data ends

CODE SEGMENT PUBLIC 'CODE'
        ASSUME CS:CODE, DS:DATA
start proc far
     push    ds
     PUSH    dx
     mov     DX,data ; Set up date segment
     mov     ds,dx
     pop     dx
     mov     ah, 09 ; Set function code for DOS display string.
     mov     dx, offset enter_mag
     int 21H
     mov     ah, 09 ; Set function code for DOS display string.
     mov     dx, offset exit_mag
     int 21H
     pop     ds
     ret
start endp
CODE ENDS

data SEGMENT PUBLIC 'DATA'
cr     equ  0Dh
```

```
1f      equ  OAH
enter_msg   db  'Entering Module 2' ,cr,1f,'$'
exit_msg    db  'Exiting Module 2' ,cr,1f,'$'
Data ends
end start
```

MODULE1.EXE then does a far return, which causes the EMM to return control to *MAPCALL.EXE* and to restore the original mapping context. *MAPCALL.EXE* then releases its handle and exits to MS-DOS.

To Get EMS 4.0

If you are interested in developing application programs that use expanded memory, call Intel for a free copy of the Lotus/Intel/Microsoft Expanded Memory Specification. From the United States and Canada, call (800) 538-3373. Outside the United States and Canada, call (503) 629-7354.

IV
Operating Systems Part I:
DOS, Environments,
and UNIX

14

386 Operating Environments[*]

Ed McNierney

An important ingredient for attaining multitasking, virtual memory, and multiuser features is the 80386-based computer introduced more than a year ago. Four products, Digital Research Inc.'s (DRI) Concurrent DOS 386, The Software Link's PC-MOS/386, Microsoft's Windows/386, and Quarterdeck's DESQview 2.01, provide the necessary brains to exploit the power of the 386, DOS, with its 640KB memory limitation, and OS/2, which runs the same on 386 machines as on 286 models, do not.

The strength of Concurrent DOS, PC-MOS/386, Windows/386, and DESQview lies in their use of the 386 processor's virtual-8086 mode and their DOS compatibility. Like other products that offer advanced computing features, they build on DOS, rather than require rewriting of applications.

To take advantage of the 386, Concurrent DOS, PC-MOS/386, Windows/386, and DESQview time-share the processor among tasks and use memory-mapping capabilities to map tasks physically stored in extended memory into conventional memory addresses for the duration of their time slice (see Figure 14-1). With the

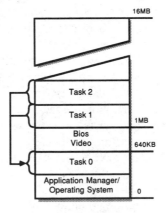

Figure 14-1: Virtual Memory

386's virtual device management capabilities, this allows time-shared execution of unmodified DOS tasks. Each product has its own application strengths and weaknesses. Features of all four are compared in Table 14-1.

	OPERATING SYSTEMS		APPLICATION MANAGERS	
	DIGITAL RESEARCH, INC.	THE SOFTWARE LINK	MICROSOFT	QUARTERBACK
PRODUCT	Concurrent DOS 386 1.1	PC-MOS/386 1.02	Windows/386 2.01	DESQview 2.01
CONCURRENCY				
Concurrent users	3	25	1	1
Concurrent tasks	255	99	32	256
MEMORY MANAGEMENT				
Minimum memory recommended	512KB	512KB	1MB	640KB
Maximum program size (EGA)	348KB	580KB	575KB	535KB
Disk swapping	No	No	No	Yes
Code/data sharing	Yes	Yes	Yes*	Yes
Expanded memory	Yes	Yes	Yes	Yes
USER INTERFACE				
Text windows	Yes	Yes	Yes	Yes
EGA graphics windows	No	No	Yes	No
Command-line interface	Yes	Yes	No	Yes
Mouse suport	No	No	Yes	Yes
Expanded keyboard buffer	Yes	Yes	Yes	Yes
Macros	No	Yes	No	Yes
FILE SUPPORT				
File sharing	Yes	Yes	Yes	Yes
Logical disks greater than 32MB	Yes	No	No	No
OTHER FEATURES				
PIFs	No	No	Yes	Yes
Cut and paste	No	No	Yes	Yes
Print spooling	Yes	Yes	Yes	No
DOS level	2x	3.2	3.3	3.3
Developer's toolkit	Yes	Yes	Yes**	Yes
Companion applications	No	No	Yes	Yes

*Among Windows 2.0 applications only.
**Windows 2.0 Software Development Kit.

Table 14-1: Comparison of Features

Concurrent DOS 386 and PC-MOS/386 are DOS-compatible multiuser, multitasking operating systems; DESQview and Windows/386 are both applications managers that work with DOS to allow a single user to run multiple DOS applications.

Concurrent DOS 386 and PC-MOS/386 are both multitasking and multiuser operating systems in their own right that replace rather than enhance DOS. They do not require purchase or use of DOS and are free to provide features that DOS inherently cannot provide. These systems support multiple users through applications run on remote terminals connected to serial ports on the host 386-based computer (PC-MOS/386 also runs on 286- and 8088-based machines). Concurrent DOS 386 supports 2 local or remote terminals; PC-MOS/386 supports 24.

Windows/386 and DESQview 2.01, on the other hand, are applications managers built on DOS, providing multitasking (but not multiuser) capabilities and allowing users to operate in a 386 control environment. By structuring themselves as shells dependent on the operating system, applications managers are inherently compatible with that operating system. They enhance normal PC single-monitor operation through a windowing environment capable of simultaneously displaying text and graphics applications. These products also provide users with a fallback mechanism; if a DOS application does not operate properly under the applications manager's control, it can always be run under DOS directly.

Concurrent Heritage

DRI has developed a long line of operating systems: first the commercially successful CP/M for Z-80 and 8088 microprocessors, then CP/M-86 and Concurrent DOS, and now Concurrent DOS 386. The company has attempted to maintain compatibility among its own operating systems almost to the point of absurdity. For example, users of Concurrent DOS 386 can read and write CP/M disks and set up a CP/M hard disk complete with user numbers and logical drive features supported by CP/M. Although a nice gesture to earlier customers, the support is not necessary in a 386-based system and only serves to confuse installation and setup of Concurrent for users who need no support for CP/M.

Getting Acquainted

Concurrent is shipped on five 360KB 5.25-inch diskettes containing a bootable version of the operating system, a set of operating system programs, and user utilities. It requires a Compaq Deskpro 386, an IBM PS/2 Model 80, or a 100-percent compatible computer with at least 512KB of memory for operation; a hard disk is recommended.

Documentation assumes users are familiar with DOS. More than that, in places, it actually advises the use of DOS commands for operations not supported in Concurrent.

For users with a DOS-formatted hard disk, installation of Concurrent is simple (the start-up screen tells users to press the F10 key to install). Eleven operating system files are copied to the hard disk's root directory. The system creates the subdirectory CON-DOS and copies Concurrent's user programs to it. Instead of directly booting Concurrent from the hard disk, DOS remains intact and the AUTOEXEC.BAT file asks users whether or not Concurrent is to be loaded. The system then returns to DOS or boots Concurrent. CONFIG.SYS on the DOS system must not specify that a device driver automatically enter protected mode when loaded, as Compaq's memory manager (CEMM) does if the ON option is set. If this happens, Concurrent resets the system instead of loading itself.

If the hard disk has not been partitioned for DOS, the automatic installation procedure will hang the system. Users must boot the system from the installation diskette without running the automatic installation program and then run the HDMAINT program, which is not on the install diskette but on a second distribution diskette.

Concurrent supports two hard disks, each with four partitions that can be formatted for DOS or CP/M and can be 512MB in size. For this review, a hard disk was set up as a single CP/M volume, and the HDMAINT program performed an apparently thorough surface analysis while formatting the disk. Although the system can be set up on DOS hard disks C:, D:, E:, and F:, CP/M choices are D: through G:. Because drive assignment of the destination disk is supplied through menu selection, users cannot choose C: for the CP/M boot disk. After removing the CP/M partition and setting up the hard disk under DOS, installation runs smoothly and creates a truly bootable hard disk devoted to Concurrent.

Concurrent provides four sessions at the main console (PC display and keyboard). Each session operates independently on its own virtual screen and executes for a time slice of one-sixtieth of a second. During its time slice, each session is mapped to the conventional memory region beginning at 256KB for a maximum program size of 348KB. Sessions start with a default memory allocation of 128KB. Users can execute the commands *ADDMEM* and *COMSIZE* before loading .EXE and .COM files, respectively, to increase or decrease the amount of memory allocated. (See Table 14-2 for a list of Concurrent-specific commands.) Keyboard input is directed to the foreground screen at all times; users move sessions to the foreground with the Ctrl key and digits 1-4 on the numeric keypad. The bottom line on the screen acts as a status line, indicating the session in the foreground and program names in each session.

At start-up, each session's window is the size of the entire screen so that switching sessions has the effect of flipping among four display screens. A window management system allows each session's window to be moved and sized and to have its own foreground and background colors. Default operation of the system can be changed so that all four sessions are partially visible at the same time.

Window layouts are defined by a command line or the WMENU interactive utility. Once WMENU is installed, users can press the Ctrl key and the + key on the numeric keypad to switch the bottom status line to a WMENU prompt line. Window positions, sizes, and other attributes are set interactively. The keyboard interface, however, is awkward, and the utility should, but does not, provide interactive mouse support. Window definitions are saved in WSETUP.BAT, using the *WMENU WRITE* command. WSETUP.BAT must be executed each time the system is initialized to restore the window layout. The user executes this file in order to set up the windows.

COMMAND	PURPOSE
8087	Indicates that a program uses the coprocessor
ADDMEM	Increases memory size for .EXE programs
AUX	Selects auxiliary port 0 or 1
BANK	Controls program mapping to extended memory
CARDFILE	Stores and retrieves names and addresses
CHSET	Changes the command header of .CMD files
COMSIZE	Sets memory size for .COM programs
COPYMENU	Copies menus from one file to another
DELQ (ERAQ)	Deletes files, upon confirmation
DREDIX	Creates and edits text files
DSKMAINT	Formats, copies, and verifies diskettes
EDITMENU	Creates, modifies, and deletes menus
FM	Allows commands to be selected from menus
FSET	Sets file and drive attributes and protections
FUNCTION	Assigns function and window switching keys
HDMAINT	Performs disk partition and verification services
HELP	Explains Concurrent commands
INITDIR	Formats CP/M directories
LOAD386	Starts Concurrent from DOS
ORDER	Changes the command file search order
PIP	Copies files between directories and devices
PRINTER	Changes the current printer number
PRINTMGR	Controls the printing of files
RETURN	Resets the system
RUNMENU	Runs a menu
SDIR	Shows director and file status information
SETPORT	Configures the serial ports
SETUP	Modifies system characteristics
SHOW	Displays information about disk drives
STOP	Terminates a program
SUSPEND	Suspends a background program
SYSDISK	Shows/sets current system disk
USER	Changes user number on CP/M media
VSET	Prevents an application's use of specific interrupts
WINDOW	Shows and modifies window characteristics
WMENU	Provides interactive manipulation of windows

Table 14-2: Concurrent DOS 386 Specific Commands

Concurrent has many commands in addition to those of DOS. They are primarily for allocating resources for multitasking and for providing CP/M media-related services. Commands also are provided for using and manipulating the menus.

Because most DOS applications are not designed to be run in small windows, Concurrent provides each window with a cursor tracking option. This permits automatic scrolling of a session's virtual screen; the display row containing the cursor is always visible in the window. Each session has its own start-up file (an AUTOEXEC.BAT equivalent). This allows path and window setup and other configuration activities to be performed automatically each time the system is started. The start-up files are named STARTUPx.BAT where x is the session number.

Concurrent DOS 386 supports expanded memory boards. It also has a built-in driver that uses 386 paging hardware and extended memory to simulate expanded memory.

Using Concurrent

At system start-up users have the option of loading Concurrent DOS 386 or the machine's native DOS, if present. If they select Concurrent, users can press F10 to see the start-up menu or Esc to enter Concurrent's command-line interface.

The interface is similar to DOS with a few improvements. Concurrent's video routines are faster; directory listings and TYPE files scroll quickly and smoothly on IBM's Enhanced Graphics Adapter (EGA). This performance is commendable in that Concurrent provides the added flexibility of built-in American National Standards Institute (ANSI) display driver support.

Concurrent provides a command-line history buffer and editing interface similar to public domain DOS enhancement programs that allow the use of up and down cursor keys to scroll through the last several command lines. Lines are edited using the cursor and control keys as with BASIC's line editor. The keyboard buffer is large, eliminating the type-ahead limitations of DOS. These features, still lacking in MS-DOS, are easy to implement and provide considerable user convenience.

Concurrent's start-up menu, invoked with F10, offers users the choice of displaying the disk subdirectory tree or activating the file or print manager, the DR EDIX editor, a card-file utility, or the help utility.

The file manager is a convenient menu-driven method for obtaining system services. It displays a directory of files and related commands. Commands are selected with cursor keys or by typing initial command letters. Cursor keys highlight commands and briefly describe their functions. Users can select files for the command to operate on in the same manner.

Concurrent supports two additional users at serial terminals connected to ports COM1: and COM2:. Sessions that run at these remote terminals are not supported by the window manager interface and cannot be viewed at the main console. Start-up files for these terminals are called STARTUP5.BAT and STARTUP6.BAT.

Use of remote terminals is not documented well. The four-page READ.ME file provides cursory information for setting up multiuser system terminals. SETUP and SETPORT, two menu-driven configuration utilities, allow the two serial ports to be configured and dedicated to remote terminals or serial printers. Remote terminals cannot be transparent to user applications that run on them; applications must be aware that they are running on terminals and use appropriate ANSI (or terminal-specific) cursor positioning and text-output commands.

Concurrent Compatibility

Concurrent suffers from a few compatibility problems. It lacks DOS version 3.x compatibility in interpreting program path names. Although it supports a search path, programs no on the path cannot be run by specifying the path name (consider *C:\BIN\MYPROG*, for example). This is a glaring omission.

Concurrent's support for character-based DOS applications is generally good; Microsoft's software development tools and Borland's SideKick and Turbo C all run without problems. Datastorm Technologies' communications program, Procomm, ran properly in one session, but an attempt to force a serial port conflict by running it in two sessions caused the system to beep and terminate the second session.

Copy-protected software and software with multiple text pages experienced problems. Lotus 1-2-3 release 2.0 cannot be installed or run on a 16-MHz 386-based system but runs well on 386 computers that allow the processor clock to be slowed to 8 MHz. Some 386 add-in boards for the AT, including Orchid's Jet 386, run exclusively at 16 MHz. Their manufacturers recommend that timing-dependent tasks, such as Lotus 1-2-3 installation be run on the AT's 286 running at either 6 or 8 MHz. This is hardly a viable option if the timing-dependent task is a process running under Concurrent.

File security is provided using a password scheme. The *FSET* command is sued to implement password protection on a disk volume, and to set passwords for access to individual files.

Concurrent does not properly handle text-page switching. Some text-based applications, such as Solution Systems' BRIEF editor, can detect a video adapter that allows multiple pages of text. When using such adapters, the editor switches to an alternate page for operation; this feature allows rapid restoration of the original DOS session screen after the editor is terminated. Concurrent, however, keeps the screen display on the original command-line page. This properly positions the cursor on the screen but prevents text output. The only way to make BRIEF work is to direct it to avoid using the alternate pages of video memory.

Graphics applications are also troublesome under Concurrent. With the exception of DRI's GEM graphics user interface, no graphics support appears in the documentation. When using an EGA and enhanced color display, a simple IBM Color Graphics Adapter (CGA) application running in black-and-white high-resolution mode appears blue on a solid-white background. Concurrent allows only one graphics application, including GEM, to be run at a time. EGA graphics can run only in a full-screen window. As applications become more graphics-oriented, Concurrent's lack of full support becomes more of a hindrance.

To its credit, DRI includes an insert on using 35 popular DOS applications under Concurrent that includes setting memory requirements and the extent of multiple-copy support. Some applications are severely limited in that they cannot be run in mapped memory, and many applications can be active only in one session at a time. Multiple copies of BASIC cannot be run; thus, multiple programs written in BASIC (such as Peachtree's General Ledger) cannot be run simultaneously. Because users are not always aware of an application's need for BASIC, unexpected problems can arise.

Concurrent's approach to machine virtualization is generally limited. Concurrent creates a virtual memory space for each DOS application but goes no further in supporting virtual hardware operation. As a result, applications directly writing to graphics memory, specifically manipulating interrupt vectors, or operating at almost any other hardware level, are likely to have difficulty running under Concurrent.

DRI has announced release 2.0 of Concurrent DOS 386. This enhanced version supports larger task size (greater than 512KB), provides DOS 3.3 compatibility, and dual-session support on remote terminals. Display of EGA graphics in a window also is supported, but not for multiple windows.

Concurrent DOS 386 provides software developers with interprocess and intertask communication facilities that can be used for applications written only for Concurrent. The product is an excellent base fo building in-house multitasking and multiuser character-based systems. But for users hoping to run multiple DOS applications with minimum effort and little or no risk, Concurrent does not provide needed flexibility and support.

Modular System

The Software Link's PC-MOS/386 is a modular operating system for 386-based computers that supports multitasking, multiple users, and remote terminals and provides total security. It mimics some features available in minicomputer environments and, like most multiuser systems, requires a system administrator for providing overall support and maintenance and setting up and deleting user names. PC-MOS also is available for use on 8088 and 80286-based computers, but requires add-in, memory-management hardware to use other than conventional memory.

Setup

PC-MOS/386 is shipped on two 360KB diskettes. Setup instructions are clear, easy to find, and detailed; a one-page READ.ME file is provided with version 1.02. A complete reference manual, including a helpful glossary and index, describes MOS commands and functions, multitasking and multiuser concepts, file and directory organization, and system security.

Unlike Concurrent documentation that frequently refers to DOS, PC-MOS documentation mentions it rarely. The Software Link correctly assumes that users are installing the operating system on a newly delivered computer and begins by describing how to partition and format the hard disk. PC-MOS/386 uses a DOS-compatible disk-partitioning scheme; hard disks formatted under either system are accessible by the other. After installation, users are guided through the more complex creation of a CONFIG.SYS file, including a description of device drivers used by the system.

Using PC-MOS/386

Like Concurrent DOS 386, PC-MOS/386 has a faster set of video display routines, allowing applications that use DOS functions for text output to run quickly. The command-line environment closely resembles DOS with the addition of command-line editing and a recall buffer for convenience; system commands generally match DOS commands with a few exceptions and enhancements.

System commands can have an optional period prefix added to them, which informs PC-MOS/386 that the command is an operating system internal command rather than the name of a program file. This feature permits system customization by allowing programs to have the same name as operating system commands. For example, the command *DIR* will run a batch file or program named DIR if one is present, while *.DIR* always runs the internal command *DIR*. Because the need for this is limited (a system in which *DIR* and *.DIR* perform two different operations is generally undesirable), users can generally ignore optional period prefix instructions.

PC-MOS/386 provides full system administration and security features, including file-by-file directory access and partition (task) access security. Each file, directory, or partition can be assigned to 1 of 26 security classes identified by letters A through Z. Each user is assigned a security file defining that person's rights (no access, execute access, read or execute access, or complete access) to each security class. Security classes for newly created tasks or files can be defined explicitly or set to the creator's default access class.

Like Concurrent, PC-MOS/386 provides an on-line help facility. Entering HELP at the command prompt displays a menu of system commands. Users are presented with a comprehensive description of the items they select. The MOS system utility command also displays a screen describing its options if the command is invoked with no operands.

PC-MOS/386 starts only one session when the system is booted; new sessions can be started using the *ADDTASK* command. See Table 14-3 for a list of PC-MOS/386-specific commands. Each task, assigned an ID number at start-up, begins on the main console or at remote terminals for which drivers have been defined in the CONFIG.SYS file. Each session runs in a virtual machine with an amount of memory specified by *ADDTASK*. Memory size of a task can range from 32 to 580KB, on systems using a VGA or an EGA, and to 644KB on systems using a CGA. Maximum task size is directly decreased by the amount of memory set aside for task supervision and device drivers; several tasks in excess of 550KB generally can execute without difficulty. Tasks can spawn additional tasks by using the *EXEC* function call to initiate the *ADDTASK* system utility.

The user can switch task displays by depressing the Alt key and typing on the numeric keypad the desired task's ID number. Because this keystroke sequence is also used to enter IBM Extended ASCII characters from the keyboard, it can be

Command	Purpose
ABORT	Stops processing within a batch file
ADDDEV	Dynamically adds a device driver
ADDTASK	Dynamically creates a memory partition for a task
ALIAS	Substitutes a drive letter for a directory name
AUTOCD	Restores drive and directory previously redirected
BATECHO	Controls the initial state of ECHO
CLASS	Assigns or changes a directory's security class
COMPFILE	Compares the contents of two files
DESNOW	Drives color display without snow pattern
DIRMAP	Displays disk directory map
DISKID	Assigns a volume identifier to a disk or diskette
ED	Creates and modifies text files
ENVSIZE	Specifies minimum environment space size
EXCEPT	Allows files to be excluded from a command
EXPORT	Creates a compressed backup copy of files
FILEMODE	Changes read-only or archive attributes of a file
FLUSH	Clears command recall buffer
FREEMEN	Defines regions above B0000H that MOS may use
HDSETUP	Sets up and maintains hard disks
HELP	Displays information about MOS commands
IMPORT	Restores compressed backup files
INSERT	Specifies insert mode for command line editing
KEY	Prompts for a keystroke
MOS	Controls memory, display, and I/O configuration
MOSADM	Controls system scheduling and disk caching
MSORT	Sorts records in a file
MSYS	Writes a boot sector to a disk
ONLY	Limits the action of a command to specific files
REL	Displays the release of MOS in use
REMDEV	Dynamically removes a device driver
REMTASK	Dynamically removes a memory partition
SEARCH	Searches one or more files for a character string
SIGNOFF	Exits a secured mode of MOS
SIGNON	Allows access to secured items
SLICE	Sets number of time slices for each partition
SMPSIZE	Sets size of system memory pool
SPOOL	Specifies where print files are to be sent
STOP	Causes an immediate exit from a batch file
TEXT	Displays a video screen from a batch file
USERFILE	Specifies the location of the system security file
VERIFY	Detects and fixes file allocation table errors
WVER	Specifies that disk writes are to be verified

Table 14-3: PC-MOS/386 Specific Commands

PC-MOS/386 provides commands for configuring the system for multitasking, resources allocation, and system security. EXCEPT and ONLY are two examples of useful commands in PC-MOS/386 that limit the action of other commands.

toggled on and off with the Alt-999 sequence.

Users at any terminal can use *ADDTASK* to create tasks and can assign tasks an ID number and a batch file to execute. Each user in a multiuser system has access to the full capability of the system at his/her terminal. The *REMTASK* command terminates a task to which the user currently has exclusive access. Because users can attach to and view other tasks (subject to security limitations), a task cannot be removed if another user is viewing it.

The time slice allocated by default to each task is approximately 1/18 of a second. This can be changed by using the *SLICE* command in CONFIG.SYS during system initialization or by dynamically using the MOS system administrator command (*MOSADM*).

Device drivers for disk caching, RAM disk, emulation of the Lotus/Intel/Microsoft Expanded memory specification (LIM EMS) using 386-page tables, and batch-file language are a few of the DOS 3.3 features that are enhanced with PC-MOS/386. Additional batch-file language features include a full-featured text-output system supporting text colors and attributes, user prompting and input, command buffer manipulation, and task control commands.

PC-MOS's PIPE device driver, which defines character devices for transferring information between tasks, is quite useful. An eight-character device name and, optionally, a buffer size defines the pipe. Any number of pipes can be defined subject to available memory. Tasks write to pipes as they do to other devices; data are retained in the buffer until read by another task.

Drivers for auxiliary tools such as pointing devices can be specified in the system CONFIG.SYS file. *DEVICE* statements for drivers using ports and interrupts (otherwise used by the system's serial device driver) must be placed after *DEVICE=$SERIAL.SYS*.

PC-MOS/386 allows device drivers to be installed and removed at runtime instead of only at boot time, as is true in DOS. Reserved memory, called the System Memory Pool (SMP) is shared by all tasks and contains system resources and device-driver code. As long as space is available in the SMP, new device drivers can be added by any task and become available to all tasks. The SMP size defaults to 64KB, and the amount of memory remaining is reported each time that a new task is added to the system. For environments requiring many device drivers, the *SMPSIZE* statement in the CONFIG.SYS file allows the SMP to be set to any size up to a configuration-dependent maximum of 440KB.

Because remote terminals are supported through device drivers (drivers for 11 different terminal types are provided), the ability to add and remove drivers without rebooting is invaluable. In addition to standard communications support for remote terminals, terminal drivers provide alternative keystroke sequences so that PC-specific keystrokes (such as F1 through F10) can be generated at terminals that use incompatible keyboards.

Compatibility and Performance

No difficulties in graphics or text modes were encountered by running DOS applications under PC-MOS/386. Graphics applications are supported in either CGA or EGA modes at the main console, assuming that the appropriate display adapter is installed; they are supported in CGA mode at remote terminals, such as remote PCs running terminal emulation software. Lotus 1-2-3 release 2.0 could be installed, removed, and run from a key disk even on a 386 running at 16 MHz—a great improvement over DRI's Concurrent DOS 386.

All software tested (the same products tested under Concurrent) ran smoothly. Because PC-MOS/386 is not a windowing system and allows only one task to be visible at a time, its job of display maintenance is relatively uncomplicated. Display modes are properly switched when moving from one task to another.

PC-MOS/386 utilities are a superset of DOS commands: system-monitoring and disk analysis utilities appropriate to the multiuser design of the system. A simple editor, called .ED, runs either as a line editor or in full-screen mode. The debugger, called .DEBUG, is compatible with Microsoft's SYMDEB debugger and has the ability to redirect the debugging session to any console on the system, allowing both application output and debugging to be visible to users simultaneously. Although .DEBUG displays the processor type as 386 and the operating system as a whole requires the 386, the debugger surprisingly does not support 386 instructions or registers.

One of PC-MOS/386's clever features is its use of the 386 to provide complete emulation of IBM's NETBIOS network protocol. The system can treat each task as a physically distinct computer connected to a NETBIOS-compatible network. Applications running in different tasks can share data files and communicate using NETBIOS's peer-to-peer communications.

For software developers who want to provide network support for applications but cannot afford a whole network setup, this feature can be valuable. Network applications can be developed and tested, using a single computer. This is one example of how The Software Link is developing virtual-device support to take advantage of the 386's special hardware features.

Unlike OS/2, PC-MOS/386 provides support for full 32-bit native mode. This feature, along with planned support for MetaWare High C and Professional Pascal 32-bit compilers, will enable the efficient development and operation of very large applications on 386-based computers.

Multiuser Asset

PC-MOS/386 is an excellent choice for small office situations that do not require the power of a minicomputer or a PC network. It is available in single-user, 5-user, and 25-user configurations. With a system administrator to set user and security partitions, the system provides users with a comfortable DOS-compatible environment. For single users, PC-MOS/386 offers a simple but fairly robust multitasking environment to support software development, background communications, or heavy applications use.

Virtual Environment

Announced in September 1987, Microsoft Windows/386 is the newest product reviewed in this chapter and comes closest to exploiting 386 hardware capabilities fully. It provides a 386 virtual machine facility controlled by a Windows 2.0 user interface.

Getting Started

The product is distributed on three 2.1MB diskettes and installed using Microsoft Windows' usual multiple-choice installation program. The copy of Windows/386 used for this review is the version distributed with, and for use on, Compaq PorTable 14-386 and Deskpro 386/20 computers. Microsoft says its generic version will support a number of 386-based computers, including the IBM PS/2 Model 80.

Documentation is nicely illustrated and is a marked improvement over previous Windows documentation. It provides voluminous explanations on how to use the product, but little information on how it works; a seven-page README file comes with version 2.01. The user's guide describes Windows Desktop Applications, Windows Paint, and Windows Write, while a smaller booklet covers Windows/386.

Using Windows/386

Started from the DOS command line, Windows/386 creates a single virtual DOS machine in which Windows 2.0 is run. Windows applications selected from the DOS Executive menu run as they do in a standard Windows session. To run non-Windows applications, however, the 386 control software intervenes. If a Program Information File (.PIF) is available for an application, Windows/386 consults it for information (such as memory requirements and screen usage) about the virtual machine environment in which it should run. If no .PIF is available, Windows/386 makes assumptions about the application's hardware and memory requirements.

It then creates a new virtual DOS machine in which it loads the applications; the environment resembles Windows 1.0's support of non-Windows software. Depending on the program's .PIF file, the application might begin in a small window or run full screen.. The Alt-Enter keystroke switches from full screen to a small window on the Windows 2.0 display surface while the application continues to run. Any number of non-Windows applications can be run in virtual DOS machine windows and are limited only by the amount of available memory because swapping is not supported (Microsoft recommends at least 2 MB of extended memory).

Compatibility and Performance

Windows/386 provides excellent display adapter virtualization. It is the only product described in this chapter that displays text mode, CGA graphics, and EGA graphics applications in windows while all applications are running and actively updating the screen. Adequate EGA virtualization is difficult and certainly the most notable technical achievement of Windows/386.

The product's value, however, lies more in ease of use than technical impressiveness. A user running Windows/386 with an EGA and enhanced color display can use all text and graphics applications without difficulty and without having to provide Windows/386 with extensive information; all windows are automatically mapped to EGA graphics mode and displayed. All application software tested, including EGA, CGA, and text programs (such as Lotus 1-2-3 at 16 MHz), run without problems.

The .PIF file editor provides information needed by Windows/386 to run non-Windows applications. Information required includes program name, minimum and desired memory requirements, and whether graphics support is needed. Desired amount of memory, if available, is allocated to the virtual DOS machine created for the application; if minimum memory is not available, the application cannot be run and Windows/386 displays an error box.

Settings in an application's .PIF also determine whether it starts in full screen or in a window, continues running when not in the foreground, and if other applications are suspended when it is in the foreground.

Windows/386 allows applications requiring a lot of processor resources to use Exclusive mode, in which the foreground application (running either full screen or in a window receiving keyboard input) is given total CPU time so that multitasking is temporarily suspended. For applications requiring little processor time except when used interactively, Windows/386 can set them to suspend automatically when in background. Text editors, for example, can be moved out of Windows/386's time-slicing schedule while in background, freeing more time for other tasks.

Windows/386 provides complete Windows clipboard support for applications, allowing both text and graphics data to be cut and pasted between non-Windows and Windows programs. In addition, an application's execution environment can be changed on the fly through the *Settings...* option, which is added to the System menu of non-Windows applications. *Settings...* dialogue also allows users to terminate a non-Windows application, destroying the virtual DOS machine in which it runs. This feature allows users to clean out the system if software goes astray or hangs up; it first warns users that abnormally terminating a virtual machine can corrupt the system.

Virtual DOS machines supported by Windows/386 are normally isolated from each other. Pop-up programs, such as SideKick, and mouse drivers, such as Microsoft's MOUSE.COM, can be installed in them. When a mouse lies in an application's window, uncertainty could exist about whether it belongs to the application or to Windows/386. However, Windows/386 resolves the issue by giving the mouse only to applications running full-screen. This limitation is minor because display adapter simulation for moving the application's mouse pointer in a window would destroy interactive user mouse control. The DOS SHARE utility lets concurrently executing applications to share and lock disk files; it must run before loading Windows/386.

Windows/386 emulates expanded memory, using the system's extended memory;

other expanded memory managers are not allowed. LIM EMS version 4.0 features are provided. Amount of memory available for expanded memory is set using the eemsize parameter in the WIN.INI file. If eemsize is not set, all available extended memory can be used as expanded memory. One problem with this setup is that an application requesting all available expanded memory could consume the extended memory needed to run other applications.

Windows/386 has a disk-caching program called SMARTDrive, for general system use as well as use with Windows/386. When used with Windows/386, it must be used with extended memory only, If configured in expanded memory, SMARTDrive's internal expanded memory manager conflicts with Windows/386's manager.

Limitations of Windows/386 are most noticeable when running multiple EGA graphics programs, each attempting to program its own 16-color palette. Windows/386 gives each full-screen application the palette it desires. For multiple applications displayed in windows sharing the same screen, it attempts to map color schemes using the EGA display driver's palette. For text-mode applications running in a window, Windows/386 tracks the cursor position so that prompts for user input are always displayed, even if most of the application's display is hidden.

Device virtualization does not come for free, and Windows/386 gives the user control over the balance between multitasking and individual application performance. EGA applications run in windows up to 50 times slower than in full screen; high-speed communications programs might require exclusive use of the CPU to avoid loss of incoming data. Windows/386 can give the entire EGA display to applications running full screen, allowing them to run almost as quickly as they could outside Windows/386. With the Alt-Tab key, users can switch from one full-screen application to another without loss if performance.

Windows/386's virtual machines, though well isolated, bump into each other when they contend for physical devices such as serial and parallel ports. If two non-Windows applications attempt to use the same port, Windows/386 displays a dialogue box explaining the difficulty and asks the user to identify the one to have access to the port. A simulated hardware error is returned to the unselected application to indicate that the device is not present. The user must then terminate that application and retry access only after the first application terminates ownership fo the port. This contention is inevitable because standard DOS applications are not designed to share communications hardware.

Impressive Environment

Microsoft Windows/386 provides a technically impressive and powerful multi-tasking environment and comes closest among the products reviewed to providing a true virtual machine environment. Windows/386 supports existing Windows applications and non-Windows applications cooperatively. Non-Windows applications can be toggled into the foreground to run full screen without the Windows user interface.

Additionally, users can migrate from running multiple DOS applications under Windows/386 to running multiple OS/2 applications under the OS/2 Presentation Manager with no change in user interface, perhaps easing the learning transition to OS/2.

Multitasking Platform

DESQview from Quarterdeck Office Systems has been available since 1985 as a multitasking environment for 8086-based PCs. Running with Quarterdeck's 386 expanded memory manager (QEMM 386) or Compaq's expanded memory manager (CEMM), DESQview 2.01 provides a multitasking virtual machine platform for 386-based computers. DESQview provides complete scheduling and interprocess communications features.

Simple Start-Up

DESQview's installation process is simple and convenient. Because DESQview requires an information file (.DVP) for each application it runs, the installation program searches the hard disk on which DESQview is being installed for familiar applications. DESQview's thorough search even discriminates among various versions of a particular product.

QEMM 386 also installs easily; an installation program automates the process, even though users need only copy the device-driver file QEMM.SYS and modify CONFIG.SYS to include it.

DESQview's documentation is generally good and professional. In tutorial format, it describes how to create .DVP files, start applications, use DESQview's cut-and-paste facilities to transfer text between windows, and use DESQview's LEARN feature to create keyboard macros. It also briefly describes DESQview's application interface for software developers who wish to create DESQview-specific applications. The 30-page appendix on expanded memory usage in standard and 386 systems is perhaps the best available description of that subject. Customer support services and warranties are clearly spelled out.

Using DESQview

Users can start DESQview at any point in a DOS session. A start-up screen is displayed, followed by a window and applications program selection menu. DESQview supports a mouse for menu selection and window manipulation, although cursor key and keyboard mnemonic commands are also provided. As users become familiar with DESQview, they most likely will find that a combination of keyboard menu selections and mouse-based window control provides the easiest operating environment. The use of a mouse is highly recommended.

For newly opened applications, DESQview uses the information—including the application's memory requirements, start-up files, and default directory—that is provided in the .DVP file. The information gives DESQview better control over the application's use of PC hardware.

Applications can have their own color scheme or use the default supplied by DESQview, which attempts to assign distinctive color schemes to windows that will readily distinguish them on the screen. Customized color for applications is a welcome relief to DESQview's default color schemes, which are often garish and hard to read.

Text-mode applications, by default, run in small windows. If a program switches to graphics mode, the window is zoomed to full screen and can later return to a small window. CGA (but not EGA) graphics applications can continue running automatically in small windows, but DESQview's documentation on how to accomplish this is unclear. It states only that the number of text pages of a CGA application running in a small window must be set to 4. Users set the number by using the Advanced Options screen in DESQview's Change-a-Program utility. The number of text pages used is specified on that screen along with information about interrupt vectors used, keyboard incompatibility levels, and other features that will certainly challenge the novice user. Although it is reasonable for DESQview to require users to identify applications using graphics, an easier mechanism is needed.

Compatibility and Performance

Lotus 1-2-3 release 2.0 could not be installed at 16 MHz using DESQview. Therefore, Lotus 1-2-3 must be installed on the hard disk before DESQview is loaded; DESQview can then be installed and Lotus 1-2-3 run in windows using a proloader provided by Quarterdeck. Multiple copies of 1-2-3 can be run (DESQview supports up to nine windows simultaneously) and properly share use of the 80287 math coprocessor for recalculations.

In general, DESQview runs all DOS applications tested when their .DVP files are set properly. EGA applications run when zoomed to full screen, but execution is suspended when switched back into small window because DESQview currently does not virtualize EGA graphics operations.

The .DVP files provide considerable application control, and DESQview comes with a large set of default files. Because DESQview can swap programs from memory to expanded memory or to disk, control features are provided to disable swapping for realtime applications (such as communications programs that might lose input characters if swapped out of memory when the characters arrive). A properly set .DVP file can give DESQview enough information to tailor an application's requirements to obtain optimum performance and compatibility.

QEMM 386, priced separately from DESQview, provides expanded memory for DESQview and other applications. Version 4.0 is an expanded-memory driver that simulates expanded memory using extended memory. The driver is compatible with LIM EMS 4.0.

DESQview provides a built-in application program interface (API) compatible with the IBM TopView 1.1 API. Programs written using DESQview's API manipulate windows and subwindows, spawn subtasks, and communicate with other programs and subtasks.

DESQview Companions 1, also separately priced, provides calculator, datebook, notepad, and communications utilities. The calculator and notepad operate on information obtained from windows using DESQview's Mark-and-Transfer feature.

DESQview can display graphics and text windows on the screen simultaneously. When the active window is in graphics mode and the user switches to a text-mode window, text is displayed in graphics mode. If a switch is made between incompatible video modes, DESQview covers the original window with a "graphics curtain" made of dither-pattern characters.

EGA Version on the Way

For character-based and CGA applications, DESQview provides a pleasing user environment and a convenient, compatible multitasking platform. Because the EGA is rapidly becoming the entry-level graphics device, support for windowed EGA graphics is planned for DESQview/386.

That version of DESQview also promises to support 32-bit protected-mode applications when used with Phar Lap Software's 386/DOS-Extender. This will allow applications that use the 386/DOS-Extender (such as Borland's Paradox 386) to run simultaneously with DOS applications.

For users reluctant to move to an total unfamiliar operating system, DESQview offers an inexpensive, compatible solution with the ability to exploit the 32-bit capabilities of the 386.

Multiple Applications Now

The four products reviewed here—Concurrent DOS 386, PC-MOS/386, Windows/386, and DESQview 2.01—admirably provide features not available under DOS. They do so in an environment that is familiar to DOS users (sometimes using helpful graphics interfaces), and they permit multitasking among applications. As with OS/2, internal multitasking within applications requires that the application be specifically designed to use interfaces provided by the product.

One advantage of OS/2 is that is runs on both 286- and 386-based machines, while some of these alternative products do not. Additionally, a large number of developers already have announced future products for the OS/2 multitasking environment, but their release is months away.

On the other hand, thousands of DOS applications, which users have invested heavily in, are available now. Unlike OS/2, Concurrent DOS 386, PC-MOS/386, Windows/386, and DESQview 2.01 can run multiple DOS applications at the same time. For users who need to run multiple applications now and who have the resources to purchase 386 hardware, these products provide a means of meeting that need without prematurely parting from DOS.

Virtual Machines on the 80386

The 386 processor supports multiple virtual 8086 machines for running applications in a multitasking environment as if each application were running on its own 8086 machine. In such an environment, applications are isolated and protected from each other through management of virtual memory and virtual devices. The 386, when operated in virtual 8086 mode by control software (operating systems/applications managers), can run multiple DOS-compatible applications.

Applications running on the 386 in virtual 8086 mode address memory as if they were in real mode; however, addresses are translated into physical addresses using the 386's memory paging mechanism. This facility allows the 1MB address space of each virtual 8086 task to be mapped to a different portion of the physical memory available. Where a precise simulation of DOS operation is desired, each application can be provided with is own RAM image of the operating system as it would expect to find it on a single-tasking PC.

Control software supervises access to all system devices. Depending on the characteristics and operating behavior of the device, sharing or serialization can be provided. Device sharing involves the use of a single device and management of virtual devices (software-created simulations or hardware devices) that might or might not map onto a device physically present in the system.

Device serialization, whereby a device is dedicated as long as required—first to one task and then another, is usually employed with sequential access devices such as tape drives, printers, and serial ports.

Shared use of a single device is by far simpler and more common than serialization; it is an approach well suited to hardware, including keyboards and pointing devices. Such devices are considered to be wholly dedicated to the application currently running under the control software and do not need to provide services for other idle applications.

Each virtual device is a portion of the control software's code activated by memory or I/O accesses to addresses associated with the physical device. Control software traps those accesses and modifies the state of the simulated device to reflect the new activity. The 386 provides complete hardware support for such device virtualization, but the software required to implement it can be the most expensive and difficult part, because all the hardware quirks must be adequately duplicated by the software.

The 386 supports device virtualization using its privileged instruction and I/O permission map features. The 8086 instructions *CLI*, *STI*, *LOCK*, *PUSHF*, *POPF*, *INT*, and *IRET* are privileged on the 386 while running in virtual 8086 mode. Because these instructions can modify flags affecting the global state of the processor, they are always trapped by the processor. Control software can allow them to continue as normal, but more likely their operation will be simulated.

I/O operations are governed by the I/O permission bitmap, which the 386 maintains for each task state segment (TSS). This TSS component allows the trapping of the *IN*, *INS*, *OUT*, and *OUTS* instructions on an address-by-address basis. Because hardware devices are usually controlled by I/O accesses, the trapping of I/O reads and writes provides control software with information needed to determine the proper behavior of the simulated device. Because each task has its own bitmap, it is possible for different virtual machines to have different devices simulated.

The most powerful and visible device to virtualize is the display. Each application can write to what it believes to be the dedicated display adapter while the control software mediates access between virtual devices and the physical display itself. Access to the display can be toggled among the virtual displays, each of which is shown full screen when selected by the user, or it can be shared among virtual displays in a windowing environment.

Although the windowing environment displays all applications at the same time, it suffers because each application works in a virtual display at all times and experiences the performance degradation associated with such virtualization. The toggled display can, when an application is brought to the screen, substitute the physical device for the virtual device used by that application. While the application is on-screen, it continues to run at the same speed it would in a normal single-tasking environment. Because performance degradation is experienced only by applications not visible, users are not so aware of the slowness of the virtual display.

Devices such as the EGA present an extremely complex and interrelated set of interfaces. Data displayed depend on the contents of the Color Compare, Read Mode, Map Enable, and other EGA hardware registers (some of which cannot be read by the CPU) as well as the contents of the video buffer. As a result, software simulation of an EGA is a complex process that must be shifted into a new state at every control register access. As in virtual memory support, powerful device virtualization is a difficult and expensive task and should be looked for as a hallmark of sophisticated 386 control programs.

15
Microsoft Windows/386 Creating a Virtual Machine Environment *

_____Ray Duncan_____

The past year has seen the emergence of a new class of personal computers, based on the IBM® PC AT® architecture but incorporating an Intel 80386 microprocessor with a 32-bit memory path for increased performance. The pioneer in this category was the Compaq® Deskpro 386™, which has since been joined by the IBM PS/2™ Model 80, as well as a score of machines from other clone vendors. Until now, the primary benefit associated with these machines has been their formidable speed. However, 32-bit operating systems and programming tools for the 80386 are still in the development stage, while 32-bit applications software waits in the wings until the tools stabilize.

Microsoft Corp.'s new product, Windows/386, unmasks the larger potential of 80386 machines while protecting the user's investment in MS-DOS®-compatible hardware and software. The key features of Windows/386 are:

- a graphical user interface compatible with Windows 2.0 and the OS/2 Presentation Manager

- true preemptive multitasking of MS-DOS applications, each in a private 640Kb memory space

- applications that run under Windows/386 receive much more memory than they would under Windows 2.0

- the ability to run MS-DOS applications in overlapping windows, even so-called "ill-behaved" applications that do not rely on MS- DOS or the ROM BIOS for screen output

- exchange of screen data between both standard MS-DOS and Windows

---

* © Microsoft Corporation, _Microsoft Systems Journal_, September, 1987

applications

- emulation of the Lotus/Intel/Microsoft Expanded Memory Specification version 4.0

Windows/386 requires either an 80386-based PC AT-compatible or an AT&T® 6300 computer, an EGA, VGA, or CGA monitor, at least 1 Mb of RAM (2Mb are recommended), and a fixed disk. The 80287 or 80387 numeric coprocessors are also supported.

An Intel Retrospective

Nearly all of the capabilities of Windows/386 depend on a feature of the 80386 called virtual 86 mode. To fully appreciate this particular facet of the 80386, it is necessary to digress for a moment and review the characteristics of the 80386's ancestors, the Intel 8086/88 and 80286 microprocessors. Each successive generation of Intel processors has supported the software that was written for its predecessors by means of "execution modes," and virtual 86 mode is the logical culmination of this approach to software compatibility.

The first Intel 16-bit processors, the 8086 and 8088 (announced in 1978 and 1979 respectively), can address a maximum of 1 Mb of memory. When memory is referenced, the contents of one of the four segment registers is shifted left four bits and combined with a 16-bit offset to form a 20-bit physical address; the segment registers simply act as base pointers. The 8086 and 8088 have no provision for memory protection, virtual memory, or privilege levels; any program can access any location in memory or any I/O device without restriction.

The Intel 80286 (first shipped in 1982) represents a major increase in speed and capability over the 8086/88. It can run in either of two modes: real or protected. In real mode, the 80286 acts like a fast 8086 with a few additional machine instructions. It can run virtually all 8086/88 software and is limited to 1Mb of memory.

In protected mode, the 80286's mapping of addresses is altered to add a level of indirection. The value in a segment register is a selector, which is an index to an entry in a descriptor table that contains the base address and length of a physical memory segment, segment attributes (executable, read-only, or read- write), and privilege information. Each time a program references memory, the hardware accesses the associated descriptor to generate the physical address and simultaneously checks to make sure that the memory access is valid.

COMPARISON OF CURRENT AND FUTURE WINDOWS VERSIONS			
	Microsoft Windows 1.03 & 1.04	Microsoft Windows 2.0	Windows 386	MS OS/2 Presentation Manager
Presentation Spaces	Tiled	Overlapped	Overlapped	Overlapped
More Consistent User and Keyboard Interface	–	Yes	Yes	Yes
Processor Environments	8088	8088	–	–
	8086	8086	–	–
	286	286	–	286
	386	386	386	386
Large Memory Support	–	EMS/EEMS	EMS/EEMS	16Mb
Multitasking	Nonpreemptive	Nonpreemptive	Fully Preemptive	Fully Preemptive
Enhanced Display	-	Yes	Yes	Yes
Runs Existing Windows(1.03) Application	Yes	Yes	Yes	No
Graphics API	GDI	GDI	GDI	GPI
Multiple Document Interface	–	Yes	Yes	Yes
Device Drivers	–	Enhanced	Enhanced	New Model
Old Application Support	–	Improved	Improved	Improved
Integral Part of OS	–	–	–	Yes
Protected-Mode Applications Execution	–	–	Yes	Yes
New Development API	–	–	–	Yes
New User "Shell" and Keyboard Interface	–	–	–	Yes
Virtual 86 Mode	–	–	Yes	–

This method of protected-mode address generation allows the 80286 to support memory protection and virtual memory management within a physical address space of 16Mb and a virtual address space of 1Gb. Four levels of privilege are also provided, allowing the operating system to be protected from applications programs and those programs from each other.

When the Intel 80286 was designed, the dominant software base consisted of CP/M® applications such as WordStar® and dBASE II®. At the time the 80286 was released, the IBM PC was just a few months old. Hence Intel engineers had no way of foreseeing the incredible success of the IBM PC and its compatibles, or the eventual need of an enormous user base to make a smooth transition from real-mode (8086/88) to protected-mode (80286) environments. Although the 80286 was designed to start up in real mode for compatibility with 8086 software, and although machine instructions were included to switch from real mode to protected mode, no mechanism was built into the chip to allow a return from protected mode to real mode under operating system control without halting the processor.

This single omission proved to be a hideous technical problem during the development of the Microsoft OS/2, since one of the overriding design goals for the new operating system was to allow "old" (real-mode) applications to run alongside "new" (protected- mode) applications. Although experimentation and painstaking optimization eventually led to an acceptable solution for the necessary mode switching, another drawback remains: the protected-mode operating system cannot be shielded against bad behavior on the part of a real-mode program. By the very nature of real mode, such a program has a free hand with the hardware and can easily crash the machine.

The Four Modes

The Intel 80386 (introduced in 1985) is a true 32-bit processor that supports a 4Gb physical address space and a 64Tb virtual address space. To ensure compatibility with previous processors and to solve the problems of support for real-mode applications that were encountered with the 80286, the 80386 has no less than four different execution modes. The first is the familiar real mode, wherein the 80386 functions as a fast 8086/88-compatible processor with some bonus opcodes. Like the 80286, the 80386 always powers up in real mode and can therefore run any existing 8086 operating systems and software.

Four Modes of the INTEL 80386 Microprocessor	
Real Mode	Functions as a very fast 8086/88-compatible processor.
Protected Mode (16-bit)	Functions in protected mode as an enhanced 286 processor.
Protected Mode (32-bit, native mode)	Functions in protected using full 32-bit instructions, registers, and stacks.
Virtual 86 Mode	Runs multiple, protected-mode, virtual 8086 machines, each with its own 1Mb of memory space.

In protected mode, the 80386 can take on two different personalities. It can execute a logical superset of the 80286 protected-mode instructions and run 16-bit programs, or it can run in its native mode, which offers 32-bit instructions, registers, and stacks, and allows individual memory segments as large as 4Gb. In either case, the 80386 translates selectors and the offsets to linear addresses using descriptor tables in much the same manner as the 80286. However, an additional level of address translation--supported in hardware by page tables--allows much greater flexibility in mapping the linear addresses onto physical memory.

Unlike the 80286, the 80386 allows the operating system to switch smoothly and quickly back from protected mode to real mode when necessary. But it is unlikely that this capability will find much use because of the 80386's fourth operating mode: virtual 86 mode.

Device Virtualization

A protected-mode 80386 operating system can create special memory segments-- up to 1 Mb in size--that have a remarkable characteristic: programs that run within these segments execute as though they were running on an 8086/88 in real mode. Each such segment is called a virtual 8086 machine, and each has its own address space, I/O port space, and interrupt vector table. Multiple virtual machines can be running simultaneously, each under the illusion that it is in complete control of the computer.

The crucial difference between real mode and virtual 86 mode is that memory protection, virtual memory, and privilege-checking mechanisms are still in effect when a virtual machine is running. Thus, a program executing in a virtual 8086 machine cannot interfere with the operating system or damage other processes. If the program reads or writes memory addresses that have not been mapped into its virtual machine, or if it manipulates I/O ports to which it has not been allowed access, an exception (hardware interrupt) is generated, and the operating system regains control.

The operating system's exception handler can choose to carry out the operation on behalf of the program running in the virtual machine, possibly substituting other port or memory addresses; it is also able to arbitrate requests from multiple virtual machines directed at the same I/O port or memory address. This process of intercepting I/O operations, where, for example, the operating system creates the illusion of a separate disk controller or video controller for each virtual machine while only one physical device is present in the system, is called device virtualization.

A program that runs in the 80386's native 32-bit protected mode and oversees a set of virtual machines is called a 386 control program, or virtual machine monitor. Windows/386 is such a virtual machine monitor; it also provides complete device virtualization for the PC's disk controller, video adapter, keyboard, mouse, timer chip and 8259 programmable interrupt controllers.

The User Interface

At first glance, the user interface of Windows/386 appears identical to that of Windows Version 2.0: it has the same MS-DOS Executive window, pull-down menus, "hot keys," and utilities (Cardfile, Terminal, and the like). A program is launched by selecting its executable file, its PIF file, or one of its data files with the arrow keys or by double-clicking with the mouse, just like under Windows. An open window can be brought to the foreground with Alt-Tab or Alt-Esc or by clicking on the window with the mouse; also, a window may be resized or moved by clicking and dragging its borders.

The first inkling that something different is going on comes when a standard application (that is, an MS-DOS application that is not written specifically for Windows) is started. Under Windows 2.0, only those relatively rare, "well-behaved" MS-DOS programs that perform all of their input and output through standard MS-DOS calls, strictly observe the system's memory management conventions, and avoid all direct access to hardware can run in a window. "Ill-behaved" programs that access the hardware directly for performance reasons--a category that includes nearly every popular MS-DOS application--must run full-screen: Windows 2.0 simply gets out of the way until such programs terminate, and its multitasking comes to a screeching halt.

A standard application under Windows/386 initially comes up full- screen just as it does under Windows 2.0. But if the user presses Alt-Enter, the program is suddenly running in an overlapping graphics-mode window right alongside the true Windows application. The user can use the mouse or the cursor keys to select and copy data from a window containing a standard application to any other window and can resize, move, or even "iconize" such a window. Furthermore, the user can toggle between windowed and full-screen mode with Alt-Enter at any time. When an application is full-screen, Windows/386 can place it into a text-display mode to allow faster displays, and the application's intrinsic mouse support works as though it were running under MS- DOS alone.

Windows/386 associates a drop-down control menu, activated with the keycode Alt-Space, with each standard application that can be used to affect its window size, position, and behavior. The Settings dialog box , which is reached through the control menu, allows the user to suspend or resume a standard application, specify whether it should run full-screen or in a window, and control its multitasking behavior. The initial settings for a program can also be determined by creating a PIF file for it.

There are three multitasking options available for a standard application: foreground, background, and exclusive. When foreground is chosen, the application runs only when it is displayed full-screen or when its window has been selected, but other applications are allowed to run in the background at the same time. The background option means that the application will continue to run even when some other application is selected (of course, this is not useful for word processors and other programs that have nothing to do unless they are receiving keyboard input). When the exclusive option is picked, the application runs only when it is in the foreground, but while it is active it receives all of the CPU time and no other applications are allowed to run at all. Hence the exclusive option permits the application to perform as if it were in a single-tasking MS-DOS environment.

A little experimentation leads to an additional pleasant surprise: there seems to be much more RAM left for a standard application than is usual under Windows. In fact, if COMMAND.COM and then CHKDSK are run in a window, approximately 580Kb is seen to be available--as though Windows weren't present at all. And when multiple standard applications are launched, each runs in a separate memory space as large as 640Kb, until the physical memory of the system is exhausted. As a fringe benefit, devotees of RAM-resident applications

(TSRs) can find relief from the phenomenon of "RAM cram" by starting multiple copies of COMMAND.COM to establish several MS-DOS sessions, and loading a different selection of TSRs into each session. This is the magic of the 80386's virtual 86 mode in action.

How Windows/386 Works

The Windows/386 system actually consists of three separate, mutually interdependent elements. The first is a regulation copy of MS-DOS or PC-DOS, Version 3.0 or later. The second is a copy of Windows 2.0 which is included in the Windows/386 product. The third is the core of the Windows/386 product, the Virtual DOS Machine Manager (VDMM).

The MS-DOS component supplies the routine file, time, and date, as well as memory allocations services to the application programs running in each virtual machine; the MS-DOS SHARE.EXE module can optionally be loaded for networklike file locking and sharing support if multiple applications will be accessing the same files. Windows 2.0 provides the graphical user interface and pointer device support. The VDMM runs in the 80386's native 32-bit protected mode and oversees the multitasking and protected-memory aspects of the system's operation. The VDMM also takes advantage of the 80386's paging capability to supply expanded (Lotus/Intel/Microsoft EMS) memory to applications that require it. The EMS services furnished by Windows/386 are compatible with the recently announced EMS 4.0 specification and do not require loading of any special driver.

Windows/386 is started on a system that has already been booted up under MS-DOS or PC-DOS in the usual manner. When Windows/386 gains control, it loads the Virtual DOS Machine Manager into extended memory (the memory above the 1 Mb boundary), creates an initial virtual machine (referred to as VM1), maps the existing copy of MS-DOS into it using the 80386's page tables, and then loads Windows 2.0 on top of MS-DOS in the first virtual machine. Control is then passed to Windows 2.0, which reads its configuration file (WIN.INI) and presents the familiar MS-DOS Executive to the user.

Tru Windows applications, such as Cardfile and Terminal, run together in the virtual machine containing Windows itself (VM1). Windows presents such programs with exactly the same applications program interface as in real mode, and multiple Windows applications running concurrently are scheduled for execution by the internal Windows multitasker-that is, nonpreemptively. Just as in real mode, the Windows kernel can use expanded memory pages to swap the code and data segments belonging to Windows applications, so that the number of Windows applications that can be loaded simultaneously is not limited by the 640Kb address space.

When a standard application is started, the VDMM creates a new virtual machine and maps the image of MS-DOS, the ROM BIOS data area, and other vital structures into it using the 80386 page tables, and then loads the application into the virtual machine (see Figures 15-1 and 15-2). If the application does not have a PIF file, the size of the new virtual machine is under the control of the windowmemsize= entry in the WIN.INI file and defaults to 640Kb. If a PIF file exists for the program, the size of the new virtual machine depends on the Kb required and Kb desired fields in the PIF, and on the amount of physical memory actually available (there is no demand paging in Windows/386 as in OS/2).

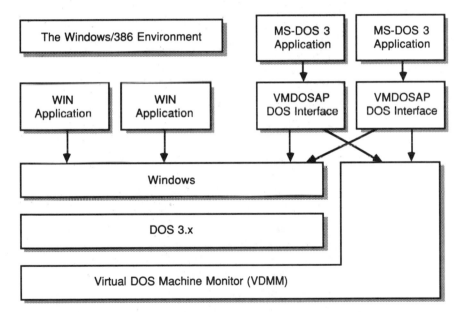

Figure 15-1: This diagram shows the relation between VDMM, MS-DOS, Windows, the VMDOSAP module, and standard applications.

While initializing a new virtual machine, the VDMM also creates a corresponding instance of a special application called VMDOSAP in VMI (multiple instances share the same code segment, so the overhead in the Windows VM for each additional standard application VM is minimal). VMDOSAP is analogous to the WINOLDAP module of realmode Windows; when the standard application is running in a window instead of full-screen, VMDOSAP is responsible for any necessary translation and clipping of its output for the window shape, size, and graphics-display mode. It also translates input on behalf of the application when necessary (for example, when data is being pasted from another window). The operation of VMDOSAP is completely transparent to the application, and VMDOSAP does not occupy any memory space within the application's virtual machine.

The final step in initializing the new virtual machine is to allocate a "shadow" video buffer for the application and select the application's initial display and multitasking status based on the contents of its PIF file. The shadow video buffer lies outside the VM's address space and holds a copy of the application's virtual screen; it is used to restore the display when the application is brought to the foreground and allows scrolling when the application is running in a window.

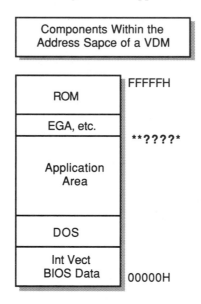

Figure 15-2: Memory occupied by the DOS and other fixed items, such as the ROM BIOS, is shared between all virtual machines. Thus the system consumes physical memory sufficient for only one copy of each of these items and shares this memory between all the virtual machines using the memory management capabilities of the 386.

If no PIF file exists for the program, it begins execution with a full-screen display and with its multitasking option set to "foreground"--that is, the application is suspended when it is in the background.

The complete isolation of VMDOSAP from the application, and of standard applications from each other, is made possible by Windows/386's virtualization of the system's input and output devices, as well as by its control over each virtual machine's interrupt vector table and I/O port address space. When an application executes a software interrupt (to invoke an MS-DOS or ROM BIOS service), reads from or writes to an I/O port, or access a memory address that lies outside its virtual machine space, an exception is generated that is fielded by the VDMM.

The VDMM disposes of the exception by examining the machine instruction that provoked it and the contents of the CPU registers. For example, requests for input and output can be funnelled to VMDOSAP, while calls for file system services revert to the virtual machine's image of MS-DOS for processing. An application that accesses the hardware to select a video mode not supported by Windows/386 is not terminated, but is forced to run full-screen.

Windows/386 Multitasking

The Windows/386 multitasking scheduler uses the standard PC AT 18.2-Hz timer tick. Its allocation of CPU cycles across multiple virtual machines is determined by the multitasking setting on each application's control menu or from its PIF file. In the simplest case, where each active program has the "background" option selected, the currently selected application gets two-thirds of the CPU cycles, and the remaining one-third are divided among the other virtual machines. Applications that hook the ROM BIOS timer tick interrupt vector (Interrupt 1CH) receive a proportionate number of timer interrupts.

There are also two extreme cases of multitasking worth mentioning. The first is when a standard application that runs under the exclusive option is selected. Such an application receives all the CPU cycles, and all other virtual machines are suspended. The other is encountered when no standard applications are running and only the Windows VM is active. In this case the internal Windows scheduler apportions the CPU cycles between various Windows applications, and the VDMM plays no multitasking role at all.

Many Machines, One DOS

One of the most interesting aspects of Windows/386 is its relationship to MS-DOS. The 80386's paging tables allow a single physical instance of MS-DOS to be mapped into each virtual machine's address space at the same apparent address.

Windows/386 uses internal knowledge of MS-DOS and Windows to maintain the integrity of the file system and to prevent different applications from executing concurrently within MS-DOS's critical regions. It also maintains a copy of the Windows and MS-DOS control structures (such as the MS-DOS system file table and the ROM BIOS video driver data area) for each virtual machine, and swaps these in and out of the MS-DOS image to supply the proper context for the application that is running. These tables and structures are referred to as the MS-DOS kernel instance data.

Since imply copying the kernel instance data back and forth on every timer tick would burn up a significant number of CPU cycles, and since applications may execute for prolonged periods (several context switches) without referencing MS-DOS or the ROM BIOS, the VDMM uses an interesting trick to reduce the multitasking overhead. Before a program is given control at the beginning of its time slice, the memory pages in its virtual machine that contain MS-DOS instance data, the interrupt vector table, and the ROM BIOS data area are marked "not present" in the CPU's page table. Only a few pages within the MS-DOS that contain instance data are marked "not present" and cause page faults. Each page is demanded independently of the others. This way many access to DOS cause no context switching overboard at all, and when an instance switch is required, its overhead is as small as possible.

If the program attempts to access these pages (for example, by inspecting the current cursor location in the ROM BIOS data area or executing an Interrupt 21H), a page fault is generated that suspends the program and transfers control to the VDMM's interrupt handler. The VDMM handles the fault for that page by moving in the MS-DOS kernel instance data, marking the MS-DOS memory page as "present" in the page table to prevent further faults during the same time slice, and restarting the instruction that caused the fault. On the other hand, if the program runs to the end of its time slice without referencing instance memory, no harm has occurred, and the overhead of moving the data needlessly has been avoided.

Communications

The techniques used in Windows/386 to virtualize the video controller and asynchronous communications controller are also particularly interesting. Since direct hardware access to these devices by standard applications for performance reasons is common, Windows/386 must stay out of the way as much as possible. This ensures that the application's throughput will not be impaired, and that other programs will not be disrupted while still providing for preemptive multitasking.

As mentioned earlier, each virtual machine is allocated a "shadow" video buffer that is used to save a copy of its complete screen image when the application is running in a window or in the background. The buffer is located in extended memory, outside the virtual machine's 1Mb address space, and may range in size from 16Kb to 256Kb depending on the display mode selected by the program.

When an application is running in the background or in a window, the VDMM uses the 80386's page tables to map the virtual machine's video refresh buffer addresses (segment A000H, B000H, OR B800H) onto the shadow buffer. The application can modify what it perceives to be the video buffer at will (see Figure 15-3), but the physical screen is not directly affected. At intervals, the VDMM checks the "dirty bits" in the page table-which are set by the hardware when an address within the page is written to--to determine if the application has modified it's video buffer. If a write is detected, the buffer is compared against an earlier copy. The changes are sent to VMDOSAP, which renders them into an appropriate pattern of pixels and displays them in the visible portion of the application's window.

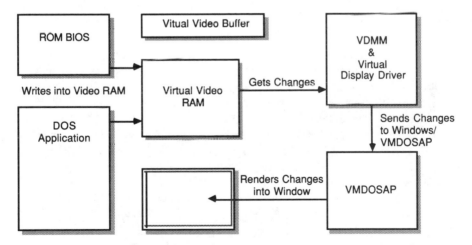

Figure 15-3: This diagram shows how a display adapter is virtualized.

When an application is running full-screen, the virtual addresses of the video refresh buffer within its virtual machine are mapped onto the physical memory belonging to the video controller, and the shadow buffer is not used as an intermediary. Thus, the program's control of the video display is direct, just as if it were running in real mode and there is no speed degradation. When the user switches away from the full screen application, the VDMM simply copies the video controller's physical buffer to the shadow buffer)the 80386's double-word string move instruction, which transfers 32 bits at a time, is used to advantage here) before restoring the screen image of the Windows/386 desktop or the next full-screen application to be selected.

Applications that run in certain EGA graphics modes receive special treatment. The virtual machine's video buffer addresses are mapped onto the second 128Kb of the EGA controller's physical refresh buffer. This lets the application use all of the EGA features without the overhead of emulation, conserves system memory, and allows a rapid switch to full-screen operation. (Instead of copying the shadow buffer to the physical buffer, the VDMM selects the second graphics page as the active display.)

In contrast to the video controller, the asynchronous communications controller, serial port, is fully virtualized at all times. The VDMM always handles all communications interrupts and input or output operations, and maintains an internal queue of serial port data and status information. Even the initialization of the serial port (baud rate, word length, parity, and number of stop bits) is virtualized, and this information is maintained separately for each virtual machine.

An application signals its intention to use the communications controller by attempting to read or write one of the controller by attempting to read or write one of the controller's data ports, change its interrupt mask bit on the 8259 Programmable Interrupt Controller, or capture its interrupt vector. Any of these operations will generate an exception that is processed by the VDMM. If the serial port is not in use by another program, the VDMM assigns "ownership" of the virtualized controller to the program that caused the exception; otherwise, a dialog box is displayed and the user is allowed to decide which program will retain access to the device.

Once a program establishes ownership of the communications controller, it can perform input and output operations, and service communications interrupts in a normal manner from its point of view. In actuality, the interrupts and I/O operations are simulated by the VDMM, which transfers data between the virtual machine and its internal queue. In this fashion, the operation of the physical device, which is asynchronous and can generate an interrupt at any time, is decoupled from the virtual 86 machine-which can only execute during its time slice.

Portents for the Future

In summary, Windows/386 exploits the 80386's unique capabilities to furnish preemptive multitasking, a windowing user interface, data exchange between any two applications, and efficient use of large amounts of RAM in conjunction with existing MS-DOS and Windows applications. In doing so, it overcomes the two most common objections to real-mode Windows: the latter's inability to coexist with popular ill-behaved programs such as Lotus 1-2-3 or Microsoft Word, and its hunger for memory. In addition, although Microsoft bills Windows/386 as an interim product, it has some interesting implications-both short-term and long-term.

In the near future, until protected-mode applications appear for OS/2 that fully exploit its virtual memory management, multitasking, and interprocess communications facilities, Windows/386 offers more to 80386-based PC owners than does OS/2. Windows/386 allows multiple MS-DOS applications to run concurrently, while OS/2 supports only one real-mode application at a time. In addition, the Windows/386 memory overhead in each virtual machine is typically 80 to 100Kb less than the OS/2 overhead in the DOS 3 x Box. Finally, since Windows/386 uses the "real" MS-DOS as a substrate--unlike OS/2, which in effect emulates MS-DOS--Windows/386 is compatible with a broader range of existing applications than is OS/2.

Taking the longer view, the availability of a true 32-bit version of OS/2 and the Presentation Manager for the 80386 will probably threaten Windows/386's market niche. However, Windows/386 has an important role to play here too. It serves as a technology testbed for memory management, multitasking, device virtualization, and MS-DOS virtual-machine techniques that can eventually be absorbed into its successor--a system that will run multiple MS-DOS applications, 16-bit 80286 protected mode applications, and 32 bit 80386 protected-mode applications simultaneously.

16
Choosing an Operating System[*]

_____ *Ed McNierney*_____

Five or six years ago, the combination of a PC and Microsoft DOS was considered the epitome of microcomputing power. Today, however, developers and end users find the single-task, single-user environment of DOS restrictive, largely because of the 640KB memory limitation and inability to run more than one application at a time. IBM and Microsoft's new operating system, OS/2, has been heralded as a solution to these problems, but it is not the only answer.

The excitement stirred by OS/2 likely will give users and developers the momentum needed to break away from DOS, but they should realize that OS/2 might not be the best choice for their specific needs. Alternative products are available, and informed decision makers will want to examine them before choosing a direction. These products and their features are summarized in tables 16-1 and 16-2.

The Range of Features

When assessing alternative systems to DOS and OS/2, users and developers must consider what combination of features best provides them with the functionality they seek. Operating system features that are most sought today are application availability, multitasking, large address space, multiuser support, realtime capacity, files larger than 32 MB, and graphics and communications support systems.

Application Availability

What applications an operating system can run is of prime importance to a user. As alternatives to OS/2, systems such as UNIX or QNX can be worthwhile; a reasonable number of applications are available for such systems, especially in the UNIX environment. DOS compatibility is an important issue facing users and developers who want to run existing DOS applications alongside their new applications on an enhanced operating system without incurring the time and expense required in conversion. For those users whose current investment in DOS applications is considerable, an incompatible operating system might be out of the question.

For this reason, many operating environments allow DOS- executable files to be run without modification. Such compatibility is usually found in multitasking systems that allow one or more DOS tasks to run concurrently with native-mode software. In these systems, a subenvironment is created that looks and acts like DOS. The effectiveness of this subenvironment to run DOS applications varies with the implementation. Some environments do not run ill-behaved programs that write directly to the hardware or that use undocumented Microsoft DOS (MS-DOS) system calls. The best test of compatibility is for the software developer or user to run desired applications and confirm they execute as expected.

Both OS/2 and Microport's Merge 286 allow one DOS application to run at a time. In OS/2, the DOS task executes only when it is in the foreground. When the DOS task is moved to the background—when control of the screen and keyboard is given to an OS/2 task—the DOS task is suspended. Under Merge 286, the DOS application is treated as a separate task and can run in the foreground concurrently with UNIX System V tasks. Similarly, under Quantum's QDOS II, a DOS application runs as a task under QNX.

Multitasking

Multitasking is a requirement of all viable modern operating systems; it is a feature of all operating systems described in this chapter, including OS/2. Multitasking takes two forms: intraprocess (or internal), and interprocess (or external). With internal multitasking, programs are composed of multiple tasks executing independently. These programs must be written to the application program interface (API) of the operating system. Normally, the operating system provides system calls for spawning and killing tasks, and for communications among tasks to synchronize their execution, to coordinate control of resources, or to share common data.

In operating systems that support internal multitasking, support for external multitasking flows naturally. The API of the operating system usually allows one program to spawn another program and either suspend execution until the child program completes or continue executing in parallel with the child program. Messages and data can be sent between programs and execution can be synchronized through interprocess communications such as semaphores, pipes, shared memory, queues, and signals.

Table 16-1: Alternative Operating Systems

	OS/2		UNIX 286		UNIX 386	
	Base	DOS Env.	Base	Merge 286	Base	Merge 386
Multitasking support	•		•		•	
Multiuser support	o		•		•	
Task greater than 640KB	•		•		•	
Large linear addresses	o		o		•	
Runs DOS applications						
Single	o	•	o	•	o	•
Multiple	o		o		o	•
Requires 80286	•		•		o	
Requires 80386	o		o		•	

Table 16-1 (continued)

	QNX		CONCURRENT	PC-MOS/
	Base	QDOS2	DOS 386	386
Multitasking support	•		•	•
Multiuser support	•		•	•
†ask greater than 640KB	•		•ᵃ	•ᵃ
Large linear addresses	o		o	o
Runs DOS applications				
Single	o	•	•	•
Multiple	o		•	•
Requires 80286	o		o	o
Requires 80386	o		•	•

• = Yes   o = No

ᵃ Using expanded memory

Some operating environments, such as Windows 386 and DESQview, support external multitasking of existing DOS applications, sometimes referred to as "old apps." These operating environments offer users the ability to run several DOS applications now, rather than wait for applications developers to convert their applications to a new operating system's API. Execution of such programs is controlled by the user who starts multiple applications through the user interface. Although these programs run concurrently with other programs, they cannot communicate or coordinate resources unless they are modified to use the API of the operating environment. Normally, data can be passed manually from one application to another through the clip-board; the user marks data that are outputted from one application and pastes them into the input stream of another application.

Large Address Space

It is becoming increasingly difficult to cram all the features that users demand into DOS's memory limit of 640KB. DOS itself grows larger with each new release, plus many users load up memory with their favorite terminate-and-stay resident (TSR) utilities. Developers are forced to resort to extensive overlay schemes in order to add features while limiting the size of their programs.

Expanded memory delivers some relief, especially for handling large data structures like spreadsheets. The Enhanced Expanded Memory Specification and the Expanded Memory Specification version 4.0 make it possible to execute code in expanded memory. This bank-switching of memory is similar to using overlays yet without the performance penalty of loading overlay code from the disk.

Neither of these solutions allows the developer to exploit the address spaces of the 80286 or the 80386. OS/2 gives the developer access to the 286's 16 MB real address space and 1GB virtual address space. So-called DOS extenders (Phar Lap's 386/DOS-Extender and AI Architect's OS/286 and OS/386) give the developer access, under DOS, to the full real and virtual address spaces of the 286 and 386. Using 32-bit addressing on a 386, developers have access to 4GB of real address space and 64TB of virtual address space.

Multiuser Support

Costs of upgrading to a 286- or 386-based operating system can sometimes be offset if the system selected supports more than one user through serial-port-connected terminals. Because PC- compatible terminals cost only a few hundred dollars, a 386-based PC with four terminals can provide a less expensive system than five 8086-based PCs. The major disadvantage of serial terminals in a multiuser system is that they rarely support graphics applications; as graphics applications and related user interfaces become more popular, the use of terminals become less desirable.

Multiuser systems are most popular in vertical applications where data need to be shared. Sharing of data requires that the operating system strictly control access to files. A systems administrator establishes an account for each user, which allows the user to log on to the system and defines what file privileges that user will enjoy—which files he will be allowed to read, write, and execute. The operating system then monitors file activity, enforcing the privileges granted or denied each user.

Another consideration in choosing whether or not to go with a multiuser system is the cost of a systems administrator to back up the system, service user requests, and maintain user accounts and security features. OS/2 has no multiuser support.

Realtime Capacity

Another feature desired in many vertical applications, such as process control or point-of-sale, is realtime response. Not only does realtime response require multitasking, but it also requires that tasks be prioritized and that the task scheduler preempt an executing task when a higher-priority task becomes ready. Since OS/2 has no guaranteed task-switching time, it makes a poor candidate for critical realtime applications. On the other hand, QNX, with its promised worst-case task-switching time of 200 microseconds on a 10-MHz PS/2, guarantees the response time that is necessary for realtime applications.

Files Larger Than 32MB

DOS's file system is serviceable, but suffers from limitations that can be severe in some environments. For example, the 32MB disk volume limitation hinders large databases. OS/2 Standard Edition 1.0 retains the DOS 32 MB barrier, but Microsoft has announced that the barrier will be removed in a later release of the operating system. Methods exist to improve file systems, but by necessity they are at the expense of DOS compatibility. Operating systems that provide such improvement might supply a DOS file import/export facility for facilitating transfers between the two systems.

Table 16-2: Application Managers, DOS Extenders, and EMS

	APPLICATION MANAGERS		DOS EXTENDERS	
	DESQview 2.0	Windows/386	286	386
Multitasking support	•	•	o	o
Multiuser support	o	o	o	o
Task greater than 640KB	•a	•a	•	•
Large linear addresses	o	o	o	•
Runs DOS applications				
Single	•	•	•	•
Multiple	•	•	o	o
Requires 80286	o	o	•	o
Requires 80386	o	•	o	•

Table 16-2 *(continued)*

	EXPANDED MEMORY	
	LIM EMS 4.0	QEMM 4.0
Multitasking support		
Multiuser support		
Task greater than 640KB	•	•
Large linear addresses	o	o
Runs DOS applications		
Single	•	•
Multiple	•	•
Requires 80286	o	o
Requires 80386	o	•

• = Yes   o = No
a Using expanded memory

Graphics Support

Built-in operating system graphics services are valuable. As the number and complexity of PC graphics displays and printers increase, the need among developers for device-independent graphics grows as well. Such graphics features, however, are often neglected in an operating system's design so that developers must either use the low-performance PC BIOS routines provided or they must develop their own routines.

OS/2's Presentation Manager provides a graphics user interface as an integral part of the operating system, but the software will not be available until OS/2 Standard Edition 1.1 is shipped in November 1988. For DOS, Microsoft Windows and similar products are available for use as graphics interfaces. Designers of systems that are not DOS-compatible should consider providing a standard graphics system as part of their product; UNIX systems, for example, are served by X-Windows, which is still relatively unknown but growing in popularity.

Communications Support

In addition to serial communications necessary for multitasking systems, more general modem and network communications can be built into PC operating environments. Applications software needs to work with files and message buffers without concern for whether they are local or remote—connected via cable, microwave, or modem. Data transfer must be independent of system technology or the operating systems of the communicating computers.

Communications support can be categorized as either standard or optional and implemented separately. Most important to users is that new devices are supported via software-transparent system upgrades after the original systems is installed.

Sweeping Approaches

Although OS/2 offers some of the desired features, it does not support all features potentially available to users with the 386 processor, although it runs on either 286- or 386-based computers. Another shortfall might be that OS/2 has just recently been released, while many other options have been available for some time.

Software designers attempting to provide OS/2-equivalent features to DOS users are taking three basic routes: new or enhanced operating systems, applications managers, or applications environments.

Enhanced Operating Systems

Several years ago, the number of viable choices for PC operating systems was small. IBM's continued endorsement of MS-DOS made it the overwhelming favorite, but small pockets of support for Digital Research, Inc.'s CP/M and University of California San Diego's (UCSD) p-System products remained. Over time, UNIX- compatible systems appeared and gathered a noticeable following with the introduction of the PC/AT. Although DOS remains the most popular operating system for IBM-compatible machines, the last several months have seen an explosion in the number of viable alternatives being offered by competing systems software developers. OS/2's introduction in April 1987 legitimized the scramble. Because user investment in DOS software is great, huge deviations might threaten market acceptance unless these new operating systems provide sufficient new value or new software developer support to compensate.

Newly released enhanced operating systems include The Software Link, Inc.'s PC-MOS/386, Digital Research, Inc.'s Concurrent DOS/386, and, of course, OS/2. Both of these operating systems were designed to overcome limitations of DOS and to add new features to improve upon features found in DOS. In addition, Concurrent DOS/386 also provides CP/M compatibility.

An operating system's design is intimately tied to the processors it supports. The current DOS environment is based on the Intel 8086-type processors (including 8088, 80186, and 80188) found in the IBM PC, XT, Portable, Convertible, and compatible computers as well as the IBM Personal System/2 Models 25 and 30.

Intel 8086-type processors provide no hardware support for multitasking, memory protection, or other features associated with sophisticated operating systems. Nevertheless, some developers squeeze considerable functionality from the 8086 and they can simulate, with varying degrees of success, the features provided in hardware from the more powerful processors.

OS/2 itself cannot run on 8086-based machines; therefore, operating systems built on these machines are not considered OS/2 alternatives. However, these systems might provide added functionality over DOS for owners of current PCs who want to avoid the expense of upgrading to a computer that runs OS/2.

The complex features demanded of operating systems today require either 286- or 386-based machines, including AT, XT/286, and AT- compatibles as well as PS/2 Models 50, 60, and 80.

OS/2 is built on the 286 processor. While in protected mode, the processor offers task management, limited virtual addressing, and segment-based protection, and it is this environment that OS/2 effectively exploits. The 286 processor has some deficiencies that OS/2 is forced to pass on to its applications. The 64KB maximum segment size still requires the developer to manage multiple code and data segments. Support for 8086 software is limited to real mode; although the 286 can be switched to protected mode under software control, a return to real mode requires a hardware reset and it is undesirably slow.

The newer 386 processor supports enhanced memory protection and execution of multiple 8086 applications, with each application running its own virtual 8086 machine, isolated and protected from other applications. 386-based computers support page-mapped virtual memory systems, improved task management facilities, large linear address space (maximum segment size is 4GB), 32-bit operations, and an I/O protection bit map to prevent direct access of devices by applications.

Although the installed base of 386 computers is still relatively small when compared to the 286, the 386 is currently the most powerful and significant member of the Intel processor family. One shortcoming of OS/2 is that it treats the 386 as it does the 286, without tapping the added features of the newer processor. Competing vendors can really exploit this OS/2 weakness by providing 386-specific products. For users planning to upgrade hardware, 386-based machines might be better choices than 286- based ones because they offer significantly increased speed and functionality with only a small increase in cost.

Control Programs (Application Managers)

Control programs operate under an existing operating system but radically change its character. Products such as Windows/386 and DESQview run under DOS, but the provide a new user interface, and they exploit the virtual 8086 mode of the 386 processor to run multiple DOS applications concurrently. Such control programs help to ease DOS's memory limitations by supporting the Lotus/Intel/Microsoft expanded memory specification (LIM EMS). In addition, DESQview/386 will run applications that are written for Phar Lap's 386/DOS-Extender that run in protected mode on the 386.

Application Environments

Application environments are those that last only for the duration of a single program. These environments are based on the premise that applications interact with an operating system only for clearly defined services and that the operating system is oblivious to the state of the processor when it is not active. DOS operates in either real or virtual 8086 mode on a 386-based machine, but if an application switches into and out of protected mode between system calls, DOS is not affected.

Control software such as Phar Lap's 286 and 386 DOS Extenders and AI Architect's OS/286 and OS/386 provide such functionality, constructing an interface between the application and the operating system.

These DOS extenders allow an application to exploit the address space of the 286 and 386 processors while still running under DOS. The advantage is that th user is not required to buy a new operating system in order to run the enhanced application. Once the application receives control, it is in a full protected-mode environment; because interaction with DOS is trapped by control software, the processor can return to real mode for the length of the required system call.

The Choice is Yours

No existing products (operating systems or extensions) offer all of the improvements over DOS that have been described here. (See tables 16-1 and 16-2 for a summary of features found in current operating systems, application managers, DOS extenders, and EMS.) Additional products are expected as software designers hasten to take advantage of the opportunities that exist, including those that result because of shortcomings in OS/2.

Deciding whether another system offers sufficient features to warrant use over OS/2 is a complex and user-specific process; OS/2 is a sophisticated operating system that excels in many areas. Perhaps more important to developers and users is the fact that OS/2 has been endorsed by IBM, Compaq, Tandy, and other computer manufacturers, a level of support and commitment not yet shared by any alternative. However, for users whose requirements differ from those of the PC mainstream, more suitable and effective solutions than OS/2 might already exist.

17

Marrying UNIX and the 80386 *

_____*Carl Hensler* and *Ken Sarno*_____

A CRITICAL ISSUE in designing a multitasking operating system such as UNIX is how to protect the programs that are sharing system memory. This is called memory management.

The UNIX executive program, called the kernel, solves the memory protection problem by giving each program its own virtual address space seen by a program into the physical memory that has been allocated to the program, and must prevent access to memory that has not been allocated to it.

The Intel 80386 processor provides powerful, flexible, and extremely fast memory management hardware that makes implementing UNIX relatively easy. It provides paged virtual memory with all the segment translation and protection architecture of the 80286 and can execute in a 16-bit mode to maintain backward compatibility with 80286 versions of UNIX.

In virtual 8086 mode, the 80386 emulates the 8086, making it possible to run MS-DOS programs under UNIX. In the standard 32-bit mode, segments can be made so large that only one segment is needed, simplifying programming and eliminating cycle-wasting segment register loading.

How can the 80386's memory management hardware be best used in a UNIX kernel? We will discuss a series of design issues and the alternatives. The design we describe is not identical to any existing implementation of the UNIX kernel on the 80386, but it is quite similar to the ones with which we are familiar.

However, before leaping into kernel design, let's briefly review the multistep process through which an 80386 translates a program's virtual address into the corresponding physical memory address.

---

* © McGraw-Hill Information Systems Company, *BYTE,* April, 1988, p. 237

Address Translation

A virtual address generated by instruction fetching or execution is translated by segmentation hardware into a 32-bit, intermediate linear address, which is in turn translated by paging hardware into a 32-bit physical memory address, as shown in Figure 17-1.

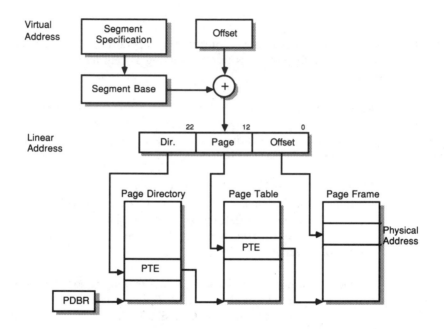

Figure 17-1: The 80386 uses segmentation and paging to translate a virtual address into a physical memory location.

In the 80386, a virtual address has two components: a segment register specification and an offset in the memory segment described by the segment register. A virtual address is translated into a linear address by adding the offset component to the segment base value in the specified segment register.

Pages are 4096-byte memory units, and page frames are pages of physical memory. The processor's page directory base register (PDBR) points to the page directory, entries in the page directory point to page tables, and entries in the page tables point to pages of physical memory. The page directory and the page tables are each one page in size, and each contains 1024 4-byte page table entries (PTE). A PTE contains a page frame address and some page attribute bits.

The processor translates a linear address by breaking it into directory, page and offset fields. The 10-bit directory field is used as an index into the page directory to select a PTE that points to a page table. The 10-bit page field is used as an index into the page table to select a PTE that points to the page that contains the linear address. The 12-bit offset field is combined with the address of the page to form the physical address.

Thus, each entry in the page directory maps a 4-megabyte (1024 x 4096 bytes) section of the linear address space to a page table, and each entry in a page table maps a 4096-byte section to a memory page, as shown in Figure 17-2. Note that the mapping between virtual and physical addresses can be changed incrementally by changing a PTE, or it can be changed completely by loading the address of a new page directory into the PDBR.

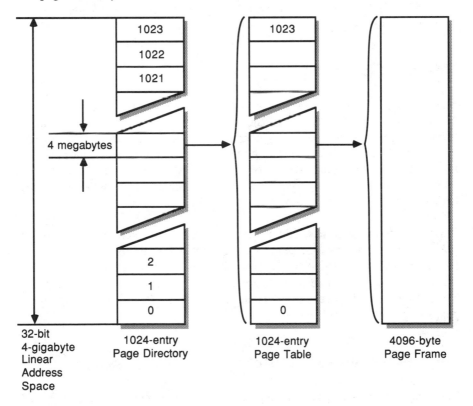

Figure 17-2: The 80386's page translation uses page directories, page tables, and page frames.

Page Faults

Each PTE has a present bit that indicates whether the entry can be used for address translation. If the present bit is not set in a PTE when it is used for translation, execution of the instruction that caused the translation is terminated as if it had not begun; the address that was being translated is put in a register where it is accessible to operating system software; and a page fault exception is generated.

The software that handles the page fault exception can correct the fault by allocating a page frame, loading the appropriate data into the page frame, putting the page frame address into the PTE, setting the present bit, and returning from the exception to the instruction that caused the fault. This time, the present bit is set and the translation succeeds. The ability to correct page faults by allocating a page that was not present and then restarting the instruction is essential for implementing demand paging.

Memory Protection

The 80386 provides memory protection during segment and page translation. The processor runs at a current privilege level that is compared to the privilege levels of segments and pages during address translation. The processor completes a segment or page address translation only if it is running at a current privilege level as high as that of the segment or page. UNIX runs at two privilege levels: a lower level when running user programs, and a higher level when running the kernel.

In addition to privilege restrictions, the 80386 checks segment offsets against a segment limit in the segment register to verify that the virtual address is within the segment's boundaries. Segments and pages can be marked read-only, so that they are protected from writing. Unfortunately, read-only protection for pages works only when the processor is running at user level. Read-only protection for pages is ignored at kernel level.

Segmented versus Nonsegmented Addressing

There are two addressing models, segmented and nonsegmented, that can be used on the 80286 and 80386. The segmented model allows a program to use many segments. Before a program can access a variable, it must load a segment register, unless it knows that a register already specifies the segment that contains the variable. This means that a C language pointer variable must include both a segment selector and an offset. Dereferencing a segmented pointer is very slow on the 80886 and 80386 because the selector must be loaded into a segment register, and loading a segment register takes 8 times longer than loading a data register.

The alternative is the nonsegmented model, in which a program uses only one segment, and virtual addresses are simply offsets in that segment. All the segment registers have the same segment base and limit and are never reloaded while the program is running. This limits the program size to the maximum segment size, but the maximum segment size on the 80386 is 4 gigabytes, the full 32-bit linear address range.

Thus, we can use the faster nonsegmented addressing model and still have an address space much larger than the amount of memory that could be installed in any contemporary computer. This is the simplest and most efficient way to use the 80386, and our design will assume it.

A special case of the nonsegmented model on the 80386 is the flat model, which uses segments that have a segment base value of 0. Since offsets arc added to 0 to produce linear addresses, virtual and linear addresses are identical in the flat model, and segmentation becomes invisible unless we use segment limits for protection. This simplifies some things, and both 80386 UNIX kernels with which we are familiar use the flat model.

Separate or Combined User and Kernel Address Spaces

A UNIX process is the environment in which a user program runs under control of the kernel. A process runs in either user mode or kernel mode. When user program instructions are being executed, the process is in user mode and can access only the memory allocated to the user program. It cannot access memory allocated to another process or to the kernel.

When kernel program instructions are being executed to provide a service for the user program, the process is in kernel mode, and it has access to both the user program's data and the kernel program's data. A process switches from user mode to kernel mode when it requests an operating system service, and it switches back to user mode when the service has been performed.

Our first design issue is whether to separate the user and kernel mode linear address spaces. It is possible to run the user program and the kernel in entirely different linear address spaces, so that the user program could not possibly access the kernel's memory. This would require having two different page directories for user and kernel modes, and making the transition from use to kernel mode through a task gate, because that is the only way to get a new page directory base pointer loaded automatically.

The simpler and more efficient solution is to have a single linear address space that is shared by both the user process and the kernel. Most of the linear address range is reserved for the user program, and only a small part is used by the kernel. Thus, a process can user the same page directory in use mode and kernel mode, and it can switch from user to kernel mode without reloading the PDBR. When you have 4 gigabytes to play with, taking a small fraction of it away from the user program is a small price to pay for simplicity.

Who's on Top?

The next issue is how to divide up the linear address space. The kernel could be at the lower end or the higher end of the linear address space. This issue is decided for you if you wish to be able to use the 80386's virtual 8086 mode, which lets you run 8086 programs in protected mode, and thus run MS-DOS programs under UNIX. In this mode, the 8086's 1-megabyte address range is translated to the low end of the linear address space, bypassing the usual protected-mode segment translation. If we want to be able to use virtual 8086 mode, we must therefore put the user program at the low end.

If we do not care about virtual 8086 mode, we might choose to put the kernel at the low end of the linear address space because then we could run the kernel without out page translation enabled during start-up. However, the implementations with which we are familiar both place the kernel at the high end, and we will assume the same arrangement here.

User and Kernel Segment Layout

Now we must decide how to lay out the user and kernel segments. Since the user program is at the lower end of the linear address space, we base the user segments at linear address 0, and we set their limits so that they do not extend into the kernel's part of the linear address space. This protects the kernel from user programs without using page protection.

We can base the kernel segments at 0 so that they overlap the user segments, or we can base them at the linear address at which the kernel starts so that the segments do not overlap. If the segments overlap, we run the risk that a bug in the kernel code will accidentally access a location in the user program without causing a protection exception.

Thus, from a protection standpoint, it is better to keep the segments separate, but it is simpler and more efficient to base them all at 0, so that a piece of data in the user program is at a kernel virtual address that is the same as the user virtual address. Then, when a user program passes an address in a system call to the kernel, the kernel can access that address without loading the user data segment selector into a segment register.

Kernel Sections

How is the kernel's part of the linear address space to be mapped to physical memory? The kernel has three sections that use fundamentally different page mappings:

- Statically mapped physical memory.
- Dynamically allocated kernel memory.
- The U area.

The kernel text and static data are loaded from the kernel executable file during UNIX start-up. They are typically loaded as contiguously as possible into low physical memory by the boot loader, though the hole between 640K bytes and 1 megabyte on AT clones presents an obstacle. Thus, the lower end of physical memory contains the kernel code and static data.

It is convenient if all physical memory is mapped into the kernel virtual address space so that the kernel can get to any of it without changing page tables. One or more page directory entries and page tables can map the low end of the kernel's section of the linear address space to all physical memory. This maps the virtual address range of the kernel's code and static data into the physical memory address range in which they are loaded, and also gives the kernel easy access to all physical memory. The virtual address of a byte of physical memory is its physical address plus the base linear address of the kernel.

Usually, most of the memory needed by the kernel for its own internal use is statically allocated at the time the kernel is linked. In addition, the kernel must be able to dynamically allocate pieces of memory for its own use. Since the page frames of physical memory that are free for allocation at any point are unlikely to be adjacent in memory, the kernel must be able to map a contiguous section of its virtual address space, of the size needed, into randomly located pages. This means that the kernel must have one or more page directory entries and page tables it can use for mapping dynamically allocated memory.

The U area, which contains the kernel stack and process information that is needed only when a process is running, is mapped into the kernel address space at a fixed location. When the kernel switches from one process to another, it changes the mapping of the virtual U area to the physical memory that contains the U area of the new process. We can dedicate a page directory entry and a page table to the U area, but this wastes most of the page table, because the U area is probably only one or two pages in size. It is more efficient to map the U area through the first few pages of the dynamically allocated kernel memory section. Then the virtual address of the U area is the base address of the dynamically allocated memory section.

So how big a piece of the linear address space should we reserve for the kernel? The biggest potential requirement is for mapping physical memory. Even if we reserve 256 megabytes for the kernel, that is still only 1/16 the linear address space.

Figure 17-3 shows our layout of the kernel part of the virtual address space. All addresses are in hexadecimal. The kernel occupies addresses F0000000 through FFFFFFFF. The statically mapped physical memory section takes up most of that, from addresses F0000000 through FEFFFFFF. The dynamically allocated memory area occupies FF000000 through FFFFFFFF, and the U area is at FF000000.

The page table overhead for a typical kernel is minimal. For a machine with 4 megabytes of physical memory, we need one page table each for the statically mapped physical memory and dynamically allocated memory sections. This is less than the page table overhead for a single process.

User Program Sections

A UNIX process must have three distinct sections of memory:

- A text section that contains the program instructions and can be shared with other processes running the same program.
- A data section containing stating and dynamically allocated data.

- A stack section containing function call linkage and automatically allocated local variables.

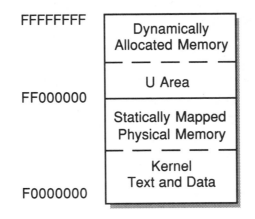

FFFFFFFF — Dynamically Allocated Memory

FF000000 — U Area / Statically Mapped Physical Memory

F0000000 — Kernel Text and Data

Figure 17-3: The kernel's virtual address space.

In addition, a process can also have an arbitrary number of shared memory and shared library sections. How should these be laid out in the user virtual address space?

A fundamental consideration is that both the data and stack sections can grow in size, and we want to leave room for them to grow. Most applications will use only a small fraction of the 32-bit address space, and most use a lot more data than stack. Yet we want to avoid layout decisions that will interfere with the efficient execution of future applications whose needs we can only guess.

UNIX assumes that the data section grows upward toward higher addresses. The 80386 stack must grow downward, because the PUSH instruction decrements the stack pointer. Only the text section is fixed in size. Our layout, shown in Figure 17-4, has the text section starting at virtual address 0, and the data section starting at the next multiple of 4 megabytes above the top of the text.

The gap between text and data is necessary because the two sections are mapped by different page tables, and each page table must be mapped by a different page directory entry. The stack is near the high end of the user address space, so that there is plenty of room for the data section to grow upward and the stack to grow downward.

Exactly where we put the stack depends on where we put shared memory and shared library sections. We can put them between the data and the stack, or we can put them above the stack. There are things to be said for and against both arrangements, and with such a big address space, it is not clear that it makes much difference. In Figure 17-4, we show shared libraries at E0000000, shared memory at D0000000, and the stack starting down from CFFFFFFF.

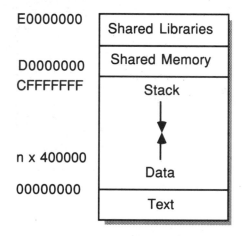

E0000000	Shared Libraries
D0000000	Shared Memory
CFFFFFFF	Stack
n x 400000	Data
00000000	Text

Figure 17-4: The user program's virtual address space.

Memory Management Data Structures

Thus far our design has focused on abstract issues of address space layout. Now it is time to turn to the more concrete task of deciding how to organize the part of the kernel program that manages memory. We have already discussed the basic building blocks: processes, sections, page directories, page tables, and page frames. Figure 17-5 shows how we put them together.

Processes and Sections

Shared text, shared memory, and shared library sections can all be attached to more than one process. Since a section can exist independently of any single process, information about sections must be kept separate form the process information in the process table and the U area. Thus, we assume that there is a section table with an entry for each section that currently exists.

An entry contains information about the type and state of the section, the number of processes to which it is attached, its size, and a way to find its page tables. Note that page tables are associated with sections, not processes, because the page tables that map a section to physical memory are the same for every process that shares that section, and it would be silly to duplicate them. Since there is only one page directory per process, it is associated with the process.

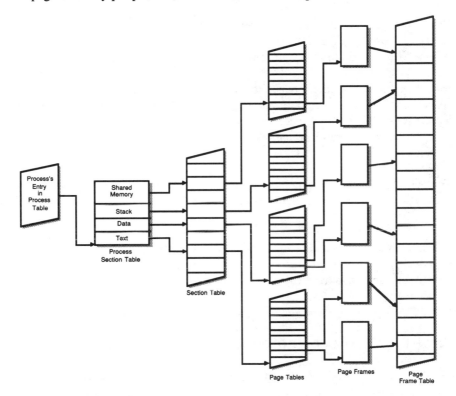

Figure 17-5: The entire memory management organizational hierarchy.

How do we associate a process with its sections? We must keep in mind that a shared memory section can appear at different virtual addresses in the processes to which it is attached, and it can be attached as either read/write or read-only. Thus, we need to distinguish between information about a section that is the same for all processes that share it, and information that differs among those processes. The former information goes in the section table, and the latter is kept in the process's process section table.

This table could be located in the process's entry in the process table or in the U area, or it could be allocated separately and linked to the process table entry or U area. Each entry in the process section table points to a section table entry.

Page Table and Page Frame Management

It must be possible for a section to map a large virtual address area so that we can run those few applications that use a large amount of memory. Thus, we must be able to attach an arbitrary number of page tables to a section.

However, because a single page table can map 4 megabytes of virtual address space, most sections have only one page table, and that is the case we wish to handle most efficiently. Each section table entry contains the first (and usually only) element of a list of pointers to page tables. Pages for page tables are dynamically allocated as needed.

The page frames at the low end of physical memory are dedicated to kernel code and static data when the kernel is loaded. Page frames above these can be allocated as needed.

Information about these allocatable page frames is kept in a page frame table established by the kernel at start-up after it has determined how much memory it has. Page frames available for allocation have their table entries linked on a free list so that it is easy to find the next one to be allocated.

Pages in Memory and on Disk

A page of a user program's virtual address space can be in memory, where it is accessible to the program, or it can be on disk, in either an executable file or the page swapping area. If a page is not in memory when it is referenced by the program, the page fault handler allocates a page frame and reads in the page from disk. Both the memory and disk forms of a page can coexist. For example, a text page always has an image in the executable file, even if it is in memory, because text pages are read-only.

Because a page can reside both in memory and on disk at the same time, we must be able to keep track of both of them. The straightforward solution to this problem is to use arrays of disk page descriptors that parallel the page tables. Each PTE has a corresponding descriptor that tells whether the page is on swap, is in a file, or is a demand 0 page. If the page is on swap or in a file, the descriptor specifies where it is on disk. A demand 0 page is cleared to 0s when it is allocated, and it has no image on disk. Demand 0 pages are used for uninitialized data, the stack, and dynamically allocated memory.

The trouble with the disk page descriptor solution is that it increases the page table overhead. A process has at least three sections-text, data, and stack-and unless we engage in some complex trickery, each as its own page table. On a processor with 512-byte pages, this would be only 1.5K bytes of page tables per process. But the 80386 has very large 4096-byte pages, requiring 12K bytes of page tables per process. If we allocate a page of disk page descriptors for each page table, which is the straightforward thing to do, we double this already large memory overhead.

The alternative is to put the disk information in the PTE when the page is not in memory, and put it in the page frame table entry when the page is in memory. Using the PTE for both memory and disk information is a bit more complex than the disk page descriptors but uses much less memory.

Page Caching

When a page frame contains data that is also on disk, its entry in the page frame data table shows where its image is on disk. When a page frame is put on the free list, it retains its disk identity until it is reallocated for a different use. If the page with that identity is needed again before the page is reallocated, it can be reused without reading from disk, because it already contains the needed data. Being able to locate a page frame with a particular disk identity is called page caching. It improves system performance by avoiding unnecessary disk reading.

Page frames that do not have a disk identity, such as the modified data and stack pages of a defunct process, are placed at the head of the free list when they are freed, and those that do have a disk identity are placed at the tail. That way, page frames that cannot be reused are reallocated first, and those that can be reused are reallocated in least-recently used order.

How it All Works

Now that we have presented our memory management design for UNIX on the 80386, let's briefly discuss how it work. When the kernel executes a program, it creates text, data, and stack sections and allocates page tables for them. The PTEs in the text section and in the initialized part of the data section are set up to point to the corresponding pages in the program executable file. The PTEs in the uninitialized part of the data section and in the stack section are marked demand 0.

When the process first starts to run, it immediately accesses the text page containing its entry point, causing a page fault. The page fault handler corrects the fault by bringing in the page of text from the executable file. The first instruction accesses the tack, causing another fault. Stack pages are demand 0, so the page fault handler simply allocates a page frame and clears it to 0s. Another instruction accesses an initialized static variable, causing a fault on a page in the data section, and the page fault handler brings in the data page from the executable file. This process continues until all the pages accessed by the program have been faulted in.

As long as there is enough physical memory so that the pages needed by all the processes can be in memory at the same time, the kernel can run without paging out. But when the kernel runs out of free page frames, it must free some for reallocation. This is sometimes called page stealing.

The prime candidates for stealing are pages belonging to processes that are waiting for events that may not occur for a while, such as a keystroke at a keyboard. If a process is waiting for a "slow" event, it is swapped out entirely. Otherwise, the kernel frees the pages least likely to be accessed again soon.

Text pages, and initialized data pages that have not been modified, can be freed without writing, because their images are in an executable file. Stack and modified data pages must be written out to the swap area on the disk before they can be freed. The PTEs for the stolen pages are changed to point to the pages on disk.

If a page frame is stolen away from a process and reallocated, the page must be read in from disk when it is accessed again. But if the process accesses the page before it is reallocated, the page frame is found in the page cache, and no I/O is necessary.

A Happy Marriage

UNIX and the 80386 are a happy marriage. The processor is fast, has a large address space, and provides on-chip memory management that supports demanding paging. Everything you need to implement UNIX efficiently is there. Carl Hensler and Ken Sarno are software engineers at Interactive Systems Corp., Santa Monica, California.

18

Intel's 386 Unites UNIX and DOS Software [*]

Clif Purkiser

UNIX workstation manufacturers, having recognized the importance of providing access to both UNIX technical and MS-DOS commercial software, have tried various ways to merge the system utilities and applications of the two operating systems. One popular approach has been to develop an add-in board that allows MS-DOS software to run on the UNIX workstation. Although better than buying two microcomputers for each user, this approach has several disadvantages—particularly in the areas of price, performance and compatibility.

The addition of a separate CPU board complicates the hardware and operating-system designs in such a dual-processor system. This added complexity increases both design and production costs while compromising performance. For example, such add-in boards typically perform at less than 80 percent of the speed of a 6-MHz IBM Corp. PC/AT and add several hundred dollars to the manufacturing cost and over $1,000 to the end-user price. Often, these add-in boards are only MS-DOS (not PC-DOS) compatible and, therefore, are unable to run the most popular PC-DOS applications. In addition, DOS coprocessor cards based on the Intel Corp. 80286 microprocessor run past and present DOS software but will not allow access to future 32-bit DOS applications.

The Intel 80386 microprocessor offers a simpler method for workstation vendors and system integrators to merge technical UNIX applications with PC-DOS applications. It provides an upwardly compatible hardware architecture and a UNIX operating system (Intel's System V/386) with hooks that allow software developers to construct virtual 8086 machines on top of UNIX. The virtual 8086 machines supports the execution of existing 8086 applications as System V/386 processes. This eliminates the need for cumbersome, performance-degrading multiprocessor solutions and provides multitasking capabilities for PC-DOS or MS-DOS.

---

[*] © Cahner's Publishing Company, *Mini-Micro Systems*, April 1987, p. 36

Supports Virtual Machines

In general, a virtual machine provides an environment that allows operating systems and applications designed for one type of computer to be run on a different type of computer. It supports the different operating systems and applications because it acts exactly like the different computers' CPU and peripheral devices (disk drives, displays) via either direct execution or software emulation. Of these two techniques, software emulation is inherently slower.

Achieving an acceptable performance level is the biggest problem for a virtual machine. Unless the virtual machine runs at least as fast as the original machine, there is little reason to buy the new computer.

For this reason, the 80386 microprocessor is designed to support fast virtual 8086 machines. As a result, 80386 systems can create a virtual IBM PC that executes all PC-DOS software much faster than does the PC. This is true even if the 80386 system has peripherals that are totally incompatible with the PC.

To achieve this speed and compatibility, the 80386 directly executes the instructions of the 8088 and 8086 microprocessors. To achieve such direct execution, the 80386 is designed with what is known as a Virtual 8086 Mode (V86). The V86 Mode is a subset of the protected mode of the 80386 and is selectable on a per-task basis. When the 80386 operates in V86 Mode, it executes 8086 programs in the same manner as an 8086 would, as opposed to emulating the 8086.

V86 Accelerates DOS Execution

For example, in the V86 Mode, the 32-bit 80386 processor assumes that instructions, registers, and data types are only 16 bits in length. But it generates a 20-bit linear address just like an 8086 does. Because the V86 Mode is a subset of the 80386's protected mode, however, its tasks are run in a fully protected, demand-paged environment under a host 32-bit operating system, such as System V/386. In fact, there are only two major differences between the V86 and an 8086 or 8088: 90 percent of the instructions execute 15 to 20 times faster, and programmers and applications have control over the execution of privileged instructions.

Privileged instructions are instructions used by the operating system. There are three main classes of privileged instructions: I/O, interrupt-related, and operating system support. Control over all these instructions is important because a single-tasking application's privileged instructions are potentially disruptive in a multitasking environment.

The interrupt-related instructions are especially important to trap because almost all 8086 applications were written for single-tasking computers. Many 8086 applications disabled interrupts for relatively long periods of time. When these applications execute in the System V/386 multitasking environment, the disable interrupts prevent other processes from running until the V86 application re-enables the interrupts.

I/O instructions, also, can cause problems for a multitasking operating system. The problem is that typical 8086 applications think they own the disk. Although these 8086 applications are likely to be running side-by-side on the 80386, one of them may operate as though it were in a single-tasking, single-user environment and reprogram the disk controllers accordingly. This would create a potentially disastrous situation if another application is waiting for data from the disk. Software is needed to control what the application can do.

However, the common solution of trapping instructions may not, by itself, solve the problem effectively. In many 8086 applications, which routinely manipulate time-sensitive peripherals (such as CRT controllers), trapping every I/O instruction would degrade performance. So, the 80386 provides a higher degree of protection via the I/O Permission Bit-Map.

The I/O Permission Bit-Map allows the 32-bit operating system to specify exactly, on a per-task basis, which peripherals an MS-DOS application can access directly without causing an exception. System V.386 can use these maps to allow foreground processes to access the screen without trapping requests for a resource, while background processes would trap requests and write to a virtual screen. Page-based protection can be used in an analogous way to manage memory-mapped I/O.

Whenever a V86 application attempts to execute a privileged instruction, if trapping is enabled, an exception occurs. This causes control to pass from the V86 task to the 80386's operating system and also causes the processor to switch from V86 Mode to protected mode. After the System V.386 (or other host operating system) handles the exception, it returns from the exception handler and switches the processor back into V86 Mode.

VM Monitor Translates 8086 Calls

The simple trapping of privileged instructions prevents a number of operating system problems, but it does not solve the V86 application's need to execute these instructions. In order to execute privileged instructions, an optional piece of software, called a virtual 8086 monitor (VM monitor), can be added to System V/386. Two such monitors are VP/ix, developed jointly by Interactive Systems Corp., Santa Monica, Calif., and Phoenix Technologies Ltd., Norwood, Mass,; and OS/Merge 386, developed by Locus Computing Corp., Santa Monica. The VM monitor translates 8086 operating system calls into 32-bit operating system calls and emulates hardware devices that are present on the 8086 computer but not on the 80386 computer.

With a VM monitor, users can execute UNIX applications and one or more 8086 operating systems and their applications. Any 8086 operating system can be run; MS-DOS, CP/M-86, and proprietary 8086 operating systems are examples. User can also create virtual I/O devices, such as disk drives, graphic adapters and memory-expansion cards.

How to Create a VM Monitor

Each combination of a 32-bit operating system and an 8086 operating system needs its own VM monitor (even though much of the code is common between monitors). Because the greatest market demand is to merge the UNIX and PC-DOS software bases, consider what is needed to sketch out such a VM monitor.

A VM monitor usually consists of three logical partitions: a V86 interrupt handler, a DOS-to-UNIX system-call translator, and an optional peripheral emulator. The V86 interrupt handler is closely tailored to the base 32-bit operating system, and many of the handler's functions are built into System V/386. The DOS-to-UNIX system-call translator interprets DOS system and function calls and translates them to UNIX system calls. The peripheral emulator is a set of software routines that mimic all of the user-programmable peripheral devices on the IBM PC. It is used when the 80386-based computer contains peripherals that are different from an IBM PC's.

Interrupt Handler Directs Traffic

The V86 interrupt handler serves as a "traffic cop" for all of the 80386 system's interrupts. It identifies a V86 interrupt, and then either reflects (returns) the interrupt back to DOS or redirects it to the appropriate routine (Fig. 18-1).

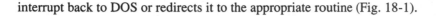

V86 Interupt Handler Controls Traffic

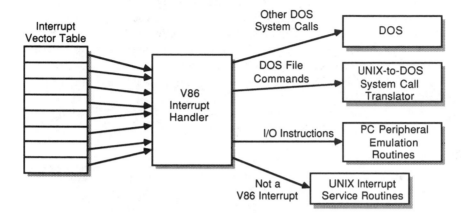

Figure 18-1: The Virtual 8086 Mode (V86) interrupt handler identifies
V86 interrupts and then either reflects them back to DOS
or redirects them to the appropriate routines.

When a V86 task attempts to execute a privileged instruction, it causes a general protection fault (exception 13). Information about the faulting instruction and the state of the processor at the time the fault occurs is pushed on to the stack, (flag and instruction pointer and other registers) and control passes to the routine pointed to by the exception 13 vector. The interrupt service routines for exception 13 will call the V86 interrupt handler.

The V86 interrupt handler determines if the fault was generated by a V86 program by checking to see if the VM bit is set in the EFLAGS image on the stack. If the exception was not generated by a V86 task, then control is passed to the System V/386 handlers. If the fault was generated when executing a V86 task, however, the V86 interrupt handler must determine what type of instruction caused the interrupt: an I/O instruction, an explicitly stated "INT n" instruction or an interrupt enable/disable instruction.

If the faulting instruction is an I/O instruction from either a background task or from any task in a system with non-PC peripherals, then the appropriate emulator routine is called. Interrupt enables and disables can be ignored for most systems; UNIX systems do not normally allow user programs to disable interrupts. INT n instructions are used by DOS applications to initiate system calls and are handled in one of two ways: reflection or emulation.

Emulation is appropriate for some DOS system calls, like "Open File" or "Read File," that can easily be mapped into a corresponding System V/386 operating system call. When a V86 task requests DOS to open a file, for example, it generates an Interrupt 21 instruction and passes the function code for "Open File" in the AX (a general purpose) register. The Interrupt 21 vector switches control to the V86 interrupt handler. The V86 handler then calls the DOS-to-UNIX call translator. After the DOS call is translated, control passes back to the DOS application (Fig. 18-2).

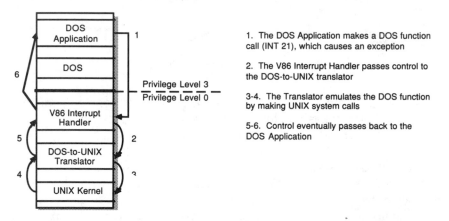

Figure 18-2: For some DOS system calls, such as "Open File" or "Read File," it is necessary to map the DOS calls into corresponding UNIX System V/386 calls via emulation.

Reflection occurs for other DOS function calls, like "Terminate and Remain Resident," that are best handled by DOS. In this case, the V86 interrupt handler modifies the return stack so that control is passed back to DOS. Then, DOS will service the request and pass control back to the application (Fig. 18-3).

Translator Operates Functions

The Dos-to-UNIX translator maps most DOS functions and some BIOS functions to the equivalent UNIX function. The DOS-to-UNIX translator can be as large or as small as desired, or it can be nonexistent. If it is nonexistent, the V86 handler would redirect all DOS function calls back to the copy of DOS that is loaded with each application. All of the emulation would then be performed by the PC peripheral-emulator routines. Assuming that the translator exists, the only requirement for the DOS-to-UNIX translator routines is that they look identical to DOS at the system-call level.

The main advantage of the DOS-to-UNIX translator is performance. It is faster to translate the system call from the virtual 8086 application being run to the UNIX format than it is to execute the hardware devices that DOS expects. It is also relatively easy to directly translate many of the DOS functions, such as the file routines (open, close, read, write) into the equivalent UNIX operating system calls.

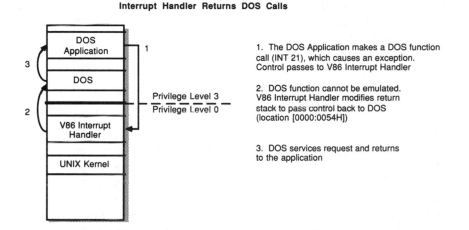

Interrupt Handler Returns DOS Calls

1. The DOS Application makes a DOS function call (INT 21), which causes an exception. Control passes to V86 Interrupt Handler

2. DOS function cannot be emulated. V86 Interrupt Handler modifies return stack to pass control back to DOS (location [0000:0054H])

3. DOS services request and returns to the application

Figure 18-3: When emulation is not possible, it is necessary to return, or "reflect," DOS calls back to the DOS operating system, which then services the request and passes control back to the application.
An example of a call that is best handled by this method is "Terminate and Remain Resident."

The IBM PC's ROM BIOS also contains many functions. Like the DOS functions, these too can either be emulated or reflected back to a copy of the BIOS that is loaded in RAM.

Emulator Simulates Peripherals

The PC peripheral emulator provides software simulation of peripheral devices that exist on an IBM PC but do not exist on the 80386 system. The PC peripheral emulator routines would not need to exist if all DOS applications were well behaved. Unfortunately, many popular DOS applications bypass MS-DOS and call the ROM BIOS and/or write directly to the PC's peripherals.

The PC peripheral-emulator routines are unnecessary for two types of computers. With the one, MS-DOS, rather than PC-DOS, compatibility is sufficient. Here, there is no need to run software that works only with the IBM PC and compatible. The second type is of those computers that contain peripherals identical to an IBM PC (i.e., an 80386 PC/AT clone).

The peripheral components most commonly manipulated directly on an IBM PC are the 6845 CRT controller, the 765 disk controller, and the 8237 DMA (direct-memory access) controller. Most 80386 UNIX workstations tend to have higher resolution displays, higher performance disk controllers and higher bandwidth and addressability DMA devices than does a PC. Therefore, emulators will likely be needed for these devices.

Virtual Machine Speeds Execution

The speed of a virtual IBM PC on an 80386-based workstation running the System V/386 operating system should be between 3 to 12 times the speed of a PC. This increase is possible, in spite of the need to perform slow operations like emulating certain privileged instructions, because in typical PC-DOS applications (such as Lotus Development Corp.'s 1-2-3) only 5 percent to 10 percent of the instructions executed are V86 privileged instructions that need to be emulated. The remaining 90 percent to 95 percent of the instructions execute about 17 times faster than they would on the 8088-based PC, simply because they run at the 80386's 16-MHz clock speed (compared to 4.77 MHz for the 8088), and they take advantage of the improved implementation of the instruction set on the 80386.

The impact of privileged-instruction traps can be reduced by writing efficient DOS-to-UNIX translator routines. Additional performance will also be gained because UNIX, unlike DOS, can run other processes while waiting for I/O operations like disk reads or writes. The faster peripheral devices of 80386-based advanced workstations will more than compensate for the slightly slower speed of I/O instructions.

The 80386 as a UNIX Engine

Intel Corp.'s 80386 microprocessor is a true 32-bit microprocessor that can execute 3 to 4 million instructions per second. Its achievement of 6,000 to 7,000 Dhrystones per second at 16 MHz puts it in the performance class of the Digital Equipment Corp. VAX 8600. The 80386 can also address tremendous quantities of memory with its 4G-byte physical, 4G-byte linear, and 64-terabyte virtual, address spaces. Furthermore, its on-chip memory-management unit allows the full performance of the processor to be realized in demand-paged virtual-memory systems.

The 80386 is fully compatible with previous Intel microprocessors: the 8086, 8088 and 80286 real and protected modes. What's more, the 80386 can run 8086 operating systems and their applications concurrently with 80286 and 80386 applications in a fully protected multitasking environment under a 32-bit operating system like Intel's System V/386.

The 80386 architecture also supports the needs of the UNIX System V operating system—for example, the MMU's support of demand-paged virtual memory. The 80386's two-level paging scheme operates in a manner similar to that of a VAX, the most popular UNIX host.

Each System V/386 operating system process has its own set of page directories and page tables, giving every process 4G bytes of virtual address space. The 80386's paging mechanism supports the sharing of page tables and pages between processes, which simplifies code- and data-sharing between applications. (The UNIX operating system minimizes physical memory requirements by having only one copy of a program loaded into memory even though numerous users are running it.)

The MMU also reduces the performance penalty associated with paging schemes implemented with an external MMU. The translation of a virtual address to a physical address is overlapped (pipelined) with other operations. In addition, the 386 contains a 32-entry page-address translation cache. The large cache, coupled with an efficient 4K-byte page size, handles over 98 percent of all memory accesses.

The System V/386 operating system uses a combination of segment- and page-based protection to increase the system's integrity. The kernel's code and data are in separate segments, which are isolated from user processes. A page directory for each process provides protective isolation between user processes.

System V/386 also fully supports the high-performance numeric processing needs of 32-bit applications. The operating system supports two types of numeric coprocessors: the Intel 80287/387 and the Weitek Corp. 1167 chip set. The 80287 and 80387 are binary-compatible with the industry standard 8087 and offer a full implementation of the IEEE P754 standard for floating-point math. The Weitek 1167 is a high-performance floating-point coprocessor that can execute up to 4 million Whetstones per second when coupled with a 386.

In order to facilitate the development of 32-bit applications, a large number of independent software vendors are developing tools to run on the System V/386 operating system. These tools include highly optimized C, FORTRAN, Pascal, COBOL, Lisp, Prolog, RPG II and BASIC compilers developed by major UNIX software vendors.

The System V/386 operating system also provides powerful debugging tools such as SDB (a source-level debugger). Due to the 80386's hardware debug registers, SDB for the future versions of System V/386 operating system will allow breakpoints to be set not only on instructions but also on data reads or writes and in ROM. This allows an application programmer to easily determine why variables are being corrupted, normally a tedious task without hardware debug support.

19

Programming Considerations in Porting to Microsoft System V/386 [*]

_____*Martin Dunsmuir*_____

XENIX System V/386 is the Microsoft version of the UNIX Operating System ported to the Intel 386 microprocessor. The product, which was released to OEMs in the summer of 1987, is the first from Microsoft to take full advantage of the features of the Intel 386 microprocessor. In particular, XENIX allows 32-bit applications to be written for the first time.

Microsoft has been active in the UNIX business since its inception, and in fact, XENIX predates even MS-DOS as a Microsoft product. Since 1983, the XENIX development effort has concentrated on the Intel microprocessors—the 286 introduced by Intel in 1983 and more recently the 386. By concentrating on one instruction set and chip architecture, Microsoft has been able to develop the world's largest installed base of binary-compatible UNIX systems. Currently, XENIX accounts for about 70 percent of all UNIX licenses sold, or roughly 250,000 units, and more than 1,000 different applications are available. Although these numbers may sound small when compared with the numbers quoted for MS-DOS, the majority of these systems are used in multiuser configurations supporting between two and 16 users.

Most of the current XENIX installed base is on 286-based PCs such as the IBM PC AT. XENIX is used primarily as a cost-effective solution for small businesses that require multiuser access; it has sold particularly well in vertical markets that lend themselves to a customized "systems solution." Two such markets are dentistry and accounting.

There was great excitement when Intel informed Microsoft that it was planning the 386 chip—and Microsoft set out to find a way to take advantage of the chip's features within the XENIX environment. In particular, Microsoft wanted to give developers the ability to create 32-bit applications and provide support within the operating system for virtual memory and demand paging—features that can greatly increase the throughput of a computer system.

Another major design goal was to be sure that existing XENIX 286 users were not prevented from moving up to the 386. Microsoft wanted its installed base to be able to take advantage of the increased performance without having to buy new versions of their applications. Since the 386 chip supports both 16- and 32-bit segments in its architecture, Microsoft has been able to create an environment in which both 16- and 32-bit programs can be executed simultaneously. The features of demand paging and virtual memory are available transparently to both 16- and 32-bit applications.

Implementing support for segments independently of the paging subsystem provides full performance for old applications without slowing down the execution of the new 32-bit programs (see Figure 19-1).

Mapping 286 Programs under XENIX 386

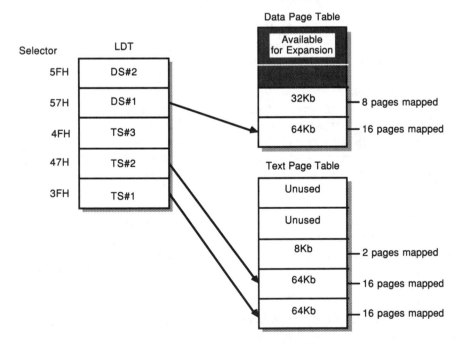

Figure 19-1: Mapping 286 Programs Under XENIX 386

Page table entries are maintained in groups of 16. This allows a 286 segment to expand to 64Kb without moving existing page table entries.

Support for 32-bit applications is the key to the continued success of XENIX. It opens the door to the creation of much more powerful programs, as well as making it easier for developers to move existing UNIX applications onto XENIX. UNIX 32-bit programs being ported to XENIX 286 often needed extensive rewriting to make them work well in a 16-bit environment. This chapter outlines the considerations that will help programmers in choosing between 16- and 32-bit program models when developing applications or migrating to XENIX System V/386.

Small-Model Programs

In 16-bit mode, as used on XENIX 286, a program is composed of two segments up to 64Kb in size. One segment contains program code; the other segment contains data (the stack is of fixed size and resides in the data segment). An example of a small-model program is shown in Figure 19-2.

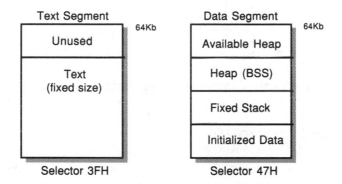

Figure 19-2: A Small-Model 286 Program

The program in Figure 19-2 has only one data and one code segment, so it is not necessary to change the contents of the segment registers while the program is running. At load time, the operating system initializes them to point to the memory in which the program executes (via the LDT). In particular, the compiler or assembler programmer does not have to take account of changing segment registers during the program execution.

Also of note is the fact that in the small model, both integers and pointers to data objects are 16-bit quantities and therefore interchangeable. This is important because many programs implicitly make this assumption. Unfortunately, although many commands and utilities are less than 64Kb in size, most third-party applications are larger than this; they require multiple code and/or data segment support. Figure 19-3 shows a multisegment program.

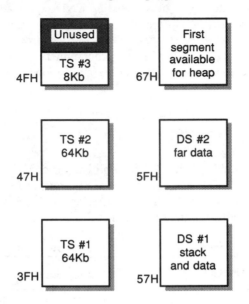

Figure 19-3: Large-Model 286 Program Layout

Large- and Middle-Model

Programs can overflow the 64Kb limit with their code or their data, or both at the same time. Programs that exceed 64Kb of code but still have less than 64Kb of data are called middle-model programs. Large-model programs exceed 64Kb in both their code and data segments.

Large Code

The program is broken down by the linker into pieces that will fit into 64Kb. If a program's code exceeds 64Kb, then it is necessary to place different parts of it in different segments. (Because the breaks occur on function boundaries, each piece can be less than 64Kb in size.) The compiler must also generate code that automatically reloads the CS register when the thread of execution moves from one segment to another. This results in a program that is slightly slower than the equivalent small-model image. The effect is not too drastic because within each subroutine CS remains constant so the frequency of segment register reloads is relatively low in comparison with the number of instructions executed.

Large Data

Data structures are spread among a number of different segments when data exceeds 64Kb. Again, the linker fills each segment with data structures as fully as possible. The performance penalty to be paid for going to large data is much larger than in the case of code because the frequency of intersegment data accesses is generally much greater than that of intersegment branches. The C compiler does not know which segment a particular data structure resides in at compile time; this causes a large number of unnecessary intersegment calls to be generated. Another problem in moving to large model is the fact that the size of data pointers increases to 32 bits. This means that the size of an integer is no longer equal to the size of a pointer, and programs that rely on this equality, either implicitly or explicitly, break. This is one of the primary problems developers experience when porting existing 32-bit UNIX programs to XENIX 286. A summary of the different models can be seen in Table 19-1.

Name of Model	Max. Text	Max. Data	Stack	Heap	Performance
Small	<=64Kb	<=64Kb	Fixed (<64Kb)	In Data (<64Kb)	Best
Middle	>64Kb	<=64Kb	Fixed (<64Kb)	In Data (<64Kb)	Good
Compact	<=64Kb	>64Kb	<=64Kb	>64Kb	Poor
Large	>64Kb	>64kb	<=64Kb	>64Kb	Poorest
Hybrid Data	<=64Kb	>64Kb	Fixed (<64Kb)	<64Kb	Good

Table 19-1: Comparison of 286 Program Models

Hybrid Model

Using the 286, where 16-bit segments are the norm but most useful applications exceed 64Kb in size, it is important for programmers to understand how to design their programs to reduce the effect of the multiple segment accesses. One way of doing this is to select specific data structures to be placed in separate far segments, while keeping indiscriminately accessed data structures (and the stack if possible) in a single near segment. The code generated by the Microsoft C compiler in this case is much more efficient because the far keyword, used to mark specific data structures, gives the compiler a hint as to when it should reload segment registers.

Use of a hybrid model with carefully designed programs comes close to the performance of small-model programs, even though they exceed 64Kb in size. However, there is a down side to this approach—it makes programs inherently less portable between XENIX 286 and other UNIX environments. Also, converting an existing 32-bit UNIX application to a hybrid model is complicated by the differences in pointer and integer size that make large-model ports such a problem.

32-Bit Programming

In contrast to the complexity of a multisegment 286 program, the native 386 program structure is very simple (see Figure 19-4). Each program consists of one code segment along with one data segment, and each segment can be very large in size. (The exact limit depends on the availability of real memory and swap space and is typically a few megabytes).

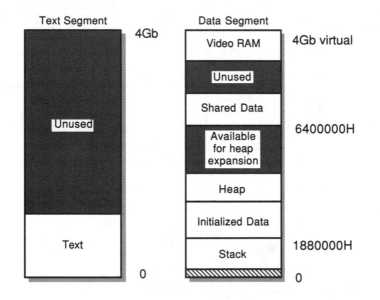

Figure 19-4: Program Layout in 386 Mode

The stack grows down to 0 virtual, while the heap grows up. The sum of the mapped text, data, and stack cannot exceed the installation dependent limit (typically the sum of installed RAM plus the size of the paging area on the disk).

Because the address space is large, it is not necessary to support multiple segments in 32-bit mode, either in the operating system or in the C compiler. When a program is loaded, all the segment registers are initialized to static values and remain unchanged while the program is executing. In 32-bit mode, the stack lives in the data segment and grows down to lower addresses, while the data segment extends upward to higher addresses.

XENIX 386 programs are truly 32-bit; they support 32-bit integers and all pointers are 32 bits in length. This eases the problems of porting existing 32-bit applications to XENIX 386 in 32-bit mode.

Other advantages offered by the 32-bit mode of the 386 are more orthogonal registers and addressing modes, which allow better code generation and more register variables, plus extra instructions that improve in-line code generation. Thirty-two-bit programs generally exhibit a significant performance advantage over the 16-bit versions.

New XENIX Applications

The introduction of XENIX 386 no longer constrains the developer to the 16-bit architecture. If he chooses, he can develop his application in 32-bit mode. However, the choice between a 16- and 32-bit architecture for a new application is not as simple as it appears at first glance. Thirty-two-bit programs will only execute on XENIX 386, whereas 16-bit applications will execute on both XENIX 286 and XENIX 386. The installed base of XENIX 386 is still small, but it is almost certain to exceed that of XENIX 286 in time. A 16-bit application may be a better choice for developers who want to address the largest possible installed base. Let's look at the trade-offs that must be considered when making the choice between 16 and 32 bits.

The developer should ask himself the following questions:

- What is the size of the application, both code and data?

- Is the application an existing UNIX program being ported to XENIX?

- Is the application an existing MS-DOS program or aimed at the MS-DOS, OS/2, and UNIX markets?

- For new applications, what is the target market for the application?

- Is it limited to XENIX or does it have wider appeal in other UNIX or DOS markets?

- What are the application's performance requirements?

Application Size

In many ways size is the most important consideration; unfortunately for new applications it is most likely the hardest to answer. For a simple application it is probably wise to build the application first as a 32-bit program and then see if it will fit into 16 bits. At this point it should be remembered that large data is a much more serious performance limitation to 16-bit programs—programs with more than 16 bits of code but less than 16 bits of data can be built as 16-bit middle-model programs without serious performance degradation.

Another approach that can be used to fit a more complex program into the 64Kb address space is to break it down into a number of separate, communicating processes, each of which fits into the smaller address space. Not all programs are amenable to such an architecture. Breaking an application into pieces can also limit portability into the MS-DOS world.

Portability

Many developers of UNIX applications for UNIX systems other than XENIX 286 have programs that are designed implicitly for the 32-bit world. This is because XENIX 286 is one of the few UNIX systems to run on a 16-bit processor. Even if size is not a consideration, the work required to port UNIX applications from 32 to 16 bits has often deterred developers from doing the port.

Such developers are best advised to build their applications for XENIX 386 only. Debugging those problems summarized earlier in this chapter is often too great an effort to warrant porting a program to XENIX 286. This extra development effort can be considered for a later release if market pressure is felt.

When porting existing MS-DOS applications to UNIX, it is usually more feasible to build an application in 16 bits. This is certainly the best and easiest option if the application contains a significant amount of assembler code. Since the XENIX and MS-DOS macro assemblers accept the same source syntax in 16-bit mode, assembly code that is not environment-specific should port directly to XENIX.

Traditionally, UNIX and MS-DOS applications markets have been separated by a wide gap in complexity. This is because the architecture of real-mode MS-DOS programs is very different from UNIX. With the advent of OS/2, the underlying support provided by the two operating systems is now comparable, so it may make sense for new applications to be developed that can easily be hosted in both XENIX and OS/2 environments. If this is the case, it makes more sense to build the application for the 16-bit environment common to both XENIX and OS/2 and to delay the development of a 32-bit application until a 32-bit version of OS/2 becomes available.

Another consideration for simpler applications is the use of the C library calls supported by the Microsoft C Compiler under MS-DOS. These calls, which embody a subset of the UNIX C library calls, can make it relatively easy to build a program that can be simply rehosted in both XENIX and MS-DOS environments. A good example of this approach would be the Microsoft 286 C compiler itself, which is recompiled and linked with different run-time libraries for execution on MS-DOS or XENIX 286. The task of creating a common source code for both MS-DOS and XENIX versions of the compiler is greatly facilitated by the fact that the XENIX and MS-DOS linkers both accept the same relocatable format as input (although they generate a different executable file format).

XENIX and UNIX Markets

Building applications that port easily between XENIX 286 and other UNIX platforms has generally been difficult. It is prudent—if a source portable application is desired—to remain within the 32-bit world. The 32-bit XENIX 386 environment is completely compatible with the System V Interface Definition (SVID), and thus there should be very little difficulty in moving a carefully designed program from XENIX 386 to other UNIX platforms.

Performance

Although performance is a combination of factors, it is most strongly linked to the architecture of the program and to the inherent speed of the host computer. All architectural considerations being equal, a 32-bit program will execute faster than a 16-bit program on the same 386 CPU. Applications that are being ported from the earlier 286 or 8086 worlds onto the 386 will experience an increase in raw 16-bit performance, simply by running the code on a 386, that more than offsets the need to consider rehosting into 32-bit mode.

For new XENIX applications, especially those being ported from other 32-bit processors, where a 16-bit port is a serious possibility, it is important to understand the performance degradation seen on the 386 between 16-bit and 32-bit code. The operating system itself runs in 32-bit mode, and some part of a program's execution time is spent in this code. The decrease in speed when moving to 16 bits is not as great as a simple comparison of CPU-bound 16 and 32 performance might indicate. Table 19-2 shows the relative execution times of two small C programs. "Cpubound" and "IObound," built as small-16, middle-16, large-16, and small-32 programs on XENIX 386. Listings 19-1 and 19-2 show the source code of these programs.

Listing 19-1: Cpubound.c

```
/*
 *              Cpubound.c
 */
#define IMAX 100
#define JMAX 1000

int id[IMAX];
int jd[JMAX];

main()
{
        int i, j;

        for (i=0;  i<IMAX;  i++) {
                id[i] = i;
                for (j=0;  j<JMAX;  j++){
                        jd[i] = j; calli (id, jd, j);
                }
        }
        exit(0);
}

calli(i, j, c)
int *i, *j;
int c;
{
        int t;
        int ti = i[c];
        int tj = j[c];

        while(ti-)
                t += (*(i++))+(*(j++))+(tj-);

        return(t)
}
```

Listing 19-2: IObound.c

```
/*
 * IObound.c
 */

#define IMAX 100
#define JMAX 100
```

```
#define BFS 2
char buffer[BFS];

main()
{
        int i, j;
        int fd;

        /* Create a Disk File */
        fd = creat("scratch", 0600);

        for(i=0; i<IMAX; i++){
                sync();
                for(j=0; j<JMAX; j++){
                        write(fd, buffer, BFS);
                }
        }

        sync();
        /* Return to Beginning of the File */
        lseek(fd, 0, 0);

        for(i=0; i<IMAX; i++){
                sync();
                for(j=0; j<JMAX; j++){
                        read(fd, buffer, BFS);
                }
        }

        /* Remove the File */
        unlink("scratch");
        exit(0);
}
```

An analysis of Table 19-2 shows that the 32-bit architecture offers a significant performance advantage for CPU-bound programs that do a mix of arithmetic, pointer processing, and function calls. There is no performance difference among the various 16- and 32-bit models chosen for I/O-bound activities where the processing is all within the kernel. Although the performance of a 16-bit application on XENIX 386 falls short of the 32-bit performance, it is still between two and three times greater than the performance when that program is run on an 8-MHz 286. The difference in performance between the 386 host and the 286 target must be factored in when measuring 16-bit performance on XENIX 386.

Demand Paging and Virtual Memory

Demand paging is a feature of the XENIX 386 operating system, built on top of the 386 chip architecture that allows a program to run even though all of its pages have not been loaded into memory. Instead, only those pages from the executable image stored on disk that are actually referenced by the program as it runs are loaded into memory.

Whenever the program references a page that is not in memory, it causes a "page fault." The XENIX kernel acts in response by loading the requested page from the disk and restarting the faulting program. The effect of demand paging is to

reduce the memory usage of a given program to those pages that it actually references during a particular invocation. This set of pages is called the "working set"
and is usually smaller than the full size of the program, especially if that program
is large.

Cpu Bound Performance (normalized)			
	Real time	User time	System time
Small-Model 286	32.4 (0.59)	32.2	0.0
Middle-Model 286	40.6 (0.47)	40.5	0.0
Large-Model 286	57.5 (0.33)	57.4	0.0
Small-Model 3286	19.0 (1.00)	18.9	0.0
I/O Bound Performance (normalized)			
	Real time	User time	System time
Small-Model 286	38.5 (1.00)	0.3	13.3
Middle-Model 286	38.6 (1.00)	0.7	12.8
Large-Model 286	42.4 (0.91)	0.4	14.8
Small-Model 386	38.4 (1.00)	0.2	12.4

Table 19-2: Performance Table

Demand paging occurs without any knowledge on the part of the application.
For example, the second pass of the Microsoft 386 C compiler is approximately
300Kb; however its working set on a typical program is closer to 80Kb, depending on which Microsoft C language features are used.

The effect of demand paging is to improve the throughput of the system on
smaller memory configurations, and because it is not necessary to load programs
into memory before they start execution, the latency of command execution can
be greatly reduced.

Virtual memory allows the real memory associated with a program's heap
(allocated via *malloc* or *sbrk* calls) to be allocated on demand rather than at the
time of the *malloc* or *sbrk* function call. A program can be assigned a large address space without incurring additional overhead for pages that would remain unused.

When a program makes a memory allocation call, the kernel recognizes the
change in the end of the virtual heap. However, it allocates no memory between

the end of the old heap and the new location. It is only when a program accesses pages in the new heap region and causes a page fault that the kernel allocates empty pages of real memory. This feature is also called "zero-fill on demand."

Entry Point	Function
chsize	adjust file size
creatsem nbwaitsem opensem sigsem waitsem	semaphore operation semaphore operation semaphore operation semaphore operation semaphore operation
execsem unexecseg	execute data execute data
ftime	obsolete UNIX time function
locking	XENIX file locking
nap	sleep for a short time
procti	process specific control function
rdchk	check for input without reading
sdenter sdfree sdget sdgetv sdleave sdwaitv	XENIX shared data extension XENIX shared data extension XENIX shared data extension XENIX shared data extension XENIX shared data extension XENIX shared data extension
shutdn	shutdown system
swapon	control paging devices

Table 19-3: XENIX System Call Extensions to be avoided for portability

Conclusion

When designing an application for the XENIX 386 environment, the developer must weigh a number of conflicting criteria. The foremost problem is whether to build the program in 16- or 32-bit mode. Further questions must address the intended market as well as the performance and portability required of the completed product. Lastly, it is important to consider future compatibility requirements.

Microsoft and AT&T are currently working together to merge XENIX 386 and AT&T's UNIX system V/386 Release 3.2 into a single UNIX system that will be marketed jointly by the two companies. This Merged Product (MP) will support all the existing 286 and 386 executable formats common to UNIX and XENIX on the 386, thereby allowing all existing applications to run.

The emphasis for developers using the MP will be to establish the UNIX/386, 32-bit mode program interface as the standard for new applications. This standard will be a superset of the current XENIX System V/386 program interface, without the support for XENIX-specific system call extensions. This means that in the long run there will be one binary standard, developed and supported by Microsoft and AT&T, which will run on all 386 machines running UNIX, thereby stabilizing the market.

Developers who would like their programs to be source compatible with the new binary standard may want to avoid the use of XENIX system call extensions before the MP becomes available in mid-1988. This applies particularly to the use of 32-bit applications (see Table 19-3). Although kernel support is provided for XENIX extensions in the MP, minimal development tools will be provided. Debugging support will be limited to the UNIX system V/386 Release 3.2 binary standard. Without exception, the functionality of the XENIX call extensions is supported within the framework of the UNIX program interface.

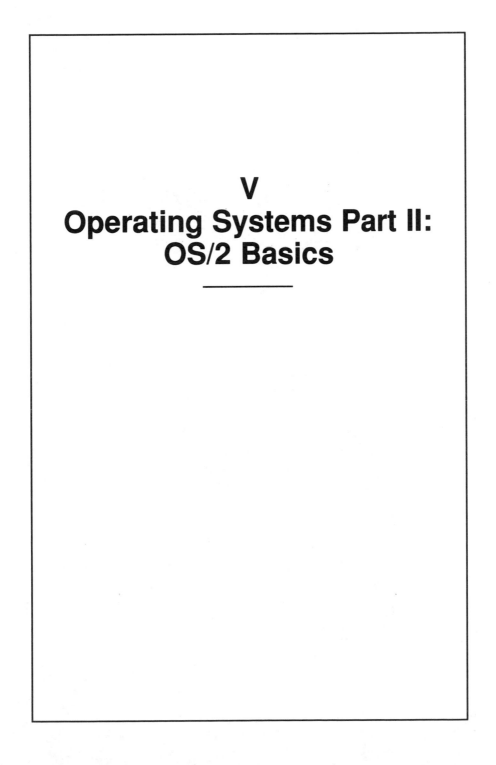

V
Operating Systems Part II:
OS/2 Basics

20
An Architecture for the Future [*]

Martin Heller

The Operating System/2 (OS/2) is the latest, most ambitious project ever under-taken by Microsoft, towering well over MS-DOS, Windows, Word, and other major languages. Its features are reminiscent of operating systems such as UNIX, MULTICS, VMS, and RSX-11M; at the same time, it remains largely compatible with MS-DOS.

Like the above-mentioned operating systems for much larger computers, OS/2 unleashes all the power inherent in the hardware while keeping a tight rein on the applications tapping that power. But unlike most of these systems, OS/2 has, as a primary design consideration, the convenience of the single user, not the maxi-mum utilization of the hardware. Faced with a choice between responding to the user or getting the maximum MIPS out of the CPU, OS/2 favors the user.

In that dim prehistoric era (until a few years ago) when computer iron was expensive and user time was cheap, operating systems primarily were driven by the need to get the maximum throughput from expensive hardware. A big OS/MVS system operator would try to balance the running of I/O-bound and CPU-bound jobs to maximize the number of CPU-minutes and I/O operations billed per day.

Today, user and programmer time costs more than computer time. OS/2 matches this new perspective with an innovative approach to system scheduling that gives top priority to whatever task the user brings into the foreground, regardless of its effect on overall system throughput. In OS/2 minimizing the loop was not a primary design consideration.

Unlike DOS, OS/2 is built in layers, as shown in Figure 20-1. Sandwiched be-tween applications at the top and hardware at the bottom are three system layers: the subsystems, the kernel, and the device drivers. While the three system levels interact, their purposes are distinct: subsystems supply the applications program interfaces (APIs), the kernel provides basic system services, and device drivers manage the intricacies of hardware. This design reflects the modern

---

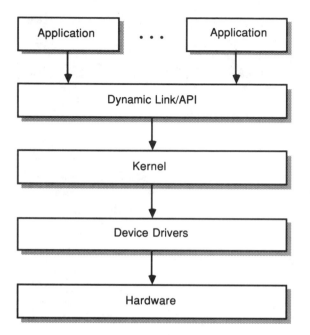

Figure 20-1: OS/2 Overall System Structure. The structure is more lay-ered and modular than that of DOS. Not only device drivers but entire subsystems such as the video and the file system can be expanded, en-hanced, or replaced outright without changing the kernel.

software-tools approach; each piece of the system performs its specialized task and passes information to another piece. The modular design makes subsystems and device drivers easy to replace. Plug in a new hardware device, copy its driver file, make a change to the CONFIG.SYS file, reboot the system, and a new ver-sion is up and running! In contrast, minicomputer systems require a time-con-suming system generation to install a new device or update any part of the oper-ating system.

The kernel constitutes the "nerve center" of OS/2: memory management, task scheduling, interprocess communication, file I/O, timer services, environment management, and basic text message facilities. For the programmer, kernel ser-vices are an arm's length away; the API implemented in dynamic-link libraries (DLLs) is at his fingertips. The API is implemented quite differently from DOS. Service functions have names instead of numbers and are entered with calls rather than interrupt instructions. Parameters are passed on the stack rather than in reg-isters. The calling protocol is the same as produced by many compilers, so OS/2 functions can be called from high-level languages such as C, Pascal, or FORTRAN.

A more significant difference between the OS/2 API and DOS is that API routines are not an integral part of the kernel but are separated into DLLs. These are similar to link-time libraries in that they contain executable code of modules called from other modules. This code, however, is not bound into the main module by the linker but brought into memory either at load time or at call time. Implementing the API by dynamic linking is quite advantageous to the operating-system designers, chiefly because the system lends itself to modification and extension. API services can be replaced simply by providing a new DLL containing modules that perform these services.

Dynamic linking presents opportunities for applications developers as well as for Microsoft. General-purpose utility libraries for database, graphics, or communications management can be distributed as DLLs instead of link-time libraries. In addition to easy upgrades and extensions, this approach's advantages are twofold. First, the distributed .EXE files are smaller. Second, several applications running concurrently can share one copy of the dynamically linked code in memory, provided that the routines are reentrant.

While the kernel encases the core of the operating system and the DLLs hold interfaces and extensions, the device drivers are the hardware-specific parts. These can be as simple as a system clock driver, and run the gamut with drivers for the keyboard, mouse, screen, and disk drives. As in DOS, device drivers permit hardware manufacturers to tailor OS/2 to their system in a way transparent to applications. Drivers can provide low-level access to the system for special applications, as they have system privileges.

OS/2's modular and expandable design allows add-on enhancements that can alter user and application system interfaces. This feature allows additions to OS/2 of a graphic user interface (the Presentation Manager, based on Microsoft Windows, announced for version 1.1) and significant enhancements to the API (database and communications services of IBM's future Extended Edition).

The Hardware Environment

OS/2 runs on the 80286 and 80386 CPUs but not on the 8088, 8086, or 80186. Therefore OS/2 runs neither on the IBM PC and PC/XT nor on the IBM Personal System/2 (PS/2) Model 30. In marked contrast to UNIX, which is designed to run on a variety of systems with different architectures, OS/2 is optimized for its

CPU and is unlikely to be ported to a non-Intel architecture. The operating-system architecture and capabilities are intrinsically linked to the 80286's architecture, with some room for enhancements to support the 80386. Therefore, understanding OS/2 requires some knowledge of the underlying hardware architecture.

Both the 80286 and the 80386 CPUs can operate in either the *real* or the *protected* mode. In real mode, the CPUs simply behave as fast 8086 chips and are limited to a 1MB memory address. Memory is addressed by the physical address, and any program, be it an application or the most crucial part of the operating system, can access any part of memory space.

Protected mode makes a larger address space available. The 80286 can address 16MB of real memory (RAM connected to the machine) and 1GB of virtual memory (address space implemented by swapping segments to and from disk.) The 80386 can address 4GB of real memory and 64TB—that's 64 *trillion* bytes— of virtual memory. Of course, there are other constraints: few personal computers today come equipped with more than 1 or 2MB of RAM and 30 or 40MB of hard disk space. Protected mode's salient quality is that is protects memory from being overwritten by an errant program. This is an invaluable tool in debugging and is the only way to preserve system integrity in a multitasking environment.

The first method of protection is to allocate each task a memory space completely disjoint from that of any other task. The hardware, not the operating system, checks that all memory references are within a task's allotted space. Any attempt to access, even to read from, a location outside this space is suppressed and causes a *protection exception* interrupt. This returns control to the operating system, which terminates the task. The result is clean isolation of tasks from one another at no cost in software overhead.

A second method of protection is to isolate the various functions of a task into four privilege levels, numbered zero through three. The privilege levels do not imply an execution priority but impose a set of validation rules for control transfers and memory accesses within a task. Level zero has highest privilege and can execute any hardware instruction; it is meant for "trusted code" such as the operating system. Level 3 has lowest privilege. For information on the hardware-level protection implemented on the 80286, see the sidebar, "How Protected Mode Protects," by Ted Mirecki, later in this chapter.

OS/2 uses level 0 for the kernel and device drivers, level 2 for special-purpose I/O routines, and level 3 for applications. Level 1 is currently unused. Applications at level 3 cannot access I/O ports nor can they set or clear interrupts. Some API calls are handled entirely within level 3; some are routed via a call gate (explained in the above-mentioned sidebar) to the kernel.

Code at level 2 can disable and enable interrupts with the CLI/STI instructions and access ports with IN/OUT instructions. This allows an application, for instance, to communicate with a data acquisition board not provided with a device driver. A program segment can be marked as intended for level 2 by declaring it an IOPL segment at link time. But at run time, IOPL is granted only if the system is booted with the statement IOPL = YES in the CONFIG.SYS file. Thus, by configuring the system appropriately, the user can choose whether to allow applications that need direct access to the hardware.

At level 0, the system is wide open; here, a process can allocate memory, build descriptor tables, adjust task scheduling, program the direct memory access (DMA)—in short, do what the operating system does. Device driver's operation is split between level 0 and application privilege; this point is discussed later in the chapter.

OS/2 supports both real and protected modes. Real mode simulates the DOS environment for compatibility with existing applications; it is discussed in the section on DOS compatibility. Protected-mode programs can benefit fully from all OS/2 services.

Mode switching on the 80286 is an interesting problem. The chip was designed to switch easily from real to protected mode (by merely turning-on a bit in a status register), but not from protected to real mode. Gordon Letwin, chief designer of OS/2, compares the mechanism that Microsoft uses to overcome this difficulty to "turning off the car to change gears," because a full system reset must be done on the fly. Doing this while running multiple tasks without losing any of them is not an easy task: it takes up to a millisecond, during which interrupts cannot be serviced. On the 80386, this is unnecessary because mode switching in either direction is done merely by setting bits. This is the one instance when OS/2 uses the 80386's special capabilities.

The Multitasking Edge

The greatest productivity gain in OS/2, compared with DOS, is its ability to run several programs concurrently. Since the user simply can switch from task to task without exiting one program and loading another, he can tailor the computer to his needs instead of trying to adjust his work schedule to the computer. One other major advantage of multitasking is that long tasks can be run in the background while other interactive work is performed in the foreground. Actually, it is an improvement over having two computers, because tasks can be synchronized and can exchange data with one another.

In scheduling multiple tasks, OS/2 uses a *prioritized preemptive* scheduling algorithm. *Prioritized* means that each time the scheduler executes, it starts up the highest-priority task ready to run (one not waiting for completion of some external event such as I/O or resource availability). If there are several such tasks with equal priority, they take turns in round-robin fashion (the next one started is the one suspended the longest).

Preemptive scheduling means that a task can be interrupted, and control given to the scheduler, by events external to the task. The alternative method, called *event-driven* scheduling, does not perform a switch until the currently executing task becomes blocked, that is, must wait for some event to occur before it can continue. In OS/2, a task obviously must be suspended when it blocks, but can also be preempted by any of three external events:

- The task calls an API service that releases some resources. If any higher-priority tasks consequently become unblocked, one of them is started.

- A hardware interrupt indicating I/O completion occurs. If some higher-priority task was waiting for this I/O, it is now started.

- A timer interrupt occurs if neither of the two events above occur in some specified time interval (which is called the *time* slice).

Note that each event merely causes the scheduling algorithm to be executed but does not cause a task switch. If the preempted task still is the highest-priority unblocked task, it resumes execution. In effect, the highest-priority task continues to run (with time-outs for scheduling interrupts), until it becomes blocked or a higher-priority task becomes unblocked.

OS/2 controls multitasking on three levels. On the top-most level is the *session*, also called a *screen group,* typically started by the user by means of the Session Manager. In most cases, each stand-alone user-level task is a separate session. For example, if a user wants to perform a database sort in the background while switching between a word processor and a spreadsheet in the foreground, he needs to start three sessions. Each session is allocated one logical screen buffer, which is displayed on the physical screen when that session is switched to the foreground.

A screen group is composed of one or more *processes*. A process is what a user thinks of a program and is associated with an executable file on disk. It can be started by the user from the operating-system prompt or by another process. In most cases, all of the processes simultaneously displaying windows on the screen must belong to one screen group.

At the lowest level, the tasks that OS/2 actually schedules are called *threads*. Each process has one or more threads or paths of execution running concurrently. The main thread of a process begins at the entry point of the program and is started by the loader; subsequent threads may be started by system calls executed within this main thread. Creating a thread is similar to calling a subroutine, but the return to the calling thread occurs as soon as the child thread is created, not when it finishes executing. OS/2 imposes a limit of 255 threads for the entire system.

This multilevel structure addresses two different aspects of multitasking. The user can control the concurrent execution of applications as sessions, while the developer has the flexibility to design applications whose functions are distributed over a set of concurrent cooperating processes and threads.

Multitasking can reach its full potential only when concurrent tasks are able to communicate with one another. The threads of one process, being part of the same program, automatically share the same data space and files (subject to the scoping rules of the language in which they are written); each process, however, is allocated a distinct set of memory and file resources. The protection mechanism of the 80286 microprocessor isolates processes from one another, unless they are designed in advance to communicate with one another. OS/2 offers abundant facilities for interprocess communications, for the dual purpose of process synchronization and data transfer.

Synchronization can be controlled by *semaphores,* named switches that can be set and tested to determine such yes/no conditions as "is this process still running" or "is the printer busy." A semaphore can be created, set, tested, and cleared by different processes, as long as all of them have been programmed to refer to the semaphore by the same identifier.

Three methods are available for data transfer among processes. The simplest and fastest of these uses a named block of *shared memory* that is mapped into the protected address space of each cooperating process. File-like I/O can be performed via in-memory structures called *pipes* and *queues*; these simulate, respectively, sequential and random-access files.

Memory Management

To many users and developers, OS/2's greatest attraction is possibly that it finally breaks the 640KB barrier. OS/2's address space corresponds to that of the 80286: 16MB of physical RAM mapped to 1GB of virtual address space. The larger address space of the 80386 is not supported by OS/2.

The general layout of OS/2 memory is shown in Figure 20-2. The resident part of the operating system is two part: *System (Lo)* and *System (Hi)*. The real-mode partition, shown in Figure 20-2 extending to 640KB, can be reduced or eliminated entirely, depending on entries in the CONFIG.SYS file. However, with System (Lo) taking up 100KB, most users with a real-mode partition will want it as large as possible.

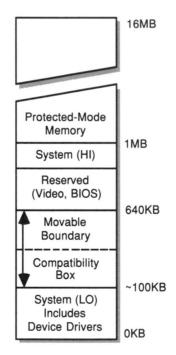

Figure 20-2: Memory Use. At last, full 80286 memory space is available. OS/2 can run most DOS programs in the compatibility box but offers less free memory than DOS as its real mode is larger.

Note that this requires 1.5MB minimum RAM and twice that for good multitasking performance. OS/2 is not designed for minimum hardware; it is no accident that the OS/2 development team at Microsoft works with 80386-based machines with lots of RAM and with big, fast hard disks.

In protected mode, OS/2 implements a virtual memory-management system based on the descriptor-table address mapping that underlies the architecture of the 80286 (see the sidebar "How Protected Mode Protects" in this chapter). If physical memory is not sufficient to satisfy an allocation request, the contents of some memory segment are swapped out to disk, and the *present* bit in that descriptor is turned off. The allocation is made from the memory that was freed as a result. When the swapped-out segment is subsequently referenced, the addressing mechanism generates a *not-present* interrupt. OS/2 blocks the task that uses this segment and starts up a system thread to read-in the missing segment (this may, in turn, cause another segment to be swapped out). After the segment has been read-in, its descriptor is updated so that it accurately reflects the new location, and the waiting task is unblocked and becomes eligible for rescheduling.

Swapping can be disabled if there is sufficient memory to load everything that needs to run at once. Swapping *should* be disabled in a realtime environment, because the delays caused by not-present faults could be unacceptable in a time-critical application.

Another possibility is that enough memory is available to satisfy a memory allocation request but that it is in several pieces scattered around the machine. In this scenario, OS/2 will move segments around until it has made a "hole" that is big enough to satisfy the request. Because the absolute location of segments is carried only in the descriptor tables (which are updated by the kernel when the movement occurs), the processes that use those segments do not require notification when segments are relocated by either swapping or moving.

In some cases, memory can be released simply by discarding a segment (marking it *not-present* in its descriptor) without writing it out to disk. Pure code is not swapped; it is discarded and later reread from the .EXE file if necessary. An application also may mark some of its data segments discardable as one way to give the operating system some flexibility in memory management. Discardable segments are useful for data that could easily be regenerated or reloaded, for instance, pieces of screen bitmap under a pop-up window or database cache buffers.

Another way to influence the system's memory-management algorithm is to link an application with some segments marked "preload" and others "load on demand." The latter delays memory allocation until it is absolutely necessary. In the meantime, more memory is available for other processes. Other suggestions for affecting memory efficiency at the source-code level are given in "Coding for Virtual Memory" later this chapter.

In order to ensure reasonable performance (see the section on timing specifications), OS/2 fixes some segments in real memory and does not allow them to be swapped out. These include the kernel code and data and the interrupt-time code for device drivers (described later). Also, the system reserves six segments of 64KB each that are allocated as a last resort when critical segments swapped out must be brought back in. All other memory is considered to be available for dynamic allocation and swapping.

OS/2 uses a least recently used (LRU) algorithm to decide what segments to swap out to disk. While this method is not important for most applications, it could, on occasion, affect optimal segment access patterns and segment sizes. The other possible swap-out algorithm, least frequently used (LFU), requires that the system track how often each segment is used, a larger overhead than simply tracking when each segment is used.

Memory allocation and swapping under OS/2 is done on a segment basis, not a page basis. The Intel architecture is basically segment oriented, with segments limited to 64KB each because of the 16-bit size of the 80286 registers. The 80386 has an additional mode that uses 48-bit addresses instead of segment: offset pairs; in this mode it can address up to 4GB of memory in a flat (unsegmented) address space. The 80386 also has hardware to implement page swapping. OS/2 does not support either of these features.

The difference between segment-based and page-based memory management is that a segment's size is determined by the application, whereas page size is determined by the system. A paged virtual memory-management system has only one size page to worry about, which is efficient when a fair amount of swapping takes place. A segment-based virtual memory-management system must track each segment's size and location in RAM or on disk.

While demand page swapping is the virtual memory-management method used in most minicomputer operating systems, including UNIX and VMS, it is not well supported by the 80286 hardware. Since OS/2 is designed to run well on the 80286 while allowing future enhancements for the 80386, the decision that was made to do only segment swapping, for which the 80286 hardware is especially designed, was reasonable.

Besides automatic and transparent virtual memory management, OS/2 provides a wide selection of system calls for memory management by applications. Included are services to allocate and free single segments, allocate "huge" segments over 64KB, subdivide segments into blocks, share segments among processes, and create segments to be written and executed.

Although the 80286 does not directly allow huge segments, OS/2 has its own mechanism for their allocation. When a huge segment is requested, the system allocates several maximum-size segments, creates descriptors for each one, and returns the selector for the first one. To access the next segment, the system returns a selector spacing value that can be added to the base selector to obtain the next selector. Note, however, that the several physical segments making up a huge segment need not be contiguous in memory.

Because segment allocation incurs substantial overhead, OS/2 has a mechanism for intrasegment memory suballocation, using a classical linked list of storage descriptors. C programmers will recognize this as the same method used by the standard *malloc()* function provided in most C compiler libraries. The system-level memory suballocation functions of OS/2 give an efficient alternative that can be used by MASM and high-level languages other than C.

Although normally the protection mechanism hides the memory allocated to one process from other processes, in OS/2 memory can be shared in two ways among processes designed to cooperate with one another. One is for the process owning a shared memory segment to pass it to another process whose task identification is known (usually, this means that the sending process created the receiving one). The other is for the owning process to create a named shared segment; then any other process that knows the name can have access to it.

Hardware protection is ideal for preventing accidental attempts to overwrite code or execute data. Situations can arise, however, in which this level of protection is undesirable. Consider the following two cases: it might be necessary to compile a bit of code and run it; then a program loader must perform segment fix-ups before it runs the code. OS/2's response to this is the *DosCreateCSALias* function, which accepts a data segment selector and returns a code segment selector for the same physical segment.

DOS Compatibility

OS/2 addresses both sides of the compatibility coin with the DOS environment. In the first place, most well-behaved DOS programs run in the OS/2 real mode. Secondly, programs can be written to run both under DOS and in the OS/2 protected mode.

Real mode (also called *DOS compatibility mode* or the *compatibility box*) can be started as an OS/2 session. It provides a reasonable facsimile of the DOS 3.x environment and includes support for all documented DOS 3.3 system services as well as a few commonly used undocumented services. (For instance, Borland's SideKick can be run under OS/2 in real mode, even though it uses undocumented system calls.) The real-mode session is suspended when it is put into the background, since OS/2 expects DOS programs to blithely write directly to video RAM; if they were allowed to time-share, they would overwrite the screen being used by protected-mode programs. However, starting up a real-mode process does not totally disable multiprocessing; protected-mode programs continue to run in the background when the compatibility box is operating in the foreground.

DOS users will feel at home with OS/2's real mode; however, they must be aware of several differences. Writing directly to the screen is possible, but the DMA ports cannot be reprogrammed. BIOS interrupts are supported, but addresses in ROM cannot be called directly. Interrupt 26H (direct disk write by absolute sector) is supported only to diskettes, not to hard disks. When a real-mode program is suspended in the background, it could lose interrupts, including clock ticks. Therefore, communications programs and programs with timing dependencies probably will fail. Table 20-1 gives a summary of the DOS features that are and those that are not supported in OS/2 compatibility mode.

Table 20.1
DOS Features in OS/2 Compatibility Mode

Supported	Not Supported
File sharing (always in effect)	DOS 3.2 Network features
Documented DOS services	Most undocumented DOS services
ROM data area	Reprogramming 8259 interrupt vectors
ROM BIOS interrupt services	Direct calls to ROM BIOS
Hardware interrupts	Realtime clock interrupt
VDI and CON device drivers	Block device drivers
Spooler interrupt (INT 28H)	Some functions of the INT 24H Critical Error Handler
Reprogramming the 8253 clock/timer	Reprogramming the disk controller
Reprogramming the COM ports	Reprogramming the DMA controllers

Although OS/2's DOS compatibility mode closely approximates the DOS 3.3 environment, it does not duplicate it. Programs that rely on unsupported features may run improperly or may not run at all.

A broad distinction also should be made between real mode and *virtual 8086 mode,* an advanced feature of the 80386 that is absent on the 80286. It provides several 1MB memory spaces, each protected from the other, in the virtual address space of the 80386. Each of these spaces can run a real-mode environment such as DOS, and the spaces can execute concurrently. In effect, the 80386 can execute simultaneously in both protected and real modes and can multitask existing DOS applications. OS/2, whose lowest common denominator is the 80286 architecture, does not support this feature—it has only one compatibility box, in the lowest 640KB of physical memory.

The other aspect of compatibility is the running of OS/2 applications under DOS. This is possible if the OS/2 application is written to use only 8086 machine instructions and call only the *Family API,* a subset of the OS/2 system services. After linking, a family application is processed with the OS/2 bind utility, adding a *stub loader* and *bindings* package to the executable file.

When a family application is started in protected mode, only the application proper is loaded from disk, and the system calls are fielded by the standard OS/2 API DLL. In compatibility mode and under DOS, the stub loader attaches the bindings to the application and performs the necessary load-time fix-ups so that API calls refer to entry points in the bindings.

The bindings translate OS/2 system API calls to DOS system function interrupts. So, in effect, the bindings are an OS/2 simulator for DOS or a call-based library to the DOS system functions.

A few other restrictions must be obeyed to build a family application. If a family application is to run in real mode, it cannot be bigger than a DOS application; it must fit into 640KB. None of the OS/2 multitasking features can be used, and certain functions must be restricted to subsets—for instance, all the features of *DosOpen* cannot be used in a family application.

Not every OS/2 function is made compatible between real and protected mode in family applications. The function *DosGetMachineMode* can be used to determine the CPU mode, and *DosVersion* to distinguish between DOS and OS/2 (the latter returns 10). Then conditional code can be employed to handle incompatibilities. For instance, the mouse library has no family binding, so sequences such as the following pseudocode are required:

```
CALL DOSGETMACHINEMODE
    (addressof(mode_flag))
if(mode_flag = 0) /* real mode */
    do INT 33H function
```

```
else                /* protected mode */.
   CALL MOUxxxx(parameters . . . )
endif.
```

Family applications are somewhat bigger on disk (by 10 to 30KB) than ordinary applications because of the presence of the stub loader and the API bindings. No speed or size overhead exists for a family application in protected mode—the bindings drop off at load time. A modest cost is incurred for running speed, load time, and size in real mode. For compilers, sort packages, or other traditional applications that would like to run in both of these modes and operating systems, family API seems a reasonable approach. Applications that need more memory, multitasking, or a graphics interface will do better with separate executable files for DOS and OS/2.

I/O Services

The API provides a complete set of services for I/O on character and block devices. Subsystems implemented in DLLs put these services into effect, allowing easy enhancement without rewriting the OS/2 kernel.

The video, keyboard, and mouse subsystems generally follow the structure of the corresponding services available under DOS. (DOS does not directly support the mouse, but most vendors supply device drivers that implement a set of functions called via interrupt 33H.) All three subsystems provide significant extensions to what is available under DOS; the best news, however, is that OS/2 video services are much faster than BIOS interrupt 10H. In addition, applications can gain direct access to both logical and physical video buffers.

One I/O service that is new to OS/2 is the character device monitor. This background-only task monitors and processes the data stream to or from a character device. One device may have several monitors; in which case each of them passes the data stream (after transforming it, if appropriate) to the next one. This is the OS/2 equivalent of DOS terminate-and-stay-resident (TSR) utilities that hook interrupts (not allowed in protected mode) and can implement keyboard macroprocessors and hot-key pop-up utilities. As support, the API includes services for writing to the physical screen even from the background.

Monitors can be used for both input and output streams. The print spooler supplied with OS/2 is a monitor that processes the stream of characters sent to the printer.

The OS/2 file system is, for all practical purposes, identical to the one in DOS. Hard disks and diskettes formatted under OS/2 can be read under DOS and vice versa. A compatible file system is good news if OS/2 and DOS are to be kept on the same hard disk. It is bad news if partitions bigger than 32MB need to be supported. A promised future enhancement, the Installable File System, will break the 32MB barrier; until then, multiple partitions must be used on large disks. The multiple-positions support is the same as the one in DOS 3.3.

Like other OS/2 services, file system functions are called by name through the standard API. Calls such as *DosOpen* and *DosWrite* will be familiar to UNIX or DOS programmers. A major innovation is that file reads and writes can be asynchronous: the system will actually create a thread to do the I/O while the calling process continues to perform other tasks.

A multitasking system, like a network, must control concurrent file access to maintain integrity of data files. In this regard, OS/2 provides the same capabilities as the SHARE option of DOS 3.1 and later versions.

Dynamic Linking

As discussed in the section on system structure, DLLs are important for keeping OS/2 modular and allowing code to be shared by multiple processes. In this section, dynamic linking is explained in some detail.

In a static link, all the target code must be present when the executable is built and incorporated into the .EXE module on disk. This makes the .EXE larger, freezes the target code, and prevents sharing of the target code. With dynamic linking, only a definition record for the target code is present at link time and incorporated into the executable file; the code itself is kept in a separate .DLL file. The target code can be changed at any time without this affecting the .EXE file, the .EXE is smaller, and the target code will be shared automatically among the multiple threads and processes.

When loading a file with calls to DLL routines, the OS/2 loader determines whether the called modules are already in memory; if not, it loads them from .DLL files. Then it resolves and fixes up call addresses, much as the DOS loader does with statically linked code. Loading of dynamically linked code can be either slower or faster than statically linked code: if .DLL code is already in memory, loading is faster; if it must be loaded, the process is slower, since .EXE files are contiguous and .DLL files require library directory lookups.

The .DLL files can be used in a number of special ways to tune application performance. Dynamic linking is simplest at load time, as described above. However, it may not be desirable to have all dynamically linked code loaded at once: there might be rarely used sections of the program requiring the loading of large libraries, which could take the program an unacceptably long initialization time, or the program could have a number of different, mutually exclusive options. In this case, dynamic linking should be done at run time instead of at load time. The routine names would be generated at run time, then loaded with explicit calls to the function *DosLoadModule*. Afterward, these could be released with calls to the function *DosFreeModule*.

OS/2 automatically takes care of data segments in shared modules. Data specific to a particular process calling a shared module is called *instance data*: memory for it is allocated and values are initialized for each calling process at each call. Data that is common to all users of the module is called *global data* and is initialized only at the point when the module is loaded.

As previously mentioned, OS/2 subsystems are generally implemented as DLLs, which makes them easy to replace, up to a point. Whereas many of the services are performed by routines that execute at privilege level 3, some of the more important ones, such as memory allocation and task control, must be performed at level 0, the kernel. The replaceable portions of these services merely invoke a call gate to transfer to entry points in the kernel.

Dexterous Drivers

As discussed in the section on system structure and shown in Figure 20-1, device drivers provide the interface between OS/2 and system peripherals. Here drivers are discussed in moderate detail; full details can fill up at least an entire book. Developers and OEMs who need to write device drivers also should request a supplemental kit (costing $150) that is available from Microsoft to owners of an OS/2 SDK. The kit includes special software that may render debugging protected-mode device drivers merely difficult instead of next to impossible.

OS/2 uses device drivers in much the same way as DOS uses BIOS—as a hardware-dependent layer between the device-independent operating system and the hardware. One obvious difference is that DOS drivers can use the ROM BIOS that comes with the hardware; for their part, the OS/2 device drivers are contained totally in software and may come with either the operating system or the hardware.

For OS/2, the ROM BIOS fulfills only two functions: to start the OS/2 bootstrap loader and to provide services to the DOS 3.x box. Since BIOS code, in general, will not run in protected mode, OS/2 ignores BIOS in protected mode and uses device drivers to go directly to the hardware. The outcome can be good and bad. On the plus side, device drivers are easier to change than BIOS chips. The drawback is that the built-in customization provided by ROM BIOS extensions in devices such as Enhanced Graphics Adapter (EGA) cards no longer exists.

The new IBM Personal System/2 (PS/2) hardware provides a partial correction for this. IBM has added an Advanced BIOS that can work with the device driver in real and protected modes. Although this innovation is not strictly an OS/2 feature, OS/2 can support it when running on a PS/2.

The device driver provides basic services directly to the operating system and indirectly to applications. It performs reads and writes on physical devices and I/O control (such as device resets and mode changes). It also isolates the OS/2 kernel from the hardware; in turn, the kernel isolates the device driver from applications, system structures, and events.

All device drivers have a standard interface. The OS/2 kernel does not know or care whether a given device uses DMA or programmed I/O, it just asks the device driver to transfer the information. Neither is the kernel concerned with the disk's geometry. On the other hand, the kernel provides a number of services to device drivers, called device helps (*DevHelps*).

The structure of an OS/2 device driver is similar to that of a DOS driver; there are both strategy and interrupt entry points. But because OS/2 is a multitasking system, this division makes sense at last. The flow of control through a device driver is as outlined in the paragraphs below.

When an application requests a device I/O, it calls the system API; the request reaches the kernel, which blocks the requesting thread, and, in turn, calls the device-driver strategy routine. This routine queues the request, and, if the device is not busy, starts it. The strategy routine then terminates, and control returns to the kernel, which dispatches the next thread.

When the device completes the I/O request, it issues a hardware interrupt that asynchronously preempts whatever thread is executing. The interrupt is handled by the device driver's aptly named interrupt routine, which marks the previous queued request complete, unblocks any threads waiting for this request to complete, and restarts the device with the next I/O request packet in the queue. At the device-driver level, all I/O requests are synchronous, that is, at least one thread always awaits every request. For asynchronous requests from applications, the kernel creates a system thread that waits for completion and signals by resetting a RAM semaphore.

The device driver is an OS/2-format .EXE file on disk, with the same structure as any protected-mode program with dynamic links to OS/2 services. It can have multiple segments in the file, but only the first two, DATA followed by CODE, are kept after initialization. A special header is located at the beginning of the DATA segment that is used for system management. This header is similar to the one used in DOS device drivers; it includes a bit-encoded device attribute word, an offset to the strategy routine, and the name of the device (for a character device driver) or the number of units (for a block device driver). As in DOS, OS/2 device drivers are kept in a linked list in memory.

Although OS/2 allows direct access to API functions from high-level languages, writing device drivers in compiled languages is not practical. The start-up routine inserted by the typical compiler is suitable only for application-level programming, and parameters are passed to the *DevHelp* routines in machine registers.

A device driver executes in one of the following four modes: *Init, User, Kernel,* and *Interrupt.*

Init mode operates at privilege level 3 with but with I/O privilege. This is operating-system boot time, and it is the device driver's chance to initialize the hardware in a synchronous way, as part of the thread of the system initialization process. As in DOS, the initialization code is called through the strategy routine as an Init request package. The driver can hook both hardware and ROM BIOS interrupts and allocate any memory it will need to service I/O requests. To do so, it can use the kernel *DevHelp* services and a subset of the OS/2 API calls. The initialization code can be discarded once that it has been implemented.

User mode is used for handling real-mode BIOS ROM requests from the compatibility box. Real-mode applications can perform device I/O through the DOS interrupt 21H function interface, through a ROM BIOS interrupt, or through direct access to the device. Requests through interrupt 21H are converted to request packets by the kernel, but BIOS interrupts must be intercepted by the device driver.

Because the ROM BIOS was never intended for a multitasking environment, the device driver must screen requests to the BIOS. First, it must serialize access to the device typically via "device-busy" semaphores. Second, it has to protect critical sections of ROM code from being preempted. For instance, the printer, screen, and disk ROM BIOS service routines are time critical and cannot tolerate being suspended—thus, the device driver has to lock the real-mode session in the foreground while I/O is in progress.

The device driver can hook ROM BIOS interrupts with the *SetROMVector* device help. It can protect critical BIOS code from being blocked with the *ROMCrit-Section* device help function, which will prevent the user from switching away from the real-mode screen. On the other hand, if the user has a TSR application that takes control while the CPU is executing ROM BIOS code with *ROMCrit-Section* set, it might not be possible to switch away from the real-mode session until the TSR application is stopped.

Kernel mode is in effect when the device-driver strategy routine (also known as the task-time routine) is called. The strategy routine will not be preempted by a task switch but can be interrupted by incoming hardware interrupts. It must actually protect itself against its own interrupt routine by disabling interrupts when it checks for an active device as well as when it examines the device queue.

The task-time routine should be fully reentrant in order for it to support multiple concurrent requests. Although it will not be preempted, this routine may become blocked (for example, by referring to a segment that was swapped out), or it may voluntarily yield control to a time-critical thread. Microsoft suggests checking for a time-critical process every 3 milliseconds and yielding control if one is found. If the task-time routine is suspended for any reason whatsoever, there is, of course, no guarantee that this routine will be resumed before the next request comes along.

The strategy routine is called with a pointer to a request packet, which contains 13 bytes of request header and a variable-length data section. The pointer is bi-modal (valid in either real or protected mode) and can be used directly as a 32-bit physical address for linking the request into the queue.

The task-time routine is responsible for queuing request packets and mapping addresses for the interrupt time routine (the reason for this is explained below). I/O control operations are generally done immediately and synchronously; reads and writes are generally queued. It is up to the strategy routine whether queued I/Os are FIFO or sorted by sector: character devices are almost always FIFO, and block devices are often sorted. Sorted block access on disks is sometimes called "elevator seeking."

Interrupt mode refers to the time when the hardware interrupt hands control to the device driver's interrupt entry point. This routine must confirm that the interrupt is indeed for this driver (in case that hardware interrupts are being shared) and, if this is the case, restart the device for the next I/O request in the queue.

Because the machine mode and addressing context may be different at task time from what they are at interrupt time, device drivers must be *bimodal,* that is, able to operate equally well in both real and protected modes. Because real-mode addresses are, in general, not the same as protected-mode addresses, segment arithmetic is inappropriate. And, as the contents of local descriptor tables need not remain the same from task time to interrupt time, the storing of segment descriptors also is inappropriate.

The solution is to store only 32-bit physical addresses. There are *DevHelp* routines to convert physical addresses to and from virtual addresses and user virtual addresses. For instance, the *PhysToVirt* function converts a 32-bit address to a segment:offset pair in real mode and a valid selector:offset pair in protected mode (creating descriptor-table entries as appropriate). This relieves the device driver from the responsibility of having to do mode-dependent addressing by recognizing the CPU mode. The call *UnPhysToVirt* is used as a signal that the device driver has finished with the temporary selectors that were set up with its calls to *PhysToVirt*. The *VirtToPhys* device help is used by the strategy routine to convert the virtual buffer addresses passed by the client routine to the 32-bit physical addresses that will be valid at interrupt time.

Bimodal addressing may seem more like voodoo than programming. But some of the confusing bits are actually simple in practice. For example, suppose that a buffer is in extended memory and an interrupt comes in real mode. The interrupt-time routine cannot access extended memory in real mode, but it does not have to: all it has to do is mark the I/O packet complete, restart the device, and exit.

Other considerations in designing device drivers are that protected-mode objects are usually movable and their location may change between task and interrupt times. *DevHelps* serve to lock and unlock memory and to allocate and deallocate physical memory. However, tying up too much static memory could increase the number of swapping operations that the system must perform to run applications—this is a trade-off between the extra code to handle moving objects and the overall system performance.

Timing Specifications

The announced critical OS/2 timing specifications are for a standard 6-MHz AT. All timings should be faster on higher-clock-speed 80286 machines and on 80386 machines. These numbers are targeted by Microsoft for their software and developers should strive to attain them in order to maintain acceptable overall system performance.

Interrupt latency. The maximum time from the occurrence of a hardware interrupt to its acknowledgement by a device driver is 400 microseconds.

Mode switching. It takes a maximum of 1 millisecond to switch from protected mode to real mode on an 80286 machine. Switching back to protected mode is faster; mode switching on an 80386 machine is much faster.

Critical thread latency. The highest-priority thread should have to wait no more than 6 milliseconds from the time that it is unblocked up to the time that it starts running. Thread latency includes, as well, 1 millisecond of possible context switching.

Timer resolution. OS/2 resets the system timer to operate at 32 Hz. Time intervals, although they can be specified in milliseconds, are restricted to the resolution of a timer tick, approximately 32 milliseconds.

In the final analysis, regardless of specifications or any adherence to them, OS/2's performance will be measured in real-world end-user applications. A complete exploration of this subject must await the introduction of significant applications whose performance can be measured.

From all the evidence available, OS/2 constitutes a complicated operating system whose true dimensions will come to light only through actual hands-on experience. Although much remains to be learned about the system, OS/2's capabilities certainly make the effort worthwhile. The three salient features of OS/2 architecture are the following: a design basis that favors interactive response, close optimization to the underlying hardware, and a modular, expandable system structure.

At the moment, the system has (finally!) realized the full potential of the AT-class machine. Although an 80286 machine is hardly state of the art, it represents a quantum leap over the most prevalent personal computer configuration, a wheezing antique of an 8088 CPU running DOS.

OS/2's main attraction, however, is the promise that it harbors for the future. Microsoft has announced that OS/2 is poised to become the bedrock upon which several generations of software for ever more powerful Intel-based machines will be built.

How Protected Mode Protects

A review of the principles of hardware protection is important because OS/2 uses protected mode on the 80286. The 80286 hardware design provides protection on three levels.

First, it isolates concurrently running tasks by limiting memory space that is separately defined for each task.

Second, it isolates various functions performed within a task by assigning them to one of four privilege levels and enforcing rules for memory access across level boundaries. Figure 20-3 illustrates the relationship between intertask and interprivilege protection. A code executing at level zero has the highest privilege, which means that it can perform any instruction in the 80286 instruction set and access memory at any level. Code at a less privileged (numerically greater) level cannot execute certain instructions and cannot directly access segments at more privileged levels. The chip designer's intention (honored by OS/2) was that only the kernel should run at level zero, whereas applications run at level three, which has the lowest privilege.

Third, the protection mechanism imposes memory typing to prevent writing over code and executing data. When the memory space is defined (as explained below), every segment is identified as either executable (code) or readable (data). Code segments also can be declared readable and data segments writable, but writable and executable characteristics are mutually exclusive.

The implementation of all three levels is tightly intertwined within the mechanism for generating physical memory addresses.

In real mode, the addressable memory space of the 80286 is predefined at 1MB, and any instruction in any program can access any location in this space. In protected mode, the addressable memory space is defined in tables containing a descriptor for each memory segment of 64KB or less. Every task is provided with two descriptor tables: a global descriptor table (GDT) that is available to all tasks in the system and a local descriptor table (LDT) specific to each task. At any given time, only one GDT and one LDT are accessible. Because memory can be accessed only through a descriptor, a task cannot access any memory outside of the space that is defined by its particular pair of descriptor tables.

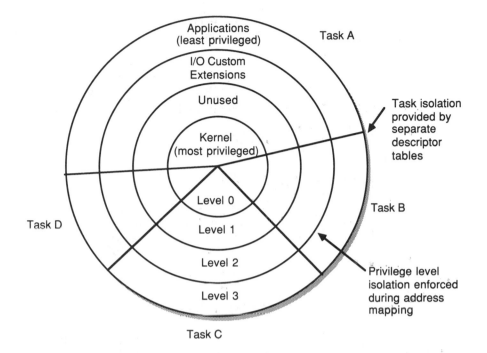

Figure 20-3: Intertask and Interlevel Protection. The protection mechanism totally isolates each task in a separate address space; within each task, it enforces strict rules of interaction between the code and data segments at different privilege levels.

A descriptor table can be up to 64KB; therefore it can contain up to 8192 eight-byte descriptors, each defining a segment of up to 64KB. With two tables of maximum size, each task can be provided with an addressable memory space of twice 8192 times 64KB, or 1GB (a billion bytes). Of course, the physical memory of the system (limited by the 24-bit address bus to 16MB) limits how many of these segments can be resident in physical RAM at any given time, but, as explained below, a mechanism is available for recording whether a particular segment is or is not resident.

The format of a descriptor is shown in Figure 20-4. The high-order two bytes are solely to provide compatibility with the eight-byte descriptors of the 80386; they must be zero. The 24-bit base address locates the start of the segment in the 16MB physical memory space; the 16-bit limit field holds the length of the segment minus one, or the offset of the last byte within the segment. The access byte specifies the type, and privilege level of the segment and whether it is currently in memory. Some descriptors do not define memory segments but contain special pointer values for validating intertask and interlevel control transfers. One type of control descriptor is described later in this sidebar.

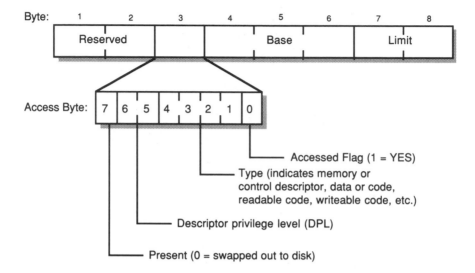

Figure 20-4: Segment Descriptor Format. Only memory defined by segment descriptors is accessible in protected mode (two descriptor tables define a task's memory space). The contents of a descriptor locate the segment in physical memory and validate access.

Descriptor tables are built in memory, but memory cannot be accessed until descriptor tables are built. In order to break this chicken-and-egg impasse, the GDT is created by the operating system before the switch to protected mode, when the lower 1MB of memory is directly accessible through physical addresses. Furthermore, the descriptor defining the memory for the GDT is kept not in a memory-based table but in a 40-bit GDT register within the CPU. This register holds the 24-bit physical base address and 16-bit length of the GDT; no access byte is needed because the table cannot be swapped out to disk, and its type and privilege (level zero) are invariant. LDTs are created in protected mode, in memory defined by descriptors in the GDT. The operating system builds an LDT for a task at load time, creating an initial set of descriptors based on information inserted in the load file by the linker. Additional descriptors within an LDT are created and destroyed in response to memory-allocation requests from the task. All access to descriptor tables is limited to code executing at privilege-level zero.

Protection checks are applied by the hardware at two points during execution: first, when a segment register is loaded, then at each reference to memory location. If a violation of the protection rules is detected at any point during the testing process, the hardware generates one of several processor interrupts known as protection exceptions. The operating system must provide interrupt handlers for each exception to process each type of protection violation appropriately.

The instructions that change the contents of registers DS, ES, and SS are LDS, LES, MOV, and POP; for the CS register they are the intersegment form of JMP, CALL, and RET. In protected mode, the value loaded into a segment register is called a segment selector; it is an index into one of the two descriptor tables available to the task. Because each descriptor is eight bytes long, the low-order three bits of its index are known to be zero and can be used to hold other information, as shown in Figure 20-5.

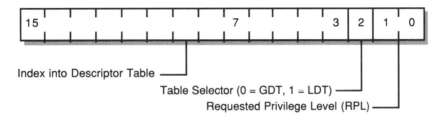

The 13-bit index value is multiplied by eight to give an offset to an eight-byte descriptor in one of the two tables selected by bit 3

Figure 20-5: Segment Selector Format

Figure 20-6 illustrates the mechanism of translating a selector into a segment address using the GDT (the LDT is used in a similar fashion). The index value from the selector first is converted to an offset by zeroing out the low-order three bits, then compared to the length of the GDT in the limit field of the GDT register. A protection exception occurs if the offset is greater than the limit. Otherwise, the offset is added to the base address, giving the 24-bit physical address of the desired descriptor.

The selected descriptor's access byte is used to determine the type, privilege level, and presence in memory of the target segment. In most cases, the type must indicate a memory, not a control, descriptor (but see a special case below), and the segment must be marked executable for loading into CS, readable for DS and ES, and writable for SS.

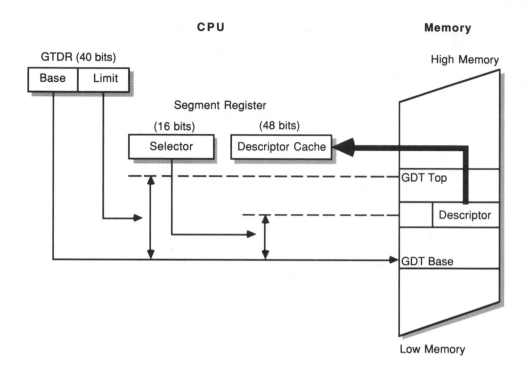

Figure 20-6: Logical-to-Physical Address Mapping. The selector points to a descriptor, which, if it passes certain checks, is loaded into the hidden cache portion of the register. A memory address is generated by adding the offset to the segment base loaded from the descriptor.

Privilege-level rules are different for loading CS and other segment registers. For CS, a jump or call instruction is legal if the descriptor privilege level (DPL) in the access byte is equal to the current privilege level (CPL) of the segment currently executing. This means that transfers of control are allowed only within the same privilege level, but a mechanism, (described later) is supplied to allow calls (but not jumps) to more privileged levels. A return is allowed to a level of equal or lesser privilege.

For data and stack segments, the target segment DPL cannot have higher numeric privilege level than the numeric maximum of the CPL and the requested privilege level (RPL) of the new segment selector. This test is intended for the validation of data selectors passed to a routine at a more privileged level; the RPL indicates the privilege level from which the selector originated. In this way, a program at a low privilege level cannot request a privileged program to overwrite privileged memory.

A protection exception occurs if any of the above type or privilege rules are violated. Otherwise, the *present* bit is tested, and a *not-present* exception occurs if the bit is zero. The hardware does not directly implement virtual memory management, but supports its implementation in the operating system by issuing an interrupt when a missing segment is referenced. The operating system is responsible for turning off the present bit when a segment is swapped out, to keep track of its location on disk, and to provide an exception handler that reads the missing segment back in and updates the present bit and base address in its descriptor.

If no exceptions are generated by the type, privilege, and presence checks, the new selector is now moved into the segment register, and the low-order six bytes of the descriptor are copied from the descriptor table into the segment register's descriptor cache. Each of the four segment registers has this 48-bit extension (not accessible by any instructions) that is automatically loaded whenever a valid sector is loaded into the 16-bit part of the register that is visible to programs. Its purpose is to keep the physical segment address and length on-board the CPU so that the subsequent protection checks can be made without reference to any of the tables that are in memory.

Whenever a descriptor is moved to a segment cache, the *accessed* bit in its descriptor in the table is turned on. The hardware neither tests this bit nor resets it when the cache is overwritten; this feature is meant merely to aid the operating system in deciding which segments to swap out by identifying those that were never loaded into segment registers.

Another protection test is applied at each reference to a memory location. The offset portion of the address is compared with the limit value in the cache; a protection exception occurs if the offset if greater. Otherwise, the offset is added to the base value from the cache in order to produce a 24-bit physical address of the location that was referenced.

It was mentioned that descriptors not only can define memory segments but also can provide information for enforcing protection when control transfers are required among tasks and among privilege levels.

As described above, the protection mechanism requires that the privilege level of a segment targeted by a far call be the same as the level of the calling segment. But interlevel calls are useful to invoke highly privileged "trusted code" to perform system-level services (such as memory allocation) for applications. An inter-level call is possible, provided that the selector portion of the far-call address points to a control descriptor known as a *call gate*. Its format is similar to that of a segment descriptor (see Figure 20-4), but the base field contains a 16-bit selector instead of a 24-bit base address, and the limit field contains the offset of the entry point called. The call-gate DPL must be the same as the calling-segment CPL, or a protection exception occurs.

When the hardware determines that the target address refers to a call gate and not a memory segment, it performs an additional level of address translation. The selector and offset from the original call instruction are replaced with the corresponding values from the call gate (note that the original offset value is ignored), and a modified address generation process is performed with the new values. This second process follows the same steps as the first, except that the privilege checking is relaxed: no exception is generated if the target segment is at a more privileged level than the segment issuing call. However, calls to less privileged levels still are not allowed.

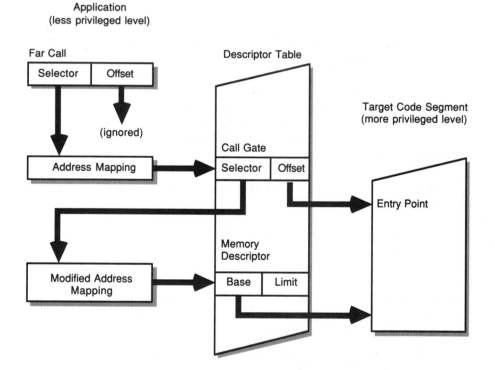

Figure 20-7: Transfer through a Call Gate. A direct call to a procedure in a more privileged segment can be transferred via a call gate with a privilege level similar to the caller's. Level checking is relaxed to allow a call, not a jump, to a segment of higher privilege.

The overall process of transfer through a call gate is illustrated in Figure 20-7. Here, the call gate is shown with a selector to its own descriptor table, but it could equally well refer to the other table. Besides the capability of performing privileged services from the applications level, this mechanism provides two additional benefits. First, it ensures that less trusted code cannot be used to provide services for (which implies writing data into) more privileged segments. Second, because the call gate hides the entry point in memory inaccessible to the calling program, it ensures that execution transfers to a valid entry point in the more privileged segment, not to mid-procedure or, worse yet, to mid-instruction.

—Ted Mirecki

Coding for Virtual Memory

Because OS/2 performs segment swapping, choice of segment size and access patterns must be a consideration for optimum performance. For instance, hundreds of tiny segments will entail a lot of overhead in memory allocation time and header space—each segment has about 30 bytes of header. On the other hand, if 64KB segments are available for constant swapping, substantial overhead is incurred every time the system performs that 64KB disk transfer.

Controlling the order in which memory is accessed determines the amount of swapping within the application. For instance, if two large arrays are in separate segments and the following code is written:

```
for i = 0 to size
  array1(i) = <expression1>;
  array2(i) = <expression2>;
next i
```

segments will be switched inside the loop and, in the worst-case scenario, both segments might be swapped each time through the loop. On the other hand, if the code is written as

```
for i = 0 to size
  array1(i) = <expression1>;
next i
for i = 0 to size
  array2(i) = <expression2>;
next i
```

localized access within each segment is guaranteed, instead of flipping between them. Of course, if array1 and array2 were in the same segment, the first method would be more efficient than the second, because, as in this case, there would be only one set of index overheads in existence.

The above paragraphs provide suggestions for affecting memory efficiency at the source-code level.

21

A Programmer's
Introduction to OS/2 *

Ray Duncan

OS/2 is Microsoft's multi-tasking, virtual-memory, single- user operating system for personal computers based on the Intel 80286 and 80386 microprocessors. Variously referred to in the press during the last two years as DOS 5, NewDOS Advanced DOS, ADOS, and 286 DOS, OS/2 is the first software product born of the Microsoft/IBM joint development agreement of August 1985.

OS/2 falls between Microsoft's MS-DOS single-tasking operating system and the XENIX multiuser, multitasking operating system. Although it is compatible with MS-DOS file systems and can run many existing MS-DOS applications, and although it has a hierarchical directory structure, I/O redirection, and some interprocess communication mechanisms similar to XENIX, it is neither an over-blown MS-DOS nor a stripped-down XENIX. It is a completely new operating system designed to support high-performance, intensely interactive, "personal-productivity," and networking applications in a business environment.

The retail version of the basis OS/2 operating system will not reach users until early 1988, and the graphic user-interface layer (the protected-mode Windows/Presentation Manager) will arrive even later. However, to help programmers get familiar with the new system as quickly as possible and encourage the early port of existing applications to the new protected-mode environment, both Microsoft and IBM are directing earnest evangelical efforts at the software-development community.

Both companies have announced an aggressive schedule of seminars for developers throughout the summer of 1987, and both have shipped software-development kits containing prerelease versions of the operating system and programming tools.

---

* © McGraw-Hill Information Systems Company, *BYTE*, September 1987, p. 101

Key Features of OS/2

MS-DOS runs the 80286 processor in real mode, which is essentially an 8086-emulation mode. Even though the benefits of the 80286's higher clock rates and more efficient instruction set were not insignificant, both programmers and users found the persistence of the real mode's 1-megabyte-addressing limitation frustrating. OS/2 runs the 80286 in its preferred protected mode, with a physical address space of 16 megabytes and a virtual address space of 1 gigabyte. This use of protected mode has important implications for the structure of the operating system itself and for the design and operation of applications programs. (You can find a more detailed introduction to protected mode in Ross Nelson's article "A Protected-Mode Program for the PC AT" in the *Fall 1986 Inside the IBM PCs*, or in *Intel's iAPX 286 Operating System Writer's Guide*.)

From the programmer's point of view, the key features of software development under OS/2 are a new application program interface (API), a preemptive multi-tasking, interprocess- communication facilities, memory protection and virtual memory, dynamic linking, and compatibility with MS-DOS.

Application Program Interface

The OS/2 kernel provides about 200 services to applications programs executing under its control. Collectively they are referred to as the OS/2 API. You invoke all these services with far calls that are resolved at load time. Parameters-a mixture of values and addresses of values or structures-are pushed onto the stack prior to the call. A status code is returned in register AX: 0 if the function succeeded, or an error code if the function failed. Other returned values are placed in variables or arrays whose addresses were passed in the original call.

The OS/2 API functions fall into four major categories. DOSxxx calls are general services, including file and record I/O, device monitors, dynamic linking, multitasking, interprocess communication, memory management, times and internationalization support. VIOxxx calls display characters or strings with or without associated attributes, read back characters (and optionally, their attributes) from the display buffer, read or set cursor position and type, scroll up/down/left/right, set or get video mode, and put up or take down the pop-up window. KBDxxx calls are for keyboard status and input. MOUxxx calls read pointing-device position, status, and state of buttons; they also hide or reveal the pointer or set its shape.

A small subset of the above calls, known as the family API, has direct equivalents in MS-DOS function calls. OS/2 programs that restrict themselves to using the family API calls can be linked and abound in a special manner that lets them run in three environments: MS-DOS 2.x/3.x, the DOS 3.x compatibility box of OS/2, or protected mode under OS/2. Such programs are called family apps or bound apps; the programming tools in the software-development kits are supplied in this form.

The Windows/Presentation Manager offers applications programs another 500 or so functions that create, destroy, and control the appearance and size of windows, perform device- independent graphic output, put up and take down the pull-down menus, load resources, and so on. I'll ignore these for the present, except to note that when Windows/Presentation Manager is present, it replaced the system's default VIO and KBD routines with new services that let a well-behaved text application run in a window without its knowledge.

An interesting feature of the new OS/2 API is that it is equally efficient to call it from either a high-level language or from assembly language. Consider the function DOSSLEEP (probably the simplest useful function in the OS/2 API), which is called with a double-word value in milliseconds and suspends the caller's execution for the specified interval. The assembly -language form of the function call is

```
extern DOSSLEEP: far
    .
    .
    .
    push 0          ; push double value
                      1000
    push 1000       ; to sleep for 1
                      second
    call DOSSLEEP   ; transfer to OS/2
    or ax,ax        ; did call succeed?
    jnz error       ; jump if call
                      failed
```

To call an OS/2 API function from a C program, you simply declare it as far Pascal (i.e., parameters pushed left to right, the call routine clears the stack) and then invoke it directly:

```
extern unsigned far pascal
  DOSSLEEP(unsigned long);

  .
  .

status=DOSSLEEP(1000L);
```

The OS/2 C compiler generates the right code for the call automatically. There is no execution time or space penalty, there is no need for intermediate library functions to shift parameters around or pop them into registers before transferring to the operating system, and the source code is far more compact and readable than its assembly language counterpart.

Although the OS/2 API is a considerable architectural change from the familiar INT 21h of MS-DOS, it offers many significant advantages. The API lets OS/2 take full advantage of the 80286's ability to automatically copy parameters from the caller's stack to the receiving routine's stack. The API also enforces the separation between kernel and user-privilege levels by protected-mode call gates. The API might make subsequent conversion of applications for a true 32-bit 80386 version of OS/2 almost trivial, and it raises the possibility that the entire operating system and its applications could someday be ported to a processor with a non-Intel architecture, such as the Motorola 68020.

Preemptive Multitasking

Preemptive multitasking refers to the operating system's ability to allocate processor time between multiple tasks in a manner that is invisible to those programs. It is sometimes called time-slicing. A hardware interrupt, called the timer tick, which is generated by a programmable timer chip, lets the operating system regain control at predetermined intervals.

After updating the current data and time, control is transferred to a scheduler that maintains a list of the active tasks and their state. If the scheduler determines that the currently executing program has exhausted its time slice or that another program with a higher priority is ready to execute, the scheduler suspends (preempts) the current program and gives control to another program.

The user's interface to OS/2's multitasking capabilities is simple and easy to understand. A special supervisory program, called the session manager, lets you start up one or more copies of the system's command processor (CMD.EXE, the protected-mode counterport of MS-DOS's COMMAND.COM). Each command processor and the programs that users launch from it are collectively termed a screen group and own a virtual screen buffer that receives all the output from the programs in that group. Users can cycle from one screen group to another with the aid of the session manager's hot key; when a screen group is brought to the foreground, its virtual screen buffer is mapped to the physical screen, and the programs in that group acquire control of the keyboard.

The programmer's view of multitasking under OS/2 is somewhat more complex and involves three types of system objects: screen groups, processes, and threads. Each screen group contains one or more active processes, and each process contains one or more active threads. The simplest case of a process is conceptually similar to a program loaded under MS-DOS: The process is initiated when the operating system allocates some memory, loads the necessary code and data from a disk file, and gives it control at an entry point specified in the file. Subsequently, the process can obtain and release other resources (such as access to disk files and additional memory), perform input or output, and spawn other processes by calls to the operating system. A process's membership in a screen group depends strictly on the membership of its "parent" process; similarly, any "child" processes that it creates will belong to the same screen group.

The OS/2 concept of threads is rather novel. A thread is a point of execution within a process and is associated with a stack, general register contents, and a state (i.e., waiting for some event, ready to execute, or executing).

Each process has exactly one thread when it is created, whose initial execution point is the entry point of that process. But that thread can create additional threads than then run asynchronously from the first and share ownership of all the processes' resources and "near data segments" (DGROUP).

Threads within a process can dynamically suspend, reactivate, and vary the priorities of one another and can perform input and output autonomously: Any necessary serialization of I/O is done within OS/2. Communication between threads is fast, since it is typically performed through shared data structures and does not need to involve operating system calls.

Interprocess Communication

OS/2 supports all the major methods of interprocess communication found in other multitasking operating systems. RAM semaphores are used for local signaling or resource synchronization between multiple threads in the same process. System semaphores that are called global objects can be used for signaling or resource synchronization between processes. Pipes, as in UNIX, allow high-performance transfer of variable-length messages between closely related processes (usually a parent and its child processes).

Shared memory, named global memory segments, can be accessed by two or more processes. Queues named global objects have several features: You can order messages in the queue by FIFO (first in/first out), LIFO (last in/last out), or priority, the queue can grow to almost any size, and many processes can write messages to the queue, but only the queue creator can remove them. Event flags, similar to those in UNIX, are used to communicate between related processes and can simulate a software interrupt.

Memory Protection and Virtual Memory

All the processors in the Intel 80x86 family generate memory addresses by combining the contents of a segment register (which you can think of as a base pointer) with an absolute or relative offset. On the 8086 or the 80286 in real mode, the value in a segment register is simply a paragraph address (a 20-bit physical address divided by 16). In protected mode, an additional level of addressing indirection is added. The value in a segment register is a selector, which is an index to an entry in a descriptor table that contains the base address and length of a memory segment, segment attributes (executable, read-only, or read/write), and privilege information. Each time a program makes a memory reference, the hardware accesses the descriptor table to generate the physical address and simultaneously checks to make sure that the memory access is valid.

Protected-mode addressing completely isolates tasks from one another. The descriptor tables themselves are not accessible by applications programs; only the operating system can manipulate them. If a program attempts to read or write a memory area that does not belong to it or calls an operating system routine to which it has not been given access, a hardware interrupt is generated that lets the operating system terminate the errant program. The combination of preemptive multi-tasking and memory protection contributes to a robust environment: There is little opportunity in protected mode for an ill-behaved program to bring the entire system down by going into a loop or writing on code or data owned by another program.

The flip side of the memory-protection coin is virtual memory. OS/2 can manage up to 16 megabytes of physical memory, but the amount of installed RAM is nearly irrelevant to the average applications program running in protected mode.

When the sum of the memory owned by active programs in the system exceeds the amount of physical memory, memory segments are rolled in and out from a swap file as needed (or just discarded and reloaded in the case of code or read-only data segments). This segment-swapping is accomplished by a module of OS/2 known as the memory manager, with the aid of the processor's hardware memory-protection mechanisms, and the process is completely invisible to applications programs. The theoretical limit on the amount of memory a program can own or share is around half a gigabyte, but the practical limit is the amount of physical RAM plus the swapping space available on the hard disk.

Dynamic Linking

The 80286's support for protected virtual memory makes it possible to place frequently used procedures, including most of the OS/2 and graphic user-interface services available to applications programs, into special fields known as dynamic link (dynalink) libraries. The routines in these libraries can be shared by all the programs that require them and are not loaded from disk into physical memory until they are needed. Placing common procedures in dynalink libraries lets you alter, improve, or replace those routines without any change to the applications programs that invoke them.

The calls from a program to the routines in a dynalink library are resolved in two stages. The linker is informed that a particular external name is a dynalink routine by either an Import statement in the program's module-definition file or by finding a special "stub" record in an object-module library. It then builds the information necessary for deferred linking into the program's .EXE-file header: the names of the dynalink routines that are needed, the modules in which they will be found, and a list for each routine of all the addresses within the program where it is called. When you load the program for execution, the list of imported routines is examined, any external routines that are not already resident in memory are fetched from the disk, and the addresses within the calling program are fixed up appropriately. You can think of this as late binding.

Compatibility with MS-DOS

OS/2 provides upward compatibility and a smooth transition from MS-DOS at three levels: the user interface, the file system, and the DOS 3.x compatibility box.

The command-line interface of OS/2 version 1.0 is identical to that of MS-DOS, with the exception of a few new or enhanced commands, batch-file directives, and CONFIG.SYS file options. The session manager, which is triggered by a hot key and lets the user move from one screen group and command processor to another, is self-explanatory, and its use becomes natural very quickly. Adaptation to the Windows/PM, when it arrives, will also be easy: Its methods of operation and pull-down menus are quite similar to that of Microsoft Windows except that it uses overlapping rather than tiled windows, and you launch programs from a list of long, descriptive names rather than double-clicking on a filename in a disk-directory listing.

The file structure for both flexible and fixed disks-that is, the layout of the partition table, directories, file- allocation tables, and the files area-is exactly the same for the initial release of OS/2 as for MS-DOS. This means that you won't be escaping the 32-megabyte volume limit or the 8- character filename limit for some time yet. However, it does let developers exchange files and move back and forth between the two environments with a minimum of difficulty. OS/2's provisions for mountable file systems portend release from some of the historical MS-DOS limitations.

The DOS 3.x compatibility box is not a box at all, but a component of the OS/2 operating system that lets one "old" applications designed for MS-DOS run at a time in the 80286's real mode alongside "new" protected-mode applications. Requests by the real-mode application for MS-DOS services are trapped by OS/2 and translated into API calls, switching back and forth between real mode and protected mode as necessary to perform I/O and other services. The user can determine how much memory will be allocated to the DOS 3.x box by an entry in the CONFIG.SYS file or disable it completely.

One disadvantage of the DOS 3.x box is that it makes the system vulnerable as a whole. Ill-behaved MS-DOS programs that manipulate the hardware directly or take over interrupt vectors can cause problems or even a hard crash--this is unfortunately the trade-off for being able to use the old programs at all.

A Simple OS/2 Application

An OS/2 application is built from two basic elements: source files that can be compiled or assembled into relocatable object modules and a module-definition file that describes the program's segment behavior (see Figure 21-1).

In a traditionally trivial program that displays the message "Hello World!," the file HELLO.ASM contains the assembly language source code for the program (see Listing 21-1). It looks similar to an equivalent MS-DOS program, with a few exceptions.

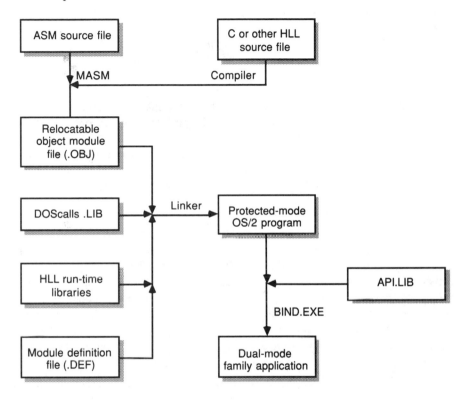

Figure 21-1: The procedure for creating protected-mode and dual-mode, or "family" applications for OS/2.

The directive .286c permits the assembly of 80286 nonprivileged instructions that are not present in the 8086 instruction set. The handiest of these is the "push immediate" instruction, which saves time and space when you set up parameters for an OS/2 API call.

References to OS/2 API entry points are accomplished with EXTRN directives, assigning a far attribute to the external name. The assembler does not know anything about the nature of the procedure represented by the external name, but only that it has to generate an intersegment call to reach it and that the final address will be fixed up later.

The declaration of DGROUP with the group directive is mandatory. This is a "magic" name that specifies the application's automatic data segment, which also contains the default stack and heap. The _TEXT and _DATA segment names are simply conventions used by the Microsoft high-level language compilers. Unlike MS-DOS, OS/2 automatically initializes the DS register to point to DGROUP before it transfers control to the program's entry point (the other conditions at entry to a protected-mode application are summarized in Figure 21-2). This is also reflected in the ASSUME directive that follows the segment declaration of _TEXT.

The remainder of the HELLO.ASM file contains nothing unexpected. Two calls to OS/2 services are demonstrated: DOSWRITE performs a synchronous write to a file or a device, and DOSEXIT terminates the application with a return code. DOSWRITE is the counterpart to MS-DOS's INT 21h function 40h, and DOS-EXIT is comparable to MS-DOS's INT 21h function 4Ch. The last line in the source file is an end directive that defines the program's entry point in the usual manner.

The file HELLO.DEF (see Figure 21-3) is the module-definition file for the program. It demonstrates only a few of the possible commands and options that can be used in this file. The name directive states that this is an executable program rather than a dynamic-link library (whose .DEF file would contain library instead). Protmode signifies that the program will run in protected mode, while the lines beginning with code and data declare a few of the many possible segment attributes. The stack size for the program's initial thread of execution is defined by the stack directive; if this were a C program, an additional heapsize command would specify the initial size of the program's local heap.

CS:IP	Points to the program's initial entry point
SS:SP	Points to the base of the program's stack
DS	Points to the program's automatic data segment (DGROUP)
AX	Contains the segment selector of the environment block
BX	Contains the offset of the command line at the end of the environment block

Figure 21-2: Conditions at entry to a protected-mode OS/2 application.

```
NAMEHELLO                    ; executable name
PROTMODE                     ; protected mode only
DATA MOVABLE
CODE MOVABLE PURE
STACKSIZE 4096
```

Figure 21-3: A module-definition file, HELLO.DEF, for the sample application file HELLO.EXE. Note that the stack size is declared here rather than in the HELLO.ASM file. If this were a C program, the heapsize would also be declared in this file.

Building the Application

To build the final executable program, you first translate the file HELLO.ASM to the relocatable object module HELLO.OBJ:

```
[C:\OS2\SOURCE\HELLO]
 MASM<Enter>

IBM Personal Computer MACRO
 Assembler Version 3.00
(C)Copyright IBM Corp 1981,
 1984, 1987
(C)Copyright Microsoft Corp
 1981, 1983, 1984, 1985, 1987

Source filename [.ASM]:
 HELLO<Enter>
Object filename [HELLO.OBJ]:
 <Enter>
Source listing [NUL.LST]:
 <Enter>
Cross-reference [NUL.CRF]:
 <Enter>
5506 Bytes symbol space free

0 Warning Errors
0 Severe Errors
```

The Microsoft segmented executable linker-the new linker supplied in the OS/2 software-development kit-combines the object module HELLO.OBJ with the module-definition file (HELLO.DEF), a library that contains special stub records for the OS/2 API dynamic links (DOSCALLS.LIB) and any applicable run-time libraries (none in this case) to create the protected-mode executable file HELLO.EXE:

```
[C: \ OS2 \ SOURCE \ HELLO] LINK
 <Enter>

Microsoft (R) Segmented-
 Executable Linker Version
 5.00.21
Copyright (C) Microsoft Corp
 1984, 1985, 1986.  All rights reserved.

Object Modules [.OBJ]: HELLO
 <Enter>
Run File [HELLO.EXE]: <Enter>
List File [NUL.MAP]: <Enter>
Libraries [.LIB]: DOSCALLS
 <Enter>
Definitions File [NUL.DEF]:
 HELLO <Enter>
```

You can also supply the assembler and linker with their parameters via the command-line or response files, or automate the process by means of a make file and the MAKE.EXE utility (see Figure 21-4).

Listing 21-1: The source file HELLO.ASM for the sample application HELLO.EXE.

```
    name    hello
    page    55,132
    title   HELLO---print Hello on terminal
    .286c
;
; HELLO.EXE utility, demonstrating a simple assembly-language; program for
Microsoft OS/2.
;
; (C) 1986 Ray Duncan
;
stdin   equ   0  ; handle for standard input
stdout  equ   1  ; handle for standard output
stderr  equ   2  ; handle for standard error
        extern  DOSWRITE:far
        extern  DOSEXIT:far

DGROUP  group       _DATA
```

```
_DATA    segment    word public 'DATA'

msg      db         0dh,0ah,"Hello Protected-Mode World!",0dh, 0ah

msg _len equ $-msg

wlen     dw         ?         ;receives number of bytes written

_DATA    ends

_TEXT    segment    byte public 'CODE'

         assume     cs: _TEXT,ds:DGROUP

print    proc       far

         push       stdout    ; file handle for standard output
         push       ds        ; long address of write buffer

         push       offset DGROUP:msg

         push       msg _len  ; size of write buffer
         push       ds        ; variable receives bytes written

         push       offset DGROUP:wlen

         call       DOSWRITE  ; transfer to os/2
         or         ax,ax     ; test returned status
         jnz        error     ; jump if write failed

         push       1         ; terminate all threads
         push       0         ; return success code
         call       DOSEXIT   ; exit program

error:   push       1         ; terminate all threads
         push       1         ; return error code
         call       DOSEXIT   ; exit program

print    endp

_TEXT    ends

         end        print
```

Figure 21-4: A make file for the sample application HELLO.EXE

```
hello.obj : hello.asm
 masm hello,hello,hello;

hello.exe : hello.obj hello.defhello
 link/map/lin hello,,,doscalls,hello
```

The output of the segmented executable linker is an .EXE file with the same structure as the .EXE files used in real-mode Windows-the so-called New.EXE format. The file has an elaborate header that contains the names of imported dynamic link routines and any attached resources and describes the locations, sizes, and attributes of the various segments within the file.

OS/2 uses the information in the header to allow for sharing of text segments between multiple instances of the same process, to discard and reload text (i.e., machine-code) segments and read-only data segments on demand, and to allocate the program's stack and heap, among other things.

Making a Family App

Since the HELLO.EXE file uses only the OS/2 functions DOSWRITE and DOSEXIT, both of which are members of the subset family API, it can be converted to a family app that runs in either the DOS 3.x compatibility box or in protected mode. To do this, you use the BIND.EXE utility and a special library named APL.-LIB as follows:

```
[C: \ OS2 \ SOURCE \ HELLO] BIND
 HELLO.EXE API.LIB<Enter>
```

The output of this process is a new HELLO.EXE file that can run in either real or protected mode on an 80286 machine. To truly generalize this program and obtain a HELLO.EXE file that could run on any 80x86-based machine under MS-DOS or OS/2, you would have to replace all 80286-specific instructions in the source code with equivalent sequences that would run on an 8086/88. For example, you would need to replace the instruction.

```
push msg _len
```

with

```
mov ax,msg _len
push ax
```

You can easily locate the 80286-specific instructions in a program by removing the .286c directive from the source file and reassembling it; each instruction that will not run on an 8086/88 processor will then be flagged as an error.

22

The OS/2 Applications Family [*]

Ray Duncan

OS/2, Microsoft's long-awaited multitasking operating system for the 80286, is designed to serve as a platform for an entirely new generation of fast, highly interactive applications with a uniform graphic user interface. It is also engineered as a crucial bridge from the 1-megabyte real-mode environment to the 1-gigabyte virtual-memory protected-mode environment.

To serve as this bridge, OS/2 can run programs with a wide spectrum of characteristics and capabilities: "old MS-DOS applications; character-oriented, dual-mode Family Apps; character-oriented, protected-mode Kernel Apps; and Windows/ Presentation Manager Apps.

This broad support has led, in turn, to much unnecessary confusion among software publishers who are trying to design and position their next wave of products and among users who are trying to reconcile their upcoming equipment purchases with their long-term software needs.

In this chapter, I will compare the types of programs that OS/2 can run (see Figure 22-1), briefly touch upon the development tools that are available during the interim period until the official retail release of the operating system, and then look at a sample OS/2 program.

"Old" MS-DOS Applications

OS/2 has a special module, the DOS 3.X Compatibility Box, that allows the user to run one old MS-DOS application at a time in real mode alongside one or more new, protected-mode applications. The Compatibility Box is not a physical box at all; it is simply a special screen group that you can enable or disable with a directive in the system's CONFIG.SYS file. Programs loaded into the

---

[*] © McGraw-Hill Information Systems Company, *BYTE*, October, 1987, p. 109

Application Type	Runs under:			
	MS-DOS 2.x/3.x	OS/2 Real-Mode Box	OS/2 Protected Mode	OS/2 Windows/ Presentation Manager
MS-DOS App	Yes	Yes	No	No
Family App	Yes	Yes	Yes	Yes
Kernel App	No	No	Yes	Yes
Windows App	No	No	No	Yes

Figure 22-1: A comparison of various types of applications that can run under OS/2.

Compatibility Box run on top of an MS-DOS emulator that traps MS-DOS and ROM BIOS function calls and converts them into calls to the appropriate OS/2 services and device drivers. It also provides a realistic-looking milieu for more hardware-dependent MS-DOS programs by supporting certain undocumented MS-DOS services and internal flags, supplying a "clock tick" interrupts at the appropriate frequency, maintaining a ROM BIOS data area at segment 40 hexadecimal, and so forth.

There are, of course, a few exceptionally ill-behaved MS-DOS programs that the Compatibility Box cannot handle. These include terminate-and-stay-resident utilities, which steal hardware interrupt vectors already belonging to a protected-mode device driver, reprogram the system's 8259 programmable interrupt controller, and perform other similarly nefarious deeds.

In any event, it is important to realize that MS-DOS applications gain nothing by being run under OS/2—in fact, they run slightly slower.

The Compatibility Box is only present as a temporizing measure, to protect users' software and hardware investments until a healthy variety of protected-mode software becomes available. It is ironic that, although the 3.X box is one of the crowning technical achievements of OS/2—and one of the major factors in the delay in OS/2's release—it is destined to fade away altogether (at least from users' consciousness, though it might still be present as a historical curiosity, just as the CP/M emulator cards and programs for the IBM PC had a brief heyday after the introduction of MS-DOS and then vanished forever).

Family Apps

A Family App program is written to conform to the new OS/2 Applications Program Interface (API). However, it restricts itself to those OS/2 functions that have direct counterparts in MS-DOS and that do not utilize the machine instructions unique to the 80286 or 80386. After a Family App is compiled or assembled and linked into a protected-mode executable (.EXE) file in the usual manner, it goes through an additional linkage step using the utility BIND.EXE and the library file API.LIB. The result is an .EXE file that can run in protected mode under OS/2, in real mode under OS/2 in the DOS 3.X Compatibility Box, or under MS-DOS 2.x/3.x on any 8086/88, 80286, or 80386-based machine. Such programs are sometimes called bound or dual-mode applications, and nearly all the programming tools supplied in the OS/2 software development kit fall into this category.

The executable file for a Family App actually contains both an old .EXE file header and an MS-DOS-compatible program called the stub loader, and a new .EXE file header (containing segmentation and dynamic-link information) and a protected-mode program image. If you invoke such a program under OS/2 in a protected-mode screen group, the OS/2 loader inspects the new .EXE file header, brings the code and data segments that are marked "preload" into memory, resolves the dynamic links to system services, and starts up the new process in the normal fashion.

If a Family App is activated in a real-mode environment, the entire file goes into memory, and the stub loader initially receives control. The stub loader patches up each OS/2 API call within the main program to point to a routine, appended to the file by BIND.EXE, that can pop the parameters off the stack into the appropriate registers and substitute an Int 21h function call to MS-DOS. It then sets up the machine registers in accordance with OS/2's conventions and jumps to the normal entry point of the application.

A Family App is the natural first target of an experienced programmer who wants to port existing MS-DOS programs to OS/2. If said programs are already segmented according to normal .EXE file conventions, are well-behaved in their use of system memory, perform all file and record I/O using Handle function calls, and do not manipulate the keyboard or video controllers directly, then conversion is a straightforward job. The MS-DOS Int 21h calls are simply rewritten as the corresponding OS/2 API calls, and any necessary variables or structures required by the OS/2 calls are added to the program's data segment. The procedures that access command-line parameters or the environment block are adjusted appropriately, and a simple module definition (.DEF) file, describing the program's segment behavior, is created for the benefit of the linker.

Thus, transformation of an MS-DOS program into an OS/2 Family App program does not require any redesign of the program's structure or internal logic. It allows the software developer to maintain a single program and manual that can be shipped to all purchasers. On the other hand, a Family App gains little from the conversion except for the ability to execute in protected mode. Since the more sophisticated OS/2 services have no MS-DOS counterparts, they cannot be used in the program unless the developer is willing to sacrifice symmetry of its operation in all three environments. When the protected-mode Windows/Presentation Manager arrives, Family Apps will run in a window (allowing cut and paste of text from one to another) but will not support graphics operation.

Kernel Apps

A Kernel App runs only in a protected-mode screen group and uses the kernel KBD, VIO and MOU subsystem services (i.e., keyboard, screen, and mouse I/O, respectively). Consequently, although such a program can run in a window under the Presentation Manager, it is ordinarily limited to character-oriented screen displays (if it has its own graphics drivers, it can't run in a window). On the other hand, a Kernel App has full access to OS/2's advanced features:

- It can create subprocesses (threads) that share the same data and files, child processes that run in protected memory spaces and have independent data and files, or whole new screen groups containing one or more processes writing to a separate virtual display.

- It can elect to perform I/O or almost any other OS/2 operation in either synchronous or asynchronous (overlapped) fashion.

- It can create either periodic or one-shot timers and use them to schedule its own operations or those of other processes.

- It can allocate huge amounts of virtual memory.

In addition, when several protected-mode applications are closely related and contain many identical or nearly identical subroutines, you can transfer those procedures to private dynamic-link (dyna-link) libraries. This reduces the size of each application's .EXE file, since the routines in dynalink libraries are bound to an application at its load time. It also allows more efficient use of memory, since concurrently executing client applications can share code segments from the library. The most important benefit of dynalink libraries, however, is simplification of code debugging and maintenance. You can modify, repair, or improve a routine in a dynalink library at any time without any change to the applications that use it, as long as you don't alter its calling sequence.

You should attempt to convert an existing MS-DOS or OS/2 Family App into a true Kernel App only after close study of both the program's fundamental mission and the services available from the OS/2 API. A clean division of the program's functionality between asynchronously executing processes or subprocesses (to fully exploit OS/2's multitasking capabilities) requires very careful planning. You must address new questions of sub-routine reentrancy and synchronization of access to shared data. But the time you invest in the design phase will be amply repaid in the user's perception of application performance.

Windows/Presentation Manager Apps

Protected-mode Windows/Presentation Manager applications, like their predecessors under real-mode Windows, have a radically different internal structure and flow of control when compared to ordinary MS-DOS or OS/2 programs. The actual work performed by the program is segregated into several relatively autonomous routines known as window processors, each associated with a specific screen region, such as a parent window, a child window, a dialog box, and so on. The main routine of a Windows App is a relatively simple loop that reads a message off the program's input queue, optionally performs some translation on the message, and then redispatches the message to a window processor within the same application or in another. The message might consist of a key press, key release, a mouse movement, a signal from the system to repaint part of a window, or a notification that the applications has been "iconized."

Conceptually, a Windows App requires a complete reversal of viewpoint on the part of the programmer. Instead of the application driving the environment, the environment drives the application. Instead of the application requesting a character from the keyboard or polling the mouse position when it is good and ready, the application is constantly being bombarded with messages from the system about events that are totally outside of its control-and it must dispose of these messages quickly (for example, most users would consider any perceptible delay between clicking on a menu bar and the appearance of the pull-down menu as intolerably poor performance).

Aside from design consideration, a move to Windows programming requires a programmer with true grit: There is no such thing as a trivial Windows program. Even the traditional "Hello, World!" program is several pages of C code, and the logic to scroll a window correctly under all possible circumstances adds a couple more pages.

For those programmers who haven't yet gotten the message about Microsoft's love affair with C, an encounter with Windows can be a real crash landing. The Windows libraries are C libraries, the manuals and example programs assume a fluent knowledge of C, and any attempt to write a Windows App in any other high-level language or even (perish the thought) in Macro Assembler are vigorously discouraged by the Microsoft support personnel.

Needless to say, those few developers who have already written real-mode Windows applications have a significant head start, but even their lot is not easy. Although protected-mode Windows/Presentation Manager has the same user interface as real-mode Windows 2.0, the system interface at the application program level is somewhat different. Developers of Windows Apps will have to maintain two sets of source code, one for protected mode and one for real mode, and just pray that the two systems don't diverge too much over the years.

What do Windows App developers get for their pains? A dramatically shortened user learning curve, access to a battery of graphic drawing and "rich text" display functions that would take years to duplicate, ready exchange of all types of data with other Windows Apps, and eternal relief from the dreary job of writing and optimizing a new device driver for every video adapter, printer, and pointing device that appears on the market. The burden of writing a general-purpose Windows driver for new hardware is shifted to the manufacturer—where it belongs.

The Tools

The Microsoft OS/2 Software Development Kit (SDK) established some historic precedents when it landed on purchasers' doorsteps with a thump on the morning of May 29. It was certainly the most formidable software package ever shipped by Microsoft, arriving in a box nearly 3 feet long and weighing roughly 30 pounds. It was the most expensive Microsoft product ever, at a cost of $3,000 per copy (to be fair, this includes automatic software updates, a year's technical support, and attendance at a three-day OS/2 seminar). It was the first time in my memory that Microsoft had delivered a product two months before its announced release date.

And last, but not least, it was the first time that Microsoft had ever asked developers to *pay* to be beta testers.

The SDK's nine high-density (1.2-megabyte) disks contain a prerelease version of the OS/2 operating system and its associated utility programs, dual-mode versions of the Microsoft C Compiler, Macro Assembler, Linker, MAKE, BIND, protected-mode Code View, source code for many example programs, and even a fully configurable visual editor. The documentation fills eight binders, totaling some 3100 pages. The first SDKs did not include the software and documentation (an additional three manuals containing another thousand pages collectively) for the Windows/Presentation Manager graphic interface that was scheduled to be delivered as part of an update by the time this chapter appears.

To use the OS/2 SDK, you need a PC AT or compatible with a hard disk and at least 1.5 megabytes of RAM, room on the disk for 10 megabytes or so of programs, libraries, and example source code, and a lot of patience. The OS/2 kernel alone supports over 200 functions that can be called by application programs, and the Windows/Presentation Manager layer adds some 500 more. The days when a PC programmer could get by with a $20 MS-DOS reference book, a run-time library manual for his or her favorite language, and a quick reference card to the Intel 80x86 instruction set are gone.

An Example Kernel App

As an example of an OS/2 Kernel App to accompany this chapter, I have written two implementations of a file-dumping utility in C and Macro Assembler. The utility accepts a filename on the command line and displays the binary contents of that file, in hexadecimal bytes and their ASCII character equivalents, on the standard output device (and may be redirected into a file or to the printer). Such a utility is indispensable when trying to decipher the format of undocumented data files, load modules, and the like. *DUMP.C, DUMP.ASM,* and *DUMP.DEF,* which contain the source code for these two implementations, are at the end of this chapter.

Although file-dumping utilities per se are common and not very interesting, these particular programs have been intentionally complicated in order to illustrate some of the powerful capabilities of OS/2. They perform overlapped I/O by creating separate threads to handle the disk reads and screen writes.

The threads use a double-buffering scheme and coordinate their access to the buffers with semaphores. Figure 22-2 shows a sketch of the general logic of the DUMP program.

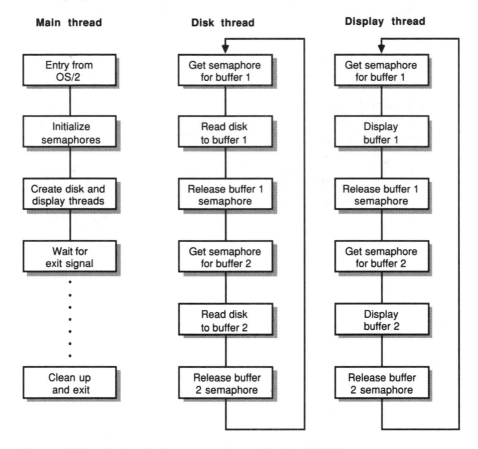

Figure 22-2: A sketch of program logic for the DUMP example program. Separate subprocesses (threads) are used to perform the disk file reads, and the formatting and display. Two semaphores provide mutual exclusion on the I/O buffers. The main thread simply waits until the other two threads are done, unless a critical error or other external event activates in the meantime.

The C example demonstrates the ease with which OS/2 services may be called directly from a high-level language. The assembly language version, DUMP-.ASM, also contains two procedures that Macro Assembler programmers should find useful in other programs. The routines are called ARGC and ARGV, and they return the number of command-tail arguments and pointers to those arguments, similar to C's argc and argv.

Assembling and Linking DUMP.ASM

First, use the Microsoft Macro Assembler to assemble the file DUMP.ASM into the relocatable object module DUMP.OBJ with the following command line:

```
[C: \ ] MASM /L/Zi DUMP
```

The optional /L and /Zi switches in the MASM command line request the creation of a program-listing file and the inclusion of symbolic debugging information in the relocatable object file, respectively.

To link the file DUMP.OBJ, the module-definition file DUMP.DEF, and the OS/2 API dynalink reference file DOS-CALLS.LIB into the executable application DUMP.EXE, enter:

```
[C: \ ] LINK DUMP,,,DOSCALLS,DUMP
```

You can then run the DUMP utility with a command of the form:

```
[C: \ ] DUMP MYFILE.DAT
```

Compiling and Linking DUMP.C

The C compiler has a control program, CL.EXE, that automatically runs the preprocessor, the various passes of the compiler, and the linker for you. To compile and link the file DUMP.C, together with the library DOSCALLS.LIB and the module-definition file DUMP.DEF, into the executable DUMP.EXE, enter the command line:

```
[C: \ ] CL /AL /Zi /Gs /F2000 DUMP.C
```

The /AL switch specifies a "large model" program, while the /Zi switch (again) specifies that the linker should include symbolic debugging information in the object module and in the final executable file. I prefer to use the large model for most of the OS/2 utility programs I write in C because the compiler then generates "long" addresses for the parameters supplied in direct calls to OS/2 services without the need for any special typecasting.

To Port a Program

If you want to port an existing MS-DOS application to OS/2, or develop an entirely new OS/2-based product, you must make some early implementation decisions based on the specific characteristics and needs of your application.

You can quickly port products that require a minimum of user interaction and have no need for graphics, such as compilers, linkers, and similar tools, to OS/2 as Family Apps. This gives you the added advantage of being able to ship a single disk and manual for MS-DOS 2.x/3.x, the OS/2 DOS 3.X Compatibility Box, and OS/2 protected mode.

You can write highly interactive applications with no need for graphics (e.g. communications programs) as character-oriented Kernel Apps and reap the benefits of OS/2's protected-mode service. While not as straightforward as a Family App port, a Kernel App is still relatively easy to write and will run in a window under the Presentation Manager, if necessary. Most of the commercial products released for OS/2 in the next year or so will undoubtedly fall into this category.

Finally, if you need to port graphics-oriented applications to OS/2, you have the choice between revamping your program as a true Windows/Presentation Manager App, or going it alone and providing your own graphics routines. If you choose the latter course, your program might be published sooner, but it will lose the ability to run in a window alongside of (and exchange data with) other Windows/Presentation Manager Apps, and your forfeit the advantages of the common graphic user interface. You will also waste time writing hardware-dependent drivers that might be better spent on user-oriented enhancements.

Listing 22-1: DUMP.C, the source code for the C version of the Kernel App example.

Here is the C code for the DUMP.C program to demonstrate semaphores, multiple threads, etc. from high level.

```
/*
        DUMP.C          Displays the binary contents of a file in
                        hex and ASCII on the standard output device.

                        Program has been deliberately complicated
                        to demonstrate direct calls from C to
                        operating system, use of multiple threads,
                        and synchronization with semaphores.
```

```
            Usage is:        C>DUMP unit:path\filename.ext [ >destination ]

            Compile with:    C>CL /AL /Zi /Gs /F 2000 DUMP.C
*/

#include <stdio.h>
#include <malloc.h>
#include <doscalls.h>

#define REC_SIZE 16                     /* size of file records */
#define STK_SIZE 1024                   /* stack size for threads */

char Buf1[REC_SIZE];                    /* first disk buffer */
unsigned Buf1Len;                       /* amount of data in buffer */

char Buf2[REC_SIZE];                    /* second disk buffer */
unsigned Buf2Len;                       /* amount of data in buffer */

unsigned Handle;                        /* file Handle from DOSOPEN */
long filptr;                            /* file offset in bytes */

unsigned long ExitSem;                  /* semaphore for process exit */
unsigned long Buf1FullSem;              /* semaphores for disk buffer #1 */
unsigned long Buf1EmptySem;
unsigned long Buf2FullSem;              /* semaphores for disk buffer #2 */
unsigned long Buf2EmptySem;

main(int argc, char *argv[])
{
    void far DisplayThr();              /* entry point for Display Thread */
    void far DiskThr();                 /* entry point for Disk Thread */

    unsigned DisplayThrID;              /* receives Thread ID */
    unsigned DiskThrID;                 /* receives Thread ID */

    char DisplayThrStk[STK_SIZE];       /* allocate stacks for threads */
    char DiskThrStk[STK_SIZE];
    int action;                         /* receives DOSOPEN result */
    int openflag=0x01;                  /* fail open if file not found */
    int openmode=0x40;                  /* read only, deny none */

    filptr=0L;                          /* initialize file pointer */

    ExitSem=0L;                         /* initialize semaphores */
    Buf1EmptySem=Buf1FullSem=0L;
    Buf2EmptySem=Buf2FullSem=0L;
    DOSSEMSET((long) &ExitSem);
    DOSSEMSET((long) &Buf1FullSem);
    DOSSEMSET((long) &Buf2FullSem);

    if (argc < 2)                       /* check command tail */
    {   fprintf(stderr,"\ndump: missing file name\n");
        exit(1);
    }
                                        /* open file or exit */
```

```
    if (DOSOPEN(argv[1],&Handle,&action,0L,0,openflag,openmode,0L))
    {   fprintf(stderr,"\ndump: can't find file %s\n",argv[1]);
        exit(1);
    }
                                    /* create Disk Thread */
    if (DOSCREATETHREAD(DiskThr,&DiskThrID,DiskThrStk+STK_SIZE))
    {   fprintf(stderr,"\ndump: can't create Disk Thread");
        exit(1);
    }
                                    /* Create Display Thread */
    if (DOSCREATETHREAD(DisplayThr,&DisplayThrID,DisplayThrStk+STK_SIZE))
    {   fprintf(stderr,"\ndump: can't create Display Thread");
        exit(1);
    }

    DOSSEMWAIT((long) &ExitSem,-1L);    /* wait for exit signal */

    DOSSUSPENDTHREAD(DiskThrID);        /* suspend other threads */
    DOSSUSPENDTHREAD(DisplayThrID);
    DOSCLOSE(Handle);                   /* close file */
    DOSEXIT(1,0);                       /* terminate all threads */
}

/*
        The Disk Thread reads the disk file, alternating between
        Buf1 and Buf2.  This thread gets terminated externally
        when the other threads see end of file has been reached.
*/
void far DiskThr()
{
    while(1)
    {   DOSREAD(Handle,Buf1,REC_SIZE,&Buf1Len); /* read disk */
        SemFlip(&Buf1EmptySem,&Buf1FullSem);    /* mark buffer 1 full */
        DOSSEMWAIT((long) &Buf2EmptySem,-1L);   /* wait for buffer 2 empty */
        DOSREAD(Handle,Buf2,REC_SIZE,&Buf2Len); /* read disk */
        SemFlip(&Buf2EmptySem,&Buf2FullSem);    /* mark buffer 2 full */
        DOSSEMWAIT((long) &Buf1EmptySem,-1L);   /* wait for buffer 1 empty */
    }
}

/*
        The Display Thread formats and displays the data in the
        disk buffers, alternating between Buf1 and Buf2.
*/
void far DisplayThr()
{
    while(1)
    {   DOSSEMWAIT((long) &Buf1FullSem,-1L);    /* wait for buffer 1 full */
        DumpRec(Buf1,Buf1Len);                  /* format and display it */
        SemFlip(&Buf1FullSem,&Buf1EmptySem);    /* mark buffer 1 empty */
        DOSSEMWAIT((long) &Buf2FullSem,-1L);    /* wait for buffer 2 full */
        DumpRec(Buf2,Buf2Len);                  /* format and display it */
        SemFlip(&Buf2FullSem,&Buf2EmptySem);    /* mark buffer 2 empty */
    }
}
```

```
/*
        Display record in hex and ASCII on standard output.
        Clear exit semaphore and terminate thread if record length=0.
*/
DumpRec(char *buffer,int length)
{
    int i;                          /* index to current record */

    if (length==0)                  /* check if record length = 0 */
    {   DOSSEMCLEAR((long) &ExitSem);  /* yes, signal main thread */
        DOSEXIT(0,0);               /* and terminate this thread! */
    }

    if (filptr % 128 == 0)          /* maybe print heading */
        printf("\n\n       0 1 2 3 4 5 6 7 8 9 A B C D E F");

    printf("\n%04lX ",filptr);      /* file offset */

    for (i = 0; i < length; i++)    /* print hex equiv. of each byte */
        printf( " %02X", (unsigned char) buffer[i] );

                                    /* space over if partial record */
    if (length != 16) for(i=0; i<(16-length); i++) printf("   ");

    printf("  ");

    for (i = 0; i < length; i++)    /* print ASCII equiv. of bytes */
        { if (buffer[i] < 32 || buffer[i] > 126) putchar('.');
          else putchar(buffer[i]);
        }

    filptr += REC_SIZE;             /* update file offset */
}

/*
        Since there is no operation to wait until a semaphore
        is set, we must maintain two semaphores to control each
        buffer and flip them atomically.
*/
SemFlip(long *sem1, long *sem2)
{   DOSENTERCRITSEC();              /* block other threads */
    DOSSEMSET((long) sem1);         /* set the first semaphore */
    DOSSEMCLEAR((long) sem2);       /* clear the second semaphore */
    DOSEXITCRITSEC();               /* unblock other threads */
}

^Z
```

Listing 22-2

```
DUMP.ASM

        name    dump
        page    55,132
        title   DUMP --- Display File Contents
        .286c
;
; DUMP.ASM --- a OS/2 utility to display the contents of a
; file on the standard output in hex and ASCII format.
;
; Copyright (C) 1987 Ray Duncan
;
; Usage:  C>DUMP path\filename.ext  [ >device ]
;
; This program has been intentionally complicated
; to demonstrate the use of multiple threads and semaphores
; in a MASM application.  For a roadmap to what is going
; on in this program, see its counterpart DUMP.C.
;

cr      equ     0dh             ; ASCII carriage return
lf      equ     0ah             ; ASCII line feed
blank   equ     20h             ; ASCII space code
tab     equ     09h             ; ASCII tab code

recsize equ     16              ; size of input file records
stksize equ     2048            ; size of stack for threads

stdout  equ     1               ; handle of standard output device
stderr  equ     2               ; handle of standard error device

        extrn   DOSOPEN:far     ; references to OS/2 services
        extrn   DOSREAD:far
        extrn   DOSWRITE:far
        extrn   DOSCLOSE:far
        extrn   DOSEXIT:far
        extrn   DOSSEMCLEAR:far
        extrn   DOSSEMSET:far
        extrn   DOSSEMWAIT:far
        extrn   DOSALLOCSEG:far
        extrn   DOSCREATETHREAD:far
        extrn   DOSSUSPENDTHREAD:far
        extrn   DOSENTERCRITSEC:far
        extrn   DOSEXITCRITSEC:far
        extrn   DOSGETENV:far

DGROUP  group   _DATA

_DATA           segment word public 'DATA'

ExitSem         dd      0               ; storage for RAM semaphores
Buf1FullSem     dd      0
```

```
BuflEmptySem    dd      0
Buf2FullSem     dd      0
Buf2EmptySem    dd      0

DisplayThrID    dw      0               ; Display thread ID
DiskThrID       dw      0               ; Disk I/O thread ID

Buf1            db      recsize dup (0) ; disk I/O buffer #1
Buf1Len         dw      0               ; length of buffer #1 data

Buf2            db      recsize dup (0) ; disk I/O buffer #2
Buf2Len         dw      0               ; length of buffer #2 data

fname           db      64 dup (0)      ; ASCIIZ name of input file

fhandle         dw      0               ; handle for input file

filptr          dw      0               ; relative address in file

status          dw      0               ; receives status of DOSOPEN

selector        dw      0               ; receives segment selector
                                        ; from DOSALLOCSEG

                                        ; formatting area for output
output          db      'nnnn',blank,blank
outputa         db      16 dup ('nn',blank)
                db      blank
outputb         db      16 dup (blank),cr,lf
output_len      equ     $-output

heading         db      cr,lf           ; heading for each 128 bytes
                db      7 dup (blank)
                db      '0  1  2  3  4  5  6  7  '
                db      '8  9  A  B  C  D  E  F',cr,lf
heading_len     equ     $-heading

msg1            db      cr,lf
                db      'dump: file not found'
                db      cr,lf
msg1_len        equ     $-msg1

msg2            db      cr,lf
                db      'dump: missing file name'
                db      cr,lf
msg2_len        equ     $-msg2

msg3            db      cr,lf
                db      'dump: memory allocation error'
                db      cr,lf
msg3_len        equ     $-msg3

msg4            db      cr,lf
                db      'dump: create thread failed'
                db      cr,lf
msg4_len        equ     $-msg4
```

```
_DATA           ends


_TEXT    segment word public 'CODE'

         assume  cs:_TEXT,ds:DGROUP

dump     proc    far                     ; entry point from OS/2

         call    argc                    ; is filename present?
         cmp     ax,2
         je      dump1                   ; yes, proceed

         mov     dx,offset msg2          ; missing or illegal filespec,
         mov     cx,msg2_len
         jmp     dump9                   ; print error message and exit.

dump1:                                   ; copy filename to local buffer
         mov     ax,1                    ; get ES:BX = filename
         call    argv
         mov     cx,ax                   ; set CX = length
         mov     di,offset fname         ; DS:DI = local buffer
dump15:  mov     al,es:[bx]              ; copy it byte by byte
         mov     [di],al
         inc     bx
         inc     di
         loop    dump15

         push    ds                      ; set ES = DS
         pop     es

dump2:                                   ; now try to open file...
         push    ds                      ; ASCIIZ file name
         push    offset DGROUP:fname
         push    ds                      ; receives handle
         push    offset DGROUP:fhandle
         push    ds                      ; receives handle
         push    offset DGROUP:status
         push    0                       ; file size (ignored)
         push    0
         push    0                       ; file attribute = normal
         push    1                       ; OpenFlag = fail if doesn't exist
         push    40h                     ; OpenMode = deny none,read only
         push    0                       ; DWORD reserved
         push    0
         call    DOSOPEN                 ; transfer to OS/2
         or      ax,ax                   ; test status
         jz      dump3                   ; jump if open succeeded

         mov     dx,offset msg1          ; open of input file failed,
         mov     cx,msg1_len
         jmp     dump9                   ; print error msg and exit.

dump3:                                   ; initialize semaphores
         push    ds
```

```
            push    offset DGROUP:ExitSem
            call    DOSSEMSET

            push    ds
            push    offset DGROUP:Buf1FullSem
            call    DOSSEMSET

            push    ds
            push    offset DGROUP:Buf2FullSem
            call    DOSSEMSET

                                        ; allocate Disk Thread stack
            push    stksize             ; size of stack
            push    ds                  ; receives selector for
            push    offset DGROUP:selector  ; allocated block
            push    0                   ; 0 = segment not shareable
            call    DOSALLOCSEG         ; transfer to OS/2
            or      ax,ax               ; test status
            jz      dump5               ; jump if allocation succeeded

dump4:      mov     dx,offset DGROUP:msg3  ; display message
            mov     cx,msg3_len         ; 'memory allocation error'
            jmp     dump9               ; and exit

dump5:                                  ; create Disk Thread
            push    cs                  ; thread's entry point
            push    offset _TEXT:DiskThread
            push    ds                  ; receives thread ID
            push    offset DGROUP:DiskThrID
            push    selector            ; thread's stack base
            push    stksize
            call    DOSCREATETHREAD     ; transfer to OS/2
            or      ax,ax               ; test status
            jz      dump7               ; jump if create succeeded

dump6:      mov     dx,offset DGROUP:msg4  ; create of thread failed,
            mov     cx,msg4_len         ; display error message
            jmp     dump9               ; and exit

dump7:                                  ; allocate Display Thread stack
            push    stksize             ; size of stack
            push    ds                  ; receives selector for
            push    offset DGROUP:selector  ; allocated block
            push    0                   ; 0 = segment not shareable
            call    DOSALLOCSEG         ; transfer to OS/2
            or      ax,ax               ; test status
            jnz     dump4               ; jump if allocation failed

                                        ; create Display Thread
            push    cs                  ; thread's entry point
            push    offset _TEXT:DisplayThread
            push    ds                  ; receives thread ID
            push    offset DGROUP:DisplayThrID
            push    selector            ; thread's stack base
            push    stksize
            call    DOSCREATETHREAD     ; transfer to OS/2
```

```
        or      ax,ax                       ; test status
        jnz     dump6                       ; jump if create failed

        push    ds                          ; now wait on exit semaphore
        push    offset DGROUP:ExitSem       ; (it will be triggered
        push    -1                          ; by routine DumpRec when
        push    -1                          ; end of file is reached)
        call    DOSSEMWAIT                  ; transfer to OS/2

        push    DiskThrID                   ; suspend Disk Thread
        call    DOSSUSPENDTHREAD            ; transfer to OS/2

        push    DisplayThrID                ; suspend Display Thread
        call    DOSSUSPENDTHREAD            ; transfer to OS/2

        push    fhandle                     ; close the input file
        call    DOSCLOSE                    ; transfer to OS/2

        push    1                           ; terminate all threads
        push    0                           ; return code 0 for success
        call    DOSEXIT                     ; final exit to OS/2

dump9:                                      ; print error message...
        push    stderr                      ; standard error device handle
        push    ds                          ; address of message
        push    dx
        push    cx                          ; length of message
        push    ds                          ; receives bytes written
        push    offset DGROUP:status
        call    DOSWRITE                    ; transfer to OS/2

        push    1                           ; terminate all threads
        push    1                           ; return code <>0 for error
        call    DOSEXIT                     ; final exit to OS/2

dump    endp


DiskThread proc far                         ; this thread performs
                                            ; the file I/O, alternating
                                            ; between the two buffers

                                            ; fill buffer #1
        push    fhandle                     ; handle for input file
        push    ds                          ; address of buffer #1
        push    offset DGROUP:Buf1
        push    recsize                     ; record length requested
        push    ds                          ; receives bytes read
        push    offset DGROUP: Buf1Len
        call    DOSREAD

                                            ; signal buffer 1 has data
        mov     si,offset DGROUP:Buf1EmptySem
        mov     di,offset DGROUP:Buf1FullSem
        call    SemFlip
```

```
        push    ds                      ; wait until buffer 2 empty
        push    offset DGROUP:Buf2EmptySem
        push    -1
        push    -1
        call    DOSSEMWAIT

                                        ; fill buffer #2
        push    fhandle                 ; handle for input file
        push    ds                      ; address of buffer #1
        push    offset DGROUP:Buf2
        push    recsize                 ; record length requested
        push    ds                      ; receives bytes read
        push    offset DGROUP:Buf2Len
        call    DOSREAD

                                        ; signal buffer 2 has data
        mov     si,offset DGROUP:Buf2EmptySem
        mov     di,offset DGROUP:Buf2FullSem
        call    SemFlip

        push    ds                      ; wait until buffer 1 empty
        push    offset DGROUP:Buf1EmptySem
        push    -1
        push    -1
        call    DOSSEMWAIT

        jmp     DiskThread              ; do it again...

DiskThread endp


DisplayThread proc far                  ; formats and displays disk
                                        ; data, alternating between
                                        ; the two disk buffers

        push    ds                      ; wait until buffer #1 full
        push    offset DGROUP:Buf1FullSem
        push    -1
        push    -1
        call    DOSSEMWAIT

        mov     si,offset DGROUP:Buf1    ; display buffer 1
        mov     cx,Buf1Len
        call    DumpRec

                                        ; signal buffer #1 is emptied
        mov     si,offset DGROUP:Buf1FullSem
        mov     di,offset DGROUP:Buf1EmptySem
        call    SemFlip

        push    ds                      ; wait until buffer #2 full
        push    offset DGROUP:Buf2FullSem
        push    -1
        push    -1
        call    DOSSEMWAIT
```

```
        mov     si,offset DGROUP:Buf2   ; display buffer 2
        mov     cx,Buf2Len
        call    DumpRec

                                        ; signal buffer #2 is emptied
        mov     si,offset DGROUP:Buf2FullSem
        mov     di,offset DGROUP:Buf2EmptySem
        call    SemFlip

        jmp     DisplayThread           ; do it again...

DisplayThread endp


SemFlip proc    near                    ; Flip status of two
                                        ; semaphores atomically

        call    DOSENTERCRITSEC         ; protect this code sequence

        push    ds                      ; set semaphore #1
        push    si
        call    DOSSEMSET

        push    ds                      ; clear semaphore #2
        push    di
        call    DOSSEMCLEAR

        call    DOSEXITCRITSEC          ; let other threads run again
        ret

SemFlip endp


DumpRec proc    near                    ; formats and displays
                                        ; contents of buffer
                                        ; DS:SI = buffer, CX = length

        or      cx,cx                   ; anything to format?
        jnz     DumpRec1                ; yes, continue

        push    ds                      ; no, clear exit semaphore
        push    offset DGROUP:ExitSem   ; (releasing wait condition
        call    DOSSEMCLEAR             ; for main thread)

        push    0                       ; and terminate this thread
        push    0
        call    DOSEXIT

DumpRec1:                               ; time for a heading?
        test    filptr,07fh             ; if 128 byte boundary
        jnz     DumpRec2                ; no, jump

        push    stdout                  ; standard output device handle
        push    ds                      ; address of heading text
        push    offset DGROUP:heading
        push    heading_len             ; length of heading
```

```
            push    ds                      ; receives bytes written
            push    offset DGROUP:status
            call    DOSWRITE

DumpRec2:                                   ; format record data...
            push    cx                      ; save record length

            mov     di,offset output        ; first clear output area
            mov     cx,output_len-2
            mov     al,blank
            rep stosb

            mov     di,offset output        ; convert current file offset
            mov     ax,filptr               ; to ASCII for output
            call    w2hex

            pop     cx                      ; get back record length
            mov     bx,0                    ; initialize record pointer

DumpRec3:                                   ; fetch next byte from buffer
            mov     al,[si+bx]
                                            ; store ASCII version of character
            mov     di,offset outputb       ; calculate output string address
            mov     byte ptr [di+bx],'.'    ; if not alphanumeric
            cmp     al,blank                ; just print a dot.
            jb      DumpRec4                ; jump, not alphanumeric.
            cmp     al,7eh
            ja      DumpRec4                ; jump, not alphanumeric.
            mov     [di+bx],al              ; else store ASCII character.

DumpRec4:                                   ; now convert binary byte
                                            ; to hex ASCII equivalent
            mov     di,offset outputa       ; calc. position in output string
            add     di,bx                   ; base addr + (offset*3)
            add     di,bx
            add     di,bx                   ; convert data in AL to hex
            call    b2hex                   ; ASCII and store into output

            inc     bx                      ; bump data pointer and loop
            loop    DumpRec3                ; until entire record converted

                                            ; now display formatted data
            push    stdout                  ; standard output device handle
            push    ds                      ; address of text
            push    offset DGROUP:output
            push    output_len              ; length of text
            push    ds
            push    offset DGROUP:status    ; receives bytes written
            call    DOSWRITE

            add     word ptr filptr,recsize ; update file pointer

            ret                             ; return to caller

DumpRec endp
```

```
argc    proc    near                    ; count command line arguments
                                        ; returns count in AX

        enter   4,0                     ; make room for local variables
                                        ; and give them names...
envseg  equ     [bp-2]                  ; environment segment
cmdoffs equ     [bp-4]                  ; command line offset

        push    es                      ; save original ES,BX, and CX
        push    bx
        push    cx

        push    ss                      ; get selector for environment
        lea     ax,envseg               ; and offset of command line
        push    ax
        push    ss
        lea     ax,cmdoffs
        push    ax
        call    DOSGETENV               ; transfer to OS/2
        or      ax,ax                   ; check operation status
        mov     ax,1                    ; force argc >= 1
        jnz     argc3                   ; inexplicable failure

        mov     es,envseg               ; set ES:BX = command line
        mov     bx,cmdoffs

argc0:  inc     bx                      ; ignore useless first field
        cmp     byte ptr es:[bx],0
        jne     argc0

argc1:  mov     cx,-1                   ; set flag = outside argument

argc2:  inc     bx                      ; point to next character
        cmp     byte ptr es:[bx],0
        je      argc3                   ; exit if null byte
        cmp     byte ptr es:[bx],blank
        je      argc1                   ; outside argument if ASCII blank
        cmp     byte ptr es:[bx],tab
        je      argc1                   ; outside argument if ASCII tab

                                        ; otherwise not blank or tab,
        jcxz    argc2                   ; jump if already inside argument

        inc     ax                      ; else found argument, count it
        not     cx                      ; set flag = inside argument
        jmp     argc2                   ; and look at next character

argc3:  pop     cx                      ; restore original BX, CX, ES
        pop     bx
        pop     es
        leave                           ; discard local variables
        ret                             ; return AX = argument count

argc    endp
```

```
argv    proc    near                            ; get address and length
                                                ; of command line arguments
                                                ; call with AX = arg. no.
                                                ; return ES:BX = address of
                                                ; argument string, CX = length

        enter   4,0                             ; make room for local variables

        push    cx                              ; save original CX and DI
        push    di

        push    ax                              ; save argument number

        push    ss                              ; get selector for environment
        lea     ax,envseg                       ; and offset of command line
        push    ax
        push    ss
        lea     ax,cmdoffs
        push    ax
        call    DOSGETENV                       ; transfer to OS/2
        or      ax,ax                           ; test operation status
        pop     ax                              ; restore argument number
        jnz     argv7                           ; jump if DOSGETENV failed

        mov     es,envseg                       ; set ES:BX = command line
        mov     bx,cmdoffs

        or      ax,ax                           ; is requested argument=0?
        jz      argv8                           ; yes, jump to get program name

argv0:  inc     bx                              ; scan off first field
        cmp     byte ptr es:[bx],0
        jne     argv0

        xor     ah,ah                           ; initialize argument counter

argv1:  mov     cx,-1                           ; set flag = outside argument

argv2:  inc     bx                              ; point to next character
        cmp     byte ptr es:[bx],0
        je      argv7                           ; exit if null byte
        cmp     byte ptr es:[bx],blank
        je      argv1                           ; outside argument if ASCII blank
        cmp     byte ptr es:[bx],tab
        je      argv1                           ; outside argument if ASCII tab

                                                ; if not blank or tab...
        jcxz    argv2                           ; jump if already inside argument

        inc     ah                              ; else count arguments found
        cmp     ah,al                           ; is this the one we need?
        je      argv4                           ; yes, go find its length
        not     cx                              ; no, set flag = inside argument
        jmp     argv2                           ; and look at next character

argv4:                                          ; found desired argument, now
```

```
                                        ; determine its length...
            mov     ax,bx               ; save param. starting address

argv5:      inc     bx                  ; point to next character
            cmp     byte ptr es:[bx],0
            je      argv6               ; found end if null byte
            cmp     byte ptr es:[bx],blank
            je      argv6               ; found end if ASCII blank
            cmp     byte ptr es:[bx],tab
            jne     argv5               ; found end if ASCII tab

argv6:      xchg    bx,ax               ; set ES:BX = argument address
            sub     ax,bx               ; and AX = argument length
            jmp     argvx               ; return to caller

argv7:      xor     ax,ax               ; set AX = 0, argument not found
            jmp     argvx               ; return to caller

argv8:                                  ; special handling for argv=0
            xor     di,di               ; find the program name by
            xor     al,al               ; first skipping over all the
            mov     cx,-1               ; environment variables...
            cld
argv9:      repne   scasb               ; scan for double null (can't use
            scasb                       ; (SCASW since might be odd addr.)
            jne     argv9               ; loop if it was a single null
            mov     bx,di               ; save program name address
            mov     cx,-1               ; now find its length...
            repne   scasb               ; scan for another null byte
            not     cx                  ; convert CX to length
            dec     cx
            mov     ax,cx               ; return length in AX

argvx:                                  ; common exit point
            pop     di                  ; restore original CX and DI
            pop     cx
            leave                       ; discard stack frame
            ret                         ; return to caller

argv        endp


w2hex       proc    near                ; convert word to hex ASCII
                                        ; call with AX=binary value
                                        ;         DI=addr to store string
                                        ; returns AX, DI destroyed
            push    ax
            mov     al,ah
            call    b2hex               ; convert upper byte
            pop     ax
            call    b2hex               ; convert lower byte
            ret                         ; back to caller

w2hex       endp
```

```
b2hex    proc    near                    ; convert byte to hex ASCII
                                         ; call with AL=binary value
                                         ;          DI=addr to store string
                                         ; returns   AX, DI destroyed

         push    cx                      ; save CX for later
         sub     ah,ah                   ; clear upper byte
         mov     cl,16
         div     cl                      ; divide binary data by 16
         call    ascii                   ; the quotient becomes the first
         stosb                           ; ASCII character
         mov     al,ah
         call    ascii                   ; the remainder becomes the
         stosb                           ; second ASCII character
         pop     cx                      ; restore contents of CX
         ret

b2hex    endp


ascii    proc    near                    ; convert value 0-0FH in AL
                                         ; into a "hex ASCII" character
         add     al,'0'
         cmp     al,'9'
         jle     ascii2                  ; jump if in range 0-9,
         add     al,'A'-'9'-1            ; offset it to range A-F,
ascii2:  ret                             ; return ASCII char. in AL.

ascii    endp

_TEXT    ends

         end     dump
^Z
```

Listing 22-3

```
-----------------------------------------------------------------
Module definition file: DUMP.DEF
-----------------------------------------------------------------

NAME DUMP
PROTMODE
DATA MOVEABLE
CODE MOVEABLE PURE
STACKSIZE 4096


-----------------------------------------------------------------
MAKE file: DUMP
-----------------------------------------------------------------

dump.obj : dump.asm
  masm /Zi dump;

dump.exe : dump.obj dump.def dump
  link /CO dump,,,doscalls,dump

-----------------------------------------------------------------


^Z
```

23

OS/2 Multitasking: Exploiting the Protected Mode of the 80286 *

_____Ray Duncan_____

Multitasking is the technique of dividing CPU time between multiple tasks so that they appear to be running simultaneously. Of course, the microprocessor is only executing one sequence of machine instructions within one task at any given time, but the switching from one task to another is invisible to both the user and the programs themselves. The operating system is responsible for allocating system resources such as memory to the various executing tasks and for resolving contending requests to such peripherals as video displays and disk drives.

The part of the operating system that allocates CPU time between tasks is called the *scheduler* or *dispatcher*, and the rotation from one task to another, or from a task to a module of the operating system, is called a *context switch*. When a context switch occurs, the dispatcher must save the current state of the task that was executing, including its registers and program counter, load the registers and program counter belonging to the next task to run, and transfer control to that task at the point where it was previously suspended.

There are two basic strategies for task scheduling that are used by modern multi-tasking operating systems: *event-driven* and *pre-emptive*.

Event-driven schedulers rely on each task to be "well-behaved" and yield control at frequent enough intervals so that every program has acceptable throughput and none will be "starved" for CPU cycles. This yielding may be explicit (the program calls a specific operating system function to give up control) or implicit (the program is suspended when it requests the operating system to perform I/O on its behalf and regains control only after the I/O is completed and other tasks have in turn yielded control). This strategy is quite efficient in transaction-oriented systems where there is a great deal of I/O and not much computation, but the system can be brought to its knees by a single compute-bound task, such as an in-memory sort.

A pre-emptive scheduler relies on the presence of an external signal generated at regular intervals, typically a hardware interrupt triggered by a real-time clock.

When the interrupt occurs, the operating system gains control from whatever task was executing, saves its context, evaluates the list of programs that are ready to run, and gives control to (dispatches) the next program. This approach to multitasking is often called "time-slicing"; this term is derived from the mental image of dividing the sweep of a second hand around a clock face into little wedges and doling out the pieces to all the eligible programs.

Modern mainframe and mini-computers, and the more powerful microcomputers, such as the Intel 80286 and Motorola 68020, include hardware features specifically designed to make mulitasking operating systems more efficient and robust. These include privilege levels and memory protection.

In the simplest use of privilege levels, the CPU is either in kernel mode or user mode at any given time. In kernel mode, which is reserved for the operating system, any machine instruction can be executed, and any location in memory can be accessed. As part of the mechanism of transferring control from the operating system to an application program, the CPU is switched into user mode. In this CPU state, any attempt to execute certain reserved instructions, such as writing to an I/O port, causes a hardware interrupt and returns control to the operating system. (Although the Intel 80286 microprocessor actually supports four privilege levels, OS/2 ordinarily uses only the highest and lowest of these.) Similarly, the hardware memory protection mechanisms detect any attempt by an application program to access memory that does not belong to it, and generate a hardware interrupt that allows the operating system to abort the offending task.

Microsoft OS/2 is designed around a pre-emptive, priority-based multitasking scheduler. Understanding OS/2 multitasking requires a grasp of three distinct, but related, concepts or system objects; processes, threads, and screen groups.

Processes

The simplest case of an OS/2 process is very similar to an application program loaded for execution under MS-DOS 2.x and 3.x. A process is started (whether by a shell or command processor or by another application) by a call to the OS/2 service DOSEXECPGM. OS/2 initiates a new process by allocating memory segments to hold that process's code, data, and stack, and then initializing the memory segments from the contents of the program's .EXE disk file.

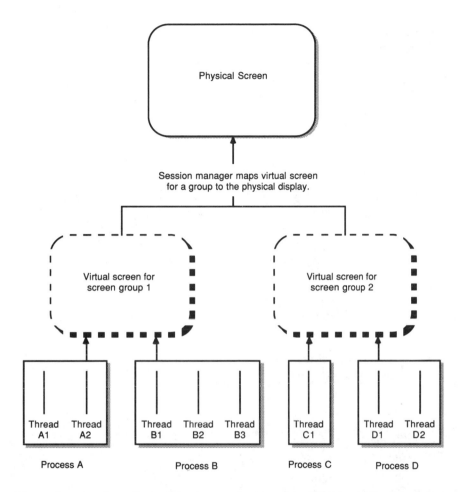

Physical Screen

Session manager maps virtual screen
for a group to the physical display.

Virtual screen for
screen group 1

Virtual screen for
screen group 2

| Thread A1 | Thread A2 | | Thread B1 | Thread B2 | Thread B3 | | Thread C1 | | Thread D1 | Thread D2 |

Process A

Process B

Process C

Process D

Three types of system objects are involved in OS/2 multitasking: processes, threads, and screen groups. A process represents an application program accessing system resources such as files, memory, and interprocess communication facilities. A process can contain multiple concurrent points of execution called threads; each thread has its own priority and stack. Processes are collected into screen groups that read and write a virtual display and keyboard; the Session Manager is used to select a screen group.

Once it is running, a process can obtain access to additional system resources such as files, pipes, semaphores, queues, and additional memory with various OS/2 function calls (see Figure 23-1). A process terminates itself with a call to the OS/2 function DOSEXIT and can also be aborted by its parent process, by an unrecoverable hardware error, or by a memory protection fault. In any case, OS/2 will automatically release all resources belonging to the process when it terminates. Ordinarily, processes are only aware of themselves, OS/2 services, and any child processes they start directly. They cannot directly access memory space or resources belonging to another process, including a child process, without the cooperation of that process.

Threads

The MS OS/2 scheduler, however, knows nothing about processes; it partitions the available CPU cycles among dispatchable entities known as *threads*. A thread has a point of execution, a priority, a stack pointer, and general register contents (see Figure 23-1). At any given time, a thread is either blocked (waiting for I/O or some other event), ready to execute, or actively executing (it has control of the CPU).

Per-Process Information
Process ID (PID)
Disk-swapping information
Local Descriptor Table (LDT) pointer
System resources owned or opened:
Files
Pipes
Queues
System Semaphores
Device monitors
Memory
Child processes

Per-Thread Information
Thread ID
Thread priority
Thread state: blocked, ready to execute, active
Time-slice
Instruction pointer
Processor state (registers and flags)
Stack pointer

Figure 23-1: Thread and process-specific information maintained by OS/2.

Each process has a primary thread that receives control from OS/2 when the process is started; it begins executing at the program's designated entry point. However, that primary thread can start up additional threads within the same process. Multiple threads within a process execute asynchonously to one another, can have different priorities, and can manipulate one another's priorities.

Although the threads within a process have separate stacks, they share the same near data segment (DGROUP) and thus the same local heap. Carefully designing code to use the stack for local variables allows procedures to be shared between threads—this happens naturally in C programs. Access to static variables or other data structures must be coordinated between threads through the use of Ram semaphores or similar mechanisms. The threads also share all the other system resources owned by the process as a whole—open files, system semaphores, queues, and pipes—but OS/2 generally provides automatic serialization of operations on these resources.

When a thread within an application program is executing, the system is in user mode; the thread can only access the resources owned by the process that contains it and cannot execute certain machine instructions. A clock tick, another hardware interrupt, or a call by the application for an OS/2 function causes a transition back into kernel mode, so that OS/2 can service the interrupt or provide the requested operation.

When OS/2 is ready to exit kernel mode, the scheduler receives control and examines its list of active threads. The thread with the highest priority that is ready to execute gains control of the machine. If the thread that was just interrupted is is one of several eligible threads and has not used up its time-slice, it receives preference. If a thread becomes starved for CPU cycles because other threads with higher priorities are getting all the attention, OS/2 will temporarily bump that thread's priority to a higher value.

Configuring the OS/2 Multitasker

There are four different directives that can be placed in the system CONFIG.SYS file to influence the operation of OS/2 multitasking. These are

```
THREADS=n
MAXWAIT=seconds
PRIORITY=ABSOLUTE
                DYNAMIC
MAXWAIT=x[,y]
```

The THREADS directive controls how many threads can be simultaneously created in the system. The parameter n may be 16-255, with a default of 16, which is sufficient for OS/2 and a few simploe processes. The upper limit of 255 cannot be expanded.

When a thread is denied the CPU for the number of seconds specified by MAXWAIT because of other higher-priority threads using up all the time-slices, the starved thread receives a temporary increase in its priority for one time-slice. The PRIORITY directive activates OS/2's mechanisms for dynamically altering the priority of each thread based on the activity of other threads within the system. When PRIORITY=ABSOLUTE, the MAXWAIT directive has no effect whatsoever.

The TIMESLICE directive controls the length of the OS/2 scheduler. The x parameter represents the normal length of a thread's time-slice in milliseconds. If a thread uses up its entire time-slice and must be pre-empted, its next time-slice will be one tick longer, up to the limit given by the y parameter. This strategy is used by OS/2 to reduce the amount of context-switching overhead when several compute bound threads are running.

Screen Groups

Processes are in turn members of screen groups, which is what the average user perceives as being OS/2 multitasking. When the user presses the SysReq key, he exits from the current session, or screen group, to a menu displayed by the Session Manager. He can then select a command processor or other program already executing in another screen group or establish a new screen group by loading a new copy of the protect-mode command processor.

OS/2 maintains separate *virtual screen* for each screen group, which receives the output of all the processes in that group. The virtual screen is mapped to the physical display whenever that screen group is selected by the user with the Session Manager. New processes are added to a screen group by being "spawned" by the command processor or another process already executing within the group.

By convention, only one of the processes within a screen group should be in the foreground at any given time, that is, writing to the screen and reading from the keyboard. The OS/2 DETACH command allows programs to be placed in the background from the command processor level. However, since OS/2 does not place any restrictions on access to the virtual display by the various processes within a screen group, DETACHing normal programs is not usually too useful since it just results in chaotic displays. Programs intended to be used as background tasks must be specially designed to use the OS/2 services for pop-up windows and keyboard monitors, so that they do not disrupt the displays or otherwise interfere with the proper operation of the foreground task within their group.

A screen group, or session, is removed from the system by first terminating any active application programs within that group and returning to the command processor prompt. Then, entry of the EXIT command terminates the command processor itself. The Session Manager regains control and displays a menu of the remaining screen groups.

OS/2 Programming

OS/2 offers a diverse set of services to application programs that allow the creation of complex and powerful multitasking applications (see Figure 23-2). These services include

- starting and stopping child processes
- obtaining the return code of a child process
- starting, suspending, and destroying threads
- altering the priorities of threads
- inter-process communication

OS/2 DOSEXECPGM is used by the *parent process* to load and execute the *child process*. This function is analogous to, but considerably more powerful than, the EXEC function (Int 2lh Function 4Bh) that was available in MS-DOS 2.x and 3.x. The child process can, in turn, load other processes and so on until system limits on threads or open files are exhausted or the system runs out of swap space on the disk.

The OS/2 DOSEXECPGM function is called with:

- the address of the filename of the child process to be executed

- a flag controlling whether the child process is synchronous or asynchronous

- the addresses of an argument string block and an environment block to be passed to the child process. (Each of these blocks consists of a series of null-terminated (ASCIIZ) strings; the block is terminated by an extra null byte. The environment block corresponds exactly to the environment block you are familiar with in MS-DOS 2.x and 3.x, while the simplest case of the argument block is simply a copy of the command line that invoked a process.)

- addresses of buffers to receive the process ID of the child and other information

Process Control	
DOSEXECPGM	Load and execute a child process
DOSCWAIT	Wait for child process to terminate
DOSKILLPROCESS	Unconditionally terminate another process
DOSPTRACE	Inspect/modify/trace a child process
Threads Controlling Threads	
DOSCREATETHREAD	Create another execution thread within the same process
DOSSUSPENDTHREAD	Suspend the execution thread
DOSRESUMETHREAD	Reactivate a thread
DOSEXIT	Terminate current thread or all threads in process
Read/Alter Thread Priorities	
DOSGETPRTY	Get the priority of specified thread
DOSSETPRTY	Set the priority of specified thread
Inter-Thread Protection	
DOSENTERCRITSEC	Disable other threads in same process
DOSEXITCRITSEC	Re-enable other threads in same process

Figure 23-2: OS/2 multitasking services at a glance.

When a child process executes synchronously, execution of the thread in the parent process that made the DOSEXECPGM call is suspended until the child process terminates, either intentionally or owing to an error condition. When the thread in the parent resumes execution, it is supplied with the return code of the child and a termination code that indicates whether the child terminated normally or was aborted by the operating system.

If the child process is asynchronous, all threads in the parent process continue to execute while the child is running. Any thread in the parent process can later use the DOSCWAIT call to resynchronize with the child process by suspending itself until the child terminates and then obtaining its return code. As an alternative, the parent can use the process ID of the child, which is supplied by OS/2 on return from the original DOSEXECPGM call, to unilaterally abort execution of the child process with the DOSKILLPROCESS call at any time. (A special usage of the asynchronous option of DOSEXECPGM, together with the DOSPTRACE function, allows the child program to be traced, inspected, and modified under the parent program's control. This combination of OS/2 services allows the creation of program debuggers that are compatible with 80286 memory protection.)

The child process automatically inherits access to certain resources of the parent process. These resources include the handles for any open files (unless the parent process explicitly opened the files with the noninheritance flag), handles to any open pipes, handles to any open system semaphores (but not ownership of the semaphores), and a copy of the parent's environment block (unless the parent goes to the trouble of creating a new block and passes a pointer to it).

Figure 23-3 is a demonstration of the DOSEXECPGM function—a synchronous execution of CHKDSK as a child process. The various options for asynchronous execution, coupled with several options that are available with the DOSCWAIT function and the DOSKILLPROCESS function, allow for very flexible execution-time relationships between parent and child processes.

Managing Threads

OS/2 has a rich repertoire of function calls for control of multiple threads of execution within a process. The use of multiple threads is particularly appropriate for cases in which a process must manage several I/O devices with vastly different I/O rates (for example, the keyboard, disk, and video display) and remain rapidly responsive to the needs of each. Multiple threads are also appropriate for cases in which a process needs to run in multiple instances, but the instances do not require separate data segments or resources, since multiple threads are started much more quickly than multiple processes and have less system overhead.

Figure 23-3: This sample code fragment demonstrates the use of the OS/2 system service DOSEXECPGM to run CHKDSK as a synchronous child process.

```
                                    .

                                    .

                                    .
              push ds               ; address of object buffer
              push offset DGROUP: ObjName
              push ObjName Len      ; length of object buffer
              push 0                ; execute synchronously
              push ds               ; address of argument block
              push offset DGROUP; ArgBlk
              push 0                ; address of envir.block
              push 0                ; (OL=inherit parent's)
              push ds               ; address to receive return
              push offset DGROUP   :PgmName
              call DOSEXECPGM ; transfer to 286DOS
              or    ax.ax           ; was EXEC successful?
              jnz   error           ; jump if EXEC failed...
                                    .

                                    .

                                    .

ObjName       db    64 dup (0)      ; receives name of dynamic link
ObjNameLen    equ   $-ObjName       ; causing EXEC failre

ArgBlk        db    'chkdsk *.*', 0; block of argument strings for child...
              db    0               ; extra null byte terminates block


                                    ; receives return codes from child...
RetCode       dw    0               ; termination code for child
                                    ; result code from child's DOSEXIT


PgmName       db    'chkdsk.eve',0 ; name of child program to run
```

As mentioned previously, each process has a single primary thread that is known to the OS/2 dispatcher when it is started up, and this thread's initial point of execution is the program's designated entry point. The primary thread can use the MS OS/2 function DOSCREATETHREAD to start up additional threads within the process, and those new threads can also start up threads and so on. Each thread is initially entered through a far call from OS/2 and can terminate through a far return or by issuing the OS/2 function call DOSEXIT. (A process is terminated when the sole remaining active thread in a process issues DOSEXIT, or when any thread issues DOSEXIT with a special parameter that indicates that all threads should be immediately terminated.)

A thread can use the function DOSSLEEP to suspend itself for a programmed period of time, or it can block on a semaphore to await reactivation by another thread or process triggering that same semaphore. Alternatively, a thread can use the functions DOSSUSPENDTHREAD or DOSRESUMETHREAD to suspend or reactivate other threads within the same process without their cooperation. Similarly, a thread can use the functions DOSGETPRTY or DOSSETPRTY to inspect or modify the execution priority of itself or other threads in accordance with execution-time requirements.

Because a thread can be unilaterally suspended by another thread without its knowledge or cooperation, the functions DOSENTERCRITSEC and DOSEX-ITCRITSEC are provided in order to protect a thread from interruption while it is executing a critical section of its code.

Figure 23-4 demonstrates the use of DOSCREATETHREAD by one thread to start up another thread that emits ten beeps at one-second intervals and then terminates. Although this is a trivial use of multiple threads, it gives an inkling of the enormous power of this concept and the ease with which asynchronous processing can be incorporated into an OS/2 application.

Figure 23-4: An example of the use of multiple threads for asynchronous execution of tasks within a single process. The main line of execution allocates memory for a new stack and then starts up another thread called beeper. The new thread uses the OS/2 service DOSBEEP to emit ten short tones at one-second intervals and then terminates.

```
stksiz      equ     1024                        ; size of new thread's stack
                         •
                         •
                         •
Selector            dw          ?               ; selector from
DOSALLOCSEG
BeeperID dw         ?                           ; Thread ID for new thread
                                                ; named 'beeper'
                              •
                              •
                              •
            push    stksiz                      ; size of new segment
            push    ds                          ; address of variable
            push    offset DGROUP: Selector     ;to receive new selector
            push    0                           ; non-shared segment
            call    DOSALLOCSEG     ;TRANSFER TO 286DOS
            or      ax,ax
            jnz     error                       ; jump if alloc failed

            push    cs                          ; execution address of
            push    offset_TEXT:Beeper          ; new thread
            push    ds                          ;address to receive new
            push    offsetDGROUP; BeeperID      ; Thread ID
            push    Selector                    ; address of base of
            push    stksiz                      ; new thread's Stack
            call    DOSCREATETHREAD ; transfer to 286DOS
            or      ax, ax
            jnz     error                       ; jump if create failed
                              •
                              •
                              •
beeper      proc    far                         ; entry point for thread

            mov     cx,10                       ; emit ten beeps...
beep1:      push    440                         ; sound a 440 Hz tone
            push    100                         ; for 100 milliseconds
            call    DOSBEEP                     ; transfer to 286DOS

            push    0                           ; now pause for one sec.
            push    1000
            call DOSSLEEP                       ; transfer to 286DOS
```

```
        loop    beep1                   ; transfer to 286DOS
        ret

beeper  endp
                                •
                                •
                                •
```

Summary

OS/2 uses a time-slicing, preemptive, priority-based multitasking strategy. The Intel 80286 microprocessor's support for privilege levels and memory protection are fully exploited by OS/2 in order to run multiple concurrent tasks and to protect those tasks from damaging each other or the operating system.

A process represents the execution of an application and the ownership of any resources—files, memory, etc.—associated with that execution. Processes can spawn other processes and can exert certain control over those child processes, but sharing of data between two processes is possible only with the cooperation of both processes. OS/2 has a wealth of facilities for inter-process communication, which are discussed in "OS/2 Inter-Process Communication: Semaphores, Pipes, and Queues."

The thread is the dispatchable element used by OS/2 to track execution cycles of the processor. Threads can start, stop, and influence the execution of other threads within the same process. Sharing of data between threads is natural and, in fact, difficult to avoid, since all threads in a process share access to the same memory, files, pipes, queues, and semaphores. In essence, the OS/2 loader knows about processes, but the OS/2 scheduler knows about threads.

24

Multiple Tasks [*]

_____*Steven Armbrust* and *Ted Forgeron*_____

Microsoft has done well to set Operating System/2 (OS/2) apart from DOS with an ability to support multitasking. In a multitasking system, the operating system manages the microprocessor so that all the independent elements appear to be executing simultaneously. Although various multitasking systems have been written for the Intel 8086 family that can operate in the processor's real mode, a protected-mode operating system such as OS/2 has a distinct advantage: the integrity of the system can be guarded by the CPU. This additional protection, however, means that the programs are obligated to use the system's formal methods for communicating with one another; OS/2 provides a cornucopia of such communication methods.

Three types of multitasking are present in OS/2: *sessions, processes*, and *threads*. Sessions, the largest overall type, designate what appears on the screen and where input from the keyboard is sent. Processes include programs and their memory resources. Threads are individual multitasking elements. Figure 24-1 illustrates the relationships among the three types of multitasking; Table 24-1 lists the different functions in each element.

The most visible benefit of multitasking in OS/2 is the Program Selector. It allows users to create, delete, and switch between multiple sessions. Developers are the primary beneficiaries of the other two types of multitasking: processes and threads. Through multitasking and the associated communication functions, a developer can design an application to increase performance as well as simplify the program design.

Sessions

A session, the highest level multitasking element, consists of one or more processes that use the same display screen and keyboard (sessions are also referred to in Microsoft documentation as *screen groups*). For example, a user could start a

_____

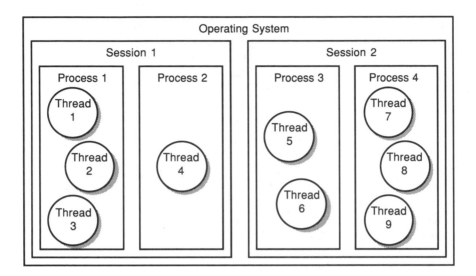

Figure 24-1: There are three entities in the OS/2 multitasking hierarchy. Sessions, the highest level, arbitrate use of the keyboard and screen. Only the foreground session may use these resources. Processes are programs (code and data loaded from an .EXE file) and any resources that are allocated by the program during execution. Each process can have one or more threads that independently execute.

word processor as one session, a spreadsheet as another, and a database program as a third. Each of these sessions displays information at a logical display and accepts input from a logical keyboard. When the user switches to a new session, OS/2 writes the new session's logical display to the physical display and directs information typed at the physical keyboard to the session's logical keyboard.

The Program Selector (see "Enter OS/2") uses standard OS/2 system calls to create and manipulate sessions. DosStartSession creates sessions, and DosStopSession destroys them. DosSetSession sets the operational characteristics of a session, and DosSelectSession chooses the session to be placed in the foreground (that is, displayed on the physical screen).

Processes

Within each protected-mode session is one or more processes. A process is an instance of an executing program, plus all the resources used by the program. A session's initial process is begun when the operating system starts the session,

TABLE 24-1: Tasking Functions

FUNCTIONS	DESCRIPTION
SESSIONS	
DosSelectSession	Select foreground session.
DosSetSession	Set session status.
DosStartSession	Start another session.
DosStopSession	Stop session started with DosStartSession.
PROCESSES	
DosExecPgm	Execute program as a child process; parent process can continue to execute.
DosCWait	Place current process in a wait state until a child process has terminated.
DosExitList	Maintain a list of routines to be executed when the current process ends.
DosGetInfoSeg	Get address of global information segment and process local information segment.
DosGetPriority	Get process or thread priority.
DosSet Priority	Set priority of a child process or thread in current process
DosPTrace	Interface to the OS/2 kernel for aid in program debugging.
DosSuspendThread	Temporarily suspend thread execution until DosResumeThread is called.
DosResumeThread	Restart thread previously stopped by DosSuspendThread.
DosKillProcess	Terminate process and return termination code to parent.
THREADS	
DosCreateThread	Create another of execution under current process.
DosEnterCritSec	Enter critical section of execution, temporarily preventing other threads in the current process from executing.
DosExitCritSecDosExit	Exit critical section of execution, reenabling other thread execution in the current process.
DosExit	Exit current thread.
OS/2 provides API functions for the creation, control, and destruction of the three types of multitasking elements, which include sessions, processes, and threads.	

and other processes are started programmatically. For example, the protected-mode command interpreter, CMD.EXE, can be started as the initial process of a session. When the user types an external command, the command interpreter calls DosExecPgm, naming the .EXE file representing that command. A new process, but not a new session, is created.

A process's resources include a process ID; a local descriptor table (LDT); and addresses of the process's code, data, and stack segments.

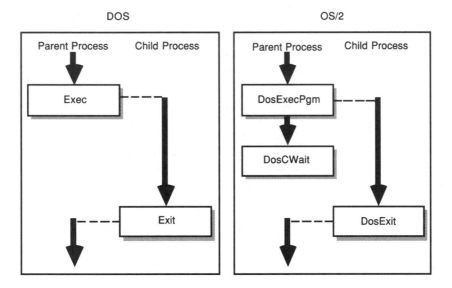

Figure 24-2: In DOS, the parent process must wait until the child process has terminated before proceeding from an EXEC call. In OS/2, the parent can start a child process with DosExecPgm but cannot block its own execution. To synchronize with the child later, the parent can call DosCWait to wait until the child terminates.

Whenever OS/2 starts a process, it loads the file containing the process's code. The DosExecPgm call is used to start a new process. It is similar to the DOS EXEC function (interrupt 21, function 4BH), except that under OS/2, parent and child processes can run concurrently. Under DOS, when a program invoked the EXEC function, the parent process waited in limbo until the child process completed. Under OS/2, the parent has the option of stopping until the child process completes, but it can also run in parallel, as shown in Figure 24-2. When the processes run in parallel, the parent process can call DosCWait at some later time to wait for the child process to complete. The parent can also call DosKillProcess in order to terminate the child process.

Threads

Within each process is one or more threads. A thread is an execution path within a process and is the multitasking element managed by OS/2.

When a process starts, only one thread exists. OS/2 starts this thread at the entry point of the program being executed by the process. This initial thread can start additional threads to gain more concurrency. Instead of invoking a thread with an ordinary procedure call, the initial thread uses the DosCreateThread call. This call specifies the address of the thread (for a call in C, this is the procedure name) and then initiates the procedure as a separate thread. Unless the procedure has been defined in a dynamic link library (DLL), the call does not load any program code from the disk (the program code was already loaded when the process was started).

OS/2 supports as many as 255 separate threads (255 per system, not per process or per session). The number that is allowed for any particular system (from 16 to 255) can be set with the THREADS = entry in the CONFIG.SYS file. For each thread, OS/2 maintains a thread priority, a stack, a processor state (copies of all the processor registers), and a thread state (blocked, ready, or active). All other resources are owned by a process and, thus, are shared among all threads in that process. For example, if one thread opens a file and obtains a file handle, another thread in that process can use the file handle to access the file.

Although OS/2 is a multitasking operating system, it has access to only one microprocessor; therefore, only one thread can be executing at any one time. The other threads are either ready to execute or blocked. When the OS/2 scheduler determines that a new thread should run, it saves the contents of all the processor registers into the processor state area for the old thread. The scheduler then loads the registers from the new thread's processor state. This enables the new thread to continue just where it left off the last time the thread was interrupted.

This saving and restoring of processor registers has a serious deficiency when OS/2 is run on 80386-based computers, because it applies only to the 16-bit registers available in the 80286. If OS/2 runs on a 32-bit 80386-based computer, it does not save the extended portions of the 32-bit registers, even though user code is otherwise free to use 32-bit 80386 instructions.

For example, in an 80386-based computer, suppose thread A performs a 32-bit operation in order to add the EBX register to the contents of the EAX register. Now suppose thread A is preempted by thread B, which proceeds to subtract EAX from itself, thereby setting the entire 32-bit register to 0. When thread A is restored, its 16-bit AX register is restored, but not the upper 16 bits, which remain set to 0. Therefore, thread A has been corrupted. This problem prevents OS/2 from being used with any application that has been designed to use 32-bit instructions.

Processes can have multiple threads running the same code. This is done by invoking DosCreateThread multiple times with the same start address. Each of the threads will have its own stack, but because the threads have access to the same memory, they must take precautions when using static variables and data structures. Mechanisms for intertask communication, such as RAM semaphores, can be used to prevent other threads from accessing these common areas until the first thread is finished. In addition, a thread about to execute a critical section of code can call DosEnterCritSec to prevent all other threads in the process from executing until the thread calls DosExitCritSec. Since Dos EnterCritSec does not prevent threads in other processes from running, this command is not an appropriate method for interprocess synchronization.

The DosSuspendThread call and the DosResumeThread call can be used by a thread to suspend and resume execution of another thread in the same process. DosGetPriority and DosSetPriority can be used to get or set the priority of a thread.

Scheduling Threads

Because only one thread at a time can be executing in the system, OS/2 uses a preemptive, priority-based approach for determining which thread will be running at any given time. When created, each thread is assigned a priority class as well as a priority number. This combination determines the overall priority of the thread. At all times, the highest priority ready-to-run thread has access to the processor. When the highest priority thread becomes not ready (when it is waiting for I/O, when it puts itself to sleep for a while with the DosSleep call, when it is waiting to synchronize with another thread, or when its time slice expires), OS/2 gives the processor to the next highest priority ready-to-run thread. When a higher-priority thread becomes ready again (when the I/O operation finishes, when its sleep time is over, or when it receives synchronization from another thread), the lower-priority thread relinquishes control of the processor.

OS/2 uses time-slicing to ensure that threads of equal priorities all have a chance to run. The time-slice value, specified with the TIMESLICE entry in the CONFIG.SYS file, designates how long OS/2 will allow a thread to continue running before checking the readiness of other threads. The minimum time-slice value is approximately 31 microseconds, which is the resolution of the system clock. If threads having higher priority are ready to run at the end of each time slice, one of those will gain access to the processor. In addition, if any other threads of equal priority are ready to run, OS/2 preempts the current thread and gives the next such thread access to the processor for its time slice. If no other threads of equal or higher priority are ready to run, OS/2 gives control of the processor back to the original thread.

This preemptive nature of OS/2 means that an application can relinquish control of the processor in two general ways. It can do so explicitly by calling an operating system service (such as waiting at a queue or putting itself to sleep). A thread can be forcibly preempted by OS/2 when its time slice expires and a thread with a higher priority is ready to run.

If no other thread wants the processor, interrupting a thread doing useful work would waste CPU cycles. To moderate the overhead from scheduling, an option is available in the CONFIG.SYS file to reduce the frequency of time-slice interruptions conditionally. The TIMESLICE entry has two parameters (TIMESLICE = x,y). The first parameter is the length of a thread's initial time slice. The second is the maximum time slice permitted. If a thread uses its entire time slice without being preempted by a higher priority thread, OS/2 increases its time slice by one clock tick. This continues up to the maximum time slice value.

Thread priority has three classes, each of which has 32 priority levels (0 through 31). The highest priority class is the *time-critical* class. All the threads in this class are of higher priority than the threads in the other two classes. Typically, the threads in this priority class would be those that handle time-sensitive areas, such as servicing high-speed data communications devices.

The next highest class is the *regular* class (also called the *normal* class in some of the Microsoft documentation). This class is used by most of the application programs and OS/2 commands invoked from the keyboard.

By default, OS/2 provides additional scheduling features within the regular class to ensure that all the threads in the class get a chance to run. Associated with the regular class is a maximum wait value (specified in units of seconds by the MAXWAIT entry in the CONFIG.SYS file). This value specifies the maximum amount of time that a thread can wait before it gets a chance to run. When the MAXWAIT time expires for any thread, OS/2 gives the thread a priority boost for one time slice. After the thread runs for one time slice, its priority reverts to its previous value. The user can disable this priority-boosting feature by placing the entry PRIORITY = ABSOLUTE in the CONFIG.SYS file.

The lowest priority class is the *idle-time* class. Threads in this class do not run unless no threads in either of the other two classes are ready to run. The idle-time class is typically used for programs such as print spoolers, automatic disk back-up programs, or any other background-running program.

Dividing Applications

Although three levels of multitasking entities--sessions, processes, and threads-- can be created, it is not always clear how to divide a single application into these elements. Should an application consist of a single session with a single process and multiple threads? Should there be multiple processes with one or more threads in each? Or, should the application consist of multiple sessions?

These questions are not answered easily, but programmers can follow some of these guidelines:

- Rarely will an application need to be divided into multiple sessions. The only obvious example of a program that needs to create multiple sessions is OS/2's Program Selector, which creates a shell for invoking multiple applications. Even OS/2's Presentation Manager will consist of a single session, because it allows multiple programs to share the same screen.

- Multiple processes are appropriate if an application has multitasking elements with a high degree of independence or those that need to be protected from one another. For example, a database management application could be divided into a user interface process that handles requests and a background transaction process that supervises the database. This arrangement allows the user interface process to be started, stopped, or killed (for example, through CtrlBreak) without compromising the integrity of the database.

- If there are many small components that execute for only a short period of time, multiple threads are a better solution than multiple processes because process creation carries a larger overhead than thread creation carries. Creating a process involves loading an .EXE file and then creating the OS/2 kernel data structures such as the LDT. The procedure for creating a thread is much quicker.

- If there are multitasking elements that need to be tied together as closely as two procedures are, they should be assigned as multiple threads in a process.

Threads in the same process can typically share data with much less overhead than threads in different processes.

- A separate thread can be used for performing any operation that would block a process when there is useful work to do. For example, a new thread could be created to open a file, which will typically block while the disk is accessed to find the file. Meanwhile, the original thread could perform other work while the new file is being opened.

Interprocess Communication

In any multitasking system, mechanisms must be available for the independent elements to synchronize and communicate with each other. In OS/2, each thread runs as if it owned the entire processor. However, threads often need to pass information to one another or to make certain that one thread has completed its operations before another thread starts operation. These mechanisms are especially useful between threads in different processes, because processes are normally isolated from each other by virtue of the processor's protected mode.

OS/2 provides the following interprocess communication (IPC) mechanisms: *semaphores, pipes, shared memory, queues,* and *signals* (see Table 24-2). In most cases, IPC requires the processes to agree upon the names and locations of the resources. Therefore, the processes must be designed and coded specifically to communicate with each other. The exception is the pipe, which allows transparent communication modeled after file I/O.

Semaphores

Semaphores are simple objects that threads can use to coordinate access to resources or to synchronize with one another. Semaphores have two states: owned and not-owned (or, depending on how they are used, set and cleared).

To coordinate access to resources (such as a sensitive area of data), a semaphore can represent ownership of the resource. To do this, all threads must adhere to the convention that before any thread can access the critical resource, it must first request ownership of the semaphore by means of the DosSemRequest call. If it is not owned when DosSemRequest is issued, the issuing thread becomes the owner and can use the resource at will. When the owning thread finishes using the resource, it calls DosSemClear in order to release the semaphore.

TABLE 24-2: Communication Functions

FUNCTIONS	DESCRIPTION
SEMAPHORES	
DosCreateSem	Create a system semaphore.
DosOpenSem	Open an existing system semaphore.
DosCloseSem	Close a system semaphore.
DosSemRequest	Obtain ownership of a semaphore.
DosSemSet	Set an owned semaphore.
DosSemSetWait	Set a semaphore and wait for it to be cleared (blocks the current thread until the next DosSemClear occurs).
DosSemWait	Wait for a semaphore to be cleared.
DosMuxSemWait	Wait for one of a number of semaphores to be cleared.
PIPES	
DosMakePipe	Create a pipe.
SHARED MEMORY	
DosAllocShrSeg	Allocate a shared memory segment (named) to a process.
DosGetShrSeg	Enable a process to access a named shared memory segment allocated by another process.
DosAllocSeg	Allocate a segment of memory.
DosGiveSeg	Give access to a segment.
QUEUES	
DosCreateQueue	Create a queue.
DosOpenQueue	Open a queue for the current process.
DosWriteQueue	Add an element to a queue.
DosReadQueue	Read and remove an element from a queue.
DosPeekQueue	Retrieve but do not remove an element from a queue.
DosQueryQueue	Return the size (number of elements) in a queue.
DosPurgeQueue	Purge a queue of all elements.
DosCloseQueue	Close a queue.
SIGNALS	
DosSetSigHandler	Define a routine to handle a signal.
DosFlagProcess	Set a process external event flag in another process.
DosHoldSignal	Disable or enable signal processing for current process.

The OS/2 abundance of interprocess and thread communication functions provides a good simplicity-versus-performance trade-off for many applications.

If a thread calls DosSemRequest to request a semaphore that is already owned, one of three things can happen (depending on the options the thread specified in the call): the call can wait forever for the semaphore to become clear; it can wait a specified number of milliseconds; or it can not wait at all. In the first case, the thread is put on hold until the semaphore becomes available. In the second case, if the semaphore becomes available in the specified amount of time, the calling thread becomes the owner of the semaphore. Otherwise, the call returns without gaining ownership of the semaphore. In the third case, the call returns immediately, indicating if the semaphore is currently owned.

Multiple threads can request ownership of the same semaphore. If the threads choose to wait (instead of returning immediately), the ones that do not immediately gain access to the semaphore continue to wait until the owning thread releases the semaphore. When this happens, the waiting threads are dispatched again, and the highest-priority waiting thread becomes the new owner, even if a lower-priority thread has been waiting longer. The other threads continue waiting. If equal-priority threads are waiting, the thread that has been waiting the longest becomes the new owner.

Using a semaphore to represent ownership of some resource enables threads to read or write sensitive data areas without fear that other threads will interrupt them before they finish. Suppose that one thread gathers information about the positions of aircraft and records their x, y, and z coordinates in a database. Another thread reads the database and displays the aircraft positions on a screen. Without a semaphore guarding the database, the thread that writes the coordinates could write an airplane's x and y coordinates but then could be interrupted by the reading thread before updating the z coordinate. If this happened, the display produced by the reading thread would not represent the airplane's actual position. The same sort of situation could happen if the reading thread was interrupted before it read all three coordinates. Using semaphores, each thread requests ownership of the semaphore before reading or writing the database. Each would clear the semaphore after accessing the database to give other threads a chance in order to use or modify the data.

Another use of semaphores is synchronizing thread activities. In this situation, a semaphore can be either set or cleared. For example, suppose a process consists of an initialization thread plus several other threads. The initialization thread must run first in order to set up the data structures needed by the other threads. After it completes those activities, however, all the other threads are free to run.

To manage this activity, the initialization thread would call DosSemSet to set the semaphore. This would designate that the initialization activity was still under way and that the other threads could not run. When the initialization thread completed its activity, it would call DosSemClear in order to clear the semaphore.

The other threads that depend on the initialization thread to finish its activities would call DosSemWait before doing anything else. This call causes the threads to wait until the semaphore is cleared before proceeding. Like the DosSemRequest call, DosSemWait allows the threads to wait forever, for a specified period of time, or not at all. Unlike the DosSemRequest call, all the waiting threads are notified when the semaphore is cleared, not just the first thread on the waiting list. In addition, the DosSemWait call does not transfer ownership of the semaphore when the semaphore is cleared. Figure 24-3 illustrates the use of semaphores in synchronizing thread activities.

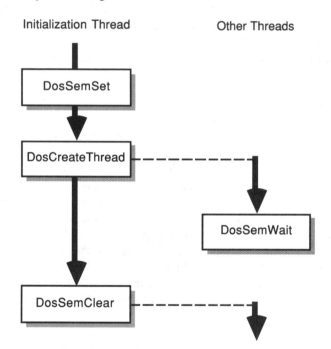

Figure 24-3: Before starting one or more threads, a master thread sets a semaphore to indicate that initialization is not complete. The other threads call DosSemWait to wait for the "initialization complete" indication. Once the master thread has finished initialization, it clears the semaphore; all of the other threads are now able to run.

Two additional OS/2 calls are available for use with semaphores in synchronizing the activities of threads. DosSemSetWait is like DosSemWait except that it sets the semaphore first before waiting for it to be cleared. This call can be used if the waiting thread knows that the thread it is waiting for will not get a chance to run first. It guarantees that the semaphore will be set so that the thread can wait for another thread to clear the semaphore. The other call, DosMuxSemWait, is also similar to DosSemWait, but it enables a thread to wait until any one of a number of semaphores is cleared.

OS/2 defines two kinds of semaphores, *system* semaphores and *RAM* semaphores. System semaphores are used for communication between threads in different processes. RAM semaphores are used by threads in the same process. The difference between the two is in how they are created and accessed, but system semaphores also provide a few more features.

In a single process, threads can share memory; therefore, threads do not need to perform a complicated procedure to create a semaphore. Instead, a double-word can be defined as the location of the semaphore and initially set to zero (meaning cleared and unowned). Threads then use the address of that double-word as the semaphore's handle in calls that manipulate the semaphore. For example, if a thread wants to establish ownership of the RAM semaphore, it simply calls DosSemRequest and specifies the address of the double-word representing that particular semaphore.

The use of RAM semaphores depends on threads being able to access the memory containing the semaphore. When two threads are in different processes, they cannot access each other's memory unless they explicitly cooperate to share a memory segment. Thus, a different mechanism must be used.

System semaphores use a named approach for creating and accessing semaphores. This mechanism is almost exactly like the one used for creating and accessing named files. To create a system semaphore, a thread calls DosCreateSem and gives and ASCII name. In response, OS/2 returns a handle that the thread can use in other calls to manipulate the semaphore.

When other threads want to use the system semaphore, they must first call DosOpenSem, specifying the ASCII name of the semaphore. If the semaphore is available, OS/2 returns a handle they can use for other semaphore calls.

When a thread finishes with a system semaphore, it calls DosCloseSem to close the semaphore. When all threads that used a system semaphore close it, OS/2 automatically deletes the semaphore. Figure 24-4 shows how two processes can use a system semaphore.

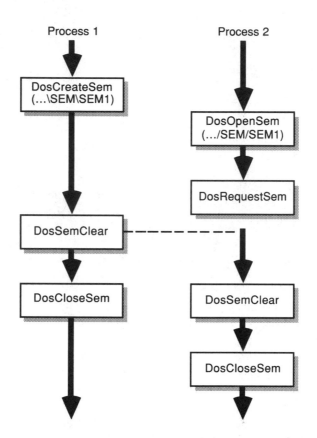

Figure 24-4: The first process that uses a system semaphore must create it. Subsequent users can open the semaphore using the agreed-upon name, in this case SEM 1. After the last thread has closed the system semaphore, OS/2 deletes the semaphore.

OS/2 maintains a directory to keep track of system semaphores. This directory is called SEM and is kept in memory rather than on disk. Whenever threads refer to system semaphores by name, they must include the \SEM\ as part of the name, just as in I/O calls a full path name is often used. Thus, the format of a system semaphore name is:

`\SEM\NAME.EXT`

where the rules for defining NAME.EXT are the same as the rules for defining the names of files.

Although a RAM semaphore placed in shared memory might seem to offer the same functionality as the system semaphore, some subtle differences can become important. OS/2 maintains information about the current owner of a system semaphore. If a process exits and still owns a system semaphore, OS/2 will notify any threads in other processes that are waiting on that semaphore by waking them and returning an error code indicating that the semaphore owner has exited. The RAM semaphores gain their simplicity by forgoing this safety mechanism.

Pipes

Pipes are another kind of object that threads in different processes can use to communicate with one another. A pipe is simply an area of memory used to store data--a circular buffer that is a RAM substitute for a file. Figure 24-5 illustrates the use of a pipe.

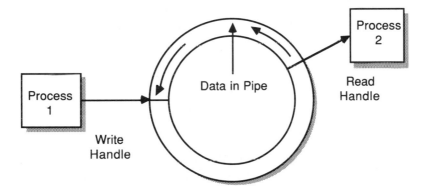

Figure 24-5: Pipes are read from and written to using standard OS/2 file I/O calls; this often makes their use transparent to the processes involved. The pipe is maintained in a memory segment as a circular buffer. When the writing process fills the pipe, it is blocked until the reading process has read some of the data from the pipe.

Using a pipe is very much like using a file. One thread writes information to a pipe using ordinary I/O calls, and another thread reads the information, again using ordinary I/O calls. Often, threads that communicate via pipes are not even aware that they are using pipes instead of files.

A thread creates a pipe by calling DosMakePipe and specifying the size of the pipe desired. A pipe is limited in size to 64KB (minus 32 bytes for the pipe header). This means that the maximum message that one thread can send to another via a pipe is 65,504 bytes. However, a pipe is a circular buffer. Therefore, once the reading thread reads some of the information from the pipe, the writing thread can continue writing data.

In response to the DosMakePipe call, OS/2 returns two handles to the pipe: the read handle and the write handle. Threads can use ordinary I/O calls to access the pipe (DosRead together with the read handle and DosWrite together with the write handle). If a thread attempts to write to a pipe and the pipe is full, the thread is suspended until another thread reads enough information from the pipe to enable the first thread's data to be written. Likewise, if a thread attempts to read a pipe and not enough data exist to satisfy the request, the thread is suspended until another thread writes additional information to the pipe. When a thread finishes using a pipe, it closes the pipe handles that are using the DosClose call. When no more open pipe handles are present, OS/2 automatically deletes the pipe.

The typical use for pipes is for a parent process to create a pipe, use DosDupHandle to substitute the pipe handles for standard ones (such as **stdin** and **stdout**), and create child processes to use the handles. When a new process is created, it automatically inherits the handles of its parents, so when the threads in the new processes read from **stdin** and write to **stdout**, they will automatically communicate via the pipe set up by their parent process.

Shared Memory

OS/2 provides several calls that enable threads in different processes to share the same data segment in memory. One mechanism for sharing segments involves using the DosAllocShrSeg and DosGetShrSeg functions. These two functions enable threads to access segments by name, much as threads access system semaphores. DosAllocShrSeg causes OS/2 to allocate a shared segment (up to 64KB in size) to the calling thread. The calling thread also specifies a name for this segment, which OS/2 stores in a SHAREMEM directory in memory. As with semaphores, the names must follow the rules for file names. DosAllocShrSeg returns a selector for the allocated segment.

When a thread in another process needs to access the shared segment, it calls DosGetShrSeg, specifying the name of the shared segment it wishes to access. This name must include the directory prefix \SHAREMEM\

DosGetShrSeg returns a selector for the segment. This selector can differ from the one received by the thread that created the segment, so threads should not pass the shared segment selectors as data to other processes. However, all selectors returned by DosGetShrSeg for the same shared segment refer to the same memory.

For shared segments allocated with DosAllocShrSeg, OS/2 maintains an internal reference counter that is incremented when the segment is allocated and each time DosGetShrSeg is called. When a thread finishes with the segment and calls DosFreeSeg, the internal counter is decremented. When all threads have freed the segment (decrementing the count to zero), OS/2 frees the segment and removes its name from the SHAREMEM directory.

Using the DosAllocShrSeg and DosGetShrSeg calls is a good way for multiple processes to access a single database. For example, in a spreadsheet program, the data that make up the worksheet portion can be kept in one or more shared segments. All the processes that need to access that worksheet (spreadsheet, print, graph, and so on) will know the names of the segments and use DosGetShrSeg to get selectors for them. Once they have the segment selectors, they can directly access the data.

Shared segments can also be used to transfer data directly from one process to another. To perform this type of activity, a thread calls DosAllocSeg to allocate a segment of memory. This call does not place a name for the segment in the SHAREMEM directory, but a parameter in the call designates that the segment can be shared.

Once a thread has allocated a shared segment and placed information in that segment, it can share the segment with another process by calling DosGiveSeg and specifying the process ID of the process that will be sharing the segment. DosGiveSeg returns something called a recipient segment handle, which is simply a selector that the other process can use to access the segment.

(The recipient's selector will be different because the segments accessible to each process are listed in its LDT, and each process uses a different LDT. Therefore, each process needs a selector that refers to its own LDT.)

After calling DosGiveSeg, the thread has a selector that a thread in a different process can use to access the shared segment, but the thread still needs to let the other process know what that selector is. To pass the selector of a shared segment to a thread in another process, another object, called a queue, is used.

Queues

A queue is simply a place that one thread can drop off a message to another thread, much like a post office box is a place where people can send messages to one another. Threads do not need to synchronize using queues, as they would when using pipes. Instead, one thread simply sends a message to the queue for safe keeping and another thread requests the message later. Queues are useful for transferring shared memory between processes, but threads in the same process can also use queues to exchange information.

When a thread sends a message to a queue (and also when a thread picks up a message), no data are actually transferred. Instead, the queue stores the address of a segment containing the message. When two processes exchange information, this segment is called a *shared* segment.

Queues use the same type of naming mechanism that system semaphores and shared segments use. A thread calls DosCreateQueue and specifies an ASCII name for the queue. OS/2 maintains this name in a memory-resident queue directory called QUEUES.

The process that created the queue is the owner of the queue. Only threads in the owning process can receive messages from the queue, purge the queue, or close the queue. Any thread can send messages to the queue. Again, this is analogous to a post office, in which the box holder is the only one who can receive mail or cancel the box, but anyone can send mail to the box.

Before a thread in another process can send messages to the queue, it must first open the queue. It does this by calling DosOpenQueue, and specifying the ASCII name of the queue. The name must include the directory name \QUEUES\. DosOpenQueue, in response, returns a handle that the thread can use when invoking other queue calls and the ID of the process that owns the queue. Having this ID is important because, in order to send a message to another process, the thread must prepare a shared segment to contain the message. Before it can send the shared segment to the queue, it must also call DosGiveSeg to obtain a selector that the other process can use. DosGiveSeg requires as input the process ID of the process that will be sharing the segment.

Once a thread opens a queue, it can send a message to it by calling DosWriteQueue and specifying the address of the message. As was mentioned earlier, this address must be one that is accessible to the receiving process. Therefore, a thread that is in a different process than the queue must allocate shared memory and call DosGiveSeg to obtain a valid address before sending to the queue.

Multiple messages can be sent to a queue; the order in which the messages are stored in the queue depends on a parameter specified when the queue was created. Messages can be maintained in FIFO order (the first one sent is the first one received), in LIFO order (the last one sent is the first one received), or in priority order (in which the sending thread specifies a priority from 0 to 15).

Any thread in the process that owns the queue can receive messages from it by calling DosReadQueue. This call removes a message from the queue and gives its address to the requesting thread. If no messages are being held in the queue, the thread can wait until a message is sent or it can return without receiving a message. Figure 24-6 illustrates the use of a queue.

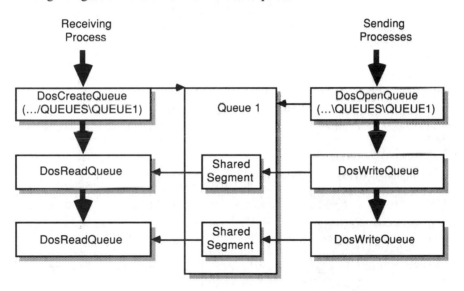

Figure 24-6: Queues are particularly good for large messages because data are not copied between processes. The queue is created by a process that wants to receive messages. One or more processes can open the queue by its agreed-upon name and send messages. Messages consist of a 16-bit number (its meaning is application-defined) and a pointer to a shared data segment allocated by the sender.

Once the receiving thread has processed the message it removed from the queue, it is responsible for freeing the segment it obtained; this is done by using the DosFreeSeg call.

Threads in owning processes can use additional calls. DosPeekQueue lets a thread read a message from the queue without removing the message. Using DosPeekQueue, a thread can browse through a queue for specific messages, then remove those messages from the queue with DosReadQueue. The DosQueryQueue call returns the number of messages being held in the queue. The DosPurgeQueue call is used to purge a queue of all messages. The DosCloseQueue call is used to close a queue and remove its name from the QUEUES directory.

Signals

Signals are another mechanism for interprocess communication. They are primarily used to handle external events, such as the operator pressing Ctrl-C or Ctrl-Break. However, signals can also be used to enable processes to communicate with each other. Using signals to analogous to using software interrupts under DOS.

The OS/2 signal facility enables a process to designate on-condition handlers that will gain control whenever a particular signal occurs. Signals occur when the following events take place: Ctrl-C is pressed, Ctrl-Break is pressed, a process is terminated by calling DosKill, or a general-purpose signal is sent by another process.

A thread sets up a signal handler by calling DosSetSigHandler and specifying the address of the routine that will handle the signal and the type of signal it will handle. The signal types are the specific ones mentioned earlier and three general-purpose signals (process flags *A, B,* and *C*). The specific signals enable an application to perform special processing when one of the interrupt keys is pressed (Ctrl-C or Ctrl-Break) or to perform clean-up operations just before the process is deleted. The general-purpose signals enable signals to be sent via software rather than by external events.

When a signal occurs while a process is active, thread one of that process (the first one started when the process was created) is diverted in a forced call to the signal handler. Because the signals often represent time-critical events, if thread one is processing a call that will not return quickly, the call will be aborted and return an error code. Slow calls are normally device I/O calls. File system calls (opening and closing, or reading and writing files) are not aborted.

Because signals are always serviced by thread one, applications that use signals may want to reserve this thread for signal processing, perhaps blocking on a RAM semaphore, and create other threads for program execution.

When a signal handler receives control, the stack is updated to contain the following information: the far return address of the thread that was interrupted, the number of the signal that just occurred, and the value of an *argument* passed to the signal handler. The argument is a word that enables the threads that cause general-purpose signals to pass small amounts of data to the signal handler. External signals (Ctrl-C, Ctrl-Break, or DosKill) do not pass any meaningful information in this particular argument.

The signal handler can then perform any operations it needs in response to the signal. For example, in response to a Ctrl-C, a signal handler could close open files, free all allocated memory, delete threads, and perform any other clean-up operations before being terminated. When it finishes, the signal handler can execute an intersegment return instruction to resume execution at the point at which it was interrupted. Or, it can manually set the stack frame to a known state and jump to a known location. Threads can send signals to signal handlers by calling DosFlagProcess. This sends one of the signals (process flag *A, B,* or *C*) to the process indicated in the call. If there is no signal handler set up for that signal in the specified process, the signal is ignored.

In addition, threads can call DosHoldSignal to disable signal processing during critical periods of operation. This is analogous to disabling interrupts under DOS. For example, if a thread is performing a time-critical operation, updating a sensitive area of data, or performing some other operation that should not be interrupted, it does not want to be interrupted by having the operator press CtrlBreak. It can use DosHoldSignal to turn off signal processing while performing the critical operations. After it finishes, it can call DosHoldSignal to turn signal processing back on. Turning signal processing back on is analogous to enabling the interrupts.

When signal processing is turned off, occurring signals are recognized but not accepted until it is turned on again. Because signals often represent critical events that should be handled quickly, signals should be treated like hardware interrupts and turned off only for short periods. OS/2 provides a full range of functions for multitasking operation and several mechanisms for communication between multitasking elements. It remains to be seen how large applications will take advantage of these features. All the tools are in place, however, to provide multitasking applications that are as sophisticated as any in the microcomputer world.

25

OS/2 Virtual Memory Management[*]

Vic Heller

Microsoft OS/2 memory management takes advantage of the 80286's fault-handling capability to support segment-based virtual memory. Programs link dynamically at load time or run time or both to library modules for system services; independent software packages can use dynamic-link library (DLL) modules to share code and data used by multiple related applications. I'll give an inside look at the design of OS/2's memory manager version 1.1 as an example of segmented virtual memory management.

Providing the virtual memory, as well as the dynamic linking and sharing of code between tasks, requires some carefully thought out data structures. The 80286 supplies hardware support for protecting tasks from each other, but we also need to keep track of allocated and unallocated memory and the status of a task's segments (e.g., present, swapped, discarded, or allocate on demand (AOD)). We need to be able to find a segment that is not present. If there isn't enough physical memory for an allocation request, the memory compactor must be able to determine whether it can move segments around to make room, or if it will have to discard or swap some segments out of memory. Providing the ability to share data among tasks adds another dimension to the complexity of the system. I'll look at the data structures OS/2 uses and explain how they work together.

Figure 25-1 shows OS/2's hardware and software data structures. Each task has a per task data area (PTDA) created by OS/2. Every executable or DLL file has a module table entry (MTE) as part of its header. The operating system reads the MTE into memory when it loads a program or library module. The PTDA contains data global to the task (local descriptor table (LDT) information, thread count, and so on) and some data specific to each thread of execution within the task (current register contents and so forth); the MTE contains each segment's size, location in the file, and other type information. The system uses the PTDA

---

[*] © McGraw-Hill Information Systems Company, *BYTE*, April, 1988, p. 227

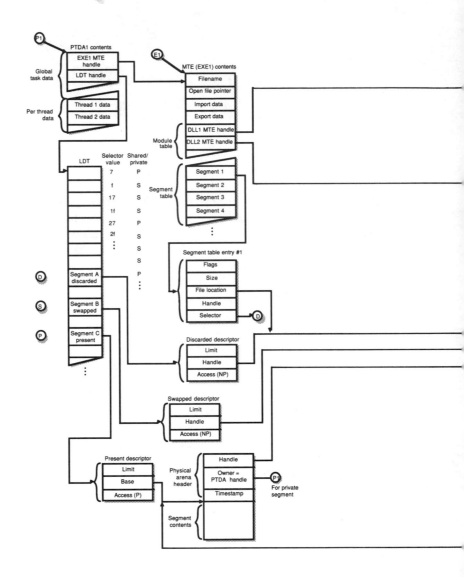

Figure 25-1: The hardware and software data structures that OS/2 uses. This example shows the state of three segments in the task EXEI. Segment A is an example of an EXE file code segment that is currently discarded. Notice it uses a private selector, and the handle table entry shows that segment A's owner is EXE1's MTE. Segment B is currently swapped to disk and has a shared selector.

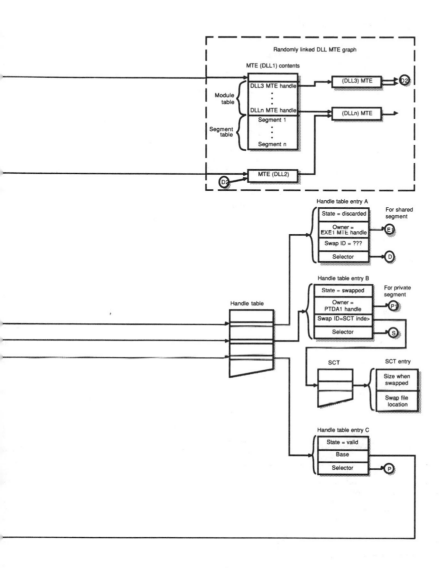

Figure 25-1 (*continued*)
The owner of segment B is EXEI's PTDA. Segment C is present in memory and
has a private selector. Since it is present in memory, its physical arena header
points to its owner, EXEI's PTDA. Notice the shared and private segment
descriptors are interleaved in a 3-to-1 ratio.

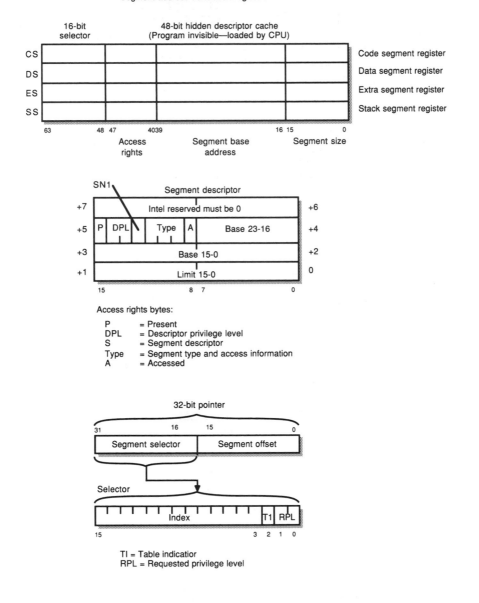

Figure 25-2: The 80286 hardware structures work together to provide memory protection. The action of loading a segment selector into a segment register causes the 80286 to use the selector to index into the LDT and use the corresponding segment descriptor for limit and access checking.

to locate a single descriptor that maps a segment so it can be edited when the state changes. The system uses the MTE to find the executable or DLL file information so it can find and read the segment contents into memory.

The 80286 hardware provides each task with an array of segment "descriptor" structures (LDT) to restrict each task's access to those segments the operating system allows. A valid descriptor entry contains a user segment's physical address, size, and access rights (read/write/execute). The operation of placing a selector into a segment register causes the 80286 hardware to use the selector to index the LDT, fetch the corresponding LDT descriptor, and allow access and limit checking during each subsequent memory reference. Figure 25-2 shows an LDT entry (descriptor), along with the format for a selector and the segment registers with their hidden descriptor cache.

The LDT descriptors work closely with two software data structures: the physical arena and the handle table. In fact, starting with any one of these structures, the system can find either one of the others.

The physical arena is a list of headers that keeps track of all available physical memory by linking free and allocated blocks of memory. A header holds a segment's handle, owner, and last detected access time (time stamp). The handle table holds more permanent information that the system must have when a segment is not present in the physical arena-information such as the segment's selector, owner, swap ID, and state.

The 80286 provides an accessed bit in each descriptor that assists the operating system in choosing which segments can be swapped out or discarded. The hardware sets this bit whenever it accesses the corresponding segment. On the order of once per second, OS/2 examines and clears these bits, and updates the physical arena time stamps for each accessed segment. When physical memory becomes scarce, OS/2 builds a simple ordered list of the segments, with the oldest time stamps first. This list is rebuilt when it is exhausted (all its entries are discarded or swapped) or when significant physical arena changes take place.

The compactor uses the handle table and owner to modify the descriptor and handle states of segments that it moves, swaps, or discards. When a segment is not present, the handle state tells whether the segment is swapped, discarded, AOD, or in transition (being swapped or moved), and part of the handle table's address field is used to identity the owner. If the segment is swapped out, the address field also contains the swap ID. A swap ID indexes the swap control table (SCT), which tells where the segment is located in the swap file. When the state of a segment is discarded or AOD, the system uses the owner ID to locate the MTE, which contains information about where to find the segment contents.

When the system swaps out or discards a segment, it moves the segment's owner into the handle table, and the handle is stored in the LDT descriptor's address field. If a descriptor's access is marked "not present," the hardware does not depend on the contents of the address field, which lets OS/2 overlay the address field with the segment's handle.

Dynamic Linking and Sharing

Executable and DLL files have relocation records that encode internal and external references that OS/2 must resolve when it loads the files. Because the system allocates selectors for each segment defined by an executable or library module when a module is loaded, internal segment or far pointer references are not resolved at link time; they must be resolved at load time. Because DLL modules can be individually replaced, all external references to library modules must also be resolved at load time. Segments can share their virtual addresses, their contents, or both. Each LDT has separate shared and private selector regions. Selectors that map to descriptors in the private region are called private selectors; those that map to descriptors in the shared region are called shared selectors. Figure 25-3 graphically depicts the difference between the two. Private and shared selectors are interleaved to allow for the smallest possible LDT size (see Figure 25-1). The selector type is independent of whether the segment contents are shared; Table 25-1 shows the four possible combinations of shared and private selectors and shared and private memory.

Table 25-1: Four combinations of shared and private selectors and shared and private memory are possible.		
Selector	**Memory**	**Origin**
Private	Private	EXE file private data segment
Private	Shared	EXE file code or shared data segment
Shared	Private	DLL file private data segment
Shared	Shared	DLL file code or shared data segment

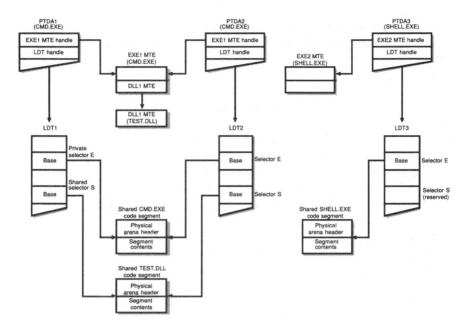

Figure 25-3: The difference between private and shared selectors. Private selector E maps the same shared (code) segment for all invocations of an executable file. Other tasks may use selector E for other purposes. Shared selector S maps the same shared (code) segment for all tasks attached to the TEST.DLL dynalink library. Shared selector S is reserved for the TEST.DLL segment; other tasks cannot use selector S for any other purpose.

Private, dynamically allocated data segments also use private selectors and private memory. Shared, dynamically allocated data segments (both named shared and unnamed shared) use shared selectors and shared memory to let an application dynamically attach to shared segment.

When the system allocates a shared selector, the corresponding descriptor is reserved in all tasks for the purpose of mapping a single segment. Shared selectors are always used for library module segments, because an application can dynamically attach to any library module. If the library module is in memory, its selectors have already been allocated, and they must be available in the caller's context to map the library's segments.

OS/2 uses private selectors for all of an executable module's segments. If shared selectors were used, large numbers of shared selectors would be reserved. Since a task can attach only to an executable module while the task is being created. OS/2 can guarantee allocation of specific private selectors, because the LDT starts out empty.

To show why an executable file must use private selectors, consider an executable file that contains 100 segments and uses shared selectors: When this executable file is active, 100 shared selectors would be reserved in every task's context, including tasks that do not (and cannot ever) reference the executable file. When new segments that require shared selectors are created (i.e., another executable file is added to the system), numerically greater selectors must be allocated, which results in the growth of every LDT that contains a reference to the new segments. LDT memory waste would increase with each executable file in use.

Executable and library module code segments always share their contents. You can declare data segments at link time as private or shared. If a segment is shared between tasks, the system duplicates the LDT descriptor contents among all tasks that reference the segment, and only one handle and physical memory segment exist for the segment. If a segment's contents are private, the system loads a new copy of the segment for each referencing task. The segment's contents may vary from one task to another over time, but each task's copy is referenced using the same selector value and has the same initial contents and size.

The owner ID of a private segment is the handle of the task's PTDA, so that when a segment's state changes, the single appropriate descriptor can be easily found and updated. The example in Figure 25-1 shows that the owner field for the two private segments points to the task's PTDA; the owner for the discarded segment can be found in the handle table entry A, while the owner for the present segment can be found in the physical arena header.

The owner ID of a shared program or library module segment is the handle of the module's MTE segment. The PTDA cannot be used as the owner because multiple LDTs can reference the same shared segment. One descriptor in each LDT must be examined to see if it maps the same segment prior to performing descriptor updates. For the shared segment in handle table entry A in Figure 25-1, the owner field points to the EXE1's MTE.

When a shared segment changes state, the system must find and update all descriptors that map that segment. To avoid the overhead of maintaining an additional data structure to enumerate the tasks that reference each shared segment, the system examines the appropriate descriptor in each LDT to see if that segment is being referenced. It then updates each descriptor that matches the search criteria.

Private segments may be allocated because of an executable or library module segment definition, or they may be dynamically allocated via a system call. Since the hardware does not support simultaneous read/write/execute access via a single LDT selector, OS/2 allows an LDT code alias selector to be created to execute code in private data segments (non-"huge" data segments only). You can use this feature to support efficient video display raster operations needed by graphics software.

Two additional types of dynamic shared memory are also available: named and unnamed shared segments. Named shared segments, allocated via a system call, allow communication between tasks that don't already share program or library references. Unnamed shared segments (also allocated via a system call) let the caller specify any combination of GIVE, GET, and DISCARD attributes.

If a segment has the GIVE attribute, any task that has access to the segment can give another task access. If a segment has the GET attribute, any task can obtain access if it knows the shared selector reserved for the segment. Finally, if an unnamed shared segment is allocated as DISCARDable, the user can change the segment back and forth between swappable and discardable. When discarded, any data stored in the segment will be lost. The application is responsible for being able to re-create the data (if necessary).

One use of discardable segments of this type is to store video display data that is temporarily overwritten and restored. If the system discards the display data due to a low-memory conditions, you can always recreate it. If the video data is still available when needed, you can easily and quickly update the display.

Since many data structures are much larger than the 64K byte segment size supported by the 80286, OS/2 provides for "huge" segment allocation. This is made up of an array of individual segments; all but the last in the array are exactly 64K bytes in length, and consecutive segments are addressable by adding a constant increment multiple to the selector of the first segment.

The constant to be added to the base selector is available to an application through a special dynamic-link reference. High-level language support for huge pointer manipulation is available that makes use of this constant; the value of the constant can change, so it could never be embedded in an application. This is the only case where an application can perform arithmetic on selector values.

Consecutive full-size data segments with consistent attributes that appear in a program or library module will be treated as adjacent huge subsegments. You can also allocate private and unnamed shared memory as huge segments.

When loaded from nonremovable media (e.g., a hard disk), the system always makes program and library module code segments discardable. Since these segments cannot be modified, you can restore their contents at any time by reading the program or library module file and performing any necessary relocation fix- ups. Program and library module writable segments and most run-time allocated segments are made swappable, since their contents may have changed from when they were initially loaded.

Some dynamic allocation requests result in allocating segments not present in physical memory. When the application first accesses the segment, the system allocates the memory. This is done when huge segments are allocated, to avoid unnecessary swapping when allocating enough memory to completely satisfy the huge allocation request.

The total of free, discardable, and swappable memory must always be large enough to let at least one task at a time reload enough segments to execute. Fixed and locked segments can reduce this total. The system performs overcommit accounting to ensure that a demand load request can be satisfied at any time. (Overcommit accounting is the allocation of more virtual memory than can be stored at once in the available physical memory.) Fixed allocation and long-term lock requests will fail if the resulting total of free, discardable, and swappable memory would be too small to reload one task's currently referenced segment.

The system swaps segments to a data file, which cannot always be grown at the time of a swap-out request; the disk space may not be available. The system must keep the swap file large enough to handle swapping out a predictable amount of memory, in advance of the need. To accomplish this, the system grows the swap file whenever it allocates new swappable segments. If a growth attempt fails, it refuses the new segment allocation request.

Some Tips On Usage

All system services are referenced via dynamic links to library modules. OS/2 kernel code supports some services directly, while others are part of bona fide library modules. A programmer references a system service as if it were a normal far procedure call with the pascal calling convention (the callee cleans parameters off the stack). Having a consistent procedure-call interface makes system services directly available to assembly language programs and several high-level languages, including Pascal, FORTRAN, and C, assuming a small amount of compiler support for the latter. The linker recognizes a dynamic-link definition in a provided library, and it turns the reference into a relocation record processed at program load time to resolve the final virtual address.

It is best to minimize the number of individual code and data segments. This is because segment allocation requests are rounded up to the granularity of the physical memory manager (32-byte multiples), and because additional memory is consumed for LDT descriptors, handles, and physical arena headers. You must separate program and library module shared and private data, so one type of data should be eliminated if it can be done without compromising the rest of the module. Reducing or eliminating library module private data is particularly useful because the effect is multiplied by the number of processes attached to the library module.

It is also helpful to put nontrivial initialization code and data into segments separate from the main code and data. Explicitly freeing these segments after initialization will release valuable memory or swap-file space if swapping is disabled or if the module is loaded from removable media. Also, rarely used code should be put into separate segments. This will reduce overall memory requirements because only the most frequently used portions of the program will be in memory.

VI
Operating Systems Part III: Porting to OS/2 and the Presentation Manager

———

26
Compatibility and Transition for MS-DOS Programs [*]

_____*Joel   Gillman*_____

Microsoft's multitasking, virtual memory operating system has finally been unveiled. Now that MS OS/2 is a reality, programmers may be wondering with some trepidation whether they'll have to rewrite all their MS-DOS programs.

The good news is that nearly all of your existing code, both commercial products and custom-made utilities, will run just fine in OS/2's MS-DOS compatibility environment, an operating mode that emulates MS-DOS 3.3. Programs that need low-level access will not run in the compatibility mode, but these are exceptions. Most spreadsheets, word processors, and many other applications programs will work just fine.

However, once you start writing code to run in the multitasking protected mode of OS/2, you will have to do some things differently. There's a silver lining in this, because you will end up with better code once you've unlearned some of the bad habits you picked up writing in MS-DOS. Multitasking implies resource sharing, so you can't be overly greedy with system resources anymore. But what you may lose in resource access you gain in the power of multitasking.

After booting OS/2, the user is greeted by the session manager, from which the user can start any number of protected-mode applications or enter compatibility mode. For each protected-mode program, the session manager creates a new protected mode execution environment, called a screen group.

Each screen group has a command processor (CMD.EXE, which corresponds to the MS-DOS 3.x COMMAND.COM), a virtual screen buffer, a virtual keyboard, and a virtual mouse, along with a virtual memory space of up to 16 megabytes (Mb) depending on the total number of screen groups.

---

[*] © Microsoft Corporation, *Microsoft Systems Journal,* May, 1987, p.19

Compatibility Mode

The MS-DOS compatibility mode in OS/2 uses the 80286 chip's real mode, which is engaged by a technique called mode switching (see "OS/2: Turning Off the Car to Change Gears," page 61). Mode switching emulates a full system re-set without disrupting operation, allowing the processor to switch from protected to real mode. The compatibility mode gives the system an 8086 interface with 1 Mb of address space and emulates MS-DOS 3.x with the MS-DOS SHARE util-ity installed. OS/2 needs up to 500 Kb of system memory in a typical configuration--substantially more than the 50 Kb required by MS-DOS 3.x.

The compatibility mode recognizes all of the documented MS-DOS services. A number of undocumented interrupt 21H services also exist under MS-DOS 3.x, but since OS/2 does not recognize most of the undocumented MS-DOS services, programs that use them won't run in the compatibility mode.

The compatibility mode supports a ROM data area and accepts service interrupts, but you cannot call ROM services directly by address. You must use the inter-rupt 10 through interrupt 1A services instead (see Figure 26-1). Applications can call any hardware interrupt except the CMOS clock/calendar interrupt or an inter-rupt already taken over by any OS/2 device driver other than the keyboard. The compatibility mode will issue interrupt 28h (spooler interrupt)--so you can still run SideKick®--and interrupt 24h (critical error handler).

A program running in the MS-DOS compatibility mode freezes up if the system places it in the background by switching to the protected mode. Programs frozen in the background receive no CPU service or interrupts. A program that deter-mines the time of day by counting clock ticks, for example, will generate inaccurate times if it goes into the background.

Version-specific applications won't run in the compatibility mode, because the MS-DOS version number of OS/2 is 10. A way around this is to modify the code so that it calls DOSGETVERSION and, if it gets back to 10, determines which mode it's executing by calling DOSGETMACHINEMODE. The program can then take the appropriate action.

When you run a driver, only programs running in the compatibility mode can use its device. The device isn't available to protected-mode applications. Device drivers cannot call user code, because they operate at a higher privilege level than the user program.

	DOS 3.3	OS/2 Compatibility Environment	OS/2 New Programs
Supported Hardware	8088 8086 286 386	---- ---- 286 386	---- ---- 286 386
Available Memory	640K	640K	16MB
Can Overcommit Memory	----	----	YES
True Multitasking	----	----	YES
Use Software Interrupts	YES	YES	NO
Use Hardware Interrupts	YES	YES	NO
Use Undocumented DOS Interfaces	YES	Some	NO
Have Direct Access to Hardware	YES	YES	NO
Can Run in the Background	NO	NO	YES
Obey 286 Segment Rules	NO	NO	YES

Figure 26-1: Hardware/Operating Environment Compatibility Chart. Hardware compatibility and support is different for DOS 3.3 and OS/2. OS/2 seeks to insulate applications software from the hardware.

Handling Devices

Most of your old device drivers will not run in compatibility mode. OS/2 doesn't support any of the MS-DOS block device drivers, such as those used with disk or tape drives. The only character device drivers it supports are VDI (video display interface) and CON (console) drivers, since character device drivers will work only if they are polled rather than interrupt-driven. The system supports all of the device driver command packets shown in Figure 26-2.

Drivers are installed the same way as in MS-DOS®, using the configuration command:

```
device = driver
    filename
```

MS-DOS device drivers are loaded and initialized in compatibility mode. Initialization is in most respects the same as in MS-DOS, except that no interrupt 21h (hardware-independent) functions can be performed from the initialization code.

Code	Command	Code	Command
0	Init	9	Output with Verify
3	IOCtl Input	10	Output Status
4	Input (Read)	11	Output Flush
5	Non-Destructive Input No Wait	12	IOCtl Output (Write)
6	Input Status	13	Device Open
7	Input Flush	14	Device Close
8	Output	15	Generic IOCtl

Figure 26-2 Device Driver Commands. Shown here are the device driver commands supported under OS/2.

Compatibility mode restricts which devices programs can manipulate. Sound-generating programs that need a higher frequency time base for more precise pitch control can remap the 8253 clock/timer chip, that is, assign different numbers to its system interrupts. Remapping the 8259 interrupt controller is not allowed. Such programs, which must remap the 8259 in order to trap keystrokes, will not run. Applications can still hook keystrokes after OS/2 gets them, however.

Programs that need low-level disk I/O access for copy protection purposes cannot remap the disk controller. Programs do have direct access to the disk controller via interrupt 13h (floppy disk services), interrupt 25h (absolute disk read), and interrupt 26h (absolute disk write). Note that interrupt 13h and interrupt 26h are not allowed for fixed media such as hard disks.

High-speed communications applications that must remap the DMA controller won't run because the operating system remaps the controller. Applications can remap the COM, AUX, and parallel ports, although using one of these ports in the compatibility mode makes it unavailable to protected mode programs and vice versa.

80286 Restrictions

Programmers writing applications for MS-DOS developed some programming techniques and coding shortcuts to enhance performance, even though the books and manuals tended to discourage using them. Many of these techniques won't work in OS/2 because of differences between the 8086 or 8088 chip and the 80286. You'll have to observe several restrictions if you want to run your applications in the compatibility environment or in protected mode.

	DOS	OS/2		
	Old Programs	FAPI Programs		New Programs
Start With	COMMAND.COM	COMMAND.COM	CMD.EXE	CMD.EXE
Can Run in OS/2 Compatibility Box	Yes	Yes	No	No
Can Run in Background	No	No	Yes	Yes
Permit Old-Style INT 21H Dos 3.x Interrupts	Yes	No		No
Permit Undocumented Dos Interfaces	No	No		No
Have IOPL	Yes	Via FAPI		Via OS/2
Obey 286 Segment Rules	No	Yes		Yes
Can Overcommit Memory	No	No	Yes	Yes
Addressable Memory	640K	640K	16M	16M
Pronto Hardware Interrupts	Yes	No		No
Permit Software Interrupts	Yes	Via FAPI	No	No
Program Residence	Below Boundary	Below Boundary	Above Boundary	Above Boundary
Permit Multitasking	No	Yes		Yes

Figure 26-3: Software Compatibility Chart. Programs may run in one or more modes depending on how they behave.

First, don't use wrap-around segment offsets. The 8086 and 8088 microprocessors translate an out-of-range address value into something recognizable, but the

80286 doesn't. You cannot address beyond the allocated size of a segment; the system aborts the program if an offset larger than the segment descriptor's limit value is used to reference that segment.

The 80286 doesn't allow writable code segments. One of the bits in the segment descriptor identifies the segment as either code or data. A code segment's descriptor doesn't have a read/write bit, so only valid code segments can be placed in the CS (code segment selector) register, and a program may not write into valid code segments. However, an alias can be used to make a data segment into a code segment to be executed.

Since different machines use different timing speeds, don't count on the CPU clock as a timing constant. This is a typical problem in copy-protected programs.

Don't allow a division-trap handler to resume execution in the original code stream unless it is able to detect and understand differences between the 8086 or 8088 and the 80286. After a division-error trap, the 80286 points to the division instruction (including prefixes) and doesn't change the register values. The 8086 and 8088 point to the instruction following the division instruction and may change the DX:AX or AH:AL register sets as well.

The 80286 CL (low-order loop/shift/repeat count) registers won't permit shift counts greater than 31. On the 80286, the shift and rotate counts are masked to 5 bits.

When executing the PUSH SP (push stack pointer onto stack) instruction, the 80286 pushes the SP value onto the stack before incrementing the value, while the 8086 and 8088 push the SP value after incrementing it. Few programs use this particular code sequence, but for those that do, Microsoft offers this way around the problem:

```
MOV AX, SP
PUSH AX
```

these two lines of code can be implemented by a macro.

The PUSHF instruction followed by a POPF may change the contents of the flag register in the 80286, since more flag bits are defined in the 80286 flag word than in those of the 8086 and 8088. Also, because of a bug in the 80286, the POPF may change the contents of the flag register in the 80286. You should use flag-specific instructions to set or test flag register values instead of setting or testing for explicit bit patterns.

FAPI

In order to permit you to write new programs guaranteed to run in MS-DOS and in OS/2's protected mode (both current and future versions), Microsoft has defined a set of system calls that are guaranteed to support both environments. This set of system calls, the Family Application Program Interface (FAPI), is a subset of the full OS/2 Application Program Interface (API).

Five types of code will run on OS/2; old programs designed for MS-DOS 3.x that run on OS/2 in the compatibility mode; presentation manager programs, FAPI programs that run on OS/2 in the compatibility mode; FAPI programs that run on OS/2 in protected mode; and new programs that run on OS/2 only in the protected mode. Figure 26-3 summarizes the characteristics valid for each of these program types.

FAPI allows a program to be linked to run in both modes and includes system calls in all categories except those specific to protected mode, such as multitasking run-time linking, and device monitors. Some restrictions apply to using the FAPI calls in the compatibility mode, which are discussed in detail in the OS/2 *Programmer's Guide*.

The protected mode does not give you direct access to the screen, as you would have with a MS-DOS 3.x BIOS call because of its memory protection. Instead, you have access to a virtual screen buffer within each screen group. The screen buffer paints the screen only when that screen group is active. For bimodal compatibility, FAPI provides a subset of the video input/output (VIO) calls for creating and writing to a virtual screen buffer.

Just using FAPI calls, however, won't guarantee protected mode compatibility. Basically, you want a well-behaved program; it shouldn't sneak past the operating system to the hardware or get too clever with the segment registers. To write code that operates in protected mode, you give up sovereignty over the hardware. Multitasking requires that the operating system, rather than your program, allocate hardware and system resources.

If you've done any programming in XENIX or UNIX, you're used to this. However, if you've only worked in MS-DOS, you'll want to adjust your thinking a little.

OS/2 uses an indirect segment addressing scheme: a segment number points to a table entry, called a *segment descriptor*, which in turn points to the memory space. OS/2's memory management service will change the memory pointer in the descriptor as the total system memory allocation changes, so there is no way of knowing where a given segment number actually puts you in physical memory. Thus, a well-behaved program doesn't try to interpret segment numbers or calculate other segment locations from a given segment number.

You can't assume that any given segments overlap or don't overlap, nor can you assume any particular relationship between segment:offset combinations and physical memory. The segment number is nothing more than a segment ID, with no particular significance apart from that.

The segment registers are intended for the storage of valid segment numbers. If you store invalid numbers there--for example, by using the segment registers as scratch-pad memory (the 8086 doesn't seem to have enough registers to suit some people)--your program will crash.

Your program cannot issue a CLI (clear interrupt) instruction in protected mode because this causes a protection trap. When in compatibility mode, IRET (interrupt return) restores the previous value of IFLG (interrupt flag), but IRET has no effect in protected mode. Protected mode programs can interact directly with hardware only by linking to a special I/O Privilege Level Segment. This allows access to the 80286 processor's Ring 2 security level.

Bimodal Device Drivers

OS/2 supports bimodal device drivers that run in either mode, obviating the need for the system to switch modes to process interrupts.

Unlike a MS-DOS 3.x device driver, a bimodal OS/2 driver has to support multiple synchronous and asynchronous requests. However, the basic structure remains pretty much the same: the driver contains a strategy routine and an interrupt routine. In addition, some device drivers may have to include a routine to trap ROM BIOS software interrupts from compatibility mode.

An application program uses a request packet to call the strategy routine, just as with a MS-DOS 3.x driver. The strategy routine determines whether a request is valid and places valid requests in a queue to the device, using the DevHlp functions to manage the queue. If the device is idle, the strategy routine starts it and returns to the operating system, which suspends the thread until the request has been executed.

When the device completion interrupt occurs, the interrupt routine sets the return status in the request packet and removes that packet from the queue. It then calls a DevHlp routine, DevDone, to tell OS/2 that the request is complete.

The strategy routine should disable interrupts when checking to see if the device is active and when examining the queue. This protects the interrupt routine from other driver request interrupts. When interrupts are reenabled, the interrupt routine will receive only ones of higher priority.

This is only a sample of some design considerations in writing OS/2 bimodal device drivers. The subject is treated at greater length in the OS/2 *Device Driver Guide*.

New Tools

A new C compiler that runs in both modes is included in the *OS/2 Software Development Kit*. However, executable files written in *Microsoft C Compiler*, Version 4.0, should have no trouble running in the compatibility mode, as long as they meet the general criteria outlined earlier for operation in OS/2. You don't need to recompile or relink them with the new OS/2 C run-time library.

The new C library is nearly identical to the Version 4.0 library, which is designed for single-thread execution only. Most of the functions are not re-entrant and therefore will not work in a multithread process. Figure 26-4 lists the re-entrant functions that may be used in multithread programs.

All the routines in Figure 26-4 will work properly in programs that use a far data model (compact and large model). However, in near-data-model-memory (small- and medium-model) programs, only some of these routines are guaranteed to function properly. The others have model-dependent pointers in their interfaces and have the potential to allocate stack space outside the default segment (SS!=DS).

The kit also contains a new macro assembler that will run in protected mode. Again, existing MASM executable files will run in the compatibility mode, subject to the general restrictions described earlier.

The MS-DOS 3.2 network function calls aren't supported in the compatibility mode, but the new Microsoft OS/2 LAN Manager will allow networking in protected mode.

Device Monitors

One problem that has plagued MS-DOS programmers is that when several terminate - and - stay - resident (TSR) programs are loaded into memory, they tend to step on each other in order to catch a reactivate keystroke from the keyboard. When you put a TSR like Borland's *SideKick*, Rosesoft's *ProKey*, or North Edge Software's *TimeSlips* into the background, the program calls interrupt 21h function 31h (Terminate and Stay Resident) and remains in memory even though you return to the system prompt. The program is still watching the keyboard, trapping keystrokes before the system gets them. When you hit a hot key combination, such as Ctrl-Alt, the program pops back onto the screen. The problem is that when two or more pop-up programs reside in the background at the same time, each wants to trap the keyboard interrupt before any other program does (see "Moving Toward an Industry Standard for Developing TSRs," *Microsoft Systems Journal*, Vol. 1, No. 2).

OS/2 solves this problem in protected mode by giving each TSR its own keyboard device monitor for reading keystrokes. Suppose you want to have several TSRs written by different vendors available within a given screen group. Each one will have its own keyboard device monitor.

The monitors receive keystrokes in the order of monitor registration, which is set when the programs are first run. Keystrokes are passed on to the first monitor registered, which can trap the keystroke and generate a response or pass the keystroke on the next monitor registered (see Figure 26-5).

Obviously, in this scheme, no two TSRs can use the same reactivate-key sequence. You can't reactivate a pop-up program in one screen group from a different screen group. By definition, a screen group is made up of a virtual screen, virtual mouse, virtual keyboard, and virtual memory space, and screen groups can't talk to each other.

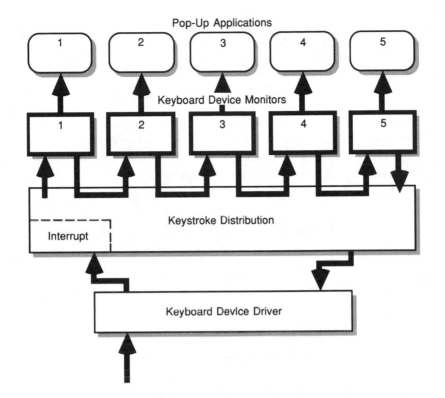

Figure 26-5: When TSR programs are run in protected mode, OS/2 assigns each a keyboard device monitor, which reads keystrokes from the keyboard. This keeps the TSRs from fighting each other to be the first to trap keystrokes.

The Tradeoff

The constraints that OS/2 imposes on the programmer may seem at first rather strict. With MS-DOS, you are pretty much free to use the system services or to leave them alone and go directly to the CPU instead. But in a multitasking system, you just can't do that. OS/2 takes over the CPU and the hardware, granting access only in certain instances.

On the other hand, a lot of old problems go away. Applications will no longer have to fight each other for system resources, because OS/2 allocates resources among them on a priority basis. Applications will have a common program interface (API) to work with, ensuring future compatibility. What you lose in resource access you gain in the new opportunities of multitasking, such as the potential for real-time multithread applications.

Similarly, the memory access restrictions are compensated for in protected mode by the greatly increased size of the memory space that you can work with and the addition of memory management capabilities. The only limitation is that you must use system calls for access rather than stuffing numbers directly into the segment registers. And the 80286 chip is fast enough that efficiency issues aren't as critical as they were on the original PCs and XTs, so programming shortcuts such as segment games just aren't necessary anymore.

Some Programming Don'ts for OS/2

When writing programs for either the compatibility mode or protected mode in OS/2, you must observe a number of restraints that weren't necessary in writing for MS-DOS. Many of these restrictions arise from differences between the 8086 or 8088 and the 80286 microprocessors.

- Don't depend on segment overlap or lack of it.
- Don't depend on any relationship between segment:offset combinations and physical memory.
- Don't use wrap-around address offsets.
- Don't use the segment registers for anything but valid segment numbers.
- Never address beyond the allocated size of a segment.
- If you have to play with the I/O ports, use only the appropriate dynamic link routines (FAPI).
- Don't mix code and data in the same segment.
- Don't use undefined opcodes.
- Don't use the PUSH SP instruction.
- Don't use the POPF instruction.
- Don't use shift counts greater than 31.
- Don't use IDIV operands to produce a most-negative number.
- Don't resume execution in the original code stream after a division trap.
- Don't use redundant prefix bytes.
- Don's use CLI instructions (in protected mode).
- Don't use CPU speed as a timing constant.
- Don't examine or set explicit flag register values.
- Don't single-step interrupt instructions in debuggers.
- Don't write self-modifying code.

OS/2 API Calls

Family API (FAPI) functions are listed in *italics*.

* Indicates that FAPI support is limited (certain restrictions are imposed)

API Function Name	Description
BadDynLink	*Bad Dynamic Link*
*DosAllocHuge**	*Allocate Huge Memory*
DosAllocShrSeg	Allocate Shared Segment
DosBeep	*Generate Sound From Speaker*
DosBufReset	Commit File Cache Buffers
*DosCaseMap**	*Perform Case Mapping on String of Binary* Characters
DosChdir	*Change Current Directory*
DosChgFilePtr	*Change File Read/Write Pointer*
DosClose	*Close File Handle*
DosCloseQueue	Close Queue
DosCloseSem	Close System Semaphore
DosCreateCSAlias	*Create CS Alias*
DosCreateSem	Create System Semaphore
DosCreateThread	Create another thread of execution
DosCreateQueue	Create Queue
*DosCWait**	*Wait for child termination*
DosDelete	*Delete File*
DosDevConfig	*Get Device Configuration*
*DosDevlOCtl**	*I/O Control Devices*
DosDupHandle	*Duplicate File Handle*
DosEnterCritSec	Enter Critical Section of Execution
*DosError**	*Enable Hard Error Processing*
*DosExecPgm**	*Execute Program*
*DosExit**	*Exit Program*
DosExitCritSec	Exit Critical Section of Execution
DosExitList	Routine List for Process Termination
*DosFileLocks**	*File Lock Manager*
*DosFindClose**	*Close Find Handle*
*DosFindFirst**	*Find First Matching File*
*DosFindNext**	*Find Next Matching File*
DosFlagProcess	Set Process External Event Flag
DosFreeModule	Free Dynamic-Link Module
DosFreeSeg	*Free Segment*
*DosGetCtryInfo**	*Get Country-Dependent Formatting Information*
DosGetDateTime	*Get Current Date and Time*
DosGetDBCSev	*Get DBCS Environmental Vector*
DosGetEnv	*Get Address of Process*

DosGetHugeShift	*Get Shift Count*
DosGetInfoSeg	Get Address of System Variables Segment
DosGetMachineMode	Return Current Mode of Processor
DosGetMessage	Get System Message and Insert Text Strings
DosGetModHandle	Get Dynamic-Link Module Handle
DosGetModName	Get Dynamic-Link Module Name
DosGetProcAddr	Get Dynamic-Link Procedure Address
DosGetPrty	Get Process Priority
DosGetShrSeg	Access Shared Segment
DosGetVersion	*Get Dos Version Number*
DosGiveSeg	Give Access To Segment
*DosHoldSignal**	*Disable/Enable Signal*
DosInsMessage	*Insert Variable Text Strings in Message*
DosIOAccess	Request I/O Access to Device
DosKillProcess	Terminate Process
DosLoadModule	Load Dynamic-Link Module
DosMakePipe	Create Pipe
DosMkdir	*Make Subdirectory*
DosMonClose	Close Connection to OS/2 Device Driver
DosMonOpen	Open Connection to OS/2 Device Driver
DosMonRead	Read Input from Monitor Structure
DosMonReg	Register Set of Buffers as Monitor
DosMonWrite	Write Output to Monitor Structure
DosMove	*Move File or Subdirectory*
DosMuxSemWait	Wait for one of n semaphores to be cleared
DosNewSize	*Change File Size*
*DosOpen**	*Open File*
DosOpenQueue	Open Queue
DosOpenSem	Open Existing Semaphore
DosPeekQueue	Peek Queue
DosPurgeQueue	Purge Queue
DosPutMessage	*Output Message Text To Handle*
DosQCurDir	*Query Current Directory*
DosQCurDisk	*Query Current Disk*
DosQFHandState	Query File Handle State
*DosQFileInfo**	*Query File Information*
DosQFileMode	*Query File Mode*
DosQFSInfo	*Query File System Information*
DosQHandType	Query Handle Type
DosQueryQueue	Query Queue
DosQVerify	*Query Verify Setting*
DosRead	*Read from File*

DosReadAsync	Asynchronous Read from File
DosReadQueue	Read from Queue
DosReAllocHuge*	*Change Huge Memory Size*
DosReAllocateSeg*	*Change segment Size*
DosResumeThread	Restart Thread
DosRmdir	*Remove Subdirectory*
DosSelectDisk	*Select Default Drive*
DosSemClear	Clear (release) Semaphore
DosSemRequest	Request Semaphore
DosSemSet	Set Semaphore Owned
DosSemSetWait	Set Semaphore and wait for next Clear
DosSemWait	*Wait for Semaphore to be Cleared*
DosSetDateTime	*Set Current Date and Time*
DosSetFHandState*	*Set File Handle State*
DosSetFileInfo	*Set File Information*
DosSetFileMode	*Set File Mode*
DosSetMaxFH	Set Maximum File Handles
DosSetPrty	Set Process Priority
DosSetSigHandler*	*Handle Signal*
DosSetVec	Establish Handler for Exception Vector
DosSetVerify	*Set/Reset Verify Switch Delay Process Execution*
DosSubAlloc	*Suballocate Memory within Segment*
DosSubFree	*Free Memory Suballocated within Space*
DosSubSet	*Initialize or Set Allocated Memory*
DosSuspendThread	Suspend Thread Execution
DosSystemService	Dos System Process Services
DosTimerAsync	Start Asynchronous Timer
DosTimerStart	Start Periodic Interval Timer
DosTimerStop	Stop Asynchronous or Interval Timer
DosPTrace	Interface for Program Debugging
DosWrite	*Synchronous Write to File*
DosWriteAsync	Asynchronous Write to File
DosWriteQueue	Write to Queue
KbdCharIn	*Read Character Scan Code*
KbdFlushBuffer	*Flush Keyboard Buffer*
KbdGetStatus	*Get Keyboard Status*
KbdPeek*	*Peek at Character-Scan Code*
KbdRegister	*Register keyboard Subsystem*
KbdSetStatus	*Set Keyboard Status*
KbdStringIn	*Read Character String*
MouClose	Close Mouse Device For Current Screen Group
MouDrawPtr	Release Screen Area For Device Driver Use

MouGetDevStatus	Get Current Pointing Device Driver Status Flags
MouGetEventMask	Get Current Pointing Device One-Word Event Mask
MouGetNumButtons	Get Number of Buttons
MouGetNumMickeys	Get Number of Mickeys-Per-Centimeter
MouGetNumQueel	Get Current Status for Pointing Device Event Queue
MouGetScaleFact	Sets Scale Factors for Current Pointing Device
MouOpen	Open Mouse Device for Current Screen Group
MouReadEventQue	Read Pointing Device Event Queue
MouRegister	Register Mouse Subsystem
MouRemovePtr	Reserve Screen Area for Application Use
MouSetEventMask	Assign New Event Mask to Current Pointing Device
MouSetHotKey	Set System Hot Key
MouSetPtrShape	Set Pointer Shape and Size
MouSetScaleFact	Set Scale Factors for Current Positioning Device
VioEndPopUp	Deallocate a Pop-up Display Screen
VioGetAnsi	Get ANSI State
VioGetBuf	*Get Logical Video Buffer*
VioGetCurPos	*Get Cursor Position*
VioGetCurType	*Get Cursor Type*
VioGetPhysBuf	*Get Physical Video Buffer*
VioPopUp	Allocate Pop-up Display Screen
VioPrtScreen	Print Screen
VioReadCellStr	*Read Character-Attribute String*
VioReadCharStr	*Read Character String*
VioRegister	Register Video Subsystem
VioSavReDrawWait	Screen Save RedrawWait
VioScrLock*	*Lock Screen*
VioScrollDn	*Scroll Screen Down*
VioScrollLf	*Scroll Screen Left*
VioScrollRt	*Scroll Screen Right*
VioScrollUp	*Scroll Screen Up*
VioScrUnLock	*Unlock Screen*
VioSetAnsi	Set ANSI On or Off
VioSetCurPos	*Set Cursor Position*
VioSetCurType	*Set Cursor Type*
VioSetMode	*Set Display Mode*
VioShowBuf	*Display Logical Buffer*
VioWrtCellStr	*Write Character-Attribute String*
VioWrtCharStr	*Write Character String*
VioWrtCharStrAttr	*Write Character String with Attribute*
VioWrtNAttr	*Write N Attributes*
VioWrtNCell	*Write N Character-Attributes*
VioWrtNChar	*Write N Characters*
VioWrtTty	*Write TTY String*

27

Converting DOS Programs to OS/2 Protected Mode[*]

David A. Schmitt

My company, Lattice, Inc., has been working with pre-release copies of IBM's OS/2 Standard Edition 1.0 since June 1986. During that time, we've converted large amounts of C and assembly language code to run in the OS/2 protected mode, and I'd like to share some of our experiences with you.

Let me begin by saying that our relationship with IBM and OS/2 has been consistently very positive. We agreed to be a test site for OS/2 with some trepidation, since testing a new operating system is usually tedious and frustrating. However, IBM answered all of our questions promptly and accurately, and with each update, OS/2 has become better and better.

By April 1987, when IBM formally announced the availability of this new operating system, it was reliable enough to be routinely used in several of our programmers' workstations, which at that time were IBM PC/AT systems. The major deficiency that prevented us from switching completely to OS/2 was its lack of LAN support, which is a vital part of Lattice's software development environment.

The few remaining problems that we observed after the announcement date were all corrected when OS/2 was officially released in December, and we remain unabashed OS/2 boosters. I can't imagine a software developer not getting excited by this major improvement over DOS, and I think we're going to see some significant applications built on top of OS/2.

Let's take a look at the most immediate problem many programmers are now facing: Can I move my DOS software to OS/2 protected mode, and if so, how do I do it? We've already come up with some guidelines that are particularly appropriate for C and assembly language, but can probably be adapted for other languages as well.

---

[*] © Microsoft Corporation, *Microsoft Systems Journal*, March 1988, p. 24

Programmers, Know Thy Code!

The first few rules are rather obvious, but I've seen several OS/2 porting efforts derailed because one of these "obvious" steps was overlooked:

- Make sure you have all of the source modules that comprise your application. If you depend on somebody else's code and it's only available in object form, you'll probably be roadblocked. If the object code is a library product that you purchased without source code, you might be able to convince the publisher to give you the source code if you agree to send back the changes that you make for OS/2. On the other hand, if the library is really complex, you might try offering to pay the publisher so he'll do the work.

- Make sure you know how to build the application. Some of the executables (i.e., .EXE files) have been floating around for some time, and the folks who originally built them may have disappeared without leaving any tracks.

- Go ahead and actually build the application under DOS to see if it still works. Use the latest version of the C compiler and assembler that you can, since old source code sometimes doesn't make it through the more recent language translators because of improved syntax checking.

- If the source code you're using produces a flawed executable, debug it under DOS since you probably work more efficiently in that environment.

- Once you have a clean version running under DOS, save the source and executable. You'll probably need to refer back to this baseline version when you evaluate the performance of the converted program under OS/2.

Remember that porting to OS/2 is a lot like painting a room: If you do a good job of preparation, the actual work is much easier and the result usually turns out better.

Programs: The Good, the Bad, and the Ugly

The next step is *triage*, or classifying your application according to the likelihood that it will survive the operation. We've identified the following four classes:

1) Well-Behaved Programs

Well-behaved programs use very few operating system services except for the File Manager, which they access through the C library via functions such as *fopen*, *getchar*, *read*, and so on. Since OS/2 has essentially the same file system as DOS, the OS/2 C library can provide exactly the same services, which makes well-behaved programs really easy to convert. In fact, most of the time you can just run the source code through the OS/2 compiler or assembler and then build an executable with the OS/2 linker.

This sounds so simple that you probably wonder if there are any significant programs in this category. Actually there are quite a few. We found that most of our programming tools, e.g., compilers, assemblers, *GREP*, *DIFF*, and so on, are well-behaved and moved to OS/2 with few problems. Of course, the Lattice MS-DOS C Compiler needed many changes in order to produce proper code for OS/2, but no changes were needed to make the original MS-DOS compiler run under OS/2 and produce MS-DOS code.

To be more specific, a well-behaved C program has the following characteristics:

- All DOS interfaces are handled through the standard library.

- The program does not use low-level DOS interface functions from the library, such as *int86*, *intdos*, *bdos*, or *BIOS*.

- The program does not hook into any DOS hardware or software interrupts.

- Keyboard and screen interactions use the simple UNIX command line protocol, or else the ANSI.SYS driver is used for any complex screen operations.

- The program always treats 32-bit pointers as atomic objects, i.e., it does not manipulate the segment and offset portions separately.

These same rules apply to assembly language functions called by C programs, although it's usually more difficult to tell if such functions are well-behaved by just "eyeballing" them. So, in addition to the items listed above, you should also look out for these coding practices, which will complicate the conversion:

- *INT* instructions, which generate software interrupts;

- *IN* and *OUT* instructions, which directly access the I/O ports;

- *CLI* and *STI* instructions, which change the state of the interrupt enable flag;

- Instruction sequences that change segment register contents, such as

```
MOV     AX,ES  ;  advance to next paragraph
INC     AX
MOV     ES,AX
```

which are guaranteed to fail because segment register arithmetic is different in protected mode; and

- Timing loops, such as

```
        MOV     CX,1000  ; wait awhile
DELAY:  LOOP    DELAY
```

which are risky, even under DOS because they often become invalid when you upgrade to a faster computer.

The first three of these latter five coding practices will cause protection violations because OS/2 does not allow normal processes to execute *INT*, *IN*, *OUT*, *CLI*, and *STI* instructions. The fourth will usually cause addressing exceptions because the process will attempt to load an invalid selector into a segment register. The fifth just causes the program to behave erratically, since the time delay varies depending on how heavily OS/2 is loaded.

We discovered that much of our assembly-language code had none of these problems and was written at that level just to achieve the maximum speed and minimum size. The Lattice floating point library is an example; it moved to OS/2 with no changes at all.

If, however, you find any of these transgressions, you'll have to do some re-designing. Fortunately, such functions are usually simple, and you can often rewrite them in C, making direct calls to the OS/2 Application Program Interface (API). That is, many of these errant assembly-language routines were originally written just to get at the DOS API in some fashion not otherwise supported by the standard C libraries. But under OS/2, you can usually find an equivalent API function and call it directly from C.

So, if you're lucky enough to have only well-behaved programs, with just a few assembly-language changes to worry about, stop reading here and start converting. Of course, well-behaved programs are typically command-line oriented, and are often somewhat boring to use. So, you'll pay your OS/2 dues later if you decide to spiff these programs up by adapting them to the Presentation Manager—a not-so-trivial task.

2) Highly Interactive Programs

The DOS world is full of programs that do all sorts of magic with the keyboard, screen, and mouse. In fact, one of the things that has made DOS so popular is the ease with which such software can be written. Of course, this has less to do with DOS than it does with the de facto hardware standards caused by the IBM PC. The undeniable influence of IBM has simplified many of the aspects of interactive programming that were quite chaotic in the earlier CP/M world, such as memory-mapped video techniques, keyboard scan codes, and extended character sets.

Nonetheless, DOS programs that have a lot of user interaction generally present more OS/2 conversion difficulties than the well-behaved programs discussed above. This is because all interfaces with the BIOS and video RAM must be changed. However, if you've followed the recommended practice of isolating these into a few modules, you'll only be dealing with a small percentage of the code.

For example, the Lattice Unicalc Spreadsheet (about 25,000 C source lines) and the Lattice Screen Editor (about 15,000 C source lines) are both highly interactive, screen-oriented programs that write directly to the video buffers. Yet, each required less than one person-week to convert, mainly because the human interfaces were designed in a very modular way. Surprisingly, there was no perceivable loss of performance relative to the DOS versions, as long as OS/2 was not running other tasks.

To convert an interactive program, you must replace all BIOS interrupts with calls to the corresponding OS/2 keyboard (*Kbd*), mouse (*Mou*), and video (*Vio*) functions listed in Tables 27-1, 27-2, and 27-3. These interrupts are usually generated directly by assembly-language functions, or indirectly from C programs via the *int86* function. Then you must modify all routines that directly address the video RAM.

Table 27-1: OS/2 Keyboard Functions

FAM	BIOS INT 16H	NAME	DESCRIPTION
F	00H	KbdCharIn	Read character and scan code
—	—	KbdClose	Close logical keyboard
—	—	KbdDeRegister	De-register keyboard subsystem
—	—	KbdFreeFocus	Free keyboard focus
F	—	KbdFlushBuffer	Flush keystroke buffer
—	—	KbdGetFocus	Get keyboard focus
F	01H	KbdGetStatus	Get keyboard status
—	—	KbdGetCP	Get keyboard code page ID
—	—	KbdOpen	Open logical keyboard
R	02H	KbdPeek	Peek at character and scan code
—	—	KbdRegister	Register keyboard subsystem
—	—	KbdSetCP	Set keyboard code page ID
—	—	KbdSetCustXt	Set custom translate table
—	—	KbdSetFgnd	Set foreground keyboard priority
F	—	KbdSetStatus	Set keyboard status
—	—	KbdShellInit	Initialize shell
F	—	KbdStringIn	Read character string
—	—	KbdSynch	Synchronize keyboard access
—	—	KbdXlate	Translate scan code

F = Full family-mode support, R = Restricted family-mode support

Table 27-2: OS/2 Mouse Functions

INT 33H	NAME	DESCRIPTION
—	MouClose	Close mouse device
—	MouDeRegister	Deregister a mouse subsystem
01H	MouDrawPtr	Draw a pointer
—	MouFlushQue	Flush mouse event queue
—	MouGetDevStatus	Get mouse device status flags
—	MouGetEventMask	Get mouse event mask
—	MouGetHotKey	Get mouse hot key definition
—	MouGetNumButtons	Get number of mouse buttons
—	MouGetNumMickeys	Get number of mickeys per centimeter
—	MouGetNumQueEl	Get number of mouse event queue elements
03H	MouGetPtrPos	Get mouse pointer position

—	MouGetPtrShape	Get mouse pointer shape
—	MouGetScaleFact	Get mouse scaling factors
—	MouInitReal	Initialize real-mode mouse driver
00H	MouOpen	Open mouse device
05H,06H	MouReadEventQue	Read mouse event queue
—	MouRegister	Register a mouse subsystem
02H	MouRemovePtr	Remove mouse pointer from a screen area
—	MouSetDevStatus	Set mouse device status flags
0CH	MouSetEventMask	Set mouse event mask
—	MouSetHotKey	Set mouse hot key definition
04H	MouSetPtrPos	Set mouse pointer position
09H,0AH	MouSetPtrShape	Set mouse pointer shape
—	MouSetScaleFact	Set mouse scaling factors
—	MouShellInit	Initialize shell linkage
—	MouSynch	Synchronize mouse subsystem

F + Full family-mode support, R = Restricted family-mode support

Table 27-3: OS/2 Video Functions

FAM	BIOS INT 10H	NAME	DESCRIPTION
—	—	VioDeRegister	De-register video subsystem
—	—	VioEndPopUp	De-allocate pop-up display screen
—	—	VioGetANSI	Get ANSI status
F	—	VioGetBuf	Get logical video buffer
—	—	VioGetConfig	Get video configuration
—	—	VioGetCp	Get video code page ID
F	03H	VioGetCurPos	Get cursor position
F	—	VioGetCurType	Get cursor type
—	—	VioGetFont	Get font
F	0FH	VioGetMode	Get display mode
F	—	VioGetPhysBuf	Get physical display buffer
—	—	VioGetState	Get video state
—	—	VioModeUndo	Cancel mode wait
—	—	VioModeWait	Wait for mode change
—	—	VioPopUp	Allocate pop-up display screen
—	—	VioPrtSc	Print screen
—	—	VioPrtScToggle	Print screen key operation trap
F	08H	VioReadCellStr	Read cell string
F	—	VioReadCharStr	Read character string

—	—	VioRegister	Register video subsystem
—	—	VioSavRedrawUndo	Cancel save-redraw wait
—	—	VioSavRedrawWait	Wait for save-redraw
—	—	VioScrLock	Lock the screen
F	07H	VioScrollDn	Scroll down
F	—	VioScrollLf	Scroll left
F	—	VioScrollRt	Scroll right
F	06H	VioScrollUp	Scroll up
—	—	VioScrUnLock	Unlock the screen
—	—	VioSetANSI	Set ANSI mode on or off
—	—	VioSetCp	Set video code page ID
F	02H	VioSetCurPos	Set cursor position
F	01H	VioSetCurType	Set cursor type
—	—	VioSetFont	Set font
F	00H	VioSetMode	Set display mode
—	0BH	VioSetState	Set video state
F	—	VioShowBuf	Display logical buffer
F	09H	VioWrtCellStr	Write cell string
F	0AH	VioWrtCharStr	Write character string
F	—	VioWrtCharStrAttr	Write character string with attribute
F	—	VioWrtNAttr	Write N attributes
F	—	VioWrtNCell	Write N cells
F	—	VioWrtNChar	Write N characters
F	0EH	VioWrtTTY	Write a TTY string

F = Full family-mode support, R = Restricted family-mode support

2.1) Converting The Keyboard Interface

Adapting to the OS/2 keyboard interface is usually fairly straightforward and has no noticeable effect on performance. Listing 27-1 is a piece of DOS-based C code that obtains a character and scan code via BIOS interrupt 16H, using *int86:*. The same operation in OS/2 can be coded as shown in Listing 27-2.

Listing 27-1: DOS-based C code that obtains a character and scan code via BIOS interrupt 16H.

```
union REGS r;           /* define register set */

r.h..ah = 0             /* use code 0 in AH to get next character */
int86(0x16,&r,&r);      /* generate INT 16H */
scancode = r.h.ah;      /* save scan code from AH */
charcode = r.h.al;      /* save character code from AL */
```

Listing 27-2: OS/2-based C code that obtains a character and scan code via BIOS interrupt 16H.

```
extern far pascal KbdCharIn();

struct CHARDATA        /* structure to hold data from KbdCharIn */
  \{
  char acode;          /* ASCII character code */
  char scode;          /* scan code */
  char status;         /* device status */
  char nls;            /* shift state for National Language Support */
  short shift;         /* keyboard shift state */
  long time;           /* timestamp */
  \} key;

int error;             /* error code */

error = KbdCharIn((far char *)(&key),0,0);  /* call OS/2 keyboard service */

if(error == 0)
  \{
  scancode = key.scode;     /* save scan code */
  charcode = key.acode;     /* save character code */
  \}
else ...                    /* error handler goes here */
```

Although the OS/2 version looks more complicated, it actually is not. Most of the OS/2 statements are declarations that would normally be coded once and kept in header files. In fact, the OS/2 Programmer Toolkit includes such header files for both C and assembly language.

The call to *KbdCharIn* probably seems mysterious if you are unfamiliar with the OS/2 Application Program Interface (API). I won't cover the API in detail here, but a few words of explanation should enable you to understand the remaining examples.

First, note that the function is declared with the "far'" and "pascal'" keywords. The former tells the compiler to use a "far call," while the latter specifies the so-called "pascal calling sequence." This means that arguments are pushed on the stack from right to left and that the function pops the arguments before it returns.

KbdCharIn takes three arguments. The first is a 32-bit pointer to the structure in which OS/2 will return information about the next keystroke. The OS/2 API requires that all addresses be passed in full 32-bit form, and so you must make sure that your C code expands 16-bit pointers to that form. The cast operation

```
(char far *)(&key)
```

does exactly that to the address of the key structure.

The second argument tells *KbdCharIn* what to do if no keystroke is ready. A value of 0 causes the function to wait until the user presses a key.

The third argument is the "logical keyboard handle," which should be 0 for the default keyboard. When OS/2 is managing several applications (called "session") at the same time, it gives each one its own keyboard buffer, called "logical keyboard 0," which will receive input characters when that application is in the foreground, i.e., is visible to the user. In some cases an application can request additional logical keyboards, which will have handles greater than 0.

2.2) Converting The Mouse Interface

If you access the mouse under DOS via software interrupt 33H, the OS/2 conversion is very similar to the keyboard work described above. Table 27-3 shows which *Mou* calls in OS/2 correspond to the interrupt 33H operations.

However, if you rely upon a special mouse interface provided by a DOS driver or pseudo-driver, you're in for some redesign. Most DOS mice on the market today include the necessary software to handle the interrupt 33H protocols, and I'd suggest that you change your DOS code to use that approach. Then it should be a straightforward job to convert that code to OS/2 using the *Mou* functions.

2.3) Converting Video BIOS Calls

If your DOS program accesses the video subsystem through BIOS interrupts, then the conversion to OS/2 is, once again, very similar to the keyboard work described above. For example, Listing 27-3 is a DOS code snippet that clears the screen and moves the cursor to the upper left corner. The same operation in OS/2 can be accomplished by the sequence shown in Listing 27-4.

Listing 27-3: DOS code to clear the screen and return the cursor to the upper left corner.

```
union REGS r;          /* define register set */

r.x.ax = 0x0619;       /* AH=6 for scroll up, AL=25 for entire screen */
r.h.bh = 7;            /* BH=7 for white-on-black attribute */
r.x.cx = 0;            /* (CH,CL) is upper left (row,col) */
r.x.dx = 0x184F;       /* (DH,DL) is lower right (row,col) */
int86(16,&r,&r);       /* generate video interrupt */

r.h.ah = 2;            /* AH=2 to set cursor position */
r.h.bh = 0;            /* BH=0 for page 0 */
r.x.dx = 0;            /* (DH,DL) is (row,col) */
int86(16,&r,&r);       /* generate video interrupt */
```

Listing 27-4: OS/2 code to clear the screen and return the cursor to the upper left corner.

```
extern far pascal VioScrollUp();
extern far pascal VioSetCurPos();
int error;

error = VioScrollUp(0,0,24,79,25,0x0720,0);
if(error) ...

error = VioSetCurPos(0,0,0);
if(error) ...
```

VioScrollUp accepts seven arguments. The first four define the scrolling area, that is, the upper left and lower right corners of the block being scrolled. Here we're dealing with the entire screen of 25 rows and 80 columns, and so the upper left and lower right corners are (0,0) and (24,79), respectively. The fifth argument specifies the number of lines to scroll, 25 in this case. The sixth argument is the attribute and character used to fill the new lines on the screen. The attribute value here is 7 for white-on-black, and the character value is 0x20, which is a blank.

The final argument to *VioScrollUp* and most other *Vio* calls is the "logical screen handle." As with the keyboard, the OS/2 session manager provides a separate video buffer for each active session. The handle for this default buffer is 0. The application program can create additional video buffers if necessary, and these will have handles greater than 0.

VioSetCurPos is much simpler. It positions the cursor to the row and column specified by the first two arguments. The third argument is the logical screen handle.

2.4) Converting Video RAM Accesses

If your program paints the screen by writing directly into the video RAM, you must deal with the fact that OS/2 severely restricts your access to this special area of memory. When you run in protected mode, the video RAM doesn't even appear in your memory map, and so if you try something like writing into the monochrome video buffer at *segment:offset* B000:0000, OS/2 will abort your process with an addressing exception. Listing 27-5 is an example of some non-portable DOS C code for clearing the monochrome screen. The strange-looking "union" is used to form a valid *segment:offset* pointer to the video buffer, then the loop simply resets that area to blanks with white-on-black attributes.

Listing 27-5: Non-portable DOS C code for clearing the monochrome screen.

```
int i;
union
  \{
  unsigned short x[2];
  unsigned short far *p;
  \} q;

q.x[0] = 0;          /* form segment:offset pointer to video RAM */
q.x.[1] = 0xb000;

for(i = 0; i < 2000; q.p[i++] = 0x0720);
```

Now, if you try to run this code in OS/2 protected mode, you'll see a prime example of an OS/2 abort message. But text-mode programs like this one can be easily converted to OS/2; you just write into the logical video buffer and let OS/2 update the physical buffer. This technique is really nothing new; it's exactly what you have to do in DOS-based multitasking systems such as IBM Topview and Microsoft Windows. For example, the code in Listing 27-6 offers a Topview-compatible example. Here we use video BIOS function 254, which leaves ES:DI intact if Topview or some other session management system is not installed. Otherwise, ES:DI is loaded with the *segment:offset* pointer to the logical video buffer. Then, after the buffer is cleared, we use video BIOS function 255 to update the screen. If no session manager is active, function 255 does nothing, since we've actually been writing to the physical buffer.

Listing 27-6: Topview code to clear the screen.

```
int i;
union REGSS r;          /* define register set with segments */
union                   /* used to make video RAM pointer */
  \{
  unsigned short x[2];
  unsigned short far *p;
  \} q;

r.x.di = 0;             /* set ES:DI to video buffer */
r.x.es = 0xb000;
r.h.ah = 0xfe;          /* use BIOS function 254 */
int86s(16,&r,&r);       /* ask BIOS for logical buffer pointer */

q.x[0] = r.x.di;        /* form far pointer to logical buffer */
q.x.[1] = r.x.es;

for(i = 0; i < 2000; q.p[i++] = 0x0720);  /* clear the buffer */

r.x.di = q.x[0];        /* set ES;DI to start of logical buffer */
r.x.es = q.x[1];
r.x.cx = 4000;          /* set size to 25 rows, 80 columns */
r.h.ah = 255;           /* use BIOS function 255 */
int86s(16,&r,&r);       /* ask BIOS to update screen */
```

The equivalent OS/2 code (Listing 27-7) looks quite similar, except that the BIOS interrupts are replaced with *Vio* calls. *VioGetBuf* returns a pointer to the logical video buffer. The pointer is stored into the 32-bit area whose 32-bit address is given by the first argument. That's the reason for the *(long far *)* cast in that argument position. The second argument is a 32-bit pointer to a short integer where the buffer length (in bytes) will be returned, and again, a cast operation is needed. The logical video handle completes the argument list, as we've already discussed.

Listing 27-7: Topview code to clear the screen adapted for OS/2.

```
extern far pascal VioGetBuf();
extern far pascal VioShowBuf();

int i,error;
short far *p;
short size;

error =                     /* get logical video buffer ptr */
  VioGetBuf((long far *)(&p),(short far *)(&size),0);
if(error) ...

for(i = 0; i < (size/2); p[i++] = 0x0720); /* clear the buffer */

error = VioShowBuf(0,size,0);             /* update the screen */
if(error) ...
```

After clearing the logical buffer, you must use *VioShowBuf* to get the physical screen updated, which will actually occur only if your program is running as the foreground session. The first argument is the offset into the logical buffer, and the second is the number of bytes being updated. So, if you were prudent enough to incorporate this type of Topview logic into your screen-oriented programs, you'll have an easy time moving them to OS/2. However, if you scattered absolute addresses of video buffers throughout your code, you'll have to do some cleanup first. I'm ashamed to admit that we had a few programs like that, and we found it worthwhile to first clean them up under DOS using the techniques already described. After that, the move to OS/2 was painless, and we improved our DOS versions as well.

2.5) Converting Graphic Programs

So far, we've only discussed text-oriented programs, that is, those programs that use the non-graphical video display modes. While OS/2 Standard Edition 1.0 provides excellent support for such applications, it has little to offer if your programs generate graphical displays.

However, the situation is not completely hopeless. Contrary to what some would have you believe, you do not have to wait for the Presentation Manager before you can move graphical programs to OS/2. The new operating system does provide the means to gain direct access to the physical video buffer and the display adaptor's I/O ports, both of which are necessary for generating graphical displays. This is not too surprising, since the Presentation Manager is itself an application on top of the OS/2 base, and it needs these capabilities.

A detailed discussion of low-level graphics programming under OS/2 would be too lengthy for this chapter, but Listing 27-8 offers a small example of how you can directly access the physical video buffer. *VioGetPhysBuf* maps the specified video buffer into your address space, if possible, and returns one or more selectors that you can use to form 32-bit pointers for protected-mode access. One selector is returned for each 64 kilobytes of video buffer area. The mapping, however, is only valid when your program is executing in the foreground, that is, when it has control of the actual display screen. So, you must call *VioScrLock* before accessing the buffer and *VioScrUnlock* when you are finished. The former, as used in this example, does not return until the user brings the program to the foreground via the session manager. Then it locks the screen so that the user cannot switch to another session until the current program unlocks the screen via *VioScrUnlock*.

Listing 27-8: A program to directly access the physical video buffer.

```
extern far pascal VioGetPhysBuf();
extern far pascal VioScrLock();
extern far pascal VioScrUnlock();

int i,error;
struct physdata
  \{
  unsigned long real;              /* physical video buffer address */
  unsigned long length;            /* buffer length */
  unsigned short prots[2];         /* protected-mode buffer selectors */
  \} x;

union                            /* used to make video RAM pointer */
  \{
  unsigned short x[2];
  unsigned short far *p;
  \} q;


x.real = 0xb0000;                /* load physical address of buffer */
x.length = 4000;                 /* load buffer length */
error = VioGetPhysBuf((struct physdata far *)(&x),0); /* Map buffer */
if(error) ...

q.x[0] = 0;                      /* form far pointer to buffer */
q.x[1] = x.prots[0];
```

```
error = VioScrLock(1,(char far *)(&i),0);      /* lock the screen */
if(error) ...

for(i = 0; i < 2000; q.p[i++] = 0x0720);        /* clear the buffer */

error = VioScrUnlock(0);                         /* unlock the screen */
if(error) ...
```

Now, even though the example in Listing 27-8 writes to the physical video buffer in text mode, you can use this same technique to draw graphic images. I won't present an example here because there are so many subtle points that this topic deserves a chapter of its own; however, the general approach is:

- Use *VioGetConfig* to determine the type of display adaptor equipped. *VioGetMode* and *VioGetState* might also be needed to determine the current display mode and state.

- Use *VioSetMode* and, if necessary, *VioSetState* to establish the appropriate graphical mode.

- Create separate execution threads using *VioModeWait* and *VioSavRedrawWait* to re-establish the display mode and save or restore the display data when a session switch occurs.

- Use *VioGetPhysBuf*, *VioScrLock*, and *VioScrUnlock* as above to gain access to the physical video buffer in order to draw the graphic images.

If you need to access the display adaptor's I/O registers, as is often the case with EGA displays, then you'll also have to create a function with I/O privileges that you can then call from your program. This is necessary because normal OS/2 processes are not allowed to execute I/O instructions.

As I said, graphic programming can be done in OS/2 without relying upon the Presentation Manager. It isn't as easy as displaying text alone, but if you study the OS/2 Technical Reference thoroughly and try a few simple experiments, you'll quickly get the hang of it.

3) Terminate-Stay-Resident (TSR) Programs

TSR programs are a special category of highly interactive DOS applications. The typical TSR, such as Borland SideKick or Lotus Metro, is dormant until the user activates it using a hot key. Then it opens a window on the screen and enters into a dialogue with the user to accomplish some task, such as updating an appointment calendar. When this dialogue is finished, the TSR restores the original screen contents and goes back to sleep. So, TSR programs typically have the same OS/2 conversion problems as the interactive programs discussed earlier, that is, their keyboard, mouse, and screen access techniques must be changed to meet the OS/2 requirements.

In addition, you need to decide if you want the TSR to become a normal OS/2 process or a "monitor" process. If the TSR is providing a data management service, such as the appointment calendar, you could simply load it as an OS/2 session and use the session manager hot keys to activate it.

However, if the TSR has to continuously monitor the keyboard input, as with a keyboard macro package such as Prokey must do, then you need to hook it into the keyboard I/O driver as a monitor process. Fortunately, OS/2 provides an elegant way that eliminates the TSR contention problems that often occur under DOS. Figure 27-1 shows how this works.

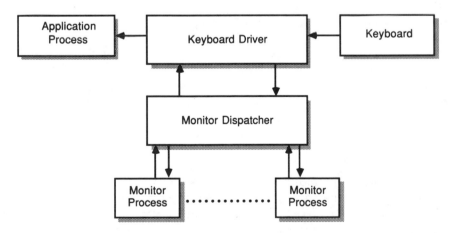

Figure 27-1: OS/2 Keyboard Monitors

The monitor process calls *DosMonOpen* and *DosMonReg* to open a monitor chain in the device driver and register itself as a monitor. Then each time the device driver receives a keystroke, it sends a "keystroke data packet" out to the first monitor in the chain. That monitor reads the packet via *DosMonRead* and chooses to absorb the keystroke, pass it on, or substitute one or more pseudo-keystrokes. These latter two operations are done via *DosMonWrite*, which sends the keystroke packet on to the next monitor in the chain. Unless everything gets absorbed in the chain, the original or substitute keystrokes eventually reach the end of the chain and are returned to the device driver, which passes them on to the application program that is waiting for keyboard data.

As with graphical techniques discussed above, there are many subtleties you must keep in mind when designing a monitor process, and so I won't attempt a thorough description here. The main thing to keep in mind, though, is that a monitor must be very fast or else the system will appear to be sluggish. Also, note that you can hook monitors into some of the other standard character drivers. For example, the OS/2 print spooler is implemented as a monitor process hooked into the printer driver.

4) I/O Drivers

I/O drivers present the toughest conversion challenges, if only because they hook into the messy guts of DOS and typically require a large amount of assembly language programming. Furthermore, as with DOS TSR programs, the rules for creating drivers have not been well documented, and so designers have had to use ad hoc techniques learned by experimentation.

Unfortunately, OS/2 drivers tend to be much more complicated than their DOS counterparts because they must operate in a multitasking environment supporting both real-mode and protected-mode processes. Because of these significant environmental differences, the typical DOS driver doesn't survive the conversion, except for small sequences of code that deal directly with the device. In other words, if you write drivers for a living, roll up your sleeves because you've got a lot of work ahead of you.

We were initially concerned that the techniques for creating OS/2 drivers would remain very unexplained and that we could not obtain the knowledge experimentally because OS/2 is so well-protected. However, IBM's documentation was a pleasant surprise, because it explains this arcane topic in great detail and includes a fairly complete example. Microsoft has also been providing a driver development kit, including an OS/2 kernel debugger, to attendees of its driver design course.

Family Mode Considerations

The final topic you must consider when converting a DOS program to OS/2 is whether you want the result to be a "family-mode application." This means that the program will be put together in such a way that its executable, i.e., the .EXE file, will run correctly in OS/2 protected mode, OS/2 real mode, or under DOS 3.x. The OS/2 Programmer Toolkit includes the BIND utility program and a special library, PI.LIB, to construct family-mode applications.

There are three simple rules for achieving family compatibility:

- Don't use any OS/2 API calls that are not part of the family-mode repertoire unless your program first tests that it is running in protected mode.

- Don't do any DOS-specific things, such as generate software interrupts, unless you verify that the program is running in real mode.

- Don't do any internal manipulation of 32-bit pointers unless you first check whether your program is in real or protected mode and choose the appropriate algorithm.

Note that the first rule requires that you know which functions in the C compiler library (and possibly other libraries) call API functions that are not allowed in family mode. When we converted the Lattice C Compiler, we were able to make most of the mainstream functions fully compatible with family mode. These are kept in the LC.LIB library. Lattice functions that only can be only in protected mode are kept in LCP.LIB, while those that can be used only in real mode are in LCR.LIB.

Tables 27-1, 27-2, and 27-3 indicate which of the keyboard, mouse, and video API functions are available in family mode. In the FAM column, an F means that the function is fully supported in the family mode, while an R indicates that there are some restrictions on family-mode use of the function. The OS/2 Technical Reference provides this information for all of the API functions.

Summary

Our experiences at Lattice in converting DOS applications to OS/2 protected mode have been much happier than we originally expected. While this exciting new operating system was designed with an eye to the future, it remains very compatible with the past. Good luck in your move to OS/2!

28
Porting to OS/2 *

Steven Armbrust

An inside look reveals how one company rapidly converted a complex data manager from DOS to the OS/2 environment.

When Microrim, Inc., became a beta site for IBM's new Operating System/2 (OS/2) in late 1986, Microrim chairman and founder Wayne Erickson knew immediately what he and his staff had to do. Not only did they have to convert R:BASE System V, Microrim's largest and most complex database manager, to run under OS/2, but the job had to be done in time to demonstrate a working product when IBM officially announced OS/2. At the time, no one knew how soon the announcement would occur (it came just six months later).

Microrim—located in the same Redmond, Washington, neighborhood as OS/2's developer, Microsoft—is a forerunner in converting to OS/2. The company internally committed to the OS/2 conversion of R-BASE System V in late 1986 and completed it in time to demonstrate the product at IBM's formal announcement of OS/2 on April 2 of this year in Miami.

"We knew the job would be big, because our program is big," Erickson said. "But with all the enhancements we wanted to make to our product, and because of the endorsements of IBM and Microsoft, we felt we couldn't ignore OS/2."

Microrim is counting on OS/2 to be a big boon in the constant battles the company must wage with competitors, most notably Ashton-Tate of dBASE fame, to add new features and otherwise improve its products. For R:BASE System V, which already s trains at the 640KB memory bounds that are available under DOS, OS/2's 16MB of memory will open the door to new features. It will also improve system performance by eliminating the need for cumbersome overlays used to squeeze numerous program elements into the overflowing 640KB memory bag. As it is now, heavy use of overlays as required by R:BASE under DOS diminishes the product's performance even on an AT-class computer.

Microrim approached the OS/2 conversion systematically and found it relatively uncomplicated, said company managers, largely because R:BASE System V (like all Microrim products) is modularly designed, thus nullifying the need for complex and interconnecting adjustments during conversions. The converted R:BASE System V is capable of running under OS/2 and using OS/2's expanded memory and some multitasking capabilities with other OS/2 applications; however, it does not yet fully tap all OS/2 features, such as multithreading and the operational doors that capability can open.

The converted R:BASE System V is not yet on the market and prices are unavailable. Microrim plans to release the product when IBM releases OS/2; meanwhile, Microrim engineers are working to enhance it with features arising out of capabilities specific to OS/2. According to Microrim, R:BASE System V will remain available in DOS for users who do not want to convert their operations to OS/2.

Planning the Conversion

As Microrim managers sat down late in 1986 to plan for the OS/2 conversion they were faced with several questions. How could Microrim engineers, who were just learning OS/2 themselves, convert an application as large and complex as R:BASE System V to the new operating system? What was the best way to proceed to optimize company resources? Should Microrim create a family application (one that could run under both DOS and OS/2 but that could not take full advantage of new OS/2 features such as extended memory and multitasking) or a separate application for OS/2 that would allow R:BASE System V to take advantage of the full extended OS/2 features? How should they proceed with the inevitable language conversion (from FORTRAN to C), and should they rewrite the program by hand or use an automatic language translator? Finally, how could Microrim accomplish the conversion in time to meet the fast-approaching (but still unknown) IBM deadline?

The company. From all observations, Microrim and its R:BASE System V product were ahead of the conversion game from the start. First, Microrim had previous experience converting products to new operating systems. Second, the modular nature of R:BASE System V allowed for the conversion to be done by making some rather simple, segregated changes as opposed to making complex and extensive modifications.

Microrim was formed by Erickson in November 1981 to develop a micro-computer version of a mainframe database product called RIM (for relational information management.) that he had created for NASA in 1978 to validate relational database technology. RIM was subsequently made available on 22 different mainframes, including those made by Control Data, Cray, Burroughs, DEC, and Prime. Microrim's first product—the minicomputer version of RIM—was named for the company and released for use on CP/M-based machines in July 1982.

Later that year, the company did two ports—one to IBM's DOS and one to Convergent Technologies' CTOS. In October 1983, Microrim did a major revision of the product and renamed it R:BASE 4000, followed by another major upgrade called R:BASE 5000 in April 1985 (reviewed in "A Data Manager with Kernel Code Generation," Steven Armbrust and Ted Forgeron, September 1985, p.82) and ultimately, the release of the current product, R:BASE System V, in July 1986. In the six years since it was founded, Microrim has grown from a company with seven people to one with 135 employees.

Decisions. Although Microrim management remains committed in the long term to enhancing R:BASE System V so that it can eventually use all applicable OS/2 features, time constraints forced the company to take a conservative approach in the beginning. Instead of redesigning the product to add the new-system-supported features, Microrim initially decided to make a direct port of the existing product in order to meet the tight schedule. With this port, R:BASE System V immediately takes advantage of OS/2's larger memory space and ability to run concurrently with other OS/2 applications; however, it still needs further enhancements to take advantage of all the other features of OS/2.

Further, Microrim decided to create a separate application for OS/2 rather than a family application; whereas a family application would have the advantage of running under both OS/2 and DOS (thus minimizing the number of different packages Microrim would have to stock, support, and maintain), it would be limited to using only OS/2 features that have counterparts under DOS. Despite the advantages of a family application, however, Microrim managers decided without hesitation to develop separate applications for OS/2 and DOS. Their goal was to create a product that does not limit OS/2 users to those features of OS/2 that are also available under DOS.

"We did not want to be unnecessarily constrained by the memory limitations of DOS, so we chose to go with two versions of the product, one for DOS and one for OS/2," explained Alan Lindsay, Microrim's computer systems engineer who performed the OS/2 conversion. Lindsay expects other developers of large applications to make the same choice, leaving the family-application approach primarily for utility programs, such as compilers, that do not require internal multitasking or large memory space.

Finally, Microrim needed a strong configuration control system. This would allow its staff both to upgrade the company's products individually and to maintain a common database for making generic changes simultaneously to all products. Configuration control is important because Microrim intends to sustain updated DOS and OS/2 versions of all its products, including Clout (a user query interface) and Program interface (a programming tool).

After examining several commercial configuration control systems, however, Microrim decided to build its own R:BASE System V because it could not find one on the market to meet its specific needs.

The Strategy. Microrim approached the OS/2 conversion of R:BASE System V in two stages. The first was a language conversion (most of R:BASE System V was written in FORTRAN, but in order to use OS/2 as it currently exists, the program had to be translated to C). The second phase was the actual conversion from DOS to OS/2.

The Switch to C

When R:BASE was developed, FORTRAN was the most portable language available and Microrim engineers knew it well—largely because R:BASE's RIM ancestor was written in FORTRAN. Thus, the original R:BASE was in FORTRAN, but enhancements to later R:BASE versions were written in C. Going into the OS/2 conversion, R:BASE System V still contained 70 to 75 percent FORTRAN code, 10 to 20 percent C code, and the remainder was in assembly language.

No FORTRAN compilers are yet available for OS/2, so Microrim had to convert R:BASE before it could start the OS/2 conversion. Such a language conversion had been on the minds of Microrim developers for some time, but they were reluctant to undertake this major project for its own sake. As Erickson explained, "We feared that the entire staff would spend two years on a conversion and the product would do nothing different from the current product." Nonetheless, Microrim engineers knew the language switch was inevitable—with or without OS/2—in order to keep R:BASE System V competitive in the marketplace, so the company started the wheels for C conversion in motion last fall. It accelerated the conversion effort a few months later when OS/2 became a reality.

The conversion to C, including hand-tweaking, required four to five people over a period of three months. To save time, Microrim engineers used Rapidtech Systems, Inc.'s FORTRIX-C, a language translator that reads source code in one programming language and produces source code in another language as output. Although the code produced by mechanical translation is not as efficient as code written by hand, the conversion package can produce an initial draft in the target language in a much shorter time. Engineer Lindsay explained that even when the translator's output required further refining by customized conversion routines or hand-tweaking, using a translator significantly reduced the time and effort of producing a finished program in the target language.

A certain amount of post-processing of the translator output was inevitable because FORTRIX-C, as a general-purpose conversion program, could not be expected to meet all of the specific requirements of a program as complicated as R:BASE System V. For example, FORTRIX-C converts a FORTRAN COMMON block into a series of pointers to an array and generates code to initialize these pointers at every entry to a function. Microrim engineers therefore had to write their own routines to convert COMMON blocks to C structures that require no address manipulation at runtime.

In addition, FORTRIX-C automatically generates all integers as long integers in C, but Microrim wanted them to be short integers; therefore, this had to be done manually. Finally, because FORTRIX-produced code is less efficient than handwritten code, Microrim engineers reviewed the FORTRIX-generated code when time allowed and manually cut out extraneous statements, reducing the size of the source code by approximately one-half.

The engineers confronted an interesting problem during the language conversion; when a math coprocessor was not present, floating-point operations were much slower in C than in FORTRAN. This was because Microsoft's FORTRAN and C compilers use two kinds of floating-point libraries. The standard library uses a math coprocessor if it is present or emulates it in software if it is not. The other, called the Alt Math library, always performs floating-point calculations in software. The efficiency of emulations in the two libraries is not always equal.

In version 3.3 of Microsoft FORTRAN, which was used to compile the FORTRAN code of R:BASE System V, the emulating routines in both libraries performed equally as fast. When the converted code was compiled with the Microsoft C 4.0 compiler, however, the emulation routines in the standard library were considerably slower than those in the Alt Math library. The Microsoft FORTRAN 4.0 compiler experienced the same problem with emulated floating-point routines.

Microrim considered using the Alt Math routines to achieve increased floating-point execution efficiency on systems without a math coprocessor (still the majority of PC systems). But this had two disadvantages. First, software routines in the Alt Math library gained execution efficiency at the expense of numeric accuracy and error checking. Second, the performance of an Alt Math product could be improved by adding a coprocessor.

In a database manager, floating-point efficiency is significant only if real-number data exist in the database; otherwise, manipulating data files is not a compute-intensive activity, and integer arithmetic is adequate for whatever computations are required. Therefore, Microrim engineers decided to accept the slower execution efficiency of the standard math library. In return, users have increased accuracy. For applications requiring upgraded efficiency, users can add a math coprocessor.

"The [language] conversion encouraged our development staff because they found they could take advantage of the C environment and decrease the code size of the product. Plus, they had a chance to clean up routines written several years ago and make the code tidier," Microrim chairman Erickson said.

Microrim's work was far from finished once the C conversion was complete, however. It still had to convert the C code to run under OS/2.

One-Man Job

The OS/2 conversion was less involved than it might have been because Microrim earlier had decided to limit its near-term efforts to producing a functionally equivalent OS/2 version of R:BASE System V without adding all the bells and whistles. Lindsay took on the job himself, using a Compaq Portable 286 computer with 2MB of extended memory. The one-man operation took three months. "In terms of effort, it was really only about half of a conversion," he said. "There weren't any big surprises; we were able to do exactly what we wanted. That probably wouldn't have been true if we were doing more than just a straight port."

Both modular programming and the structured, well-balanced code of R:BASE System V substantially expedited the OS/2 conversion. Erickson explained, "We've always tried to keep our machine—and operating-system-dependent code clearly isolated, so the number of routines we had to change for OS/2 was considerably smaller than it could have been."

Earlier conversions of Microrim products from different operating systems compelled company engineers long ago to isolate all operating-system-specific operations into a small set of procedures that other routines call whenever they need operating-system services. This set of procedures was placed into a library. Instead of making DOS calls directly, the rest of the routines in R:BASE System V called the routines in this library. As a result, the task of isolating DOS calls is easier, and fewer system-specific modules need to be rewritten.

Of approximately 2,500 total routines making up R:BASE System V, only 25 to 50 of them contained DOS calls that needed to be converted. Consequently, only about two percent of approximately 90,000 total lines of source code needed to be changed. Procedures that did not issue operating-system calls were able to function under OS/2 without change because none of them breaks rules of protected-mode operation, such as performing arithmetic on segment registers or attempting to access memory outside assigned memory space.

Any operating system functions handled by calls to standard C library routines were, for the most part, automatically taken care of simply by recompiling with the OS/2 version of the compiler. Changes were required, however, in the operating-system calls issued by assembly language routines. The majority of effort was spent isolating all DOS-style calls (placing values in registers and issuing an INT 21) and replacing them with equivalent OS/2 calls (pushing values on the stack and calling OS/2 procedures).

In some cases, the conversion could be applied at a higher level. Because of the higher-level syntax of the OS/2 applications program interface (API)—the rules for calling up OS/2 routines—some calls to assembly language routines implementing customized system interfaces were replaced with direct calls to OS/2 functions.

After isolating DOS calls and determining OS/2 equivalents, Lindsay tested each of the new system calls with a small test program. By taking this approach, Lindsay could monitor system operation and determine any operating quirks, performance problems, or bugs. He was able to determine immediately whether he would need to redesign parts of the application because of differences between DOS and OS/2.

In at least one instance, Lindsay had to make some modifications. Applications that formerly wrote to DOS video memory easily wrote to the OS/2 logical video buffer, but applications that send characters to the screen one at a time experienced a significant slowdown. To improve performance, Lindsay reprogrammed the R:BASE video procedures to write a string of characters to the logical video buffer first, then to update the screen.

The extent of IBM and Microsoft contributions to the R:BASE System V conversion effort is unclear. "We had what we needed, and we got help when we needed it," Lindsay said, but he would not elaborate because of a confidentiality agreement that Microrim signed prior to the conversion. Neither would Lindsay describe the documentation he worked from, although it is safe to assume that the material was similar to the OS/2 Software Development Kit now available commercially.

Better with OS/2

Because the conversion went smoothly, Microrim completed its prototype OS/2 version of R:BASE System V in time for the introduction of IBM's OS/2 on April 2 in Miami. The conversion was essentially a direct port of the DOS version, but it automatically takes advantage of a couple of OS/2 features.

First, the ported program is not restricted to DOS's 640KB memory limitation. Instead of being heavily overlaid as the DOS version is, the entire program (approximately 680KB worth) is loaded into memory at once. This improves the performance of the product, and it also eliminates the development burden of having to plan an overlay structure to optimize performance.

In addition, R:BASE System V and other OS/2 applications can be multitasked or a user can invoke two copies of R:BASE simultaneously to obtain multitasking features not built into the program. For example, a user can start up one copy of the program to print out a report and start another one to enter records into the database. Because OS/2 shares code segments, the memory space required by each subsequent invocation of a program is significantly less than the first. Also, because DOS's networking features are carried over to OS/2, R:BASE System V's built-in networking capabilities enable multiple invocations of the program, as well as multiple users, to update the same database without fear of corruption.

Microrim did not find that the OS/2 version of R:BASE System V runs any slower than the DOS version. Certainly, OS/2, as a multitasking operating system, has more overhead and could, in general, be expected to run slower than a single-tasking application such as DOS. However, because Microrim was able to remove the overlays required under DOS for R:BASE System V, the company actually improved the performance of the OS/2 version.

Instead of focusing on raw speed for isolated functions (i.e., sorting), Microrim believes that users should look at total throughout over time of combined functions (sorting, printing, etc.) to determine whether an OS/2 version of an application is superior or inferior to a DOS version. "It's not how long a sort takes, but how much I can get done in an hour that's important," Fred Gray, Microrim's senior vice president of research and development, said. The multitasking features of OS/2 give database users the ability to get more done per hour.

Microrim managers remain confident that the OS/2 conversion was worthwhile and has put them in an ideal position in the marketplace. If IBM releases OS/2 immediately, Microrim could release the ported R:BASE within days. Meanwhile, they have a team of developers enhancing the product with OS/2-specific features.

The upcoming Presentation Manager, being developed by IBM and Microsoft for use with OS/2, presents another opportunity to Microrim. Although sophisticated database users might not be helped much by a graphical user interface, such as the Presentation Manager, Microrim understands that effective use of graphics can help novices pick up database concepts more easily. In addition, the ability to build graphically oriented database applications could help sophisticated users build better applications for novices to use. Because the release date of the Presentation Manager is uncertain, Microrim has not made firm plans about which Presentation Manager features to put in R:BASE System V.

Even in their enthusiasm to develop an OS/2-only version of R:BASE System V, Microrim officials have not deserted their DOS customers. The company already supports its products on both CTOS and DOS, and OS/2 adds another entire operating system to the list. In addition to converting R:BASE System V, Microrim plans to update all of its products to take advantage of the new OS/2 features. All other Microrim products, except Clout, already have been converted from FORTRAN to C. Because they use a common set of library routines to perform system operations, converting other products to OS/2 should go even more smoothly than R:BASE System V.

Microrim was in the right position at the right time to do a quick conversion to OS/2. The company's database management products are well suited to quick conversion because they are not graphically based and do not break any operation-system interface rules, such as writing to unallocated memory. More importantly, Microrim was experienced in converting to other operating systems, so it knew the importance of writing modular, well-behaved code.

Lindsay cautioned against expecting to convert all DOS calls to OS/2 and have them work right away. He stressed use of modular code and recommended making poorly structured DOS programs modular first, isolating operating-system calls to a few procedures. When restructured code is working correctly under DOS, operating-specific-routines can then be recoded under OS/2 and tested. By isolating operating system calls to just a few procedures, OS/2 conversion involves changing only a small set of procedures, not searching through every line of source code. "Even if you don't have modular, well-behaved code before you start converting, you will when you finish," Lindsay concluded.

29

Preparing for Presentation Manager: Paradox® Steps Up to Windows 2.0 *

Craig Stinson

Ansa Software, the Belmont, Calif., firm recently acquired by Borland International, sells only one product, but that product, the relational database manager Paradox®, will appear in four new versions during the coming year. A fifth new version will probably be available in early 1989.

The offspring are aimed at different operating environments: Microsoft Windows Version 2.0, OS/2 systems Version 1.0, the OS/2 Presentation Manager, UNIX 5.3 and XENIX, and the 80386 running MS-DOS 3.x in protected mode with the help of a 386 MS-DOS compatibility tool. Paradox 386 was shown at last November's Comdex and will probably be available by the time you read this chapter; it won't require a compatibility tool, just a 386 machine.

All Paradox versions, old and new, will have multiuser capability and will be data-compatible. With versions for all the major personal computing environments (except Macintosh—Ansa is currently evaluating the feasibility of a Mac version). Ansa will be in a position to serve the vast majority of desktop users. And all users at various nodes of a network will be able to access and edit a common database, regardless of the hardware or operating systems they're running.

Sound Design Pays Off

What type of effort is involved in porting a large, complex MS-DOS application such as Paradox to all these different operating environments? In a recent interview with _MSJ_, Richard Schwartz, vice president for software development and a cofounder of Ansa, said that the move from one character-based system to another

---

has been relatively straightforward, thanks largely to the foresight of the original designers of Paradox.

"We designed Paradox from the beginning to be very clean and portable," says Schwartz. "We tried not to play dirty tricks getting at the operating system or creating hardware dependencies." This is not to say, of course, that the original Paradox doesn't write directly to the screen. "We do, of course, but we've isolated it. We have one module that will access the screen memory map directly. And even the BIOS dependencies are all in one place."

The move from a character environment (MS-DOS 3.x) to a graphics environment (Microsoft Windows and the OS/2 Presentation Manager) is a considerably more ambitious undertaking. Schwartz talked about the whys and hows of this move and about how the graphics-based Paradox will look, feel, and perform relative to the original.

Why Windows?

The move to Windows now, according to Schwartz, will give Ansa advantages in marketing and in implementation when the OS/2 Presentation Manager arrives.

"We think it's important to put out the Windows version, not because Windows 2.0 is going to be the primary market—certainly, Presentation Manager market will dwarf the Windows market—but because a lot of companies will be evaluating the Presentation Manager interface through Windows 2.0. And applications that run under Windows early on will have an advantage, given the long evaluation cycles that companies go through."

Second, because Windows 2.0 is here now and Presentation Manager is not, the effort required to rethink and recode Paradox for Windows is the best preparation Ansa can undertake for the eventual port to the Presentation Manager—even though the API for Presentation Manager will differ significantly from that for Windows.

The Good News

How hard was the port to Windows? According to Schwartz, all but the underlying database engine was redesigned, borrowing pieces of the previous architecture and source code. Nevertheless, he asserts, about 50 percent of the original source code emigrated to the new world intact. That's an off-the-cuff, work-in-progress estimate, but even if it is too optimistic, it is still good news for Windows developers: not all programs will have to be rewritten from the ground up to run in the new graphics environments.

Moreover, in Ansa's case the conversion will probably take about two person-years of work. That's not bad, considering that the original Paradox was a 14-person-year effort. And the company has done it without hiring a lot of specialized expertise. That's also good news, considering the current scarcity and high market value of Macintosh and Windows programmers.

"We tried to get some people with product-level graphics experience. We used a headhunter for a while, but we were very unsuccessful," says Schwartz. "And it turned out that we did very well taking good software engineers who have general computer science sophistication and having them come up to speed under Windows. We found that general computer science background was the most important factor."

A Natural Fit

Making Ansa's transition from characters to pixels easier was the fact that Paradox, despite its early origins (development for the first version began in the summer of 1981), has always been a highly visual, interactive program. From an interface design standpoint, therefore, the transfer to Windows entailed an expansion of ideas already in place rather than a wholesale reconceptualization.

"We've always had a very visual orientation, an object orientation," says Schwartz. "And it was just sort of a natural fit."

Data tables in the character-based Paradox, for example, are presented to the user in the form of visual constructs that look much like windows, except that the borders are made of text-graphic characters and don't go all the way around. Like a frame in Framework or a screenful of a spreadsheet, these objects act as portholes onto larger expanses of data, which Paradox calls images.

Paradox presents the user with a workspace, much as Windows does, on which he can keep several images visible at once. And though it doesn't support a mouse, the character-based product lets the user manipulate the sizes and locations of images, and the width of columns within them, by positioning a highlight in the right hot spot and pressing cursor keys. This ability to interact immediately with a data construct, instead of having to issue a menu command and describe what one wants, is what Schwartz calls "direct operability," an important component of the original Paradox interface.

Visual Interaction

"The idea was—as much as possible, anywhere we could—to allow visual interaction, rather than descriptive interaction," says Schwartz. "Instead of asking the user to explain or describe something, we asked him to show it to us. That's very compatible with moving to the Windows environment."

Paradox under Windows will look quite similar at first glance to the original version, except that the Lotus-style menu gives way to drop-down menus, the text comes up black-on-white, and the images are fully formed document windows, with title bars, scroll bars, control menus, and sizing icons. The direct operability will still be there, but there will be more of it. And, of course, there will be mouse support.

One new area of direct operability in Windows Paradox is in the specification of sorts. In the character-based version, the user indicated which fields he wanted to be sort keys and in which direction he wanted a field sorted by typing a field number followed by an "a" for ascending or a "d" for descending.

The Windows version simplifies this process and makes it less analytical by letting the user double-click directly on the name of each sort key field. An arrow indicating sort direction (ascending, by default) will appear to the left of the chosen field name; to switch directions, the user merely toggles the arrow by double-clicking on it.

The notion of clicking on a value to toggle it or to select from available values appears elsewhere in Windows Paradox. In creating or restructuring a table, for example, where the user is asked for a data type, he can click the mouse to get a menu showing available types. Similarly, in the create/restructure subsystem, a double-click on a field name will summon a dialog box, allowing the user to inspect current validity-check definitions or create new ones.

Implementation Advantages

Describing the conversion effort, Schwartz downplays the fearsome Windows learning curve, emphasizing instead the implementation advantages conferred by the graphics environment. In particular, he cites the greater degree of independence among the various objects with which the user interacts.

In the Windows environment, every table in the workspace, as well as every form, query, and report specification, lives in its own window and has its own message handler. That message handler is responsible for knowing only about itself, how to repaint itself and how to update itself. In the character-based version, more attention had to be paid to the "global state," that is, to the ways in which changes in a table would affect everything else in the workspace.

"At the implementation level," says Schwartz, "that means that your code can have an architecture such that everything is purely local to each image. So you can have a local handler that knows how to resize a window or how much of it to repaint. If anything in the size of that window is affected, Windows takes care of sending messages to the other windows to let them know that some other portion needs to be repainted."

Debugging Difficulties

According to Schwartz, one fairly serious hindrance to the development of Windows Paradox was the lack of debugging tools for use in the Windows environment.

"It's a harder problem anyway," Schwartz says, "because there's more going behind the scenes in the Windows environment." The moveability and discardability of Windows object code complicates matters, making bugs harder to find. Bugs tend to turn up later in the game as the result of stress on the system because a piece of code has been moved in memory.

The current version of Code View doesn't work in the Windows environment, though Microsoft is working on a Windows-specific version. *Symdeb* is provided, but Ansa didn't use it extensively, preferring instead to rely on algorithmic-level debugging by embedding *printf* statements to test values of variables at various points in the program.

"In our design environment, we have a monochrome display hooked up as well as an EGA. We've hooked things up so that we can put *printf*s in the code and have them scroll out on the monochrome display. You get the effect of traditional debugging preserved in the Windows environment."

Making debugging even more difficult was the fact that Ansa was working with early pre-release versions of Windows and the Windows development tools (the project began last April). Programmers were sometimes hard pressed to tell which problems they should attribute to their own code, which to the compiler, and which to bugs in the underlying environment.

User Advantages

The independence of screen objects provides several benefits for users. Most importantly, it means that users can have more things going on at once and still keep track of everything. Instead of being limited to the number of images that will fit one after the other on screen, the user can load up the screen with overlapping windows, thereby achieving whatever level of information density he finds most appropriate.

This facilitates such activities as moving from one table to another, copying data or structures from one table to another, discovering correlations between one set of data and another, and so on. It also means that Windows Paradox will appear somewhat less "modal" to users than its text-based ancestor. There are places in the current program where a user has to drop one context, if only briefly, to work in another. The Windows version will minimize the effects of such breaks in continuity.

For example, in the character-based version, if the user wants to modify a data-entry form on the fly while entering data, he issues a command to summon the forms subsystem. The data and form he was working on disappear at that point, becoming visible again only after he's finished changing the form spec. In the Windows version, the form subsystem will appear in a child window, with the data remaining visible in the parent window.

Other benefits the Windows Paradox user will find include the following:

1. The Windows version will automatically support any high-resolution large-screen displays supported by Windows itself.

2. The report subsystem will offer enhanced font support and will accept bit-mapped images by way of the Windows clipboard. Users can dress up Paradox reports with company logos, signatures, clip art, and the like. Windows Paradox will not accept bit-mapped images as data types, although Schwartz concedes that that's "a natural direction" for the product to evolve in.

3. Windows Paradox can exchange data with other Windows applications by way of dynamic data exchange (DDE). At the Microsoft Excel announcement, Ansa showed an early version of Paradox running as a client of Microsoft Excel, with Paradox stated up by means of the macro language and transferring data to Microsoft Excel via DDE. The finished Windows version of Paradox will allow a reversal of this scenario: you can start up and control other applications by means of scripts written in the Paradox application language (PAL).

Performance Hits

The picture sounds rosy, but Schwartz concedes that the advantages of the Windows environment will exact a few performance penalties. The hits, he suggests, will come less from Windows' need to represent text in graphics mode than from its propensity to swap program modules in and out of memory.

Because the program was still under development at this writing, Ansa was not prepared to supply benchmark data. However, Schwartz maintains the company is "quite happy with the Paradox performance on 10-MHz 286s and above." And, he says, the SMARTDrive program, a Microsoft-supplied disk-caching utility tailored to enhance the performance of Windows, speeds things up significantly on all machines.

Fears Allayed

What messages would Ansa's Schwartz pass along to another Windows application developer? The most obvious one is that the redesign of an MS-DOS program to run under Windows is not the horrendous task it's commonly thought to be, particularly if the program was well designed in the first place. A second notion involves the maintenance of individuality under conditions that seem to impose similarity.

"Some people say that all products are going to look alike, that all the creativity has been taken away from the designer in the Windows environment," says Schwartz. "So much has been standardized that everything's going to look the same and work the same. That's certainly true at some level. Still, there is a very diverse set of ways in which one can take advantage of the environment to present a particular application. You need to concern yourself first with the core model of how an application is to be constructed—with the user-level concepts and how you want to present them. And only after that you look at what the

Windows tools are and how you'll use them. The greatest effect on the user is the underlying model, and that is not affected at all by Windows. Windows is just a way to present that, to communicate it more effectively to the user."

Paradox Under Microsoft OS/2

Paradox was conceived in the days of very limited resources. Development began in the first half of 1981, months before the announcement of the IBM PC, when 64Kb was as much memory as anyone could expect to have.

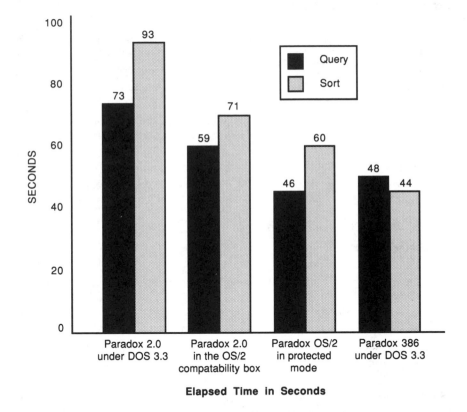

Figure 29-1: Preliminary performance statistics for three new versions of Paradox, as measured on a PS/2 Model 80. The query involved a join of a 5000-record table and a 10,000-record table; the sort was for the 500-record table. The figures for Paradox OS/2 and Paradox 386 may differ when those products are shipped.

Over the next several years, as larger-capacity machines became commonplace, Paradox grew in scope and ambition, so that by the time the product was announced in the fall of 1985, it required 512Kb to run—practically speaking, that meant a 640Kb computer.

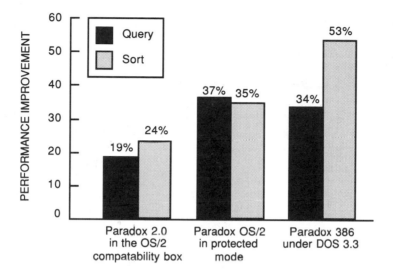

Figure 29-2: Performance improvements of three new versions of Paradox over Paradox 2.0 running in MS-DOS 3.3. These figures are preliminary and may not reflect actual performance when the products are shipped.

Like a Depression era parent, however, Paradox never forgot what it was like to live in lean times. From the beginning, the product incorporated a virtual memory manager that swapped data as necessary to the hard disk. One of the program's stronger selling points, moreover, was its heuristic approach to the processing of relational queries. An important aspect of this process was machine reasoning about what data was currently in memory and what was swapped out somewhere.

Therefore, the large address space afforded by the 80286 and 80386 chips running in protected mode represents a liberation for Paradox, demonstrated by the preliminary performance statistics shown in figures 29-1 and 29-2.

Judging by the numbers, Paradox running under the OS/2 systems in protected mode should take care of complex queries and large-scale sorts much more quickly than the MS-DOS 3.3 version. The 80386 version will do queries about as efficiently as the OS/2 versions and will be even more nimble at sorting.

Perhaps the most surprising information revealed by these early numbers is that Paradox 2.0 running in real mode under OS/2 (in the OS/2 compatibility box) outperforms the same product running on the same hardware under MS-DOS 3.3 According to Microsoft, most MS-DOS programs will run 5 percent slower in the compatibility box. Ansa's Richard Schwartz attributes the improvement to the fact that Paradox is doing a lot of random file access and is therefore able to profit significantly from OS/2's disk caching.

Performance statistics for the Microsoft Windows version of Paradox were not yet available as of this writing.

30
The OS/2 Windows Presentation Manager: Microsoft Windows On the Future *

Manny Vellon

Last April, Microsoft announced a series of new products, including a new operating system, Microsoft Operating System/2 (OS/2). An important part of this announcement was the inclusion of Microsoft Windows as a standard part of the OS/2 operating system. Currently, Microsoft Windows must be purchased separately and installed under MS-DOS.

The Windows presentation manager will be tightly integrated with OS/2 and will provide the same benefits that Microsoft Windows provides to MS-DOS: a windowed, graphical user interface and support for a variety of input and output devices. Through the presentation manager, OS/2 will replace the well-known A> prompt of MS-DOS with window-based screens.

This union of Windows with OS/2 strengthens the role of Windows in future system and application products and also addresses the ease-of-use issues that have been associated with MS-DOS and IBM PC software. Windows provides a more intuitive interface that allows novice users to learn products more quickly.

Also important is IBM's support of Microsoft Windows in its new products. This support ensures that Windows will become a standard part of the operating environment and encourages other hardware manufacturers to support it as well.

Protected Mode

The new IBM PS/2 series, the IBM PC AT, the Compaq 386, and other Intel 286- and 386-based computers are capable of running in real mode or protected mode. In real mode, they operate much like the Intel 8088-based IBM PC: they are limited to using 1 megabyte (Mb) of memory, they can usually run only one program at a time, and they are vulnerable to crashing when a program goes

---

* © Microsoft Corporation, *Microsoft Systems Journal*, May, 1987, p. 13

513

awry. In protected mode, the 286- and 386-based computers don't have those limits.

Under OS/2's protected-mode operating system, programs are no longer limited to 640K; applications can take advantage of up to 16 Mb of real memory and up to 1 gigabyte of virtual memory. OS/2 is able to perform multitasking—it can run several programs simultaneously by quickly switching among them. OS/2 is more robust than real-mode operating systems: programs run independently of each other, and if one crashes it is less likely to affect the others.

Currently, Microsoft Windows can also do many of these functions. By performing a variety of sophisticated functions, Windows can take advantage of extended memory if available and can provide rudimentary multitasking. With the OS/2 Windows presentation manager, however, these functions are much easier to implement since the underlying operating system kernel includes these capabilities.

User Interface

In addition to this symbiosis "under the hood," OS/2 Windows is integral to the operating system at the user level. The Windows presentation manager will be the standard user interface for the new operating system. Users won't have to learn about disk directories, filenames, and cryptic commands; executing programs and managing the OS/2 file system with the OS/2 Windows presentation manager will be intuitive and fast.

Although the new OS/2 Windows bears a strong resemblance to today's Microsoft Windows, there are some substantial differences between the two. Most significant are the differences in user interfaces. To eliminate these differences so as to produce a common user interface, Microsoft has announced a new version of Microsoft Windows—Version 2.0 (see Figure 30-1). This version, while still a real-mode version for MS-DOS, employs the same user interface to be used by the OS/2

When Microsoft Windows was first developed, it used tiled windows. Overlapped windows were considered too slow and unusable with low-resolution displays. In order to respond to customer requests for overlapping windows, and because optimized graphics algorithms and improved processing speeds have eliminated performance bottlenecks that are found in older technology, the new Windows uses overlapped windows instead of tiled windows.

New Windows products will also have improved keyboard interfaces. Although Windows is best used with a mouse, it is possible, and sometimes preferable, to use it solely through the keyboard. Changes in the user interface will make this easier.

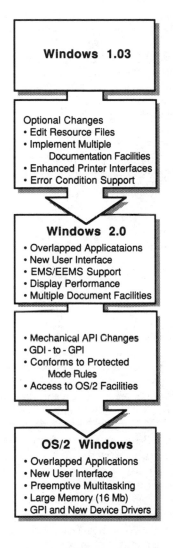

First, the keyboard interface has been improved in order to allow direct access to items in dialog boxes. The user can type Alt-F to quickly position the cursor in the filename field of the dialog box. Access to menus from the keyboard has also been enhanced by allowing the developer to select any letter from a menu command to execute the item rather than being limited to the first letter, as in the case of Windows Version 1.03 and Version 1.04. This helps to make it easier for software developers to provide meaningful command names while still providing fast keyboard access to commands.

The second significant change affects mouse operation. Currently, Windows employs pull-down menus. You click down on the menu bar to make visible a pop-up menu; then, while holding down the mouse button, you drag down to the desired command in the pop-up menu and let go of the button. This technique is fast, but it is prone to accidental selections and requires considerable manual dexterity. The new interface allows you to click and let go on the menu bar to make the pop-up menu visible and then click down on the desired command within the given menu.

Finally, the new interface employs some new terminology (for example, minimize and maximize, instead of icon and zoom) and some additional keyboard operations.

Users who are accustomed to the old keyboard interface won't be forced to learn the new one. Microsoft Windows, Version 2.0, will work in both the old and new styles to help users get accustomed to the new interface. However, the OS/2 Windows presentation manager will use this new interface only.

API

Although Microsoft Windows, Version 2.0, and the OS/2 Windows presentation manager appear to be similar and have many common functions, programs written for Microsoft Windows will have to be modified to work with the OS/2 Windows presentation manager. OS/2 restricts several operations in programs; for example, software interrupts are not allowed. Programs written for MS-DOS will also have to be modified to work in OS/2.

Besides the changes required by the new operating system, such as replacing software interrupts with operating system calls, other changes have been made to the OS/2 Windows Application Program Interface (API) in order to standardize coding practices, improve error handling, and exploit new graphics capabilities. Fortunately, many of these changes are "mechanical" in nature. To follow the new coding practices, for example, all window manager calls are preceded with "Win": "WinCreateWindow", "WinShowWindow", etc. Other changes entail reordering parameters. Applications that make heavy use of graphics will require the most changes; the OS/2 Windows presentation manager contains a new graphics library that requires a variety of changes to be made to the API.

The Future

OS/2 is not intended to replace MS-DOS. Microsoft expects that real-mode (MS-DOS) and protected-mode (OS/2) products will continue to coexist until Intel 286- and 386-based computers predominate. MS-DOS and Microsoft Windows will continue to be developed and marketed for low-end machines, while OS/2 addresses newer, more-powerful computers. The Windows user interface will serve as a bridge for users, allowing them to operate each of these classes of machines regardless of the underlying hardware. In time, Microsoft expects Intel 386-based machines to become the standard hardware environment for powerful new business and engineering applications. Microsoft will extend OS/2 to exploit the additional capabilities of the Intel 386 and will upgrade OS/2 in the future. Once more, the Windows presentation manager interface will help to keep these changes invisible to the user.

Figure 30-1: Comparison of Current and Future Windows Versions

	Microsoft Windows 1.03 P 1.04	Microsoft Windows 2.0	MS-OS/2 Windows
Presentation Spaces	Tiled	Overlapped	Overlapped
More Consistent User and Keyboard Interface	—	Yes	Yes
Processor Environments	8088 8086 286 386	8088 8086 286 386	— — 286 386
Large Memory Support	—	EMS/EEMS	16Mb
Multitasking	Non Preemptive Fully Preemptive		Non Preemptive
Enhance Display Performance	—	Yes	Yes
Runs Existing Windows (1.03) Application	Yes	Yes	No
Graphics API	GDI	GDI	GPI
Multiple Documentation∫nterface	—	Yes	Yes
Device Drivers	—	Enhanced	New Model
Old Application Support	—	Improved	Improved
Integral Part of OS	—	—	Yes
Protected Mode Execution Applications Execution	—	—	Yes
New Development API	—	—	Yes
New User "Shell" and Keyboard Interface	—	—	Yes

Figure 30-2: Microsoft Windows API. Programs written for MS-DOS will have to be modified to work in OS/2. Many of these changes are mechanical in nature—for example, all window manager calls are preceded with "Win". Compare the above *Windows 2.0* code with that shown in Figure 30-3.

```
                                   .
                                   .

int PASCAL WinMain( hInstance, hPrevInstance, lpszCmdLine, cmdShow)
HANDLE hInstance, hPrevInstance;
LPSTR lpszCmdLine;
int cmdShow;
{
        MSG    msg;
        HWND   hWnd;
        NPWNDCLASS        pHelloClass;
                                   .
                                   .
                                   .
    /* Allocate and initialize class data structure pHelloClass */
                                   .
                                   .
                                   .
      /* Create a window class */
      if (!RegisterClass( (LPWNDCLASS)pHelloClass ) )
             return FALSE;

      /* Create an application window */
      hWnd = CreateWindow ((LPSTR)"Class", (LPSTR) "Title",
                        WS_TILEDWINDOW, 0, 0, 0, 0, (HWND)NULL,
                        (HMENU)NULL, (HANDLE)hInstance,
                        (LPSTR)NULL );
                                   .
                                   .
                                   .
      /* Process messages*/
      while (GetMessage ((LPMSG) &msg, NULL, 0, 0)) {
             TranslateMessage ((LPMSG) &msg) ;
             DispatchMessage ((LPMSG) &msg) ;
             }

             return (int)msg.wParam;
}
```

Figure 30-3: OS/2 Windows presentation manager (API) (see Figure 30-2)

.
.
.

```
int cdecl main(argc, argv)
int argc;
char *argv[];
{
        QMSG qmsg;
        HAB     hab;
        HMQ     hmq;
        HWND    hwnd, hwndFrame;

        /* get an anchor block */
        hab = WinInitialize();

        /* create a message queue for the application */
        hmq - WinCreateMsgQueue(hab, 0);

        /* create a window class */
        if (!WinRegisterClass(  (LPCH) "Class",
                                WndProc,
                                WS_SYNCPAINT | WS_CLIPSIBLINGS |
                                WS_SIZEREDRAW,
                                0,
                                NULL)) return FALSE;

        /* create an application window */
        hwndFrame =
                WinCreateStdWindow (NULL,
                                FS_MENU | FS_TITLEBAR | FS_MINMAX |
                                FS_SIZEBORDER | FS_SYSMENU,
                                (LPSTR) "Class",
                                (LPSTR) "Title", OL, NULL,
                                IDM_APPMENU,
                                (HWND far *)&hwnd);
                                .
                                .
                                .

        /* process messages */
        while (WinGetMsg(hab, (LPQMSG)&qmsg, NULL, 0, 0))
                WinDispatchMsg(hab, (LPQMSG)&qmsg);

        /* destroy the resources used by the application */
        WinDestroyWindow(hwndFrame);
```

```
        WinDestroyMsgQueue(hmq);
        WinFinalize(hab);
}
```

VII
286/386 Programming
Products and Tips

31
80386 Operating System Examples [*]

Chris Crawford

This chapter will present examples on the use of operating system features of the 80386 intended for the operating-system programmer.

Syntax

We need to present a bit more syntax of the assembly language. Most of the new constructs relate to the definition of segments.

Segment/Ends

SEGMENT and *ENDS* are assembler directives that define the beginning and end of a segment. Directives such as these do not generate any code; rather, they tell the assembler how to generate code.

USE32/USE16

USE is an assembler directive that indicates whether the contents of this segment are 31-bit or 16-bit code or data. A *USE32* segment will cause the assembler to generate code assuming the descriptor for this segment has the *D* bit equal to 1.

Note that the programmer could have made an error (the assembler does not check) and not set the *D* bit for this descriptor. In this case, the program would fail, since the code or data in this segment is of incorrect size.

---

[*] © M&T Publishing, Inc., *Dr. Dobb's Journal of Software Tools*, 1988.

AT

AT is a directive that indicates the linear address (or physical address, if paging is disabled) where this segment is to be located.

ORG

ORG is an assembler directive that defines an offset within a segment.

ASSUME

ASSUME is the final directive presented here. *ASSUME* is only meaningful for code segments. It indicates when to assume the segment register contents are within this segment. Without this directive, the assembler will issue messages warning that the addressed segment may not be currently addressable. This directive does not generate any code to load the indicated segment register with the specified segment.

Syntax Example

Below is a brief example demonstrating all the above.

```
Test_Code_Seg SEGMENT USE32 AT 0FFh
ASSUME DS:My_Segment
        MOV AX, My_Segment_Sel
        MOV DS, AX
        ; Code

        ORG 0FF0h
        ; More Code
Test_Code_Seg ENDS
```

A segment name *Test_Code_Seg* is defined by the *SEGMENT* and *ENDS* directives. It is a 31-bit segment as indicated by the *USE32* directive. The segment is located at address 0FFh in the linear (or physical) address space. The segment is assembled assuming that *DS* is addressing the segment defined as *My_Segment*, which the first two lines of the code in the segment does, in fact, load. Finally, part of the code is given an origin in the segment of 0FF0h.

Initialization Example

The first example is an initialization example that takes the machine from its reset state to a 31-bit flat machine, with paging enabled to run multiple tasks.

Overview of Example 1

Before beginning a detailed description of the code, it is helpful to first present a picture of what we want the final machine state to be. After this is presented, the details of how the machine gets into this state should be easier to understand.

This initialization example provides a simple core of an operating system. A real operating system is composed of thousands, if not millions, of lines of code (and we certainly aren't going to explain a million-line example here). Many, many things are missing, but enough of the basics remain to demonstrate most of the operating-system and multiple-segment instruction semantics.

Assumptions

We make a few assumptions about the underlying hardware.

1. The operating-system code resides in a ROM (read-only memory) in highest physical memory. The ROM is assumed to be at least 64K bytes in size (begins at FFFF0000h and ends at FFFFFFFFh).
2. RAM (random access memory) begins at address 0, and the machine has at least 48K bytes of memory. Our example does not try to figure out exactly how much memory the hardware provides (a necessary thing for a complete operating system to do). It simply assumes at least 48K bytes is present.

Other than these assumptions, the example is complete and self-contained.

Multitasking and Protection

At the conclusion of the example, the necessary operating-system tables will have been developed and a single user task will be invoked. We've taken care, however, to allow multiple tasks to be executing on this machine at one time. Two protection levels are used in the example: 0 for the operating system and 3 for the application program. The operating system, however, is typically shared by all tasks within the system. Each task has its own private code and data regions, which are stored in the local address space and so are not visible to other tasks within the system. The operating system is shared by all tasks and is therefore stored in the global address space. Figure 31-1 demonstrates this. The concentric circles represent the protection levels (we make use of only 0 and 3), and the radial lines distinguish between tasks within the system.

Figure 31-1: Multiple-Task System

```
First Task
Task 2
Task 3
Task n
Protection Level
User Code
User Data
-Data
-Stack
3
2
1
0
OS Code
OS Data
- GDT,IDT,TSS
- Page Tables
- Private Data
- Stack
```

Each radial slice of the pie indicates a task boundary. Except for the global address regions of each task's virtual address space, an address in task 1 is unrelated to an equal-value address in task 2.

Virtual Address Space

Figure 31-2 depicts the virtual address space of each task. The virtual address space is composed of the global address space mapped by the GDT and the local address space mapped by the LDT. The global address space contains five segments:

1. The GDT itself, which contains descriptors that define the other four segments in this global address space.

2. The TSS of the first task. When many tasks are executing, a TSS would be defined for each.
3. The operating-system data segment.
4. The operating-system code segment.
5. The LDT of the first task, which maps the segments in the local address space. When many tasks are executing, an LDT would be defined for each.

The local address space contains two segments.

1. The user code segment.
2. The user data segment containing data and stack.

Applications see a single-segment model containing a single data segment and a single code segment, which is mapped by the segmentation mechanism to the linear address space shown in Figure 31-2.

Figure 31-2: Virtual Address Space

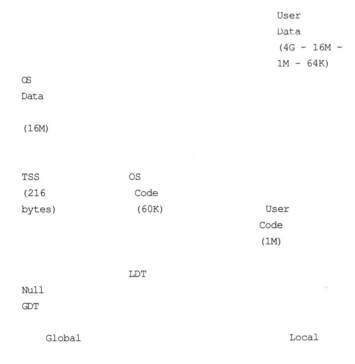

Linear Address Space

The linear address space is shown in Figure 31-3. There are four segments in the linear address space, which are described below.

Figure 31-3: Linear Address Space of Each Task

```
                          FFFFFFFFh

     16-bit OS
    Boot Code
        (4K)
                          FFFFF000h
                          FFFFEFFFh

     OS Code                           Limit =      0000Eh   G   =   1
       (60K)                           Base  =   FFFF0000h   DPL = 00b
                                       Table =         GDT   TYPE = Ah

                          FFFF0000h
                          FFFEFFFFh

    User Data
                                       Limit =      FEEEFh   G   =   1
    (4G - 16M -                        Base  =   01100000h   DPL = 11b
     1M - 64K)                         Table =         LDT   TYPE =   2


                          01100000h
                          010FFFFFh

    User Code
       (1M)                            Limit =      000FFh   G   =   1
                                       Base  =   01100000h   DPL = 11
                                       Table =         LDT   TYPE = Ah

                          01000000h
                          00FFFFFFh
```

```
OS Data
   (16M)                      Limit  =     00FFFh   G    =   1
                             Base   =  00000000h   DPL  = 00b
                             Table  =        GDT   TYPE =   2
            00000000h
```

1. Operating-system data (OS Data), a 16M segment beginning at linear address 0 and continuing to 00FFFFFFh. This segment contains the system segment tables (GDT, IDT, TSS), the page tables (directory and second-level tables), local data for the operating system, and the stack for the operating system.

2. User code, a 1M segment beginning at 01000000h and continuing to 010FFFFFh. The choice of 1M in size is arbitrary. When the task is actually loaded, the code segment size will be known exactly and the segment limit can be adjusted appropriately.

3. User data. All memory not required by the operating system or by the user's code is given to the user's program in one enormous data segment. The segment begins at linear address 01100000h and continues to FFFEFFFFh. Thus, the size of this segment is

```
4G -- 16M -- 1M -- 64K
```

   (quite a large data array indeed!). In this segment, the stack starts at the top and grows down, and the data starts at the bottom and grows up.

4. Operating-system code (OS Code). This segment begins at linear address FFFF0000h and ends at FFFEFFFFh (the top of a task's virtual memory space). The example assumes that all code within the operating system fits within a 64K ROM (not likely for a real operating system, but fine for this example).

5. The boot code segment begins at linear address FFFEFFFFh and continues to FFFFFFFFh. Thus, the upper 4K of the boot ROM are dedicated to the 16-bit start-up code. Note that this segment is not addressable in the example after protection has been enabled.

The choice of where these segments reside in the linear address space is completely arbitrary except for the boot code, which must begin at physical address FFFFFFF0h. The mapping for both the operating-system code and data are chosen so their linear and physical addresses are the same. We'll give a thorough explanation of this in the detailed discussion of the initialization code below. The linear address location of the application code and data segment is somewhat arbitrary.

Page Mapping

The linear address space—the address space after translation by the segmentation mechanism—is mapped by the page tables, as shown in Figure 31-4. The figure shows the linear address space divided into 4M regions. This is the amount of memory that is mapped by a page table (1K page entries with 4K bytes per page). Five tables with pointers from the page directory are set up. A sixth directory entry points back to the page directory itself. A directory entry pointing to the directory is a simple means of mapping the page tables back into the linear address space to allow access to them, as explained in detail below. The six-page directory entries and page tables that are set up are:

1. Common operating-system data. GDT, IDT, and TSS tables in particular.
2. Page directory and page tables.
3. Private operating-system data. Miscellaneous operating-system data and the operating-system stack.
4. User code and data.
5. User stack.
6. Operating-system code.

Figure 31-4: Page Tables Map Linear Address Space

```
                            .
              OS CODE       .   3FF
                            .
FFC00000h

                            .
              User Stack    .   3FE
                            .
FF800000h




01400000h

                            .
              User Code + Data  .   4        Page
                            .                Directory
01000000h
                            .
         Private OS Data,Stack   .   3
                            .
00C00000h
```

```
        Unallocated
00800000h
        Page Directory + Tables
00400000h
                          .
        Common OS Data    .   0
                          .

00000000h
.pa
```

Physical Address

The physical address space is given in Figure 31-5. A total of 28 pages (each page is 4K) have been allocated. The lower 12 pages are defined in the RAM area beginning at address 0, continuing up to the page starting at address 0B000h. Sixteen pages are allocated in high memory, beginning at address 0FFFF0000h. These pages match the 64K bytes ROM area in high memory exactly, which we discussed earlier in this chapter.

Figure 31-5: Physical Address Space

```
                          .
        OS CODE         .  3FF
                          .
FFC00000h
                          .
        User Stack      .  3FE
                          .
FF800000h



01400000h
                          .
        User Code + Data  .   4        Page
                          .           Directory
01000000h
                          .
        Private OS Data,Stack  .   3
                          .
00C00000h
```

```
                  Unallocated
00800000h
          Page Directory + Tables
00400000h
                                     .
          Common OS Data       .    0
                                     .
00000000h
```

Now that we've discussed both linear and physical address spaces, it is very interesting to compare them and make several observations.

1. The operating-system code region is at the high of 64K bytes in both. As the machine is being initialized, this is helpful, as we will see in the detailed code below. The code could have been at different addresses in the different address spaces, but this would have made the example more difficult to understand as well as write! This is particularly true when protection and, later, paging are enabled.

2. The GDT, IDT, TSS, and LDT tables are located at the same address in both. If this were not the case, these tables would have to be re-created or moved, and descriptors reloaded after protection was enabled and again after paging was enabled. Rather than this complication, we have kept them at the same address. Thus, we only need to load and build them once.

3. The physical addresses for the remainder of the pages do not match the linear addresses. This is done to minimize the amount of physical memory required to map the linear address space. This is one of the major benefits of paging: a linear address space that is larger than physical memory is allowed. We have, however, kept the physical pages in approximately the same order as they appear in the linear address space. Except for points 1 and 2 above, the location of the pages in physical memory is arbitrary. In fact, these pages could be moved later, as the paging mechanism replaces certain inactive pages with other active pages. Not only can we swap portions of the linear address space by paging, we can even page the page tables (this may be necessary to minimize the amount of physical memory dedicated to the operating system, since the page tables can get quite large). To page the page tables, some care has to be taken in updating the invalid page table entries and distinguishing them from simple page entries. The page directory needs to remain in the same location and must always be present. Changing the location of the page directory requires the page directory (base register R3) to be updated.

Task Switch

We do not go through the details of building and switching to a new task (such as the second task in the system), but it is helpful to point out what is needed to accomplish this.

1. An LDT needs to be built for the new task. It would be identical to the one in the example except for the different code space sizes possible. A GDT entry would have to be created for this LDT.
2. A TSS would have to be built. It is similar to the one built in the example, except that the LDT is the one described above. A GDT entry would have to be created for this TSS.
3. A page directory needs to be built. The page tables that map the global address space are identical to the first task, and these page directory entries are shared by both (and all future) tasks. The directory entries for the local page tables (user code and data and stack) are, of course, different.
4. Page tables for the local address space for the new task need to be built. They are the same as the page tables for the first task, except that they map to different physical pages.
5. To switch to the new task requires the loading of TR, LDT, and CR0.

Details of Initialization Example

With the overview of the desired final machine state given above, we are now ready to dig into the details of the example. The example in Listing 31-1 can actually be considered as many short examples that are executed in the proper sequence to form a complete initialization sequence.

Equates

The first section of the example simply defines some mnemonics for later use. All seven selectors (five in the GDT and two in the LDT) are defined. The physical addresses of all pages are also defined. Since the linear addresses and physical addresses for these tables do not all match, we define the physical address mnemonics here. Note that these physical addresses do match Figure 31-5, which shows the physical address space.

Segment Definitions

The four segments of the example are defined next (*OS_Data_Seg*, *User_Code_Seg*, *User_Data_Seg*, and *OS_Code_Seg*). These segment definitions exactly match the picture of virtual and linear address spaces given in Figures 31-2 and 31-3, respectively. The segment definitions given here enable us to use symbolic references to the segments throughout the remainder of the example. Declaring the segments in this way does not initialize these memory segments.

Also note that the *OS_Code* segment does not cover the upper 4K of memory. The upper 4K of operating-system code is contained within a separate segment (*BootRom16*). This segment is a 16-bit segment, whereas *OS_Code_Seg* is a 31-bit segment. Since the 80386 begins in a 16-bit mode of operation, we need at least a small region of code to take us from 16-bit mode into the 31-bit mode of operation. After protected mode is entered, this 16-bit segment is not addressable. The example minimizes the amount of time spent in this backward-compatible 16-bit mode of operation. The goal of minimizing 16-bit code matches the theme of the book—focus on the 31-bit 80386.

Code Sequence 1—Cold Start

At reset, the 80386 begins operation in what is termed real mode. For our purposes, real mode is simply a 16-bit machine where the maximum size of a segment is 64K bytes. In real mode, the selector is shifted left by 4 and added to the offset within the segment to form the physical address. Thus, the maximum physical address is 0FFFFFh or a total address space of 1M byte. Reference is made to the initial machine state in the following sections.

At reset, the CS register is initialized to F000h and IP is initialized to FFF0h. Thus, the first instruction fetch after reset would be done to address FFFF0h. In addition, the 80386 keeps the address bits A31 to A20 asserted such that the first instruction fetch is done to address FFFFFFF0h. So the 16-bit code segment is at address FFFFF000h and the ORG of the cold start code (JMP Start16) is to offset 0FF0h. Address bits A31 to A20 remain asserted until the first intersegment control transfer. It is common practice for machines to begin execution at the highest memory location, as the 80386 does. This allows a boot ROM to be placed in high memory.

Code Sequence 2—Miscellaneous

This sequence begins at the Start16 label. The first instruction clears the IF (interrupt enable) bit, masking all maskable interrupts. Clearing IF is not really needed, since the 80386 reset sequence clears IF also, but it is shown here for emphasis. The IDT (interrupt descriptor table) is also set to have a limit of 0. This causes any nonmaskable interrupts to generate a shutdown (discussed in Chapter 6). Since the LIDT instruction requires a memory operand, we need to first initialize the DS register to point at the *OS_Data_Seg*. Since the *DS* register is initialized to 0 and *OS_Data_Seg* is at address 0, this was not needed. But since in most cases (except a few like this one) loading a segment register is needed prior to addressing a segment, we do so here.

Table 31-1: Summary of Descriptor Contents

NAME	TABLE	LIMIT	BASE	TYPE	DT	DPL	P	D	G
Null	GDT	00000	00000000	0	0	0	0	0	0
OS Code	GDT	0000E	FFFF0000	A	1	0	1	1	1
OS Data	GDT	00FFF	00000000	2	1	0	1	1	1
User Code	LDT	000FF	00100000	A	1	3	1	1	1
User Data	LDT	FEEEF	00110000	2	1	3	1	1	1
TSS1	GDT	000D7	000000B8	9	0	0	1	0*	0
LDT1	GDT	00011	0000018F	2	0	0	1	0*	0

*Note: The *D* bit for a system segment has no meaning.

Code Sequence 3—Build GDT, LGDT

The third section of code builds the GDT (global descriptor table) and loads the GDT pseudo-descriptor into the processor. The first step is to build a pseudo-descriptor in memory. The low word is the limit of the GDT. The limit is eight times the number of GDT entries minus 1, the largest valid offset within the GDT. The upper *dword* of the pseudo-descriptor is the linear address of the GDT. This descriptor is then loaded into the processor with the LGDT instruction. The next step is to fill the GDT with the appropriate information. In the example, we have five GDT entries (*Null*, *OS Code*, *OS Data*, *LDT*, and *TSS*). Table 31-1 summarizes the contents of these five descriptors. The code shows the appropriate decomposition of this information into the descriptor format (given in Figure 5.10). Table 31-2 summarizes the descriptor types used here.

Table 31-2: Descriptor Types

```
TYPE    DT    DESCRIPTION
2       1     Memory Segment—Read/Write
A       1     Memory Segment—Execute/Read
9       0     System Segment—Available 386 TSS
2       0     System Segment—LDT
```

Code Sequence 4—Enter Protected Mode

The next step is to set the *PE* (protection enable) bit of the machine status word. After the *PE* bit is set, it is important to immediately perform a jump. This causes the on-chip prefetch and decode queues to be flushed (set to empty). This is necessary because any prefetched and predecoded information pertains to real mode, which is no longer valid. The machine is now in 16-bit protected mode. For our purposes, this mode is similar to what we have discussed so far in the book, except that all data and offsets are 16 bits.

After protected mode has been entered, a far *JMP* is executed. The *JMP* references the *OS_Code_Sel* entry of the GDT and an offset to the *Start32* location within this segment. Since the GDT entry corresponding to the *OS_Code_Sel* selector is a 31-bit code segment (as indicated by the *D* bit of the descriptor), the machine will be executing as a 31-bit machine when the call is completed.

Code Sequence 5—Load Segment Descriptors

Since the machine is now in protected mode, it is necessary to reload the segment registers to make the data segments addressable. Note the difference between the load of the DS register performed here and the one done in Code Sequence 2, when the machine was still in real mode. In the load of the DS register in real mode, the selector value loaded into DS is simply shifted left by 4 and added to the offset to form the final physical address. Now that we have enabled protected mode, loading a selector into DS causes the descriptor given in the GDT to be loaded. The selector is also loaded into ES for use by string instructions. SS will be loaded with this selector later.

Code Sequence 6—Build LDT, LLDT

The local address space of the task is mapped by the LDT (local descriptor table). The LDT contains two entries, one for the user code segment and one for the user data segment, as seen in Figure 31-2. When the GDT was built, an LDT entry was included that defined an LDT of two entries. The LDT segment is defined as a piece of the *OS_Data* segment. The initialization example uses alias locations in the *OS_Data* segment to access the LDT, while the 80386 uses the actual LDT segment. The first part of this example fills this LDT with the appropriate information for these two segments (user code and data). The code shows the appropriate decomposition of the descriptor information into the descriptor format. Table 31-2 summarizes the descriptor information for the two segments mapped by the LDT. After the LDT is built, the selector for the LDT is loaded into the LDTR.

Much of the protected model initialization (GDT, IDT, TSS) can be done either before or after entering protected mode. Since our goal was to minimize the amount of 16-bit code written, all of these except for the GDT are done after entering protected mode. Since loading of the LDTR can only be done in protected mode, we did not have a choice where to perform it.

Code Sequence 7—Build IDT

A very important part of initialization is building the IDT (interrupt descriptor table). In our example, after user mode (level 3) execution begins, the only way for the task to access the operating-system services is via the exception processing mechanism. Gates allow levels of lesser privilege to access levels of greater privilege, but we have defined no gates in our example. Also, any normal exception processing services by either the application program or the operating system, such as a demand page fault handler, require the appropriate IDT entries to be present.

The IDT entries themselves are interrupt gates. Since in our flat machine model the entire operating system is visible to the current task, we need not use a task gate for the IDT entries. The basic contents of our interrupt gate descriptor are summarized in the following table. If an exception or interrupt is taken from level 3, a privilege-level change to level 0 will occur. Each protection level (0-n-3) has a separate stack. Thus, as part of the transition from level 3 to 0, the stack is switched to the level 0 stack.

```
Field          Value
Offset         offset Default_Hand
Selector       OS_Code_Sel

DwordCount     0, copy no parameters
Type           E, 386 Interrupt Gate
DPL            0
```

Aliases in the *OS_Data* segment are used to access the IDT. Initially, all 17 interrupt gates are filled with the same information. These 17 interrupt levels are those predefined by the 80386, and we don't define any additional ones at this point. After the 17 descriptors have been set to the default, we explicitly replace this information for interrupts that have specific handlers provided for them by the operating system. In this way, many interrupts that the operating system has no interest in distinguishing between go to the same default handler. The exception handlers given at the start of the *OS_Code_Seg* are obviously trivial, and are for the purpose of demonstrating the declaration of an exception handler. A more elaborate example of an exception handler (a coprocessor device not available—exception 7) is the subject of the second example in this chapter.

Code Sequence 8—Build Page Directory

Now that the segmentation model is built, we are ready to begin setting up the paging mechanism of the 80386. As discussed in Chapter 5, the paging mechanism has two levels of memory-resident translation tables: the page directory and page tables. This code sequence discusses building the page directory, and the following section discusses building the individual page tables.

Each entry (of the 1024 possible) in the page directory points to a page table. Since each page table has 1024 entries, each pointing to a 4096-byte page, each page directory entry is mapping up to 4M of memory. If the page directory entry is marked not present, the entire 4M linear address space is not present (unmapped). The first step of this code sequence in building the page directory marks all tables not present (bit 0 of each entry is the *P* or present bit, which is set to 0). Each page directory entry that is to map a valid section of the linear address space is then updated with the pertinent information. This information is:

1. Present bit (=1).
2. User/supervisor privilege level.
3. Read/write.
4. Physical address of the page table this entry points to.

All entries are marked supervisor read-only except the user code, and data and user stack directories, which are marked user-writable. The page table address inserted into each of these is the physical address of the page table.

The second page table entry is particularly interesting. This directory entry points to the directory itself. This may seem a bit confusing at first, but this is a convenient means to map the page directory and page tables into the linear address space. Figure 31-6 demonstrates this. Page directory entry 0000000001b points to the page directory.

Figure 31-6: Page Directory Pointing to Self

```
        Linear Address
31          22 21          12 11        2              .
   3h               0h          10h                    .
                                                       .
                                                    10h
                                                    Ch
                                                    8h
                                                    4h
                                                    0h
                                           .
                                           .
                                           .
                                        0

                         .
                         .
                         .
                         3
                         2
                         1
Page                     0
Directory

        Linear Address
31          22 21        12 11          2
   1h             3h          0h
                                           .
                                           .
                                           .
                                        0

                       .
                       .
                       .
                       3
                       2
                       1
```

```
                            0
Page
Directory


        Linear Address
31          22 21      12 11         2
    1h             1h         3h


                                    .
                                    .
                                    .
                                    3
                                    2
                                    1
                                    0
Page
Directory
```

A linear address of:

```
    31                  22 21                12 11                  0
    +------------------+------------------+----------------------+
    |0 0 0 0 0 0 0 1 1|0 0 0 0 0 0 0 0 0|0 0 0 0 0 0 1 0 0 0 0|
    
    +------------------+------------------+----------------------+
```

is a normal access through page directory entry 3, through page table 0 to address 10h within this page, as is seen in the first part of Figure 31-6.

The second example:

```
    31                  22 21                12 11                  0
    +------------------+------------------+----------------------+
    |0 0 0 0 0 0 0 0 1|0 0 0 0 0 0 0 1 1|0 0 0 0 0 0 0 0 0 0 0|
    +------------------+------------------+----------------------+
```

will access the second entry (*dword*) in page table 3, as seen in the second part of Figure 31-6.

The third example:

```
31                    22 21               12 11                     0
+------------------+------------------+---------------------+
|0 0 0 0 0 0 0 0 1|0 0 0 0 0 0 0 0 1|0 0 0 0 0 0 0 1 1 0 0|
+------------------+------------------+---------------------+
```

will access the fourth entry (*dword*) in the page directory, as seen in the third part of Figure 31-6.

Code Sequence 9—Build Page Tables

After the page directory is built, tables need to be built for each valid page directory. As was the case for building the directory, the first thing to do is fill the entire table with not-present entries and then selectively insert valid entries into the tables. As discussed above, making the linear address space identical to the physical is an important consideration in building the page table. At this point, we need to keep the following addresses the same in the linear and physical address spaces:

1. The operating-system code executing out of ROM, 16 pages starting at physical address FFFF0000h, FFFF1000h ... FFFFF0000h, are given identical locations in the linear and physical address spaces. Otherwise, a *magic jump* will be executed when paging is enabled. *Magic* means that the next instruction will be fetched from the linear address that maps to a different physical address than the one prior to enabling paging.

2. GDT, IDT, and TSS, the page beginning at physical address 00000000h, is given the same linear address. Otherwise, we need to reload these registers and rebuild the associated tables.

Refer to Figure 31-5 (the physical address space) and compare the page table entries that are filled to the allocated pages in the figure. Table 31-3 summarizes the pages allocated and the access allowed to them.

Code Sequence 10—Enable Paging

The page directory and tables are ready. All that is needed to enable paging is to set the PG bit of CR0. After paging is enabled, it is important to perform a jump that will flush both the prefetch queue and the instruction decode queue. As was the case when protection was being enabled above, the information in these queues was prefetched and decoded when paging was disabled and is no longer valid.

Code Sequence 11— Load Operating-System Stack Pointer

This code segment simply loads the operating-system stack pointer. Each protection level (0-n-3) has a different stack. Since our example only uses levels 0 and 3, only two stacks are required. Note the use of the LSS instruction. LSS avoids any of the difficulties that may arise when SS and ESP are loaded separately. In this case, interrupts are disabled and no possible exceptions can occur, so using LSS would not be needed. Nevertheless, it is good practice to always use LSS rather than two separate instructions.

Table 31-3: Allocated Pages

DIRECTORY ENTRY	TABLE ENTRY	USER	WRITE	COMMENT
0	0	No	No	IDT, GDT, TSS
1	1	No	No	Page Directory
1	0	No	No	Page Table 0
1	3	No	No	Page Table 3
1	4	No	No	Page Table 4
1	3FEh	No	No	Page Table 3FE
1	3FFh	No	No	Page Table 3FF
3	0	No	No	OS Private Data
3	3FFh	No	No	OS Stack
4	0	Yes	No	User Code
4	100h	Yes	Yes	User Data
3FEh	3FFh	Yes	Yes	User Stack
3FFh	3F0-n-3FFh	No	No	OS Code

Code Sequence 12—Build TSS

During privilege-level changes or task switches, the TSS will be referenced to retrieve or store information for later use. For example, the first exception (maybe a page fault, for instance) will require a privilege-level transition from 3 (the user level) to 0 (the operating-system level). As part of this change, stacks will be changed. The 80386 expects to find the level 0 stack selector and offset at the appropriate locations in the TSS. The only information we need to put in the TSS is:

1. Level 0 stack offset
2. Level 0 stack selector
3. Page directory base *(CR3)*
4. LDT

The TR (task register) is then loaded to make the TSS visible to the processor.

Also note that the TSS has room allocated for a floating-point state. The uppermost byte of TSS is set to 0 to indicate this task has not yet used the coprocessor.

Load User Task

Almost all aspects of initialization are now complete, and we are ready to load the user's task. The example assumes the existence of a procedure *loader*, which takes the selectors for the code segment and data segment for the task. The loader routine will then read the code and data for the task from disk (for instance) into memory. Since the task may be quite large, the first page of code and data are loaded into memory while the rest of the task is kept in virtual storage on the swapping disk until the appropriate page faults force them to be read into memory. The loader routine returns the offset of the start of the task (the first instruction to be executed in the task) in the EAX register.

When the local descriptors were built (Code Sequence 6), we arbitrarily made the user code area 1M in size and gave the rest of memory (most of the 4G of linear address space) to the user data area. The loader would readjust the *User_Code_Seg* limit and *User_Data_Seg* base appropriately, as the task was loaded.

Prepare for User Task Invocation

Calls to outer levels are not allowed. Instead, returns are done to outer levels. Thus, we put an image on the stack composed of

```
&B Stack selector
&B Stack offset
```

```
&B Flags
&B Code selector
&B Code offset (returned by loader)
```

for the user task. When a subsequent *IRET* is done, it will return to the user program at level 3 to begin execution of the first user task of the system. Note that interrupts are enabled by setting the *IF* bit in the flags image on the stack. As part of the *IRET*, interrupts will be enabled, not prematurely as would be the case if a STI would be executed while still in the operating-system code.

Invoke User Task

Finally, we reach the magic *IRET*. The first user-level task is invoked, and our example is complete. The *IRET* will retrieve the information just pushed onto the stack and change machine state appropriately. In this case, the protection level, stack, *CS:EIP*, and flags are changed.

Listing 31-1: Initialization Code

```
; *************************************************************
; * Take the machine from its reset state to completely
; * initialized as a flat machine and invoke the first
; * user task. Major portions of this program are building the
; * appropriate segmentation tables and building the paging
; * tables.
; *
; * The example is composed of 15 steps:
; * 1)   Boot Address cold start
; * 2)   Misc: Disable interrupts, load DS, null IDTR
; * 3)   Build GDT, LGDT
; * 4)   Enter protected mode/32b code
; * 5)   Load segment registers
; * 6)   Build LDT, LLDT
; * 7)   Build IDT, LIDT
; * 8)   Build page directory
; * 9)   Build page tables
; * 10) Enable paging
; * 11) Load OS stack
; * 12) Build TSS, LTR
; * 13) Load user task
; * 14) Prepare for user task invocation
; * 15) Invoke user task!
; *********************************************************************

; Miscellaneous Constants
IDT_Entries     EQU     17
GDT_Entries     EQU     5        ; Null, OS Data, LDT
```

```
                                 ; OS Code, TSS
        LDT_Entries     EQU     2        ; User Code, User Data

        Page_Size       EQU     4096
        Page_Entries    EQU     1024
        Not_Present     EQU     0
        PE              EQU     1
        PG              EQU     80000000h
        Int_Flag        EQU     0200h

        ; GDT Selectors
        Null            EQU     0h
        OS_Code_Sel     EQU     8h       ; 1,GDT,RPL=00
        OS_Data_Sel     EQU     10h      ; 2,GDT,RPL=00
        LDT1_Sel        EQU     18h      ; 3,GDT,RPL=00
        TSS1_Sel        EQU     20h      ; 4,GDT,RPL=00

        ; LDT Selectors
        User_Code_Sel   EQU     7h       ; 0,LDT,RPL=11
        User_Data_Sel   EQU     0Fh      ; 1,LDT,RPL=11

        ; Physical Address Constants. Use these to initialize
        ; the page tables.
        P_OS_GData      EQU     0000h
        P_Page_Dir      EQU     1000h

        P_Page_Tab0     EQU     2000h
        P_Page_Tab3     EQU     3000h
        P_Page_Tab4     EQU     4000h
        P_Page_Tab3FE   EQU     5000h
        P_Page_Tab3FF   EQU     6000h
        P_OS_PData      EQU     7000h
        P_OS_Stack      EQU     8000h
        P_User_Code     EQU     9000h
        P_User_Data     EQU     A000h
        P_User_Stack    EQU     B000h

        TSS_Size        EQU     104  ; Minimum TSS size
        FP_Save         EQU     112  ; Save area is 108+4 (extra
                                     ; word for flag that FP used)

        ; *********************
        ; *********************
        ; ** OS Data Segment **
        ; *********************
        ; *********************
        ; Contains the segmentation and paging tables.
        OS_Data_Seg     SEGMENT  USE32  AT 00000000h

        ; IDT_Table at Offset 0, GDT immediately above it,
        ; TSS immediately above GDT, LDT immediately
        ; above TSS.
        IDT_Table       db IDT_Entries DUP ( 8 DUP(?))
        GDT_Table       db GDT_Entries DUP ( 8 DUP(?))
        TSS1_Table      db (TSS_Size+FP_Save) DUP (?)
        LDT1_Table      db LDT_Entries DUP ( 8 DUP(?))
```

```
; *****
; ** Page Directory and Page tables area. 4M linear space for
; ** full directory and tables.
; *****
ORG              00400000h               ; Linear Address
Page_Dir        db Page_Size DUP(?)
Page_Tab0       db Page_Size DUP(?)      ; OS Common Data
                                         ;     (IDT, GDT, TSS)
Page_Tab3       db Page_Size DUP(?)      ; OS Private (stack)
Page_Tab4       db Page_Size DUP(?)      ; User Code and Data
Page_Tab3FE     db Page_Size DUP(?)      ; User Stack
Page_Tab3FF     db Page_Size DUP(?)      ; OS Code

; *****
; * OS data. 4M linear space. Not used in example.
; *****
ORG     0800000h


; *****
; ** OS data. 4M linear space for data and stack private to OS.
; *****
ORG     0C00000H        ; Linear Address
Unshared_OS_Data        dd      ?

; Unshared OS Data Area, Temps, etc.
temp    db      10 dup (?)
fptss   dw      ?

; *****
; ** OS Stack.
; *****
ORG             0FFFFFCh        ; Top of OS stack
Top_OS_Stack    dd      ?
OS_Data_Seg     ENDS

; **********************
; **********************
; ** User Code Segment **
; **********************
; **********************
User_Code_Seg  SEGMENT USE32 AT 1000000h
  ; Start of User's code segment in linear address space.
  ; Define a 1Me region
User_Code_Seg  ENDS

; **********************
; **********************
; ** User Data Segment **
; **********************
; **********************
User_Data_Seg  SEGMENT USE32 AT 1100000h
  ; Start of User's code segment in linear address space.
  ; The rest of memory (enormous) is defined for user data.
  ORG 0FEEEFFFCh
  Top_User_Stack    dd ?
```

```
User_Data_Seg  ENDS

; ****************************
; ****************************
; ** 31-bit OS Code Segment **
; ****************************
; ****************************
; 31-bit OS code.
OS_Code_Seg Segment EO   USE32 AT 0FFFF0000h
ASSUME DS:OS_Data_Seg,ES:OS_Data_Seg,CS:OS_Code_Seg

Default_Hand:
        ; < Default Handler Code >
        IRET
DNA_Hand:
        ; < DNA Handler Code: Example 2 >
        IRET
Page_Fault_Hand:
        ; < Page Fault Handler Code >
        IRET
Debug_Hand:
        ; < Debug Handler Code >
        IRET


Start32:

    MOV fptss, 0  ; This is discussed in Example 2.

    ; *****
    ; ** [5] Make OS_Data segment addressable by loading
    ; ** it into DS and ES segment registers.
    ; *****
        MOV AX, OS_Data_Sel
        MOV DS, AX
        MOV ES, AX

    ; *****
    ; ** [6] Build LDT, LLDT
    ; *****
        MOV EAX, offset LDT1_Table
        ; entry 0 --> User Code Descriptor
        ; Base=00100000h, Limit=000FFh,G=1,D=1,Type=A,DPL=3
        MOV word ptr [EAX],0000Fh      ; Limit[15..0]
        MOV word ptr [EAX+2],0000h     ; Base[15..0]
        MOV byte ptr [EAX+4],000h      ; Base[23..16]
        MOV byte ptr [EAX+5],0FAh      ; Type = data
                                       ; descriptor,DPL=11
        MOV byte ptr [EAX+6],0CFh      ; G,D,Limit[19..16]
        MOV byte ptr [EAX+7],01h       ; Base[31..24]
        ADD EAX,8

        ; entry 1 --> User Data Descriptor
        ; Base=00110000h, Limit=FEEEFh,G=1,D=1,Type=A,DPL=3
        MOV word ptr [EAX],0FEEEh      ; Limit[15..0]
        MOV word ptr [EAX+2],0000h     ; Base[15..0]
```

```
        MOV byte ptr [EAX+4],010h     ; Base[23..16]
        MOV byte ptr [EAX+5],0F2h     ; Type = data
                                      ; descriptor, DPL=11
        MOV byte ptr [EAX+6],0CFh     ; G,D,Limit[19..16]
        MOV byte ptr [EAX+7],01h      ; Base[31..24]

        MOV AX, LDT1_Sel
        LLDT AX

; *****
; ** [7] Build IDT
; *****
        ; load IDT
        MOV word ptr [offset temp],(IDT_Entries * 8 - 1)
        MOV dword ptr [(offset temp) + 2], offset IDT_Table
        LIDT pword ptr temp

        ; Fill in first 16 entries in IDT. First fill with the
        ; Default Handler, then come back and update.
        MOV EAX, offset IDT_Table
        MOV word ptr [EAX], (offset Default_Hand _AND 0FFFFh)
        MOV word ptr [EAX+2], OS_Code_Sel
        MOV byte ptr [EAX+4], 00h          ; WordCnt=0
        MOV byte ptr [EAX+5], 8Eh          ; Type=E, DPL=00

        MOV word ptr [EAX+6],
                ((offset Default_Hand _SHR 16) _AND 0FFFFh)
        ; Now that one is built, copy into rest.
        MOV ESI, offset IDT_Table
        MOV EDI, (offset IDT_Table + 8)
        MOV ECX, (IDT_Entries-1)*2
        REP MOVSD

        ; Now come back and fill nondefault pointers.
        ; entry  1: Debugger
        MOV EAX, (offset IDT_Table + (1 * 8))
        MOV word ptr [EAX], (offset Debug_Hand _AND 0FFFFh)
        MOV word ptr [EAX+6],
                ((offset Debug_Hand _SHR 16) _AND 0FFFFh)

        ; entry 7: Device Not Available
        MOV EAX, (offset IDT_Table + ( 7 * 8))
        MOV word ptr [EAX], (offset DNA_Hand _AND 0FFFFh)
        MOV word ptr [EAX+6],
                ((offset DNA_Hand _SHL 16) _AND 0FFFFh)

        ; entry 15: Page fault handler
        MOV EAX, (offset IDT_Table + (15 * 8))
        MOV word ptr [EAX], (offset Page_Fault_Hand _AND 0FFFFh)
        MOV word ptr [EAX+6],
                ((offset Page_Fault_Hand _SHR 16) _AND 0FFFFh)

; *****
; ** [8] Build Page Directory
; *****
        MOV EAX,Not_Present
```

```
        MOV ECX,Page_Entries
        CLD
        MOV EDI,P_Page_Dir
        REP STOSD              ; mark entire directory not present

        ; Entry 0: OS Shared Data Table, No user-level access.
        ; Locate at 0 so linear=physical and the loaded GDT, IDT,
        ; TR, are still valid after paging is enabled.
        MOV dword ptr [P_Page_Dir +    0],
             ((P_Page_Tab0 _AND 0FFFFF000h) _OR 001h)

        ; Entry 1: Pointer to Directory, No user-level access.
        ; This maps the PageDir and PageTables into the linear
        ; address space.
        MOV dword ptr [P_Page_Dir +    4],
             ((P_Page_Dir _AND 0FFFFF000h) _OR 001h)

        ; Entry 3: OS Private Data Table. No user-level access.
        MOV dword ptr [P_Page_Dir +    12],
             ((P_Page_Tab3 _AND 0FFFFF000h) _OR 001h)

        ; Entry 4: User code and Data
        MOV dword ptr [P_Page_Dir +    16],
             ((P_Page_Tab4 _AND 0FFFFF000h) _OR 007h)


        ; Entry 3FE: User Stack, put at highest area of user
        ; data space.
        MOV dword ptr [P_Page_Dir + 4088],
             ((P_Page_Tab3FE _AND 0FFFFF000h) _OR 007h)

        ; Entry 3FF: OS Shared Code Table, User level read only
        ; It is very important this entry is at high memory to map
        ; to the same address as is currently being executed.
        MOV dword ptr [P_Page_Dir + 4092 ],
             ((P_Page_Tab3FF _AND 0FFFFF00h) _OR 001h)

; *****
; ** [9] Build Tables: Directory has been built, now we must
; ** build each page table.
; *****
        ; Page Table 0: OS common data
        ; First thing is to clear entire table.
        MOV EAX, Not_Present
        MOV ECX, Page_Entries
        CLD
        MOV EDI, P_Page_Tab0
        REP STOSD
        ; Now allocate page for IDT, GDT, TSS, ...
        MOV dword ptr [ P_Page_Tab0 + 0000h],
             (P_OS_GData _AND 0FFFFF000h) _OR 001h)

        ; Page Table 3: OS private data
        ; First thing is to clear entire table.
        MOV EAX, Not_Present
        MOV ECX, Page_Entries
```

```
    CLD
    MOV EDI, P_Page_Tab3
    REP STOSD
    ; Allocate pages for private data and OS stack.
    MOV dword ptr [ P_Page_Tab3 + 0000h],
            (P_OS_PData _AND 0FFFFF000h) _OR 001h)
    MOV dword ptr [ P_Page_Tab3 + 0FFCh],
            (P_OS_Stack _AND 0FFFFF000h) _OR 001h)


    ; Page Table 4: User code, data and stack
    ; First thing is to clear entire table.
    MOV EAX, Not_Present
    MOV ECX, Page_Entries
    CLD
    MOV EDI, P_Page_Tab4
    REP STOSD
    ; Allocate pages for user code and data.
    MOV dword ptr [ P_Page_Tab4 + 0000 ],      ; User Code
            (P_User_Code _OR 005h)
    MOV dword ptr [ P_Page_Tab4 + 1024 ],      ; User Data
            (P_User_Data _OR 007h)


    ; Page Table 3FE: User Stack
    ; First thing is to clear entire table.

    MOV EAX, Not_Present
    MOV ECX, Page_Entries
    CLD
    MOV EDI, P_Page_Tab3FE
    REP STOSD
    ; Allocate page for user stack: highest linear address.
    MOV dword ptr [ P_Page_Tab3FE + 4092 ],    ; User Stack
            (P_User_Stack _OR 007h)


    ; Page Table 3FFH: OS code. All pages are readable to
    ; user, the upper 64K of memory are mapped such that
    ; physical and linear address match.
    MOV EAX, 0FFFFF005h        ; highest PTE,
    MOV ECX, Page_Size
    LoopTop:
        SUB ECX, 4
        MOV dword ptr [ECX + P_Page_Tab3FF], EAX
        SUB EAX, 1000H
        cmp ECX, 4032
        JNZ LoopTop

; *****
; ** [10] Enable Paging
; *****
    MOV EAX, P_Page_Dir
    MOV CR3, EAX
    MOV EAX, CR0
    OR  EAX, PG
    MOV CR0, EAX
    JMP pflush
  pflush:
```

```
; *****
; ** [11] Load the OS Stack pointer
; *****
    MOV dword ptr [offset temp + 0],offset Top_OS_stack
    MOV word  ptr [offset temp + 4],OS_Data_Sel
    LSS ESP,pword ptr temp

; *****
; ** [12] Build TSS. Only load up the parts referenced
; ** by OS. All other parts are written over on first
; ** transition to inner-level or unneeded. Also load
; ** the task register.
; *****
    ; Level 0 stack offset
    MOV dword ptr [offset TSS1_Table +  4 ],
            offset Top_OS_stack
    ; Level 0 stack selector
    MOV dword ptr [offset TSS1_Table +  8 ],OS_Data_Sel
    ; CR3
    MOV EAX, CR3
    MOV dword ptr [offset TSS1_Table + 1Ch],eax
    ; LDT
    MOV dword ptr [offset TSS1_Table + 60h],0

    MOV AX, TSS1_Sel
    LTR AX
    ; Floating-point Byte Flag
    MOV byte ptr [offset TSS1_Table +
                    (TSS_Size + FP_Save - 1)], 0
; *****
; ** [13] Load User Task
; *****
    MOV EAX, User_Code_Sel  ; Selector for user code
    MOV ECX, User_Data_Sel  ; Selector for user data
    ; The loader will fetch the first user task from disk
    ; and load it into the locations as specified by the
    ; selectors passed to it. The loader routine returns
    ; the offset of the start of the user task in the EAX
    ; register.
    CALL loader

; *****
; ** [14] Prepare for user task invocation. Push user's
; ** SS:ESP, push the flags, push the CS:EIP, and IRET
; ** will invoke the user code.
; *****
    MOV  ECX, User_Data_Sel ; Stack for user routine,
                            ; as data selector.
    PUSH ECX
                            ; Stack pointer for user.
    MOV  ECX, offset Top_User_Stack
    PUSH ECX

    PUSHF
                            ; Set IF on the stack
    OR SS: dword ptr [ESP],Int_Flag
```

```
        MOV ECX, User_Code_Sel   ; Code Segment of user routine
        PUSH ECX
        PUSH EAX                  ; Offset to start in user task

; *****
; ** [15] Invoke user task
; *****

        ; The magic IRET, switch to user routine as indicated
        ; on the stack.
        IRET

OS_Code_Seg     ENDS

; 16-bit OS code.
BootRom16  Segment EO   USE16 AT 0FFFFF000h
Start16:
    ; *****
    ; ** [2] Misc: CLI, DS, null IDT
    ; *****
        CLI                      ; disable interrupts
        MOV AX, OS_Data_Seg      ; initial Data segment

        MOV DS, AX

        ;  Set up empty IDT, will cause shutdown on any interrupts.
        MOV  word ptr [offset IDT_Table],0
                            ; set up for zero limit IDT,Base
        MOV  dword ptr [offset IDT_Table+2],0
        LIDT pword ptr [offset IDT_Table]

    ; *****
    ; ** [3] Set up GDT
    ; *****
                            ; set up GDT limit
        MOV  word ptr  [offset GDT_Table],(GDT_Entries*8 - 1)
                            ; set up GDT Base
        MOV  dword ptr [offset GDT_Table+2],offset GDT_Table
        LGDT pword ptr [offset GDT_Table]
        MOV EAX, offset GDT_Table
        ; entry 0 --> Null
        MOV dword ptr [EAX],0
        MOV dword ptr [EAX+4],0
        ADD EAX,8

        ; entry 1 --> OS Code Descriptor
        ; Base=FFFF0000h, Limit=0000Eh,G=1,D=1,Type=A,DPL=0
        MOV word ptr [EAX],0000Eh    ; Limit[15..0]
        MOV word ptr [EAX+2],0000h   ; Base[15..0]
        MOV byte ptr [EAX+4],0FFh    ; Base[23..16]
        MOV byte ptr [EAX+5],09Ah    ; Type = code
                                     ; descriptor, DPL=0
        MOV byte ptr [EAX+6],0C0h    ; G,D,Limit[19..16]
        MOV byte ptr [EAX+7],0FFh    ; Base[31..24]
        ADD EAX,8
```

```
        ; entry 2 --> OS Data Descriptor
        ; Base=00000000h, Limit=00FFFh,G=1,D=1,Type=9,DPL=0
        ; Map entire data space into OS Address Space --> this gives
        ; access to memory to load user task for instance.
        MOV word ptr [EAX],000FFh      ; Limit[15..0]
        MOV word ptr [EAX+2],0000h     ; Base[15..0]
        MOV byte ptr [EAX+4],00h       ; Base[23..16]
        MOV byte ptr [EAX+5],092h      ; Type = data
                                       ; descriptor, DPL=0
        MOV byte ptr [EAX+6],0CFh      ; G,D,Limit[19..16]
        MOV byte ptr [EAX+7],00h       ; Base[31..24]
        ADD EAX,8

        ; entry 3 --> LDT
        ; Base=(offset LDT1_Table), Limit=(LDT_Entries * 8),
        ; G=0, Type=LDT, DPL=00
        MOV word ptr [EAX],            ; Limit[15..0]
              (LDT_Entries * 8 - 1)
        MOV word ptr [EAX+2],          ; Base[15..0]
              (offset LDT1_Table _AND 0FFFFh)
        MOV byte ptr [EAX+4],          ; Base[23..16]
              ((offset LDT1_Table _SHR 16) _AND 0FFh)

        MOV byte ptr [EAX+5],082h      ; Type=LDT
        MOV byte ptr [EAX+6],000h      ; Limit[19..16]
        MOV byte ptr [EAX+7],          ; Base[31..24]
              ((offset LDT1_Table _SHR 24) _AND 0FFh)

        ; entry 4 --> TSS for this task
        ; Base=(offset TSS1_Table), Limit=(TSS_Size + FP_Save),
        ; G=0, Type=Available 386 TSS, DPL=00
        MOV word ptr [EAX],            ; Limit[15..0]
              (TSS_Size + FP_Save - 1)
        MOV word ptr [EAX+2],          ; Base[15..0]
              (offset TSS1_Table _AND 0FFFFh)
        MOV byte ptr [EAX+4],          ; Base[23..16]
              ((offset TSS1_Table _SHR 16) _AND 0FFh)
        MOV byte ptr [EAX+5],089h      ; Type=Available 386 TSS
        MOV byte ptr [EAX+6],000h      ; Limit[19..16]
        MOV byte ptr [EAX+7],          ; Base[31..24]
              ((offset TSS1_Table _SHR 24) _AND 0FFh)
; *****
; ** [4] Enter Protected Mode
; *****
        SMSW AX
        OR   AX,PE
        LMSW AX                        ; Set protection enable bit
        JMP  Flush
    Flush:
        JMP far ptr Start32            ; Jump through GDT to 31-bit
                                       ; OS code.
; *****
; ** [1] Cold Start Code!
; *****
        ORG 00FF0h
```

```
        JMP Start16
BootRom16 ENDS
```

Coprocessor Exception Handler

The second example is a coprocessor *Device Not Available* (DNA) exception handler. This example is an extension of the first. The exception handler is given in Listing 31-2.

Overview of Example 2

This example will demonstrate the details of a fault handler and specifically the coprocessor device not available handler. A device not available exception level 7 can be generated for any of the following reasons.

1. A floating-point instruction is executed and the *EM* bit in control register CR0 is a 1. *EM* indicates that a math coprocessor is to be emulated.
2. A floating-point instruction is executed and the *TS* bit in control register CR0 is a 1. TS indicates the fast task-switch mode discussed below.
3. A *WAIT* instruction is executed and both the *TS* and *MP* bits in CR0 are 1.

In our example, we deal with the fast task-switch mode. If the system is to emulate the coprocessor, a simple call to the routine *DNA_Emulate* is done. It is the responsibility of this routine to emulate the operation of the coprocessor.

The fast task-switch mode is an optimization that allows the state of the coprocessor to be saved only when it is accessed by a task. If most tasks in the system do not use the coprocessor, this can be a large benefit, since unloading and reloading the coprocessor state is quite time-consuming.

When a DNA exception occurs, the coprocessor device not available handler would be called. This handler is written to be inserted directly into the first example of this chapter, the initialization example. In fact, you could insert the DNA handler exactly at the location in the first example seen as:

```
    Several items are assumed (Example 1 meets these assumptions):
    1 - FPTSS is a selector of the TSS of the most recent task
        that used the coprocessor (e.g., the state is still in the
```

the coprocessor from this task). If none, it is 0.

2 - The TSS has an area immediately above the minimal TSS, that holds the floating-point state.

3 - The floating-point state area of the TSS is 108 (normal save area) plus 4 bytes. The highest addressed byte is a flag, indicating if the task has coprocessor state (0 indicates no state).

Several items in the first example are exclusively for the purpose of this example. For instance, the TSS has enough space allocated in it to allow the floating-point state to be stored into it.

On an exception, if a task had been using the coprocessor, the coprocessor state is stored into the TSS of the task using it (if there was one). The current task's coprocessor state (if it already made use of it) is then loaded into the coprocessor. The operating system keeps a variable containing the base of the TSS of the last task using the coprocessor. This is updated as part of loading the coprocessor with its new state. Throughout this example, interrupt latency is a concern, and will be further discussed below.

Details of Exception Handler

Before anything else is done, interrupts are enabled. Since loading and storing coprocessor state can take a while, we will disable interrupts only when absolutely needed. Interrupts need to be enabled, since all the handlers from the first example are interrupt gates that disable interrupts as they are taken.

Code Sequence 1—Emulation

If the exception was caused by the *EM* bit being set in CR0, the emulator is called. An emulator is not part of the example. After emulation, simply return.

Code Sequence 2—Current Task Base

The *fptss* variable contains the selector for the TSS of the task whose state is currently in the coprocessor. The coprocessor state is stored in the upper part of the TSS. Thus, we need to determine the selector and the base of the current task's TSS. This is done rather nicely by working backward, beginning at the TR. The TR gives the selector for the current TSS, accessing the GDT and unscrambling the base from the descriptor. The selector is kept in SI and the base in ECX for future use.

Code Sequence 3—Save Old State

The initialization sequence clears the *fptss* variable to 0. This is done to indicate that no task has yet used the coprocessor. If this is the case, the current coprocessor state need not be stored anywhere, and the coprocessor will be initialized with the *FNINIT* instruction below. If *fptss* was not zero, the coprocessor state is stored into the TSS of the old task at the appropriate location. As above, this location is determined by following the *fptss* selector to determine the base of the TSS. Another optimization is if the last task to use the coprocessor is the current task. If this is the case, do nothing and return.

Code Sequence 4—Load New State

While the new state is being loaded into the coprocessor, it is necessary to disable interrupts, since the machine is not in a valid state. Consider the case when the coprocessor state has been stored into the prior task's TSS and the state for the new task is loaded into the coprocessor, but *fptss* has not yet been updated. In this case, the coprocessor state and *fptss* are inconsistent. If an interrupt were taken at this point, a subsequent invocation of this fault handler (prior to return to this invocation) could corrupt the old task's coprocessor state.

It is unfortunate that interrupts are disabled during the loading of a new coprocessor state: interrupt latency suffers, since the *FRSTOR* instruction is very long. You can avoid the disabling of interrupts throughout this instruction, but you'd need two semaphores, and the exception handler becomes much trickier to write. Rather than complicate this example handler to the point of being unintelligible, this exercise is left to the interested and able reader.

The highest byte in the coprocessor state portion of the TSS is a byte indicating that the coprocessor state has been saved in this TSS. The part of the operating system that initiates tasks takes care to zero this byte (we did so in our initialization example). If this byte is 0, the coprocessor state need not be restored from the current task, as the current task has never used the coprocessor and the coprocessor is simply reset by the *FNINIT* instruction. If this byte is 1, this task has state to be loaded into the coprocessor. Finally, the *fptss* variable is updated, and the highest byte of the TSS coprocessor state is set to 1 to indicate the new status of the coprocessor and this task's use of it.

Listing 31-2: Device Not Available Exception Handler

```
DNA_Hand:
        STI
    ; *****
    ; * [1] Determine if fault is caused by Emulation
    ; *****
        ; Remember CR0 layout:    3
        ;                         1 ... 4 3 2 1 0
        ;                         P     E T E M P
        ;                         G     T S M P E
        MOV  EAX, CR0
        BT   EAX, 2
        JNC  DNA_Task_Ex
        CALL DNA_Emulate
        IRET


    ; *****
    ; * [2] Determine current task TSS base
    ; *****
DNA_Task_Ex:
        XOR  ESI,ESI
        STR  SI          ; ESI holds TSS selector of current task
        MOV  ECX,[ESI + offset GDT_Table + 0]
        MOV  EDX,[ESI + offset GDT_Table + 4]
        SHRD ECX,EDX,16
        AND  ECX,000FFFFFFh
        AND  EDX,0FF000000h
        OR   ECX,EDX       ; ECX now holds base of current task


    ; *****
    ; * [3] Fault is caused by task switch. If state of old task needs
    ; * to be saved, do so.
    ; *****
        XOR  EDI,EDI
        MOV  DI, fptss
        CMP  DI,0
        JE   DNA_Restor   ; No prior task used Coprocessor.
        CMP  DI,SI         ; If the last user is the current task
                           ; we don't need to save and restore.
        JNE  DNA_Save
```

557

```
        IRET
    DNA_Save:
        ; determine base of TSS of last task
        MOV   EAX,[EDI + offset GDT_Table + 0]
        MOV   EDX,[EDI + offset GDT_Table + 4]
        SHRD  EAX,EDX,16
        AND   EAX,000FFFFFFh
        AND   EDX,0FF000000h
        OR    EAX,EDX    ; EAX now holds base of prior task TSS

        FNSAVE [EAX + TSS_Size]   ; save old task's coprocessor state

    ; *****
    ; * [4] Now set fptss to this task. If needed, load up the
    ; * prior copocessor state of this task. Interrupts
    ; * must be disabled throughout.
    ; *****
    DNA_Restor:
        CLI
        ; This byte indicates that this task had prior
        ; coprocessor state.
        CMP byte ptr [ECX + (TSS_Size + FP_Save - 1)],1
        JNE DNA_Init
        FRSTOR [ECX + TSS_Size ]
        JMP DNA_Done
    DNA_Init:
        FNINIT
    DNA_Done:
        MOV fptss, SI    ; Store this task TSS selector into
        ; fptss, set byte indicating coprocessor has been used
        ; by this task, clear TS and set IF.
        MOV byte ptr [ECX + (TSS_DW + FP_Save - 1)],1
        CLTS
        STI
        IRET
```

32

80386 Software Development *

_____ _M. Steven Baker_ _____

This chapter looks at several 386 compilers and runtime environments and provides limited benchmarks to illustrate the potential speed advantages of certain programs on this new hardware.

The compiler and runtime products reviewed appear in Tables 34.1 and 34.2. They include three 80386 DOS extender programs and debugger runtime environments and several C and FORTRAN compilers. In addition, I used an 80386 assembler, linker, and librarian from Phar Lap and an 80386/387 Hummingboard (coprocessor hardware board) for the PC from A.I. Architects.

	PharLap	**IGC**	**A.I. Architects**
Product	386/DOS Extender	X-AM	OS/386
Version	1.1V	1.1	1.9.09
Price	$995	$595	$495+

Table 32-1: 80386 Runtime Environments Reviewed

The MetaWare C and Pascal compilers (I tested only the C compilers) are reasonably mature products, having been available for about a year. The three 386 DOS runtime environments are more recent and are changing rapidly to meet market demand. For the 386 FORTRAN compilers, this is really a preview. I used mostly Beta test copies of these compilers, and my comments should be viewed in this light. The AI Hummingboard 80386/387 coprocessor has been out for about a year and appears to be a stable product. The software tests were conducted in two environments: (1) a 16 MHz Compaq 386/387 with a 70 megabyte hard disk and 2 megabytes of memory, and (2) an AT&T PC6300 (with Nec V30 chip) with a Seagate 277R (60 megabyte) hard disk using the A.I. Architects 20 MHz 80386/387 Coprocessor board with 4 megabytes of memory.

	MetaWare	MetaWare	LPI	MicroWay	SAIC
Product	High C	highC-386	LPI-FORTRAN	FORTRAN-386	SVS
FORTRAN					
Version	1.4	1.4	02.07.03	1.3B	2.7
Price	$595	$805	$695	$595	$895

Table 32-2: 80386 DOS Compilers Reviewed

Why Bother with the 386 Anyway?

That's what the CP/M Z80 and 8085 folks said about the 8086. Time marches on, and in hardware and software, product differentiation and marketing are driving forces. As long as speed and power spur marketing, the powerful features of the 80386 just can't be neglected. The 386 DOS extenders serve in the interim to allow large 386 applications to be run under DOS until a true 386 operating system (UNIX, OS/3, CDOS-386, VMS) is well established. In November, I felt that these DOS extenders would have maybe a two year lifetime. Others, including the developers of these products, agreed, but as the muddling wars continue, with OS/2's various versions and extended editions, I now feel that the life of these products may be much longer, perhaps up to five years.

80386 DOS Runtime Environments

The 80386 can almost be considered several different chips in a single 132-pin package. Most 386 PC machines are running the 80386 chip in its real mode to emulate the 8086 chip. Actually, the 80386 handles the *LOCK* prefix and the *PUSH SP* instruction differently, but these aren't normally used by DOS applications. In real mode, memory is limited to 1 megabyte and some instructions are not available. On the plus side, DOS programs run just fine and much faster. On the negative side, programmers have to deal with those ?#@ 64K segments of the original 8086. But the 386 has other modes: (1) a protected mode (native mode) that supports both 286 and 386 memory protection and segmentation, and (2) a virtual 8086 mode to provide emulation of the 8086 when in protected mode.

Only the protected mode takes full advantage of the power of the 386. In protected mode, the physical and virtual memory space is seemingly unlimited (4 gigabytes and 16 terabytes). (Oops—back to the real world, where available hardware limits physical memory to 16 megabytes or less). In the protected mode on the plus side is this large memory space. On the negative side (depending on your perspective), memory protection is enabled—you can no longer write into code segments, muck about with interrupt vectors, and do other fun things. And to use the protected mode, software must first set up the prerequisite memory management tables, including segmentation and paging tables if paging is enabled (the 386 has built in support for 4K physical to logical memory paging). These include (in Intel jargon) global (GDT), local (LDT), and interrupt descriptor tables (IDT). Setting one bit in the LDT for a program converts all 16-bit register accesses to similar 32-bit instructions. For example, the instruction opcode that meant *PUSH AX* (push the 16-bit register onto the stack) now means *PUSH EAX* (push the 32-bit register). The most common memory model in this mode is a flat one (the small model) with all segment selectors pointing to the same chunk of memory.

No more segments—just 4 gigabytes of 32-bit address space! All is not free, however; memory management imposes some software penalties on 386 instruction times. Because of memory protection, instructions that modify segment registers take longer in protected mode. Enabling paging can also slow down memory access. Although the 80386 has a built-in, on-chip cache of 32 most recently used page table entries to speed memory access, that represents only 128K of memory. Intel's simulations suggest that this should catch about 98 percent of normal memory accesses, but this depends on the code. If a page table entry is not in the cache, the 386 must read two double word entries from the page translation table in memory before accessing the memory location of interest.

In addition, some gateway or bridge to DOS must be constructed—the task of the 386 DOS runtime extenders. These control programs set up the required memory management structures including a gateway to DOS and other operating system and hardware services, load a 386 program into memory, and start it. In general, these runtime extenders set up an emulation of the DOS and BIOS calling conventions using INT instructions. They intercept DOS calls, transform them for passing to the real DOS kernel that waits in low memory, pass the call to the real DOS and BIOS, and pass the returned information back to your 386 program.

The subtle differences are in this emulation of DOS and BIOS that your application sees and in facilities to allow a 386 protected mode program to call an 8086 real mode procedure (say a graphics routine or a TSR) sitting down in low memory, load other 80386 programs, and provide helpful development environments.

Some General Observations

I worked with the three major 386 DOS extenders. They all include a debugger, utility programs, and examples of their use to create and execute protected mode 386 programs. My first observation relates more to the programming process than to the specifics of these various runtime environments. Let's take a typical application and divide the time spent on various tasks. You might spend 20 percent on planning and design, 40 percent for programming, and 40 percent for debugging. When you decide on a runtime environment, you are also choosing a debugger and technical support. Because of software differences among them, a debugger from one vendor will not work under another 386 environment.

All three DOS extenders emulate DOS and the BIOS to a substantial degree. If we rank runtimes, A.I. Architects' OS/386 is the closest to DOS while IGC's X-AM is the furthest. The Phar Lap DOS Extender lies somewhere in between. The three runtimes support three different executable file formats, and Phar Lap has proposed two more. From a programmer's perspective, I wish these three runtimes were closer together in their DOS and BIOS emulation and EXE file formats and in the way they handle other hardware issues (e.g., the Weitek chip). I'd rather choose 80386 compilers and development tools without being forced to make a choice of development and runtime environments at the same time. With the exception of the MetaWare compilers, if I choose a 386 compiler, I'm also unfortunately choosing an associated DOS extender and debugger.

These DOS extenders are not ideal candidates for fast file I/O. Whenever a DOS call is made by a protected mode application, the machine state is saved twice— once by the DOS extender and once by the underlying DOS system. Also, under normal circumstances, file I/O is handled by the real DOS and BIOS down low in physical memory and block moved by the DOS extender to your program's disk buffers in high memory. This additional block move and state save is bound to impose a performance penalty on file I/O. Therefore, you're best off minimizing DOS calls and doing I/O in large chunks if possible. Onward to specifics.

A.I. Architects OS/386

A.I. Architects (AIA) sells a Developer's Kit that includes the OS/286 or OS/386 kernel, a symbolic debugger, and an EXPRESS utility to generate a protected mode executable file from Microsoft or Phoenix DOS linker output. The runtime included in the Developer's Kit can be used solely for development. Runtime licensing starts at $40 each and decreases with quantity for distribution of the OS/386 runtime with your application. AIA's OS/x86 runtime kernel differs substantially from the other vendors'. OS/286 supports a multiple segmented memory model on the 286, allowing applications to break the 640K memory barrier under DOS. Language support and library files are provided for use with Microsoft C and FORTRAN 4.0, MetaWare High C, Lattice C, and Lahey F77L-EM to create 16-bit protected mode programs. The same memory map is also supported on the OS/386 runtime along with the more common flat, unsegmented (small) memory model. AIA's protected mode programs use the file extension EXP (EXecutable Protected mode) for both 16-bit and 32-bit programs. Unfortunately, this is the name adopted by Phar Lap for their default executable files even though the files have different structures. AIA calls the Phar Lap 32-bit files PLX (Phar Lap eXtended) and can run them. A strength of the AIA product is its support for larger applications under DOS on the 286.

Among the three runtime environments, OS/386 offers the closest emulation of DOS and BIOS. Its manual is the clearest of the three DOS extenders, describing both compatible and slightly incompatible DOS calls supported. Primary variances from DOS are that FCB I/O calls support records up to 16K, DOS memory allocation, and EXEC calls. Otherwise, all DOS calls are fully supported except that 32-bit registers are used.

OS/386 switches from protected mode to real mode for DOS calls and does not use paging. Only memory above the 1 megabyte barrier is available for use in the protected mode. AIA based their decision to forego paging for the time being on a bug in current versions of the 80386 with 80387 math chip errors (the infamous Intel ERRATA #21). The Weitek math chip is to be supported in the next version. Extended DOS calls are supported ($AH >>= E0h$) for calling real mode procedures, setting arbitrary interrupt vectors, creating code and data segments, getting segment information, and block transfers to low memory. Execution of a 386 program is preceded by the *UP* command on the command line. The AIA debugger (CP—Command Processor) is a powerful command shell that can execute DOS-like built-in commands and batch files, as well as be used as an assembly language symbolic debugger. The shell includes a history command and a built-in command-line editor using key bindings similar to the standard EMACS editor defaults. The shell has a powerful macro processor that allows invoking a batch file of macros to make the debugger or shell look similar to SYMDEB—although other user interfaces are only a macro file away. This shell is easily the most powerful of the debugging environments provided with the runtimes. Currently, the only 80386 compilers that work under the OS/386 runtime and produce 32-bit code are MetaWare's C and Pascal. The next revision of OS/386 should support LPI and Green Hills compilers.

IGC X-AM Development Environment

Last May, IGC acquired the 80386 development team from Softguard Systems (the copy protection folks). IGC now offers two 80386 system products— VM/386 (a powerful multitasking control program similar to Microsoft's Windows-386 and Quarterdeck's DESQview) and X-AM, their 386 DOS extender. Of the multitasking programs I've seen so far, VM/386 looks very powerful. X-AM is its lesser cousin. The IGC X-AM (eXtended Address Mode) runtime, called VM/RUN, is a different model of the machine than OS/386. The VM in these product names stands for Virtual Machine (the IGC development team comes from the IBM mainframe VM world). Although neither of these products currently implements virtual memory, the overall design concept is based on creating virtual machines with complete protection of the operating system from damage by an errant program.

The other two DOS extenders run DOS in real mode and 386 applications in protected mode. VM/RUN puts the entire system in protected mode and runs the DOS kernel in lower memory in the Virtual 8086 mode. VM/RUN provides a completely flat memory model for the system, with applications loaded at the 32 megabyte address. No segment registers are used. DOS is down low in memory where you would expect it. For example, monochrome screen video memory is mapped at B0000h, and BIOS data at 400h—their actual physical addresses. All of this is done with paging. VM/RUN is the largest DOS extender (200K) and takes up the most memory. After it's loaded and has allocated buffers for I/O, EXECing other applications, and TSRs, memory below 640K is pretty much used up. These memory protection features are justified for VM/386; their necessity for the single-tasking X-AM system is arguable. X-AM supports the Weitek math chip memory-mapped up high in the 386 address space at the same location UNIX chose on the 386. X-AM looks the least similar to DOS—FCB I/O calls are omitted, and a number of other functions are different. On startup, X-AM passes a global data structure (GDA) with system information to your application.

X-AM requires a REX (Relocatable EXecutable) file extension for 386 programs. The REX file can be generated by the Phar Lap 386 linker and includes relocation information. The runtime consists of four REX files and a main (VMRUN.COM) loader file. The REX files must be available along the current path. For debugging, a special debug REX file must be substituted for one of these standard REX files. The main COM file is a program loader used to make profiles for the executable 386 program. Similar to a feature found in UNIX, the loader uses *arg[0]* (the name of the command invoked) under DOS 3.x to determine the REX file to load. A more recent version of the runtime concatenates these files, but this then requires an additional 110K loader file with the same name as your 386 REX application file. This makes a lot more sense under UNIX, where multiple links (with different names) to the same physical file can exist. Under DOS during the development stage, each one of your REX programs carries around this extra file.

One awkward feature of development with X-AM is that the stack is completely protected (the IGC model of the machine). The COM file has locations that may be changed that determine the amount of stack to allocate, whether the debugger should be available, etc. The stack does not grow from this default value. After creating a REX file, the Make Profile utility (MP) must be used regularly to modify these default values. IGC is working on correcting this problem in the next revision. The assembly language debugger is the weakest of the three products. It is *window oriented* if you consider a fixed line across the top of the screen with a register display and a fixed line across the bottom of the screen with a prompt for your commands a windowing system. The 16 lines of the display area are used for dumps and unassembly, but this is done in a maximum of only 16 line dumps at a time. The X-AM manual I received was also the weakest of the three runtimes—no index and an incomplete list of error messages. The Weitek chip was not mentioned (at least I didn't find it) although I know it is supported. The X-AM environment is currently supported by compilers from MetaWare, SVS, and LPI.

Phar Lap 386IDOS Extender

Phar Lap includes in its 386 assembler/linker package RUN386, their 386 DOS Extender. This version can be used solely for development. In order to distribute this runtime to end users of your product, you must buy a runtime license ($995). The unlimited runtime license comes with BIND386 and CFIG386 utilities. The binder binds the 386 system kernel to the front end of an application, turning it into a DOS EXE file—really a mere concatenation process. Under development, a 386 application is invoked by prefixing the command line with RUN386 followed by the application to invoke and its command line. RUN386 supports two different file formats—the Phar Lap EXP and the IGC REX. Although RUN386 can load a REX file (Phar Lap wrote the assembler/linker currently used by all three vendors), it cannot in general execute REX programs because of differences in the Phar Lap and IGC runtime environments. I was not able to execute REX files supplied with or created by the SVS FORTRAN compiler with RUN386.

The Phar Lap runtime is a flat memory model with several hardwired segment selectors for memory mapping. For example, your program CS has a segment selector of 0Ch while DS and ES have a selector of 14h—all pointing to the same block of physical memory. RUN386 uses about 100K of low memory aside from DOS, leaving about 500K of low memory plus any extended memory above 1 megabyte available for protected mode use. RUN386 uses memory paging on the 386. This is the only DOS extender that easily makes any sizable quantity of low memory available for 386 programs. This may be a consideration for low memory (2 megabyte) machines.

The DOS protected mode function calls are reasonably similar to normal DOS calls with a few exceptions. Of course, registers used are 32-bit instead of 16. The DOS *get_version (AH=30h)* is used to return information about the runtime. The DOS *getint (AH=35h)* and *setint (AH=25h)* calls are not supported. FCB type file I/O calls are not supported. Memory management and EXEC calls are slightly different from their DOS counterparts. The Weitek math chip is supported by mapping it into a 64K block of memory pointed to by segment register GS (the 386 has six segment registers—FS and GS and the 4 registers available on earlier chips). This requires a segment override and address length override prefix instruction in order to access the math chip although timing and opcode length end up the same when accessing the math chip with a full 32-bit address. But loading a register with the start of the Weitek chip address and using register indirect addressing would require an extra segment override byte.

The latest versions of RUN386 are to incorporate support for DESQview and the Compaq Extended Memory Manager (CEMM). Applications developed with Phar Lap's DOS Extender will be able to multitask under DESQview for the 386. The Beta test version (1.1W) had a few bugs, so I subsequently did my testing with Version 1.1V, which does not include DESQview support. RUN386 comes with a solid 200-page manual describing in detail all DOS and BIOS functions supported. To registered users, Phar Lap sends out free software updates and a technical newsletter documenting changes in all of their products. The Phar Lap debugger 386DEBUG is not included with the assembler or runtime and must be purchased as a separate product ($195). The debugger feels much like Microsoft's SYMDEB, featuring many of the same commands and support of symbolic names. The MetaWare 80386 compilers, along with LPI and NDP compilers, run under and generate code to operate using Phar Lap's DOS Extender.

MetaWare High C and High C-386

MetaWare was the first to supply compilers under DOS for the 80386, with Pascal and C compilers out for over a year now. These products are currently the most mature in the DOS environment (they support DOS's quirks). MetaWare offers two sets of compilers—High C and Pascal for creating DOS programs and High C-386 and Pascal-386 for protected mode 80386 programs. The 386 compilers could almost be considered cross compilers since they operate on an 8086 (or the 80386 in the real mode) and do not require an 80386 for compilation. This is a convenient feature because they can be run under the normal DOS environment and aren't limited to a particular 386 DOS extender. Without these compilers, most of these runtimes wouldn't be available. Both the AIA and Phar Lap 386 DOS extenders and debuggers were written in MetaWare C—a pretty strong recommendation. IGC wrote their runtime and debugger in assembly language although you wouldn't know it by the executable size.

MetaWare supports all three 386 runtime environments fully, and the source code to the INIT module is provided for customization. MetaWare also provides the source code for other parts of the runtime for embedded applications. The compiler generates code for the 80287, 80387, and Weitek chips and comes with libraries for the math chips and an emulation library. These compilers are highly optimizing and offer excellent code generation. A large array of command-line and inline *pragma* options in the source code are supported, as well as the current draft of ANSI C including prototyping, the new preprocessor directives, standard header files and libraries, and not promoting floats to doubles. This last option provides a means for C to compete in the numerically intensive programming market generally dominated by FORTRAN.

The 8086 DOS C compiler supports code generation for the 8086, 80186, 80286, NEC V30, and 80386 CPUs. In the real mode, certain 80386 instructions are used for long int divides, block moves, bit routines, etc., but memory addressing is still limited to *segment:offset* addressing. This is more a limit of the existing DOS linkers and EXE relocation schemes than of the compiler technology. The MetaWare High C compiler (DOS) also supports both the Phoenix PLINK86 linker and the INTEL object module format for embedded applications or other environments. High C also supports linking routines from about the widest variety of other compilers I've seen—from most Microsoft languages to Lattice C. Various *pragma*s specify the order of arguments, who pops arguments, and the registers used to return values. The compiler can generate object files compatible with Microsoft's CodeView debugger and the INTEL PSCOPE-86 debugger.

The High C-386 compiler generates object code for the Phar Lap 386|LINK program using the easy-OMF format as defined by Phar Lap. This format has become a defacto 386 linker standard under DOS. Both compilers support a variety of options—to enable and disable various optimizations, generate a mixed pseudo assembly language and C source listing, enable prototypes, emit line numbers and procedure names for postmortem debugging—the list goes on. The compilers may be configured using a utility with some of these options as defaults. In addition, the compilers support a handy feature given all these options—a Profile file. Upon invocation, the compiler looks for a file called HC.PRO (a command-line option can change the Profile filename to be used). The Profile file can contain #*def*ines, *pragma*s, prototypes, etc., necessary for a particular compilation. This is convenient given the large number of options, and it's also nice when porting software from one environment to another. In this latter case, main source code modules can be maintained with target dependent compiler options placed as *pragma*s in the profile. This is much more convenient than trying to squeeze this information into the DOS environment space as is done with Microsoft C and other compilers. Your C code is often a lot more readable without the myriad #*ifdef*s and #*else* clauses. MetaWare also supports using the DOS environment space for the location of include files.

Documentation includes a *Program* manual describing compiler operation and use, a *Library Reference* manual, and a *Language Reference* manual. Each is about 200 pages with an individual table of contents and index. I have one complaint with the *Library Reference*: The material is organized into sections by the library header file. I would much rather see an alphabetized list of library functions by name. The library is fairly complete, but not as comprehensive as the Microsoft C 5.0 libraries for DOS. Certain UNIX compatible DOS library routines are not currently provided for file time stamping, mode setting, and determining file size. A set of some low-level UNIX I/O calls is provided in a separate file, but these are not documented in the *Library Reference*. MetaWare does provide object file and library support for FlexOS, Concurrent DOS, and some other 80x86 system environments.

I used some standard integer and floating point benchmarks to get a feel for the impact of moving from the real mode to the protected mode. Table 34.3 shows a comparison of execution results of simple integer benchmarks using High C and Microsoft C 5.0 and the High C-386 compiler. In the best case for these simple programs, putting the 386 into its 32-bit mode about doubles execution speed. The performance difference of about 500 percent is more dramatic going from the AT&T PC6300 with 8 MHz V30 to the 20 MHz Hummingboard coprocessor. Comparing High C with Microsoft C 5.0 for some of these benchmarks, each is faster. For floating point, the results indicated about a 100 percent speed up in going to the 386 protected mode. Using the Weitek math coprocessor with the 80386 as supported by MetaWare would show even more dramatic improvements. Be mindful that these benchmarks are all for small applications that don't require overlays. As soon as we squeezed a large application into the DOS real mode memory limitation with overlays, the comparison with a protected mode program would become dramatic indeed. I was able to port 32-bit C code from the GNU project using C-386 when the DOS compilers would not execute it properly. It's surprising how much supposedly portable C code is dependent on integer size.

	MetaWare C-386	MetaWare C	Microsoft C	MetaWare C	Microsoft C
Dhrystones (k/sec)	8,116	4,374	4,540	878	890
Execution time (secs)					
Fibonacci	38.1	51.7	54.3	256	216
Sieve	4.2	6.9	6.7	41	42
8 Queens	3.6	5.8	7.4	35	46

Note: MetaWare C and Microsoft C 5.0 compiled for large model and 80186, with no stack probes and optimizations to simulate larger programs.

Table 32-3: Standard C Benchmarks

LPI FORTRAN

Because quality C and Pascal compilers have been available from MetaWare, most vendors have focused on FORTRAN and other languages for their first releases on the 80386. Language Processors (LPI) has ported their FORTRAN, COBOL, and BASIC compilers to the 80386 under DOS. LPI has already ported the same compilers and PL/I, RPG C, and their source code debugger to XENIX and UNIX on the 80386. LPI FORTRAN currently supports the 80287 and 80387 math chips, and Weitek math chip support is in the works. The LPI compilers are written in PL/I. The user has access to the compiler developers for support. LPI has tried to structure their compilers to look much like their UNIX products and support using several of their compilers. The FORTRAN compiler executes under the Phar Lap 386 DOS Extender and produces code for either the Phar Lap or IGC 386 runtime environments. The compiler is bundled with the Phar Lap linker and runtime. The code produced senses at runtime which DOS extender it is operating under—an attractive feature. The compiler generates object files directly for the Phar Lap linker.

LPI FORTRAN supports options for optimization, listing control, cross reference, floating point, SAVEall, etc., on the command line. Three levels of optimization may be turned off in stages. This is a handy feature since probably 90 percent of porting problems are from compiler code optimizers. When you move a mainframe program, say, between an IBM and a VAX, the first thing that's usually done is to turn off all optimization. The LPI FORTRAN compiler can also generate a listing file with pseudo assembly language statements. The generated assembly language does not use standard Intel mnemonics. LPI supports a convenient feature whereby the command-line options and file names to the compiler may be taken from a file—allowing you to get around the DOS command-line limit and build an option file to literally compile and build a 250-module program in one swoop. LPI's post processor then builds the LNK file for the Phar Lap linker.

The documentation includes a *User's Guide* and a *Language Reference*, each with table of contents and index. The *User's Guide* is short but adequate, and does briefly cover mixed language data type considerations for linking with other LPI languages. LPI's compiler operated more slowly than the other 386 FORTRAN compilers. This was partly a result of LPI's decision to mimic the LPI UNIX compiler interface, and they plan to revisit this decision. The LPI compiler generated fast code, but was not quite equal to the other 80836 compilers. The optimization level had to be reduced in order to get the Linpack benchmark to return correct results.

MicroWay NDP FORTRAN-386

MicroWay has been working with minicomputer compiler vendor Green Hills Software (Glendale, California) to provide Green Hills' family of C, Pascal, and FORTRAN compilers under DOS for the 386. MicroWay has traditionally specialized in math coprocessor hardware and software for the PC. They have been working with Green Hills to add Weitek support and other DOS features. These compilers are globally optimizing—they require lots of memory for compilation. The compilers are written in Pascal. FORTRAN-386 supports the 80287, 80387, and Weitek chips and comes with libraries for each math chip. FORTRAN-386 executes under the Phar Lap 386 DOS Extender and produces code for this same runtime environment. The compiler generates assembly language files for the Phar Lap assembler, but this additional step slows the speed of compiles. The Phar Lap assembler and linker must be purchased separately.

FORTRAN-386 supports a large range of command-line options and can use part of the 80387 stack or some of the Weitek registers for register variables. The compiler is also conservative about using variables in registers when other procedure calls take place. This compiler demonstrated the case in which creating temporary FORTRAN variables can generate faster code because of the register allocation scheme. The excellent compiler documentation includes a *User's Manual* and a *Reference Manual* of several hundred pages each with separate tables of contents and indices. The *User's Manual* is by far the best of the three 386 FORTRAN compilers considered, clearly documenting the compiler switches, FORTRAN-386 extensions and peculiarities, interfacing with other languages, compatibility with the UNIX f77 compiler, optimization, porting issues, intrinsic functions, and numeric coprocessor support. Stephen Fried from MicroWay has written probably the best piece on numerics and optimization I've seen as one chapter of the *User's Manual* (see his earlier *BYTE* articles, too).

FORTRAN-386 sports one feature not available from the other vendors—it figures out which FORTRAN variables must be *SAVE*d and allocates globals for them. This makes porting from IBM and VAX much easier. The other compiler vendors do allow making all variables *SAVE*d, but with a noticeable performance penalty. MicroWay is working on improving the numeric code generator. The version I tested thinks that the math chips have registers, as opposed to a stack, and as a result generates much better code for the Weitek chip than it does for the 80387. This can represent up to a 20 percent speed penalty. For the benchmarks I ran, the compiler generated fast times although all of these compilers generated fast code compared with the real mode DOS compilers. But FORTRAN-386 also needs lots of memory for operation. One benchmark program (Superlite) with one program unit of 2,000 lines ran out of memory during compilation even on a machine with 3 megabytes.

SAIC FORTRAN-386

Science Applications International Corporation (SAIC) has been working with Silicon Valley Software (SVS) of Cupertino, California, to market SVS's FORTRAN, Pascal, and C compilers under DOS. SAIC's Los Altos, California, office needed a 386 FORTRAN compiler for its own use and ultimately decided to offer the same product in the DOS market. SVS traditionally markets their compilers, written in Pascal, to the UNIX world. The SVS FORTRAN compiler executes under the IGC DOS extender and generates code for this same runtime. The compiler supports the 80287, 80387, and Weitek chips. SVS FORTRAN-386 comes bundled with the Phar Lap linker and is also the only compiler to come bundled with a source level debugger. After seeing the rather primitive nature of the 386 assembly language debugging, SAIC insisted that SVS port their source debugger to the DOS environment. The SVS debugger works only with the SVS compilers since the compiler back end generates the DBG file. IGC added two features to X-AM so that SVS could port its debugger to their environment—the ability for one program (the source debugger) to load another program and the ability to take over the breakpoint interrupt vector.

The SVS compiler supports a variety of command-line and inline (source) options, but no control over optimization; it's always on. The listing options don't provide any assembly language output. A *SAVE*all option can be used to allocate globals for all variables. Otherwise, SVS FORTRAN will allocate variables on the stack. Even common blocks in the main program are allocated on the stack at entry. Invoking *SAVE*all exacted a 15 percent performance decrease on some of the benchmark programs I used. The LPI FORTRAN compiler exhibited similar behavior. This is an example of differences between the 8086 and 80386. In the 86 world, accessing absolute memory locations was faster; on the 386 register, indirect data access is quicker.

The SAIC documentation includes a brief *User's Guide*, the *SVS FORTRAN Reference Manual*, and the *Debugger Reference Manual*. None has an index. The little DOS-specific information is buried in two appendices in the *FORTRAN Reference*.

The SVS compilers generate an intermediate file that goes through two other program steps before becoming an object file suitable for the Phar Lap linker. Despite these steps, this compiler executed the fastest of the three FORTRAN compilers, and the executable file sizes were usually the smallest of the three compilers. File execution speed was very fast on the 80387, often the fastest of the three compilers. The source debugger allows setting breakpoints or trace-points using source line numbers or procedures. The debugger can be used to look at both local and global FORTRAN variables, including those allocated to registers, but it does not provide disassembly of the code generated.

The IGC runtime was awkward to use because the first attempt to execute any sizable FORTRAN program would crash me into the IGC debugger. The culprit was the fixed size stack in combination with the SVS code generator. As noted above, common blocks and variables are allocated on the stack on entry to main at runtime. Each program has to have its IGC runtime profile adjusted to allow an adequate stack for these variables. The next IGC revision should remove this problem.

A.I. Architects' Hummingboard Coprocessor

A.I. Architects manufactures a series of 80386/387 coprocessor boards for the PC XT and AT. These boards provide a separate 80386 CPU and optional math chip and from 2 to 24 megabytes of memory in both 16- and 20MHz versions. The board I used was a 4 megabyte, 20MHz unit that performed flawlessly. This had to be the easiest board I've installed. Four dip switches set the ports used by the coprocessor board. Using the default settings, I dropped the board into an AT&T PC6300 and was running in fewer than two minutes. The Hummingboard (HB) uses a 64K window of memory into the PC or AT address space along with several I/O ports for communication. This memory window can be in one of four locations—9000h, A000h, D000h, or E000h. A CONFIG.386 file specifies the default window address and total memory on the board.

These boards provide an excellent environment for developing and debugging 80386 software. The 80386 CPU can crash on the HB, yet the main PC CPU will still be active to view a postmortem dump or disassembly. The HBs use a 12K memory cache. The coprocessor boards don't have to respond to the PC's timer interrupts, and processing can be performed in parallel on the two CPUs. The designers obviously did something right since the 16MHz HB outperforms a 16MHz COMPAQ 386 machine by 10 percent or more. (The Compaq/20 is slightly faster than the 20MHz HB.) OS386 running on the HB can also be used to run normal DOS programs although they run blindingly fast. Execution times compared with my base 8MHz AT&T 6300 were about 500 percent faster on the HB. This board should be considered an alternative to the Definicon 68020 Coprocessor Board.

And the Envelope, Please

Don't pay attention to the 386 executable file sizes—the bloat is mostly from uninitialized data. The compiler writers are revising the way they handle this. As demonstrated by the benchmarks, the 386 protected mode offers benefits to both integer and numeric programming (when using the 80387). C programs requiring the large model or 32-bit ints should show a substantial benefit using the protected mode. These simple benchmarks indicate a decrease in execution times of 30 to 70 percent of the real mode equivalents. The math chip operates at the same speed in either real or protected mode, but array indexing is improved by the 386. The reason these compiler vendors are rushing to support the Weitek chip for numeric programs is that it promises to double or triple numeric performance over the 80387. MetaWare with High C-386 and Pascal-386 compilers offers an easy entry into the 386 protected mode. Both SAIC and MicroWay will offer C and Pascal compilers, but MetaWare has had a year's head start, and its libraries are based on several years of experience in the DOS environment.

This preview of FORTRAN compilers demonstrates the benefits of using any of these products over their real mode counterparts. All three vendors are working hard to improve code generation and adjust to the DOS environment. These vendors need to either support all three DOS extenders or supply their own INIT modules as MetaWare has done. The three DOS extenders are all functional, but more divergent than I like to see. There needs to be some agreement on EXE file formats and a set of uniform calling conventions on a minimal set of DOS calls. Programmers will also need better tools, such as profilers and debuggers that show the 80387 stack and Weitek registers and provide source and symbolic debugging capabilities.

33

Developing 80386
Applications ... Today *

_____ *Richard Relph*_____

The arrival of the Intel 80386 (386 for short) promises a new level of sophistication in applications. With its speed and multi-gigabyte virtual, physical, and segment address spaces, developers can create applications requiring the resources of a mainframe, but usable on personal computers. In addition to being able to run these new, sophisticated applications, the 386 can also play host to several "old" 8086 programs, each believing it has the whole CPU to itself. It is this promise of being able to run newer, more powerful applications without losing the use of existing programs that makes the 386 so exciting.

But for many software developers, it is difficult to take advantage of the availability of a new CPU like the 386. There is not an operating system supporting the 386 that people are willing to buy. Even when Microsoft's 386 DOS becomes real, the Lotuses of the software world will get first crack at it, taking away the small developer's edge of being able to react more quickly. It seems as if there is no way for a small company or individual to develop the first spreadsheet (for example) to take advantage of the 386's capabilities.

Well, that isn't the case anymore. Just about any programmer can develop code today that takes advantage of the full resources of the 386, using what I call an "environment". An environment is a layer of software that looks like an 386 DOS to your 386 application, but acts like a standard 8086 application to the host operating system, MS-DOS. This chapter describes two such environments that were available in March 1988; at least two more should be available by the time you read this.

The environments described here limit your 386 application to physical memory and must be written in either Pascal or C (unless you feel up to developing multi-megabyte programs in assembler). Over the next few months, these restriction may be eased. Environments supporting virtual memory and other languages will certainly be ported to the 386. Two environments supporting

_____

multitasking were planned for release in April.

Before an environment can be used, a compiler that supports the environment (and its host processor, the 386) must be found. First you select your compiler, then an environment, and finally, the hardware to run it on. All three ingredients are available today.

The Compiler

The only vendor supplying 386 compilers for any environment I know about is MetaWare. They are shipping both Professional Pascal and High-C. Phar Lap was the first company to ship an environment—DOS-Extender. Softguard followed soon after with VM/RUN, the pieces of VM/386 needed to run 386 programs. The Software Link provided PC/MOS 386, a multiuser, multitasking OS for the 386. The version of PC/MOS I tested only supported 8086 tasks, although documentation and release dates were provided for the 386 tasking version. The hardware I used was the Compaq Deskpro 386.

Compiling your source code is the starting point for creating 386 programs. I used MetaWare's High-C 386 to perform this task. High-C 386 itself runs on any MS-DOS computer with a hard disk. In fact, no 386 is required anywhere in the development process until you actually need to execute (and debug) your code. Of course, like any MS-DOS program, High-C runs significantly faster on a well- designed, 386-based computer.

MetaWare High-C is a complete (and then some) implementation of the C language, regardless of which standard you choose to hold it up to. The ANSI C language specification, though not yet a standard, is supported in one of two similar languages accepted by High-C. The other language is perhaps best referred to as extended ANSI C. This is the default language. The strict ANSI language is supported in the form of different parse and scan table files supplied, which can be fed to the compiler in lieu of the ones built into it.

Some of the MetaWare extensions to ANSI C include case ranges, nested procedures (like Pascal), named parameter association (borrowed from ADA), access to unnamed members of unions (taken from C++), and interleaved declarations and statements.

Two unusual features allowed by ANSI and used by MetaWare are pragmas and intrinsic functions. Pragmas allow the programmer to tell a compiler something about his code. MetaWare uses them to change calling conventions, specify segments for objects, enable various optimizations, and other very unusual, but sometimes needed features. Intrinsic functions are function calls that the compiler recognizes and generates code for inline (without a procedure call), using any special instructions the processor may support (such as *rep*, *scans*, *movs*, etc). MetaWare provides intrinsics for absolute value, minimum and maximum of lists, common string and memory functions, and, if the 387 option is used, some transcendental functions. Support for Intel's 80387 numeric coprocessor (a faster, extended 80287) wasn't tested since the Compaq Deskpro 386 can't use one, but 287 support is also provided and was tested.

To do language testing, MetaWare provided me with their test suite, which they also sell as a separate product. The test suite includes many strange but valid and mostly compiler independent constructs in the C language. It consists of roughly 2,000 lines of code and includes both a language test and a library test. I expected MetaWare to pass the suite (since they had provided it) and they did. I was convinced by looking at the test suite that a compiler would have to be pretty sound to run it, but just to provide a basis of comparison, I stripped the suite of High-C specific code and ran it through some other well-known compilers. The other compilers all failed, in various and surprising ways, but that is not the subject of this chapter.

The library provided with High-C is intended to conform to the ANSI specification, and it does. Additional, nonstandard (but common) functions are also supported via utility "packages". These packages are in the form of header files much like the normal ones, only with the extension .CF. Packages are provided for stack dumping, interrupt trapping (yes, trapping), for using the MS-DOS Int 21 functions, and for calling other system dependent services. As an additional feature of the library, all portable, but system dependent, functions rely on a core of functions that the programmer may replace in order to support embedded or hostless applications.

The documentation provided with High-C is, to say the least, complete. Some 700 or more pages in length, there is probably no question about the product not answered within its volume. The documentation is divided into five sections, each a manual itself, each with a table of contents and an index. The manuals are *License, Installation, Program, Library*, and *Language*. Each is typeset, with the exception of the *Language* manual, which is printed on a dot-matrix printer (presumably awaiting final ANSI approval of the C standard). It will take a new user some time to get familiar with the structure of the manuals and to feel at ease with them. This is especially true of the language manual, which is precise but not particularly easy to read or understand.

When it comes to support for High-C, it is hard to imagine any better. Questions about the product are routed directly to the person who wrote the compiler. This ensures that you are talking to someone who has some familiarity with the product. MetaWare is always improving its compilers, both by fixing any bugs they know about and by adding new little features. I always found MetaWare to be very cooperative when it came to providing updates, although MetaWare's official policy is three month's of free updates with additional support at 15 percent ($135) per year.

High-C is more expensive than MetaWare's other DOS compilers, but not unreasonably so. The version I tested was 1.3, although this is not enough to exactly specify a particular set of compiler characteristics since MetaWare often tinkers with the compiler without changing the version number.

Installation of the compiler is easy if you proceed as MetaWare suggests. The first step is to run a batch script called, oddly enough, *install*. This will place a number of files and directories in the current directory. It is unfortunate that most of these files are packed in a single archive file spread across the four diskettes. This makes customized installations a two-step process: first installing per MetaWare guidelines, then rearranging for individual tastes. To MetaWare's credit, the entire installation section of the manual is duplicated on the first diskette for easy reference.

Besides the compiler, include files, and necessary libraries, a number of other utilities are also included. The utilities include some standard UNIX-style file manipulators. More unusual is a set of utilities that allow editing and detailed examination of .OBJ files, and utilities for producing cross-references of multiple source files.

Compiler Performance

The compiler isn't going to win any contests in speed of compilation, but users should find performance adequate for most programs. Most of the slowness comes from the size of the compiler and the time it takes to load from disk, so performance will appear particularly bad on small source files. The compiler does generate a lot of information about your program, and issues many useful warnings where it finds questionable code, such as using a variable before assigning anything to it, or failing to specify a return value from a nonvoid function. Listings, with or without generated assembly code, can be produced via a command-line switch.

The generated code is good considering that no global optimizations are being made. Of course, the 386's more regular architecture doesn't hurt either, although there are nuances there as well. For instance, the fastest way to multiply something by 5 is to use the *LEA* instruction, of all things! High-C supports three register variables, and they are used by default, unlike High-C for the 8086 and 80286, which only supports two and then only if you enable them. The size of integers is 32 bits in High-C. I didn't spend a lot of time benchmarking the compiler, since it is the only game in town right now. But I did compare programs compiled under 386 mode and under 286 mode and found general improvements of 5 to 10 percent in the 386 version. In programs in which long arithmetic was used often, more dramatic increases were apparent.

The Linker

After compiling your program, you'll need to link it. I used Phar Lap's assembler and linker, although you can get the same assembler and linker from Softguard, (which licenses them from Phar Lap). I did not play with the assembler much beyond running the installation test, but based on comments in the update notice, it seems fairly sound. The linker, on the other hand, I used a great deal.

386LINK, as it is called, is fairly slow, mostly due to the way libraries are managed. Unlike Microsoft's DOS linker, which uses an (undocumented) index table, Phar Lap simply searches the library by scanning it. Doing all the arithmetic in 32 bits using 8086 instructions doesn't help performance either. The input form is something Phar Lap calls Easy OMF-386, a simple extension to OMF-86, the .OBJ form both Intel and Microsoft use for 8086 objects. Easy OMF-386 extensions are documented in an appendix of the linker manual. The linker can produce several output forms. .EXE files are the default, although the format is not exactly compatible with DOS .EXE files because it doesn't use 8086-style segments. Intel Hex and Motorola S-records may also be generated. A special output form is .REX, which is what the Softguard environment uses.

The Environments

If you buy the assembler and linker from Phar Lap, you also get MINIBUG and RUN386. The total package lets you develop programs to run on the 386. If you want to sell those programs, you must purchase a redistribution license. You can then bind RUN386 to your program and sell it. In this bound form, 386 programs are invoked just as normal DOS applications.

MINIBUG is a debugger for 386 programs, similar to MS-DOS DEBUG. Missing are the Assemble command, the Load command, and the Name command. The Dump and Enter commands are enhanced to support SYMDEB-style size specifiers for ASCII, word, and double-word quantities. The *RX* command displays all 80386 registers, while the *R* command displays just the registers used by normal programs. You can modify any 80386 register, including all of the protected registers (which include the debug registers).

RUN386 is Phar Lap's 386 execution vehicle. It is a single, standard MS-DOS program that accepts the name of a 386 .EXE file, loads it, and runs it, passing any additional command-line parameters on to the 80386 application. RUN386's job has really only begun when your 386 program gets control, hwever. Presumably, your program wants to do I/O and probably through the MS-DOS that was running just before. The problem is that it is an 8086 program and yours is not. Furthermore, you can address gobs of memory, and MS-DOS and its underlying hardware can only get at the first megabyte of physical memory. RUN386 handles the details of getting your data through to DOS and letting DOS get to its hardware. It does this by intercepting your *INT 21*s, examining the registers, translating them and moving data if necessary, and finally passing control to MS-DOS in real mode. When MS-DOS finishes, RUN386 regains control and again translates registers accordingly. RUN386 also fields hardware interrupts and forwards them to their real-mode handlers.

Softguard's VM/RUN does pretty much the same thing as RUN386. VMRUN is a .COM file that loads many other Softguard-supplied files (all of which must be in the current directory) and then the application's .REX file. Each application must have a profile, a description of how the programmer would like certain features of the environment configured. Mainly, these parameters specify how much memory to allocate for specific uses. Memory may be allocated for program-managed, low-physical address buffers (thus avoiding the expensive block move), for DOS *exec* calls, and for the stack. All other memory is given over to the 80386 application code and its data.

Another bit of information in the profile is whether to start up in debug mode or not, and whether to debug using the display or a separate terminal connected to a COM: port.

Softguard's debugger is much different than Phar Lap's and is in many ways better. It uses the 80386's debug registers to set execution and data breakpoints. It is screen-oriented when running locally, and can use a remote terminal as the debug console (in which case it does start to resemble DEBUG). When running locally, screen swapping is used to avoid the normal problems associated with one screen being used for two purposes. The debugger is more or less always present. If a trap occurs during execution of your program, the debugger is invoked.

One major difference between the environments presented by these two packages is the memory model. Phar Lap continues to use segments whereas Softguard is based on a flat-memory model. While it is accurate to say that Phar Lap is supporting the large model compared to Softguard's small model, it is perhaps a bit misleading. The small model, after all, supports up to 4 gigabytes per object or program. One place this dichotomy of models is apparent is in direct screen I/O (I do not recommend doing direct screen I/O, but both environments support it and it does provide a useful example of the difference between flat and segmented models). For Softguard, you merely compute what the address would have been on the IBM PC bus (which depends on what display adapter is in use), put that in an index register, and access screen memory through it. So Softguard would have screen addressed with *EDX* (for example) equal to 000b8000. Phar Lap, on the other hand, provides a segment descriptor that points at the base of the display adapter, so merely computing the offset and accessing through the segment with the offset does the equivalent thing. Segment 1c points at the screen memory, so to access the first location in it, one loads a segment selector (register) with 1c and uses an offset of 0. Phar Lap's 1c:0 is equivalent to Softguard's 000b8000, assuming a color graphics adapter. If a monochrome adapter is used, Phar Lap still accesses it using 1c:0, but Softguard uses 000b0000. It should be noted that Phar Lap does provide a segment selector (34) that works the way Softguard's *DS* does for the low 1 Megabyte.

Softguard's VM/RUN is compatible with its future VM/386, a multitasking 386 control program. VM/386 is not an operating system, but rather a layer between other operating systems and the hardware (VM/370 programmers should recognize this picture immediately). Under (or over, depending on how you view things) VM/386, several different 8086 operating systems may be running, each believing it owns the machine. One virtual machine may even be rebooted without affecting any other virtual machine.

The Software Link has taken a different tack. Its PC/MOS 386 is a single 80386 operating system that can run several DOS programs at one time. PC/MOS will also support 80386 native mode programs, but this feature was not available at the time I wrote this review (it was due to be released in April 1988). Documentation provided by The Software Link indicates that PC/MOS will support large-model 386 programs, like RUN386 does, although it doesn't appear that they will be compatible.

When comparing RUN386 and VM/RUN in use, RUN386 seems to be more friendly. Only one new file is introduced (RUN386.EXE) and it may be anywhere along the path, although the 386 .EXE file must be in the current directory. VM/RUN requires at least five other files, four of which must be in the current directory, along with the 386 application's .REX file. VM/RUN takes longer to load these files and to get to the task at hand (running your program) than RUN386. RUN386 seemed to cooperate with my editor (Epsilon) whereas VM/RUN did not. Both VM/RUN and RUN386 did run under my make utility (Polymake). VM/RUN also clears the screen during initialization, which did not seem appropriate. And finally, VM/RUN is between 7 and 15 percent slower executing identical code on the same Compaq Deskpro 386. This is presumably because of hardware interrupt handling or overhead associated with running at CPL 3 rather than CPL 0 as RUN386 does. (CPL is the current processor level and represents the level of privileges that should be granted to a program—0 is the most privileged level.) Other explanations are possible and the results may not repeat on non-Compaq 386 machines.

Softguard's product does outperform Phar Lap's in one important area—memory allocation. In addition to being more flexible (through the profile discussed above), Softguard's also seems to end up with more memory available. Running a binary search between 0 and MAXINT (2 billion), Softguard's reported 1,656,288 bytes available in a 2-megabyte system, where Phar Lap's reported only 1,496,912 bytes available. Of course, the more memory you have in the machine, the more memory will be available for 386 programs (until you hit that 4 gigabyte limit).

The Hardware

None of this discussion would matter if there were not computers on which to run these new environments. The Compaq Deskpro 386 proved to be an excellent performer on all counts. It was a joy to use. Everything about this machine is fast, except the tape drive. The machine has four speed modes— common, fast, auto, and high. Common speed is 4 Mhz and is comparable to a 6-Mhz IBM AT. Fast is 8 Mhz and is a bit faster than an 8-Mhz IBM AT. High is 16 Mhz and is unlike anything you have had on your desk before. Auto mode switches between high and fast depending on the diskette motor-on signal, attempting to ease speed incompatibilities in such areas as floppy disk access. I ran in high-speed mode exclusively and had no problems, although I did not run any copy protected software. The bus version of Microsoft Mouse also worked well.

Unless you believe the rumors about Intel building a 386 with 286 pinouts (shaving address bus and data bus pins in the process), I believe your next MS-DOS machine should have a 386 in it. I know mine will. And more software developers have announced 386 specific applications in the six months since Compaq introduced its Deskpro 386 than all the 286 specific applications announced since, well, ever.

Summary

The point of this chapter is to convince you that you can get started developing 386-based applications now, without waiting for 386 DOS to arrive, whenever that may be. If you develop in a high-level language, such as MetaWare's High-C or Professional Pascal, you will at most have to recompile and relink your application to get it to run under some new environment.

The tools to do these things are still young but certainly adequate for conventional application development. They will undoubtedly get better as time goes on. I hope that anyone who wishes to do development for the 386 will contact each of the vendors mentioned here and listed below to get more up-to-date information.

Vendors

High-C 386
MetaWare Inc.
903 Pacific Ave., Ste. 201
Santa Cruz, CA 95060
(408) 429-6382

386ASM, 386LINK, RUN386, MINIBUG
Phar Lap Software Inc.
60 Averdeen Ave.
Cambridge, MA 02138
(617) 661-1510

VM/RUN
Softguard Systems Inc.
2840 San Thomas Expressway, Ste. 201
Santa Clara, CA 95051
(408) 970-9240

PC/MOS 386
The Software Link, Inc.
8601 Dunwoody Pl., Ste. 632
Atlanta, GA 30338
(404) 998-0700

VIII
Coprocessors

34
Peripherals Enhance 80386
Design Options [*]

V. Siva Kumar

A numerics coprocessor, a 32-bit direct memory access controller and a cache controller let system designers create a variety of compatible 80386 systems.

Today's 32-bit microprocessors are accelerating the trend toward a standard computer architecture spanning a range of market segments, from personal computers to workstations and minicomputers. Most of these 32-bit microprocessors have the horsepower for the raw performance requirements of these segments. The 80386, however, has the unique ability to simultaneously run applications from different industry standard operating systems such as UNIX and DOS. This capability brings to 80386-based systems the large existing software base of the 8086/286 family of microprocessors as well as all UNIX-based technical and commercial software.

The 80386's on-chip hardware supports multitasking, a pipelined architecture, an address translation cache, a high-speed bus, and memory management, including protection mechanisms. These features provide for fast instruction execution and as well allow compact system design. At 20 MHz, the 80386 executes at 4 to 5 Mips, offering CPU performance greater than that of the Digital Equipment Corp VAX 8600 minicomputer. The cost-effective 16-MHz version provides 3 to 4 Mips performance.

The high-speed external bus of the 80386 is optimized for efficient interface to a variety of memory and I/O devices. Only two clocks are needed for the processor to perform a full 32-bit access, allowing for a throughput of 40 Mbytes/s at 20 MHz. Even with this fast bus, however, economic high performance systems can be built with inexpensive dynamic RAMs by using cache memory techniques or through address pipelining.

The 80386 bus can also accommodate slower memory and peripherals through a Ready input to the processor that indicates when a bus access has been completed. Since the bus can be dynamically configured to support both 16- and 32-bit devices, the 80386 can be coupled with a range of 8-bit, 16-bit and newer 32-bit peripherals.

After choosing the 80386 as the system CPU, designers still have various options to consider for hardware as well as for the operating system software. Choices for critical system functions include coprocessors, memory subsystems and direct memory access (DMA) controllers.

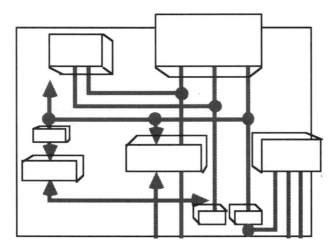

Math Coprocessors Speed Floating-Point Performance

Three math coprocessors can be used to accelerate floating-point performance of 80386 systems. Two of these—the 80287 and its superset, the 80387—extend the 80386-supported data types to support single-, double- and extended-precision operations. The 80287 and the 80387 have high-precision 80-bit architectures and are software-compatible with many popular software packages such as Lotus 1-2-3, dBASE III + and AutoCAD. The third choice for a floating-point unit (FPU) is the 1167 three-chip set from Weitek (Santa Clara, CA), which offers higher performance but isn't software-compatible with the large PC software base.

Compatible with the IEEE 754 floating-point standard, the 80287 performs 16-bit transfers and, with the proper interface, can be used with the 80386. With the lowest performance of the three options, the 80287 is useful in cost-sensitive applications with the 80386. With a 10-MHz clock speed, the 80287 provides a 0.3-MWhetstone/s performance. It's software-compatible with PC software packages that support floating-point coprocessors. Support for the 80287 is also included in the UNIX System V/386 Release 3.0 operating system and optimizing compilers.

The 80387 is the companion numerics coprocessor to the 80386 and provides full 32-bit data transfers. The 80387 has a tightly coupled interface to the 80386 and operates synchronously on the 80386's two-clock bus. It provides minicomputer-like floating-point performance of 1.5 MWhetstones/s for 16-MHz 80386/87-based systems.

This chip fully implements the IEEE 754 standard with support for trigonometric, exponential and logarithmic functions. Entirely software-compatible with the DOS software base, the performance of an 80386/87 system is four to six times greater than a 80286/87 system running the same software. Support for the 80387 is also included in the UNIX System V/386 Release 3.0 operating system and optimizing compilers.

The Weitek 1167 FPU consists of three VLSI chips. This chip set does not fully implement the IEEE 754 standard but is compatible with it. The 1167 performs only the four basic arithmetic functions with 64-bit precision, and it's not software-compatible with DOS software. Nevertheless, performance of over 3 MWhetstones/s can be realized in an 80386 system with this coprocessor unit. Applications such as solids modeling, flight simulation and three-dimensional graphics require this level of floating-point performance. The UNIX System V/386 Release 3.0 also provides for optimizing compiler support for the 1167.

Floating-Point Coprocessors for the 80386

	Number of Chips	Performance in MWhetstones/s	PC Software Compatibility	Built-in Transcendental Functions	IEEE 754 (Rev. 10) Floating-point Standard	UNIX V/386 C compiler Support	Precision
80287	1	0.3 (10 MHz)	yes	yes	compatible	yes	80-bit
80387	1	1.5 (16 MHz)	yes	yes	full implementation	yes	80-bit
1167	3	3.2 (16 MHz)	no	no	compatible	yes	64-bit

When choosing an FPU, designers should examine trade-off's in raw performance, software compatibility and system design ease and cost. The 1167 provides the highest performance, but only the 80387 and the 80287 can run the existing PC software base. The 80287, being the more mature IC, offers the best choice for cost-sensitive applications, while the 80387 has the highest single-chip numerics performance. The 80287 and the 80387 are single chips and offer greater ease of design, and save board real estate compared to the 1167.

High-end systems, such as minicomputers, typically use the 1167 along with the 80387 to provide software compatibility and performance. Mid-range systems, such as workstations, typically use the 80387 with optional 1167 support, while lower-end systems, such as PC's, would likely use either the 80387 or the 80287.

Match Memory Bandwidth to Processor Cycle

A fast processor such as the 80386 performs only as fast as its memory subsystem allows. For maximum performance, the memory subsystem must let the CPU operate at its full potential, providing code and data as fast as is needed. Performance requirements are weighed against memory and support circuitry costs in memory system design.

With its high-speed, two-clock bus, the 80386 can put out an address in one clock and get data back in the next clock. The object of memory subsystem design for the 80386 is to economically match the memory bandwidth to the processor cycle. At 16 MHz, each clock cycle is 62.5 ns. For zero-wait-state operation, however, the memory access time should be faster than 50 ns. Static RAMs alone have similar fast access times, but they're usually considered too expensive to use for large arrays. A cost-effective solution is to use a small but fast SRAM cache memory and a larger but slower DRAM main memory.

Another method of memory interface on the 80386 is the use of its Next Address pin, which allows address pipelining. With pipelining, the processor outputs the next memory address before the current memory access cycle is completed. This feature provides an extra clock (62.5 ns at 16 MHz) to access main memory, allowing memory design with 100-ns access time DRAM. The performance of a pipelined zero-wait-state 80386 system is 91 percent of that of an ideal zero-wait-state system. Wait states are extra clock cycles added to the 80386 bus cycle. By adding wait states, one can use slower memories but with performance degradation. When using one wait state without address pipelining, 81 percent of ideal memory system performance is achievable.

Wait States and Pipelining Effects on Performance		
Number of Wait States	Without Pipelining (%)	With Pipelining (%)
0	100	91
1	81	76
2	66	63

Designing an efficient memory subsystem for a high-performance microprocessor requires an understanding of the cost/performance trade-offs involved. Slower memories are more cost-effective but require the insertion of wait states. As wait states are added to the subsystem, performance declines at roughly 20 percent per wait state.

Even with address pipelining, a pure DRAM system can't be interfaced to the 20-MHz 80386 without providing for at least one wait state. This makes a cache memory system the best alternative for near zero-wait-state performance.

In designing a cache memory system, price/performance, system real estate and cache coherency implications are the factors considered. When using DMA or in multiprocessing systems, the cache data can become stale; the main memory can change while the cache retains older data. The cache subsystem needs to monitor the bus via bus watching so that the processor can update the cache when data is modified.

Another important consideration is the software support required for the cache. The cache system must be software-transparent for compatibility with existing software and ease of upgradability in the future.

The relation of cache size and organization to system performance is a hotly debated topic at system design reviews. The structure of a cache depends entirely on the programs the system will most often run. Good system design practice is to tune the cache with address traces of the most common applications that the system will execute. In general, a larger cache is better than a smaller one, and greater cache associativity leads to a higher hit rate and better cache performance.

The 82385 is a high-performance cache controller that's specifically designed to interface with the 80386 and that can address the entire 4-Gbyte main memory address range. Because tag memory and control logic are on-chip, design of a cache memory subsystem is greatly simplified when using the 82385. The device stores a copy of frequently accessed code and data from main memory in a fast local cache memory. Integrating the cache directory on-chip, the 82385 supports a 32-kbyte two-way set-associative cache that has bus-watching capability. The 82385 prohibits stale data and guarantees cache coherency of data and code in systems in which other bus masters have access to the same memory space. Because it requires no special software initialization and is software-transparent, the 82385 is compatible with existing software and future software.

DMA Controller Takes Over Data Transfer

Of all the peripheral requirements of a computer system, DMA control is the most performance-critical function. A DMA controller is used to offload the processor from data transfer tasks and greatly improve system performance. Data needs to be moved between main and secondary storage areas (DRAM to disk), between main memory and I/O devices (DRAM to printer, or DRAM to local area network) or between two I/O devices. Since a DMA controller relieves the processor of the I/O transfer duties, system performance increases since the CPU doesn't have to switch context for every transfer.

The data transfer rate is the most important aspect to consider when choosing a DMA controller. The data transfer rate must be weighed against the bus utilization, since the DMA controller must not monopolize the processor bus. There are several secondary items to consider in addition to the data transfer rate. A number of 16-bit and 8-bit peripherals are found in 80386 systems. In particular, I/O devices are often 8 bits wide. The DMA controller, therefore, must be able to transfer any combination of bytes, words or double words (32 bits). The number of DMA channels supported and the capability for alignment of misaligned data and for address increment/decrement are other important considerations.

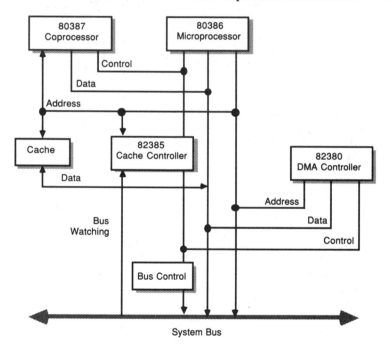

The microprocessor (80386), coprocessor (80387), and VLSI microperipherals (82380 and 82385) form the core of high-performance 80387-based systems. The 80387 accelerates floating-point operations, while the 82385 controls a 32-kbyte cache memory with advanced features such as bus watching. The 82380 integrates several system functions, including dynamic RAM refresh, interrupt and timers, and 32-bit direct memory access control.

The 80386 system can utilize a number of DMA controllers, such as the 8237A, the 82258 and the new 82380. The 8237A is an 8-bit chip that transfers data at 1.6 Mbytes/s; two of these can be used in an 80386 system, doubling the data transfer rate of 8 Mbytes/s. Both these chips are mature devices, having been introduced as companion DMA chips to the 8086/8088 and the 80286 microprocessors, respectively.

The 82380 is the newest generation DMA controller that also integrates a number of other common system peripheral functions such as DRAM refresh control, programmable timers and interrupt control and wait-state generation. These functions are all supersets of earlier peripherals such as the 8237, the 8259 and the 8254, so software compatibility with the previous generation is preserved. Systems using the 82380 can therefore be designed for software compatibility with the large PC software base. The 82380 can transfer data through eight individually programmable channels at the full bus bandwidth of the 80386—40 Mbytes/s at 20 MHz.

The 8237A and the 82258 require external logic to be used with a 32-bit CPU, while the 82380 can be directly coupled to the 80386. The 82380 has the highest performance of the three. Since it integrates DMA control with several useful system peripherals, it provides cost effectiveness (replaces up to 20 LSI/VLSI devices) and software compatibility.

System Hardware Examples

Since the 80386, along with its many peripherals, provides a family of products with complete software compatibility, system designers can design a range of compatible hardware with different price/performance capabilities. Examples of 80386 design can be used to examine compute engine designs in light of the applications for those systems. The first wave of 80386-based personal computers were built on the IBM PC AT standard and used a number of peripherals that are common to the PC AT class of machines.

The typical compute engine for this 80386 PC class consists of a 16-MHz 80386 supported by a 10-MHz 80287 numerics coprocessor (some of these machines have sockets for optional 80387s). The DMA tasks are handled by two 8237A DMA controllers. The memory subsystem uses address pipelining with interleaved DRAM memory. Some machines have a cache subsystem to allow close to zero-wait-state performance. Many of the system design choices for this class of machines were based on software compatibility with previous-generation MS-DOS systems and on design time and cost.

A higher performance system than the PC, the Multibus CPU card uses a 16-MHz 80386 supported by a 64-kbyte DRAM cache. The cache is controlled by a controller made up of LSI components that provides zero wait states on memory reads for up to 16 Mbytes of dual-port memory. Designed with 80387 support, the board also allows use of a daughter board supporting the 1167 FPU chip set if higher performance numerics solutions are needed. DMA tasks are handled by the 82258 DMA controller, which is better suited to the bus bandwidth than the

8237A. Compatibility with Intel's iRMX real-time operating system and with previous-generation Multibus CPU cards is important in a design. Also, low chip-count can accommodate tight board real estate.

For high-performance applications, the 20-MHz 80386 is coupled to both the 80387 and 1167 FPUs for maximum floating-point flexibility and performance. The full bus bandwidth 82380 DMA controller is also used to maximize performance. The large main memory, fast disk drives and high-speed communications channels such as Ethernet require a high-bandwidth DMA performance.

The 20-MHz 80386 is fed by a cache memory subsystem that uses a 32-kbyte, two-way set-associative cache controlled by the 82385. The system can run UNIX System V/386, Release 3.0, and simultaneously execute DOS applications, which is a task that would require an additional CPU on non-80386-based systems.

Software Compatibility Brings Huge Selection

Once they've selected hardware for the 80386 system, system vendors consider the software choices open to their customers. Here, just as with the hardware, there are many options.

Because it's software-compatible with the previous generations of 8086/286 family microprocessors, the 80386 can run the software written for the earlier versions. Operating systems such as MS-DOS and XENIX have a large installed base in the commercial marketplace that 80386-system OEMs can leverage. Newer versions of these operating systems tailored to the 80386 will soon appear on the market. Toolkits that let programmers write applications for the 80386-specific version of XENIX are already available, and several software houses are working on porting their applications.

A number of highly optimized compilers are being developed for the UNIX System V/386, Release 3.0, operating system that will allow high-performance execution of scientific and commercial applications in a multiuser, multitasking environment. Several new products that combine UNIX System V/386 with the MS-DOS world are also now appearing, such as Merge 386 from Locus Computing and VP/ix from Interactive Systems/Phoenix Technologies. These systems make use of the virtual mode hardware feature of the 80386 to provide the simultaneous execution of applications from UNIX and DOS.

Other systems that make use of the virtual mode hardware feature of the 80386, but in a DOS environment, are Softguard Systems' VM/386 and Quarterdeck Office Systems' Desqview 80386. These are control programs that let multiple DOS 3.x sessions be run simultaneously, providing a multitasking environment that's software-compatible with existing applications.

Since designers don't have to choose the operating system and attendant applications packages when they design the system hardware, the vendor can offer a number of these alternatives on a common hardware platform.

35

Increase the Performance of Your Programs with a Math Coprocessor[*]

Marion Hansen and _Lori Sargent_

The microprocessor in your personal computer's CPU is powerful, but it wasn't designed to handle complex math operations rapidly. Whether it's an 8086, 8088, 80286, or 80386, your microprocessor will perform floating-point and transcendental calculations far more quickly and with greater precision if a math coprocessor is linked to it. Coprocessors also have capabilities useful for business computing. A coprocessor can process binary coded decimal numbers up to 18 digits long without round-off errors, perform arithmetic on integers from 2×10^{-9} through 2×10^9, and carry out math functions on real numbers as small as 3.4×10^{-4932} or as large as 1.1×10^{4932}.

When software written to use a coprocessor performs certain types of math, it engages the coprocessor rather than the microprocessor. The coprocessor performs the calculation and returns the answer to the microprocessor. This entire process takes a fraction of the time required by the microprocessor executing alone. To give you an idea of how fast a coprocessor is, Figure 35-1 compares spreadsheet recalculation times with and without an 8087 math coprocessor.

Besides performing certain kinds of math faster, coprocessors also save programming time. Because trigonometric, logarithmic, and exponential functions are built into the coprocessor's hardware, the programmer doesn't have to write these routines. And with the routines in the chip instead of in the code, programs are smaller. Coprocessors generate instructions for many numeric operations such as number conversions, arithmetic operations, and transcendental functions (tangents, exponents, and logarithms).

A coprocessor is the most cost-effective way to increase number-crunching power. For a fraction of the cost of an accelerator board, a coprocessor can dra-

---

[*] © Microsoft Corporation, _Microsoft Systems Journal,_ July, 1987, p. 59

matically speed up floating-point calculations. And it won't consume a precious expansion slot (or two), since it fits in a socket already on the motherboard.

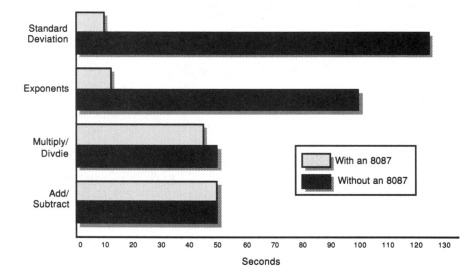

Figure 35-1: Recalculating Lotus 1-2-3™ spreadsheets on an IBM® PC can usually be done much more quickly with an 8087 coprocessor.

Math coprocessors come in three varieties: the 8087 (for 8086- and 8088-based computers), the 80287 (for 80286-based computers), and the 80387 (for 80386-based machines). The 8087 and 80287 are both available in three different speeds. The speed you need depends on how fast your computer drives the coprocessor socket, not on the speed of your microprocessor. For example, some 10-MHz computers drive the socket at 8 MHz and thus need a coprocessor that runs at 8 MHz, not 10 MHz. If you aren't sure which speed is correct for your computer, contact the manufacturer.

Hundreds of application programs have been written to take advantage of the co-processor's speed and precision, including business, engineering, graphics, statistical, and econometric packages. Many compilers and assemblers can benefit from a coprocessor as well. Using a coprocessor with one of these programs couldn't be easier, because all interfacing between microprocessor and coprocessor is built in. The only difference you'll notice is the increased speed.

Development Tools

Most of today's compilers and assemblers can generate coprocessor code. This includes all recent versions of Microsoft C, Pascal, and FORTRAN compilers, as well as Borland's Turbo Pascal. No matter which of these languages you're writing in, incorporating complex math into programs is not difficult with a coprocessor.

In a high-level language, using the coprocessor is quite painless. Coprocessor instructions such as sine, square root, hyperbolic tangent, and log are built into manufacturer-supplied library routines.

Assembly language programmers using Microsoft's Macro Assembler Version 1.25 or later have the option of writing code that explicitly references coprocessor instructions or implicitly does so by linking in a math library such as those supplied with the Microsoft C, Pascal, or FORTRAN compilers. In addition, a number of other software vendors market specialized math libraries that perform many math functions and can be linked to programs written in a variety of languages. Although programs can usually call math library routines with or without a coprocessor, programs running on systems with a coprocessor will execute significantly faster. Figure 35-2 illustrates how much faster an 8-MHz computer performs floating-point instructions on typical spreadsheet data when a coprocessor is installed.

Figure 35-2: Calculation times for floating-point instructions decrease dramatically when a coprocessor is added to an 8-MHz IBM PC.

Instruction	Approximate Execution Time (in microseconds)	
	With an 8087	Without an 8087
Add/Subtract	10.6	1,000.0
Multiply (short real nos.)	11.9	1,000.0
Multiply (temporary real nos.)	16.9	1,312.5
Divide	24.4	2,000.0
Compare	5.6	812.5
Load (long real nos.)	6.3	1,062.5
Store (long real nos.)	13.1	750.0
Square Root	22.5	12,250.0
Tangent	56.3	8,125.0
Exponentiation	62.5	10,687.5

Most high-level languages link an emulation library into any program that contains floating-point instructions or data. Code to check for the presence of the coprocessor is generated at run time. If a coprocessor is detected, it is used. If a coprocessor is not present, the emulation library is used. This way, programs written to take advantage of a coprocessor can run on systems without one.

Debugging code that contains coprocessor instructions is not much different from debugging code written for the microprocessor alone. A good debugger, such as the CodeView facility included in Microsoft's C Compiler Version 4.0, lets you examine and change all the coprocessor registers, including status and control registers. CodeView displays data register contents in both their 80-bit internal hexadecimal form and their decimal equivalents. This makes debugging floating-point instructions no more difficult than debugging microprocessor instructions.

Synergy

The coprocessor is an extension of the microprocessor. (In fact, Intel calls the coprocessor the numeric processor extension, or NPX.) They share the same buses and memory. The microprocessor's status lines and queue status lines are directly connected to the coprocessor, so the coprocessor is able to track the microprocessor's instruction queue. The coprocessor monitors and decodes instructions without any overhead. It reads each instruction into its queue but executes only its own instructions, treating each microprocessor instruction as a no-operation (NOP) command. In turn, the microprocessor treats each coprocessor instruction as a NOP and executes only its own instructions. The microprocessor controls programs execution, and the coprocessor controls numeric operations.

Instead of the 8-bit registers in the 8088, the 16-bit registers in the 8086 and 80286, or the 32-bit registers in the 80386, the coprocessor has 80-bit data registers, which allow it to hold more information. The coprocessor's registers were designed to hold specific types of data and are significantly different from the microprocessor's general-purpose registers. Nonetheless, the two chips can still share data through common memory.

Data Types

Coprocessor registers were designed to store 80-bit floating-point numbers. This format, which Intel calls temporary real, is compatible with the proposed IEEE 754 floating-point standard. A temporary real number is composed of a sign bit, a 15-bit exponent, and a 64-bit significand. Although the coprocessor stores all data as temporary real numbers, it can also read and write data in six other formats: packed decimal, long real, long integer, short real, short integer, and word integer (see Figure 35-3). Coprocessor load and store instructions automatically convert the other six data types to temporary real format and back again. Microsoft's Macro Assembler allows these formats to be declared with the directives DW (word integer), DD (short integer and short real), DQ (long integer and long real), and DT (packed binary coded decimal and temporary real).

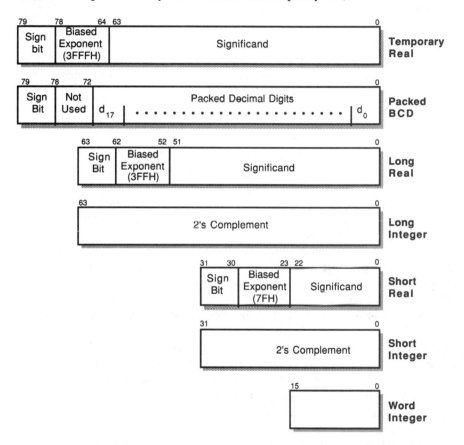

Figure 35-3: The coprocessor can recognize seven numeric formats, which make use of up to 80 bits.

The coprocessor stores numbers in normalized format (scientific notation). A number is normalized by shifting the 1 that's furthest to the left up or down until is occupies bit 63. The coprocessor assumes the number in the significand is a real number between 1 and 2. The exponent field specifies how far the digits must be shifted to get the correct number back. Because the exponent is stored as an unsigned value, an offset (bias) is added to it so negative numbers can be represented. This lets the coprocessor compare the magnitude of two numbers without first performing arithmetic on the exponents, and execution time is thus shortened.

Registers

Coprocessor computations occur in eight data registers. The registers can be accessed as a LIFO (last-in-first-out) stack, with instructions operating on the top one or two stack elements. Or the registers can act as a fixed register set, with instructions operating on explicitly designated registers.

Unlike those of the microprocessor, the coprocessor's data registers don't have unique names. They're treated as indexed entries in a stack, with the top of the stack designated as register ST(0) and the others designated ST(1) and so on. Values are loaded into the coprocessor by pushing them onto the stack, and some (but not all) are retrieved by popping them off. Many coprocessor instructions operate only on the top of the stack. Most other instructions default to operating on the stack's top. All register addresses are relative to the top of the stack.

A 3-bit top-of-stack pointer in another type of register—the status word register—identifies the current top-of-stack register. A push decrements the value in this pointer by 1 and loads a value into the new top register. A pop increments the value in the pointer by 1 and removes the value from the register currently at the top. The stack is circular and can be overwritten if not managed properly.

All the coprocessor's numeric opcodes (as opposed to control opcodes) use the top of the stack as at least one operand. Some instructions operate only on the top of the stack, while others operate on both the top and the second stack register. Some take their second operand from another stack register, and others can take their second operand from memory.

Besides the eight data registers, the 8087 has five other registers accessible to the programmer, each 16 bits in size: status word, control word, tag word, operand pointer, and instruction pointer.

The status word can be thought of as a flag register (see Figure 35-4). It contains a busy indicator, a top-of-stack pointer, condition codes, and exception indicators. To read the status word from Microsoft C, call the built-in _status87 function. To read the status word from the coprocessor in assembler, execute an FSTSW instruction to write the status word to memory where the microprocessor can examine it.

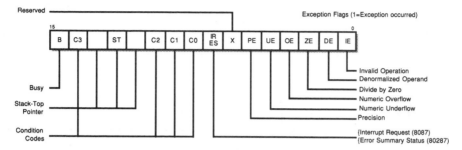

Figure 35-4: The coprocessor's 16-bit status word register serves as a flag register.

The control word defines how the coprocessor should react to different exception conditions (see Figure 35-5). It also defines the precision, how the results will be rounded, and whether signed or unsigned infinity will be used. The control word register has three control fields and six exception masks. Masking the exception bit tells the coprocessor to handle all occurrences of this exception; leaving it unmasked means that the programmer will have to handle the exceptions.

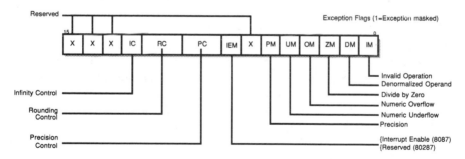

Figure 35-5: The control word register governs how the coprocessor reacts to exception conditions.

In assembly language, control words are sent to the coprocessor by writing them to a memory location and having the coprocessor execute an instruction that reads in the control word from memory. Programmers using a high-level language can check their library reference guide to see how this is implemented in the library they are using. For programmers who do not care to set these fields, Intel provides a set of default control conditions. The default settings are: exceptions masked, interrupts masked, 64-bit precision, rounding to the nearest number, and projective infinity.

The tag word contains information about the contents of each data register (see Figure 35-6). This information is used by the coprocessor primarily to optimize performance. The coprocessor stores 2 bits for each data register, for a total of four possible tag values.

15							0
Tag (7)	Tag (6)	Tag (5)	Tag (4)	Tag (3)	Tag (2)	Tag (1)	Tag (0)

Tag values: 00 = valid (i.e., any finite nonzero number)
01 = zero
10 = invalid (i.e., NaN or infinity)
11 = empty

Figure 35-6: The tag word holds information about the contents of each data register.

The coprocessor uses the tag word to keep track of the contents of each of its data registers and to report invalid results. The coprocessor also uses the tag word to maintain stack integrity information. For example, if a register tagged as empty (tag value = 11) is popped from the stack, the coprocessor detects stack underflow. Similarly, the coprocessor uses the tag word to detect stack overflow when new data is stored in a register that wasn't previously empty. Stack underflow and overflow trigger an invalid operation exception. Programmers can mask or unmask this exception (the default is masked). If either stack underflow or overflow occur and the invalid operation exception is masked, the coprocessor adjusts the stack pointer and returns a standard result to indicate that the value is not meaningful.

The operand pointer and instruction pointer registers provide information about the instruction and data that caused an exception and are used with user-written error handlers. Most programmers do not employ these registers, however, preferring to let the coprocessor handle exceptions.

Unlike the status word and control word, the tag word, operand pointer, and instruction pointer cannot be accessed directly. These registers are accessed indirectly by writing to memory either the coprocessor's environment (using FSTENV) or the coprocessor's state (using FSAVE). The 14-byte coprocessor environment consists of the status word, control word, tag word, instruction pointer, and operand pointer. The 94-byte coprocessor state includes everything in the environment plus the eight coprocessor data registers (see Figure 35-7). The format of the coprocessor state and environment depends on the coprocessor's operating mode.

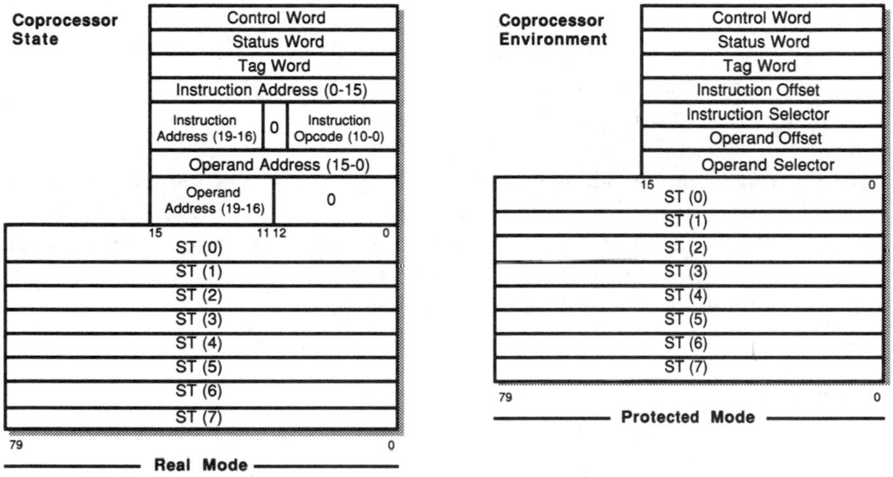

Figure 35-7: The coprocessor environment consists of the contents of all registers but the data registers. The coprocessor state includes all registers.

When an exception occurs while the coprocessor is in real mode, it supplies the 20-bit addresses of the offending instruction and its memory operand (if any), plus the 11 low-order bits of the opcode. In protected mode (with the 80287 and 80387 only), the coprocessor supplies the selectors and offsets of the offending instruction and its memory operand (if any). Although the 80287/80387 real-mode exception pointers have the same format as the 8087 exception pointers, the 80287/80387 instruction pointer indicates any prefixes preceding the opcode. In contrast, the 8087 instruction pointer indicates the escape (ESC) instruction opcode.

Exceptions

The coprocessor recognizes six exception conditions: invalid operation, denormalized operand, division by zero, numeric overflow, numeric underflow, and inexact result. The coprocessor's exception masks give programmers the choice of trapping exceptions themselves or having the coprocessor return a fixed value. When an exception occurs during execution of a coprocessor instruction, the coprocessor sets the appropriate bit in its status register. The coprocessor then checks its control register to determine whether or not that type of exception is masked. If the exception is masked, then the coprocessor uses its on-chip logic to return a result. The exception indicator bits in the status register will hold their value until they are explicitly cleared with either a FINIT or FCLEX instruction. Consequently, with exceptions masked, programmers do not have to check the status register after every instruction. Checking the exception indicator bits periodically ensures accurate results.

The other method of handling exceptions is to unmask one or more of the exception bits and clear the coprocessor's interrupt enable mask. Under these conditions, an exception will trigger an interrupt request. It is up to the programmer to write the interrupt handler that will respond to such requests. The coprocessor contains a lot of built-in support for writing such routines.

Instructions

Coprocessor instructions fall into six categories: data transfer, loading constants, transcendental calculations, comparison, arithmetic, and processor control. A coprocessor instruction can be written in assembler in either of two ways: as a microprocessor ESC instruction followed by a number (for example, ESC 0BH) or as a specific coprocessor mnemonic (FSTP). All versions of Microsoft assemblers later than 1.25 accept coprocessor mnemonics; ESC instructions are needed only for older assemblers that do not, and are thus rarely used. Programmers writing in high-level languages needn't worry about the format of coprocessor instructions—the compiler will take care of everything.

A coprocessor mnemonic takes the form of a sequence of letters beginning with an F. Figures 35-8 and 35-9 give examples of these instructions incorporated into assembly language programs. Figure 35-10 is a sample of code created by Microsoft's C Compiler Version 4.0. While the coprocessor instructions are not apparent in the source code, you will see them if you compile the program with the /Fc option and look at the .COD file.

If an instruction starts with 11011 the microprocessor recognizes it as a coprocessor instruction and responds by generating any necessary operand addresses, putting them on the address bus, and ignoring the coprocessor opcode. The microprocessor then continues fetching and executing instructions unless it is instructed to wait for the coprocessor to complete its task.

Since the microprocessor and the coprocessor can work on separate tasks simultaneously, they can overwrite each other's data or miss instructions unless they're synchronized. All high-level languages automatically synchronize the activity of the two chips, while assembly language programmers must do so explicitly. In exchange for the extra programming effort, however, assembly language programmers get more flexibility (carefully managed concurrency) and faster performance.

The 80286 and 80386 have instruction synchronization built in, but this is not true of the 8088 and 8086 or any of the coprocessors. Consequently, programmers must on occasion insert an FWAIT after a coprocessor store instruction.

When you are using escape sequences, specify the FWAIT instruction when the microprocessor must wait for data from the coprocessor. All floating-point mnemonics have an FWAIT as their first byte, so it isn't necessary to code one explicitly. (A few coprocessor instructions assume an FN<op> form, which keeps the assembler from generating an FWAIT instruction.)

In addition to synchronizing data, the 8086 and 8088 must also synchronize 8087 instructions. Because the coprocessor gets its instructions by monitoring them as they go into the microprocessor prefetch queue, the 8087 can miss an instruction if it is busy executing while the 8086/8088 is fetching and executing.

Any program that uses a coprocessor should also be able to run without one. Before the software tries to use the coprocessor, it should check to see if there is one. It can easily do this by attempting to initialize the coprocessor and then attempting to read the coprocessor's control word after the initialization. (If a coprocessor is present, the control word will be set to the default value specified by Intel. Many software libraries have this checking function built in. If a coprocessor is not found, the program should call an emulation library to handle coprocessor instructions or should gracefully exit. Figure 35-11 provides an example of this type of program.

Real vs. Protected

The 8087 operates only in real mode, while the 80287 and 80387 can operate in either real or protected mode. All programs written to use the 8087 are compatible with the 80287 and 80387 in real mode. Executing the privileged SETPM instruction will place the 80287 or 80387 in protected mode. They can then be returned to real mode only by a hardware reset.

The microprocessor's operating mode affects coprocessor code in two areas: exception handling and memory accesses. The memory image of the instruction pointer and data pointer following an FSTENV or FSAVE instruction depends on the coprocessor's operating mode (see Figures 35-8 and 35-9). Any code that examines this information must consider the operating mode for accurate interpretation. In protected mode, Interrupt Vector 16 is dedicated to the numeric exception handling routine. Coprocessor instructions that result in exception conditions will trigger an Interrupt 16 if the exception is unmasked. Protected mode also has a built-in mechanism for handling coprocessor instructions when a coprocessor is not present (or it its absence is being emulated). Interrupt 7 is automatically triggered if a coprocessor ESC sequence is executed and the emulation bit (EM) of the microprocessor's machine status word is set. This built-in trapping can help programmers systematically include emulation code in their programs.

MS® OS/2, Microsoft's new protected-mode version of MS-DOSR, offers basic exception handling for coprocessors by supporting the exception handling capabilities of the 80287 and 80387. It doesn't supply a standard emulation library for coprocessors; this must be provided by the compiler.

When in protected mode, the microprocessor checks all memory accesses (including coprocessor operands) for violations of protection rules. Coprocessor applications running in protected mode must comply with protected-mode memory management regulations. Any violations cause either dedicated Interrupt 13 (when the violation occurs on the first word of the numeric operand) or dedicated Interrupt 9 (when the violation occurs on subsequent words).

If you want to port an 8087 program to a protected-mode system, consider reassembling the program on an 80286/80386 assembler. This removes the redundant FWAITs and usually gives you a more compact code image. In addition, make the following changes to the 8087 program:

- Delete interrupt-controller-oriented instructions in numeric exception handlers.

- Delete 8087 instructions FENI/FNENI (enable interrupts) and FDISI/FNDISI (disable interrupts). The 80287 and 80387 ignore these instructions, so none of the 80287/80387 internal states will be updated.

- Be sure Interrupt Vector 16 points to the numeric exception handling routine.

- Include a microprocessor exception handler for an Interrupt 7, which will occur during the execution of coprocessor instructions if the microprocessor's machine status word contains the settings TS=1 (task switched) or EM=1 (emulation).

- Include a microprocessor exception handler for Interrupt 9 (which occurs when the second or later word of a floating-point operand fails outside a segment) and Interrupt 13 (caused by the starting address of a numeric operand falling outside a segment).

Figure 35-8: This assembly language program uses coprocessor instructions to calculate the circumference of a circle with a given radius. Each of these instructions begins with an F.

```
title     circumference

.287            ; Tell MASM there are coprocessor instructions
                ; in the program.

data      segment
    radius              DD  2.468
    circumference       DD  ?
data      ends

code      segment
    assume cs:code, ds:data
start:
    mov     ax, data        ; Initialize data segment
                            ; register
    mov     ds, ax
    finit                   ; Initialize coprocessor
    fldpi                   ; ST = pi
    fadd    st, st          ; ST = 2pi
    fld     radius          ; ST = radius
                            ; ST(1) = 2pi
    fmul    st, st(1)       ; ST = radius*2pi
    fstp    circumference   ; store result and pop
    fwait                   ; wait for store to complete
    mov     ah, 4ch         ; return to DOS
    int     21h
code ends
    end start
```

Figure 35-9: This program uses coprocessor instructions to calculate the square root of each element in an array of binary coded decimal integers. The results are stored in another binary coded decimal array and can easily be converted to ASCII strings for output.

```
.287                    ; Indicate to MASM program
                            contains npx code.

bcd_data    segment
    array_1 DT  1234567890, 82, 769823, 84165
            DT  246809, 1526374859, 199, 41290
            DT  98654210, 340126, 2400, 371849
    array_2 DT 12 DUP (?); storage for results
bcd_data    ends

code segment
    assume  cs:code, ds:bcd_data
start:
    mov ax, bcd_data
    mov ds, ax
    finit           ; initialize coprocessor
                    ; assume default control word

    mov cx, length array_2  ; initialize loop counter
    mov si, 0               ; initialize index

process_array:
    fbld    array_1[si]  ; st(0) = array_1[index]
    fsqrt                ; st(0) = sqrt (st(0))
    frndint              ; round at(0) to integer
    fbstp   array_2[si]  ; store bcd result in
                         ; array_2[index] and
                         ; pop coprocessor stack
    add     si, 10       ; increment index to point
                                to next DT array element
    loop    process_array  ; DO WHILE
                                loop counter <= length array_2
exit:
    fwait               ; make sure last store completed
    mov ah, 4ch         ; exit to dos
    int 21h

code    ends
    end start
```

Figure 35-10: Using Microsoft C library functions to calculate sine and co-sine, this program in C draws a circle on the screen of a system equipped with a graphics adapter. The coprocessor instructions are apparent only after compilation.

```c
#include "stdio.h"
#include "math.h"

extern set_graph_mode();
extern set_text_mode();
extern plot_point();

#define VERTICAL_CENTER 99.5
#define HORIZONTAL_CENTER 319.5
#define PI 3.1415927

main()
    {
    char ch;
    float radians,radius,aspect_ratio;

    aspect_ratio=2.1; /* adjusts horizontal scaling to account */
                      /* for PC's "tall and skinny" pixels     */
    radius=90;

    set_graph_mode(); /* set screen to 640x200 graphics mode */

    /* step around the circle in 1/100th radian increments */
    for (radians=0; radians < 2*PI; radians=radians + 0.01)
        {
        long x,y;

        x=HORIZONTAL_CENTER+radius*aspect_ratio*cos(radians);
        y=VERTICAL_CENTER+radius*sin(radians);
/* call routine to write a pixel on the screen */
        plot_point((int)x, (int)y);
        }

/* wait for user to hit a key before erasing screen  */
    ch=getchar();

/* restore user's screen to text mode */
    set_text_mode();
    }
```

Figure 35-11: This routine performs the same multiplication function with or without a coprocessor. First the program checks for the presence of a coprocessor. If it finds one, it executes the imul_32 procedure. If not, it jumps to the emulation procedure, emulate_imul_32.

```
title        math_module

.287                      ; Tell MASM that there are coprocessor
                          ; instructions here.
public  init_math
public  imul_32

    present      EQU    0
    missing      EQU    1


code     segment    public     'code'
         assume  cs:code

    cp_flag        DB   1      ; local flag
    ctrl_word   DW   0         ; for storing '87 control word


;------------------------------------------------------------;
;   init_math: Detects math coprocessor and sets global flag  ;
;       which is used to determine whether or not to use      ;
;       coprocessor instructions or emulation code.           ;
;                                                             ;
;   This procedure must be called before the coprocessor can  ;
;   be used by math routines in this module.                  ;
;------------------------------------------------------------;

init_math        PROC        FAR

    fninit                            ; initialize coprocessor
    fnstcw  cs:ctrl_word              ; store '87 control word
    test    byte ptr cs:[ctrl_word+2], 03 ; if bits 8 and 9 are set
    je      yes_cp                    ; then coprocessor present
    mov     cs:cp_flag, missing       ; else no coprocessor
    jmp     init_math_exit

yes_cp:
    mov     cs:cp_flag, present

init_math_exit:
    ret
init_math    ENDP
```

```
;----------------------------------------------------------;
;  imul_32:  Performs signed multiplication on two 32 bit   ;
;            integers.  (Note: can also be used to perform  ;
;            fixed point 32 bit decimal multiplication)     ;
;                                                           ;
;      Input:   Two 32 bit integers                         ;
;               ds:si pointer to integer A                  ;
;               ds:di pointer to integer B                  ;
;                                                           ;
;      Output:  64-bit result returned at [es:bx]           ;
;                                                           ;
;----------------------------------------------------------;

imul_32      PROC    FAR

    cmp      cs:cp_flag, missing    ; IF coprocessor missing
    je       emulate_imul_32        ; THEN emulate
                                    ; ELSE use coprocessor
    fild     dword ptr [si]         ; st(0)= A
    fimul    dword ptr [di]         ; st(0)=A*B
    fistp    qword ptr es:[bx]      ; store result and pop stack
    fwait                           ; wait for store to complete
    jmp      imul_32_exit           ; coprocessor done, exit

emulate_imul_32:


;---------------------------------------------------------------;
;                                                               ;
;    The following code computes A x B where                    ;
;                                                               ;
;            A is a 32 bit integer composed of                  ;
;                a low word (A0) and a high word (A1) and        ;
;            B is a 32 bit integer composed of                  ;
;                a low word (B0) and a high word (B1)            ;
;                                                               ;
;    The result is calculated by summing the partial products of ;
;    individual 16 bit unsigned multiplies.  The final result is ;
;    sign adjusted.                                             ;
;                                                               ;
;---------------------------------------------------------------;
;
    push     ax                     ; save caller's state
    push     cx
    push     dx
    push     bp

A0_x_B0:
    mov      ax, [si]               ; ax=A0
    mul      word ptr [di]          ; dx=A0B0H, ax=A0B0L
    mov      esL[bx], ax            ; store A0B0L - 4th column sum
    mov      cx, dx                 ; cx=A0B0H
A1_x_B0:
    mov      ax, [si+2]             ; ax=A1

    mul      word ptr [di]          ; dx=A1B0H, ax=A1B0L
    push     bx                     ; running out of registers,
                                    ;    reuse bx
    mov      bx, ax                 ; bx=A1B0L
    mov      bp, dx                 ; bp=A1B0H

A0_x_B1:
    mov      ax, [si]               ; ax=A0
    mul      word ptr [di+2]        ; dx=A0B1H, ax=A0B1L
```

```
          add     cx, bx              ; cx=A0B0H+A1B1L
          adc     cx, ax              ; cx=A0B0H+A1B1L+A0B1L+carry
          pop     bx                  ; need pointer back
          mov     es:[bx+2], cx       ; store 3rd column sum
          push    bx                  ; still short of register space
          xor     bx, bx
          adc     bx, 0               ; save carry information
          mov     cx, dx              ; cx=A0B1H
A1_x_B1:
          mov     ax, [si+2]          ; ax=A1
          mul     word ptr [di+2]     ; dx=A1B1H, ax=A1B1L
          add     cx, bx              ; cx=A0B1H+stored carry
          adc     cx, bp              ; cx=A0B1H+A1B0H
          adc     cx, ax              ; cx=A0B1H+A1B0H+A1B1L+carry
          pop     bx                  ; restore pointer
          mov     es:[bx+4], cx       ; store 2nd column sum
          adc     dx, 0               ; dx=A1B1+carry
          mov     es:[bx+6], dx       ; store 1st column sum
; now adjust for negative numbers
test_A:
          mov     ah, [si+2]          ; ah=high byte of A
          or      ah, ah              ; IF A is negative
          js      subtract_B          ; THEN subtract B from
                                      ;      high DD of result

test_B:
          mov     ah, [di+2]          ; ah=high byte of B
          or      ah, ah              ; IF B is negative
          js      subtract_A          ; THEN subtract A from
                                      ;      high DD of result

          jmp     emulate_done
subtract_B:
          mov     ax, [di]            ; ax=B0
          mov     cx, [di+2]          ; cx=B1
          sub     es:[bx+4],ax        ; adjust the two high words
          sbb     es:[bx+6],cx
          jmp     test_B
subtract_A:
          mov     ax, [si]            ; ax=A0
          mov     cx, [si+2]          ; cx=B1
          sub     es:[bx+4], ax       ; adjust the two high words
          sbb     es:[bx+6], cx
emulate_done:                         ; restore caller's state
          pop     bp
          pop     dx
          pop     cx
          pop     ax

imul_32_exit:
          ret
imul_32 ENDP

code ends
          end
```

36
The 80387 and its Applications *

David Perlmutter and *Alan Kin-Wah Yuen*

In today's microprocessor systems, floating-point coprocessors are becoming the standard option. This trend began with a need for more floating-point processing power, the industry standardization that came about with the introduction of the 8087 floating-point coprocessor for the 8086, and the subsequent support by popular software. Intel Corporation contributed further to this trend when it introduced the 80287 coprocessor as an option for the 80286 microprocessor.

The 80387 coprocessor, designed to complement the 80386 32-bit microprocessor, represents the highest floating-point performance in the 8087 family. It offers four to six times the performance of the 80287. Implemented in the CHMOS III double-metal process, the same fabrication process for the 80386, the 80387 achieves 16- and 20-MHz performance levels. The combined microsystem provides the most powerful, closely coupled microprocessor configuration with the largest software base available on the market.

Since the advent of the 8087, two major classes of on-chip floating-point solutions have emerged. One class borrows the RISC concept from microprocessor design, performing very fast basic operations (Add/Subtract, Multiply, Divide, Compare) in single or double precision. This class requires software to support exception handling and data format conversions (integer or BCD to floating-point formats and vice versa). Complex trigonometric, logarithmic, and exponential operations are not supported in hardware. All these operations entail a significant amount of software development, maintenance cost, and additional product development time.

The second design approach presents a more comprehensive solution on chip. These floating-point coprocessors provide more complex instruction extension for the CPU and automatically take care of exceptional cases, rounding, and precision control. Such solutions usually keep intermediate results in 80-bit, extended-precision format, thus reducing the chances of overflow and underflow and preserving precision. The extended format gives better accuracy. Because their microcode is written to take the best advantage of the hardware, these coprocessors perform floating-point instructions much faster than software emulators. Therefore, in addition to the reduction of complexity and cost of software development, speed increases significantly. Intel numeric processor extensions pioneered this class of floating-point solutions.

IEEE standard implemented. The 80387 fully supports the *ANSI/IEEE Standard 754-1985 for Binary Floating-Point Arithmetic*, which defines the basic algorithms and implementation-independent rules for performing floating-point operations. This standard supports software portability and interfacing between different machines. It also defines the data types to be supported, their accuracy, rounding control, and exception-handling support.

The 80387 fully supports all basic floating-point operations and all precision and rounding modes required by the standard. It also handles internally all exceptions defined by the standard, thus freeing external software from filtering and handling the exceptional cases. A recommendation of the standard to round constants is also fulfilled.

In addition to basic operation support, the 80387 converts data types from integer and BCD to floating-point and vice versa and variables from one precision to another. It calculates remainders, SQRT, and scaling of operands and supports basic trigonometric, logarithmic, and exponential (base 2) operations. Such a variety of instructions gives the programmer a lot of flexibility.

Family compatibility. The 80387 executes object codes compiled for its predecessors. This means that any compiled program written for 8087/80287 can be run without the need for recompilation. All operating modes of the 80386 are supported. Both 16-bit and 32-bit programs can take advantage of the high performance of the 80387. For example, the 80387 (operated at 16 MHz) executes the Whetstone benchmarks in double precision at 1.5 M Whetstones/s (versus 0.3 M Whetstones/s for the same program on the 8-MHz 8087/80287). On a clock count basis, the 80387 Floating Add operation requires 23 to 31 clocks, while the 80287 requires 70 to 100 clocks. Moreover, a virtual 8086 mode of the 80386 allows DOS programs to use the full performance of the 80387 in a 32-bit operating system environment.

The 80387 supports a super set of the 8087/80287 instructions with a variety of enhancements such as increased operand range for transcendental functions. It connects directly to the 80386 through an optimized and dedicated coprocessor interface in a similar fashion to the way the 8087 and 80287 are connected to their host processors. The 32-bit external interface allows faster operand transfers and larger memory for access.

External Architecture

The 80387 interfaces to the 80386 CPU as a slave coprocessor. The CPU writes opcodes and operands to the coprocessor and performs memory transactions for it. All memory accesses for numeric operands use the full 80386 memory management hardware. Therefore, the integrity of the 80386 memory protection mechanism is preserved, and the user's memory management scheme is simplified. Figure 36-1 illustrates this interface; Table 36-1 describes the pins and their functions.

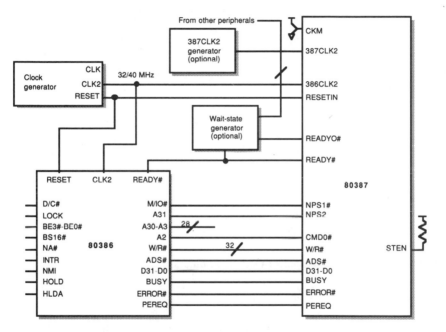

Figure 36-1: 80386/80387 system configuration.

The address and data buses are 32 bits wide to match the high bus bandwidth of the 80386. The following signals select the coprocessor:

- NPSI # (connected to M/IO# of 80386) and

- NPS2 (to A31 of 80386) with STEN pulled high.

CMDO# (connected to A2 of 80386) distinguishes between opcode and data cycles initiated to the 80387. Other system control signals include W/R# (write/read), ADS# (address/data strobe), and READY#, READYO# is the active-low ready output from the 80387. BUSY#, ERROR#, and PEREQ denote when the 80387 is busy executing the current instruction, when an error occurs, and when the 80387 is ready for operand transfer for the 80386, respectively. A key signal, the CKM, indicates to the 80387 that the synchronous mode of operation is desired. In such a case, the internal execution unit uses the same clock as does its bus interface and the 80386. Otherwise, a separate clock is required to connect to the 387CLK2 input.

System interface. In defining the system architecture, we concentrated on optimizing two major factors: overall system performance and system cost.

The 80387 resides on the 80386 local bus to serve 80386 requests. It directly decodes the control signals and traces all bus cycles on the bus. Bus cycle tracing is required to recognize pipelined data cycles to the 80387. ADS#, READY#, and control signals must be monitored to recognize such cycles.

A synchronous interface is required to correctly sample the ADS# and READY#. No glue logic is required. This not only reduces system cost but also increases system reliability. The simplicity of the interface eases the system design.

The 80387 can be envisioned as two different devices in one package:

- the Bus Control Logic unit, which serves as a dedicated bus controller for the 80387, and

- the 80387 core, which performs the computations.

A block diagram of the 80387 is shown in Figure 36-2.

The use of a 10-byte-deep FIFO between Bus Control Logic and the core permits the 80386 to process Reads/Writes with the minimal wait states possible (0 in Writes, 1 in Reads). It also facilitates the pseudosynchronous mode of operation in which the execution unit runs asynchronously to the bus interface. However, the 80387 bus interface always runs synchronously with the 80386. This mode of operation is effected by the input signal CKM.

Table 36-1
80387 I/O pin description.

Pin	Function
386CLK2	80386 CLocK 2 clocks the bus interface of the 80387, which is always synchronous to the 386 local bus. If the 80387 runs in synchronous mode, this clock is also used to clock the execution and the rest of the circuits. It uses the same system clock as the 80386. For a 16-MHz system, it operates at 32-MHz frequency.
387CLK2	80387 CLocK 2 clocks the execution unit of the 80387 if running in asynchronous mode. It has to use a separate clock in this mode. At the execution speed of 16 MHz, it operates at 32-MHz frequency.
CKM	ClocKing Mode is a strapping option. When tied high, the 80387 is intended to run in synchronous mode, when tied low, in asynchronous mode.
RESETIN	System reset.
PEREQ	Processor Extension Request indicates whether the 80387 is ready for data transfer or not.
BUSY#	Indicates that the 80387 is busy executing an instruction.
ERROR#	Indicates that a math error has occurred.
READYO#	Ready Output from the 80387 for opcode and data transfers between the 80386 and 80387.
READY#	Bus Ready input.
STEN	STatus Enable; when active, all 80387 outputs are enabled.
NPS1#	Numeric Processor Select #1.
NPS2	Numeric Processor Select #2.
CMDO#	CoMmanD distinguishes between opcode and data transfers.
ADS#	ADdress Strobe, the 80387 uses this 80386 output to monitor bus activities. It indicates the beginning of any new bus cycle.
W/R#	Write/Read.
D31-DO	A 32-bit data bus is connected directly to the 80386 data pins.

Interface Protocols

The 80387 instructions are an integral part of the 80386 instruction set. When the 80386 recognizes an 80387 instruction, it partially decodes it and initiates bus transactions for and with the 80387. The 80386 differentiates among the following instruction categories (only major categories are listed):

1. *Instructions that load an operand from the memory with the operand length in the range of two to 10 bytes.* These include all the load instructions as well as all arithmetic operations that need one operand from memory. The destination for a load operation and the second operand for a two-operand arithmetic operation is assumed to be at the top of the floating-point stack. Examples are FILD MEMORY[SI], FADD[BP].UPPERLIMIT, and FBLD BCD_NUMBERS. This category is referred to as "load type" instructions.

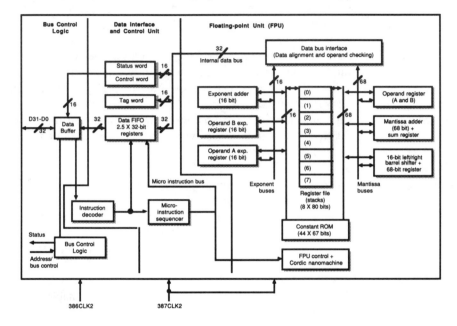

Figure 36-2: 80387 block diagram.

2. *Instructions that store an operand in the memory with the operand length in the range of two to 10 bytes.* These store instructions also convert internal, 80-bit extended format to the precision format as implied by the variable type. Examples of this category are FIST MEMORY[SI] and FBSTP BCD_NUMBERS. We call this category "store type" instructions.

3. *Numeric instructions that involve only the stack elements.* ST, the top of the stack, is always the implied stack element when omitted from an instruction. Examples of this category are FPATAN, FSTP ST(2), and FMULP ST(5),ST. We call this category "nonoperand transfer type" instructions.

4. *Administrative instructions that support the operating systems and exception handlers.* These instructions do not involve any operand transfer from any

source. Examples are FNINIT (FINIT without WAIT prefix) and FNCLEX (FCLEX without WAIT prefix). This category is referred to as "administrative type" instructions.

5. *Other categories exist that involve saving and restoring the 80387 state or its partial state.* These instructions are basically similar to the load type and store type instructions. They differ in their longer operand length. Examples of these instructions are FLDENV [BP] and FNSAVE [BP] (FSAVE without WAIT prefix). This category is referred to as "state save/restore type" instructions.

(See Table 36-2 for a list of the instructions discussed here.)

Synchronization becomes necessary when both the CPU and the coprocessor execute instructions concurrently. This state includes instruction and data synchronization and error handling. The 80386/80387 synchronization is implemented in three hierarchical levels:

- *Instruction synchronization.* Since the duration of the 80387 instructions is relatively long, the 80386 could try to write the next 80387 instruction before the previous one in completed. The 80386 and 80387 handle synchronization automatically.

- *Data synchronization.* Within the execution of an 80387 instruction, data transfer between the 80386 and the 80387 must be synchronized. The system also handles these transfers automatically.

- *Error synchronization.* When an exception is unmasked and an error condition is detected by the 80387, the corresponding exception bit and error summary bit in the 80387 status word are set. This step causes the ERROR# output to become active and hence gets the attention of the CPU. Since the error pointers to the failing floating-point instruction and operand are saved in the 80386, application software can locate the error point.

The FWAIT instruction and three signals, BUSY#, PEREQ, and ERROR#, are all that would be required to preserve the various types of synchronization.

Instruction synchronization. BUSY# is used to synchronize the parallel instruction execution between the 80386 and the 80387. The 80387 signals that it is busy by activating the BUSY# signal and that it is ready to execute the next instruction by deactivating the BUSY# signal. By testing its BUSY# input, the

80386 can decide whether it can write the next 80387 instruction or wait until the 80387 is ready. While waiting, the 80386 honors interrupt requests.

In the case of load type instructions (excluding transfers of two or 10 bytes), the 80386 writes the next (floating-point) opcode in line before the 80387 completes the current instruction. It waits until BUSY# has been deactivated before transferring the operand for the new instruction. On the other hand, once the 80387 frees itself from the current instruction, it starts executing the new instruction. The execution is prohibited from proceeding any further only if it has to wait for a memory operand. The 80387 will activate its BUSY# output only when the last operand word has been written to it (in contrast to the other cases where BUSY# is activated when the instruction is written). The execution of the new instruction can be aborted by the 80386 (by writing a new opcode instead of an operand) in case any exception has occurred in executing the current instruction.

Table 36-2
Partial list of 80387 instructions (used in the text).

Instruction	Function
FLD	Loads real numbers from memory/stack to stack top (ST) or ST(0); ST(1) is the next to the top of the stack.
FILD	Loads integer numbers from memory/stack to ST.
FBLD	Loads BCD numbers from memory/stack to ST.
FST	Stores ST to memory/stack in real format.
FSTP	Similar to FST—also pops ST off the stack.
FBSTP	Similar to FSTP—also stores in BCD format.
FIST	Stores ST to memory/stack in integer format.
FADD	Adds ST and memory/stack operand. For stack-stack operations, the first operand after mnemonics is the destination.
FMUL	Multiplies ST with memory/stack operand similar comment for stack-stack operations.
FMULP	Similar to FMUL—also pops ST.
FSIN	Calculates the sine of ST, including operand reduction.
FCOS	Calculates the cosine of ST, including operand reduction.
FSINCOS	Generates sine and cosine in one instruction.
FPATAN	Partial arc tangent of ST(1)/ST.
FSTENV	Saves the internal state of the 80387 in memory.
FLDENV	Restores the internal states from memory.
FSAVE	Saves the internal states and stack contents in memory.
FRSTOR	Restores the internal states and stack contents in memory.
FINIT	Initializes the 80387.

FCLEX   Clears the exception flags in the status word.

FWAIT   Ensures the completion of the current floating-point instruction before executing any other instruction; also makes the CPU check the status of its ERROR# input.

Most arithmetic operations use two operands, both of which could be stack elements; however, at least one of them must be the top of stack ST. The implied destination is always the ST, unless otherwise indicated. The complete list of 80387 instructions is documented in the 80387 Datasheet and the *80387 Programmer's Reference Manual*.

Administrative type instructions do not use this protocol, and the 80386 does not check its BUSY# input before writing the opcode to the 80387. The 80387 processes these instructions in parallel with any other instruction already being processed by the core at that time.

Data synchronization. PEREQ is used to synchronize the data transfers. By testing the state of PEREQ, the 80386 can tell whether the 80387 is ready for operand transfer or not. As soon as the 80387 is ready for operand transfer, it activates PEREQ. It deactivates the signal only when its FIFO becomes full (in the case of load type instructions) or empty (in the case of store type instructions). A good example is a store type instruction in which the 80387 performs data type conversion for the data on the stack before storing it and hence is not ready to transfer. In this case PEREQ is deactivated.

Another situation in which the use of PEREQ is essential is the 80387 execution of state save/restore type instructions. The transferable data is much longer than the depth of the data FIFO can accommodate. In this situation PEREQ regulates dataflow into and out of the FIFO. In load type instructions (excluding loads or two or 10 bytes), the 80387 FIFO is always ready to accept data, and the use of PEREQ is not needed.

Error synchronization. On some occasions users would like to handle a numeric exception in a different way than the default handling of the 80387. To support such applications, the 80387 drives its ERROR# output whenever it encounters an unmasked exception (that is, an exception users want to handle differently). The 80386 samples this signal whenever it encounters an exception-checking 80387 instruction, for example, FWAIT. If activated, the 80386 is interrupted. This ERROR# signal can be deactivated only by a user application using FNCLEX or FNINIT instructions.

Most store instructions must be followed by an FWAIT so that the ERROR# signal will be sampled by the CPU in case of an error in storing the result. Otherwise, the next instruction might use invalid data. An example of the use of an FWAIT instruction is:

```
FST mem      ; store single-precision floating-point result
FWAIT        ; check 80387 ERROR#
MOV eax, mem; before using the result
```

If no FWAIT is inserted after FST, the MOV instruction might end up using the invalid data stored in mem if there were indeed a math error.

Bus cycles. We describe the bus operation in terms of an abstract state machine shown in Figure 36-3. Bus cycles are more complex because of the 80386 pipelined bus. The pipelined bus allows more time to respond to new bus cycle addresses. Nonpipelined cycles are bus cycles that get started after the previous bus cycle has been terminated by READY#. Pipelined cycles get started before the end of the previous bus cycle.

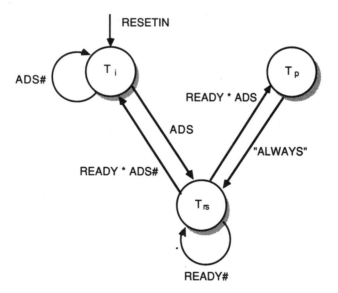

Figure 36-3: Bus state diagram.

- T_i is the idle state. This is the state of the bus logic after RESET, the state to which Bus Control Logic returns after every nonpipelined cycle, and the state to which bus logic returns after a series of pipelined cycles. New cycles start with new addresses.

- T_{rs} is the READY# sensitive data. Different types of bus cycles may require a minimum of one or two successive T_{rs} states. The bus logic remains in the T_{rs} state until READY# is sensed, at which point the bus cycle terminates. Any number of wait states can be implemented by delaying READY#, thereby causing additional successive T_{rs} states.

Illustrated in figures 36-4 and 36-5 are the nonpipelined bus cycles and the transitions to and from pipeline bus cycles. Both the read and write cycles can be seen. The sequence of events for a typical nonpipelined cycle is:

1. Sampling the ADS# input to sense the beginning of a bus cycle while various bus controls and addresses are latched as needed at the end of the first clock.

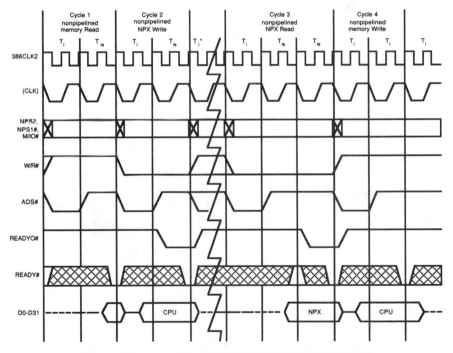

Cycles 1 and 2 represent part of the operand transfer cycle for instructions involving either 4-byte or 8-byte operand loads.
Cycles 3 and 4 represent part of the operand transfer cycle for a store operation.
Cycles 1 and 2 could repeat here or T i states for various nonoperand transfer cycles and overhead.

Figure 36-4

2. At the end of the second or a later clock, the READY# input is sampled to sense the end of the current cycle. If READY# is sampled active, go to Step 1 on the next clock.

A pipelined cycle involves sampling the ADS# active again before READY# is found active to terminate the current cycle. The pipelined mode allows the next cycle to start as soon as the second clock of the pending cycle is entered.

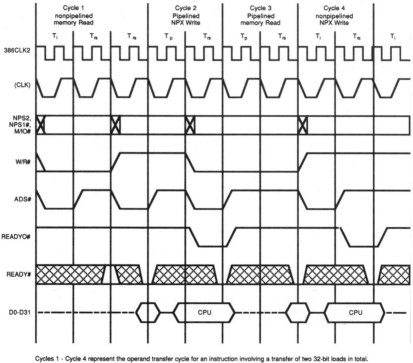

Cycles 1 - Cycle 4 represent the operand transfer cycle for an instruction involving a transfer of two 32-bit loads in total. The opcode write cycles and other overhead are not shown.

Note that the next cycle will be a pipelined cycle if both READY# and ADS# are sampled active at the end of a T rs state of the current cycle.

Figure 36-5: Fastest transitions to and from pipelined cycles.

Internal Architecture

Figure 36-2 (shown earlier) illustrates the internal architecture of the 80387 coprocessor. The three major functional units in the 80387 are the:

- Bus Control Logic,
- Data Interface and Control, and
- Floating-Point Unit.

In general, the 80387 core is the combination of the Floating-Point Unit and the Data Interface and Control Unit. Bus Control Logic communicates solely with the CPU using I/O bus cycles, which are initiated automatically by the CPU when executing floating-point instructions. This unit relies on the CPU to perform all the memory cycles. Bus states are decoded to recognize data transfers to/from the 80386. All 80386 pipelined bus cycles are supported (refer to Figure 36-5).

The instruction decoder inside the Data Interface and Control Unit decodes the floating instructions to direct the dataflow in the FIFO. This unit generates the bus synchronization signals, BUSY#, PEREQ, and ERROR#, to reduce the delay through the Bus Control Logic. It is also responsible for sequencing the microinstructions to control the Floating-Point Unit as well as the rest of the core.

The Floating-Point Unit executes all the instructions that involve the register stack, for example, the arithmetic, logical, transcendental, constant, and data transfer instructions. The data path in the unit is 84 bits wide (68 significant bits, 15 exponent bits, and a sign bit). This width allows internal operand transfers to be performed at very high speeds.

Features and Major Enhancements

The 80387 floating-point coprocessor features additional instructions not present in the 8087 and 80287 and an increased range of operands for several instructions.

New instructions. Two types of new instructions appear in the coprocessor. One type better supports the requirements and recommendations of the *ANSI/IEEE Standard 754-1985 for Binary Floating-Point Arithmetic*. Examples of such instructions are FPREM1, which supports a partial remainder as required by the standard, and FUCOM(P)(P), which performs unordered comparison. The other type of new instructions includes the trigonometric functions that are not already implemented in the 8087/80287, for example, FSIN (sine), FCOS (cosine), and FSIN-COS (sine and cosine in one instruction). FPTAN (partial tangent) and FATAN (arc tangent) available on previous numeric processors are also supported.

With the new built-in sine and cosine functions, calculating the inverse of the trigonometric functions becomes easier and faster.

```
ASIN(Z) = ATAN2[Z,SQRT(1-Z2)], when Z=SIN(Theta)
ACOS(Z) = ATAN2[SQRT(1-Z2),Z], when Z=COS(Theta)
```

Note: The ATAN2 function uses two operands (Y and X) and computes the arc tangent, ATAN of Y/X; for example, ATAN2(y,x) = ATAN(y/x).

Wider operand ranges. In the 8087/80287 some instructions restrict operand ranges. Such restrictions require application software to verify that operands are in range before performing a desired operation. The 80387 widens the range for most of these limited instructions. For example, the arc tangent function is unlimited in operand range while tangent, sine, and cosine are now almost unlimited in range (2^{63}). For large operands, the range improvement not only reduces the programming overhead mentioned above but also improves accuracy. More accuracy results because large operands are reduced with a more-precise, built-in PI (in 84-bit internal extended format versus 80-bit extended format for external PI). Since the trigonometric functions are periodic, for very large operands, the error accumulated as a result of using a less-precise PI value can result in significant accuracy degradation as illustrated here.

```
Let PI be the external PI and
   MPI be the PI available to the machine performing the reduction.
Let E = PI - MPI.

If SIN(N*PI + Theta) needs to be calculated, the accumulated error will be:
   (for the ease of calculation, let N be an even number)
SIN(N*PI + Theta) = SIN[N*(MPI + E) + Theta]
                  = SIN(N*E + Theta)
= SIN(Theta)*[SIN(NE)*COT(Theta) + COS(NE)]
   Relative_Error =
   [SIN(NE)*COT(Theta) + COS(NE)]
```

It is obvious that for a large enough N, the computed result is very inaccurate.

Another enhancement permits the 80387 to support Denormal as an operand in many other instructions that might not otherwise be supported by the 8087/80287.

Applications

The compatibility of both the 80386 and the 80387 at the object-code level allows existing application software to run on the system without modification.

Established uses of the 8087 and 80287 include math accelerators in personal computers, multiuser microsystems, and multiprocessing systems such as the iPSC Intel Personal Supercomputer.

The 80387's speed improvement of four to six times over the 80287 extends math applications to such new areas as workstations and real-time and embedded systems. Examples of real-time and embedded applications are process control, robotic, navigational, and guidance systems.

Typical hardware configuration. The 80386/80387 interface shown in Figure 36-1 represents the simplest interface. One key feature permits the CKM input to the 80387 to be strapped low so the 80387 can run in the asynchronous mode of operation. When running asynchronously, the 80387 core can run at a different speed than the system interface. In this case, an external oscillator meeting the AC timing requirements for the 387CLK2 input is needed. This mode of operation offers design flexibility during the design phase and numerics performance upgrading in the future without having to redesign the overall system interface.

This interface is typically used in most of the 80386-based systems (such as those to be described shortly). PC AT-compatible systems use a slightly different 80386/80387 interface as described later.

Single-board computers. A single-board computer using the 80386/80387 with on-board cache and/or a large amount of static RAM, DMA controller, interrupt controller, and timers could be used in stand-alone or embedded systems. Stand-alone systems include workstations and expert systems; embedded systems could be used for process control, robotics, navigation, and phototypesetting purposes. The 80387 is particularly useful in embedded systems with positional and rotational matrix calculations involving a lot of accurate floating-point computations. The 84-bit internal computing hardware provides the needed accuracy for recursive computations and precise control of distance, position, and motion. The built-in FSIN, FCOS, and FSINCOS functions (generating both the sine and cosine) significantly reduce computing time. This feature is especially important for complex robotic applications.

A block diagram of a typical 80386/80387, single-board iSBC386/20 computer appears in Figure 36-6. The board contains 64K bytes of cache and executes with less than one wait state. It serves as the CPU board in various engineering workstations and embedded systems. The system is expandable in hardware configuration using the Multibus and various local bus extensions. Major system software is targeted around this board.

Each of the iPSC processing nodes is connected to a host processor called the Cube Manager, which provides programming and system management. The Cube Manager allows the iPSC system to operate as a stand-alone system or a computational server within a distributed processing environment. It could be another 80386-based microcomputer system. A block diagram of a node board can be seen in Figure 36-7.

Multiprocessing systems. In a hypercube multiprocessor system, such as the iPSC Personal Supercomputer, each node in the cube is an independent, single-board computer. The node can contain an 80386/80387 pair and some dual-port local memory for initialization, kernel loading, interprocess communication, and user programming. The two key factors in the design are the computing power of each node and the efficiency of interprocessor communication. The needed computing power is provided by the 80386/80387, while dedicated communication hardware supports the low-level internode message routing. The use of 80386/80387 reduces the cost of each node, increases nodal performance, and allows the use of readily available software development tools and languages. Existing system software for the 80286/80287-based iPSC computer can be run on the new system. The 80387 floating-point coprocessor greatly increases the numeric processing power.

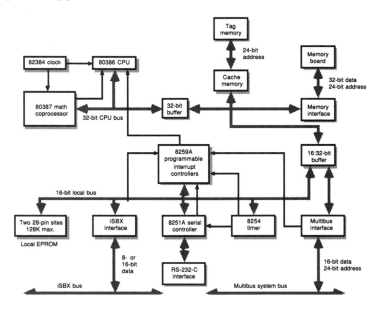

Figure 36-6: Block diagram of the single-board computer, the iSBC386/20.

The diagram shows that the 80386 and 80387 are closely tied together as a single piece of hardware integrated into a multiprocessor system. The 80386 LOCK instruction and atomic page table updates allow multiple CPUs to share data and page tables.

Distributed processing. A distributed process control system consists of many distributed nodes controlling the different processing functions in a factory. Functions such as temperature sensing and controlling, valve opening and closing, and stepper motor control require local intelligence. A complex system can contain over a hundred nodes or drops.

Each node contains the central processing module, which may be implemented with an 80386/80387 system such as an iSBC386/20 board or a distributed controller. The 80387 offers fast, real-time floating calculations to effect environmental and robotic control. Application software for existing 8086/8087- and 80286/80287-based distributed systems runs directly on the new 80386/80387-based distributed systems. This capability significantly reduces software development cost and time.

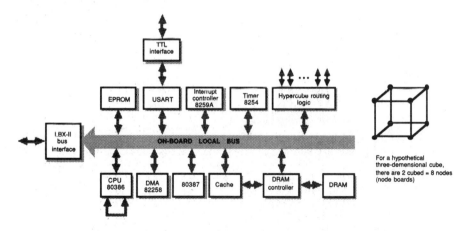

Figure 36-7: Node board block diagram (a) and hypercube structure (b).

IBM PC AT-compatible interface. Just as the PC AT personal computer has become a versatile system for a variety of applications, the use of an 80387 in an 80386-based personal computer could significantly improve the numeric performance, opening up many new applications. For example, the 80387 could accelerate signal processing to the performance range of many existing array-processor-based PC accelerator cards, which would cost as much as 30 times that of an 8087. In addition, the 80386/80387 could be used in artificial intelligence or other accelerator add-on cards on a PC AT platform. For computation-intensive systems, the 80387 should be configured to run in asynchronous mode. In this case, the internal number crunching could be clocked at a faster rate than that of the bus interface. This cuts down the cost of having to design and implement a faster overall system.

Conceptually depicted in Figure 36-8 is the IBM PC AT-compatible 80386/80387 interface. The external interface logic serves as error-signaling hardware. In this configuration, the ERROR# output of the 80387 is not connected to the 80386 directly but rather to interrupt logic (8259A), which in turn drives the INTR input of the 80386.

The use of interrupts for math-error signaling is a technique that was carried over from the design of the 8088-based personal computer. The 8088 contains no ERROR# pin, and hence INTR signals math error. To be able to run existing PC software, the PC AT also signals math error via interrupts, although the 80286 used in the PC AT also has the same ERROR# as the 80387. This explains the need for the additional hardware to simulate the error-signaling hardware in the PC AT.

The segment of the code that calculates the matrix elements is shown in the box above. Although only 64-bit memory operands are used, the internal operations are carried out in the 80-bit extended format.

The 80387 fully complies with the *ANSI/IEEE Standard 754-1985 for Binary Floating-Point Arithmetic* in addition to being fully compatible with the previous generations of floating-point processors. The CPU/coprocessor interface has been improved, especially for operations that involve 32/64-bit memory operands. For those instructions, the CPU can start writing the new opcode into the coprocessor before the 80387 finishes executing its current instruction. The asynchronous mode of the 80387 allows flexibility in design and future upgrading.

The improvement in performance of four to six times over the 80287 opens up many new applications for the 80387, especially in real-time, embedded systems, which require fast and high-precision numerics processing. For existing applications, the fast 80387 speeds up existing software and makes other time-consuming software feasible.

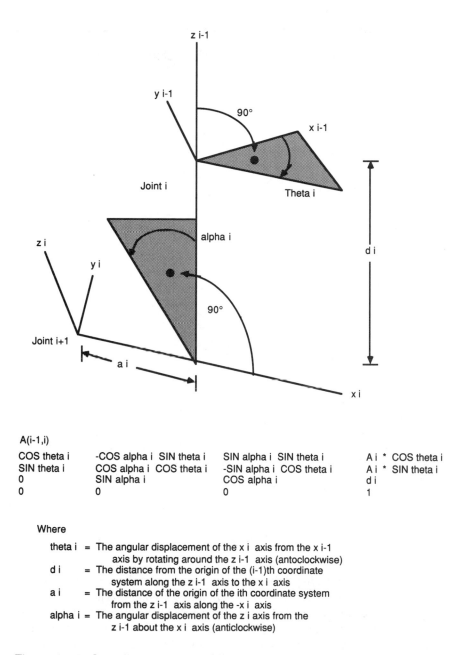

A(i-1,i)

COS theta i	-COS alpha i SIN theta i	SIN alpha i SIN theta i	A i * COS theta i
SIN theta i	COS alpha i COS theta i	-SIN alpha i COS theta i	A i * SIN theta i
0	SIN alpha i	COS alpha i	d i
0	0	0	1

Where

theta i = The angular displacement of the x i axis from the x i-1
          axis by rotating around the z i-1 axis (antoclockwise)
d i   = The distance from the origin of the (i-1)th coordinate
          system along the z i-1 axis to the x i axis
a i   = The distance of the origin of the ith coordinate system
          from the z i-1 axis along the -x i axis
alpha i = The angular displacement of the z i axis from the
          z i-1 about the x i axis (anticlockwise)

Figure 36-9: Coordinate relationships between adjacent joints.

Code Segment of the Denavit-Hartenberg Transformation Matrix

```
TRANS_PROC proc far                          ;a14 = A * cos theta
                                              a21 = sin theta
                                              a22 = cos alpha * cos theta
; Calculate alpha and theta in radians       ;a23 = -sin alpha * cos theta
; from their values in degrees               ;a24 = A * sin theta
  fldpi                                       ;a32 = sin alpha
  fdiv    d180                                ;a33 = cos alpha
                                              ;a34 = D
; Duplicate pi/180                            ;a31 = a41 = a42 = a43 = 0.0
  fld     st                                  ;a44 =1

    fmul    qword ptr ALPHA_DEG[ecx*8]        ;ebx contains the offset for the matrix
    fxch    st(1)
    fmul    qword ptr THETA_DEG[ecx*8]          fsincos  ;cos theta in ST
                                                         ;sin theta in ST(1)
; theta(radians) in ST and                      fld  st ;duplicate cos theta
; alpha(radians) in ST(1)                        fst [ebx].a11 ;cos theta in a11
                                                 fmul  qword ptr A_VECTOR[ecx*8]
; Calculate matrix elements                      fstp  ebx].a14 ;A * cos thetain a14
; a11 = cos theta                                fxch  st(1)  sin theta in ST
; a12 = 0 cos alpha * sin thet                   fst [ebx].a21 ;sin theta in a21
; a13 = sin alpha * sin theta                    fld     st  ;duplicate sin theta

    fmul   qword ptr A_VECTOR[ecx*8]             fstp    [ebx].a22 ;stored in a22
    fstp [ebx].a24;A * sin theta in a24          fmul  st,st(1) ;cos alpha  sin theta
    fld  st(2)   ;alpha in ST                    ;
    fsincos      ;cos alpha in ST                ; To take advantage of parallel operations
                 ;sin alpha in ST(1)             ; between the CPU and NPX
                 ;sin theta in ST(2)             ;
                 ;cos theta in ST(3)             push   eax ; save eax
    fst [ebx].a33;cos alpha in a33               ;
    fxch st(1)   ;sin alpha in ST                ; also move D into a34 in a faster way
    fst [ebx].a32;sin alpha in a32               mov    eax, dword ptr D_VECTOR[ecx*8]
    fld  ST(2)   ;sin theta in ST                mov    dword ptr [ebx + 88], eax
                 ;sin alpha in ST(1)             mov    eax, dword ptr D_VECTOR[exc*8 + 4]
    fmul  st,st(1);sin alpha * sin theta         mov    dword ptr [ebx + 92], eax
    fstp [ebx].a13;stored in a13                 pop    eax ;restore eax
    fmul  st,st(3);cos theta * sin alpha         fchs         ;and all nonzero elements
    fchs         ;-cos theta * sin alpha         fstp   [ebx].a12;stored in a12
    fstp [ebx].a23;stored in a23                         ;and all nonzero elements
    fld  st(2)   ;cos theta in ST                        ;have been calculated
                 ;cos alpha in ST(1)
                 ;sin theta in ST(2)             ret
                 ;cos theta in ST(3)
    fmul st,st(1) ;cos theta*cos alpha     TRANS_PROC endp
```

While an error is signaling through the interrupt logic, the CPU must be prevented from passing another math instruction to the 80387. The error latch, as triggered by the low-going edge of the 80387 ERROR# output, serves to extend the active time of the BUSY# signal to the CPU. The PEREQ is reactivated when ERROR# occurs. This action brings the CPU out of any wait state for pending data transfer, if any, to complete. The error latch is cleared once the CPU starts executing the interrupt service routine via the signal OUT_PORT_F0).

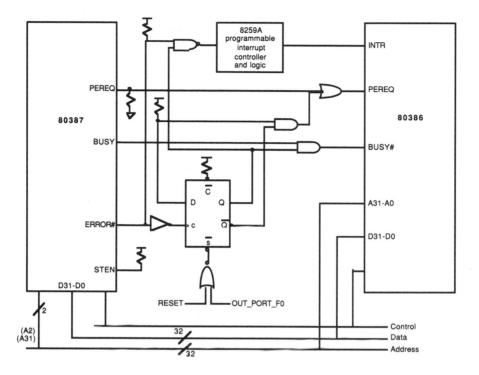

Figure 36-8: Block diagram of a conceptual IBM PC AT-compatible 80386/80387 interface.

Although this configuration does not take full advantage of the most-efficient-possible interface between the 80386 and 80387, it provides a PC AT-compatible interface for the personal computers. A similar interface can be found in the new IBM PS/2 systems.

Numerics Programming Example

Numerics programming can be illustrated with the following example showing the way some common 80387 instructions are used. The new, built-in FSIN-COS function calculates both the sine and cosine values for the given angle in radians, saving hundreds of clocks in the computing time. The possibility for parallel execution of the 80386 and 80387 instructions is also highlighted. The parallel operations balance and improve overall system performance.

Consider the calculations of matrix elements for the Denavit-Hartenberg transformation matrix used to model the kinematics of a robot arm. Shown in Figure

36-9 are the local coordinate systems originated at adjacent joints of a robot arm. The matrix A(i-1,i) transforms the *i*th coordinate system to the (*i*-1)th coordinate system.

Additional Reading

A Proposed Radix and Word Length Independent Standard for Floating-Point Arithmetic, (Draft 1.0 of IEEE task P854), IEEE Micro, Aug. 1984, pp. 86-100.

ANSI/IEEE Standard 754-1985 for Binary Floating-Point Arithmetic, Inst. Electrical and Electronics Engineers, New York, 1985.

Denavit, J., and R. Hartenberg, "A Kinetic Notation for Lower-Pair Mechanisms Based on Matrices," *J. Applied Mechanics*, June 1955, pp. 215-221.

8087 and 80287 Programmer's Reference Manuals, Intel Corporation, Santa Clara, Calif., 1985.

80386 Programmer's Reference Manual, Hardware Reference Manual and Datasheet, Intel Corporation, 1986.

80387 Datasheet and *80387 Programmer's Reference Manual*, Intel Corporation, 1987.

Lee, C.G., "Robot Arm Kinematics, Dynamics, and Control," *Computer*, Dec. 1982, pp. 63-80.

Nave, R., "Implementation of Transcendental Functions on a Numeric Processor," *Microprocessing and Microprogramming*, 1983, pp. 221-225.

Palmer, J., et al. "Making Mainframe Mathematics Accessible to Minicomputers," *Electronics*, may 1980, pp. 114-121.

Technical Reference Manual for Personal Computer AT, IBM Corporation, Boca Raton, FL 33432, 1985.

37

Programming the 80387
Coprocessor[*]

Prakash Chandra

THE 80387 CHIP is a math coprocessor for the 32-bit 80386 microprocessor. The 80387—actually called a Numerics Processor Extension (NPX) by its maker, Intel Corp.—implements the IEEE 754-1985 Standard for Binary Floating-Point Arithmetic and provides numerics capabilities that include support for floating-point, extended-integer, and binary-coded-decimal (BCD) data types. The 68-pin 80387 operates independently of the real, protected, and virtual-8086 modes of the 80386.

While maintaining upward object-code compatibility with the 8087 and the 80287, the 80387 contains a variety of new instructions, including instructions to compute sine and cosine functions, and it extends the capabilities of many existing instructions. Object-code compatibility ensures that any program running on the 8087 or the 80287 will run on the 80387 without recompilation.

Let's look at the key differences between the 80387 and the earlier 8087/80287 floating-point units (FPUs).

Architectural Overview

The 80287 was designed before the final IEEE-754 standard was approved. The 80387, on the other hand, fully conforms to the standard, including automatic normalization of denormal operands, support of only the affine interpretation of infinity (the 80287 supports both affine and projective interpretations), and IEEE 754-compatible unordered and partial remainder instructions.

The programmer of an 80386/80387 computer system can view the 80387 as a means to add extra registers, new data types, and trigonometric, exponential, and arithmetic instructions to those of the 80386.

---

[*] © McGraw-Hill Information Systems Company, _BYTE,_ March, 1988, p. 207

- Register set: as Figure 37-1 shows, an 80387 contains a set of eight 80-bit general-purpose registers that are individually addressable, plus three 16-bit registers and two 48-bit registers. The general-purpose registers are organized in the form of a stack. The top of the stack is designated by the TOP field of the 80387 status-word register (described later). Numeric instructions address the eight general-purpose registers relative to the top of the stack. In the rest of this article, I'll use ST to indicate the top of the stack and ST(i) (with i = 0,...,7) to represent the *i*th register from the top of the stack.

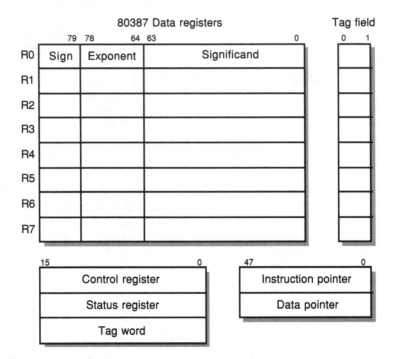

Figure 37-1: The register and model of the 80387.

The three 16-bit registers in the 80387 are known as status-word, control-word, and tag-word registers. The overall state of the 80387 is stored in the status word. The control-word register is used to control processing options in the 80387. The tag word indicates the contents of each register in the general-purpose register stack.

The function of the tag word is to optimize the 80387's performance and stack handling by making it possible to distinguish between empty and nonempty register locations. It also allows programmers of exception handlers to check the contents of a stack location without the need to perform complex decoding of actual data.

The 48-bit instruction and data-pointer registers provide for user-written exception handlers. These registers, which are actually located in the 80386, can be referenced only by a subset of 80387 instructions and are used by the 80386 to save the instruction address, the operand address (if any), and the instruction op code whenever the 80386 decodes an 80387 instruction.

Data formats	Range	Precision	Most significant byte ... Highest addressed byte
Word integer	10^4	16 bits	(Two's complement)
Short integer	10^2	32 bits	(Two's complement)
Long integer	10^{19}	64 bits	(Two's complement)
Packed BCD	10^{18}	18 digits	S X d17 d16 d15 d14 d13 d12 d11 d10 d9 d8 d7 d6 d5 d4 d3 d2 d1 d0
Single precision	$10^{\pm 38}$	24 bits	S Biased exponent Significand
Double precision	$10^{\pm 308}$	53 bits	S Biased exponent Significand
Extended precision	$10^{\pm 4932}$	64 bits	S Biased exponent Significand

(1) S = Sign bit (0 = positive, 1 = negative)
(2) d n = Decimal digit (two per type)
(3) X = Bits have no significance; 80387 ignores when loading, zeros when storing
(4) Δ = Position of implicit binary point
(5) | = Integer bit of significand; stored in temporary real, implicit in single and double precision
(6) Exponent bias (normalized values): single: 127 (7FH); double: 1023 (3FFH); extended real: 16383 (3FFFH)
(7) Packed BCD: (-1) to the S power (D 17...D 0)
(8) Real: (-1) to the S power (2 to the E-Bias) (F 0 F 1...)

Figure 37-2 : The data types supported by the 80387.

- *Data types:* As Figure 37-2 shows, the 80387 supports seven data types in three different formats–binary integer, BCD integer, and binary real. Internally, all numbers are stored in the extended-precision real format.

- *Special numeric values*: A real number in the 80387 has three parts–sign, significand, and exponent. The 1-bit sign indicates whether the number is positive or negative. The number's significant digits are held in the significand field. The exponent field determines the location of the "decimal" point within the significant digits.

The data format of the 80387 also permits representation of special numeric values. A significand of 00...00B (B=binary) and a biased exponent of 00...00B represent the value 0. A 0 can be positive or negative. Infinity is another special numeric value, represented by a significand of 1.00...00B and a biased exponent of 11...11B. The 80387 allows both positive and negative infinities. A third special case represents denormal numeric values that occur in computations involving extremely small numbers. Use of denormal values allows the gradual loss of precision in computations on small numbers.

The class of real numbers represented by an exponent of 11...11B and a significand of anything except 21.00...00B is termed a NaN (not a number). The 80387 uses two classes of NaNs–signaling NaNs (SNaNs) and quiet NaNs (QNaNs). The 80287, on the other hand, employs only one type of NaN–the equivalent of QNaN in the 80387.

A signaling NaN has a 0 in the most significant bit of its significand. Although the 80387 never generates a signaling NaN itself, it recognizes signaling NaN operand.

For example, a compiler could use the signaling NaN to detect the use of a variable in a program before the variable has been initialized. This can be done by initializing all variables declared in a program to be a signaling NaN. If a variable is used in an arithmetic operation before it has been initialized, it will cause the operation to be performed on a signaling NaN. If the invalid operation exception would occur to identify the offending variable.

A quiet NaN in the 80387, which contains a 1 in the most significant bit of its significand, behaves the same way as a NaN in the 80287.

New Instructions in the 80387

The 80387 contains seven new instructions not in the 80287. Of these, three are transcendental instructions, three are unordered compare instructions, and one is an IEEE-754 partial-remainder instruction. Table 37-1 summarizes these new instructions.

- *Trigonometric instructions:* The trigonometric functions accept a practically unrestricted range of operands. The instruction *FCOS* computes the cosine of the contents of ST and replaces it with *COS(ST)*. The value contained in ST must be in radians, and its absolute value must be less than 2^{63}. If the operand is within this range, the C2 bit (the eleventh bit) of the status word is cleared. The C2 bit is set to 1 if the operand of *FCOS* is outside the range and ST remains unchanged. The instructions *FPREM* and *FPREM1* can be used to reduce the operand to a specified range.

The *FSIN* instuction works the same way as the *FCOS* instruction. It replaces the contents of ST, which must be expressed in radians, with *SIN(ST)*. The operand range restriction for *FCOS* also applies for *FSIN*. The *FSINCOS* instruction computes both the sine and the consine of the contents of ST. First, the contents of ST are replaced by *SIN(ST)*, and then *COS(ST)* is pushed onto the stack. The operand range requirements for *FCOS* apply to *FSINCOS*, too.

Table 37-1: The new instructions added to the 80387 instruction set.

Instruction	Function
FCOS	Cosine
FSIN	Sine
FSINCOS	Sine and cosine
FUCOM	Unordered compare real
FUCOMP	Unordered compare real and pop
FUCOMPP	Unordcred compare real and pop (twice)
FPREM1	IEEE Standard partial remainder

- *Unordered compare instructions:* In addition to all the compare, test, and examine operations of the 80287, the 80387 offers three new instructions– *FUCOM, FUCOMP,* and *FUCOMPP*–to perform unordered comparisons. The *FUCOM* instruction operates like the *FCOM* (compare real) instruction in that it compares the value on the top of the stack to the source operand, where the source operand can be in a register or on the stack, or a single- or double-real memory operand. This instruction will not, however, generate an invalid-operation exception if one of the operands is a NaN. Table 37-2 shows the values of the condition code bits in the status word (bits 9, 10, 11, and 15) for various situations. If either operand is a NaN, the condition bits of the status word are set to unordered.

FUCOMP and *FUCOMPP* behave like *FUCOM* and also pop the stack once and twice, respectively.

Table 37-2: The values of the condition code bits in the 80387 status word for various conditions.

Order	C3(ZF) (Bit 15)	C2(PF) (Bit 11)	C0(CF) (Bit 9)	80386 Conditional branch
ST>operand	0	0	1	JA
ST<operand	0	0	1	JB
ST=operand	1	0	0	JE
Unordered	1	1	1	JP

- *IEEE 754-compatible remainder instruction:* The IEEE 754-compatible partial-remainder instruction in the 80387, *FPREM1*, computes the remainder of the division of ST by ST(1). The result is stored in ST. The instruction finds a remainder r and a quotient q such that

```
r = ST - ST(1) x q,
```

where *q* is the integer nearest to the exact value of ST/ST(1). *FPREM1* always produces exact results, and therefore the 80387's rounding control mode has no effect on the result.

If the *FPREM1* instruction is used on operands that differ greatly in magnitude, it can consume large amounts of time and will also increase the computer's interrupt latency, since the 80387 can be interrupted only between instructions. The instruction, therefore, may terminate before the calculation has been completed. If this happens, the C2 bit of the status word is set, indicated incomplete calculation. The contents of ST in this case contain only the partial remainder. *FPREM1* can reduce the exponent of ST by up to (but not including) 64 in one execution. If the reduction is complete, the C2 bit of the status bit is set to 0, and C3, C1, and C0 contain the least-three significant bits of the quotient generated. The *FPREM1* instruction differs from the 8087/287 instruction *FPREM* in two ways:

1. Remainder *r* produced by the instruction *FPREM* is in the range $0 \leq r < |ST(1)|$, or $-|ST(1)| < r \leq 0$, depending on the sign of the dividend. *FPREM1*, on the other hand, produces a remainder r such that $-|ST(1)|/2 < r < |ST(1)|/2$. 2. The low-order three bits of the quotient as reported in the

status word bits C3, C1, and C0 may differ by 1 in some cases because *FPREM1* and *FPREM* choose the value of quotients differently.

Extended Operand Range

The 80387 has extended the operand ranges of four instructions: *FPTAN*, *FPATAN, F2XM1,* and *FSCALE*. Table 37-3 compares the operand ranges for the 80387 with those for the 80287.

The allowed operand range for the *FPTAN* (partial tangent) instruction in the 80387, which computes the function y = TAN(ST) (ST is in radians), is $|ST(0)| < 2^{63}$. The corresponding range for the 80287 is $|ST(0)| < \pi/4$. The *FPTAN* instruction reduces the operand internally using an internal $\pi/4$ constant, which is more accurate than the value obtained using a constant instruction like *FLDPI.*

Table 37-3: The operand ranges for the 80387 compared to the 80287.

Instruction	Function	80387 Operand range	80287 Operand range
FPTAN	Partial tangent	$|ST(0)| < 2**$	$|ST(0)| < \pi/4$
FPATAN	Arctangent	Unrestricted	$|ST(0)| < |ST(1)|$
F2xM1	2*-1 -	$1 \leq ST(0) \leq 1$	$0 \leq ST(0) \leq 0.5$
FSCALE	Scale	Unrestricted	Undefined in $0 < |ST(1)| < 1$

The *F2XM1* instruction in the 80387 computes the function $y = 2^x - 1, -1 \leq x \leq 1$. This represents an increase in the range from $0 \leq x \leq 0.5$ in the 80287.

Instructions *FPATAN* (arctangent) and *FSCALE* in the 80387 have unrestricted operand ranges. The arctangent instruction *FPATAN* computes the function $0 = ARCTAN(y/x)$, where x and y indicated the contents of ST(0) and ST(1), respectively. Although the range of the operands is unrestricted, the range of the result depends on the relationships between the operands, as shown in Table 37-4.

FSCALE, which scales the top of the stack by the power of 2 given in ST(1), has no restriction on the range of value in ST(1) as the 80287 did. If $0 < |ST(1)| < 1$, the scaling factor is taken to be 0 in the 80387. This contrasts with the 80287, which produces an undefined result.

Rounding Control

Constants 0, 1, π, log*10, log*e, log*2, and In 2 can be loaded onto the 80387 stack using *FLDZ, FLD1, FLDPI, FLDL2T, FLDL2E, FLDLG2, and FLDLN2* instructions, respectively. These constants have full extended-real precision (64 bits) and are accurate to approximately 19 decimal digits. The 80387 allows rounding of these internal constants according to the rounding control (RC) bits (bits 11 and 12) of the control word. If the RC bit is set to the Nearest rounding mode, the 80387 produces the same constant as produced by the 80287.

Denormal Operations

The 80387 allows the use of denormal operands with *FBSTP* (packed decimal BCD store and pop), *FDIV* (divide real), *FIST* (integer store), *FISTP* (integer store and pop), *FPREM* (partial remainder), and *FSQRT* (square root) instructions. This differs from the 80287, which raises an invalid-operation exception when denormal operands are passed to these instructions.

Table 37-4: The result range of operands depends on the relationship between the operands

Sign(y)	Sign(x)	$|y|<|x|$?	Final result
+	+	Yes	$0<\text{atan}(y/x)<\pi/4$
+	+	No	$\pi/4<\text{atan}(y/x)<\pi/2$
+	-	No	$\pi/2<\text{atan}(y/x)<3x\pi/4$
+	-	Yes	$3x\pi/4<\text{atan}(y/x)<\pi$
-	+	Yes	$-\pi/4<\text{atan}(y/x)<0$
-	+	No	$-\pi/2<\text{atan}(y/x)<-\pi/4$
-	-	No	$-3x\pi/4<\text{atan}(y/x)<-\pi/2$
-	-	Yes	$-\pi<\text{atan}(y/x)<-3x\pi/4$

Exceptions occur whenever the 80387 receives an invalid operand or produces a result that cannot be represented. When an exception occurs, the 80387 does one of the following:

1. Handles the exception itself by invoking the default exception handler. This happens when the exception is masked (i.e., the corresponding mask bit in the control word is set to 1).

2. Signals the host (80386) that an exception has occurred and invokes a user-supplied exception handler. This is the case when the exception is unmasked–that is, the mask bit in the control word is set to 0.

Types of Exceptions

The 80387 recognizes six types of exceptions: (1) invalid operation; (2) divide-by-zero; (3) denormal operand; (4) numeric overflow; (5) numeric underflow; and (6) inexact result. These six types are described in detail below.

*   *Invalid operation*: An invalid-operation exception occures in two situations: An arithmetic instruction encounters an invalid operand, or a stack operation results in a stack overfow or underflow. As described earlier, the 80387 recognizes two kinds of NaNs–signaling and quiet. An invalid-operation exception is usually raised only upon encountering a signaling NaN. The instructions *FCOM, FIST*, and *FBSPT*, however, flag an invalid-operation exception on quiet NaNs. The 80287, on the other hand, signals an invalid-operation exception upon encountering any kind of NaN, since it does not differentiate between two NaNs.

    While the 80287 defines and supports special handling for pseudozero, pseudo-NaN, pseudoinfinity, and unnormal formats, the 80387 neither generates nor supports these formats and raises an invalid-operation exception whenever it encounters them in an arithmetic operation.

*   *Divide-by-zero*: A zero-divide exception is reported whenever an attempt is made to divide a finite number by 0. This can happen in instructions like *FDIV, FDIVP, FIDIV, FDIVR, FDIVRP*, and *FIDIVR* that do explicit divides or in instructions that do divides internally, such as *FYL2X (yxlog*x)* or *FXTRACT* (extract exponent and significand). If the zero-divide exception is masked, the 80387 responds by returning infinity signed with the exclusive-OR of the signs of the operands in the case of divide (*FDIV*, etc.) and *FYL2X* instructions. For *FXTRACT*, ST(1) is set to negative infinity and ST is set to 0 with the same sign as the original operand. In the event of an unmasked divide-by-zero exception, the operands remain unchanged.

*   *Denormal operand:* The 80387 reports a denormal-operand exception whenever an attempt is made to operate an arithmetic instruction on a denormal operand. The masked response for the instruction is to set the DE-bit (bit 2) of the status word and to then proceed with the instruction.

The 80387 does not raise an invalid-operation exception when it encounters a denormal operand in *FSQRT, FDIV,* or *FPREM,* or upon conversion to BCD or to integer. The operation proceeds by first normalizing the value. The 80287 will raise an invalid operation in such cases. Furthermore, the 80387, in contrast with the 80287, reports a denormal exception if a denormal operand is found in transcendental instructions and in *FXTRACT.*

- *Numeric overflow and underflow:* Numeric overflow and underflow exceptions occur when the exceptions occur when the exponent of a numeric result is too large or too small, respectively, to be represented in the destination format.

The masked response to the numeric overflow exception depends on the rounding mode. Table 37-5 shows the results of the computation for various rounding modes. The masked response in the case of rounding mode set to chop (i.e., toward 0) is to produce the most positive or the most negative number. The 80287 will not report an overflow exception in a similar situation. It will, in fact signal overflow only when the rounding control mode is *not* set to round to 0.

If the overflow exception is not masked in the 80387, it raises the precision exception (inexact result). When the result is stored on the stack, the significand is rounded according to the precision control (PC) bits (bits 9 and 10) of the control word, or according to the op code. In the 80287, on the other hand, the precision exception is not reported, nor is the significand rounded.

Table 37-5: The rounding modes of the 80387.		
Rounding mode	**Sign of true result**	**Result**
To nearest	+	$-\infty$
	−	$-\infty$
Toward $-\infty$	+	Largest finite positive number
	−	$-\infty$
Toward$+\infty$	+	$+\infty$
	−	Largest finite negative number
Toward 0	+	Largest finite positive number
	−	Largest finite negative number

The underflow exception is flagged by the 80387 if the true result is so small that it cannot be represented in the destination format. When the underflow exception is masked, it is signaled when there is a loss of accuracy in the result. The 80287 will report the underflow exception on underflow if rounding is toward 0, regardless of loss of accuracy.

If the underflow exception is unmasked and the result is to be stored on the stack, the significand is rounded according to the precision control bit of the control word in the 80387. The 80287 does not round the significand on the stack.

- *Inexact result:* If an operation produces a result that cannot be represented exactly in the destination format, the inexact-result exception is reported. The inexact exception is also raised in the event of an underflow exception with a loss of accuracy.

The 80387 does not give precedence to the denormalized exception, whether it is masked or not. In the 80287, the unmasked denormal exception takes precedence over all other exceptions.

Programming Examples

Listing 37-1 shows an example of 80387 code to compute $y=e^z$ Note that $e^z = 2z^{x\log_2 e}$. The program first checks to find out whether an 80387 or an 80287 is present. This is done by examining the value stored at *SS:FFFEH*. If an 80387 is present, the code takes advantage of the fact that the instruction *F2XM1* accepts operands in the range $-1<=z<=1$. First, the largest integer X that satisfies the condition $zx\log_2 e = x + y$ is found. Note that all values of y satisfying the above condition must lie in the range $-1<=y<=1$. The expression $2^{ax\log_2 e}$ is computed by computing the expression $2^x x[(2^y-1) + 1]$. Slightly different code is used to compute e^z if an 80287 is present, since the *F2XM1* instruction in the 80287 supports only operands in the range $0<=z<=0.5$.

An example of how to compute the function ARCSIN(z) is illustrated in Listing 37-3. It makes use of the relationship ARCSIN(z) = ARCTAN(z/SQRT(1-z)).

Listing 37-1: A code sample illustrating the use of 80387 instructions.

```
; compare ez, assume Z is in ST
FLD1
CMP SS:BYTE PTR 0FFFEH,1 ; 80287 or 80387?
JE USE_287
 ; 80387 found
FLDL2E ; load log2e
FMUL ST, ST(2) ; ST = z * log2e
FST ST(2)
FPREM ; reduce ST between -1 and 1 F2XM1
FADD
FSCALE
FSTP ST(1)
RET
USE_287:  ; 80287 found
FCHS
FLDL2E
FMUL ST, ST(2)
FST ST(2)
FTST
JB NEG_VAL
FPREM
FSCALE ; postitive value
F2XM1
FSUBR
FMUL ST, ST(0)
FSCALE
FSTP ST(1)
RET
NEG_VAL:  ; negative value
FPREM
FCHS
FSCALE
F2XM1
FSUB ST,ST(1)
FMUL ST,ST(0)
FDIV
FCHS
FSCALE
FSTP ST(1)
RET
```

Listing 37-2: Sample code illustrating the use of built-in transcendental functions.

```
; compute ARCSIN(Z), assume Z in ST
FST ST(1) ; ST(1) = ST = Z
FMUL ST, ST(0) ; ST = Z2
FLD1
FSUBR ; ST = 1-Z2
```

```
FSQRT ; ST = SQRT(1-Z2)
FPATAN ; ST = ARCTAN (Z/SQRT(1-Z2))
RET
```

New Look

The 80387 provides the system designer with significant enhancement in features and speed over the 80287. It fully conforms to the IEEE 754-1985 Standard for Binary Floating-Point Arithmetic. While maintaining object-level compatibility with the 8087 and the 80287, it provides the 80287 set of floating-point instructions with additional trigonometric, unordered comparison, and partial-remainder instructions. The operand ranges for some 80287 instructions have been expanded in the 80387.

Processor Initialization and Control

During initialization of an 80386 system, system software must recognize the presence or absence of an FPU and set flags in the 80386 machine status word to reflect the state of the numeric environment. If an 80387 is present, it must also be initialized.

Listing 37-3 shows a routine to determine the presence of a coprocessor (8087, 80287, or 80387). The algorithm first tries to dertermine if a coprocessor is present by examining the status and control words. An affirmative test confirms the presence of a coprocessor. To test for the presence of an 80387, both positive and negative infinities are generated and their values compared. Since the 80387 differentiates between positive and negative infinities, this comparison indicates that the two infinities are different. The 80287, however, does not differentiate between the two infinities.

This program sets the word at SS:FFFEH to 0 if no FPU is present, to 1 if an 8087 or 80287 is present and to 2 if an 80387 is present. Once this test has been performed and the word at SS:FFFEH appropriately set, a program needs to just examine the value at SS:FFFEH to determine which FPU is present. This can also be used to execute different code, depending on whether an 80287 or 80387 is present.

There is a difference in FPU initialization between the 80287 and the 80387. Either the *FINIT* or *FNINIT* instruction initializes teh 80387 to a state compatible with the state of the 80287 after *FINIT* or a hardware *RESET*. A hardware *RESET* of the 80387, however, leaves it in a state that is *not* the same as its state after a *FINIT* or *FNINIT* instruction. The two states have these differences:

1. The mask bit for the invalid-operation exception is reset.
2. The invalid-operation exception flag of the status word is reset.
3. The exception-summary bit of the status word is set.

These settings cause the FPU to assert the *ERROR#* output to indicate that an 80387 is present. It is, therefore, necessary to execute an *FNINIT* instruction after a hardware reset of the 80387.

Listing 37-3: A routine to check for the presence of a math coprocessor.

```
dgroup      group     data
cgroup      group     code

code  segment  public 'code'
 assume    cs:cgroup,ds:dgroup
;
;Look for an 8087, 80287, or 80387 NPX.
;Note that we cannot execute WAIT on 8086/88 if no 8087 is
                              present.
;Set word at SS:FFFEH to 0 for no NPX, 1 for 8087 or 80287, 2
                              for 80387
;
test_npx:
 fninit                  ;Init NPX, must use non-wait form!
 mov si,0fffeh          ;set offset of status variable
                  ; SS:FFFEH can be accessed at any time
 sub si,bp             ; [BP+SI] points at SS:FFFEH
 xor dx,dx             ; Clear NPX status flag
 mov word ptr [bp+si],5A5AH ; Initialize temp to non-zero
                              value
 fnstsw   [bp+si]       ; Must use non-wait form of fstsw
                  ; It is not necessary to use a WAIT
                              instruction
                  ; after fnstsw or fnstcw.  Do not use one
                              here.
 cmp [bp+si],dl         ; See if correct status with zeroes was
                              read
 jne  set_flags         ; Jump if not a valid status word,
                              meaning no NPX
;
;Now see if ones can be correctly written from the control
                              word.
;
 fnstcw   [bp+si]          ; Look at the control word do not use
```

```
                         WAIT form
                   ; Do not use a WAIT instruction here!
     mov ax,[bp+si]       ; See if ones can be written by NPX
     and ax,103fh     ; See if selected parts of control word
                         look OK
     cmp ax,3fh           ; Check that ones and zeroes were
                         correctly read
     jne set_flags        ; Jump if no npx is installed
;
;Some numerics chip is installed. NPX instructions and WAIT
                     are now safe.
;See if the NPX is an 8087/287 or 80387.
;This code is necessary if a denormal exception handler is
                     used or the
;new 80387 instructions will be used.
;
     inc dx              ; Indicate 87/287 by default status=1
     fld1                ; Must use default control word from FNINIT
     fldz                ; Form infinity
     fdiv                ; 8087/287 says +inf = -inf
     fld st              ; Form negative infinity
     fchs                ; 80387 says +inf <> -inf
     fcompp                 ; See if they are the same and remove
                         them
     fsysw    [bp+si]       ; Look at status from FCOMPP
     mov ax,[bp+si]
     sahf                ; See if the infinities matched
     je  set_flags         ; Jump if 8087/287 is present
;
;An 80387 is present. If denormal exceptions are used for an
                     8087/287,
;they must be masked.  The 80387 will automatically normalize
                     denormal
;operands faster than an exception handler can.
;
     inc dx              ; Set status variable to 2
     set_flags:
     mov [bp+si],dx
```

80387 Performance

The 80387 provides a considerable speed improvement over its predecessor, the 80287. This has been accomplished by using a higher clock speed, an optimized core that takes fewer clocks per instruction than the 80287, and new transcendental instructions. Benchmark results on a system using a 20-MHz 80386 is 1.8 megaWhetstones. Whetstone is a measure of the number of floating-point computations that can be computed by the processor per unit time.

Using an 80387 in a Compaq Deskpro 386/20 Model 30 reduces the time to remove hidden lines from a sample drawing of the space shuttle using the Auto-CAD version 2.62 *HIDE* command by a factor of 2.6 over the 80287 used in a Compaq Deskpro 286 Model 40. (Source: Compaq Deskpro 386/20 Personal Computer Features/Specifications).

Compilers available for the 80386 from Green Hills, MetaWare, Silicon Valley Software, Language Processors, and Austec provide a switch for the 80387 that allows the compiler to generate in-line 80387 instructions.

38

How to Get Better
Floating-Point Results [*]

_____*Carl Byington*_____

Floating-Point Coprocessor units (FPUs) are the key to getting good number-crunching performance out of personal computers, and yet they are usually extra-cost options. To be fair to users who haven't added one to their computers, a software designer has to write software that will use an FPU if one is present or perform the necessary operations using the main processor otherwise. In a compiler system, the component that takes care of this is called a floating-point emulator.

Unfortunately, all emulators are not alike. They do not behave identically nor always emulate the hardware exactly. This means that a given program may produce different results, depending on whether an FPU is present, and, if not, depending on which emulator is used.

But you can solve or at least control the problem by designing the high-level algorithm carefully, based on a few principles that derive from an elementary understanding of the emulation process and floating-point representation systems.

This article discusses some of the trade-offs involved in emulating floating-point hardware and explains the implications for programmers. All the specific examples in this article apply to the Ryan-McFarland RM/FORTRAN version 2.4 8087 emulator, which I helped design and implement. Previous versions of the compiler had used the emulator provided by Intel. We (the compiler design team) knew we could significantly speed up the emulation by writing a new emulator with a different set of design goals. The Intel emulator was designed to produce an exact emulation of the 8087 chip. It calculates results more precisely (and therefore more slowly) than is required by the RM/FORTRAN compiler. The Intel emulator also fails to take full advantage of the 8086 instruction set. For instance, many internal variables are maintained in memory, rather than in registers.

_____

The 8087 chip can work with numbers in three basic formats: the 32-bit (24-bit significand) single precision; 64-bit (53-bit significand) double precision; and 80-bit (64-bit significand) temporary. I will refer to these various formats by the number of significand bits (24, 53, and 64).

The version 2.4 emulator was designed to produce results accurate to 60 bits. The primary design goals was to increase the speed of floating-point computations subject to the 60-bit precision requirement. A secondary goal was to increase the precision beyond 60 bits whenever possible so long as the speed was not reduced. A third goal was to make the emulator as small as possible, but this was not allowed to interfere with the first two goals. The speed objective is easily understandable, but why choose 60-bit precision when both the 8087 hardware and the Intel emulator calculate results to 64-bit precision? We did this because it doesn't affect the precision of the results produced by a FORTRAN program.

Precision and How to Keep It

Three factors control the precision of the results produced by a FORTRAN program: the algorithm (sequence of operations) and input data the program uses, the order of those operations after the compiler has optimized and rearranged the code, and the precision of individual operations within the FPU or emulator.

The entire FORTRAN system (compiler and emulator) has no control over the first factor; that is left up to the programmer. The second and third factors are related in that the choice of precision in the emulator needs only to match the precision requirements of the compiler.

RM/FORTRAN assumes that intermediate results need to be calculated to only 24 (REAL) or 53 (DOUBLE PRECISION) bits. Intermediate results will be calculated to a greater precision if there is no performance penalty. The emulator calculates the standard add, subtract, multiply, and divide functions to 64-bit precision; and it calculates the square root, tangent, arctangent, exponential, and logarithm functions to 60-bit precision.

Only two things can be done with the result of an arithmetic operation: It can be stored in a FORTRAN variable or used as an operand of another arithmetic operation. In the former case, the result's precision will be reduced to 53 bits. In the latter case, two further possibilities apply. The result may be used directly with its full precision, or the compiler optimizer may choose to store it in a compiler-generated temporary variable for later reuse, in which case the temporary variable will have a maximum precision of 53 bits.

Consider the FORTRAN statements

```
DOUBLE PRECISION A,X,Y,Z
A=X+(Y+Z)
```

One possible 80x87 FPU code sequence to calculate A is

```
FLD  X ;floating point load X
FADD Y ;floating point add Y
FADD Z ;floating point add Z
FSTP A ;floating point store A
```

The register operand for the second FADD can have up to 64 significant bits, since it was calculated by the first FADD.

Now consider a second code sequence that might be generated if the subexpression *Y+Z* appeared in more than one expression in the FORTRAN program:

```
FLD  Y;floating point load Y
FADD Z;floating point add Z
FST  T;save subexpression in temp T
...
FLD  T;floating point load T
FADD X;floating point add X
FSTP A;floating point store A
```

Here the precision of *T* is only 53 bits (a double-precision temporary generated by the compiler), and the results may not be identical to those produced by the first code sequence.

The compiler and emulator guarantee that each elementary arithmetic operation is accurate to at least 53 bits. You can still write FORTRAN code that is exact in the mathematical sense and yet produces very imprecise results. Two common causes for this loss of precision are subtraction of two numbers that are almost identical and addition of two numbers of widely different magnitudes. As an example of the first situation, consider the problem of finding the roots of the quadratic equation $x^2 + 2bx + c = 0$.

The standard formula gives us

$$x_1 = -b + \sqrt{(b^2-c)}$$
$$x_2 = -b - \sqrt{(b^2-c)}$$

If these were implemented with infinitely precise arithmetic and the coefficents b and c were known exactly, they would produce the exact roots of the quadratic equation. But when they are used in a FORTRAN program, several things happen. Here are the FORTRAN statements:

```
x1 = -b + Sqrt (b**2 - c)
x2 = -b - Sqrt (b**2 - c)
```

First, the coefficients can be known exactly but represented only imprecisely in FORTRAN variables with 53-bit precision. Second, the individual arithmetic operations are implemented with only 53-bit precision. Let us see what effect this has on the precision of the result when b is approximately -2^{26} and c is approximately 1. The result x1 will have 53 bits of precision; $x2$ will have only a few bits of precision (note that we're now using FORTRAN rather than algebraic variables). Why did this happen?

Consider the computation of $x2$. The expression $b**2$ will be calculated to 53 bits and is approximately 2^{52}. The value of $b**2-c$ is calculated to 53 bits, but only a few high-order bits of c take part in this calculation. The expression $Sqrt(b**2-c)$ is calculated to 53 bits and is almost exactly the same as $-b$. The final step in the calculation of $x2$ is a subtraction involving operands that are almost identical; the result of this subtraction has only a few bits of precision.

Look at the FORTRAN numbers A, B, C, and D in Table 38-1. A and B share 50 high-order bits. $A-B$ is C, which has 50 high-order 0s. D is the result of normalizing C, so the high-order bit of D is 1. But the low-order 0s in D are an artifact of the floating-point arithmetic, and they have no significance. D is really known to only three bits of precision, even though its representation in a FORTRAN variable will have 53 significand bits.

This is essentially what has happened in the final subtraction in the calculation of $x2$ above. An alternate formula is $x2=c/x1$, which can be calculated to 53 bits of true precision. The quad program in Listing 38-1 demonstrates the different results obtained using these two approaches. Note that the computation of the error in $x1$ is itself an ill-posed computation with no significant bits. The compiler has calculated that error (variable $x3$) twice with two different results.

a) C=A-B and D=C (normalized).

A=0.xxxxxxxxxxxxxxxxxxxxxxxxxxxxxxxxxxxxxxxxxxxxxxyyy x 2^{26}
B=0.xxxxxxxxxxxxxxxxxxxxxxxxxxxxxxxxxxxxxxxxxxxxxxwww x 2^{26}
C=0.00000000000000000000000000000000000000000000zzz x 2^{26}
D=0.zzz0000000000000000000000000000000000000000000000 x 2^{-24}

b) A and B are to be added; C=B(normalized); D=A+C.

A=0.xxxxxxxxxxxxxxxxxxxxxxxxxxxxxxxxxxxxxxxxxxxxxxxxxxxx x 2^{3}
B=0.yyyyyyyyyyyyyyyyyyyyyyyyyyyyyyyyyyyyyyyyyyyyyyyyyyyy x 2^{-50}
C=0.00000000000000000000000000000000000000000000000000 x 2^{3}
D=0.xxxxxxxxxxxxxxxxxxxxxxxxxxxxxxxxxxxxxxxxxxxxxxxxx x 2^{3}

Table 38-1: Results of computations involving (a) subtraction of nearly equal numbers and (b) addition of numbers of widely different magnitudes.

Now we will look at an example where you lose precision by adding numbers that are very far apart. Consider the numbers in Table 38-1b. The magnitude of A is very different from the magnitude of B. C is B modified so that the exponent will match the exponent of A. Note that in order to make the exponents match, all the bits of B have been lost. D is A+C, which is the same as A. In this case, you have not lost any precision, since the sum is still correct to 53 bits.

Listing 38-1: (a) A FORTRAN program illustrating ill-formed and well-formed calculations of the quadratic formula, followed by (b) a sample run of the program.

(a)

```
       program quad
       double precision b, c, x1, x2, x3, x4
10     write (6, 1)
       write (6, *) 'Enter coefficients b and c separated by
                                 spaces: '
       read (5, *) b,c
       if (c .eq. 0.0) stop
```

```
        write (6, 1)
        write (6, 3) b, c
c
        write (6, *) 'Method one.'
        x1 = -b + sqrt(b**2-c)
        x2 = -b - sqrt(b**2-c)
        x3 = x1**2 + 2*b*x1 + c
        x4 = x2**2 + 2*b*x2 + c
        write (6, 2) x1, x2, x3, x4
c
        write (6, *) 'Method two.'
        x1 = -b + sqrt (b**2-c)
        x2 = c/x1
        x3 = x1**2 + 2*b*x1 + c
        x4 = x2**2 + 2*b*x2 + c
        write (6, 2) x1, x2, x3, x4
c
        goto 10
c
1       format (1x)
2       format (' x1 solution  ', D25.18 /
     $          ' x2 solution  ', D25.18 /
     $          ' error in x1  ', D25.18 /
     $          ' error in x2  ', D25.18)
        format (' b            ', D25.18 /
     $          ' c            ', D25.18)
        end
```

(b)

```
Enter coefficients b and c separated by spaces: -3e7 1

b               -0.300000000000000000D+08
c                0.100000000000000000D+01
Method one.
x1 solution      0.599999999999998510D+08
x2 solution      0.149011611938476563D-06
error in x1     -0.800024414062500000D+01
error in x2     -0.794066971630857155D+01
Method two.
x1 solution      0.599999999999998510D+08
x2 solution      0.166666666666667067D-07
error in x1     -0.794067382812500000D+01
error in x2     -0.220580931992175877D-14
```

```
Enter coefficients b and c separated by spaces: -3e8 1

b               -0.300000000000000000D+09
c                0.100000000000000000D+01
Method one.
x1 solution      0.600000000000000000D+09
x2 solution      0.000000000000000000D+00
error in x1      0.000000000000000000D+00
error in x2      0.100000000000000000D+01
Method two.
x1 solution      0.600000000000000000D+09
x2 solution      0.166666666666666670D-08
error in x1      0.100000000000000000D+01
error in x2      0.281892564846231153D-17

Enter coefficients b and c separated by spaces: -3e9 1

b               -0.300000000000000000D+10
c                0.100000000000000000D+01
Method one.
x1 solution      0.600000000000000000D+10
x2 solution      0.000000000000000000D+00
error in x1      0.100000000000000000D+01
error in x2      0.100000000000000000D+01
Method two.
x1 solution      0.600000000000000000D+10
x2 solution      0.166666666666666660D-09
error in x1      0.100000000000000000D+01
error in x2      0.000000000000000000D+00

Enter coefficients b and c separated by spaces: 1 0
```

Now consider the problem of calculating the sum of the power series $1 + r + r^2 + r^3 + r^4 + ...$, where r is in the interval (0,1). If r is .99, then the sum of the infinite series is 100. If the first 2000 elements are added in the order indicated, starting with the first and largest element, the partial sum will eventually become much larger than subsequent series elements, producing a problem similar to that illustrated in Table 38-1, part (b).

This problem can be partially solved by summing the series starting with the smallest elements first. The loss of precision is then not so severe, although it still occurs. The only way to eliminate this problem is to use an array of accumulators and add the next series element into the appropriate accumulator. A far better algorithm in this case is to throw away the series expansion and calculate the mathematically equivalent expression $1/(1-r)$.

The series program in Listing 38-2 demonstrates these techniques. The *do 15* loop initializes the *sumx* array. The array element at that position should either be 0 or have a value close to the value of the series element $r**i$. The *do 16* loop checks for array elements that have become too large and effectively propagates the carry. The *do 25* loop finally adds the *sumx* array elements to arrive at *sumw*. Note that this algorithm works only when all the series elements have the same sign. For an alternating series, you need separate arrays for the positive and negative elements; merging the two arrays produces the final answer.

Listing 38-2: (a) A FORTRAN program illustrating various approaches to the calculation of a power series, followed by (b) a sample run of the program.

(a)

```
        program series
        double precision r, sum, sumup, sumdown, x
        double precision sumx(30), sumw
        index(x) = 4 + int(-log10(x))
c       sumx(i) < 10**(4-i)
c
        km = 30
c
10      write (6, 1)
        write (6, *) 'Enter r and n separated by spaces:'
        read (5, *) r, n
        if (r .eq. 0) stop
c
        sum     = (1-r**n) / (1-r)
        sumup   = 0
        sumdown = 0
        do 15 j = 1,km
           sumx(j) = 0
15      continue
c
        do 20 i = 0, n-1
           sumup   = sumup + r**i
           sumdown = sumdown + r**(n-1-i)
           j = index(r**i)
           sumx(j) = sumx(j) + r**i
```

```
         do 16 k = j, 2, -1
           if (sumx(k) < 10**(4-k)) goto 20
           sumx(k-1) = sumx(k-1) + sumx(k)
           sumx(k)   = 0
16       continue
20     continue
c
       sumw = 0
       do 25 j = km, 1, -1
         sumw = sumw + sumx(j)
25     continue
c
       write (6, 2) r, sum, sumw, sumup, sumdown
       goto 10
c
1      format (1x)
2      format (' r                        ', d25.18 /
      $           ' correct partial sum    ', d25.18 /
      $           ' calculated with array ', d25.18 /
      $           ' added from largest     ', d25.18 /
      $           ' added from smallest    ', d25.18)
       end
```

(b)

```
Enter r and n separated by spaces: .99 40
r                     0.989999999999999991D+00
correct partial sum   0.331028241430319454D+02
calculated with array 0.331028241430319454D+02
added from largest    0.331028241430319312D+02
added from smallest   0.331028241430319454D+02

Enter r and n separated by spaces: .99 2000
r                     0.989999999999999991D+00
correct partial sum   0.999999998136242567D+02
calculated with array 0.999999998136242567D+02
added from largest    0.999999998136241004D+02
added from smallest   0.999999998136241857D+02

Enter r and n separated by spaces: 0 1
```

Note that the calculation using the array of accumulators matches the accuracy of the exact solution. If an exact solution is not known, then this method can be used to avoid loss of precision, although it is very slow.

The design goals for an emulator are influenced by the data types available in the language, the code sequences generated by the compiler, and the compiler and run-time system's assumptions regarding precision. The 80x87 emulator we designed for RM/FORTRAN achieved our design goals of dramatic speed improvement (approximately a factor of 5) with no loss of precision at the FORTRAN level. Although the emulator produces results different from those produced by the 8087 hardware, they are no less precise.

To analyze a FORTRAN program to determine the precision of its output, you need to know the size of the input numbers. As the quadratic-roots problem demonstrated, the standard formula works fine for some argument ranges but is terrible for others. You must then analyze each subtraction operation (or addition of numbers with opposite signs) to determine if the operands of that subtraction might ever be almost identical; if so, you should find another way to solve the problem, or at least be aware of the resulting loss of precision. In general, the addition of two numbers that are far apart doesn't result in precision loss, unless you calculate a series of such additions.

If your FORTRAN program produces significantly different results on the 8087 hardware versus the emulator, then you are using an algorithm that depends on 64-bit precision arithmetic. Any small change to that program may cause the compiler optimizer to reorder the object code such that the precision will drop to 53 bits, even on the 8087 hardware. This is a simple though incomplete test for imprecise results.

As the quadratic-root and series-sum problems showed, changing the numerical algorithm at the FORTRAN level can have a larger effect on the precision than any compiler or emulator change. There is no substitute for analyzing the numerical accuracy of the FORTRAN code.

39
Avoiding Coprocessor Bottlenecks[*]

Mauro Bonomi

Numerics performance in the millions of floating-point operations per second (MFLOPS) is vital to workstation tasks such as high-quality graphics, stress analysis, CAD, and electrical or mechanical simulations. With the increasing sophistication of business software, MFLOPS are fast becoming a necessity in many office applications as well. Linear programming, used to solve complex optimization problems in business and industrial planning, relies largely on floating-point computation. So does statistical analysis, employed in market research, product quality analysis, capacity planning, and stock portfolio analysis. The high-resolution graphics found in computer-aided drafting and desktop publishing make copious use of floating-point arithmetic.

While high-end microprocessors such as the Intel 80386 provide general-purpose horsepower in the 3- to 4-MIPS range, their arithmetic performance lags far behind, delivering only thousands of floating-point operations per second–far too slow for compute-intensive personal workstation applications.

For higher numerics performance, system designers must turn to coprocessors and numerics accelerators. By relieving the CPU of floating-point math, these arithmetic engines can increase system performance markedly. A range of numerics accelerators are available, from conventional coprocessor chips, like Intel's 80387 and Motorola's 68882, to very fast bit-slice array processors.

Conventional coprocessors are relatively inexpensive and run standard software but offer performance levels suitable only for low-intensity numerics applications, such as spreadsheet recomputation and two-dimensional graphics. Array processors, on the other hand, are often expensive and difficult to program. They execute special operations, such as matrix multiplications and vector calculations, very rapidly. But because of their complex architectures, often featuring multiple memory banks, pipelined stages, and multiple address generators, they are not

---

[*] © McGraw-Hill Information Systems Company, _BYTE_, March, 1988, p. 197

supported by standard compilers. Simple recompilation of existing software is not possible.

A variation on the conventional coprocessor is the memory-mapped coprocessor. These coprocessors reach a middle ground between conventional coprocessors and array processors; they provide standard software support like the conventional coprocessors but move up the performance curve toward array processors. Memory-mapped coprocessors vary from conventional coprocessors in one vital respect: Memory mapping attempts to deal with the bus bandwidth bottleneck.

Sun, Apollo, and Masscomp all make proprietary memory-mapped floating-point accelerators for workstations; in the personal computer world, the Weitek 1167 is the only example of a memory-mapped coprocessor.

Bottlenecks Limit Performance

The vast majority of arithmetic calculations performed by any computer employ real numbers and so require floating-point processing. Such processing is, however, a good deal more complex than integer math. The computer must keep track of a mantissa and an exponent for every operand and perform scaling after each arithmetic operation to reduce the result to a normalized format.

Owing to silicon space limitations, microprocessors, such as the 80386 and the 68020, feature integer-only ALUs. Floating-point operations are accomplished through software subroutines. Each such operation is carried out by the integer hardware as a lengthy series of ALU steps (adds, subtracts, and shifts).

This type of software implementation places a significant drag on performance in numerics-intensive tasks. Numerics coprocessors provide dramatic gains in speed by implementing floating-point functions in specialized hardware. Coprocessors work in close conjunction with the microprocessor.

Assuming, for example, the two single-precision numbers, A and B, stored in two 80386 registers must be added and the result C stored back in the 80386, the following actions must be carried out: The microprocessor must instruct the coprocessor to execute an addition, pass the two operands, and then store the result after the completed operation. Clearly, the resulting system performance depends on two main factors: the raw speed of the floating-point hardware and the efficiency of the interface between the microprocessor and the numerics coprocessor. Even if the floating-point unit (FPU) latency–the time required to generate a result from two input operands–could be reduced to 0, an inefficient interface protocol could limit system performance.

Low-Latency Data Paths

The 80386/80387 combination illustrates conventional coprocessor function. The 80387, connected to the system data bus, monitors the same program instruction stream as the microprocessor does. The microprocessor is responsible for generating all addresses for both code and data. Operands and op codes are transmitted to the coprocessor from memory via the data bus. Whenever the microprocessor detects a coprocessor instruction, it waits until the coprocessor becomes idle, lets the coprocessor begin the instruction, and then moves on to the next instruction. If the 80387 is still busy by the time the 80386 encounters another coprocessor instruction, the microprocessor waits until the coprocessor is done. This process is invisible to the programmer; it appears as though there is only a single processor.

Despite this tight coupling and ease of programming, the performance of conventional numerics coprocessors suffers both from some inherent processing limitations and from interface bottlenecks. To begin with, simple operations such as adds and multiplies may require multiple passes through the hardware. This is due to limited silicon space for ALUs. Similarly, the number of on-chip registers is often relatively small. But a bigger problem is that both data and instructions are sent to conventional coprocessors via a data bus of limited bandwidth.

Memory-mapped coprocessors accelerate floating-point operations in two ways: They use dedicated 64-bit floating point multiplier and ALU data paths, and they provide an interface that lets the coprocessor acquire data and instructions by using both the address and the data bus simultaneously.

For example, consider the simplified block diagram of the Weitek 1167 memory-mapped coprocessor and its interface to the Intel 80386 (Figure 39-1). The multiplier and ALU data paths execute such operations as single-precision adds, subtracts, and multiplies in a single pass through the silicon. The 1167 multiplier and ALU flow-through time is under 200 nanoseconds for a single-precision operation. In contrast, conventional coprocessors usually require over 1.5 microseconds (7 to 8 times slower) to carry out the same operation.

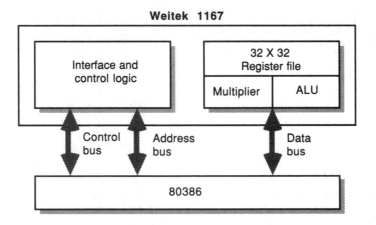

Figure 39-1: A block diagram of the 80386/Weitek 1167 interface.

The coprocessor is connected to the 80386 via the control, data, and address buses. Instructions (op codes) are sent to the coprocessor using the system address bus, while data (operands) are sent over the data bus. As the address bus specifies the instruction to be performed, the data bus can pass a 32-bit operand simultaneously. This parallelism reduces bus bottlenecks that otherwise significantly limit system performance.

View of the System Address Bus

The microprocessor treats a memory-mapped coprocessor as a distinct region of physical memory. Data-moves to and from this memory region select the coprocessor and specify both the floating-point op code, the location of the two operands, and the destination of the computational result. At the same time, the data on the data bus can provide any operand not already present in the coprocessor's registers.

Figure 39-2 shows the Weitek coprocessor view of the 80386 address bus. The coprocessor is mapped into the physical memory area ranging from C0000000h to C000FFFFh. A given address in this area selects the coprocessor, indicates the instruction for the coprocessor to perform, and specifies the operand locations (Source 1 and Source2/Destination). The most significant 16 bits of the physical address identify a coprocessor instruction. If the upper bits of the address are not equal to C000h, the address does not specify a Weitek command and is ignored by the coprocessor. The next 6 bits of the address specify the coprocessor instruction to be executed. The least significant 10 address bits specify the registers that will provide sources and destination for the instruction.

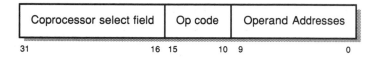

Coprocessor select field	Op code	Operand Addresses

31   16 15   10 9   0

Figure 39-2: The Weitek 1167 view of the 80386 address bus.

Source2 and Destination always coincide. When Source1 is set to 0, the Source1 data is provided by the system data bus. Source2 and Destination, on the other hand, always specify one of the remaining 31 32-bit registers (1 to 31) of the co-processor register file. This means that one of the two operands always resides in the coprocessor register file.

Generating Instructions

Coprocessor instructions for the Weitek 1167 are specified via simple 80386 memory moves. Assuming that the two single-precision operands in the 80386 registers EAX and EBX need to be added and the result is to be stored back in register EAX, the following three memory move instructions will execute the operation:

```
1) mov ADDR1,eax    ; load content of
                      EAX (A) into the
                      Weitek 1167 reg-
                      ister file.
2) mov ADDR2,ebx    ; load content of
                      EBX (B) into Wei-
                      tek register file
                      and add it to A.
3) mov EAX,ADDR3    ; store result C
                      back into 80386
                      register EAX.
```

Addresses *ADDR1*, *ADDR2*, and *ADDR3* are derived by filling the address fields, shown in Figure 39-2, with the proper values. The most significant 16 bits of all the addresses are set to C000h in order to select the coprocessor. The next 6 bits are filled with the op code for *LOAD*, *ADD*, and *STORE*, respectively. Finally, the least significant 10 bits will be filled with the operand addresses.

As all the above operations involve one operand coming from the bus, Source1 will always be set to 0. Source2 can instead specify any of the remaining 31 registers (1 to 31) in the Weitek 1167 register file. With the move to *ADDR2*, the 80386 passes a 32-bit operand (B) to the coprocessor on the data bus and specifies the floating-point instruction that needs to be executed (*ADD*). This is an example of the parallelism provided by the memory-mapped interface.

To hide the details of the memory-mapped interface from the programmer, memory-mapped coprocessors feature macros, one for each coprocessor instruction. Using Weitek 1167 macro notation, for example, the addition sequence above becomes

```
1) wfldws1,EAX      ; load EAX (A) into
                      Weitek register 1.
2) wfaddws1,EBX     ; add Weitek regis-
                      ter 1 (A) to EBX
                      (B).
3) wfstEAX,ws1      ; store result from
                      Weitek register 1 to
                      EAX.
```

The instruction stream assumes that register 1 has been used to accumulate the result inside the coprocessor.

Large Register Sets

Memory-mapped coprocessors commonly offer large internal register sets that can be used to store constants and to accumulate partial results. The accumulation of partial results in internal registers lets the coprocessor minimize the number of loads and stores between the microprocessor and the FPU.

When performing a three-dimensional graphics transformation, for example, requiring the multiplication of a large number of vectors of four elements each by a 4-by-4 transformation matrix, the programmer can store all 16 matrix coefficients in the coprocessor register file and then use them to transform all the vectors.

C programmers can define all variables processed by the coprocessor as temporary variables. The compiler will then allocate such variables to coprocessor internal registers, thus holding the number of store and load operations between microprocessor and coprocessor to a minimum.

Compiling: An Example

A picture of a beach ball was generated on a 20-MHz Compaq Deskpro 386/20 with an EGA graphics card. The C code for this simple graphics example is presented in listing 1. The program uses the Phong shading technique to compute the intensities and colors of the surface of the ball. The idea behind this technique is to compute normal (perpendicular) vectors to each point on the surface using an interpolation scheme and then apply the shading model at each pixel displayed.

The program involves a large number of floating-point computations on single-precision numbers, including the four basic instructions (add, subtract, multiply, and divide), as well as special functions (sine, cosine, and square root). The C program was compiled with a MetaWare High C compiler that supports both the Weitek 1167 and the 80387 coprocessor. The compiler generates either 80387 or Weitek 1167 object code. Users choose the desired coprocessor by setting a special switch on the command line when giving the compile command.

Listing 39-1: The C code to generate a picture of a beach ball. (Code written by Bruce Holloway of Weitek.)

```
#include <math.h>
#include <stdio.h>
#include <time.h>

clock_t start,stop;
float pi;
int colors[]={3,6,10,13,6,3,10,13,6,3,13,1
    0},d[]={640,350,1},i,k,
  palatte[]={000,010,001,011,020,002,022
    ,077,040,004,044,060,006,066,007,077},
  x,y,x_min,x_max,y_min,y_max;
unsigned short random;

main()
{
  float a,b,c,10,11,12,1n,1n1,n0,n1,n2,p,q,r=1 28,s,t,v,[12][3];
  int n;

  /* Put EGA in hi-res graphics mode & initialize pallette. */
  video_int(0x10);
  for (n=0;n<16;n++)
    video_int(0x1000,n+(palette[n]<<8));

  /* Print title & start timing. */
#ifdef Intel
  printf("\n\n\t\t      80387 Phong Shading Demonstration\n");
```

```
#else
  printf("\n\n\t\t    Weitek 1167 Phong Shading
      Demonstration\n");
#endif
  printf("\n\n\n\n\n\n\n\n\n\n\n\n\n\n \n\n\n\n\n\n\n");
  start=clock();

  /* Pixel aspect ratio. */
  a=1.3;
  /* Screen center coordinates. */
  b=.5*(d[0]-1);
  c=.5*(d[1]-1);
  /* Unit length light source vector. */
  10=-1/sqrt(3.);
  11=10;
  12=-10;
  /* Ratio of circumference to diameter of a circle. */
  pi=4*atan(1.);
  /* A dozen vertices evenly spread over a unit sphere. */
  v[0][0]=0;
  v[0][1]=0;
  v[0][2]=1;
  s=sqrt(5.);
  for (i=1;i<11;i++) {
    p=pi*i/5;
    v[i][0]=2*cos(p)/s;
    v[i][1]=2*sin(p)/s;
    v[i][2]=(1.-i%2*2)/s;
  }
  v[11][0]=0;
  v[11][1]=0;
  v[11][2]=-1;

  /* Loop to Phong shade each pixel. */
  y_max=c+r;
  y_min=2*c-y_max;
  for (y=y_min;y<=y_max;y++) {
    s=y-c;
    n1=s/r;
    1n1=11*n1;
    s=r*r-s*s;
    x_max=b+a*sqrt(s);
    x_min=2*b-x_max;
    for {x=x_min;x<=x_max;x++) {
      t=(x-b)/a;
      n0=t/r;
      t=sqrt(s-t*t);
      n2=t/r;
      /* Compute dot product and clamp to positive value. */
      1n=10*n0+1n1+12*n2;
      if (1n<0) 1n=0;
      /* cos(e.r)**27 */
      t=1n*n2;
      t+=t-12;
      t*=t*t;
      t*=t*t;
```

```
        t*=t*t;
        /* Nearest vertex to normal yields max dot product.  Get
        its color. */
        for (i=0,p=0;i<11;i++)
          if (p<(q=n0*v[i][0]+n1*v[i][1]+n2*v[i][2])) {
            p=q;
            k=colors[i];
          }
        /* Aggregate ambient, diffuse, & specular intensities &
        do dither. */
        i=k-2.5+2.5*1n+t+(random=37*random+1)/65536.;
        /* Clamp values outside range of three color levels to
        black or white. */
        if (i<k-2) i=0; else if (i>k) i=15;
        draw_dot();
      }
    }
    stop=clock();
    reg_reset();
    printf("\t\t\t\tTime = %3.2f seconds",((double)(stop-
        start))/CLK_TCK);
    while (clock()-stop<5*CLK_TCK);
    /* Put EGA in 80-column mode. */
    video_int(0x03);
}
```

Running without a floating-point coprocessor, with the 80386 emulating 80387 instructions, the program takes 8 minutes to complete. Adding a 20-MHz 80387 reduces the execution time to a little more than 28 seconds. Finally, the Weitek memory-mapped coprocessor cuts execution time by about three times, down to only 10 seconds. The 200 percent performance improvement was achieved by simply recompiling the source code with no hand-coded optimizations.

Samples of the compiler output for both the 80387 and the Weitek 1167 are provided in listings 39-2 and 39-3. When compiled for the 80387, the code line $s=r*r-s*s$ is translated into the code stream in Listing 39-2.

Listing 39-2: Sample of compiler output for the 80387.

```
                        ;    s=r*r-s*s;
0214  d9 46 c8          fld    dword ptr -56[bp]
0217  d8 c8             fsqr
0219  d9 46 c4          fld    dword ptr -60[bp]
021c  d8 c8             fsqr
021e  de e9             fsub
0220  d9 5e c4          fstp   dword ptr -60[bp]
                        ;    x_max=b+a*sqrt(s);
0223  d9 46 c4          fld    dword ptr -60[bp]
0226  d9 fa             fsqrt
```

```
0228  d8 4e fc              fmul    dword ptr -4[bp]
022b  d8 46 f8              fadd    dword ptr -8[bp]
022e  e8 ----e              call    _mwtrunc
0231  a3 0054r              mov     @FONGBALL+84,ax
```

The same equation is translated into 1167 memory moves by the compiler when
the Weitek coprocessor is selected. The Weitek object code shown in Listing 39-
3 makes efficient use of coprocessor registers. The equation result *s (s=r*r-s*s)*,
for example, is not stored back into the 80386 but is left in the coprocessor
register file and is then used by the instruction *(x_max=b+a*sqrt(s))*, thus minimizing the data transfers between the microprocessor and the coprocessor and
freeing up the system bus.

Listing 39-3: Sample of compiler output for the Weitek 1167.

```
              ;    s=r*r-s*s;
0388  64:a2 0719       wload   .s fr2,fr25    ; mov al,fs:[]
038c  64:a2 081a       wmul    .s fr2,fr2     ; mov al,fs:[]
0390  64:a2 0b7a       wmul    s fr26.fr26    ; mov al,fs:[]
0394  64:a2 107a       wsub    .s fr26,fr2    ; mov al,fs:[]
              ;    x_max=b+a*sqrt(s);
0398  64:a2 471a       wcvtsd .s fr2,fr26     ; mov al,fs:[]
039c  66:64:ff 36 0c18  push    .s fr2        ; push fs:[]
03a2  66:64:ff 36 0c1c  push    .s fr3        ; push fs:[]
03a8  e8 ----e       call    sqrt
03ab  64:a2 45a1       wcvtsd .S fr4,fr13     ; mov al,fs:[]
03af  64:a2 45a8       wcvtsd .S fr6,fr12     ; mov al,fs:[]
03b3  64:a2 889a       wmul    .D fr2,fr6     ; mov al,fs:[]
03b7  64:a2 8098       wadd    .D fr2,fr4     ; mov al,fs:[]
03bb  64:a2 bc1a       wfix    .D fr2,fr2     ; mov al,fs:[]
03bf  66:64:a1 8c18 wstor  .D fr2,eax     ; mov eax,fs:[]
03c4  66:0f a4 c2 10          shld    edx,eax,16
03c9  a3 0054r                mov     @FONG1167+72,ax
```

Programming for Performance

When writing high-level language code for a memory-mapped coprocessor, some
simple techniques can lead to significant performance improvements in the compiled code. First, variables used only in specific subroutines can be defined as
local variables. The compiler then allocates such variables to coprocessor registers and will not store them back to main memory at the end of each instruction.

In the case of the 1167, the assembly language programmer has access to special instructions not otherwise available to compiler users. The multiply-accumulate (*wfmac*) instruction is an example. This instruction, useful in implementing matrix multiplications, specifies the multiplication of the two input operands, followed by the addition to a previously calculated partial result. A single memory move can then specify two floating-point instructions (multiply and add), further decreasing the burden on the system bus.

Additional assembly-level instructions that can improve the system performance are block moves–that is, moves of blocks of data to or from adjacent memory locations. A block move effectively encodes a stream of floating-point instructions. It is useful in loading and unloading the entire contents of the coprocessor register file, as well as in implementing vector adds and multiplies.

Boiling Down

Accelerating floating-point performance boils down to more than just clock rates and the size of machine words. We need the hardware assistance of dedicated ALUs and multipliers. But equally important is the need for efficient ways to move data and instructions between the main processor and the math coprocessor.

Removing the coprocessor instruction stream from the data bus–using the address bus to transmit op codes–leaves more room for passing operands. This strategy is one way to increase data bus bandwidth and improve processor/coprocessor interaction.

40

New Issues in PC Graphics [*]

Ed McNierney

Display boards incorporating third-generation graphics controllers have provided software developers with a highly sophisticated set of capabilities. Along with those capabilities comes a level of complexity previously unknown in the PC graphics industry; in order to use these new hardware tools effectively, programmers need to become familiar with the new issues they raise and with the new techniques associated with those issues.

The chief features of these new controllers, which include the Intel 82786 and the Texas Instruments 34010, include hardware graphics primitives, which give them the ability to draw circles, lines, and bit-mapped text at high speed. The controllers also have true microprocessor architectures that allow the development and execution of complex graphic algorithms in parallel with the host CPU's execution; the ability to address large amounts of memory (up to 512 megabytes) in support of multiple pages of screen memory and large amounts of off-screen graphics storage memory; and hardware windowing capabilities that, for the first time, completely separate the physical layout of graphics memory from the data displayed on the screen.

Two Examples

Although they are both graphics coprocessors, the Intel 82786 and the TI 34010 are not head-to-head competitors in the graphics market. The 82786 is able to address 4 megabytes of memory and display that memory in hardware windows at a resolution of up to 640x480 pixels. Internally, the 82786 is structured as three distinct processors: a graphics processor that performs drawing, a display processor that extracts bit-map data from memory and generates a display from it, and an interface unit that mediates requests for access to display memory. The graphics processor is capable of executing a simple command list stored in graphics memory. Although the command set supports subroutine call and jump instructions, there are no conditional branch opcodes. The command list, therefore, cannot be executed intelligently and must be constructed and managed by an ex-

---

[*] © M&T Publishing, Inc., *Dr. Dobb's Journal of Software Tools,* November 1986, p. 30

ternal intelligent processor—usually the host CPU. These features combine to make the Intel 82786 an excellent choice for general-purpose, high-resolution graphics systems, such as might be used in business graphics, graphic user interfaces, and desktop publishing systems.

The architects of the TI 34010 have taken a slightly different approach. The 82786 is capable of only simple (but very fast) drawing and complex display manipulation, whereas the 34010 is the reverse. It provides no hardware windowing, and it is only capable of generating a display that shows different portions of graphics memory by splitting the screen into horizontal strips. It does not have as high a clock speed as does the 82786, but it is capable of executing extremely complex graphic algorithms. Its strength lies in drawing rather than in display generation.

Algorithms for drawing complex figures can be coded and executed directly by the 34010, which operates as a 32-bit processor capable of addressing 512 megabytes of memory. It is therefore suited to high-resolution, drawing-intensive applications such as computer-aided design, drafting, and high-end publishing and page composition.

Optimized for Graphics

The execution of graphics primitives by either of these graphics processors provides two direct benefits: Unlike the host CPU, the graphics processor is designed to draw efficiently and quickly, and the presence of a coprocessor frees up the host to perform other tasks while the drawing is being performed. Current host CPU instruction sets are optimized toward the manipulation of numeric and string objects, not graphics; they allow instructions that update pointers to move through linear blocks of memory (such as strings or buffers) rather than through rectangular areas suitable for graphic applications. CPUs are being forced into a service they were never designed to perform, whereas graphic processors address memory properly and also contain silicon implementations of drawing algorithms. Both features greatly reduce the amount of code required to execute a figure. Listing 40-1, for example, contains three versions of a routine that draws a 10x10 rectangle—one on a CGA in an 8086 system, one in an 82786 system, and the last in a 34010 system. Note that in the second two cases, the host processor is not executing the algorithm but is instead free to prepare for the next graphic output sequence. A system incorporating a graphics processor can have its software tuned to achieve real-time performance increases of 50 to 100 times compared to a host CPU/display buffer system.

Listing 40-1

Draw a rectangle with an 8086 on CGA.
```
;
;               Draw a rectangle in the upper
;               left corner of a CGA display
;               in high-resolution mode.  The code EODone
;               is hardwired to a 10x10 rectangle.
;
;
; Set up segment and offset registers
; to point to display memory.
;
        mov         AX, 0B800H
        mov         ES, AX
        mov         BX, 0
;
; Draw the top line by stuffing one byte
; and the first two bits of the next byte.
;
        mov         byte ptr [BX], 0FFH
        mov         byte ptr [BX+1], 0C0H
;
; Draw the bottom line the same way.
;
        mov         byte ptr [BX+800], 0FFH
        mov         byte ptr [BX+801], 0C0H

;
; Draw the first and last pixels on the
; next 4 even scan lines, then do the same
; on the odd scan lines.
;
        mov         SI, 50H
        mov         CX, 4
EOLoop: mov         byte ptr [BX+SI], 80H
        mov         byte ptr [BX+SI+1], 40H
        add         SI, 80
        loop        EOLoop
        cmp         SI, 2000H
        jg          EODone
        mov         SI, 2050H
        mov         CX, 4
        jmp         EOLoop
        label       byte
;
; Rectangle is finished.
;
****************************************************************
```

Same rectangle drawn by 34010

```
;
; Draw a line from 0,0 to 0,10.  The start
; point is in register B2 and the end point
; (delta X and delta Y) is in register B7.
;
; The > sign precedes a 32-bit hex constant.
;
        MOVI    >0,B2
        MOVI    >00100000,B7
        LINE    0
;
; Repeat the process for the other sides.
;
        MOVI    >00100000, B2
        MOVI    >00000010, B7
        LINE    0
        MOVI    >0, B2
        MOVI    >00000010, B7
        LINE    0
        MOVI    >00000010, B2
        MOVI    >00100000, B7
        LINE    0
;
; Finished!
;
*****************************************************************

Same rectangle drawn by 82786


;
; Move to the upper left corner and
; draw a 10x10 rectangle.
;
        ABS MOVE 0,0
        RECT     10,10
;
; All finished!
;
```

For cases in which the graphics primitives are insufficient for the task at hand, the TI 34010 provides a true microprocessor instruction set, with arithmetic instructions, conditional test and branch instructions, and software and hardware interrupt control. Not only does this provide the developer with a general-purpose coprocessor but it also permits the 34010 to be used as the only processor in the system. Intelligent terminals or printers can be driven by only one CPU, reducing hardware cost and simplifying software development. Although the TI processor is slower in terms of clock speed and in the types of memory accesses it can perform than the Intel 82786, its programmability can allow a greater synergy between it and the host CPU, resulting in greater application throughput. A graphic processor is not a panacea that will cure a sluggish graphic implementation, however, because the task of creating a system in which both processors are used optimally is an extraordinarily difficult one. The complexity of such coprocessor systems is suggested in Figure 40-1 in which sample 34010 and sample 82786 system memory layouts are compared.

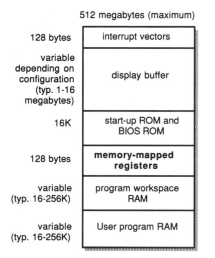
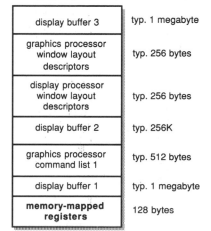

34010 Memory Map
Up to 512 megabytes of RAM and ROM, with registers and interrupt vectors occupying fixed addresses. Display buffers must be contiguous. Graphic code in ROM is typical.

82786 Memory Map
Contains up to 4 megabytes of RAM that can be used freely in any manner needed. Little if any ROM is present.

Figure 40-1: Comparison of sample 34010 and
82786 system memory layouts.

Both the TI and Intel processors are capable of addressing large amounts of graphics memory. Although more memory is required simply to support high-resolution and high-color displays, these processors require access to additional objects in their memory—graphic software (both in ROM and in RAM), memory-mapped register sets, control areas, and graphics source data all reside in the processor's address space. One of the more difficult issues facing developers is the management of all this memory because neither the Intel nor the TI processors supports explicit memory management other than reserving certain portions of their address spaces for some specific uses.

Graphics memory also has to accommodate many new types of objects whose presence springs directly from the fact that they support off-screen graphics data. No application developers really want to store fonts, icons, cursors, and temporarily hidden portions of the display in system memory; they have, however, been forced to do so because there has been no other place to put them. All the housekeeping efforts that currently have to be exerted in the host address space in order to keep track of these objects must now be transferred to the graphics processor. The host is equipped with the operating system's normal memory allocation, deallocation, and management functions, all of which need to be duplicated and executed by the graphics coprocessor to manage its own memory. Although display memory grows in complexity, it is at least performing a task for which it is intended, freeing system memory for the execution of host CPU code and the storage of host CPU data.

The management of graphics memory becomes especially complex in the case of the 82786 because it has full hardware windowing support. As graphics-based user interfaces become more common, the 82786 will prove a great benefit to application developers and to the underlying windowing systems that support them. An 82786-based system is entirely freed from any association between physical memory addresses and screen displays—any graphics data residing anywhere in its address space can be displayed at any point on the screen by creating a window, positioning it on the screen, and defining the bit-map address from which that window should take its data. This system provides greater flexibility for the application as well as increased performance in windowing environments. On an IBM Enhanced Graphics Adapter, for example, moving a 400x300-pixel rectangle in 16-color mode to another position on the screen requires moving up to 60,000 bytes more to fill the hole uncovered by the moved rectangle. In an 82786 environment, however, the same operation requires updating only about a dozen bytes, performing the same task up to 10,000 times faster!

The fundamental benefit derived from a hardware-based windowing system is that the covering of one window by another does not destroy any display information but simply hides it. Moving the covering window then reveals that graphic data again, without the application having to store a temporary copy of it and replace it—panning, smooth scrolling, and the repositioning of windows all become much faster and much more practical to implement in graphical user interfaces. Not only do these windows save graphics memory by obviating the need for maintaining duplicate copies of display data, but they also save memory by allowing data in different windows to be displayed at different pixel depths.

In a high-color paint package using an 8-bit-per-pixel display, there is no need for a pop-up window containing a list of picture file names to be displayed in anything but black and white. By creating a new 1-bit-per-pixel window in which to display the text, the application reduces both the memory required for the display and the time required to print the text in the window by a factor of 8. This greater flexibility means that display memory resources can be used more prudently and in a manner more appropriate to the particular display application at hand.

New Expertise Is Needed

All these wonderful advantages are not without their price. As with any new hardware or software technology, a whole new area of expertise has to be developed. The examples set by the Apple Macintosh and the IBM EGA are good parallels to the graphic coprocessor environment. Both of these technologies represented significant advances over what was previously available in the market, and they both ran into difficulties because of the long lead time required for software development to take place. The new graphic coprocessor systems are complex, and it will take a while before sufficient expertise is acquired to use them well or at all.

Although software development efforts are simplified at the microscopic level in that a developer is spared one more implementation of Bresenham's circle algorithm, the overall environment is more demanding and more detailed, and the development overhead required may prevent smaller software firms from undertaking any development until a significant market leader has become apparent. The ability to take an intelligent graphics board and use it to run existing applications faster will help break the hardware/software development deadlock in which software developers won't port to new boards until they sell and hardware developers can't sell boards until the software support is there. As a result of this complexity, the first coprocessor systems will probably do nothing more than execute current software packages more quickly. There will be a definite development lag before the coprocessors are used fully and effectively for new, innovative applications.

Hindering the ability of developers to work with these products is the current state of graphic software standards. In different respects they provide too much and too little. The graphic software world has too many "primitive" standards, and a developer often has to make a difficult choice between VDIs, CGIs, GKS, and PHIGS systems, not to mention new systems being proposed. A standard just isn't a standard when a developer has to support six of them to cover 50 percent of the market! On the short side, none of the present standards addresses the issue of windowing, although an ANSI committee is working on a windowing proposal. Unfortunately, it will almost certainly take a while for standards committees to propagate new proposals for these new processors, and by that time several independent interfaces will exist and the standards will occupy the same role they do now.

Communication and Synchronization

On the more practical side, some implementation problems need to be addressed by any application that attempts to use a graphic processor well. Because each processor has its own instruction set and opcode syntax, commands need to be translated from the format in which the application program generates them to a format intelligible by the graphic processor. A well-thought-out communication syntax is necessary in order to minimize the overhead required to send the desired command to the graphic processor, or the application may end up taking longer to perform the drawing than if the host CPU had executed the graphic algorithm itself. Going hand in hand with an efficient communications protocol is a careful synchronization of the tasks being performed by the host and graphic processors. Because a PC with an 82786 or 34010 is a true multiprocessor system, the architecture of the graphics board may require full status information to be provided to the host CPU. If a command is sent to the graphics processor to draw a circle, and then the host CPU wishes to read the value of a pixel along the circumference of that circle, the host needs to be able to tell whether the circle has been completed, lest the incorrect value be read.

An extreme approach to synchronization is to wait for any command or program sent to the graphic processor to complete before returning control to the host application. Although "lockstepping" will work and will execute faster than a host CPU without the processor, the capabilities of the processor are largely ignored in this case. Synchronization schemes can include mutually interruptible systems in which each processor signals the other when it is ready for new material, critical flags that tell one processor that the other is in a possibly unstable state, and polling mechanisms in which each processor registers a request to the other and then polls for a status flag to be set indicating that the request can be honored. Figure 40-2 illustrates these schemes.

Black Boxes

Additional issues are brought up by the blurring of certain traditional boundaries in PC environments. There is less and less of a distinction between "graphic" and "system" memory; packages such as Microsoft Windows require that a display driver be able to perform drawing in precisely the same manner on a given block of graphic data, no matter where it resides in the system. Drawing may be performed in traditional system memory, in bank-selected expanded memory, or in on-board graphic memory.

Host CPU
Execution

Graphic Coprocessor
Execution

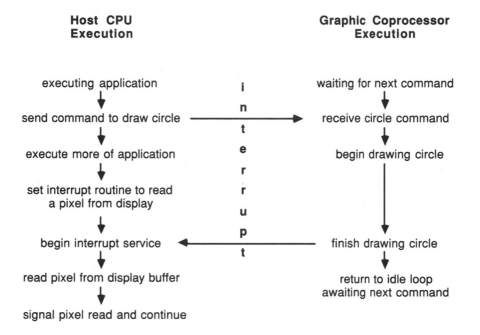

Host CPU Execution	interrupt	Graphic Coprocessor Execution
executing application		waiting for next command
send command to draw circle		receive circle command
execute more of application		begin drawing circle
set interrupt routine to read a pixel from display		
begin interrupt service		finish drawing circle
read pixel from display buffer		return to idle loop awaiting next command
signal pixel read and continue		

Figure 40-2: Synchronization of dual processors through
a mutual interrupt system.

The difficulty here comes from what in other cases is a benefit—the graphic algorithms embodied in the graphic processor are "black boxes," opaque to the user. If the graphic processor is not capable of performing drawing in system memory because of limitations of software or hardware design, then the application much provide an algorithm that duplicates the one contained in the black box in every respect. If the algorithm cannot be duplicated precisely, the graphic processor becomes useless in that system—unfortunately, the IBM PC's architecture prevents a graphics board residing in an expansion slot from modifying system memory in any way. This restriction has been lifted in the PC/AT, but it still presents an obstacle blocking access to a large installed base of machines. In addition, because the graphics board may contain far more memory than the host CPU system does, that memory may be made available for nongraphics use by other applications such as RAM disks, disk caches, and expanded memory drivers. Developers need to avoid painting themselves into corners by clinging to old assumptions that were valid on IBM Color Graphic Adapters but that are no longer appropriate.

Dealing with Text

Aiding the battle against rapidly multiplying display modes but clouding the implementation battle is the growing awareness and appreciation of the fact that text in any form is nothing more than a special type of graphic data. Text can be zoomed, scaled, colored, italicized, or displayed in many different fonts all on the screen at once, and that same text must be able to be read back from the screen. Character recognition on a monochrome screen is straightforward, but the extraction of ASCII data from a highly complex graphical bit map is a very challenging task.

The further hardware and software manufacturers can go in removing constraints on the use and appearance of text, the closer they will come to an ideal user interface. The application of multiple scaled fonts to WYSIWYG word processing is obvious, and the growing desktop publishing market will certainly benefit form these new processor technologies. Average users are becoming more sophisticated and more demanding about the text they see every time they turn on the PC. High-quality text must be provided without an excessive speed penalty on the part of users; no matter how pretty it looks, if it is not fast it won't be liked.

Both the TI and Intel processors provide sophisticated text support, allowing for color bit-mapped text to be generated at speeds approaching those of hardware character generators. Fonts can be stored in graphic memory, freeing precious system memory from the task, and special attributes such as underlining and boldfacing can be synthesized on the fly, obviating the need for storing multiple copies of the same font. Fonts are not tiny objects, and extremely large amounts of memory may be required to store and format them. The effective use of font storage may be the most critical issue in the apparent performance of a graphics application because poorly managed font memory translates into slow text performance and text performance is the one area in which users are most sensitive and critical. Judgment and clever implementation here can certainly make the difference between a popular package and a failure.

Fortunately, as the silicon available becomes more complex, the tools available become more powerful. Already function libraries that perform three-dimensional graphics, floating-point arithmetic, text generation and scaling, and object filling and shading are being provided, both by chip manufacturers and by third parties. In addition, TI even offers a C compiler for the 34010, allowing the direct conversion of algorithms developed on earlier systems. These libraries and compilers are no longer the convenient graphics toolkits offered for existing graphic display boards but are essential steps to application development.

Virtual Displays

Because it provides hardware windowing directly, the 82786 can create a virtual-display environment that directly parallels the 80386's Virtual 86 execution mode—each Virtual 86 task can think it is running on an IBM Color Graphics Adapter, while each virtual CGA is being displayed in a distinct hardware window. This chip companionship not only allows existing applications to run unmodified on an 80386 but also allows them to execute unmodified in a windowing environment (see Figure 40-3).

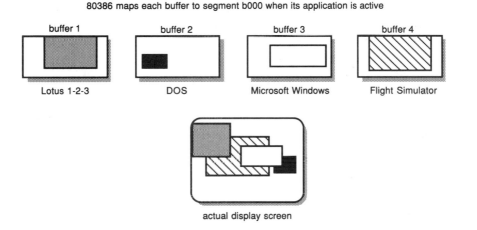

80386 maps each buffer to segment b000 when its application is active

| buffer 1 | buffer 2 | buffer 3 | buffer 4 |

| Lotus 1-2-3 | DOS | Microsoft Windows | Flight Simulator |

actual display screen

Window management software controls display of each buffer. Each application can read and write directly to the display buffer without causing screen conflicts.

Figure 40-3: 82786 managing multitasking display.

Along with the essential ability to execute current applications, the 82786 introduces the concepts of visual hierarchy and privilege in direct parallel to the software execution controls provided by the 80386. A truly integrated multitasking system must be able to treat graphic and visual information with the same protection and control as it treats any other portion of its execution environment. Imagine an 82786 graphic application running in a multitasking environment. When the application starts up, it wants to display itself in the top window, centered on the screen and occupying three-quarters of the visible area of the screen. Although it is quite reasonable to expect that the application considers itself important enough to merit all that room, the operating system knows that there are several other applications active that may require attention. By making the window positioning and sizing commands privileged system calls, the operating system can act as an intermediary between what the application wants and what resources it considers appropriate to supply. The request can be examined, modified to fit the state of the system at the moment, and the application notified of the modifications required to fulfill the request. Alternatively, the application could be allowed to test the manner in which a specific request would be fulfilled and modify or cancel the request entirely depending upon the results.

The concept of visual hierarchy and privilege can be the beginning of another step forward in user-interface design. By providing the means to manipulate shared bit-mapped displays in a multitasking system, a graphics processor frees application designers from one more level of hardware constraint—instead of designing to be cooperative with other applications sharing the same screen, designers can work with a true virtual system in which they appear to own not only all of memory (and then some) but also to own an entire dedicated display. This freedom, combined with the ability to produce higher-color and higher-resolution displays and the freedom gained by off-loading the host CPU from graphics work, will allow remarkable growth in the sophistication and ease of use of software; the tools are finally becoming available to catch up with the dreams of software designers.

The Next Generation

Where will the first fruits of graphic processor technology appear? Right away systems will incorporate them into high-speed versions of current products. The chief problem with graphical operating environments (Windows, GEM, and the like) is that they incur vast overhead in maintaining the screen. Ports of these environments (and similar graphics-intensive applications, such as CAD packages) to faster, graphics-processor-based systems will become available almost immediately—some may even have been introduced by the time this chapter is printed. Graphics toolkits and libraries, especially the popular ones such as MetaWINDOW and HALO, will follow soon after. Some of the more foresighted of these libraries have been emulating the capabilities of graphic processors in software for quite a while; applications that have taken advantage of those emulations will benefit most greatly. In parallel with the porting of graphic operating environments will come the development of enhancements to those environments, especially in the field of font and text development. The ability to generate text at high resolutions with acceptable speed will spur consumer demand for more powerful text systems and displays that begin to approach the flexibility and resolution available in their laser printers. Operating system and memory management products will lag behind. When available, however, they will be the sources of the largest direct benefit to users.

Conclusion

Intel and TI have produced two very different but remarkable processors. The software industry will reap many benefits from them both, in part because each company has been very responsive to the concerns and needs of developers. The Number Nine Pepper Series of graphics boards includes products that use both the TI and Intel coprocessors. In addition to providing powerful hardware, the Pepper Series addresses the software issues raised here through the Number Nine Intelligent Operating System (NNIOS).

As the technology of visual displays is brought to a price and performance level that can make it available to the mass market, the opportunity for software of high perceived value increases. Public awareness of the quality and craftsmanship inherent in excellent software will certainly increase, and developers who make the necessary investments in time and effort to use these new graphic systems effectively will become a prominent part of that awareness.

41

High-performance Graphics: Intel 82786 *

Ed McNierney

New high-performance graphics processors, once restricted to professional work-stations and expensive PC graphics controllers, are now generally available for business, design, and home applications. As prices have dropped, demand has increased for sophisticated graphics processors such as the Intel 82786.

Intel's new graphics processor is a highly integrated component that, in one chip, provides graphics-display functions that traditionally have required discrete components or external microprocessor support; this not only lowers the cost and size of the processor, but also increases its reliability and performance.

The Intel 82786 is packaged as an 88-pin, ceramic pin grid array. Power, ground, and external-control signals are supplied to it, and address and data lines for controlling graphics memory are provided as outputs. Video signals can be configured either as outputs or as inputs slaved to an external video-synchronization source.

The 82786 executes many drawing operations and provides sophisticated hardware windowing. These windows allow the placement of any portion of graphics-display memory onto any portion of the screen, entirely eliminating traditional hardwiring between display addresses and pixel positions on the screen. The 82786 supports screen resolutions of 640-by-480 pixels at eight bits per pixel, and even higher resolutions if display depth is reduced. Multiple 82786 processors can be combined in applications requiring high resolution and color depth.

For example, an 82786 implementation might include one or more megabytes of dynamic RAM (DRAM), the 82786 itself, normal palette and output support, and a small amount of ROM. Because the 82786 executes graphics using fixed commands, relatively little ROM is needed. A much larger amount (32KB or more) of host-computer ROM may be included in the system for such uses as a subroutine package for calculating display parameters or constructing graphics-instruction

---

sets. This kind of implementation is particularly well suited to a multitasking text and graphics workstation arrangement.

The 82786 sets graphical boundaries between tasks in the same way that multitasking systems such as the Intel 80386 use hardware to separate tasks. A task running in a specific window is entirely self-contained; it has a specified display size and depth and a data buffer at a particular address in display memory. Because it does not know what other tasks are in the system—or the location of critical parameters—it is hindered from interfering with them.

A difficult problem for the operating system in managing multitasking DOS applications is controlling arbitration between various programs that all write directly to display memory. The 82786 solves this problem by providing each application with its own private bitmap, contiguous memory representing a rectangular area of specified pixel depth.

The application can write to that bitmap whenever it desires, because its data are shared by no other application. The data are positioned dynamically in a screen window as the display is refreshed, a process that is transparent to the applications modifying graphics memory.

The 82786 uses three independent processors: the display and graphics processors contained in the 82786 itself and the host CPU. The display processor extracts graphics data from the 82786's local memory and converts it to video-data output that appears in windows on the monitor. The graphics processor is responsible for performing all of the 82786's drawing operations.

The three processors communicate with each other and are coordinated by means of an on-chip bus called the bus-interface unit (BIU). Together, these processors, possibly coupled with one or more external microprocessors, perform the complete set of Intel 82786 functions (see Figure 41-1).

The entire system is driven by two independent clocks: CLK and VCLK. CLK is a general CPU clock that controls all processor operations; VCLK is the fundamental pixel clock that controls all video-output signals. Because the two clocks operate independently, video rates may be modified without affecting overall graphics performance.

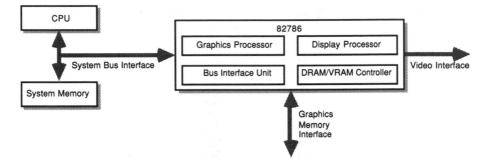

Figure 41-1: 82786 Functional Overview. The BIU acts as coordinator between the independent graphics processor and display processor on the 82786 and the host CPU.

BIU Control

The BIU not only arbitrates among multiple requests for bus access from the 82786's display and graphics processors and the CPU, but also provides a complete memory-controller system for either video RAM (VRAM) or conventional DRAM chips. The 82786 itself has an address space of 4MB that is divided between dedicated-graphics memory and the host CPU's memory spaces. When the host CPU accesses graphics memory, the BIU acts as a slave to the host, providing graphics data directly from the 82786's memory space. Conversely, the BIU also can act as a bus master in the host CPU's address space, allowing the 82786 processor to draw directly into the host CPU's memory.

Operation of the BIU itself is controlled by local registers occupying 128 bytes of memory and including BIU control, relocation, refresh control, VRAM/DRAM control, and three programmable priority registers (see Table 41-1). These registers, like all others in the 82786, can be mapped into the host CPU's memory- or I/O-address space. They also can be programmed to access either an 8-bit or 16-bit host interface, allowing the host CPU to configure its access to suit the PC's bus size.

The BIU's relocation register controls the location of the register block. At RESET, this register block appears to occupy the entire I/O space of the 82786: any I/O anywhere in the 82786's memory is written to it. Once this register is written, the register set is anchored in the address space at whatever location has been specified.

Mnemonic	**Function**	**Description**
BIU CONTROL		
WP2	Write-protect 2	Write-protects entire BIU register set
WP1	Write-protect 1	Write-protects certain BIU registers
DI	Display interrupt	Display processor causes interrupt
GI	Graphics interrupt	Graphics processor causes interrupt
BCP	Byte control	Determines if host accesses are 8/16 bits
WT	Wait	Wait states on host accesses of 82786 memory
VR	Video RAM	Selects video RAM refresh cycles
RELOCATION		
REL	Relocation	Sets location where register set is addressed
REFRESH		
REF	Refresh	Controls frequency of RAM refresh cycles
VRAM/DRAM CONTROL		
HT	Height	RAM device height (8K-by-N to 1M-by-N)
DC	DRAM control	Selects RAM interleave and page mode accesses
RW	Row	Number of rows of RAM devices
PRIORITY		
GPRIOR	Graphics	Priority of graphics processor bus cycles
DPRIOR	Display	Priority of display processor bus cycles
XPRIOR	External	Priority of external CPU bus cycles

Table 41-1: BIU Register Set: The overall operation of the BIU is governed by the BIU control, relocation, refresh, VRAM/DRAM control, and three programmable priority registers.

A flag bit in the register determines whether it is mapped into memory or I/O. If the register is memory-mapped, the host CPU reads the registers instead of the graphics memory when it accesses the register's addresses. Thus, any physical memory is hidden from the host CPU. Drawing operations can still be performed on that memory, and display- or graphics-processor instruction sets may be stored there.

The BIU's memory interface is controlled by two of its internal registers: refresh control and VRAM/DRAM control. The six-bit refresh control register determines the frequency of memory refresh cycles; its programmed value is decremented every 16 clock cycles, and a refresh is generated when the value reaches zero. Because another 82786 memory cycle may be active when the refresh is signaled, refreshed must occur with sufficient frequency to tolerate any delay-causing latency.

TABLE 41-2: Display Processor Status Registers

Mnemonic	Function	Description
ECL	End of command list	Set when processor finishes command list
ODD	Odd Field	Interlaced display is showing odd field
EVEN	Even Field	Interlaced display is showing even field
BLANK	Blank status	Video output is currently being blanked
FMT	FIFO empty	Display FIFO has run out of video data
DOV	Descriptor overrun	Tiles define too many pixels on one line
RCD	Reserved command	An undefined opcode is encountered
FRI	Frame interrupt	Set when a frame count has elapsed
The display processor status and interrupt mask registers are mapped parallel to one another, thus allowing events to be polled or interrupt-signaled.		

The VRAM/DRAM control register defines the size, type, and number of memory devices supported in the 82786's graphics-memory space. Because this information defines the actual amount of display RAM installed, it sets the boundary between the 82786's graphics- and system-memory spaces.

The BIU's three priority registers (graphics, display, and external) determine the relative priorities assigned to competing processors during memory arbitration. The BIU can get bus requests from three separate sources: the display and graphics processors within the 82786 itself, each operating as an independent processor, and the external host CPU. In addition, both the display processor and graphics processor may wish to transfer blocks to and from graphics memory. These competing demands are arbitrated on the basis of programmable priorities that are assigned to each competitor for its first request and any subsequent requests.

Certain performance functions, such as display refresh, impose restrictions on setting these priorities: the display processor retrieves the data to refresh the screen; if it is denied a bus request for too long it will run out of video data and be forced to display field (background) on the screen. Because the first priority of a graphics system is to maintain an undisturbed image on the screen, such disruptions are unacceptable to the user. Therefore, display refresh has a fixed priority higher than all programmable priorities.

The external CPU also can impose constraints on the amount of latency permitted to a device in the I/O channel: in the IBM PC, any request made to memory in an external, plug-in device must receive a response in 2.7 microseconds or less. Excessive bus latency can cause unpredictable behavior and corrupt the PC's local memory. Fortunately, the graphics processor is flexible; so long as it gains access to graphics memory to perform its drawing operations, it may be delayed for long periods without causing problems.

Each processor also has a priority register, in which 6 bits are used to assign two 3-bit priorities. Bits 5 through 3 determine the priority of a processor's first request for a bus cycle, and bits 2 through 0 determine the priority for subsequent requests made in a block transfer. Because the external CPU is not permitted to initiate block transfers, the low-order 3 bits in the external priority register are not used.

By adjusting the values used in the first priority level and the subsequent priority level, a trade-off can be obtained between maximum block-transfer performance and maximum bus latency is a given system, with each system—or even each application program—tuned to its particular needs.

Display Processor

The display processor extracts bitmap information from graphics memory and displays it in hardware windows on the graphics monitor, supplying all video-timing and synchronization signals from information stored in programmable video-control registers. It provides normal display data, zoomed displays, and hardware cursor control, plus an instruction set for defining new display formats. The display processor also fetches the descriptor information used to determine the size and position of hardware windows on the screen; this is done transparently.

The hardware windows displayed on the monitor are arranged as a number of horizontal strips, each running the entire width of the screen. Each strip is composed of tiles the height of the strip. A strip can be as small as one scan line high; ut to 16 tiles the height of the strip. A strip can be as small as one scan line high; up to 16 tiles can be placed horizontally across a single strip.

The display processor is controlled by a set of internal registers: display opcode, display address, default video, interrupt mask, and display status. The display opcode and display address registers allow the processor to execute its command set; the opcode indicates which operation, and the address is set to point to the data used by that operation. The low-order bit of display opcode is called the display-end-of-command-list bit; when cleared to zero, it informs the display processor that a legal opcode is then executed at the next vertical blank period, using the data that are identified in the display address register. When the command has been completed, the display processor sets the display-end-of-command-list bit and continues with display output.

The display processor uses the default video register to define the data to be driven on the video-data output pins during blanking periods. These data can be used as an overscan color or to signal other portions of the graphics system, such as a palette-load facility, that a blanking period is active.

The interrupt mask and display status registers are exact duplicates of each other (see Table 41-2). When the host CPU requests that it be interrupted under a particular condition, the corresponding bit is set in the interrupt mask register; setting that bit in the display status register causes the interrupt. The host CPU reads the display status register to determine which even caused the interrupt. This reading clears any interrupt flag that was set.

A much larger register block within the display processor—display control—provides video and cursor control and defines where in graphics memory the hardware-window data descriptors can be read (see Table 41-3). The display opcodes supported by the display processor are simple: load register, dump register, load all registers, and dump all registers. Each display opcode executes during the next vertical blank period, allowing modifications to window arrangement on the screen to occur smoothly and without interruption.

Only one register defines the layout of hardware windows on the display screen: in fact, it is only a pointer to the actual window-descriptor list. The descriptor list is arranged in memory as a linked list of strip descriptors, each of which points to its own list of tile descriptors. The strip descriptors and tile descriptors together define the display's hardware windows, which are set dynamically during the display refresh cycle (see Figure 41-2).

TABLE 41-3: Display Control Registers

Mnemonic	Function	Description
VSAT	Video status	Controls cursor and video display enable
INTMSK	Interrupt mask	Selects conditions that cause interrupts
TRIPPT	Trip point	Controls frequency of FIFO fill accesses
FRINT	Frame interrupt	Number of frames between interrupts
CRTMODE	CRT mode	Flag bit register
IL	Interlace	Selects interlaced/noninterlaced display
W	Window status	Selects output of window status pins
S	Sync slave	Selects sync pins as inputs or outputs
B	Blank slave	Selects blank pins as inputs or outputs
AA	Acceleration	Number of pixels emitted each dot clock
HSYNSTP	Horizontal sync stop	Width of horizontal sync signal in dots
HFLSTRT	Horizontal field start	Time from sync to active video in dots
HFLDSTP	Horizontal field stop	Time from start to end of active video
LINELEN	Line length	Length of each scan line in dot clocks
VSYNST	Vertical sync stop	Width of vertical sync signal in lines
VFLSTRT	Vertical field start	Time from sync to active video in lines
VFLDSTP	Vertical field stop	Time from start to end of active video
FRMELEN	Frame length	Height of entire display in scan lines
DAP	Descriptor pointer	Addresses of first strip/tile descriptor set
ZOOMX	X-zoom scale	Amount zoomed tiles are X-zoomed
ZOOMY	Y-zoom scale	Amount zoomed tiles are Y-zoomed
FLDCOLR	Field color	Color when no window is present
BDRCOLR	Border color	Color of window borders
1BPPPAD	1 bit/pixel pad	Padding 1-bit data to 8 output bits
2BPPAD	2 bit/pixel pad	Padding 2-bit data to 8 output bits
4BPPPAD	4 bit/pixel pad	Padding 4-bit data to 8 output bits
CSRMODE	Cursor mode	Flag bits controlling the cursor
S	Size	Selects 8-by-8 or 16-by-16 pixel cursor
X	Crosshair	Selects a block or crosshair cursor
T	Transparency	Controls whether cursor is transparent
CST	Cursor status	Value on window status pins under cursor
CSRPAD	Cursor pad	Padding cursor to 8 output bits
CSRPOSX	Cursor position	X coordinate of cursor position on screen
CSRPAT0	Cursor patter O	First word of 16-word cursor pattern
CSRPATF	Cursor pattern F	Last word of 16-word cursor pattern

Header

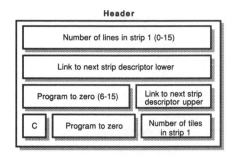

First Tile Descriptor

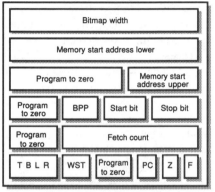

Second Tile Descriptor

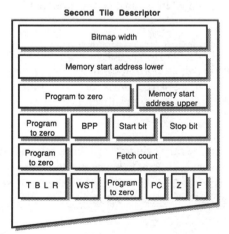

Figure 41-2: Strip and Tile Descriptors. The combination of the strip and tile descriptors defines the display's hardware windows, which are set dynamically during the course of the display refresh cycle.

Each tile descriptor defines a horizontal strip of uniform vertical format across the screen. To help reduce the bus bandwidth required for reading descriptors, the tile descriptors used with a given strip descriptor occupy consecutive memory locations immediately following the strip descriptor.

The first strip descriptor whose address is in the register is read during vertical retrace. This descriptor is used for as many scan lines as are specified in its definition; the next strip descriptor is fetched during the horizontal retrace preceding its first scan line.

The strip descriptor begins with a simple four-word header block. The first word of the descriptor defines the number of scan lines occupied by the entire strip. This number must match the height of the screen as defined by the video-control registers in the display processor. The next two words contain the address to be used beneath the current one. The last word defines the number of horizontal tiles in the strip—and therefore the number of tile descriptors that follow the header.

Each tile descriptor is a six-word definition of a single tile on the display. These tiles are the fundamental unit of screen output; each displays data from one bitmap in graphics memory. The first word of the descriptor defines the width of the displayed bitmap in bytes. Because the actual bitmap can be much larger than the tile used to display it, the display processor needs this value to determine how much the display-data fetch address must be incremented for each scan line of the tile.

The next two words specify the start address for the bitmap data being displayed; the start address controls which portion of the bitmap is displayed in the tile. By properly calculating the offset-start address for a given tile, it can be made to pan and scroll across a bitmap, displaying different portions of graphics data (see Figure 41-3).

The fourth word determines the window's pixel depth and defines the start and stop bits to be used in each scan line. Because the addresses and fetch counts used by the display processor must all be even word counts, these start- and stop-bit fields are needed to give single-pixel resolution to the staring position and width of the window.

The fifth word—the fetch count—lets the display processor know the number of bytes of data to fetch for the display of the tile. Along with the pixel depth and start- and stop-bit fields, it also determines the actual displayed width of the tile in pixels.

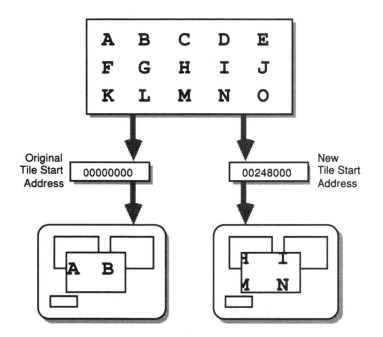

Figure 41-3: Graphic Bitmap Panning. The tile's bitmap start address controls which portion of the bitmap is displayed in the tile. By changing the start address, the tile can be panned across the bitmap.

The last word of each tile descriptor contains an assortment of flag bits. The four high-order bits control the display of a single-pixel border along any of the tile's four edges; a bit set to 1 turns on the border along that tile edge. Two window-status bits provide output on the window-status pins while this tile is being displayed. These bits are not used by the 82786, but are provided only for possible use by external display-board logic.

The zoom bit indicates whether the window should be zoomed by the factors defined in the display processor's ZoomX and ZoomY registers. The field bit determines whether actual bitmap data should be displayed in the window or whether no bitmap data should be fetched, leaving the window filled with the current field color.

The remaining two bits in the flag word determine the format of the bit-map data displayed by the tile. The 82786 can display data in formats compatible with a number of currently popular display adapters. The native 82786 format consists of data bytes stored sequentially and linearly in graphics memory; a single word is defined with its high-order byte appearing at a lower address than its low-order byte. The Intel 8086 microprocessors do not use this format; instead, they store words as low byte followed by high byte. In addition, the Hercules Graphics Card (HGC), the IBM Color Graphics Adapter (CGA), and the IBM PCjr interleave banks of display data, with consecutive lines of data in memory appearing every second or every fourth scan line on the screen, depending on the display adapter and the display mode.

The 82786's graphics processor can perform drawing operations only on bitmap data defined in its own native format: However, it can easily emulate current display adapters because each tile on the display is able to define its own memory format.

On power-up, the display processor does not execute any commands; all display outputs and interrupts are disabled and default video is generated on the video-data output pins. At a minimum, the host CPU must program the video-control registers for the 82786 to start generating synchronization signals to display a stable, if empty, image. The strip descriptors and tile descriptors need not be programmed until the applications software (or operating system) begins to define windows for its use. Because the strip descriptors are read and interpreted dynamically, the format of the entire display can be changed instantaneously.

Graphics Processor

The graphics processor, which is responsible for all 82786 drawing operations, provides graphics primitives for drawing lines, rectangles, arcs, and circles; incremental procedures for rapidly drawing or filling in complex figures; as well as a complete set of 16 binary Boolean drawing operations. The graphics processor also supports rectangular clipping and picking, in which pointing devices of some kind are used to select a portion of the display.

The processor operates on bitmaps of programmable size and characteristics. It can draw on any number of distinct bitmap areas in memory, each of which can have its own pixel depth. It also can execute general bit-block-transfer (bit-BLT) operations plus specialized character-BLTs that convert a one-bit-per-pixel source-character mask into a multiple-bit colored character.

Overall operation of the graphics processor is controlled by six memory-mapped registers: opcode, link address (two words), status, and instruction pointer (two words). These registers direct execution of commands and allow monitoring by the host CPU.

The graphics processor has 22 internal registers, two of which are status mask registers: graphics poll mask (GPOEM) and graphics interrupt mask (GIMR). The GPOEM and GIMR have flag bits corresponding to the bits in the graphics status register (see Table 41-4). If a bit is set in GIMR, then a graphics-processor interrupt to the host CPU is generated whenever the corresponding flag bit is set in the graphics status register. If a flag is set in graphics status, and its corresponding bit is also set in GPOEM, the graphics processor immediately enters the poll state, in effect aborting the current command list.

Mnemonic	Function	Description
GIBMD	Illegal bitmap	Current bitmap definition is not valid
GCTP	Character trap	Signals character larger than 16-by-16 pixels
GBMOV	Bitmap overflow	A drawing command crossed the clip rectangle
GBCOV	Character overflow	Text or bit-BLT crossed the clip rectangle
GPSC	Pick successful	Drawing in PICK mode found desired object
GINT	Graphics interrupt	82786 generated a software interrupt
GP GRCD	Reserved opcode	82786 found an undefined opcode
GPOLL	Graphics poll state	Commands finished and 82786 is idle

Table 41-4: Graphics Processor Status Register. The status register is written to by the 82786 and is read by external devices; the GPOEM and GIMR are written to by external devices and read by the 82786.

The graphics count (GCNT) register provides a count of characters being drawn during a character-string draw, and the graphics stack pointer (GSP) register is used while executing command lists. Because blocks of graphics commands can be defined as subroutines and called from other graphics-command lists, a stack pointer, defined by the application, is used to indicate the region of memory to be used for storing return addresses. If no subroutines are used, this register does not have to be initialized.

The instruction set of the graphics processor is divided into four functional groups: drawing-environment control, geometric drawing, BLT, and execution-control instructions (see Table 41-5). The graphics processor usually fetches commands from a sequential list in memory with its starting address programmed into the graphics control register. In order to begin executing a command list, the graphics control opcode must contain a LINK (or GOTO) command. LINK is followed by the address of the new command list; as soon as execution begins, the graphics processor jumps to the new command list.Each instruction consists of an opcode word followed by a varying number of words of data specific to that opcode. The opcode itself occupies only the high eight bits of the opcode word; the low-order bit is the graphics-end-of-command-list (GECL) bit. Whenever an opcode with the GECL bit is fetched, the command is considered to be last on the list. Its parameters are fetched and the command is executed, but the GECL bit is copied into the graphics poll (GPOLL) bit in the graphics status register and the graphics processor enters a poll state. It remains in that state until a new link address is programmed into the graphics control register and the GPOLL bit is reset to 0. Once the graphics processor has established the graphics environment, drawing can take place. Each application must initialize all aspects of its drawing environment. As a graphics-processor instruction list is executed, the flow of control from one group of graphics commands to another is governed by execution-control instructions. The 82786 provides no conditional test-and-branch instruction, but can jump to new addresses only to fetch instructions and call other blocks of instructions as subroutines. The host CPU is responsible for determining which graphics operations are to be performed and for programming the 82786 appropriately.

TABLE 41-5: Graphics Processor Instruction Set

Mnemonic	Function	Description
ENVIRONMENT		
DEF_BIT_MAP	Define bitmap	Set drawing area size and depth
DEF_CLIP_RECT	Define clip rectangle	Set size of clip rectangle
DEF_COLORS	Define colors	Foreground and background colors
DEF_TEXTURE	Define texture	Pattern used in line drawing
DEF_LOGICAL_OP	Define logical	Boolean raster operation used operation in drawing
DEF_CHARSET	Define character set	Address of character set to use
DEF_CHARORIENT	Define character orient	Path and rotation of characters
DEF_CHARSPACE	Define character spacing	Added spacing between characters
ABS_MOV	Absolute move	Move drawing pointer absolutely
REL_MOV	Relative move	Move drawing pointer relatively
ENTER_PICK	Enter pick mode	Stop drawing, select objects
EXIT_PICK	Exit pick mode	Leave pick mode, resume drawing

(continued on next page)

GEOMETRIC DRAWING

POINT	Point	Draw a single pixel
INCRPOINT	Incremental points	Draw a complex figure of pixels
CIRCLE	Circle	Draw a circle
LINE	Line	Draw a single line segment
RECT	Rectangle	Draw a rectangle
POLYLINE	Polyline	Draw a set of line segments
POLYGON	Polygon	Draw an outlined polygon
ARC	Arc	Draw a circular arc
SCANLINES	Draw horizontal	Fill a set of adjacent scan lines

BLOCK TRANSFER

BIT_BLT	Bit-BLT	Copy rectangle inside a bitmap
BIT_BLT_M	Bit-BLT between	Copy data between two bitmaps
CHAR	Draw character string	Draw a series of characters

CONTROL

LINK	Link	Unconditional jump to new address
CALL	Call subroutine	Jump to graphics subroutine
RETURN	Return from subroutine	Return from graphics subroutine
INTR_GEN	Generate interrupt	Cause a graphics software interrupt
DUMP_REG	Dump register	Store a graphics processor register in memory
LOAD_REG	Load register	Load a graphics processor register from memory

The graphics processor's instruction set is broken down into four groups: environment, geometric drawing, BLTs, and control.

Local Memory

The 82786's 4MB address space contains no dedicated or reserved locations for special data. Each processor uses local registers to store pointers to its current command lists. Local graphics memory holds the actual bitmap-display data, as well as the bitmaps required by a multitasking workstation.

Local 82786 graphics memory extends from the beginning of the address space to a memory size programmed by the host processor at power-up. Addresses within this local range refer to memory locations controlled by the BIU and are accessed at high speed by either the graphics processor or the display processor. The 82786 makes the assumption that any addresses exceeding the programmed memory size are in external memory, which is controlled by the host CPU.

When the 82786 generates an address that exceeds its memory, the BIU requests system memory from the CPU. This allows the 82786 to retrieve display data, execute command lists, or draw upon bitmaps stored in system memory rather than graphics memory.

This feature is also a good alternative to other methods: traditional systems using graphics controllers for drawing either must use the host CPU to precisely emulate the controllers, or they must copy system memory to display memory, allow the controller to draw on it, and then copy the modified data back to their original location. For example, the Enhanced Graphics Adapter (EGA) display driver in Microsoft Windows includes two transparent routines to set a pixel, both of which are required: one sets a pixel in the EGA memory, and the other sets a pixel in the system memory.

The 82786 can support up to 32 VRAM and DRAM devices. Its flexible memory interface supports a variety of RAM technologies, memory organizations, and device densities, allowing the designer to trade-off cost with performance to build the system most appropriate to the application.

It also supports standard-page and fast-page modes, static column, and Intel's Ripplemode DRAMs, providing cycle times of 100 nanoseconds for the faster devices. Memory can be interleaved or noninterleaved. Devices can have one, four, or eight bits in sizes from 16KB to 1MB per chip. Even more memory devices can be installed if external drivers are there for support.

Slaves and Masters

The host CPU and the 82786 can exchange information by reading and writing data in each other's address space. The exchanges may vary from simple command lists or instructions to large chunks of data. In a multitasking system, the host CPU can implement virtual bitmap memory by moving display data to local address space and then writing the data to disk for later retrieval into the 82786's memory.

The 82786 operates in slave mode when it responds to a request form the host CPU either to read or to write graphics memory. This interface can be synchronous or asynchronous, with either an 8-bit or 16-bit interface. The host CPU can access the 82786's memory by asserting the Chip Select Low input line on the 82786; the 82786 activates the Slave Enable output line, which indicates the 82786 is ready to accept write data from the data lines or provide read data to the lines. Slave Enable is brought high by the 82786 when the slave transfer is complete. The host CPU's request is arbitrated according to the setting of the external priority register and is not queued by the BIU; if the host CPU wishes to initiate several slave transfers, it must assert the Chip Select Low input line for each one, wait until the 82786 completes its current cycles and arbitrates in favor of the external CPU, perform the operation, and then restart the process.

The 82786 processor also can act as a bus master to access memory not under its control; usually this memory resides in the host CPU's address space. Local and external memory are differentiated on the basis of installed memory in the 82786 system—all addresses beyond the configured size of graphics memory initiate transfers in which the 82786, acting as a master, requests memory from the host CPU.

The 82786 pulls the Hold Request line high to the host CPU or bus arbiter to indicate that it wishes to become the bus master. The 82786 waits for a Hold Acknowledge and then drives the address, data, read or write lines, and Master Enable High to initiate the cycle and indicate that it is now controlling the bus. Master Enable High is asserted for as long as the 82786 requires the bus; Hold Request is deactivated as soon as the transfer is complete.The 82786 still responds to slave accesses by the host CPU when it is waiting for acknowledgment of a Hold Request. This prevents a lockout if the 82786 starts a master request at the same time the host CPU initiates a slave request; the host CPU does not respond with a Hold Acknowledge until its slave cycle has been completed.

Normally the 82786 processor can occupy the external bus for an extended period, particularly if the graphics processor is performing a drawing operation on system memory. It is interrupted only by local memory-refresh requests. If the 82786 occupies the bus for too long, the host CPU can withdraw the Hold Acknowledge to interrupt the 82786. The 82786 then removes its Hold Request after completing the current cycle to indicate it has freed the external bus. After waiting two cycles, the 82786 again attempts a Hold Request to complete its operation. If the host CPU cannot respond in less than two cycles, external logic must be supplied to extend the delay time.

Heart of Multitasking

The Intel 82786 provides a powerful, low-cost approach to graphics-display system design. Its high level of integration and design makes it especially suitable for coupling with other Intel 8086-family microprocessors. Although geometric and character-graphics operations are fully supported, the 82786's strongest advantage is its hardware-windowing capability.

For the first time in PC graphics, restrictions have been removed between graphics memory and display output. A powerful graphics presentation system is the result of this progressive move. As PCs begin to provide more sophisticated multitasking environments, the 82786 offers a display-management facility that supports the same concepts of display-memory management and protection that the multitasking operating system provides to the application program.

The popularity of these multitasking environments is growing; expect to see the 82786 processor at the heart of the low-cost multitasking PC workstations in the very near future.

42

Inside the 82786 Graphics Chip *

Bill Nicholls

Intel's 82786 graphics processor is another step in the continuing conflict between the demand for higher resolution, more colors, and faster display. By improving the performance of current programs, such as Microsoft's Windows or Digital Research's GEM, it gives users more flexibility with the programs they already have. And by expanding display speed and resolution, it gives software developers more latitude in designing new systems.

Intel defines 82786 windows as "portions of bit maps. . .output by the display processor." The 82786 can display a large number of windows simultaneously. It can have up to 16 horizontal window segments on any single scan line, and as many vertical window segments as there are scan lines.

With the system clock running at 10 megahertz and the video clock at 25 MHz, the 82786 executes line draws at 2.5 million pixels per second, circles at 2 MPS, and area fills at 30 million bits per second.

The graphics coprocessor's bus interface does bus block transfers (BBLTs) at 24 million bps and draws 25,000 characters per second regardless of font or orientation. Internal hardware handles character fonts up to 16 by 16 pixels. Larger fonts require both software and hardware, or BBLT transfers. The 82786 can perform vertical and horizontal scrolling immediately, without external hardware, and enlarge (zoom) up to 64 times in either direction (in this case, zoom is a pixel-replication function).

The 82786 internal graphics processor and display processor each use 22 address bits, yielding an address range of 4 megabytes shared by the host processor and the graphics display processor. The 82786 can display up to 1024 colors simultaneously and supports resolutions of from 640 by 480 pixels by 8 bits, to 1024 by 1024 pixels by 2 bits with 60-Hz non-interlaced refresh.

By using video RAMs, you can boost resolution to 2048 by 1536 pixels by 8 bits, up to a maximum of 4096 by 4096 pixels by 1 bit. In addition, you can

* © McGraw-Hill Information Systems Comapny, *BYTE,* August, 1987, p. 135

synchronize multiple 82786 chips to produce higher-performance systems with more colors, higher resolution, and greater bandwidth.

Graphics Coprocessor Architecture

The principal components of the 82786 graphics coprocessor architecture are the graphics processor, display processor, bus interface, RAM refresh unit, and graphics memory space (see Figure 42-1). The graphics processor executes instructions placed in RAM by the host CPU and updates the bit map in graphics memory for the display processor.

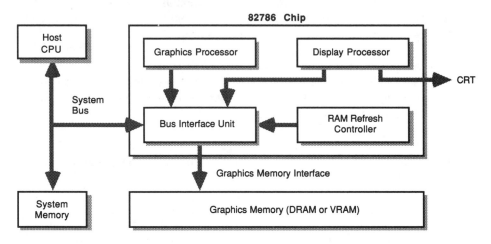

Figure 42-1: The 82786 graphics coprocessor architecture.

The display processor transforms the bit maps created by the graphics processor into the raster sequences required by the system display. The bus interface comprises four logical interfaces: external, memory access for the graphics processor, host-processor access to processor registers and graphics memory, graphics-processor access to the graphics memory, and requests for video RAM refresh.

The Graphics Processor

The graphics processor executes linked lists of graphics commands residing in the host processor's memory, accessing them via the bus-interface logic. The host processor first builds the list of graphics instructions and their parameters. Then, the host processor initializes the graphics processor by writing the upper and lower bytes of the link address in the graphics processor's control register and setting the link-command bit.

After a reset, the graphics processor starts up in poll mode and checks the value of bit 0 (the end-of-instruction-list flag) of its instruction register. When the host processor loads an instruction that has bit 0 cleared, the graphics processor begins executing instructions, starting with a link address to the beginning of an instruction list in memory.

Once started by the host processor, the graphics processor executes instructions without being synchronized to either the host processor or the display processor. The host processor can write graphics-processor instructions anywhere in the graphics processor's 4-megabyte address space.

Pixel drawing is done in the graphics memory only. The graphics processor can update bits in any bit map in the graphics memory, regardless of whether the display processor is actively displaying that bit map.

The graphics processor can also operate in pick mode. Instead of updating the graphics memory, the graphics processor executes the instructions and checks to see if the pixels they address are in the clipping window defined in the window descriptor block (see the section, "Managing Windows," on page 716). If these objects are within the clipping window, a flag is set to speed up the selection of objects on the screen.

The Display Processor

The display processor controls the pixel output to a CRT, laser printer, or other raster output device. The display processor transforms the bit map created by the graphics processor into the sequence of pixels and control signals required for the attached device. The display processor is optimized for data in packed bit-map form but can switch while in a window to IBM Color Graphics Adapter mode and byte-swapped addressing. You can also synchronize the display processor to external video sources.

Program instructions also drive the display processor, but in a unique fashion. Once for each frame, the display processor can load a new instruction into its registers for execution during the following frame. This highly complex instruction specifies everything except the windows on the screen. The instruction (see Figure 42-2) points to another block of memory, which specifies the windows.

The program parameters specify functions such as hardware zoom, cursor display, windows, video pixel rates, and CRT timing signals.

Display Control / Address

Legend:

# of frames between interrupts

C = Cursor on
D = Display on
IL = Interlace
W = Window status enable
S = Sync slave mode
B = Blank slave mode
AA = Accelerated video

S   = Cursor size
X   = Cross hair mode
T   = Transparent/opaque mode
CS = Cursor status
CSC = Cursor status control

Bit positions: 15 14 13 12 11 09 | 8 7 6 5 4 3 2 1 0

Address	Field
0	C D (bits 1, 0)
1	Interrupt mask
2	Trip point
3	Frame interrupt
4	Reserved
5	IL W S B AA
6	Hsync clock count
7	Hfeild start count
8	Hfield stop count
9	Line length clock count
A	Vsync clock count
B	Vfield start count
C	Vfield stop count
D	Frame line count
E	Lower window descriptor pointer
F	Upper window descriptor pointer
10	Reserved
11	Xzoom | Yzoom
12	BG color
13	Border color
14	1-bit pixel pad
15	2-bit pixel pad
16	4-bit pixel pad
17	S X T CS CSC − | Cursor pad
18	Cursor X position (lower)
19	Cursor Y position (upper)
1A – 29	16 words of cursor pattern

Figure 42-2: Graphics coprocessor display-control block.

The display processor can zoom the display screen horizontally and vertically by a factor of from 1 to 64, affecting all windows. (This is a pixel-replication function, as opposed to recalculating endpoints and redrawing lines.) At the normal video rate of 25 MHz and 8 bits per pixel, you can locate windows on the screen with single-pixel resolution. You can set the cursor to display as 8 by 8 or 16 by 16 pixels with single-pixel resolution. The cursor can be opaque, transparent, a block, or full-screen cross hairs. You can program cursor color, pattern, and blinking, and turn off the cursor. CRT timing signals are programmed at single-pixel resolution, allowing up to 4096- by 4096-pixel displays.

You can change the display processor's mode to trade off bits per pixel for pixel draw rate. Thus, you can exchange the basic 25 MHz at 8 bits per pixel for 50 MHz at 4 bits per pixel, 100 MHz at 2 bits per pixel, or 200 MHz at 1 bit per pixel. At the higher rates, horizontal resolution decreases to 2-, 4-or 8-pixel boundaries.

The display processor controls the video RAMS by loading the shift registers during the retrace time between each scan line. Additional processing is required for each display line containing windows or cursor display before the line loading into the VRAM shift register.

Memory-Access Priorities

The bus-interface logic performs arbitration between four logical interfaces: external host memory access for the 82786, host-processor access to internal registers and graphics memory, 82786 access to graphics memory, and, most importantly, RAM refresh.

The refresh unit generates and queues RAM refresh requests to the bus interface, which executes them at top priority. The host processor, graphics processor, and display processor contend for memory access according to a 3-bit priority system.

The priorities break down further into first (FA) and subsequent access (SA). Default priorities are (high to low) RAM refresh, display processor, graphics processor, and host processor. RAM refresh is always the highest priority, but you can change the others under program control. This allows you to program performance trade-offs into the chip to take advantage of the 82786 for various types of applications.

The default priorities after a reset are Host (FA) 7, Display (FA) 6, Graphics (FA) 5, Display (SA) 3, and Graphics (SA) 2. Since the graphics processor and display processor usually access more than one word in sequence, the bus interface provides maximum throughput when accessing sequential words. However, if sequential access locks out a first access from another processor, that might affect overall performance.

This adjustable priority scheme lets software maximize the 82786's performance for specific circumstances by balancing access priority of the host processor, graphics processor, and display processor in relation to their need for first and sequential access.

The refresh-controller parameters, which the software sets at start-up, schedule the DRAM refresh, although the bus interface unit performs the actual refresh cycles. Because of the contention for graphics memory access, you can queue three refresh requests internally. The longest acceptable delay without refresh is 225 cycles at 10 MHz (about 45 microseconds).

Manipulating Bit Maps

The graphics processor converts host-processor graphics commands into a specific bit representation as specified by the drawing parameters contained in the graphics-processor instructions. The instruction-execution process starts by loading the graphics processor's link address registers (upper and lower byte) with an address that points to the beginning of a list of instructions. The graphics processor executes instructions until stopped by a flag (bit 0 set to 1) in an instruction word.

During its execution, the graphics processor shares memory access (with the display processor and host processor) to the 4-megabyte address space. The bus-interface logic controls this sharing according to parameters set by the host processor at start-up.

The graphics processor draws a bit map into graphics memory. You can think of this bit map as a rectangular array of display pixels (up to 32K by 32K pixels in size) with the [0,0] coordinate located at the display's upper left corner. Pixels are packed linearly in the bit map.

The system stores 4-bit pixels as four pixels per 16-bit word, each line consisting of (the number of pixels divided by four) words, with the lines stored sequentially. Thus, the bit map is packed into the minimum memory required for a given display size and number of bits per pixel. Graphics-processor performance depends heavily on frequent access to graphics memory. Ignoring the overhead for instructions, each updated word requires a read-modify-write (RMW) cycle of graphics memory. An 8-bit-per-pixel resolution requires a word access for every two pixels.

The two predominate factors affecting performance are graphics-memory bandwidth and the amount of display-processor overhead involved in an operation. If you use VRAMs, the graphics processor will be able to use up to 99 percent of the available memory-bus bandwidth. Using DRAMs, the memory bandwidth available to the graphics processor depends upon the access required by the display processor and can be from 50 percent to 90 percent.

Graphics Memory

One of the 82786's key high-performance graphics features is its dynamic-memory interface. This interface lets the 82786 take full advantage of both dual-bank and page modes of using dynamic RAMs for a maximum speed of 40 megabytes per second.

The 4-megabyte linear address space of the graphics processor begins at address 00 hexadecimal of the graphics memory. If less than 4 megabytes of graphics memory is implemented, the remaining addresses access system memory. You can move these system addresses by setting the top 2 address bits externally to point anywhere in the host processor's 4-megabyte address space.

The 82786 was designed to support a wide range of DRAM configurations: one or two banks for interleaving with one to four rows per bank; 16K-bit to 1-megabit RAMs in by-1, by-4 and by-8 width; and page or fast-page modes for performance. (Fast-page-mode RAMs can be cycled in 100 nanoseconds instead of the 200 ns required for page-mode RAMs.)

The memory interface will support up to 32 DRAMs without external logic, within the total 4-megabyte addressable memory. The 82786 can also use video RAMs in its overall memory scheme. VRAMs contain a shift register and a serial output that allows high-speed shifting of the video data without repeated memory access. The use of VRAMs for graphics memory decreases the display overhead from a maximum of 50 percent to approximately 1 percent.

Using VRAMs makes more memory cycles available for the host and graphics processors, but some features are restricted. The 82786 can zoom VRAM-supported displays vertically, but horizontal zoom requires external circuitry because the 82786 doesn't have access to the bit map to replicate the pixels once the bit map has been moved into the shift register.

The DRAM access can be single or multiple cycle. A single cycle is a single 16-bit word; a multiple cycle is two or more. A single read or write is 300 ns at 10 MHz, RMW is 400 ns. Multiple-access data rates can run from 10 megabytes per second for noninterleaved page mode to 40 megabytes per second for interleaved fast page mode. (To minimize processing overhead the display processor uses multiple access whenever possible.). The graphics processor uses single RMW cycles for pixel updates and multiple RMW cycles for block moves, while the host processor uses only single cycles.

The Programmer's Model

Software configuration controls the 82786 chip. Host software can program the graphics processor and display processor and set the bus-interface-control parameters. Host software accesses the 82786 through a 128-byte block of addresses that can be memory- or I/O-mapped anywhere in the 4-megabyte address space. The 128 bytes are divided into three areas, one each for the graphics processor, the display processor, and the bus interface. Intel has reserved the unused words in this 128-byte space for future use.

The bus interface controls access to system and graphics memory. The eight bus-interface registers contain the most critical information for 82786 operation. These registers set up the access to all 82786 control registers, interrupts, and their status, DRAM refresh and configuration, and the relative priorities that the display, graphics, and host processors will have when accessing graphics memory.

Before the host processor can use the 82786, it must first set up the memory relocation and mapping, configure the graphics memory, and set refresh parameters and graphics-processor priorities. After allowing sufficient time for all DRAMs to refresh, the host creates screens by programming the graphics processor and displays them by programming the display processor. Within a bit map, the graphics processor will draw lines, circles, polygons, and arcs. BBLTs can manipulate any rectangular block of bits. Character block transfers (CBLTs) move character matrices into the bit map with four rotations or directions. The four categories of graphics-processor instructions are nondrawing, drawing-control, geometric-drawing, and bit- and character-block moves.

Nondrawing instructions allow graphics-processor-register access and control-instruction execution, and set up macros of instruction sequences. NOP performs nothing, LINK directs the graphics processor to the next instruction, and INTR_GEN generates an 82786 interrupt to the host processor. You can save the graphics-processor registers that are not directly addressable (registers 1 through 22) and restore them for program swapping by DUMP_REG and LOAD_REG. You can build subroutines of instructions by using the ENTER_MACRO and EXIT_MACRO instructions.

Each drawing operation is subject to the parameters set by the drawing-control commands. The major controls are definition of the memory location of the bit map and clipping rectangle, and entry to and exit from pick mode. The memory location and size define the boundaries of the bit map to be operated on. The clipping rectangle restricts pixel updates to a rectangular subset of the bit map. Pick mode allows execution of the display-processor instructions without updating the bit map. Instead, a flag is set when an instruction points to a pixel inside the current clipping rectangle. This allows for quick location of an object selected on the screen.

Other commands control the foreground and background colors, line texture, color-bit mask, and raster operations.

Raster Operations

The color and texture controls let you draw dotted or dashed lines as opaque or transparent. The bit mask can restrict drawing to a subset of color bits, letting you overlay different planes of information on the same screen. Raster operation defines the logical combination of bits during BBLT and CBLT operations. Control commands also define the character set, the character orientation, and the intercharacter spacing. Both relative and absolute move commands are provided for positioning in the bit map. Geometric commands are the simplest to describe. The instructions draw points, incremental points, lines, circles, arcs, rectangles, polylines (open multisegment lines), and polygons (closed multisegment lines). A scan-line instruction is for fast-fill operations once the host processor determines the boundaries. Block-transfer instructions can transfer within a single bit map for simple moves or logical overlays. BBLTs can also transfer across different bit maps to combine separately drawn images.

Character transfers move character matrices into the bit map with any of four orientations or directions. Operating within these design parameters, the display processor can switch windows or displays as fast as once every frame, typically 30 to 60 times per second, with minimal overhead. Instead of rapidly executing simple instructions, the display processor can execute complex instructions at a slower rate. This approach is well-matched to the nature of the display process.

Future Impact

The Intel 82786 will clearly improve the performance of windowing systems, especially systems with slower processors and those performing multitasking.

Microsoft's Windows and Digital Research's GEM are two obvious beneficiaries of the graphics coprocessor. But so is every user who loads up a system only to find that more speed, higher resolution, and more windows are needed. In addition to operating systems, applications such as CAD and desktop publishing will benefit significantly from higher performance graphics.

One of the side effects of unloading the host processor and speeding up the display will be to extend the usable lifetime of current systems, especially the 8088-based systems. Manufacturers of new systems might view this with some concern, but they can rest assured that users and software developers will manage to dispose of the extra capacity easily. In fact, experience with high-performance systems typically builds demand for even higher performance. The 82786 is another step in this continuing process.

Managing Windows

Most of the effort in programming the display processor involves setting the window strip descriptors as windows are moved and overlaid. The host processor must determine which windows are visible on the screen, in what order they appear vertically, and in what sequence they appear horizontally. From this information, the host processor builds one or more linked windowstrip descriptors that specify how to display each window segment or "tile". Descriptors for each strip link together in a list forming a complete description of the screen in tile-by-tile sequence. Since the list is linked, you can update it on the fly if you're careful. The window descriptor block shows a display header and multiple tile descriptors, organized in the sequence in which they will appear on screen.

Each tile is a horizontal segment of a window that is not obstructed on the display. A tile can be anything from a scan line to a full window in height, and from one pixel to the full screen in width. The only limitation is that there can be no more than 16 tiles per scan line. Each tile can specify a separate bit map, bits per pixel, and several other window parameters.

The display processor ties its execution of instructions to the display's refresh rate. During the vertical-blanking interval, the display processor will load a new command into an internal control block (if its control registers point to one). The internal control block is not directly accessible; it is loaded or stored by instructions in a six-register section of the main graphics-coprocessor registers. Display-processor commands generate external signals for horizontal and vertical timing, blanking signals, and the chip's eight video output pins. Internally, it controls interlace, synchronization, window and cursor generation, colors, and pixel bit-padding.

During each frame, the display processor executes the command (actually a macroinstruction) contained in the 42-word internal control block and a variable-length window descriptor block. It can execute only one command during the frame, which prevents interference with display refresh. Under control of the parameters set in the control and window blocks, the display processor retrieves portions of one or more bit maps from graphics memory and out-puts them to the display as pixels.

This process is somewhat complex. Here's how it works: The display processor fetches the window-strip-descriptor header for the first set of tiles.

Using the tile count, the display processor then loads the first tile descriptor, which contains the pointers to the actual memory containing the image and the dynamic window parameters. The display procssor then builds the pixel output from the specified memory areas until the tile (created by this tile descriptor) is completed.

The display processor then links to the next window-strip descriptor (the first header specifies the link), and it repeats this process until all the tiles comprising the screen have been built. The display processor can then load a new macroinstruction at vertical-retrace time and begin the process of creating the next screen.

While the display processor is busy displaying a screen of windows, the graphics processor can update images and the host processor can set up new windows for display. The new set of windows is linked by the macroinstruction, or a link to a new set of window strip descriptors. The cost of all these capabilities is the significant amount of programming required. Streamlining this process will require new parameter sets that control the 82786 to avoid reinventing fast-line drawing. The 82786 represents a functional step upward, but it will take a little time for the programmers to take full advantage of this added capability.

Appendix
IBM PC Family BIOS
Comparison *

Jon Shiell

This chapter presents an expanded and updated BIOS Table. Except for the Model 30, the PS/2 systems actually have two versions of the BIOS in their ROMs. The first version, for use in real mode and compatible with the BIOS in the prior PCs, is covered in this chapter. The other BIOS is for use with the OS/2 operating system and will not be covered here.

As the PC family has grown, there have been additions and deletions to the basic hardware set of the machines. (Because the Model 25 was only recently introduced, detailed information on its BIOS was not available for this chapter.) This chapter attempts to provide a comparative perspective of the various Basic I/O System (BIOS) features. If you wish to program on one machine, this chapter can help determine which functions apply across all machines in the family.

Table 1 gives the system configurations for IBM PC computers, with the exception of the 3270 PC. Table 2 describes the ROM BIOS interrupt vectors; Table 3 lists BIOS video modes; and Table 4 lists low-memory reserved addresses. Table 5 describes hardware interrupt request lines; Table 6 covers Expanded Memory Specification (EMS) function-call interfaces. Table 7 covers multitasking hooks using interrupt 15; Table 8 gives BIOS extension addresses; and Table 9 lists the NETBIOS modifications and additions to DOS.

The purpose of the BIOS is to present a common interface to the program, be it an applications program or an operating system, to minimize the amount of code that must be rewritten when using different machines. The BIOS lets the programmer isolate hardware dependence to a single set of primitive routines. What you gain from this is portability and compatibility between different hardware environments. At the same time, you retain almost all the speed and control of direct hardware access.

---

* © McGraw-Hill Information Systems Company, *BYTE,* 1987, Extra Edition, p. 173

The BIOS is made up of the code and programs that provide the device-level control for the major I/O devices in the system. In the IBM PC family, the BIOS is contained in ROM on the system board, along with cassette BASIC and a set of routines (called POST, for power-on self test) that check out the machine when you turn it on.

The BIOS creates hardware independence by providing a level of indirection and separation from the hardware. For example, when using a BIOS call to send a character to a printer, a programmer doesn't need to know what the I/O address of the printer port is or how to control it.

The BIOS is normally invoked via a set of interrupts vectored into various BIOS entry points. Other interrupt vectors are used to service hardware interrupts, such as "disk operation finished." In practical terms, the software invokes the BIOS by loading the appropriate registers in the microprocessor and issuing an *INT* instruction. For example,

```
MOV AH,O    ; Load AH with the BIOS
              function code for
              "print the character
              in register AL"
MOV AL,'B' ; Character to be
              printed, in this case
              a `B'
MOV DX,O    ; Print it on LPT1
              (Printer number minus 1)
INT 17      ; Printer BIOS entry
              interrupt.
```

The BIOS is extensible. When the POST routines run, as part of their operation they scan the ROM address space for add-on routines, which are then invoked so that they can install themselves. The IBM EGA, for example, extends the video interrupt INT 10, as indicated in Table 2.

The rule for BIOS entries is one software interrupt per device. There may also be one or more hardware entries, and entries that point to Tables or blocks of data used by the device driver.

The interrupt vectors, used as pointers to data instead of code, allow easy alteration to the environment, such as changing the character set displayed for 80 to FF by the CGA.

According to IBM, the only time you safely bypass the BIOS is when you access the following I/O ports: 21-interrupt mask registers; 61-sound control; 40-, 41-

(Note: Don't change this port.), 42- (timer frequency will remain fixed at 1.19 MHz), and 201-game control adapter.

Regarding absolute memory locations, note the following: Some functions have been added to interrupt vectors (0:0 to 3FF), but no functions have been redefined. The video display memory maps (A000:0, B000:0, and B800:0) will not change for a given video BIOS mode of operation. If the bit map is altered, a new mode is defined to support it. ROM BIOS data areas (starting at 40:)) will retain their current definitions as long as the corresponding functions are defined. In other words, the definitions can change at the whim of IBM.

Table 1: *System configurations for the IBM PC family of computers.*

Feature	PC	PC XT	PCjr	PC AT	PC AT 3x9	XT/2	XT/ 286	PC CVT	PS/2 30	PS/2 50	PS/2 60	PS/2 80	Comments
Model byte	FF	FE	FD	FC	FC	FB	FC	F9	FA	FC	FC	F8	@ FFFFE
Type byte	N/U	N/U	N/U	N/U	01	01	02	00	00	04	05	00	
BIOS level	N/U	N/U	N/U	N/U	00	00	00	00	00	00	00	00	
Hardware configuration	N/U	N/U	N/U	N/U	70	D0	70	38	FA	F6	F6	F6	Note 1
Processor type	8088	8088	8088	80286	80286	8088	80286	80C88	8086	80286	80286	80386	
Processor speed	4.77	4.77	4.77	6	8	4.77	6, 0 WS	4.77	8	10	10	16/20	Note 2; 1 wait state (WS) unless otherwise noted.
Num coprocessor speed	4.77	4.77	4.77	4	5.3	4.77	6	4.77	8	10	10	16/20	
DMA speed	4.77	4.77	4.77	3	4	4.77	3	4.77	4	10	10	8/10	
Bus width	8	8	8	16	16	8	16	8	8	16	16	32	Note 3
Maximum memory (in bytes)	640K	640K	640K	15M	15M	640K	15M	512K	640K	16M	16M	>16M	Note 4
8-bit DMA channels	4	4	0	4	4	4	4	3	4	4	4	4	Note 5
16-bit DMA channels	0	0	0	3	3	0	3	0	0	3	3	3	
Timer channels 0 and 2	●	●	●	●	●	●	●	●	●	●	●	●	Note 6
Timer channel 1	●	●	●	●	●	●	●	○	●	●	●	●	Note 7
System clock	○	○	○	●	●	○	●	●	●	●	●	●	Note 8
Number of function keys	10	10	10	10	10/12	10/12	10/12	12	12	12	12	12	Note 9

Notes:

All memory addresses and interrupts are in hexadecimal. The PC AT 3x9 models are the 319 and 339. The older models are the 099, 068, and 239. The PS/2 Model 25 has the same system configuration as the Model 30, except it has no hard disk and a different model version in the BIOS.
● = Yes; ○ = No; N/U = not used.

1. Configuration parameters, INT 15 (AH=0C0) returns a pointer to a block with the following format:

DW	8	Length of following table
DB	Model_byte	System model; see hardware table for specific values
DB	Type_byte	System model type
DB	BIOS_level	BIOS revision level
DB	HW_config	10000000 = DMA channel 3 used by fixed disk BIOS
		01000000 = Cascaded interrupt Level 2
		00100000 = Real-time clock available (RT/CMOS RAM chip)
		00010000 = Keyboard scan code hook 1A (PC AT and XT 286)
		00010000 = Keyboard intercept (INT 15, AH=41) supported (PC CVT and PS/2)
		00001000 = Wait on external event (INT 15, AH=41) supported (PC CVT); reserved on PS/2 systems
		00000100 = Extended BIOS data area allocated
		00000010 = Micro Channel system
		00000001 = Reserved
DW	0	Reserved
DW	0	Reserved

The PC XT 2 (Model 5160, model = FB, type = 01, BIOS date 01/10/86) returns an incorrect value for the configuration parameter. The incorrect value indicates that the level 2 interrupt is cascaded into another interrupt controller, and that DMA channel 3 is not used by the system BIOS when a hard disk is installed.

2. In the PCjr, the video is mapped into the lower 128K bytes of memory. Accesses to that area tend to be 50 percent slower than accesses for a normal PC. The PC CVT uses static CMOS RAM, so it needs no refresh cycles; thus, programs may run slightly (up to 5 percent) faster than expected. The PS/2 Model 80 comes in two speeds—16 MHz and 20 MHz, both with one wait state.

3. The PS/2 Model 30's memory is 16 bits, but the I/O bus is the 8-bit PC bus.

4. The PCjr has up to 128K bytes of internal memory; full expansion requires sidecars. The PS/2 Model 80 supports 32-bit memory addresses, so in theory you could put up to 4 gigabytes in one.

5. The PC CVT doesn't need to use one channel for dynamic RAM refresh, so its channel 3 acts like a PC's channel 4.

6. The PC CVT supports only modes 0, 2, 3, and 4 on channel 0.

7. Use depends on model (mostly refresh timing).

8. RT/CMOS RAM chip; PC CVT does not save configuration here.

9. The PC XT Models 089, 268, and 278 have the new keyboard; the other three models have the old keyboard. The PC AT Model 339 has the new keyboard, and the Model 319 has the old keyboard. The PC CVT generates function keys F11 and F12 with multiple keystrokes.

Table 2: *ROM BIOS interrupt vectors.*

Interrupt	Function code	PC	PC XT	PCjr	PC AT	XT /2	XT /286	PS CVT	PS/2 30	PS/2 other	BIOS	Comments
0	N/A	●	●	●	●	●	●	●	●	●		Divide by zero trap
1	N/A	●	●	●	●	●	●	●	●	●		Single-step mode (used by debug)
2 NMI	N/U	●	●	○	●	●	●	○	●	●		Parity check routine
	N/U	●	●	○	○	●	○	○	●	○		Coprocessor interrupt (directly)
	N/U	○	○	○	●	○	●	○	○	●		Coprocessor interrupt (via redirection from Int 75, IRQ 13)
	N/U	○	○	●	○	○	○	○	●	○		Keyboard interrupt routine (with data ready)
	N/U	○	○	○	○	○	○	○	●	●		I/O channel check
	N/U	○	○	○	○	○	○	●	○	○		Disk-controller power-on request
	N/U	○	○	○	○	○	○	●	○	○		System suspend
	N/U	○	○	○	○	○	○	●	○	○		Real-time clock (periodic, update-ended, or alarm interrupt)
	N/U	○	○	○	○	○	○	○	○	●		System watchdog timer, time-out interrupt (IRQ0 interrupt missed)
	N/U	○	○	○	○	○	○	○	○	●		Uchannel DMA timer, time-out interrupt (DMA burst greater than 7.8 microseconds)
3	N/A	●	●	●	●	●	●	●	●	●		Breakpoint (used by debug)
4	N/A	●	●	●	●	●	●	●	●	●		Overflow trap
5	N/A	●	●	●	●	●	●	●	●	●		Print-screen function (uses address 50:0 for status)
6	N/U	○	○	○	○	○	○	○	○	○		Reserved
7	N/U	○	○	○	○	○	○	○	○	○		Reserved
8 (IRQ 0)	N/A	●	●	●	●	●	●	●	●	●		Timer interrupt handler (entered about 18.2 times per second)
9 (IRQ 1)	N/A	●	●	●	●	●	●	●	●	●		Keyboard interrupt handler
A (IRQ 2)	N/A	○	○	○	●	○	●	○	○	●		Cascade for IRQ8 to IRQ15
	N/A	○	○	○	○	○	○	○	○	●	EGA	Vertical retrace interrupt for EGA and VGA
B (IRQ 3)	N/A	●	●	●	●	●	●	●	●	●		COM2: controller (e.g., serial port) hardware interrupt entry
C (IRQ 4)	N/A	●	●	●	●	●	●	●	●	●		COM1: controller (e.g., serial port) hardware interrupt entry
D (IRQ 5)	N/A	●	●	○	●	●	●	○	●	○		Alternate printer LPT2: (PC AT's 80287 initial-interrupt entry)
	N/A	○	●	○	○	●	○	○	●	○		Hard disk controller
	N/A	○	○	●	○	○	○	○	○	○		Vertical retrace interrupt (display)
E (IRQ 6)	N/A	●	●	●	●	●	●	●	●	●		Disk-controller interrupt entry
F (IRQ 7)	N/A	●	●	●	●	●	●	●	●	●		Parallel printer, LPT1:
10	0	●	●	●*	●	●	●	●	●	●	EGA	Set CRT mode
Video I/O	1	●	●	●	●	●	●	●	●	●		Set cursor type
	2	●	●	●	●	●	●	●	●	●		Set cursor position
	3	●	●	●	●	●	●	●	●	●		Read cursor position
	4	●	●	●	●	●	●	●	○	○		Read light-pen position
	5	●	●	●*	●	●	●	●	●	●		Select active display page
	6	●	●	●	●	●	●	●	●	●		Scroll active page up
	7	●	●	●	●	●	●	●	●	●		Scroll active page down
	8	●	●	●	●	●	●	●	●	●		Read attribute/character at current cursor position
	9	●	●	●	●	●	●	●	●	●		Write attribute/character at current cursor position
	0A	●	●	●*	●	●	●	●	●	●		Write character only at current cursor position
	0B	●	●	●*	●	●	●	●	●	●		Set color palette
	0C	●	●	●	●	●	●	●	●	●		Write dot
	0D	●	●	●	●	●	●	●	●	●		Read dot
	0E	●	●	●	●	●	●	●	●	●		Teletype write to active page
	0F	●	●	●	●	●	●	○	●	●		Return current video state
	10	○	○	○	○	○	○	○	●	●	EGA	Set palette registers
	11	○	○	○	○	○	○	○	●	●	EGA	Character-generator routine
	12	○	○	○	○	○	○	○	●	●	EGA	Alternate select
	13	○	○	○	●	○	●	○	●	●	EGA	Write string (with optional attributes)
	14	○	○	○	○	○	○	●	○	○		Load LCD character font or set LCD high-intensity substitute
	15	○	○	○	○	○	○	●	○	○		Return active-display type and parameters
	1A	○	○	○	○	○	○	○	●	●		Read/write display combination code
	1B	○	○	○	○	○	○	○	●	●		Return functionality/state information

Interrupt	Function code	PC	PC XT	PCjr	PC AT	XT /2	XT /286	PS CVT	PS/2 30	PS/2 other	BIOS Comments
	1C	○	○	○	○	○	○	○	○	●	Save/restore video state
11	N/U	●	●	●	●	●	●	●	●	●	Equipment determination; returns the EQUIP__FLAG from BIOS data area
12	N/U	●	●	●	●	●	●	●	●	●	Memory size determination; returns amount of memory in the system
13 Disk	0	●	●	●	●	●	●	●	●	●	Reset disk system
	1	●	●	●	●	●	●	●	●	●	Read status of last operation
	2	●	●	●	●	●	●	●	●	●	Read sectors into memory
	3	●	●	●	●	●	●	●	●	●	Write sectors from memory
	4	●	●	●	●	●	●	●	●	●	Verify sectors
	5	●	●	●	●	●	●	●	●	●	Format a track
	8	○	○	○	3x9	○	●	●	●	●	Return the current drive parameters
	15	○	○	○	●	○	●	●	●	●	Read disk type (none, disk-no-change line, disk, hard disk)
	16	○	○	○	●	●	●	●	●	●	Disk-change line status
	17	○	○	○	●	●	●	●	●	●	Set disk type for format
	18	○	○	○	3x9	●	●	○	●	●	Set media type for format
	N/A	●	●	●	●	●	●	●	●	●	Uses BIOS data area DISK__POINTER
	N/A	○	○	○	●	○	●	○	●	●	Uses disk-drive-media-type bytes at 40:90 and 40:91
	N/A	○	○	○	●	○	●	○	●	●	Uses rest of disk "state machine" at 40:92 to 95
13 Hard disk	N/U	●	○	●	○	○	○	●	○	○	Not used by PC, PCjr, or PC CVT
	0	○	●	○	●	○	●	○	●	●	Reset disk system
	1	○	●	○	●	○	●	○	●	●	Read status of last disk operation
	2	○	●	○	●	○	●	○	●	●	Read sectors into memory
	3	○	●	○	●	○	●	○	●	●	Write sectors from memory
	4	○	●	○	●	○	●	○	●	●	Verify sectors
	5	○	●	○	●	○	●	○	●	●	Format a track (not enhanced-small-device-interface [ESDI] disks)
	6	○	●	○	N/U	○	N/U	○	N/U	N/U	Format a track and set bad-sector flags
	7	○	●	○	N/U	○	N/U	○	N/U	N/U	Format the drive starting at the desired track
	8	○	●	○	●	○	●	○	●	●	Return the current drive parameters
	9	○	●	○	●	○	●	○	●	●	Initialize drive-pair character (uses INT 41 and 46, not ESDI disks)
	0A	○	●	○	●	○	●	○	D	D	Read long
	0B	○	●	○	●	○	●	○	D	D	Write long
	0C	○	●	○	●	○	●	○	●	●	Seek to desired track
	0D	○	●	○	●	○	●	○	●	●	Alternate disk reset (not ESDI disks)
	0E	○	●	○	N/U	○	N/U	○	D	D	Read sector buffer
	0F	○	●	○	N/U	○	N/U	○	D	D	Write sector buffer
	10	○	●	○	●	○	●	○	●	●	Test drive ready
	11	○	●	○	●	○	●	○	●	●	Recalibrate
	12	○	●	○	N/U	○	N/U	○	D	D	Controller RAM diagnostic
	13	○	●	○	N/U	○	N/U	○	D	D	Drive diagnostic
	14	○	●	○	●	○	●	○	D	D	Controller internal diagnostic
	15	○	○	○	●	○	●	○	●	●	Read disk type (none, disk-no-change line, disk, hard disk)
	19	○	○	○	○	○	○	○	●	●	Park heads
	1A	○	○	○	○	○	○	○	○	●	ESDI disks only; format unit
14 RS-232C I/O	0	●	●	●	●	●	●	●	●	●	Initialize communications port
	1	●	●	●	●	●	●	●	●	●	Send a character
	2	●	●	●	●	●	●	●	●	●	Receive a character
	3	●	●	●	●	●	●	●	●	●	Get port status
	4	○	○	○	○	○	○	○	●	●	Extended initialize
	5	○	○	○	○	○	○	○	●	●	Extended communications port control
		2	2	2	2	2	2	2	4	4	Number of serial ports supported (four ports via extended control functions)
15 Cassette I/O	N/U	○	●	○	●	○	○	○	○	○	Not used on PC XT
	0	●	○	●	○	○	○	○	○	○	Turn cassette motor on
	1	●	○	●	○	○	○	○	○	○	Turn cassette motor off
	2	●	○	●	○	○	○	○	○	○	Read from cassette
	3	●	○	●	○	○	○	○	○	○	Write to cassette
and System services	0F	○	○	○	○	○	○	○	○	●	ESDI drive only; format unit periodic interrupt (invoked once per cycle)
	20	○	○	○	●	○	●	○	○	●	AL=10, setup of SYSREQ routine $ (software only)

Interrupt	Function code	PC	PC XT	PCjr	PC AT	XT /2	XT /286	PS CVT	PS/2 30	PS/2 other	BIOS	Comments
		○	○	○	●	●	●	○	○	●		AL=11, completion of SYSREQ function $ (software only)
	21	○	○	○	○	○	○	○	○	●		Power-on self-test error log
	40	○	○	○	○	○	○	●	○	○		Read or write system (AL= 0,1) or modem (AL= 2,3) profile
	41	○	○	○	○	○	○	●	○	○		Wait on external event
	42	○	○	○	○	○	○	●	○	○		Request system power off (system suspend)
	43	○	○	○	○	○	○	●	○	○		Read current system status information
	44	○	○	○	○	○	○	●	○	○		Activate or deactivate internal modem power
	4F	○	○	○	3x9	●	●	●	●	●		BIOS keyboard interrupt hexadecimal 9 intercept
	80	○	○	○	●	●	●	○	●	●		Device open $
	81	○	○	○	●	●	●	○	●	●		Device close $
	82	○	○	○	●	●	●	○	●	●		Program termination $
	83	○	○	○	●	●	●	○	●	●		Event wait
	84	○	○	○	●	●	●	○	●	●		Joystick support
	85	○	○	○	●	●	●	●	●	●		AL=0, system request key has been pressed $
		○	○	○	●	●	●	●	●	●		AL=1, system request key has been released $
	86	○	○	○	●	●	●	●	●	●		Wait (for n microseconds)
	87	○	○	○	●	○	●	○	●	●		Move block of memory (can move to and from extended memory)
	88	○	○	○	●	○	●	○	●	●		Return amount of memory above 1 megabyte
	89	○	○	○	●	○	●	○	●	●		Switch processor to virtual mode
	90	○	○	○	●	●	●	●	●	●		Device busy loop $
	91	○	○	○	●	●	●	●	●	●		Interrupt complete flag set $
	C0	○	○	○	3x9	●	●	●	●	●		Return system parameter pointer; see table 1 for definitions
	C1	○	○	○	○	○	○	○	●	●		Return extended-BIOS data-area segment address
	C2	○	○	○	○	○	○	○	○	●		Pointing-device BIOS interface
	C3	○	○	○	○	○	○	○	○	●		Enable/disable watchdog time-out
	C4	○	○	○	○	○	○	○	○	●		Programmable option select
16 Keyboard	0	●	●	●	●	●	●	●	●	●		Read next ASCII character
	1	●	●	●	●	●	●	●	●	●		Set Z flag if buffer not empty
	2	●	●	●	●	●	●	●	●	●		Read shift status
	3	○	○	●	339	○	●	○	●	●		Set typematic rates
	4	○	○	○	○	○	○	○	○	○		Turn on/off keyboard click
	5	○	○	○	339	●	●	○	●	●		Place ASCII character/scan code combination in keyboard buffer as if from keyboard
	10	○	○	○	339	●	●	○	●	●		Extended read interface for the enhanced (101-/102-key) keyboard
	11	○	○	○	339	●	●	○	●	●		Extended ASCII status for the enhanced (101-/102-key) keyboard
	12	○	○	○	339	●	●	●	●	●		Return extended shift status in AX register (101-/102-key keyboard)
17 Printer	0	●	●	●	●	●	●	●	●	●	NB	Print a character
	1	●	●	●	●	●	●	●	●	●	NB	Initialize printer port
	2	●	●	●	●	●	●	●	●	●	NB	Return printer-port status
	3	3	3	3	3	3	3	3	2	2		Number of printer ports supported
18 BASIC	N/A	●	●	●	●	●	●	●	●	●		Points to resident (ROM) BASIC
19	N/A	●	○	○	○	○	○	●	○	○		Bootstrap loader, IPL the system from a disk
	N/A	○	●	○	●	●	●	○	●	●		Bootstrap loader, IPL the system from a disk or hard disk
	N/A	○	○	●	○	○	○	○	○	○		Bootstrap loader, IPL the system from a disk or cartridge
1A Time of day	0	●	●	●	●	●	●	●	●	●		Read current clock setting
	1	●	●	●	●	●	●	●	●	●		Set the current clock
	2	○	○	○	●	○	●	●	●	●		Read the real-time clock
	3	○	○	○	●	○	●	●	●	●		Set the real-time clock
	4	○	○	○	●	○	●	●	●	●		Read date from real-time clock
	5	○	○	○	●	○	●	●	●	●		Set date into real-time clock
	6	○	○	○	●	○	●	●	●	●		Set the alarm (24 hour maximum, goes off and causes an INT 4A)
	7	○	○	○	●	○	●	●	●	●		Reset the alarm
	8	○	○	○	○	○	○	●	○	○		Set real-time clock alarm activated power-on mode
	9	○	○	○	○	○	○	●	●	○		Read alarm time and status

continued

Interrupt	Function code	PC	PC XT	PCjr	PC AT	XT /2	XT /286	PS CVT	PS/2 30	PS/2 other	BIOS	Comments
Sound select	0A	○	○	○	○	●	○	○	●	●		Read system-timer day counter
	0B	○	○	○	○	●	○	○	●	●		Set system-timer day counter
	80	○	○	●	○	○	○	○	○	○		Set up sound multiplexer
1B	N/U	●	●	●	●	●	●	●	●	●		Keyboard break address
1C	N/U	●	●	●	●	●	●	●	●	●		Timer tick
1D	N/U	●	●	●	●	●	●	●*	●	●		Video parameters for 6845 initialization
1E	N/U	●	●	●	●	●	●	●	●	●		Disk parameters
1F	N/U	●	●	●	●	●	●	●	●	●		Graphics character extension for modes 4, 5, and 6
20		○	○	○	○	○	○	○	○	○		DOS program terminate
21		○	○	○	○	○	○	○	○	○	NB	DOS function call
22		○	○	○	○	○	○	○	○	○		DOS terminate address (don't issue this INT)
23		○	○	○	○	○	○	○	○	○		DOS control-break exit address (don't issue this INT)
24		○	○	○	○	○	○	○	○	○		DOS fatal-error vector
25		○	○	○	○	○	○	○	○	○		DOS absolute disk read
26		○	○	○	○	○	○	○	○	○		DOS absolute disk write
27		○	○	○	○	○	○	○	○	○		DOS terminate, stay resident (instead, use INT21, AH=31)
28		○	○	○	○	○	○	○	○	○		Used internally by DOS
29		○	○	○	○	○	○	○	○	○		Reserved for DOS
2A		○	○	○	○	○	○	○	○	○		Used by NETBIOS
2B		○	○	○	○	○	○	○	○	○		Reserved for DOS
2C		○	○	○	○	○	○	○	○	○		Reserved for DOS
2D		○	○	○	○	○	○	○	○	○		Reserved for DOS
2E		○	○	○	○	○	○	○	○	○		Reserved for DOS
2F		○	○	○	○	○	○	○	○	○	NB	Interprocess multiplex interrupt (see notes)
	1	○	○	○	○	○	○	○	○	○		Call resident part of PRINT
	2	○	○	○	○	○	○	○	○	○		Call resident part of ASSIGN
	10	○	○	○	○	○	○	○	○	○		Call resident part of SHARE
	B7	○	○	○	○	○	○	○	○	○		Call resident part of APPEND
30 to 3F		○	○	○	○	○	○	○	○	○		Reserved for DOS
40	N/U	○	●	○	●	●	●	○	●	●		Points to disk BIOS entry
41	N/U	○	●	○	●	●	●	○	●	●		Pointer to first hard disk, parameter block (not ESDI disks)
42	N/U	○	○	○	○	○	○	○	●	●	EGA	Points to screen BIOS entry
43	N/U	○	○	○	○	○	○	○	●	●	EGA	Pointer to EGA initializing parameters
44	N/U	○	○	○	○	○	○	●	●	●	EGA	Pointer to EGA graphics character table
	N/U	○	○	●	○	○	○	●	●	●		Pointer to lower graphics character table
45	N/U	○	○	○	○	○	○	○	○	○		Reserved
46	N/U	○	○	○	●	○	●	○	○	●	○	Pointer to second hard disk, parameter block (not ESDI disks)
47	N/U	○	○	○	○	○	○	○	○	○		Reserved
48	N/U	○	○	●	○	○	○	○	○	○		Cordless keyboard translation
49	N/U	○	○	●	○	○	○	○	○	○		Nonkeyboard scan-code translation table address
4A	N/U	○	○	○	○	○	○	●	●	●		Real-time clock alarm
4B to 4F	N/U	○	○	○	○	○	○	○	○	○		Reserved
50	N/U	○	○	○	○	○	○	○	○	○		Periodic alarm interrupt from timer
51 to 59	N/U	○	○	○	○	○	○	○	○	○		Reserved
5A	N/U	○	○	○	○	○	○	○	○	○	CLU	Cluster adapter BIOS-entry address
5B	N/U	○	○	○	○	○	○	○	○	○		Reserved
5C		○	○	○	○	○	○	○	○	○	NB	NETBIOS entry point
5D to 5F	N/U	○	○	○	○	○	○	○	○	○		Reserved
60 to 66	N/U	○	○	○	○	○	○	○	○	○		Reserved for user program interrupts

Interrupt	Function code	PC	PC XT	PCjr	PC AT	XT /2	XT /286	PS CVT	PS/2 30	PS/2 other	BIOS Comments
67	N/U	O	O	O	O	O	O	O	O	O	Reserved for user program interrupts, LIM EMS interrupt entry
68 to 6B	N/U	O	O	O	O	O	O	O	O	O	Not used
6C	N/U	O	O	O	O	O	O	●	O	O	System resume vector
6D to 6F	N/U	O	O	O	O	O	O	O	O	O	Not used
70 (IRQ 8)	N/U	O	O	O	●	O	●	O	O	●	Real-time clock INT
71 (IRQ 9)	N/U	O	O	O	●	O	●	O	O	●	Redirected to IRQ2
72 (IRQ 10)	N/U	O	O	O	●	O	●	O	O	●	
73 (IRQ 11)	N/U	O	O	O	●	O	●	O	O	●	
74 (IRQ 12)	N/U	O	O	O	●	O	●	O	O	●	PS/2 others: mouse interrupt
75 (IRQ 13)	N/U	O	O	O	●	O	●	O	O	●	Coprocessor, BIOS redirect to NMI interrupt (INT 2)
76 (IRQ 14)	N/U	O	O	O	●	O	●	O	O	●	Hard disk controller
77 (IRQ 15)	N/U	O	O	O	●	O	●	O	O	●	
78 to 7F		O	O	O	O	O	O	O	O	O	Not used
80 to 85		O	O	O	O	O	O	O	O	O	Reserved by BASIC
86 to F0		O	O	O	O	O	O	O	O	O	Used by BASIC when the BASIC interpreter is running
F1 to FF		O	O	O	O	O	O	O	O	O	Reserved for user program interrupts

Notes:

tv	= Topview function.	O	= Not supported.
NB	= NETBIOS alters this function.	●	= Supported.
EGA	= Enhanced graphics adapter	●*	= A superset is supported.
	(and video graphics array) function.	$	= These INT 15 functions are just operating system hooks. They perform no BIOS-level functions.
N/U	= Not used.		
D	= Used for diagnostics only.	3x9	= Only on PC AT Models 319 and 339.
		339	= Only on PC AT Model 339.

All PC AT interrupts are valid for real mode only.
The PC Portable, PC/370, and 3270 PC all use the PC XT BIOS.
The AT/370 uses the PC AT BIOS.
PS/2 other systems are the Micro Channel systems and the Models 50, 60, and 80.
The Typematic rate of the 84-key PC AT keyboard is programmable, but no explicit BIOS support is provided. Also, the AT's keyboard has an internal 16-key buffer.
When a hard disk is present, the INT 13 disk interrupt is rerouted to INT 40 and INT 13 points to the hard disk BIOS.
For the multiplex interrupt (INT 2F), AH contains the identification of the routine to be called, where IDs 00–7F are reserved for DOS and C0–FF are reserved for user applications. AL contains the function code.

Table 3: *BIOS video modes.*

Mode	Type	Max colors	Alpha format	Buffer start	Display size	Box size	Max pages	Supporting cards
0, 1	A/N	16	40×25	B8000	320×200	8×8	8	PCjr, CGA, PC CVT, EGA, and PS/2 others
					320×350	8×14	8	EGA and PS/2 others
					320×400	8×16	8	PS/2 Model 30
					360×400	9×14	8	PS/2 others
2, 3	A/N	16	80×25	B8000	640×200	8×8	4	PCjr, CGA, and PC CVT
					640×200	8×8	8	EGA and PS/2 others
					640×350	8×14	8	EGA and PS/2 others
					640×400	8×16	8	PS/2 Model 30
					720×400	9×16	8	PS/2 others
4, 5	APA	4	40×25	B8000	320×200	8×8	1	PCjr, CGA, EGA, and all PS/2 systems
6	APA	2	80×25	B8000	640×200	8×8	1	PCjr, CGA, EGA, and all PS/2 systems

continued

Mode	Type	Max colors	Alpha format	Buffer start	Display size	Box size	Max pages	Supporting cards
7	A/N	Mono	80×25	B0000	720×350	9×14	1	MDA and PC CVT
					720×350	9×14	8	EGA and PS/2 others
					720×400	9×16	8	PS/2 others
					640×200	8×8	4	PC CVT
8	APA	16	20×25	B8000	160×200	8×8	1	PCjr
9	APA	16	40×25	B8000	320×200	8×8	1	PCjr
A	APA	4	80×25	B8000	640×200	8×8	1	PCjr
B, C			-Reserved-					
D	APA	16	40×25	A0000	320×200	8×8	8	EGA and PS/2 others
E	APA	16	80×25	A0000	640×200	8×8	4	EGA and PS/2 others
F	APA	Mono	80×25	A0000	640×350	8×14	2	EGA and PS/2 others
10	APA	16	80×25	A0000	640×350	8×14	2	EGA and PS/2 others
11	APA	2	80×30	A0000	640×480	8×16	1	All PS/2 systems
12	APA	16	80×30	A0000	640×480	8×16	1	PS/2 others
13	APA	256	40×25	A0000	640×480	8×8	1	All PS/2 systems

Notes

APA = All points addressable (i.e., graphics mode)

A/N = Alphanumeric (i.e., text-only mode)

CGA = Color Graphics Adapter

MDA = Monochrome Display Adapter

EGA = Enhanced Graphics Adapter

The cursor is not displayed in APA modes.

Modes 0, 2, and 5 are identical to modes 1, 3, and 4, except color burst is not enabled. (This doesn't affect RGB displays.)

Table 4: *Low-memory reserved addresses.*

00000–002FF	System interrupt vectors
00300–003FF	System interrupt vectors, power-on and bootstrap stack area
00400–004EF	BIOS data area
00400–00406	COM1: to COM4: I/O port base addresses, one word each.
00407–00408	LPT1: to LPT4:* I/O port base addresses, one word each.
00409–0040F	Reserved
00410–00411	Equipment flag word, returned in AX register by INT 11.

Bits	Meaning
14-15	Number of printers attached (0 to 3, LPTs)
13	Internal modem installed (PC CVT) or serial printer installed (PCjr)
12	Joystick installed
9-11	Number of COM devices (0 to 4, COMs)
8	Unused (PCjr only; DMA chip present on system)
6-7	Number of disk drives (if bit 0 is 1; 00=1, 01=2, 10 and 11 not used)
4-5	Initial video mode
	00 Unused
	01 40 × 25 BW using color card
	01 80 × 25 BW using color card
	11 Monochrome card
2-3	Unused, or, in the PC, old PC XT, and PCjr, planar RAM size; 00=16K bytes, 01=32K bytes, 10=48K bytes, 11=64K bytes
1	Math coprocessor installed (unused on PCjr and PC CVT)
0	IPL disk installed.

00412	Reserved, except in PC CVT power-on self-test status
00413–00414	Memory size in K bytes (0 to 640)
00415–00416	Reserved
00417	Keyboard Control

Bits	Meaning
7	Insert locked
6	Caps Lock locked
5	Num Lock locked
4	Scroll Lock locked
3	Alt key pressed
2	Control key pressed
1	Left shift key pressed
0	Right shift key pressed

00418	Keyboard Control

Bits	Meaning
7	Insert key pressed
6	Caps Lock key pressed
5	Num Lock key pressed
4	Scroll Lock key pressed
3	Pause locked
2	System request key pressed
1	Left Alt key pressed
0	Left Control key pressed

00419	Alternate keypad entry
0041A–0041B	Keyboard buffer head pointer
0041C–0041D	Keyboard buffer tail pointer
0041E–0043D	32-byte keyboard buffer
0043E–00448	Disk drive data area
00449–00466	Video-control data area 1
00467–0046A	Reserved, except PS/2 others, 00472=pointer to reset code upon system reset when memory is preserved.
0046B	Reserved
0046C–0046F	Timer counter
00470	Timer overflow
00471	Break key state
00472–00473	Reset flag

Bits	Meaning
1234	Bypass memory test
4321	Preserve memory (PS/2 other only)
5678	System suspended (PC CVT only)
9ABC	Manufacturing test mode (PC CVT only)
ABCD	System POST loop mode (PC CVT only)

```
00474-00477   Hard disk drive data area
00478-0047B   LPT1: to LPT4:* time-out values, 1 byte each.
0047C-0047F   COM1: to COM4: time-out values, 1 byte each.
00480-00481   Keyboard buffer start offset pointer
00482-00483   Keyboard buffer end offset pointer
00484-0048A   Video control data area 2
0048B-00495   Disk drive/hard disk drive control-data area
              (XT/2, AT, XT/286, and all PS/2s)
    00496     Keyboard mode state and type flags
    00497     Keyboard LED flags
00498-00499   Offset address to user wait complete flag
0049A-0049B   Segment address to user wait complete flag
0049C-0049D   User wait count in microseconds, low word
0049E-0049F   User wait count in ms, high word
    004A0     Wait active flag
              Bits   Meaning
               7     Wait-time elapsed and posted flag
              6-1    Reserved
               0     INT 15, AH=86, Wait, has occurred.

004A1-004A7   Reserved
004A8-004AB   Pointer to video parameters and overrides
004AC-004EF   Reserved
004F0-004FF   Applications program communication area
    500       Print screen-status flag
    504       Single-drive mode status byte
00510-00521   Used by BASIC
00522-0052F   Used by DOS for disk initialization
00530-00533   Used by MODE command
00534-005FF   Reserved for DOS
```

* PS/2 systems don't support LPT4:.

Table 5: *Hardware interrupt request lines.*

Hardware interrupt request line	PC and PC/XT and PS/2 Model 30	PCjr	PC CVT	PC AT and XT/286	PS/2 Models 50, 60, 80
NMI	See notes	Keyboard interrupt	See notes	Parity errors	See notes
IRQ 0	Timer	Timer clock interrupt	Timer output 0	Timer output 0	Timer output 0
IRQ 1	Keyboard	I/O channel (reserved)	Keyboard (buffer full)	Keyboard (buffer full)	Keyboard (buffer full)
IRQ 2	Reserved	I/O channel	Reserved	Cascade for 8 to 15	Cascade for 8 to 15
IRQ 3	Serial port 2	Serial port 2	Serial port 2	Serial port 2	Serial port 2
IRQ 4	Serial port 1	Modem or serial port 1	Modem or serial port 1	Serial port 1	Serial port 1
IRQ 5	Hard disk (not PC)	Display vertical retrace	Reserved	Parallel port 2	Reserved
IRQ 6	Disk control	Disk	Disk control	Disk control	Disk control
IRQ 7	Parallel port 1	I/O channel (parallel printer)	Parallel port 1	Parallel port 1	Parallel port 1
IRQ 8*				Real-time clock	Real-time clock
IRQ 9				Redirected to IRQ2	Redirected to IRQ2
IRQ 10				Reserved	Reserved
IRQ 11				Reserved	Reserved
IRQ 12				Reserved	Mouse
IRQ 13				Coprocessor	Coprocessor
IRQ 14				Hard disk controller	Hard disk controller
IRQ 15				Reserved	Reserved

* Interrupts 8 to 15 are not available on the PC, PC XT, PCjr, PC CVT, and PS/2 Model 30.

Notes:

PC, PC XT, and PS/2 Model 30 use NMI for parity errors and numeric coprocessor interrupt.

PC CVT uses NMI for I/O channel check, disk power-on request, keyboard, real-time clock alarm, or system suspend.

PS/2 Models 50, 60, and 80 use NMI for parity errors, I/O channel check, watchdog timer, and arbitrator time-out.

IRQ 3 and 4 (except in the PC CVT) may be used by SDLC or bisynchronous communication cards instead of serial ports.

Table 6: *Expanded EMS function-call interfaces. This covers version 3.2 and is accessed via interrupt 67.*

AH =	Function
40	Get manager status
41	Get page frame segment
42	Get number of pages
43	Get handle and allocate memory
44	Map memory
45	Release handle and memory
46	Get EMS version
47	Save mapping context
48	Restore mapping context
49	Get I/O port address
4A	Get logical-to-physical-page mapping
4B	Get number of EMM handles
4C	Get pages owned by handle
4D	Get pages for all handles
4F–5F	Reserved
60	Get physical window array

Table 8: *BIOS-extension (ROM-area) addresses.*

C0000-C3FFF	16K bytes EGA BIOS
C4000-C5FFF	
C6000-C63FF	256 bytes PGA communication area
C6400-C7FFF	
C8000-CBFFF	16K bytes hard disk BIOS
CC000-CFFFF	
D0000-D7FFF	32K bytes cluster adapter BIOS
D8000-DBFFF	
DC000-DFFFF	
E0000-EFFFF	64K bytes expansion ROM space (PC AT)
F0000-FFFFF	64K bytes ROM BASIC and simple BIOS

Note: PCjr uses D0000-DFFFF for expanded cartridges and E0000-EFFFF for standard cartridges.

Table 7: *Multitasking hooks using Interrupt 15.*

Wait Function (AH=90, AL=type code). Used to tell the OS task dispatcher to dispatch another task while the current task waits for its I/O operation to finish.
Post Function (AH=91, AL=type code). I/O operation complete, which can be used to inform the OS task dispatcher that an I/O operation for a waiting task has completed, and the task should now be moved to the ready queue.

Type codes for Wait and Post functions

00–7F Serially reusable device; OS must serialize access.
    00   Disk (time-out)
    01   Disk (time-out)
    02   Keyboard (no time-out)
    03   Pointing device (time-out)

80–BF Reentrant devices; ES:BS points to a unique control block.
    80   Network (no time-out), ES:BX points to network control block.

C0–FF Wait-only calls, no complementary Post function. Time-out on nonoccurrence of event.
    FC   Fixed-disk reset, PS/2 only (time-out)
    FD   Disk drive motor start (time-out)
    FE   Printer (time-out)

Table 9: *NETBIOS modifications and additions to DOS functions. This covers version 1.10.*

INT	AH	AL	
21	3D		Open file with sharing specified
	44	09	IOCTL, is device redirected?
		0A	IOCTL, is handle local or remote?
		0B	IOCTL, change sharing retry count
	59		Get extended error
	5A		Create temporary file with unique name
	5B		Create new file
	5C	00	Lock byte range
		01	Unlock byte range
	5E	00	Get machine name
		02	Set up printer-control string
	5F	02	Get assign list entry
		03	Redirect device to network
		04	Cancel redirection
2A	00		NETBIOS installation check
	03		Get device-shared status
	04		Execute NETBIOS
	05		Get network resource information
	06		Network print-stream control
2F	87	00	Append installation check
		02	Append version check
	88	00	Network command installation check
		03	Get server post address
		04	Set server post address
		09	Network version check

More Programming Tools from M&T Books

Programming Languages

C

C Chest and Other C Treasures from *Dr. Dobb's Journal*
Edited by Allen Holub
Item #40-2 $24.95 (book)
Item #49-6 $39.95 (book/disk)
This comprehensive anthology contains the popular "C Chest" columns from *Dr. Dobb's Journal of Software Tools*, along with the lively philosophical and practical discussions they inspired, in addition to other information-packed articles by C experts. The software in the book is also available on disk with full source code. MS-DOS format.

Turbo C: The Art of Advanced Program Design, Optimization, and Debugging
Stephen R. Davis
Item #38-0 $24.95 (book)
Item #45-3 $39.95 (book/disk)
Overflowing with example programs, this book fully describes the techniques necessary to skillfully program, optimize, and debug in Turbo C. All programs are also available on disk with full source code. MS-DOS format.

C Programming for MIDI
Jim Conger
Item #86-0 $22.95 (book)
Item #90-9 $37.95 (book/disk)
For musicians and programmers alike, here is the source that will help you write programs for music applications. The author begins by outlining the features of MIDI (Musical Instrument Digital Interface) and its support of real-time access to musical devices. An introduction to C programming fundamentals as they relate to MIDI is also provided. The author fully demonstrates these concepts with two MIDI applications: a patch librarian and a simple sequencer.

A Small C Compiler: Language, Usage, Theory, and Design

James E. Hendrix

Item #88-7 $23.95 (book)

Item #97-6 $38.95 (book/disk)

A full presentation of the design and theory of the Small C compiler (including source code) and programming language. The author has implemented many features in this compiler that make it an excellent example for learning basic compiler theory. Some of these features are: recursive dissent parsing, one-pass compilation, and the generation of assembly language. Here is a look into a real compiler with the opportunity for hands-on experience in designing one.

Dr. Dobb's Toolbook of C

Editors of *Dr. Dobb's Journal*

Item #89303-615-3 $29.95

From *Dr. Dobb's Journal of Software Tools* and Brady Communications, this book contains a comprehensive library of valuable C code. *Dr. Dobb's Journal of Software Tools'* most popular articles on C are updated and reprinted here, along with new C programming tools. Also included is a complete C compiler, an assembler, text processing programs, and more!

The Small-C Handbook

James E. Hendrix

Item #8359-7012-4 $17.95 (book)

Item #67-4 $37.90 (book and CP/M disk)

Also from *Dr. Dobb's Journal of Software Tools* and Brady Communications, the handbook is a valuable companion to the Small-C compiler, described below. The book explains the language and the compiler, and contains entire source listings of the compiler and its library of arithmetic and logical routines.

Forth

Dr. Dobb's Toolbook of Forth

Edited by Marlin Ouverson

Item #10-0 $22.95 (book)

Item #57-7 $39.95 (book/disk)

This comprehensive collection of useful Forth programs and tutorials contains expanded versions of *Dr. Dobb's Journal of Software Tools'* best Forth articles and other material, including practical code and in-depth discussions of advanced Forth topics. The screens in the book are also available on disk as ASCII files in the following formats: MS/PC-DOS, Apple II, Macintosh, or CP/M: Osborne or 8" SS/SD.

Dr. Dobb's Toolbook of Forth, Volume II
Editors of *Dr. Dobb's Journal*
Item #41-0 $29.95 (book)
Item #51-8 $45.95 (book/disk)
This complete anthology of Forth programming techniques and developments
picks up where the Toolbook of Forth, First Edition left off. Included are the
best articles on Forth from *Dr. Dobb's Journal of Software Tools,* along with the
latest material from other Forth experts. The screens in the book are available on
disk as ASCII files in the following formats: MS-DOS, Macintosh, and CP/M:
Osborne or 8" SS/SD.

BASIC

**The New BASICs: Programming Techniques and Library
Development**
Namir Clement Shammas
Item #37-2 $24.95 (book)
Item #43-7 $39.95 (book/disk)
This book will orient the advanced programmer to the syntax and programming
features of The New BASICs, including Turbo BASIC 1.0, QuickBASIC 3.0,
and True BASIC 2.0. You'll learn the details of implementing subroutines,
functions, and libraries to permit more structured coding. Programs and subrou-
tines are available on disk with full source code. MS-DOS format.

Turbo Pascal

The Turbo Pascal Toolbook
Edited by Namir Clement Shammas
Item #25-9 $25.95 (book)
Item #61-5 $45.95 (book/disk)
This book contains routines and sample programs to make your programming
easier and more powerful. You'll find an extensive library of low-level routines;
external sorting and searching tools; window management; artificial intelligence
techniques; mathematical expression parsers, including two routines that convert
mathematical expressions into RPN tokens; and a smart statistical regression
model finder. More than 800K of source code is available on disk for MS-DOS
systems.

Programming Tools and Utilities

Small-Windows: A Library of Windowing Functions for the C Language
James E. Hendrix
Item #35-X $29.95
Small-Windows is a complete windowing library for C. The package includes video functions, menu functions, window functions, and more. The package is available for MS-DOS systems for the following compilers: Microsoft C Version 4.0 and 5.0; Small-C; Turbo C 1.0 and 1.5; and Lattice C 3.1. Documentation and full C source code is included.

Small Tools: Programs for Text Processing
James E. Hendrix
Item #78-X $29.95 (manual/disk)
This package of text-processing programs written in Small-C is designed to perform specific, modular functions on text files. Source code is included. Small Tools is available in both CP/M and MS/PC-DOS versions and includes complete documentation.

Small-Mac: An Assembler for Small-C
James E. Hendrix
Item #77-1 $29.95 (manual/disk)
Small-Mac is a macro assembler designed to stress simplicity, portability, adaptability, and educational value. Small-Mac is available for CP/M systems only and includes source code on disk with complete documentation.

NR: An Implementation of the UNIX NROFF Word Processor
Allen Holub
Item #33-X $29.95
NR is a text formatter that is written in C and compatible with UNIX's NROFF. *NR* comes configured for any Diablo-compatible printer, as well as Hewlett Packard's ThinkJet and LaserJet. Both the ready-to-use program and full source code are included. For PC compatibles.

Statistical Toolbox for Turbo Pascal
Namir Clement Shammas
Item #22-4 $39.95 (manuals/disks)
Two statistical packages in one! A library disk and reference manual that includes statistical distribution functions, random number generation, basic descriptive statistics, parametric and nonparametric statistical testing, bivariate linear regression, and multiple and polynomial regression. The demonstration disk and man-

ual incorporate these library routines into a fully functioning statistical program. For IBM PCs and compatibles.

Turbo Advantage
Lauer and Wallwitz
Item #26-7 $29.95
A library of more than 200 routines, with source code sample programs and documentation. Routines are organized and documented under the following categories: bit manipulation, file management, MS-DOS support, string operations, arithmetic calculations, data compression, differential equations, Fourier analysis and synthesis, and much more! For MS/PC-DOS systems.

Turbo Advantage: Complex
Lauer and Wallwitz
Item #27-5 $39.95
This library provides the Turbo Pascal code for digital filters, boundary-value solutions, vector and matrix calculations with complex integers and variables, Fourier transforms, and calculations of convolution and correlation functions. Some of the *Turbo Advantage: Complex* routines are most effectively used with Turbo Advantage. Source code and documentation included.

Turbo Advantage: Display
Lauer and Wallwitz
Item #28-3 $39.95
Turbo Advantage: Display includes an easy-to-use form processor and thirty Turbo Pascal procedures and functions to facilitate linking created forms to your program. Full source code and documentation are included. Some of the *Turbo Advantage* routines are necessary to compile *Turbo Advantage: Display*.

Time and Task Management with dBASE III
Timothy Berry
Item #09-7 $49.95 (manual/MS-DOS disk)
Like an accounting system for time and tasks, this package helps users organize hours, budgets, activities, and resources. Providing both a useful time-management system and a library of dBASE III code and macros, this package has practical as well as educational value. To be used with dBASE III. Source code and documentation is included. MS-DOS disk format.

Sales Management with dBASE III
Timothy Berry
Item #15-1 $49.95 (manual/MS-DOS disk)
Sales management works with dBASE III to provide a powerful information system that will help you to keep track of clients, names, addresses, follow-ups, pending dates, and account data. This system organizes all the day-to-day activities of selling and includes program files, format files, report files, index files, and data bases. Documentation and full source code is included.

Operating Systems

OS/2

The Programmer's Essential OS/2 Handbook
David E. Cortesi
Item #82-8 $24.95 (book)
Item #89-5 $39.95 (book/disk)
Here is a resource no developer can afford to be without! Cortesi succinctly organizes the many features of OS/2 into related topics and illuminates their uses. Multiple indexes and a web of cross referencing in the margins provide easy access to all OS/2 topic areas. Equal support for Pascal and C programmers is provided. *The* essential reference for programmers developing in the OS/2 environment.

UNIX

UNIX Programming on the 80286/80386
Alan Deikman
Item #83-6 $24.95 (book)
Item #91-9 $39.95 (book/disk)
A complete professional level tutorial and reference for programming UNIX and XENIX on 80286/80386 based computers. Succinct coverage of the UNIX program environment, UNIX file system, shells, utilities, and C programming under UNIX are covered. The author also delves into the development of device drivers; some examples of these are video displays, tape cartridges, terminals, and networks.

On Command: Writing a UNIX-Like Shell for MS-DOS
Allen Holub
Item #29-1 $39.95
Learn how to write shells applicable to MS-DOS, as well as to most other programming environments. This book and disk include a full description of a

UNIX-like shell, complete C source code, a thorough discussion of low-level DOS interfacing, and significant examples of C programming at the system level. All source code is included on disk.

/UTIL: A UNIX-Like Utility Package for MS-DOS
Allen Holub
Item #12-7 $29.95
This collection of utilities is intended to be accessed through SH but can be used separately. It contains programs and subroutines that, when coupled with SH, create a fully functional UNIX-like environment. The package includes a disk with full C source code and documentation in a UNIX-style manual.

MS-DOS

Taming MS-DOS, Second Edition
Thom Hogan
Item #87-9 $19.95
Item #92-5 $34.95
Described by reviewers as "small in size, large on content," and "fun." The second edition promises to be just as readable and is updated to cover MS-DOS 3.3. Some of the more perplexing elements of MS-DOS are succinctly described here with time-saving tricks to help customize any MS-DOS system. Each trick is easily implemented into your existing tools and for programmers, Hogan includes many complete source code files that provide very useful utilities. All source code is written in BASIC.

Program Interfacing to MS-DOS
William G. Wong
Item #34-8 $29.95
Program Interfacing to MS-DOS will orient any experienced programmer to the MS-DOS environment. The package includes a ten-part manual with sample program files and a detailed description of how to build device drivers, along with the device driver for a memory disk and a character device driver on disk with macro assembly source code.

Other

Tele Operating System Toolkit
Ken Berry
This task-scheduling algorithm drives the Tele Operating System and is composed of several components. When integrated, they form an independent operat-

ing system for any 8086-based machine. Tele has also been designed for compatibility with MS-DOS, UNIX, and the MOSI standard.

SK: THE SYSTEM KERNEL
Item #30-5 $49.95 (manual/disk)
The System Kernel contains an initialization module, general-purpose utility functions, and a real-time task management system. The kernel provides MS-DOS applications with multitasking capabilities. The System Kernel is required by all other components. All source code is included on disk in MS-DOS format.

DS: WINDOW DISPLAY
Item #32-1 $39.95 (manual/disk)
This component contains BIOS level drivers for a memory-mapped display, window management support and communication coordination between the operator and tasks in a multitasking environment. All source code is included on disk in MS-DOS format.

FS: THE FILE SYSTEM
Item #65-8 $39.95 (manual/disk)
The File System supports MS-DOS disk file structures and serial communication channels. All source code is included on disk in MS-DOS format.

XS: THE INDEX SYSTEM
Item #66-6 $39.95 (manual/disk)
The Index System implements a tree-structured free-form database. All source code is included on disk in MS-DOS format.

Chips

Dr. Dobb's Toolbook of 80286, 80386 Programming
Editors of *Dr. Dobb's Journal*
Item #42-9 $24.95 (book)
Item #53-4 $39.95 (book/disk)
This toolbook is a comprehensive discussion on the powerful 80X86 family of microprocessors. The editors of *Dr. Dobb's Journal of Software Tools* have gathered their best articles, updated and expanded them, and added new material to create this valuable resource for all 80X86 programmers. All programs are available on disk with full source code.

Dr. Dobb's Z80 Toolbook
David E. Cortesi
Item #07-0 $25.00 (book)
Item #55-0 $40.00 (book/disk)
This book contains everything users need to write their own Z80 assembly-language programs, including a method of designing programs and coding them in assembly language and a complete, integrated toolkit of subroutines. All the software in the book is available on disk in the following formats: 8" SS/SD, Apple, Osborne, or Kaypro.

Dr. Dobb's Toolbook of 68000 Programming
Editors of *Dr. Dobb's Journal*
Item #13-216649-6 $29.95 (book)
Item #75-5 $49.95 (book/disk)
From *Dr. Dobb's Journal of Software Tools* and Brady Communications, this collection of practical programming tips and tools for the 68000 family contains the best 68000 articles reprinted from *Dr. Dobb's Journal of Software Tools,* along with much new material. The book contains many useful applications and examples. The software in the book is also available on disk in the following formats: MS/PC-DOS, Macintosh, CP/M 8", Osborne, Amiga, and Atari 520ST.

X68000 Cross Assembler
Brian R. Anderson
Item #71-2 $25.00
This manual and disk contain an executable version of the 68000 Cross Assembler discussed in *Dr. Dobb's Toolbook of 68000 Programming,* complete with source code and documentation. The Cross-Assembler requires CP/M 2.2 with 64K or MS-DOS with 128K. The disk is available in the following formats: MS-DOS, 8" SS/SD, and Osborne.

General Interest

Interfacing to S-100/IEEE 696 Microcomputers
Mark Garetz and Sol Libes
Item #85-2 $24.95
This book helps S-100 bus users expand the utility and power of their systems. It describes the S-100 bus with unmatched precision. Various chapters describe its mechanical and functional design, logical and electrical relationships, bus interconnections, and busing techniques.

Public-Domain Software: Untapped Resources for the Business User
Rusel DeMaria and George R. Fontaine
Item #39-9 $19.95 (book)
Item #47-X $34.95 (book/disk)
Organized into a comprehensive reference, this book introduces the novice and guides the experienced user to a source of often overlooked software—public domain and Shareware. This book will tell you where it is, how to get it, what to look for, and why it's for you. The sample programs and some of the software reviewed is available on disk in MS-DOS format. Includes $15 worth of free access time on CompuServe!

Dr. Dobb's Journal Bound Volume Series

Each volume in this series contains a full year's worth of useful code and fascinating history from *Dr. Dobb's Journal of Software Tools*. Each volume contains every issue of *DDJ* for a given year, reprinted and combined into one comprehensive reference.

Volume	1: 1976	*Item #13-5*	*$30.75*
Volume	2: 1977	*Item #16-X*	*$30.75*
Volume	3: 1978	*Item #17-8*	*$30.75*
Volume	4: 1979	*Item #14-3*	*$30.75*
Volume	5: 1980	*Item #18-6*	*$30.75*
Volume	6: 1981	*Item #19-4*	*$30.75*
Volume	7: 1982	*Item #20-8*	*$35.75*
Volume	8: 1983	*Item #00-3*	*$35.75*
Volume	9: 1984	*Item #08-9*	*$35.75*
Volume	10: 1985	*Item #21-6*	*$35.75*
Volume	11: 1986	*Item #72-0*	*$35.75*
Volume	12: 1987	*Item #84-4*	*$39.95*

To order any of these products send your payment, along with $2.95 per item for shipping, to M&T Books, 501 Galveston Drive, Redwood City, California 94063. California residents, please include the appropriate sales tax. Or, call toll-free 800-533-4372 (in California 800-356-2002) Monday through Friday between 8 A.M. and 5 P.M. PST. When ordering disks, please indicate format.